Barron's 巴朗

AP 美国历史

（第3版）

Barron's AP
United States History
(3rd Edition)

［美］瑞斯尼克（Eugene V. Resnick） 编著

世界图书出版公司

北京·广州·上海·西安

图书在版编目（CIP）数据

Barron's 巴朗 AP 美国历史：第3版 = Barron's AP United States History，3rd Edition：英文 /（美）瑞斯尼克（Eugene V. Resnick）编著. —影印本. —北京：世界图书出版公司北京公司，2017.2
ISBN 978-7-5192-2403-5

Ⅰ.①B… Ⅱ.①瑞… Ⅲ.①美国—历史—高等学校—入学考试—自学参考资料—英文 Ⅳ.①K712

中国版本图书馆CIP数据核字（2017）第 034759 号

书　　名	Barron's 巴朗 AP 美国历史（第3版）
	BARRON'S BALANG AP MEIGUO LISHI（DI 3 BAN）
编　　著	［美］瑞斯尼克（Eugene V. Resnick）
责任编辑	梁沁宁　张晓梅
出版发行	世界图书出版公司北京公司
地　　址	北京市东城区朝内大街137号
邮　　编	100010
电　　话	010-64038355（发行）　64037380（客服）　64033507（总编室）
网　　址	http://www.wpcbj.com.cn
邮　　箱	wpcbjst@vip.163.com
销　　售	新华书店
印　　刷	三河市国英印务有限公司
开　　本	880 mm × 1230 mm　1/16
印　　张	33.25
字　　数	728千字
版　　次	2017年5月第1版　2017年5月第1次印刷
版权登记	01-2017-1402
国际书号	978-7-5192-2403-5
定　　价	78.00元（含1张CD-ROM）

目 录

第一部分 引言

第二部分 复习部分——历史时期

第三部分　模拟考试

Contents

As you review the content in this book and work toward earning that **5** on your AP U.S. HISTORY exam, here are five things that you **MUST** know above everything else.

Barron's Essential 巴朗五大 要点提示

1 **Thinking like a historian.** The questions on the AP U.S. History exam are all built around historical thinking skills. The College Board has identified nine skills that are central to the exam and to the broader field of history. The first five skills—Historical Causation, Patterns of Continuity and Change over Time, Periodization, Comparison, and Contextualization—encourage you to develop the habits of mind required for a critical examination of the past. The other four skills—Historical Argumentation, Appropriate Use of Relevant Historical Evidence, Interpretation, and Synthesis—focus on constructing and evaluating historical arguments about the past. These skills encourage students to go beyond memorization and to engage with the past in complex and sophisticated ways.

2 **Reading documents.** Documents are the building blocks of history and are central to the AP exam. All of the multiple-choice questions and the short-answer questions are built around primary or secondary documents. In addition, the document-based essay question asks you to analyze a series of documents as you construct a response to the question. Focus on how documents relate to the question and on how documents often relate to one another. Remember that historical documents contain a point of view. You should be able to read a diary entry, a newspaper article, a speech, or an argument by a historian and ascertain the point of view and intent of the author.

3 **Growth and conflict in American history.** The rapid growth of the United States—territorially, economically, and demographically—is unprecedented in world history. On the one hand, this growth decimated Native American cultures; on the other, the nation has provided a haven for immigrants. The territorial growth of the country—inspired by the spirit of "manifest destiny"—intensified the debate over slavery in the antebellum period. The series of compromises over expansion eventually unraveled and helped bring about the Civil War. The economic and territorial growth of the United States continued in the period following the Spanish-American War, as the United States joined the other imperialist powers of the world. Be familiar with the causes of American expansion as well as the profound impacts.

4 **The changing nature of the American experiment in democracy.** The United States had made major contributions to the literature and the practice of modern representative government. However, be aware that democracy did not emerge fully formed with the birth of the nation. Americans have struggled over the meaning of democracy throughout American history. Abigail Adams encouraged her husband, John, to "remember the ladies" at the time of the creation of the United States. Slavery and the "Jim Crow" system excluded African Americans from the American experiment in democracy. The civil rights movement struggled to fully include African Americans in the democratic system. These conflicts over the meaning of democracy are crucial to understanding the evolution of the United States.

5 **The dynamic nature of history.** Traditional historians saw history as unidirectional—emanating from the minds and priorities of the elites in society. More recently, historians have seen events as part of a more dynamic process. Social and cultural historians have explored "history from below." As you study, look for such connections and interactions in history. For instance, while it is important to remember that President Lyndon Johnson endorsed and pushed for passage of the 1964 Civil Rights Act, you should be able to connect that with the growth of the grassroots civil rights movement, with the violent backlash against the movement, with shifts within the major political parties and with the dynamics of the Cold War. Historical events do not occur in isolation of one another. Therefore memorizing discreet events in American history is not sufficient for success on the AP exam.

PART ONE
Introduction

第一部分
引言

Introduction: Preparing for the Advanced Placement Exam in United States History
引言：为美国大学预修课程考试之美国历史考试做准备

Congratulations on taking the Advanced Placement course in United States History. If taken seriously, the class and the exam will develop your critical thinking skills and your ability to understand the world in nuanced ways. The class and the exam ask more of you than merely memorizing facts. You are asked to think through problems, to engage in debates, to organize your thinking, to develop your communication skills, and to take thoughtful stands on important issues.

The College Board introduced a major redesign of the AP United States History program in 2014–2015. Since then, the College Board has made some minor revisions to the AP United States History Curriculum Framework and to the exam. The 2014–2015 redesign represents a significant change in the way United States history is organized and taught. This book is designed to prepare students for all of the changes to the AP United States History program that the College Board has introduced.

The College Board identifies nine periods in United States history. Within each period, the curriculum framework uses a thematic rather than a strictly chronological approach. Each of the nine periods is broken down into two or three "Key Concepts" and several supporting concepts and historical developments. These key concepts (identified with numbers), supporting concepts (identified with Roman numerals), and historical developments (identified with letters) form the structure of each of the nine periods in this book. The College Board has also identified specific skills and themes that students must show proficiency in to earn high scores on the AP exam.

The skills and themes in the framework reflect the College Board's desire to align the AP curriculum and exam with history courses at the university level. The College Board has put more of an emphasis on developing the historical thinking skills that will deepen your understanding and appreciation of history, and less of an emphasis on memorizing hundreds of seemingly unrelated facts. Yes, you still must be familiar with a wide variety of developments in United States history. However, the exam focuses on your ability to use this historical content in analyzing and developing arguments, in making connections across time, in understanding the broader context of particular developments, in identifying major turning points, in assessing causation, and in challenging interpretations and developing new ones. The course and exam will push you toward greater intellectual growth and will help you think in new and more sophisticated ways about the world we live in.

USING THIS BOOK TO HELP YOU PREPARE FOR THE EXAM
使用本书帮您准备考试

This book has been written and revised with the explicit aim of helping you succeed on the AP United States History exam. In the following chapter you will find descriptions of the historical thinking skills and thematic learning objectives that are central to the exam. The book provides examples of how these skills and themes apply to the content of American history. These descriptions are followed by a detailed description of the exam. Each of the four sections of the exam are explored, along with tips, strategies, and approaches for achieving high scores on the exam.

Next, the book contains nine chapters of historical content corresponding to the breakdown of United States history in the College Board's concept outline. In addition to describing each of the points of the concept outline, these chapters provide you with a wealth of illustrative examples. This additional content is designed to illustrate and bring to life the points of the outline. Although the multiple-choice questions on the exam are based on the main points and developments of the concept outline, the written sections of the exam invite you to draw on the wealth of American history. This book has condensed the vast content of American history into the illustrative examples that are most relevant to the points in the concept outline and will be most useful to you as you prepare for the AP exam.

Each of the nine content chapters concludes with a "Subject to Debate" section. These sections are designed to call your attention to important debates about historical interpretation. Often, essays can be strengthened by a discussion of how historians have addressed a question. For example, the exam might ask, "To what degree was Reconstruction a turning point in regard to conditions for African Americans?" The student should discuss his or her view of the period, but could also discuss the nature of the historical debate over interpretations of the period. The student might write: "Historians have held dramatically different views of the period. Many southern historians in the late nineteenth and early twentieth centuries looked at the Reconstruction period as a bitter failure. They were dismissive of any attempts to extend basic rights to African Americans. However, since the Civil Rights era of the 1950s and 1960s, historians have reexamined the record of the period and acknowledged its successes as well as its shortcomings." In this way, the student is recognizing the contentious nature of historical interpretation. Students should be prepared not only to recognize these ongoing debates about the past, but also to participate in them.

Finally, the book contains two practice exams, with two additional exams contained on a CD-ROM (if you purchased a copy of this book with the accompanying CD-ROM). It is suggested that you time yourself as you take these exams. In this way, you will get used to the pacing required for the actual Advanced Placement exam. The exams are followed by explanations for the multiple-choice questions. Please consult these explanations if the material in the question is not clear to you.

Good luck as you prepare for the AP exam.

Historical Thinking Skills and Thematic Learning Objectives

历史思维技能 与主题学习目标 1

In the redesigned Advanced Placement United States History Curriculum Framework, the College Board identifies Historical Thinking Skills and Thematic Learning Objectives that shape the new curriculum framework and the new exam. These skills and themes are central to all the questions on the redesigned exam. The skills transcend American history and are important in the practice of history in any region or topic. The skills outlined by the College Board reflect the skills used by professional historians in their day-to-day work. The themes are windows to help students see continuities and enduring debates and challenges in United States history.

Below, these skills and themes are described and discussed; it is crucial to be familiar with them during the AP course and, of course, as you prepare for the AP exam.

HISTORICAL THINKING SKILLS　历史思维技能

In redesigning the Advanced Placement United States History curriculum and exam, the College Board is making explicit nine specific skills that are commonly used by those who participate in the field of historical study. These nine skills are grouped into four skill-type categories. The skills outlined by the College Board for the AP United States History exam are the same as those used on the AP World History exam, since its redesign as of the 2016–2017 academic year, and on the redesigned European History exam, which went into effect in 2015–2016. Therefore, familiarity with these skills can aid you in other AP history courses you may take. These skills are at the heart of the practice of history—in college, in graduate school, and in the field. At least one of these skills is built into every question on the Advanced Placement exam. Therefore, an understanding of these skills is essential to success on the AP exam.

Skill Type 1: Analyzing Historical Sources and Evidence
技能类型一：分析历史根源与史料
ANALYZING EVIDENCE: CONTENT AND SOURCING　分析史料：内容与来源

Evidence is a basic building block in the study of history. Students must be able to carefully describe and evaluate evidence about the past from a variety of different sources. Historical evidence can include written documents, artifacts, oral traditions, works of music and art, and other primary sources. This skill requires students to understand the content of a piece of evidence, but also to go beyond the content and investigate the purpose, point of view, argument, limitations, format, authorship, and intended audience of different sources. In addition, students must be able to make supportable inferences and draw reasonable conclusions from analyzing and evaluating historical evidence.

A sophisticated use of evidence is central to writing responses to the document-based question (DBQ). Documentary evidence is also central to the multiple-choice questions and the short-answer question. Students should be proficient in "reading" a variety of sources, including documents from the point of view of traditionally underrepresented groups and cultures. For example, in understanding the impact of Protestant missionary work in nineteenth-century Irish-Catholic immigrant neighborhoods, students might be asked to look at different types of evidence—from the point of view of the Protestant missionaries as well as from the point of view of the Irish immigrants. The exam might also invite students to analyze historical evidence beyond the written word; students might have to evaluate archeological evidence or geographical analyses. In addition, students should be prepared to examine popular culture in gaining an understanding of a period, such as the 1950s or 1960s. Finally, not all relevant evidence will be from an American point of view; in examining the role of the United States in the world, it is important to be able to understand evidence offered by non-American actors.

INTERPRETATION　解读

Students of history will confront a wide variety of interpretations of the past. This skill requires students to first analyze diverse historical interpretations. Second, students must evaluate how a historical interpretation is shaped, both by the perspective of the historian and by the time and context in which the historian wrote.

This skill encourages students to be familiar with the historiography of various historical topics, such as the historiography of American imperialism. If students examine the work of various historians of American imperialism, they will see that interpretations change over time and are influenced by the social setting in which the historians wrote. For instance, historians writing during the World War II era might see American interventions abroad in a positive, even heroic, light, while historians writing a generation later, during the aftermath of the Vietnam War, might see American interventions abroad as misguided impositions of American economic priorities on weaker nations. Of course, the era in which historians live and write is not the only factor that determines the content of their interpretation. Many factors shape historical interpretations. Historians writing during the same period can come up with widely divergent interpretations of events in the past.

As students come to understand the diversity of interpretations, they will learn to create their own interpretations of the past. When interpreting events students should be cognizant of "presentism"—a mode of historical analysis in which the writer introduces anachronistic contemporary perspectives into interpretations and depictions of the past.

Skill Type 2: Making Historical Connections　技能类型二：进行历史关联

COMPARISON　比较

Students should be able to look at two or more different historical developments or processes and note similarities and differences. They should also be able to compare different perspectives on a particular process or development. This skill is often presented in history class as the directive to "compare and contrast."

The Advanced Placement exam might ask students to compare developments or processes across time and place. The developments might be from different societies or from within the same society. A sophisticated analysis might compare different developments and processes across more than one variable—such as across time and across space. In any case, a successful comparison will demonstrate the ability to describe, compare, and evaluate different historical developments or processes.

There is a wide variety of comparison-based questions that students might encounter on the AP exam: How similar and how different were the antebellum reform movements and the Progressive–era reform movements? Or: How does the anti-imperialism movement of the early twentieth century compare to the antiwar movement of the 1960s and 1970s? Students might be asked to compare thematic developments in different time periods, such as how ideas and debates around gender in the 1920s compare to those in the 1950s.

CONTEXTUALIZATION 联系有关背景

This skill requires students to look at historical events and processes and to be able to evaluate how they connect with other things happening at the same time. The context of a particular event can be regional, national, or global. In addition, students should be able to explain and evaluate how a phenomenon, event, or process connects to similar processes across space and time.

Contextualization deepens our understanding of how and why particular events and developments occur. In trying to understand why, for example, the civil rights movement occurred in the 1950s and 1960s, it is important to go beyond the stories of the individuals and organizations involved. Although finding continuities with earlier movements of African-American resistance might lead to fruitful insights, it is also important to understand what is happening contemporaneously in the South, in the United States, and even in the world. To help understand the origins of the movement, students could look at the context of economic changes in the South in the post–World War II period or the experiences of African-American veterans. More broadly, an understanding of the origins of the movement might lead one to examine changes in the Democratic Party as it distanced itself from the ideology of its base in the white South. Students could also look at the context of America in the Cold War to understand why calls for civil rights found a receptive audience; many leaders found it difficult to accuse the Soviet Union of denying democracy to peoples within its orbit while the United States practiced Jim Crow segregation. These layers of context help students of history to more fully understand a particular event or phenomenon.

SYNTHESIS 整合

This final skill involves the ability to use all the other historical thinking skills in developing meaningful and compelling new understandings of the past. Students must be able to combine and make sense of a variety of types of evidence from primary and secondary sources. In addition, students should be able to apply understandings and insights about the past to other contexts and circumstances, including the present. The practice of creating syntheses of historical narratives is fraught with difficulties. Traditional narratives of the past often leave out certain perspectives. Students should examine, for instance, whether interpretations of industrialization in the Gilded Age include evidence from the perspectives of working people or women, or whether interpretations of the World War II home front include the perspectives of women or African Americans. As they attempt to create new syntheses, students should be prepared to challenge traditional narratives and ask what voices and perspectives might be missing.

Skill Type 3: Chronological Reasoning 技能类型三：按时间顺序进行推理

HISTORICAL CAUSATION 历史上的因果关系

This skill involves thinking about the causes and effects of historical events. It requires students to see that events in history do not happen in a vacuum—that they are connected to and influenced by previous events in history. Students should be able to distinguish and compare causes and effects and to analyze both long-term and short-term causes of events. Further, historical events generally have multiple causes—rarely is there a direct linear relationship between one event and another. Students, therefore, should be able to evaluate the relationship of multiple causes and effects.

This skill also requires students to assess *historical contingency*. Historical contingency presumes that each event in history depends on a whole array of events and circumstances—that each event is contingent on this universe of previous conditions. If one or more of the antecedent conditions were absent, perhaps a historical event would have occurred differently or not at all. Understanding historical causation requires students to interrogate and dissect the myths of inevitability that have shaped many people's thinking about the past. The events that led the United States to expand its borders, for example, were contingent on earlier events—expansion was not simply the "manifest destiny" of the American nation.

Thinking about historical contingency requires students to distinguish among coincidence, causation, and correlation in looking at different events. Perhaps two events happening around the same time are not related to each other in any significant way—they are merely coincidental. Perhaps one can be seen as the cause of the other. Or, perhaps, the two events are related, but one cannot clearly be seen as the cause of the other. Teasing out the relationship of events in history is key to historical interpretation and key to critiquing existing interpretations of causality.

PATTERNS OF CONTINUITY AND CHANGE OVER TIME 延续和变迁的模式

Recognizing patterns of continuity and change requires students to see patterns and trends in history and at the same time to see that not all events can fit neatly into existing patterns. Students of history can readily see change over time—that our predecessors functioned with different technologies, lived under different laws, participated in different cultural pursuits. This skill requires students to understand these changes over time, but also to see continuities as well. Students must be able to evaluate and analyze these patterns and to connect patterns of continuity and change with larger historical processes and themes.

Let us look at a specific occurrence in history to explore the skill of continuity and change. The implementation of restrictive quotas on immigrants in the 1920s can certainly be seen in light of continuities with earlier episodes of vocal nativist sentiment. One can explore thematic continuities between the anti-immigrant sentiment that led to the Emergency Quota Act of 1921 and the earlier "Know-Nothing" Party of the 1840s or the movement preceding the Chinese Exclusion Act of 1882. At the same time one can look at and evaluate the actions of prominent nativist writers and activists of the first decades of the twentieth century, such as Madison Grant. One can also look at the broader context of the Emergency Quota Act of 1921, including World War I and the "Red Scare" (see more on Contextualization, page 7). In this way, the student can also note discontinuities with earlier nativist movements. Finally, the student might be asked to weigh continuities and change over time and to cite evidence to best understand the implementation of immigration restrictions in the 1920s.

PERIODIZATION　时期划分

A sophisticated understanding of history involves the ability to organize historical events into discrete periods. Students should be able to explain the ways that historical events and processes can be organized into blocks of time, and they should also be able to evaluate competing strategies and models for organizing these historical periods. This process of periodization requires that historians evaluate historical events and processes and determine which ones are most significant—which ones can be considered turning points, signaling the beginning of a different direction in the development of the country. This allows historians to create an overall narrative to make sense of the flow of history. Of course, different historians can come to different conclusions about the important turning points in history and, consequently, about the periodization of American history.

With its redesigned Advanced Placement curriculum, the College Board has divided the history of North America and the United States into nine discrete periods. In order to familiarize students with this periodization, this book follows the breakdown of the College Board narrative by utilizing the same nine periods. However, students should be prepared to question and challenge any particular breakdown. For instance, many historical narratives, including the College Board's, mark the 1890s as the beginning of the period of U.S. imperialism. The arguments for such a beginning point are persuasive—the U.S. annexation of Hawaii and the Spanish-American War (both in 1898) open an era of U.S. military and imperial efforts throughout the Americas and Asia. However, one can see continuities between the earlier Mexican-American War (1846–1848)—a war that involved an expansion of American hegemony over another country—and the Spanish-American War. The beginning and ending periods are not, therefore, self-evident; they are determined by the judgment and the point of view of the historian.

Skill Type 4: Creating and Supporting a Historical Argument
技能类型四：提出历史观点并进行论证

HISTORICAL ARGUMENTATION　历史论证

A basic skill in the field of history is the construction of an argument. Students should be able to frame a question about the past, then develop an argument. A convincing argument contains a compelling and comprehensive thesis and draws on relevant evidence. In addition, students should understand that historians have been addressing major interpretative questions for generations. In constructing an argument, a student, therefore, is entering and interacting with a community of scholars.

This skill has three discrete parts. First, students should be able to analyze historical arguments. This requires students to explain how commonly accepted historical arguments are constructed from available evidence. Second, students should be able to construct compelling interpretations of the past through analyzing evidence. Finally, students should be able to construct persuasive arguments after evaluating and synthesizing conflicting historical evidence.

The skill of constructing a historical argument often operates in conjunction with course themes that involve students being able to transcend several periods of time and use other skills. For instance, in conjunction with the theme of migration and settlement, students might be asked to construct an argument about the reasons for territorial expansion in the decades before the Civil War. This requires students to use the skill of historical causation in conjunction with the skill of argumentation to construct a coherent thesis. Students will have to include evidence from different periods of time, developing a sophisticated analysis of a variety of factors. Evidence might be found in the following: the Puritan belief in establishing a "city set upon a hill"; political ideas about the superiority of republican ideals; the evolution of American ideas about American Indians; and the economic, technological, and demographic changes that affected America in the first half of the nineteenth century.

THEMATIC LEARNING OBJECTIVES　主题学习目标

The redesigned Advanced Placement curriculum highlights seven themes that are dealt with throughout the Advanced Placement course and that are reflected in the questions on the Advanced Placement exam. Within each of the seven themes are several specific thematic learning objectives. All the questions on the exam are designed to assess your proficiency in one or more of these thematic learning objectives.

Below is a list of the seven themes in the redesigned Advanced Placement curriculum, followed by a description of each theme and a description of the learning objectives for each theme. There are five to eight specific learning objectives for each theme. Familiarity with the thematic learning objectives is crucial for success on the Advanced Placement exam.

The seven themes are:

American and National Identity
Politics and Power
Work, Exchange, and Technology
Culture and Society
Migration and Settlement
Geography and the Environment
America and the World

American and National Identity　美国人与国家认同

This theme encourages students to analyze both the identity of the American people as a national entity as well as to explore the ways that various groups of individuals have sought to define their identities within the broader American culture. This theme requires students to understand that identity changes over time and that participants in these various groups themselves play an important role in reshaping and redefining identity. Groups have sought to define themselves along lines of gender, class, race, and ethnicity.

The concept of national identity involves topics such as citizenship, foreign policy, constitutionalism, and assimilation. In addition, this theme invites us to grapple with the idea of American exceptionalism. This idea stresses the unique character of the United States, based on democratic ideals and individual liberty. It sees the United States as unique in that it was formed around a creed, rather than around a shared history or common ethnicity. Others view these "American" qualities as manifestations of broader developments in global history.

The College Board has identified four specific thematic learning objectives related to American and national identity. Students should be able to:

1. Explain how ideas about democracy, freedom, and individualism have found expression in the development of cultural values, political institutions, and American society.
2. Explain how interpretations of the Constitution and debates over rights, liberties, and definitions of citizenship have affected American values, politics, and society.

3. Analyze how ideas about national identity have changed in response to U.S. involvement in international conflicts and the growth of the United States.

4. Analyze relationships among different regional, social, ethnic, and racial groups and explain how these groups' experiences contributed to national identity in the United States.

Politics and Power 政治与权力

This theme expands on the traditional theme of political history, which has been at the center of standard American history curricula for decades. The understanding of the theme of politics and power in the redesigned Advanced Placement curricula goes well beyond the traditional focus of elections, presidents, parties, and policies. This theme invites students to explore the interactions between power, on the one hand, and popular participation, on the other. Attempts have been made to limit participation by certain groups throughout American history; likewise, reform movements have attempted to expand avenues for participation in the political process. This theme also examines the debates about the proper role of government in society. Students should be familiar with changes in the relationship among the three branches of government and between the national government and the state governments. Finally, this theme invites students to explore the ongoing tensions between liberty and authority in American history.

There are three specific thematic learning objectives related to politics and power. Students should be able to:

1. Explain how and why political ideas, beliefs, institutions, party systems, and alignments have developed and changed.

2. Explain how popular movements, reform efforts, and activist groups have sought to change American society and institutions.

3. Explain how different beliefs about the federal government's role in American social and economic life have affected political debates and policies.

Work, Exchange, and Technology 就业、贸易与技术

This theme expands on the traditional theme in the American history curricula of "economic history." The theme looks broadly at the development of the American economy from the colonial period through the present. The College Board identifies agriculture, commerce, and manufacturing as the basis of the American economy.

There are three specific thematic learning objectives related to work, exchange, and technology. Students should be able to:

1. Explain how different labor systems developed in North America and the United States, and explain their effects on workers' lives and on American society.

2. Explain how patterns of exchange, markets, and private enterprise have developed, and analyze ways that governments have responded to economic issues.

3. Analyze how technological innovation has affected economic development and society.

Culture and Society 文化与社会

In traditional history courses, cultural history often occupies a marginal place, relegated to the random song or poem introduced as a precursor to the more "serious" history. Over the last generation, historians have worked to integrate cultural, religious, moral, and intellectual history into the mainstream of historical study. The College Board's redesigned curriculum framework recognizes this shift in the Ideas, Beliefs, and Culture theme. The theme explores the roles that ideas, beliefs, social mores, and creative expression have played in the ongoing development of the United States. Part of understanding the identity of the United States is understanding the development of aesthetic, religious, scientific, and philosophical principles. In addition, students should be prepared to examine how these principles have affected individual and group actions. Beliefs and value systems do not exist in isolation—they intersect with ideas about community and economics, and with movements for social change.

There are four specific thematic learning objectives related to culture and society. Students should be able to:

1. Explain how religious groups and ideas have affected American society and political life.
2. Explain how artistic, philosophical, and scientific ideas have developed and shaped American society and institutions.
3. Explain how ideas about women's rights and gender roles have affected society and politics.
4. Explain how different group identities, including racial, ethnic, class, and regional identities, have emerged and changed over time.

Migration and Settlement 移民与殖民

The theme of migration and settlement covers migration into the United States, out of the United States, and within the United States. Further, this theme recognizes the impact that the adjustments of borders have had on the people who did not migrate. Migrants bring with them ideas, beliefs, technologies, gender roles, and traditions. This theme explores the ways in which people adapt to new settings, and how these adaptations have shaped American society.

There are two specific thematic learning objectives related to migration and settlement. Students should be able to:

1. Explain the causes of migration to colonial North America and, later, to the United States, and analyze the effects of immigration on American society.
2. Analyze causes of internal migrations and patterns of settlement in what would become the United States, and explain how migration has affected American life.

Geography and the Environment 地理与环境

The inclusion of this theme represents a coming together of two traditionally discrete disciplines—history and geography. In the last decade, geographers have become increasingly interested in the historical patterns of the human imprint on the physical world, and historians have become increasingly interested in the degree to which the physical environment has shaped human patterns of behavior over time. The theme focuses on interactions. Specifically, how have interactions between the physical environment and various North American groups shaped their institutions and values? In addition, the theme invites students to examine decisions and policies related to the environment.

There is only one specific thematic learning objective related to geography and the environment. Students should be able to:

1. Explain how geographic and environmental factors have shaped the development of various communities, and analyze how competition for, and debates over, natural

resources have affected both interactions among different groups and the development of government policies.

America and the World   美国与世界

Traditional United States history curricula have certainly focused on the diplomatic and military history of the United States. Such traditional history courses have focused almost exclusively on the decisions made by leaders and on the impact of those decisions. The College Board, however, goes beyond this traditional approach by looking at the United States in a global context and looking at a wide range of factors that have shaped the role of the United States in the world. The primary focus is no longer on the diplomatic and military decisions of American political leaders. Rather, students are asked to put the United States in a global context. Students should be able to look at the broad array of factors and motives that have shaped specific decisions in relation to American military, economic, and diplomatic interventions abroad. This theme places foreign policy in the broader context of American social, economic, and political history.

There are two specific thematic learning objectives in relation to America in the world. Students should be able to:

1. Explain how cultural interactions, cooperation, competition, and conflict between empires, nations, and peoples have influenced political, economic, and social developments in North America.
2. Analyze the reasons for and results of U.S. diplomatic, economic, and military initiatives in North America and overseas.

Navigating the Redesigned Advanced Placement United States History Exam
掌握新编美国大学预修课程考试之美国历史考试

2

The AP United States History exam is focused explicitly on assessing students' achievement with the thematic learning objectives and on students' use of historical thinking skills. Familiarity with these themes and skills, discussed in the previous chapter, are essential to success on the exam.

The Advanced Placement exam has two sections; each section has two parts. Section I consists of the multiple-choice and the short-answer questions. Part A of Section I consists of 55 multiple-choice questions. Students have 55 minutes to complete this part; it accounts for 40 percent of the total exam grade. Part B consists of four short-answer questions. Students have 50 minutes for this part; it accounts for 20 percent of the total exam grade. Section II consists of the free-response section. Part A of Section II consists of a document-based question. Students have 55 minutes for this part; it accounts for 25 percent of the total exam grade. Part B requires students to complete one of two long-essay questions. Students have 35 minutes for this part; it accounts for 15 percent of the total exam grade. The exam is 3 hours and 15 minutes long; students have 105 minutes for the multiple-choice and short-answer section and 90 minutes for the free-response section.

In terms of content, the questions focus on the points in the concept outline in the College Board's AP United States History Curriculum Framework. These points are described in this book within each of the nine chronological periods. There are two or three numbered "Key Concepts" in each period. Under each key concept, you will find several supporting concepts, identified with Roman numerals. Finally, under each supporting concept, you will find several historical developments, identified with capital letters. Multiple-choice questions on the AP exam are based on the points in the concept outline. However, the written portions of the exam invite you to introduce illustrative examples from history to add depth and insight to your responses. As you respond to the short-answer and essay questions, you have the flexibility to introduce illustrative examples that are appropriate and compelling.

The approximate breakdown of time periods for exam questions is as follows: About 5 percent of the exam deals with Period 1: 1491–1607. This represents an increased focus on the period before the first English settlements in North America. Approximately 45 percent of the exam focuses on the four periods between the founding of the Jamestown colony (1607) and the period of the Civil War and Reconstruction. An additional 45 percent focuses of the three periods beginning with the economic developments following the Civil War and ending in 1980. The final 5 percent focuses on the period from 1980 to the present; again this represents an increased focus on the recent past. Note: No long-essay question or document-based essay question focuses exclusively on the first period (1491–1607) or the last period (1980–Present). Essays, however, could span two or more periods and require students to address events or documents from the first or last period in conjunction with other periods.

MULTIPLE-CHOICE QUESTIONS 选择题

Section I, Part A of the exam consists of 55 multiple-choice questions. You have 55 minutes to complete this part of the exam; 40 percent of your grade on the exam is based on this section. The multiple-choice questions focus on your ability to reason about different types of historical evidence. In a departure from the previous format of the exam, each question refers to a primary source, secondary source, a historian's argument, or a historical problem. Questions are organized in sets of 2–5, with each set referring to specific stimulus material. Each multiple-choice question has four choices.

All of the multiple-choice questions require you to show proficiency in one or more of the thematic learning objectives and require you to apply one or more of the historical thinking skills. The questions require you to reason about the stimulus material. The stimulus material could be graphs or charts, maps, paintings or political cartoons, historical interpretations, letters or diary entries—virtually any primary or secondary source. The multiple-choice questions ask you to draw on the stimulus material as well as on your knowledge of the concepts and historical developments in the College Board's curriculum framework. As indicated above, these concepts and developments are all described in this book. Events and topics beyond the key concepts, supporting concepts, and historical developments (the numbered and lettered entries in this book) do not appear in multiple-choice questions unless they are introduced and explained in the stimulus material.

Bring a watch with you and try to work at a steady pace. You have about a minute for each question. This means that you cannot get hung up on difficult questions. If the answer does not immediately come to you, make a notation in the test book and come back to it if you have time. Make sure you leave yourself time to get to all the questions.

Sample Multiple-Choice Questions 选择题示例

The following is a sample set of multiple-choice questions. In this case, students are presented with a political cartoon and then four questions related to the cartoon.

Questions 1–4 refer to the following quotation: 根据下列引用的材料，回答第1—4题

—Thomas Nast, "This Is a White Man's Government,"
Harper's Weekly, September 5, 1868

1. The political cartoon shown above makes the point that

   (A) northern capitalists benefit as much from the institution of slavery as southern plantation owners do.
   (B) Reconstruction was brought to an unfortunate end by a coalition of forces in the North and South.
   (C) African Americans were incapable of effectively participating in the political process.
   (D) nativist politicians were unfairly presenting Irish Americans as ignorant and brutish.

2. Which of the following would most likely support the perspective of the cartoon?

   (A) Radical Republicans.
   (B) Southern Democrats.
   (C) Working-class Irish immigrants.
   (D) Northern opponents of the Civil War.

3. The sentiments expressed in the cartoon most directly contributed to which of the following?

    (A) The compromise ending Reconstruction.

    (B) The rise of the Ku Klux Klan in the South.

    (C) The enactment of segregation laws in Southern states.

    (D) The passage of the Fifteenth Amendment.

4. The ideas expressed in the cartoon most directly reflect which of the following continuities in United States history?

    (A) Debates about immigration policy.

    (B) Debates about the regulation of big business.

    (C) Debates about access to voting rights.

    (D) Debates about nullification and secession.

Answers and Explanations to Multiple-Choice Questions
选择题的答案与解析

1. **(B)** This evocative political cartoon requires you to read a whole host of clues before you can understand its meaning. The man on the left is an Irish immigrant; the "5 Points" on his hat refers to the Irish neighborhood in New York City. Note his almost ape-like face. This was typical of representations of Irish immigrants as drawn by nativist cartoonists. The man in the middle has "C.S.A." on his belt buckle: Confederate States of America. His knife says "Lost Cause," an allusion to the southern nostalgia for the noble fight the South put up in the Civil War. The man on the right has "Capital" written on the object he is holding; he is a northern capitalist, ready to use money to purchase votes. These three sinister forces are working together in the Democratic Party to deny African Americans the right to vote. Note the ballot box contents strewn on the ground in the lower right hand corner of the cartoon. Nast intended the cartoon as a warning about the dangers of a Democratic victory in the upcoming presidential election. The cartoon does not allude to the slave system or cotton production (A). The cartoon is drawn sympathetically toward African Americans; there is no allusion that the man on the ground is ignorant or debased (C). It is true that Irish immigrants were presented as ignorant, but the cartoonist is not critiquing that. In fact, he himself is presenting an Irish immigrant in an unflattering manner (D).

2. **(A)** The sentiment in the cartoon is that of the Radical Republicans. In the years after the Civil War, they grew alarmed at the assertiveness of the old plantation-owning class and the supporters of secession. This cartoon, published in the weeks before the 1868 presidential election, was intended to warn voters of the dangers of a victory by the Democratic Party. The cartoon depicts working-class Irish immigrants (C) in a stereotypically brutish manner; they would be unlikely to support the overall point of the cartoon. The cartoon is meant as a critique of the Democratic Party's agenda in the South (B); they would certainly not support the sentiment of the cartoon. Northern opponents of the Civil War (D), a war that undid the system of slavery, were unlikely to embrace the cause of suffrage for African Americans.

3. **(D)** The sentiments expressed in the cartoon most directly contributed to the passage of the Fifteenth Amendment. The Fifteenth Amendment states that the vote may not be denied to someone based on "race, color, or previous condition of servitude." Voting

rights for African Americans was a key element of the Reconstruction program of the radical Republicans. The cartoon shows empathy for African Americans, depicted being pushed to the ground and having the vote denied them. The other choices all reflect the point of view of white southern opponents of Reconstruction. The compromise in 1877 that allowed Republican Rutherford B. Hayes to assume the White House also led to the end of Reconstruction, allowing Democrats in the South to reestablish power (A). One factor in pushing African Americans from meaningful participation in the political process was the rise of the Ku Klux Klan in the South (B). After Reconstruction southern states enacted segregation laws (C), further solidifying the second-class status of African Americans.

4. **(C)** The ideas expressed in the cartoon most directly reflect debates about access to voting. The Constitution left voting procedures up to each state. This lack of a federal mandate on voting opened the door to an ongoing debate about equal access to the ballot box. Initially, many states had property qualifications for voting. By the 1820s and 1830s, however, most states had eliminated these qualifications. Throughout the 1800s, most states had not extended the right to vote to women. After debates on the state level, the U.S. Constitution was amended in 1919 to extend the right to vote to women. Access to voting for African Americans has been an ongoing source of debate and struggle. Though the Fifteenth Amendment barred racial discrimination in voting, southern states devised strategies to suppress the African American vote. The debates about access to voting rights led to passage of the Voting Rights Act in 1965, removing many impediments to African Americans voting.

SHORT-ANSWER QUESTIONS　简答题

Section I, Part B of the exam consists of four short-answer questions. You have 50 minutes to complete this part of the exam; 20 percent of your grade on the exam is based on this section. Each short-answer question has three parts, with each part given a grade of 0–1. Therefore, the maximum grade for each of the short-answer questions is 3. At least two of the questions have some degree of internal choice, so you will be able to focus on what you know best. Each question focuses on one or more of the thematic learning objectives. These questions include some sort of source material. You are required to apply one or more historical-thinking skills in responding to the source material—primary documents, historians' arguments, secondary sources, or general propositions about United States history. In each of these questions you are asked to identify and analyze historical evidence relevant to the task at hand. The following is an example of a short-answer question:

Question 1 is based on the following two passages:　根据以下两个段落，回答第1题

"I shall show how wrong they are in fact, with great harm to their own souls. For the Creator of every being has not so despised these peoples of the New World that he willed them to lack reason and made them like brute animals, so that they should be called barbarians, savages, wild men, and brutes, as they [Sepúlveda et al.] think or imagine. On the contrary, they [the Indians] are of such gentleness and decency that they are, more than the other nations of the entire world, supremely fitted and prepared to abandon the worship of idols and to accept, province by province and people by people, the word of God and the preaching of the truth. . . .

"Long before they had heard the word Spaniard they had properly organized states, wisely ordered by excellent laws, religion, and custom. They cultivated friendship and, bound together in common fellowship, lived in populous cities in which they wisely administered the affairs of both peace and war justly and equitably, truly governed by laws that at very many points surpass ours, and could have won the admiration of the sages of Athens."

—Bartolomé de Las Casas, *A Short Account of the Destruction of the Indies*, 1542

"War against these barbarians can be justified not only on the basis of their paganism but even more so because of their abominable licentiousness, their prodigious sacrifice of human victims, the extreme harm that they inflicted on innocent persons, their horrible banquets of human flesh, and the impious cult of their idols. Since the evangelical law of the New Testament is more perfect and more gentle than the Mosaic law of the Old Testament (for the latter was a law of fear and the former is a law of grace, gentleness, and clemency), so also [since the birth of Christ] wars are now waged with more mercy and clemency. Their purpose is not so much to punish as to correct evils. What is more appropriate and beneficial for these barbarians than to become subject to the rule of those whose wisdom, virtue, and religion have converted them from barbarians into civilized men (insofar as they are capable of becoming so), from being torpid and licentious to becoming upright and moral, from being impious servants of the Devil to becoming believers in the true God? They have already begun to receive the Christian religion, thanks to the prudent diligence of the Emperor Charles, an excellent and religious prince. They have already been provided with teachers learned in both the sciences and letters and, what is more important, with teachers of religion and good customs."

—Juan Ginés de Sepúlveda, *The Second Democrates*, 1547

1. Use the two passages above and your knowledge of U.S. history to answer parts A, B, and C.
    A. Explain how Bartolomé de Las Casas and Juan Ginés de Sepúlveda disagree with each other?
    B. Provide evidence from history to explain the context of the debate between Bartolomé de Las Casas and Juan Ginés de Sepúlveda.
    C. Explain the impact the debate had on Spanish policies in the Americas.

Explanation and Discussion of Sample Short-Answer Question
简答题示例的分析与讨论

This question is based on two primary sources from the period of the Spanish conquest and settlement of areas of the Americas in the 1500s. The redesigned AP curriculum puts additional emphasis on the period of European colonization of the New World before the settlement of Jamestown by the English, so be prepared to answer questions relevant to the first period of the outline of United States history: 1491–1607. This question revolves around a debate that occurred in the 1500s, primarily by the two men cited in the question, and called the Valladolid debate (named after the city in which the two men debated face to face).

Part A of the question requires students to note that the debate centers on the Spanish treatment of native peoples in the New World and, more broadly, on the colonization of the Americas. The Dominican Friar Bartolomé de Las Casas argued that the Indians were free people in the natural order and deserved the same treatment as others. He argued that before the arrival of the Spaniards, "they had properly organized states, wisely ordered by excellent laws, religion, and custom." Opposing him was fellow Dominican Juan Ginés de Sepúlveda, who insisted that because of their "barbarian" nature the Indians should be punished and therefore reduced to slavery. Such treatment, he argued, was in keeping with Catholic theology and natural law. He asserted that they were less than human and that they required Spanish masters in order to become civilized. Las Casas maintained that they were fully human and that forcefully subjugating them was unjustifiable.

Part B asks students to provide evidence to explain the context of this debate. The debate occurred in the context of Spanish conquest and settlement of the New World. More specifically, the context of Spanish treatment of the native peoples of the Americas must be discussed. Evidence could include a discussion of the forced conversion of native peoples to Christianity, the importance of the extraction of gold and silver, and the harsh details of the *encomienda* system. Part C asks students to explain the impact of the debate. Students should discuss how the debate led to limited changes. King Charles V of Spain created the position of Protector of the Indians to oversee the treatment of native peoples and appointed Las Casas to the position. There were limits placed on the *encomienda* system, with the *repartimiento* system essentially replacing actual slavery with slave-like labor forced on the Indians. The change, however limited, had one major effect on subsequent history: it led to a growth of the African slave trade, as African slavery gradually replaced Indian slavery.

DOCUMENT-BASED QUESTION 材料分析题

Section II, Part A of the redesigned AP exam consists of one document-based question. You will have 55 minutes to complete this part of the exam; 25 percent of your grade on the exam comes from the document-based question. The DBQ evaluates your ability to assess, analyze, and synthesize a wide variety of types of historical evidence and to construct a coherent essay. Your response to the document-based question is judged on your ability to formulate a thesis and support it with relevant evidence. The documents can include written materials, charts, graphs, cartoons, and pictures. The documents are carefully chosen to allow you to explore the interactions and complexities of the topic at hand.

The document-based question centers on a particular historical thinking skill. Each document-based question will focus on one of the following historical thinking skills: historical causation, patterns of continuity and change over time, comparison, interpretation, or periodization. In addition, every document-based question assesses four additional thinking skills: argumentation, analyzing evidence, contextualization, and synthesis.

HISTORICAL NEUTRALITY 历史中立

Try to avoid using the words "us," "our," and "we," when discussing the United States. Refer to the United States in a neutral manner. Strong essays should be intellectually engaged, but not emotionally invested in a particular outcome or position. Such personal investment tends to undermine one's argument.

INTEGRATE THE DOCUMENTS INTO YOUR RESPONSE　结合材料回答问题

As you develop your skill in constructing responses to the document-based question, it is important to work on integrating documents into your overall response. You are on the wrong track when the paragraphs of your essay begin as follows: "According to Document 1 . . ." or "As Document 3 indicates . . ." This has the makings of a very low-scoring essay—one that merely describes the content of the documents rather than illustrating the targeted historical thinking skill. Try to begin paragraphs with *your* ideas. Then, within the paragraph, mention the appropriate document or documents that illustrate that paragraph's idea. For example, in an essay comparing the temperance movement with the abolitionist movement in the pre–Civil War period, you might have a paragraph that leads with the following sentence: "Both the temperance movement and the abolitionist movement drew on middle-class Protestant fears of licentiousness; both stressed the importance of individuals possessing self-control." Within the paragraph, you might discuss an image of an out-of-control slave owner violently whipping a defenseless slave, as well as a newspaper article describing an out-of-control drunkard. By contrast, a weak lead to a paragraph in this essay might read like the following: "Document 3 shows a slave owner whipping a slave. This image made people oppose slavery. . . ." The paragraph is not addressing the historical learning skill of comparison.

NOTICE CONNECTIONS BETWEEN DOCUMENTS　注意不同材料的关联之处

Often in document-based questions, two or more documents "talk to one another." That is, one responds to something in another one. One document might amplify an earlier one or, more likely, offer a different perspective. In a document-based question on southern and northern home-front issues during the Civil War, one document might defend the New York City draft riot as a justified response to the "$300 rule" in the draft law; the next document might condemn the rioters as misguided and racist. Your job is to let the documents communicate with each other. Bring out the tensions implicit in these two documents. Begin a paragraph with these tensions: "New Yorkers had markedly different reactions to the draft riot. . . ." Do your best to make sense of the tensions between documents; do not simply avoid the documents that do not immediately conform to your thesis.

AUDIENCE, PURPOSE, CONTEXT, AND POINT OF VIEW　读者、目的、历史背景与观点

Higher scoring essays need to go beyond simply analyzing a source and fitting it into an argument (see rubric). Try to situate a document in its time and place, noting its intended audience, purpose, historical context, and the author's point of view. Do not take every document at face value. Note the origins and dates of particular documents as you use them, and take that knowledge into consideration. A report about the corruption and inefficiencies of Reconstruction governments in the South should be questioned if it was written by a former Confederate official. His purpose might be to discredit Reconstruction governments rather than merely describe their functioning.

OUTSIDE EVIDENCE　外部证据

A strong response must have significant outside evidence. You cannot get the highest score on a document-based question by only citing evidence in the documents themselves (see rubric). You must introduce relevant outside information and evidence. A document-based question looking at changes in the civil rights movement from the 1950s to the 1960s might provide you with a reading from a Black Panther platform in 1967, illustrating a more militant direction for the movement in the 1960s. Outside evidence could include a speech by Malcolm X or by Stokely Carmichael.

Scoring Rubric for the Document-Based Question 材料分析题的评分规则

The maximum score you can receive for the document-based question is 7. This grade is based on the following rubric:

Thesis and Argument Development (Skill assessed: Argumentation): 0–2 points.
论点及论证发展（技能评估：论证），0—2分

To earn 1 point, the thesis of your essay will be assessed on your proficiency in argumentation. You must develop a historically defensible claim around a specific historical thinking skill, such as historic causation or continuity and change over time. Your thesis must directly address all parts of the question. The thesis must consist of one or more sentences located in one place, either in the introduction or the conclusion. You must do more than restate the question.

To earn a second point, you must develop and support a cohesive argument that recognizes and accounts for historical complexity by explicitly illustrating relationships among historical evidence such as contradiction, corroboration, and/or qualification.

Document Analysis (Skills assessed: Analyzing Evidence: Content and Sourcing, and Argumentation): 0–2 points.
材料分析（技能评估：分析史料的内容与来源，并进行论证），0—2分

To earn 1 point, students must utilize the content of at least six of the seven documents to support the stated thesis or a relevant argument. To earn the second point in this section of the rubric, you must, in addition to meeting the criteria for 1 point, also offer plausible analysis of at least one of the following for at least four of the documents: intended audience, purpose, historical context, and/or the author's point of view.

Using Evidence Beyond the Documents (Skills assessed: Contextualization and Argumentation): 0–2 points.
使用给定材料之外的材料（技能评估：联系有关背景进行论证），0—2分

Contextualization: This element of the rubric assesses your ability to place your essay in a broader context. To earn the first point for this element you must accurately and explicitly connect historical phenomena that are relevant to the argument to broader historical events and/or processes. Contextualization requires using knowledge not found in the documents. The element requires an explanation, consisting of multiple sentences or a full paragraph—not simply a word or a phrase.

Evidence beyond the documents: To earn the second point for this element, you must provide an example or additional piece of evidence beyond those found in the documents to support or qualify the argument. Again, this must consist of more than a word or phrase; you must explain how the outside evidence you have chosen supports or qualifies your argument.

Synthesis (Skill assessed: Synthesis): 0–1 point. 整合（技能评估：信息整合），0—1分

To earn 1 point in this final element of the rubric, you must tie up the elements of your essay and then go beyond the immediate question at hand and connect your argument with one of the following: a development in a different historical period, situation, era or geographical area; or a course theme and/or approach to history that is not the focus of the essay (such as political, economic, social, cultural, or intellectual history).

The following is an example of a document-based question.

1. Compare the mobilization efforts by local, state, and federal authorities in the United States during World War I with mobilization efforts during World War II.

DOCUMENT 1

Source: Announcement, The War Industries Board, June 6, 1918, reprinted in *The New York Times*, June 7, 1918.

Be it Resolved, by the War Industries Board, That the following agreement reached as a result of several conferences between a committee of the board and the American Iron and Steel Institute, be and the same is hereby ratified, confirmed, and approved, to become effective at once:

Whereas, A careful study of the sources of supply in connection with the present and rapidly increasing direct and indirect war requirements for iron and steel products has convinced the War Industries Board of the necessity for (1) a strict conservation of the available supply of iron and steel products, on the one hand, and (2) the expansion of existing sources and the development of new sources of supply of iron and steel products, on the other hand; and

Whereas, the producers iron and of iron and steel products in the main concur in this conclusion reached by the said board, and have expressed their willingness to cooperate wholeheartedly with the said board. . . .

Source: Poster, United States Food Administration, L. N. Britton (artist), 1917.

Source: "Another Tar and Feather Party Is Staged," *Ashland* [Wisconsin] *Daily Press*, April 11, 1918.

Adolph Anton, residing at 1100 Sixth Avenue West, was taken from his home at about nine o'clock last night by a party of five or six who came to the house in an auto, carried to a spot on the Beaser Avenue road known as the Chequamego Ice Company's farm, and given a coat of tar and feathers for alleged pro-German sentiments. He was then released and told to beat it for home. Stark naked and covered with a profuse coat of tar and feathers, he walked the distance to his home, about a mile.

Source: Portion of the amendment to Section 3 of the Espionage Act of June 15, 1917, United States, *Statutes at Large*, Washington, DC, 1918.

SECTION 3. Whoever, when the United States is at war, shall willfully make or convey false reports or false statements with intent to interfere with the operation or success of the military or naval forces of the United States, or to promote the success of its enemies, or shall willfully make or convey false reports, or false statements, . . . or incite insubordination, disloyalty, mutiny, or refusal of duty, in the military or naval forces of the United States, or shall willfully obstruct . . . the recruiting or enlistment service of the United States, or . . . shall willfully utter, print, write, or publish any disloyal, profane, scurrilous, or abusive language about the form of government of the United States, or the Constitution of the United States, or the military or naval forces of the United States . . . or shall willfully display the flag of any foreign enemy, or shall willfully . . . urge, incite, or advocate any curtailment of production . . . or advocate, teach, defend, or suggest the doing of any of the acts or things in this section enumerated and whoever shall by word or act support or favor the cause of any country with which the United States is at war or by word or act oppose the cause of the United States therein, shall be punished by a fine of not more than $10,000 or imprisonment for not more than twenty years, or both. . . .

Source: Printing Office for the Office of Price Administration, 1943.

Source: "We Can Do It!" by J. Howard Miller, produced by Westinghouse for the War Production Board, 1943.

Source: Al Waxman, editor of the *Eastside Journal*, June 1943.

At Twelfth and Central I came upon a scene that will long live in my memory. Police were swinging clubs and servicemen were fighting with civilians. Wholesale arrests were being made by the officers.

Four boys came out of a pool hall. They were wearing the zoot-suits that have become the symbol of a fighting flag. Police ordered them into arrest cars. One refused. He asked: "Why am I being arrested?" The police officer answered with three swift blows of the night-stick across the boy's head and he went down. As he sprawled, he was kicked in the face. Police had difficulty loading his body into the vehicle because he was one-legged and wore a wooden limb. Maybe the officer didn't know he was attacking a cripple.

At the next corner a Mexican mother cried out, "Don't take my boy, he did nothing. He's only fifteen years old. Don't take him." She was struck across the jaw with a night-stick and almost dropped the two and a half year old baby that was clinging in her arms. . . .

Rushing back to the east side to make sure that things were quiet here, I came upon a band of servicemen making a systematic tour of East First Street. They had just come out of a cocktail bar where four men were nursing bruises. Three autos loaded with Los Angeles policemen were on the scene but the soldiers were not molested. Further down the street the men stopped a streetcar, forcing the motorman to open the door and proceeded to inspect the clothing of the male passengers. "We're looking for zoot-suits to burn," they shouted. Again the police did not interfere. . . . Half a block away . . . I pleaded with the men of the local police substation to put a stop to these activities. "It is a matter for the military police," they said.

Answering the Document-Based Question 回答材料分析题

This document-based question asks you to compare the mobilization efforts of World War I with those of World War II. As you look at the documents, several themes should emerge. One theme that quickly emerges is that in both World War I and World War II, the role of the federal government grew. We can see this in the conservation efforts in both wars. In World War I, we see this in Document 2, a poster from the Food Administration urging a change in diet to prevent shortages of certain commodities (meat, sugar, and fat) for the war effort. In World War II, we see a similar effort at conservation in Document 5; commuters are urged to carpool so as to save fuel for the war effort.

In addition to conservation, we can see that in both wars authorities put a good deal of effort into filling defense-industry plants with workers. For World War I, we see this implied in Document 1—the efforts of the War Industries Board. For World War II, we see this effort in Document 6, urging women to take industrial jobs, assuring them that they could handle such jobs. The World War II efforts to find employees are alluded to in Document 7 as well. This document describes one of the "zoot suit riots" that occurred in Los Angeles and elsewhere during the war. These anti-Mexican riots occurred after the federal government instituted the Bracero program, allowing thousands of Mexicans to legally enter the United States as temporary guest workers.

Another theme that emerges in the comparison is the treatment of different ethnicities. In World War I, we see violence against German Americans in Document 3. This document should remind students of the rise in xenophobia and anti-German violence during World War I. In World War II, in addition to the violence against Mexicans in the "zoot suit riots" (Document 7), we can go beyond the documents and cite discrimination against Japanese Americans with their relocation to the interior of the United States. In both wars, ugly expressions of ethnic hatred were unleashed by the war.

The final area of comparison to examine is the limits placed on civil liberties in both conflicts. In World War I, the government passed the Espionage and Sedition Acts, limiting free-speech rights. These acts are referenced in Document 4, an excerpt from the Espionage Act. During World War II, the government limited the civil liberties of the entire population of West Coast Japanese Americans by issuing Executive Order 9066, calling for the internment of people of Japanese descent in a series of camps. In both wars, the government expanded its power to limit civil liberties. Students can judge the merits of each action, noting similarities and differences.

A successful essay would earn two points for developing a strong thesis and then developing a cohesive argument in ways that recognize and account for historical complexity. In this case, argument development could include looking at differences between the government's response in the two wars, noting contradictions, corroborations, and/or qualifications. The essay can earn two additional points for document analysis. For the first of these two points, the essay must successfully use at least six of the documents. For the second point, the essay must go beyond the content of the documents and examine authorship, audience, and context for at least four of the documents. For instance, the essay could inquire about the authorship and audience of the poster encouraging women to work in factories during World War II (Document 6.) The fact that the document was created by the government might show that the positive depiction of the female factory worker might not be fully accurate. The poster is an advertisement not a description. Many women, in fact, experienced discrimination and hostility at the workplace.

Two additional points can be earned by using evidence *beyond* the documents. For the first point, the student must put the government mobilization efforts into a wider context. For instance, this essay could refer to the broader efforts to expand the role of the government. In the case of World War I, this would involve discussing the efforts of the progressive movement; in the case of World War II, this would involve invoking the ideology of the New Deal. The seventh, and final, point of the essay can be earned by extending the argument—to either a different period, situation, or geographic area, or to a different approach to history (such as political, economic, social, cultural, or intellectual history). This skill of synthesizing your argument could involve extending the argument to other national crises in American history, such as the Civil War or the Great Depression and drawing conclusions about the growth of federal power during times of crisis.

LONG-ESSAY QUESTIONS　论述题

Section II, Part B of the exam gives students a choice between two comparable long-essay questions. You will have 35 minutes to complete this part of the exam; 15 percent of your grade on the exam is based on the long essay. Since you have a choice in deciding which of the two questions to write about, you have the opportunity to demonstrate what you know best. The long essay is assessed on your use of specific historical thinking skills in explaining and analyzing important issues as defined by the thematic learning objectives. The long essay requires you to develop a thesis or argument and to support your thesis with an analysis of specific and relevant historical evidence.

Scoring Rubric for the Long-Essay Question　论述题的评分规则

The maximum score you can receive for the long-essay question is 6. This grade is based on the following rubric:

Thesis (Skills assessed: Argumentation and targeted skill): 0–1 points.
论点（技能评估：论证及目标技能），0—1分
To receive the 1 point for this element of the rubric, you must state a thesis that directly addresses all parts of the question. The thesis must do more than restate the question. Your thesis must address the thinking skill specified in the question.

Argument Development: Using the Targeted Historical Thinking Skill (Skills assessed: Argumentation and targeted skill): 0–2 points.
论证发展：使用目标历史思维技能（技能评估：论证及目标技能），0—2分
This element of the rubric is determined by the specific historical thinking skill cited in the question. These skills can include Continuity and Change Over Time, Comparison, Causation, or Periodization.

For Continuity and Change Over Time questions, you will receive 1 point for describing historical continuity *and* change over time. For the additional point you must also analyze specific examples that illustrate continuity *and* change over time.

For Comparison questions, you will receive 1 point for describing similarities *and* differences among historical developments. For the additional point, you must also provide examples and do one of the following, depending on the prompt: Either analyze the reasons for the similarities *and/or* differences among historical developments, or analyze the relative importance of the historical developments.

For Causation questions, you will receive 1 point for describing causes *and/or* effects of a historical development. For the additional point, you must also analyze specific examples that illustrate causes *and/or* effects of a historical development.

For Periodization questions, you will receive 1 point for describing the ways in which the historical development discussed in the prompt was different from *or* similar to developments that came before *and/or* afterward. For the additional point, you must analyze the extent to which the historical development discussed in the prompt was different from *and* similar to developments that came before *and/or* afterward, providing specific examples to illustrate the analysis.

Argument Development: Using Evidence (Skills assessed: Argumentation): 0–2 points.
论证发展：使用论据（技能评估：论证），0—2分
To receive 1 point, you must support your thesis with specific evidence. To receive 2 points, you must also clearly and consistently state how the evidence you have introduced supports the thesis or argument and establishes clear linkages between the evidence and the thesis or argument.

Synthesis (Skills assessed: Synthesis): 0–1 points. 整合（技能评估：信息整合），0—1分

To earn 1 point, this final element of the rubric requires you to tie up the elements of your essay and then go beyond the immediate question at hand and connect your argument with one of the following: a development in a different historical period, situation, era, or geographical area; or a course theme and/or approach to history that is not the focus of the essay (such as political, economic, social, cultural, or intellectual history).

The following are examples of long-essay questions:

Questions 1–2: These questions ask students to analyze patterns of continuity and change from the late 1800s to the 1930s. The first question focuses on organized labor; the second question focuses on the relationship between major corporations and government. Students must develop an argument and support that argument with appropriate evidence. *Historical Thinking Skill: Patterns of Continuity and Change over Time.*

1. Analyze continuities and changes in workplace conflicts between organized labor and management in the United States from the 1880s to the 1930s?

2. Analyze continuities and changes in the relationship between major corporations and the federal government from the 1880s to the 1930s?

Explanation and Discussion of Sample Long-essay Question
论述题示例的分析与讨论

Both questions invite students to examine continuity and change over time from the Gilded Age of the late 1800s to the era of the Great Depression and New Deal of the 1930s. In both cases, students are invited to describe the changes and continuities that occurred and to give examples to illustrate those changes and continuities. Also, in both cases, strong essays should place these historic changes in the context of the times.

In Question 1, a key change to note in terms of workplace conflicts, when looking at the Gilded Age and the age of the New Deal, is that organized labor was far stronger during the New Deal. Students could compare the defeats of organized labor in the Homestead Strike and the Pullman Strike in the 1890s with the remarkable growth of the Congress of Industrial Organizations (CIO) in the 1930s. A major factor in understanding the change involves government policies toward unions. In the Gilded Age, government was generally on the side of management. Students could cite ample evidence for this—the use of the Sherman Antitrust Act against unions, the Supreme Court decision on the Pullman Strike and Eugene V. Debs, the use of federal troops. During the New Deal era, President Franklin Roosevelt pushed for legislation that recognized the right of organized labor to collective bargaining. Students could cite section 7A of the National Industrial Recovery Act (NIRA) or the Wagner Act. Students must also look at continuities between the two periods. These could include hostility in the mainstream press, similarities in the work process, and ethnic divisions. These continuities shaped the workplace conflicts of both periods in similar ways.

A thesis statement must account for both continuities and changes over time. The following is an example of a thesis that would earn two points: "In both the 1890s and the 1930s organized workers faced similar challenges in pressing for improvements—a weak economy, competition for jobs, and racial and ethnic divisions. These factors made success difficult. However, organized labor was able to achieve some key victories in the later period because of a shift in government policies, as the pro-business ideology of the 'robber baron' era gave way to the demand-side ideology of the New Deal era."

In Question #2, students again must note changes and continuities from the Gilded Age to the era of the New Deal. In terms of changes, we can contrast the laissez-faire approach of the government during the first period with the interventionist approach of the New Deal. In the early period, the government generally let major corporations have a free hand in conducting business. Laissez-faire ideology was supported by Social Darwinism, by the sociological writings of William Graham Sumner, and even by the dime novels of Horatio Alger, Jr. Both the Sherman Antitrust Act and the Interstate Commerce Commission were circumvented by big business. By the 1930s, the ideology of laissez-faire no longer resonated as it had a generation earlier. The realities of the Great Depression and the pragmatism of Franklin Roosevelt made possible a far more active federal government when it came to major corporations. Students could cite the Securities and Exchange Act, the National Industrial Recovery Act, or the Glass-Steagall Act in illustrating this shift. In terms of continuities, students could note that the Supreme Court in both periods sided with corporations. In both periods, the court made regulation of business and industry difficult. In the first period, the decision in *Santa Clara County v. Union Pacific Railway* established the concept of "corporate personhood" and shielded corporations from onerous regulation. In the later period, the decision in *A.L.A. Schechter Poultry Corp. v. United States*, the court declared the National Industrial Recovery Act unconstitutional, making regulation of industry more difficult. Now, let us put these ideas together to develop a thesis statement: "The administration of President Franklin Roosevelt, abandoned the laissez-faire, pro-business ideology of the Gilded Age and implemented a sweeping series of reforms that dramatically increased the role of the federal government in regulating big business. At the same time, certain factors remained the same—in both periods, the Supreme Court limited the ability of the government to regulate business."

PART TWO
Review Section—Time Periods

第二部分
复习部分——
历史时期

Period 1: 1491–1607 The Meeting of Three Peoples
第一个时期（1491—1607）：三个民族的汇聚

3

TIMELINE 大事年表

1492 Christopher Columbus (Italian, in the service of the Spanish monarchy) sails to the New World, beginning era of European colonization of the Americas

1498 Vasco da Gama (Portugal) sails to India

1517 Martin Luther challenges Roman Catholic beliefs and practices; initiates Protestant Reformation

1521 Spanish forces, led by Hernan Cortes, defeat the Mexica people, led by Montezuma

1530 John Calvin breaks with the Catholic Church

1532 Spanish forces, led by Francisco Pizarro, defeat the Inca people

1542 Bartolomé de Las Casas writes *A Short Account of the Destruction of the Indies*

1549 The *repartimiento* reforms begin to replace the *encomienda* system

1587 Founding of the "lost" English colony of Roanoke

1588 English defeat of the Spanish Armada

1597 Juanillo's Revolt in Florida

1598 Acoma Pueblo Massacre in New Mexico

INTRODUCTION 简介

> The meeting of three peoples—American Indians, Europeans, and West Africans—on land held by American Indians on the North American continent created a "new world." From the late 1400s to the early 1600s, a remarkable series of events led to a broad transformation of much of the world.

The age of exploration and colonization brought peoples together from far-flung corners of the globe. The local and regional systems of an earlier era gave way to a global system. The encounters of peoples from the Americas, Europe, and Africa led to a reordering of the world and created great wealth for some and utter destruction for others. Out of these encounters, new settlements and colonies emerged in the New World. People from all three regions had to adapt to one another as they developed new cultural patterns.

KEY CONCEPT 1.1 PRE-CONTACT NORTH AMERICA
核心概念1.1：土著与外来文化接触之前的北美

A wide variety of social, political, and economic structures had developed among the native peoples in North America in the period before the arrival of Europeans. These structures grew, in part, out of the interactions among native peoples and between native peoples and the environment.

I. Adaptations to Diverse Environments   适应多样的环境

As native peoples migrated across North America, over time they developed a great diversity of complex social structures. These peoples both adapted to the environment and transformed it.

A. SOCIETIES OF THE SOUTHWEST   西南地区的群集

Maize (corn) cultivation spread from present-day Mexico through the Southwest and across much of North America. The cultivation of maize fostered economic development and social diversification among Native Americans.

The Pueblo People of the Southwest   西南地区的普埃布洛印第安人

The Pueblo people lived in areas that are part of the current southwestern United States. The Pueblo were named by the Spanish because many lived in small towns, or *pueblos*. Ancestral Pueblo culture developed around the year 900 AD in the area that is today known as the Four-Corners region of the Southwest—where Utah, Colorado, Arizona, and New Mexico meet. These early Pueblos, sometimes called the Anasazi people, became increasingly dependent on the cultivation of maize. Their settled communities developed complex, technologically advanced societies. Many lived in architecturally sophisticated structures, including those found in the Chaco Canyon of New Mexico, some of which contained hundreds of rooms.

Because of climatic change, including volcanic eruptions and severe drought in the thirteenth and fourteenth centuries, the Pueblo people began to disperse from the complex settlements around the Four Corners region. This dispersal led to conflict with neighboring peoples. Some Pueblos united with Zunis and Hopis in western New Mexico, while others joined with settled communities in the Rio Grande valley. This movement, known as the Great Migration, led the Pueblo to abandon the sophisticated towns they had developed over hundreds of years of civilization and to join other groups in the Southwest. This development weakened Pueblo communities on the eve of European contact.

B. SOCIETIES OF THE GREAT BASIN AND GREAT PLAINS   大盆地与大平原地区的群集

The peoples of the Great Basin and the western Great Plains tended to develop mobile lifestyles in response to the lack of natural resources.

The Shoshone, Paiute, and Ute Peoples of the Great Basin
大盆地地区的肖松尼族印第安人、派尤特族印第安人以及犹特人

The Great Basin refers to the 400,000-square-mile area between the Rocky Mountains and the Sierra Nevada Mountains. The area has a great deal of environmental diversity but is characterized by a pronounced lack of natural resources. This dearth of resources was especially severe after a rise in temperatures, approximately five thousand years ago, created hot, arid conditions, leading to a series of droughts that struck the American West from approximately

900 to 1400. Historians and archeologists refer to a "desert culture" that was common among most of the pre-contact American Indian tribes of the Great Basin. "Desert culture" was characterized by seasonable mobility, as hunters and foragers searched for food throughout the year. "Desert culture" peoples often developed basketmaking, whereas more sedentary groups often developed pottery. Three large groupings of native peoples of the Great Basin were the Shoshone, the Paiute, and the Ute.

American Indians of the Great Plains　大平原地区的美洲印第安人

The Great Plains refers to the vast stretch of land in the United States and Canada that stretches from the Mississippi River to the Rocky Mountains. The Plains Indians are the native groups most commonly stereotyped in images of Indians in American popular culture. The stereotype often involves Plains Indians riding horses, wearing feathered headdresses, and hunting buffalo. In the minds of many Americans who know this stereotype from movies and television shows, this image represents not just Plains Indians, but all American Indians. The stereotype has little validity even when it comes to Plains Indians. Although many Plains Indian groups, especially those of the western Great Plains, did depend on hunting buffalo for survival, it was not until European contact that horses were introduced into Plains Indian cultures. Before that, many American Indian cultures of the Great Plains, such as the Sioux, the Blackfoot, the Arapaho, and the Cheyenne, hunted for buffalo on foot, maintaining a mobile lifestyle. Some American Indian groups of the Great Plains, especially the eastern Great Plains closer to the Mississippi River (such as the Osage, the Wichita, and the Omaha) developed more sedentary, agrarian lifestyles.

C. SOCIETIES OF THE EAST　东部地区的群集

Along the Atlantic seaboard, many native societies developed a mix of agricultural and hunter-gatherer economies. These economic developments fostered the development of permanent settlements.

The Algonquian Peoples　阿尔冈昆语族人

The Algonquian language group included hundreds of American Indian tribes along the east coast of the present-day United States and in the interior of the continent, around the St. Lawrence River and the Great Lakes. The Atlantic coast Algonquians hunted, fished, and grew corn. In northern New England and the upper Great Lakes region, the colder climate tended to make agriculture impractical, forcing Algonquians in these areas to rely on hunting and fishing.

The Iroquois Great League of Peace　易洛魁人和平大联盟

In present-day New York State, groups of Iroquoian-speaking peoples formed the Iroquois League, a confederation made up of the Mohawks, Oneidas, Onondagas, Cayugas, and Senecas. (Later, in 1720, a sixth group, the Tuscaroras, joined the league). The founding of the Iroquois League dates back to perhaps the fifteenth century (although some oral traditions assert an earlier founding date). The league formed in order to end infighting among the groups. Over time, the cohesion of the five nations grew, and the Iroquois League became one of the most powerful forces in the pre-contact Northeast.

The Iroquois lived in settled, permanent villages. They relied on farming, gathering, hunting, and fishing for their sustenance, but the majority of their food came from farming. Their three most important crops were corn, beans, and squash, the "three sisters" of crops common to many agrarian American Indian societies. The Iroquois are, traditionally, a matrilineal society—inheritance and descent pass through the mother's line.

D. SOCIETIES OF THE PACIFIC NORTHWEST 太平洋西北地区的群集

Societies in the Northwest and in areas of present-day California experienced economic development and social diversification, developing a mix of foraging and hunting. In some areas, the peoples of the Northwest supported themselves with the vast resources of the Pacific Ocean and the rivers.

Chinook People of the Pacific Northwest 太平洋西北地区的切努克人

In the Pacific Northwest, the Chinook people lived along the Columbia River in present-day Washington and Oregon. The Chinook consisted of several groups, all speaking related languages. These groups practiced foraging, hunting, and fishing and tended to live in settled communities. Chinook communities had a high degree of economic development and social stratification. A higher caste of Chinook people—shamans, warriors, and successful merchants—lived in relative isolation from Chinook commoners. Many Chinook people lived in longhouses, which contained up to fifty people.

KEY CONCEPT 1.2 EXPLORATION, CONQUEST, AND THE "COLUMBIAN EXCHANGE"
核心概念1.2：探险、征服与"哥伦布交换"

In the late 1400s and 1500s, European overseas exploration and settlement resulted in a series of interactions and adaptations among Europeans, American Indians, and Africans. Historians refer to the introduction of new products and organisms on each side of the Atlantic as the "Columbian Exchange." These developments were ushered in by the age of exploration and conquest and included social, political, and cultural changes. Contact among different groups also challenged the worldviews of those involved.

I. Europe and the Age of Exploration and Conquest
欧洲与探险和征服的时代

European expansion into the New World was fueled by a variety of factors. In time, the impact of conquest and settlement in the New World was felt in the Old World. Expansion in the Americas resulted in increased competition among the nations of Europe as well as in the promotion of empire building.

A. FACTORS CONTRIBUTING TO EUROPEAN EXPLORATION AND CONQUEST
促成欧洲人进行探险和征服的因素

A variety of factors help to explain why the age of exploration and conquest took place when it did. These factors include a desire for new sources of wealth, competition for power and status, and a push among Christian sects for new converts. Several important changes in Europe set the groundwork for exploration and conquest.

The Crusades and the Revival of Trade　十字军东征与贸易复苏

The series of religious wars known as the Crusades shook the stability of European feudal society and whet the appetites of Europeans for foreign trade goods. The wars, with the goal of securing Christian control of the "Holy Land," occurred primarily in the twelfth and thirteenth centuries. The relatively self-sufficient manorial world of feudal Europe began its long demise during this period, as trade routes and regional and international economic activity shifted power and priorities. Europeans became interested in circumventing the Italian city-states and finding new trade routes with the East.

The Black Death and the Decline of Feudalism　黑死病和封建主义的衰落

The Black Death, probably caused by a pandemic outbreak of bubonic plague in the fourteenth century, reduced the European population by from 30 to 60 percent and also played a role in weakening the feudal system.

The Impact of the Renaissance　文艺复兴的影响

The Renaissance spirit of curiosity about the world inspired people to explore and map new areas. Universities and scholarly books—also infused with the spirit of Renaissance humanism—spread knowledge of these new discoveries. Johannes Gutenberg's printing press (developed in the 1440s) helped disseminate information and stimulated interest in new discoveries.

The Protestant Reformation and the Catholic Counter-Reformation
新教宗教改革与天主教反宗教改革

Religious movements in the sixteenth century renewed many people's religious zeal and their desire to spread their gospels. The most important religious movement was the Protestant Reformation. Theologians Martin Luther and John Calvin both led breaks with the Roman Catholic Church over church practices and beliefs. Both believed that the church had drifted from its spiritual mission. The Catholic Church's practice of selling indulgences—or remissions of sin—was especially galling to Luther.

In England, King Henry VIII also led a break with Rome, but his break was more political than theological. The event that precipitated the break was the Pope's refusal to grant Henry a divorce. Some English Protestants, the Puritans, believed that the English Protestant Reformation did not go far enough. Motivated by Calvinist thinking, the Puritans argued for a complete reformation in England (see Period 2 for more on the Puritans).

The Catholic Church itself underwent a reform in the sixteenth century. This Counter-Reformation focused on a renewed sense of spirituality within the Catholic Church. Out of this movement came the Jesuits, a Catholic order devoted to spreading their gospel throughout the world.

B. THE IMPACT OF EXPLORATION AND CONQUEST ON EUROPE
探险和征服对欧洲的影响

The introduction of new sources of wealth in the form of precious metals transformed the European economy and helped facilitate the ongoing transition from feudalism to capitalism. In addition, new crops and livestock contributed to population growth in Europe.

The Impact of the "Columbian Exchange" on Europe　"哥伦布交换"对欧洲的影响

New crops and livestock that were native to the Americas were introduced to Europe in the 1500s. The list of organisms brought by Europeans back to the Old World included turkeys, corn, potato, sweet potato, cacao (cocoa), and tomatoes. These foods revolutionized agricultural and culinary traditions in Europe and supplemented the meager diets of the European peasantry. In addition, Spanish sailors brought syphilis back to Europe—the result of sexual encounters with women in the New World. Tobacco, too, was introduced and started a craze among Europeans.

The Economic Impact of Conquest　征服对经济的影响

It is assumed that since conquest brought so much hardship to American Indians as well as to Africans, it must surely have brought improvements to the status of Europeans. However, this was for the most part not the case. The position of ordinary Spaniards declined during the age of exploration and conquest. First, the influx of silver and gold into Spain set off a wave of inflation in the 1500s that made many ordinary items considerably more expensive. Second, in Spain taxes went up more than fivefold in the 1500s, so that the monarchy could pay for the military expenditures necessary to secure its New World empire. Third, Spain went into debt, as it borrowed more and more from European banks to maintain its empire. The interest on this debt also depressed the Spanish economy; in many ways, ordinary Spaniards did not recover from this period until the nineteenth century.

C. TECHNOLOGICAL ADVANCES AND NEW ECONOMIC STRUCTURES
技术进步与新的经济结构

New forms of technology and new business models facilitated extensive changes in both the economies of Europe and the Americas.

Technological Advances and a Revolution in Navigation
技术进步与航海领域的革命

A series of developments in maritime technology encouraged exploration and transformed the global economy. The compass, the astrolabe, the quadrant, and the hourglass all aided navigation, helping sailors plot direction, determine speed, and assess latitude. *Portulanos*, detailed maps, also helped navigators find their way around the world, many sailing on Portugal's maneuverable and sturdy ships, called caravels.

The Joint-stock Company　股份公司

The joint-stock company model was developed in Europe in the 1500s and became an important engine for exploration and colonization in the New World. In a joint-stock company, shareholders control part of the company in proportion to the number of shares they own. The joint-stock company model was embraced by many of the European nations embarking on risky expeditions of exploration, colonization, and trade because the risks involved would be spread out among multiple investors. Another advantage of the joint-stock company is the concept of limited liability; the shareholders can be held liable for company debts, but their liability is limited to the face value of their shareholding.

II. Contact, Conquest, and Transformations　联系、征服与变革

The Columbian Exchange and the expansion of the Spanish Empire in the fifteenth and sixteenth centuries ushered in momentous demographic, economic, and social changes.

A. THE SPANISH AND PORTUGUESE MODELS　探险先锋——西班牙人和葡萄牙人

The first explorers and settlers in the New World were sponsored by Spain and Portugal. Their presence in the New World led to deadly epidemics that decimated native populations. Over time, a racially mixed population developed in the Americas, characterized by caste distinctions that grew out of the intermixture of Spanish settlers, African slaves, and American Indians.

Portugal and Spain Lead the Way　西班牙人和葡萄牙人领路

Portugal, with the encouragement and guidance of Prince Henry the Navigator, embarked on a search for new trade routes to Asia that would bypass the Italian city-states that controlled Mediterranean trade. Portuguese explorers moved down the coast of Africa with the goal of rounding the Cape of Good Hope and crossing the Indian Ocean to arrive at India and China. Bartolomeu Dias sailed around the Cape of Good Hope in 1488 and Vasco da Gama reached India by 1498.

Spain also sought new trade routes. The Italian navigator Christopher Columbus convinced the Spanish monarchs, Isabella and Ferdinand, to fund a venture west, across the Atlantic, to reach the East. Columbus argued that the circumference of the earth was smaller than cartographers believed and that a venture in a westerly direction was both possible and feasible. (Most educated Europeans, including Columbus, believed the earth was round). Columbus's three ships, the *Nina*, the *Pinta*, and the *Santa Maria*, set sail in 1492 and, six weeks later, reached a Caribbean island that he named San Salvador. Columbus assumed that he had reached the East Indies, and he named the Taino people he encountered "Indians." The misnomer stuck. Columbus made two more voyages but never fully realized that he had voyaged to an entirely new continent. Others who followed in his footsteps made that realization, paving the way for a century of exploration, conquest, and riches.

Spanish and Portuguese Ambitions　西班牙人和葡萄牙人的野心

Spain was able to secure a dominant role in the New World following the Treaty of Tordesillas (1494) between Spain and Portugal. The treaty settled the competing claims of the two countries to the newly explored lands outside of Europe by drawing a longitudinal line through the Atlantic Ocean and South America. Portugal was granted lands to the east of the line, including Brazil in the Western Hemisphere and Africa. Spain was granted the rest of the lands of the Americas. Spain made those claims real by establishing settlements throughout Central and South America. Spanish explorers even made it as far north as California and New Mexico, the area around the Mississippi River, and Florida. Ponce de Leon reached Florida in 1513. Spaniards later established the first permanent European settlement in what would become the United States, at St. Augustine, Florida (1585).

The Conquistadores and the Defeat of Native Peoples　征服者与土著居民的战败

Within a generation of Columbus's first journey to the New World, Spanish forces wrested control of much of Central and South America from the native inhabitants, transforming the economic and social structures of the region and devastating the native population.

The sixteenth century saw brutal fighting in the Americas as Spain extended its dominance over much of Central and South America. One of the more brutal episodes of violence between the Spanish conquistadores and native peoples was the defeat of the Mexica (also known as the Aztecs, and led by Montezuma) by Spanish forces led by Hernan Cortes (1518–1521). The Incas of South America were defeated by a Spanish expedition led by Francisco Pizarro (1532).

Disease and Death　疾病与死亡

The peoples of the New World, having evolved and adapted separately from the peoples of the Old World, had no immunities to many of the germs and infectious diseases that foreign explorers and settlers inadvertently brought with them. These diseases included bubonic plague, influenza, cholera, scarlet fever, and, most important, smallpox. It is estimated that between 50 and 90 percent of the native peoples of the Americas died between 1500 and 1650. For instance, on the island of Hispaniola (the island where Haiti and the Dominican Republic are today) the population rapidly declined from over a million to a mere 500 in the years following contact with Christopher Columbus and Spaniards in the 1490s.

The rapid decline of the various peoples in the areas of Spanish conquest should not be attributed solely to disease. Spanish policies focused on subjugating the native peoples of the New World. Warfare, brutal conquest, and harsh working conditions, fueled by the desire for riches and an ideology of racial superiority, contributed to the decline of native populations. Many were killed outright; many were physically weakened under Spanish occupation and became susceptible to disease.

> ## THE IMPACT OF DISEASE　疾病的影响
> Remember that the main cause of the massive die-off of American Indians in the 1600s was disease, not warfare. Warfare was brutal, but it could not have affected the large number of people that disease did.

The Columbian Exchange Transforms the Americas　"哥伦布交换"改变了美洲

By far, the most important organisms brought from Europe to the New World were germs, which caused widespread disease and death. The exchange, however, also brought useful products to the inhabitants of the New World, where the Europeans introduced important crops, including sugar, wheat, and bananas, as well as domestic livestock, including goats, cows, and chickens. The exchange also brought the horse to the New World, which proliferated and transformed many native cultures.

B. SPANISH EXPLOITATION OF NEW WORLD RESOURCES
西班牙人对新世界资源的开发

Spaniards first turned to the forced labor of native Indians in a system known as the *encomienda*. This exploitative system was used in plantation agriculture and in the extraction of precious metals. Over time, native labor was replaced by enslaved Africans.

Silver and the *Encomienda*　银金属与"监护征赋制"

Upon gaining control of much of the Americas, Spain created a system to extract gold and silver and ship it to Spain, which soon became the wealthiest country in Europe with the influx of New World precious metals. In Spain's *encomienda* system, the initial Spanish settlers were granted tracts of land and the right to extract labor from local inhabitants. In many ways, this system of New World colonization resembled Old World feudalism. Acting as feudal lords, the *encomenderos* had a free hand to manage their holdings, as long as a percentage of gold and silver was sent back to the monarchy. The *encomienda* system led to brutal exploitation. Spurred by Spanish critics such as Bartolomé de Las Casas, the crown issued a series of reforms to the governance of Spain's New World colonies, known as the *repartimiento* (1549). Treatment of native peoples did not improve appreciably, but control of Spanish America came to be exercised more directly by the crown (see Period 2).

PARALLELS　平行系统

There are many parallels between the Spanish and English colonial systems. In both cases, the crown initially gave local governors a free hand in the New World. Subsequently, in both cases, the crown exercised direct control over its New World holdings. In New Spain, we can look at the *repartimiento*; In English America, we can look at the creation of the Dominion of New England.

C. SPAIN AND THE AFRICAN SLAVE TRADE　西班牙与非洲奴隶贸易

Soon after European settlement in the Americas, a system of outright slavery developed. Spain participated in the international slave trade to import enslaved Africans to the New World in order to labor in plantation agriculture and mining.

The Impact of the Slave Trade　奴隶贸易的影响

Even before the settlement of the New World, Europeans began taking Africans from their villages and forcing them into slavery. Slavery has existed since ancient times, but the concept of slavery changed in the 1500s. Captured Africans were thought of as slaves for life; it was not a temporary condition. Also, the children of slaves would now be considered slaves as well. This, too, was a break from tradition. African slaves were considered property, with no rights, as opposed to people who were enslaved for a period of time.

There were two main impacts of the slave trade on Africa from the 1500s onward. First, entire generations of strong, young people were kidnapped and taken out of the country. These would otherwise have become the leaders of their tribes or villages. Second, the introduction of European manufactured items undermined the traditional African economy.

SLAVERY IN HISTORY　奴隶制的历史

It is true that slavery has existed since ancient times. However, be prepared to discuss the aspects of modern slavery that differentiate it from ancient slavery.

Resistance to Slavery and the Development of the Maroon Communities
对奴隶制的反抗与逃亡黑奴团体的发展

As Africans were brought into the slavery system, they developed forms of cultural resistance that attempted, against great odds, to preserve traditional cultural patterns and to maintain a sense of autonomy. In New Spain, one notable form of resistance was the establishment of "maroon" communities.

Maroons were Africans who had escaped from slavery in the New World and established independent communities. These communities existed throughout the New World, with many in the Caribbean and Brazil. Often, these communities were formed by slaves who were the first generation brought out of Africa. The Maroons, with memories of Africa, were in the best position to preserve African traditions in the New World. These traditions included the use of medicinal herbs, often combined with special drumming and dancing as part of healing rituals. Other African healing traditions and rites have survived over the centuries through the descendants of these original Maroons. One of the most significant Maroon communities was Palmares, established in Brazil in the early 1600s. It had more than 30,000 residents and remained an independent community until it was conquered by the Portuguese in 1694. When the English took over Jamaica from the Spanish in 1655, many enslaved Africans fled into the interior and joined communities of Arawak Indians. Over time, the Maroons came to control large areas of the Jamaican interior.

D. THE SOCIAL STRUCTURE OF SPANISH AMERICA　西班牙美洲殖民地的社会结构

Spanish colonizers developed an elaborate caste system in the New World. This system incorporated American Indians and Africans, but Spaniards were careful to define the status of each group within New Spain.

The *Casta* System　"卡斯塔"制度

Despite traditional notions of the superiority of "pure blood" among Spaniards (see pages 45–46), a good deal of intermixing occurred in the Spanish colonies. In Spain's New World colonies, Spaniards were always greatly outnumbered by native peoples. Further, Spanish men greatly outnumbered Spanish women. In these circumstances, intermarriage was common. The Spanish used the term *casta* to describe the variety of mixed race people in the new world. The *casta* system included *peninsulares* (born in Spain) and *creoles* (those born in the New World of Spanish parents) at the top of the social structure. These groups usually consisted of only 1 or 2 percent of the population. Just below them in social status were *mestizos*, the children of Spanish men and Indian women. *Mestizos* comprised 4 to 5 percent of the population of Spain's New World empire. Below them were *mulattos* (children of Spanish men and African women), followed by American Indians and Africans at the bottom of the social pyramid. The Spaniards developed even finer gradations, based on the specific percentage of each background an individual possessed.

III. Divergent Worldviews of Europeans and American Indians
欧洲人与美洲印第安人迥异的世界观

In the sixteenth century, the divergent worldviews of Europeans and American Indians became increasingly evident. Both groups attempted to assert worldviews about religion, gender roles, family, land use, and power.

A. INTERACTIONS, TRADE, AND CULTURAL ADAPTATIONS IN THE NEW WORLD
在新世界的互动、贸易与文化适应

The divergent worldviews of Europeans and American Indians were evident in the first century of Spanish conquest of the Americas. Each side often misunderstood the cultural assumptions of the other. In the process of conquest and domination by the Spanish, each side adopted some useful aspects of the other's culture.

Adaptation in New Spain 对新西班牙的容纳

Some Native Americans made accommodation with the Spanish, adopting Christianity and adapting it to fit their needs and circumstances. Some native peoples adopted Catholicism completely, while others incorporated certain Spanish spiritual beliefs into traditional religious practices.

B. RESISTANCE BY AMERICAN INDIANS AND AFRICANS 美洲印第安人和非洲人的反抗

As Europeans encroached upon Native Americans' land and attempted to impose their ideas about culture, propriety, gender roles, family structure, religion, and the natural world, native peoples developed strategies for resistance and contestation. In the face of enslavement, subjugation, and defeat, Africans and American Indians attempted to maintain a sense of political and cultural autonomy.

Native American Resistance in New Spain 美洲原住民对新西班牙的反抗

The responses of American Indians to the catastrophe of conquest were varied. Some fled from the invading Spaniards, abandoning their ancestral homelands. These migrations led to population pressures and conflicts elsewhere in the Americas. Native people engaged in violent resistance as well as more passive cultural resistance. The Guale people lived near the Spanish mission in St. Augustine—one of four missions in Spanish Florida in the sixteenth century. As missionaries tried to bring Guale Indians into the mission system, a revolt, known as Juanillo's Revolt, occurred in 1597, resulting in the deaths of several missionaries.

Juan de Onate and the Acoma Pueblo People 胡安·德·奥纳特与阿科马普韦布洛人

In the western reaches of Spain's New World empire, a violent confrontation occurred with the Pueblo people in what is now New Mexico. The Spanish *conquistador* Juan de Onate and his soldiers had, in the 1590s, occupied land held by the Acoma Pueblo people. In 1598, the Acoma resisted an order by the Spaniards to hand over certain supplies that the Acoma needed to survive the upcoming winter. They attacked the Spanish occupiers, killing 15, including the nephew of Onate. Onate responded by firing cannons from a mesa above the Acoma people, killing over 800 native people. The survivors were put on trial by the Spanish, whose punishments included cutting off one foot for males over the age of 25. As many as 80 men had a foot cut off. The remaining 500 Acoma people were enslaved by the Spaniards.

C. DEBATES AROUND PERCEPTIONS OF AMERICAN INDIANS
对美洲印第安人看法的争论

Before the age of exploration, most Europeans had little or no knowledge of people who were different from themselves. Initially, Spanish and Portuguese explorers did not know what to make of the people they encountered in the Americas. Over time, debates occurred around how civilized these peoples were compared with European standards.

The Development of the Belief in White Superiority 白种人优越信念的发展

As Europeans solidified their control over the New World and brought more American Indians and Africans under their control, a set of racist ideas developed to justify the continued subjugation of nonwhite people. These racist ideas often grew out of earlier notions of race that had existed in Europe. For the Spaniards, for instance, these included traditional notions about "pure blood" (*limpieza de sangre*). In Spain, this description was used for those without Jewish or Muslim ancestry. The idea that "pure blood" was superior shaped Spanish understandings of race in the New World. As miscegenation—the mixing of races—occurred in the New World, Spaniards erected an elaborate hierarchy of racial classes. The degree of "pure blood" determined one's place in this hierarchy. Indians and Africans were at the bottom. This model drew on traditional Spanish beliefs and adapted them to a New World setting. The model was useful to the Spanish because it justified their position at the top of the hierarchy and the continued subjugation of those at the bottom.

Debates over Spain's Actions in the New World　对西班牙在新世界的作为的争论

As reports of the actions of the Spanish conquistadores and officials in the *encomienda* system reached Spain, a heated debate ensued about Spanish behavior in the New World. The priest Bartolomé de Las Casas roundly criticized Spanish actions as being among "the most unpardonable offences committed against God and mankind." His book, *A Short Account of the Destruction of the Indies* (written in 1542; published in 1552), chronicled atrocities against native peoples in the New World. He has been criticized as paving the way for the enslavement of Africans in order to replace American Indian laborers. He did advocate such a transition, but later came to believe that all forms of slavery were morally wrong.

Las Casas was challenged by another Spanish theologian, Juan Ginés de Sepúlveda. Sepúlveda defended the treatment that the Spaniards meted out to the native peoples of the Americas. He asserted that American Indians were beings of an inferior order. Because they could not be expected to perform duties beyond manual labor, he argued that they were "natural slaves." He followed in the footsteps of philosophers and theologians who argued for the existence of "natural law." He insisted that the battles of conquest in the New World were "just wars." His justifications for taking native peoples' lands and for destroying their culture—including the idea that it was in their best interests—would resonate with Spanish policymakers in their assertion of power in the New World in the coming centuries.

SUBJECT TO DEBATE　相关讨论

Most American history textbooks provide vivid accounts of the brutality of the Spanish conquistadores toward American Indians. That the Spaniards were often cruel to the native peoples of the Americas is not in question, but recently historians have begun to question the extent of Spanish brutality. The term, "Black Legend," was coined by a Spanish historian in 1914 to describe the anti-Spanish propaganda written by English, Italian, Dutch, and other European writers. Although English sources from the 1500s onward should not be discounted, it would be prudent for the student to take into account the authorship of these sources and their motives. English writers might have been trying to demonize Spanish behavior in order to portray English behavior in the New World in a more favorable light. The English portrayed themselves as altruistic, bringing God and civilization to the inhabitants of the New World, while the Spanish were portrayed as greedy and cruel. Of course, the historical record demonstrates that the English committed their share of atrocities in the New World, probably comparable to those committed in New Spain. The controversy provides us with a cautionary lesson: Look carefully at the source of documents as you use them to write about the past. The sources of documents in the document-based question on the Advanced Placement exam are clearly indicated. Do not ignore this information.

PRACTICE MULTIPLE-CHOICE QUESTIONS 选择题练习

> **Directions:** Pick the letter that best answers the following questions.

Questions 1–3 refer to the following passage: 根据下列段落，回答第1—3题

"The gold and silver mined with forced labor in Mexico and what is now Bolivia constituted a windfall that could have been used to develop Spanish agriculture, industry, and commerce. It could have helped the country catch up with northwestern Europe's more developed economies. . . .

"But Spain [in the 1500s] was in the grip of a tiny ruling class of royalty, Catholic Church hierarchy, and landed aristocracy. Two to three per cent of the population owned 97 per cent of the land in Castile, Spain's heartland. The great landowners had no incentive to modernize Spain. They just wanted to raise more sheep and sell more wool. The environmental degradation that overgrazing vast numbers of sheep entailed seems to have bothered the ruling class no more than the cutting of forests for timber to build ships and provide charcoal to smelt domestic Spanish silver ore. And so, what if the wool went to Holland to be manufactured into cloth rather than being processed in Spain itself.

"Meanwhile, successes in the New World swelled the Spanish monarchy's ambitions in the Old. The bonanza of bullion from the Americas encouraged Spain's rulers to build up the army into Europe's largest military force, setting off an arms race that forced rivals to multiply their armed forces as well.... Hegemonic wars against the French, Dutch, and English followed. . . .

"The most lasting and far-reaching effect of the increase of money in circulation was to set off a long wave of inflation that spread throughout Western Europe. To be sure, deficit spending on unproductive armies, navies, and wars as well as debasement of coinage by monarchs in search of additional royal revenue contributed to the run-up in prices."

—A. Kent MacDougall, University of California, Berkeley, March 1992.

1. Which of the following best describes a central point of A. Kent MacDougall's argument above?

    (A) During the age of exploration and conquest, a growing divide developed in Spain between the Catholic Church and the monarchy over the treatment of American Indians.

    (B) The large-scale migration of Spanish peasants to the New World left Spain with a scarcity of workers and a depressed economy.

    (C) Spanish conquest of the New World led Spain to focus its military and diplomatic efforts toward subduing resistance in the New World and removing itself from the conflicts of Europe.

    (D) The successes of Spanish conquest in the New World did not result in a general economic improvement in Spain itself.

2. The description of Spanish actions by A. Kent MacDougall contributes to an understanding of which of the following developments beyond the 1500s?

(A) The industrial growth of Spain in the seventeenth century.

(B) The growing gap between the wealthy and the poor in the seventeenth century.

(C) Spanish military domination over its European rivals in the seventeenth century.

(D) The success of independence movements in Spanish America in the seventeenth century.

3. Concerns raised in Spain in the 1540s about "forced labor in Mexico and what is now Bolivia," mentioned in the first paragraph of MacDougall's article, led to which of the following changes?

(A) Limits being placed on the *encomienda* system and a shift toward African slavery.

(B) The growth of the Spanish abolitionist movement and a royal decree ending slavery in the New World.

(C) A shift in Spanish economic activities in the New World from export-oriented activities toward production for local consumption.

(D) The establishment of a line of demarcation in Spanish-held territories in the New World between areas for American Indians and areas for Spanish colonists.

Answers and Explanations to Multiple-Choice Questions
选择题的答案与解析

1. **(D)** The successes of Spanish conquest in the New World did not result in a general economic improvement in Spain itself. The article focuses on the shortsightedness of the wealthy class and the impact of ongoing warfare. The elite class in Spain did not try to improve infrastructure or develop new forms of processing and manufacturing.

2. **(B)** The article is attempting to account for a curious outcome. With all the gold and silver coming into Spain in the 1500s, why did the standard of living for most Spaniards decline from the 1500s until, according to the article, the late 1800s? MacDougall argues that the wealth was squandered rather than reinvested. Further, taxes and inflation both increased, putting the peasantry in a deeper hole. The author states, in another part of the article, "Super-exploitation of labor on the periphery of the world capitalist economy leads to increased exploitation of workers at the core."

3. **(A)** The article focuses on the impact of Spanish colonization on Spain itself, rather than on the Americas. However, it does allude to "forced labor in Mexico and what is now Bolivia." The super-exploitation of indigenous peoples by the Spaniards was raised in the 1640s by the Dominican Friar Bartolomé de las Casas. He described the brutality of slavery under the *encomienda* system. He asserted that Indians were free people in the natural order and deserved the same treatment as others. He also suggested replacing Indian labor with African labor. In the coming decades, Spain shifted toward a reliance on African slavery for labor in its New World empire.

Period 2: 1607–1754 Patterns of Empire and Resistance
第二个时期（1607—1754）：帝国的模式与反抗

4

TIMELINE 大事年表

1588	England defeats the Spanish Armada
1607	Jamestown colony founded
1609	Henry Hudson explores area that will become New York
1609–1610	"Starving time" in Virginia
1619	House of Burgesses established
1620	Founding of Plymouth Colony
	Mayflower Compact signed
1622	Attack on Jamestown by local Algonquin Indians
1624	New Amsterdam founded by the Dutch
1630	Founding of Massachusetts Bay Colony
1630–1640	"Great Migration" of Puritans from England to Massachusetts
1632	Founding of Georgia Colony
1636	Founding of Rhode Island Colony
1638	Anne Hutchinson banned from Massachusetts
1639	The Fundamental Orders of Connecticut adopted
1649	Act of Religious Toleration passed in Maryland
1662	The Half-Way Covenant
1663	Founding of Carolina Colony
1675	King Philip's War
1676	Bacon's Rebellion
1679	New Hampshire Colony separated from Massachusetts
1680	Pueblo Revolt (Pope's Rebellion)
1681	Founding of the Pennsylvania Colony
1686	Creation of the Dominion of New England
1688	The Glorious Revolution
1689	Colonists bring down the Dominion of New England
1692	Salem witch trials
1711	Founding of North Carolina Colony
1733	Molasses Act

1735	Zenger trial
1739	Stono Rebellion
1741	Arrests and executions in the supposed "Negro Plot" in New York City
	Jonathan Edwards's sermon, "Sinners in the Hands of an Angry God"

INTRODUCTION 简介

> Throughout the seventeenth century and the first half of the eighteenth century, the major European imperial powers and different groups of American Indians maneuvered and fought for control of the North American continent. Out of these conflicts, native societies experienced dramatic changes and distinctive colonial societies emerged.

England was eager to duplicate the stunning success of the Spanish in the New World. Emerging as the most powerful nation on the high seas after defeating the Spanish Armada in 1588, England then set its sights on North America. England, Spain, Holland, and France all made attempts to establish control over different areas of North America. These efforts led to different patterns of colonization and different types of interactions with American Indian groups.

Once established, the 13 British colonies developed along diverse, but parallel, paths. We see distinct patterns of development in the three regions of colonial America. The southern colonies—Virginia, South Carolina, North Carolina, and Georgia—all moved toward an economy dominated by the institution of slavery. The New England colonies of Massachusetts, Rhode Island, Connecticut, and New Hampshire all experienced economic transformations that undermined the community cohesion and intense piety of the founding generation of Puritan settlers. The middle colonies of New York, New Jersey, Pennsylvania, and Delaware saw the development of economic and ethnic diversity as immigrants from Europe began to fill up the region. However, the 13 colonies were united by shared experiences as much as they were separated by different patterns of development. All lived under the British crown and practiced some form of Protestantism; all maneuvered within mercantilist trade rules; all pushed back and fought with American Indians; and all were exposed to new philosophical and religious ideas. We begin to see, in the eighteenth century, a pattern of development in North America distinct from Britain (by then England and Scotland had formed a union known as Great Britain). These distinctions begin to lay the groundwork for the political break that followed the intellectual break from the British.

KEY CONCEPT 2.1 PATTERNS OF COLONIZATION
核心概念2.1：殖民模式

In the seventeenth century, several European empires competed for control of North America. These colonial powers had various priorities and goals. As they sought to exert control over different parts of North America, they established distinct patterns of settlement and colonization. These patterns were shaped by environmental factors in North America and by competition for resources among the European powers and between them and the diverse American Indian groups.

I. Competing Models of Colonization 形态各异的殖民模式

The Spanish, French, Dutch, and British developed various patterns for colonizing the New World. These patterns reflected the different economic and social goals, cultural assumptions, and traditions and folkways of these major powers.

A. SPAIN'S NEW WORLD COLONIES 西班牙的新世界殖民地

Spain maintained tight control over its colonial empire in the New World. Spanish colonizers focused on converting American Indians to Christianity and on exploiting the labor of the native population.

The Evolution of Spanish America 西班牙美洲殖民地的发展

The basis of Spain's New World empire was the exploitation of the labor of native peoples. By 1550, Spain abandoned the *encomienda* system. Under this system, the initial Spanish settlers in the Americas were granted tracts of land and the right to extract labor from local inhabitants. This system led to brutal treatment of Indians. The worst excesses of Spanish behavior were chronicled by the Spanish Dominican friar, Bartolomé de Las Casas (see Period 1). The Spanish government replaced the *encomienda* system with the *repartimiento* system—banning outright Indian slavery and mandating that Indian laborers be paid wages. However, Spain's empire remained highly exploitative of native labor. Colonial authorities could still require that local people work for Spanish landlords. In many colonies the work of Indians was supplemented by African slave labor.

By 1650, approximately 350,000 Spaniards had migrated to the New World. This population was supplemented by more than a quarter million Africans. Indians were still the majority in Spanish America, but their population, by 1570, had been reduced by approximately 90 percent from what it was in 1492. Intermarriage was common in Spain's New World colonies. A complex social hierarchy resulted from the mixing of peoples of different backgrounds (see page 44).

Spain's New World empire was tightly controlled by the crown, especially after the *repartimiento* system was established. In the sixteenth and seventeenth centuries, administration of the empire was divided between two administrative units. The northern portion of the empire, called the Viceroyalty of New Spain, was headquartered in Mexico City. The southern portion of the empire was called the Viceroyalty of Peru, consisting of Spanish holdings in South America and headquartered in Lima. New Spain attempted to extend its reach into modern-day Florida and New Mexico, but failed to establish a strong presence in the northern reaches of its imperial holdings (see page 157).

Most Indians lived removed from Spanish colonists—remaining in their own communities under the authority of native leaders and speaking their own languages. Spanish priests were, however, aggressive in leaving the imprint of Catholicism on native communities. Priests converted communities en masse; Spanish efforts at conversion seemed successful. However, the Catholicism that was practiced in native communities was different from what Catholic priests had originally intended. Indians often accepted Jesus as one among many Gods and interwove Catholic practices with traditional Indian spiritual practices. At the same time, local ideas and expectations frequently reshaped Catholic practices. Catholic priests realized they had to accept certain adaptations in order to better reach native peoples.

B. FRENCH AND DUTCH COLONIES　法国与荷兰的殖民地

Both France and the Netherlands established colonies in North America, but they differed markedly from the Spanish and British models. Few French or Dutch people actually settled in the New World. Rather, the French and Dutch colonies served as trading outposts. Their colonials often intermarried with the native peoples, thereby combining new family connections to promote trade, acquiring furs and other valuable goods for export to Europe.

France's New World Empire　法国的新世界帝国

France's North American colonies were vast on paper but thinly populated when it came to French colonials. New France stretched from the mouth of the St. Lawrence River in Quebec, encompassed the Great Lakes region and the Ohio River Valley, and included the vast Great Basin of what would later become the United States and the port of New Orleans. The first permanent French settlements were Port Royal (1605), in what would later become Nova Scotia, and Quebec (1608), founded by Samuel de Champlain. In 1642, French traders established a small settlement at what would later become Montreal. It was not until the latter part of the seventeenth century that the French established settlements at New Orleans and in the southern Great Lakes region.

French–American Indian Diplomacy　法国与美洲印第安人的外交活动

Because the French had relatively few actual colonists in the New World, they had to rely on diplomacy with American Indian groups more than did the Spanish or the British. French military officers in the New World learned native languages and became well versed in American Indian diplomatic protocol, including smoking the long-stemmed calumet ("peace pipe") and giving and receiving gifts, including wampum belts. French officers and agents often married Indian wives, which promoted their efforts at maintaining good relations with native peoples. Despite these efforts, American Indians maintained actual control of the heart of the North American continent. In these areas, French agents had to adjust to Indian ways to maintain France's colonial presence. The Osages, for example, south of the Missouri River, accepted some French agents into their kinship networks. This French accommodation of and adaptation to American Indian ways was extremely rare among British colonists.

The Metis of the French Colonies　法国殖民地的混血

In many French settlements in the interior of the North American continent, French women were few and far between. In these frontier communities, a certain intermingling of French and American Indian peoples and lifeways occurred. The fort and trading post at Detroit, for instance, combined French as well as American Indian elements. The layout of the village resembled a French village, but many of the buildings were covered by bark, in the style of local American Indians. Clothing among French colonists also included European and native elements: European shirts and Indian shoes, for example. In addition, intermarriage with American Indians was common in these far-flung French colonies. The children of these marriages were known as Metis—an old French word for "mixed" or "mixed-blood." In Metis communities, American Indian women often played important roles, in contrast to traditional French family structures. These women served as cultural mediators and were an important part of the fur trade as brokers. Metis communities, combining Catholic and indigenous religious practices, continued to exist after France officially surrendered its North American colonies in 1763.

The Dutch Presence in the Americas 荷兰人在美洲的出现

The Dutch presence in the New World dates from the 1590s. Like the French, the first Dutch colonies in the New World functioned more as trading outposts rather than as populated settlements. The Dutch established forts and small settlements in Guyana in 1590, followed by a string of island settlements in the Caribbean in the early 1600s. Dutch efforts at colonization were often stymied by rival European powers. In Tobago, for example, the Dutch attempted four different times to build settlements in the seventeenth century, with each settlement destroyed by either the French, the Spanish, or the British. Later in the seventeenth century, the Dutch obtained control of the colony of Suriname, in South America. Earlier, in the 1650s, the British had established a colony there. It was captured by a Dutch expedition in 1667 and was formally transferred to the Dutch as part of the Treaty of Breda, following the Second Anglo-Dutch War, 1665–1667. By this treaty, the Dutch formally relinquished control of New Amsterdam (see page 54). The Dutch focused on sugar production in Suriname, relying on African slave labor to work the fields.

Dutch New Amsterdam 荷兰新阿姆斯特丹

In the early 1600s, the Dutch set their sights on North America. The Dutch Republic commissioned an expedition to North America led by English explorer Henry Hudson. The project was funded by the Dutch East India Company, which instructed Hudson to search for a Northwest Passage to Asia. Hudson sailed into the river that would later bear his name, and past Manhattan Island, part of present-day New York City. Continuing northward, he sailed almost as far as present-day Albany before turning back. Hudson never found a Northwest Passage, but his reports of abundant fur, timber, and fertile lands generated further interest among Dutch merchants to exploit these lands. After several more journeys of exploration and repeated attempts to find a Northwest Passage, the Dutch Republic chartered the Dutch West India Company to develop colonies in North America. The Dutch claimed a vast stretch of land from the Delaware River in the south to Cape Cod in the north. The Dutch later acquiesced to claims by the growing population of Puritan Connecticut (a 1650 treaty with the Connecticut colony formalized a new border, close to the present border between New York and Connecticut).

The administrative seat, and most important settlement of New Netherland, was New Amsterdam. A settlement was established in 1624 on what is now Governor's Island, in New York Harbor. The following year, a fort was built at the tip of Manhattan, and settlement begun around Fort Amsterdam. Legend has it that in 1626 Peter Minuit, the company director general of New Amsterdam, purchased the island of Manhattan from the local people for goods estimated to be worth $24. Almost all aspects of this transaction are in doubt—the value of the goods, the intentions of the American Indians, and even the legitimacy of the unnamed native people to "sell" the island. However, the myth of the "$24 Deal" has persisted.

The Economy of New Amsterdam 新阿姆斯特丹的经济

The Dutch West India Company did not see immediate profits, as the colony of New Amsterdam floundered during its first 20 years. Initially, few Dutch settlers came to the New World. The company tried to induce immigrants with generous land grants along the Hudson River. Slowly, settlers began to arrive—an amalgam of Europeans of diverse national and religious backgrounds (including some Portuguese Jewish colonists originally heading to Brazil). The Dutch also brought African slaves to New Amsterdam.

The colony began to thrive under the leadership of the heavy-handed Peter Stuyvesant, who was hired by the company in 1647. New Amsterdam became a center for the thriving trade in beaver furs and a growing commercial town. However, King Charles II of England soon set his sights on the "Dutch wedge," which divided England's holdings in North America. The king sent a fleet of warships to New Amsterdam. The outnumbered and outgunned Stuyvesant surrendered in 1664 without a fight. Charles II granted the colony to his brother James, the Duke of York, who renamed it New York. Formal transfer to the English occurred in 1667, as part of the settlement following the Second Anglo-Dutch War.

C. BRITISH COLONIAL PATTERNS　英国的殖民模式

Of the European empires that sought to establish colonies in the New World, the British pattern differed markedly from the Spanish, Dutch, and French. Whereas their European competitors sent relatively few colonists to the New World, the British migrated in substantial numbers to the new colonies.

The Founding of Jamestown and the "Starving Time"
詹姆斯敦的建立与"大饥荒时期"

The first settlers to Jamestown arrived in 1607. Investors in England formed a joint-stock company, the Virginia Company, to fund the expedition. King James I chartered the company and territory in the New World. The Jamestown colony nearly collapsed during its first few years of existence. The colonists were not prepared to establish a community, grow crops, and sustain themselves. They were mostly male gentlemen, unaccustomed to working with their hands. These early settlers hoped to find gold and silver and to quickly duplicate the Spanish successes in Central and South America. They did not find precious metals, nor did they plant crops. Their store of food diminished quickly and, by 1608, only 38 of the original 144 colonists were still alive. By 1610, things had not improved; only 60 settlers, out of 500 who had come over, were still alive. Many had perished during the "starving time" (winter of 1609–1610).

GEOGRAPHY AND SOCIETY　地理和社会

The "starving time" for the Virginia colony illustrates the idea that geography and biology cannot always determine the outcomes of human events. One would have expected the Puritans in bitter-cold New England to die off in large numbers, while the Virginians, in a mild climate, thrived. The opposite occurred, showing that planning and organization trump geography and biology.

Jamestown and its American Indian Neighbors　詹姆斯敦及其美洲印第安邻居

Relations with local American Indians deteriorated rapidly during the early years of the Jamestown colony. The local Algonquian people, led by their chief, Powhatan, father of Pocahontas traded corn with the settlers at first. However, when the American Indians could not supply a sufficient amount of corn for their English neighbors, the English initiated raids on Powhatan's people. These skirmishes occurred for years, until the Indians organized an assault on Jamestown in 1622. The raid did not dislodge the Jamestown settlement, but it worsened relations between the settlers and the native people. In many ways, the incidents in Jamestown foretold the history of relations between the American Indians of North America and the white settlers from Europe. Whites consistently encroached on American Indian lands and consistently defeated them in the violent encounters that resulted.

II. Geography and Regional Development in British North America 英属北美殖民地的地理和区域发展

Although the colonists who settled British North America had much in common, the varied geographic and environmental characteristics of the New World did much to shape the particularities of these colonies, which lay along the Atlantic seaboard. We see distinct commonalities among the New England colonies, the middle colonies, the Chesapeake colonies, and the lower South and West Indian colonies.

A. THE CHESAPEAKE AND THE UPPER SOUTH 切萨皮克与上南部

The upper South was the most populous part of the South, containing 90 percent of the white population and 80 percent of the black population of the South. The colonists of the Chesapeake region and North Carolina came to rely on labor-intensive tobacco, using white indentured servants and slaves as their workforce.

A Tobacco Economy 烟草经济

Following a difficult beginning, marked by disease, starvation, and resistance by native peoples, the colonists of Virginia began the successful cultivation of tobacco. Tobacco was unknown in Europe before Columbus's journeys to the New World. The Spanish had first introduced tobacco to Europe in the 1500s, but it remained a scarce luxury there. In 1612, the Jamestown planter John Rolfe began experimenting with growing tobacco. The first shipments were sent to England in 1617. With its addictive properties, tobacco soon became extremely popular in Europe and hugely profitable for the Chesapeake Bay region. By 1700, the American colonies were exporting more than 35 million pounds of tobacco a year. Tobacco became the most important crop for the Chesapeake region, accounting for nearly three-fourths of the exports by 1750, and nearly one-third of all exports from British North America.

> ### AGRICULTURE, NORTH VERSUS SOUTH
> ### 南方与北方的农业
>
> From the beginning, the northern and southern colonies developed different patterns of agriculture. The southern colonies focused on a few staple crops, grown for export. The northern colonies focused on smaller scale agriculture, and a variety of crops.

The shift to a tobacco economy profoundly affected the direction of Virginia's development and, subsequently, the rest of the Chesapeake and the northern part of the colony of Carolina (the area that would become North Carolina in the eighteenth century). First, the cultivation of tobacco required large tracts of land. Tobacco cultivation quickly exhausted the nutrients in the soil, requiring growers to seek out new tracts of land after only a few years of production. This thirst for land inevitably led to encroachments on the territory of American Indians in the interior of Virginia. Second, the success of tobacco established a pattern in the South of large-scale production of staple crops for the international market. This pattern continued with the expansion of cotton production in the nineteenth century. Finally, this reliance on the cultivation of export crops required a large number of laborers. The need for labor facilitated the development of indentured servitude and slavery.

Labor and Tobacco 劳工与烟草

The leaders of the Chesapeake colonies used a variety of methods to bring workers to the New World. New immigrants were enticed to come to the Chesapeake region with the offer of

50 acres, called a head-right, upon arrival. However, this still required a potential immigrant to scrape together the fare for passage to the New World—approximately a year's income for an agrarian worker in England. To bring lower-class agrarian workers to America, wealthy Virginians employed the system of indentured servitude. Under this system, a potential immigrant in England would agree to contract to work as an indentured servant for a certain number of years in America (usually four to seven) in exchange for free passage. An agent would then sell this contract to a planter in the colonies. The system accomplished its goal, allowing for tens of thousands of impoverished English men and women to migrate to the New World, but the system also created an entire underclass of mistreated workers. The first enslaved Africans were brought to Virginia in 1619. Slavery developed gradually; it was only later in the century that it began to grow dramatically (see more on the development of slavery, page 79).

Maryland 马里兰

Economically, the colony of Maryland bore similarities to Virginia. Maryland also focused on the cultivation of tobacco as an export crop and used indentured servants and African slaves to work the tobacco fields.

Maryland was the first proprietary colony established by England in North America. The crown was moving away from the model of granting charters to joint-stock companies. It hoped that the proprietor (owner) of a colony would be more accountable to the monarch. The proprietor of Maryland was to be George Calvert, Lord Baltimore. Calvert was Catholic and hoped to create in the New World a refuge for Catholics. He was granted a charter by King Charles I, but died just weeks before the colony was to be established. His son, Cecelius Calvert, became the actual proprietor of Maryland. Almost immediately, Protestants outnumbered Catholics, but Catholicism continued to be tolerated in Maryland.

North Carolina 北卡罗莱纳

The roots of North Carolina can be found in the divergent development of the Carolina colony. Carolina was founded in 1663 by wealthy plantation owners who had migrated from Barbados. These wealthy plantation owners created an agrarian system in the southern portion of Carolina that came to resemble the sugar economy of Barbados (see page 65). However, from the 1670s and 1680s, when the first English settlers arrived in the northern part of the Carolina colony, its economy more closely resembled that of the Chesapeake colonies. These settlers included runaway servants as well as families of modest means. Tensions between the two regions, which were remote from one another, led to a split in 1712, and the establishment of North Carolina as a distinct colony from South Carolina.

B. THE NEW ENGLAND COLONIES 新英格兰殖民地

The first colonists of the New England region were driven more by religious reasons than economic gain. These settlers were devout Puritans. Their religious motivation helps explain the unique patterns of development in New England.

Origins of Puritanism 清教主义的起源

The roots of Puritanism can be found in the Protestant Reformation of the first half of the sixteenth century. Martin Luther and John Calvin both broke with the Catholic Church for theological reasons. Both argued that the Catholic Church had strayed from its spiritual mission. The Protestant Reformation took hold in much of Northern Europe but not, initially, in England. In the 1530s, King Henry VIII of England initiated his own break with the Catholic Church. His break, however, was not over theological differences with Rome, but over political control. Henry wanted control of the vast holdings of the church in England and the power to appoint members of the church hierarchy, as well as the power to annul his marriage. Because Henry's break with Rome was not theological in nature, he did not question, nor did he change, the traditional Roman Catholic religious practices. This "halfway reformation" upset many true Protestants in England. Those who sought a full reformation in England, who wanted the Church of England to be "purified" of Catholic practices, came to be known as Puritans. Some Puritans went even further and argued for a complete separation from the Church of England.

THE RELIGIOUS SCHISMS OF EUROPE
欧洲的宗教分裂

Although the Protestant Reformation occurred in Europe, it cannot be ignored by students of American history. The religious divisions of Europe profoundly impacted colonial America and the United States.

Puritan Beliefs and Practices 清教徒的信仰与习俗

The Puritans took their inspiration from Calvinism. Calvinist doctrine taught that individual salvation was subject to a divine plan, rather than to the actions of individuals. The doctrine of predestination left true believers in a state of anxiety, since it was impossible to know God's will. To lessen this sense of anxiety, Puritans lived lives of strict piety, framed by prayer, righteous living, and hard work. Calvinism held that everyone had a "calling"—work on Earth that God intended the individual to do. Being diligent at one's "calling," therefore, was central to Puritanism.

The Puritans also put a great value on community. They believed it was God's will that members of the community take care of one another and watch that members did not go astray. Individual malfeasance could result in divine punishment for the entire community.

Finally, the Puritan approach to humanity and to God was markedly dour, even dark. The Puritans put a great deal of emphasis on "original sin" (stemming from Eve, and then Adam, violating God's injunction not to eat the forbidden fruit in the Garden of Eden) and saw humanity as tainted with this inheritance. Further, the Puritan vision of God was closer to the vengeful, jealous God found in much of the Old Testament, rather than the loving God found in much of the New Testament.

Plymouth and the Mayflower Compact 普利茅斯与《五月花号公约》

A group of separatists, known to history as the "Pilgrims," fled England in 1608 to find a more hospitable religious climate in Holland. Holland, by this time, was tolerant of different beliefs and had a strong Calvinist presence, and it seemed like the ideal location for this group of English Calvinists. Although the Pilgrims did not suffer religious persecution in Holland, their leaders became concerned about the country's material temptations. These leaders came to believe that the challenges of establishing a settlement in the New World would steel the congregants for the rigors of religious piety. William Bradford and the leadership of the separatist community got permission from the English king to settle in the land granted to the Virginia

Company. They formed a joint-stock company to fund the expedition. Slightly over a hundred separatists set sail on the *Mayflower* in 1620, arriving on Cape Cod 11 weeks later. They quickly realized that they were well north of their targeted area, and did not have legal authority to settle. To provide a sense of legitimacy they drew up and signed the Mayflower Compact, an agreement calling for orderly government based on the consent of the governed. The colony of Plymouth struggled the first year. By 1630, it achieved a small degree of success, but it failed to attract large numbers of mainline Puritans from England.

PLYMOUTH AND NEW ENGLAND
普利茅斯与新英格兰

The Pilgrims of Plymouth would remain largely on the margins of New England society. The Massachusetts Bay Colony, founded a decade later, would prove to be far more successful. One reason for the centrality of Plymouth in historical accounts is that it was the first New England colony.

Massachusetts Bay Colony—"A City Set Upon a Hill"
马萨诸塞湾殖民地——"山巅之城"

By the 1620s, many Puritans were eager to leave England. King Charles I, with the encouragement of his advisor, Archbishop William Laud, sought to suppress the religious practices of Puritans and other nonconforming sects in England. In 1629, the king, perhaps eager to rid England of Puritans, granted a charter to the Massachusetts Bay Company to establish a colony in the northern part of British North America. The charter did not specify the exact location of the company's headquarters, allowing the governance of the Massachusetts Bay Company to be located in the colony instead of in England. This gave the colony a high degree of autonomy. The leader of the Massachusetts Bay Colony was John Winthrop. Before their ship, the *Arbella*, landed in present-day Salem in 1630, Winthrop gave a sermon that is considered one of the more important in American history. He stressed the importance of the colonists' mission. They should think of their colony as being "a city set upon a hill," for, he insisted, "The eyes of all people are upon us."

"A CITY SET UPON A HILL"
"山巅之城"

This phrase is from Winthrop's sermon "A Model of Christian Charity." The sermon is very important and gives an excellent description of the Puritan mission in the New World.

CHURCH AND STATE   教会和国家

Students of American history often make a profound mistake about church and state in colonial Massachusetts. They hear in history class, "The Puritans came to America to freely practice their religion." From this they conclude that the origins of religious freedom can be found in Massachusetts. This is absolutely incorrect. The Puritans (with the exception of Roger Williams) established theocratic governments.

The "Great Migration" and the Growth of New England
"大迁徙"与新英格兰的发展

Like their fellow New Englanders in Plymouth, the settlers of the Massachusetts Bay Colony, centered in present-day Boston, had a difficult first year. However, unlike the Pilgrims' original settlement in Plymouth, Winthrop's colony was soon thriving. By 1640, a "great migration" of more than 20,000 settlers came to Massachusetts Bay Colony. The settlers arriving in

Massachusetts Bay were middling sorts—farmers, carpenters, textile workers—not the aristocratic settlers of Jamestown. While the Jamestown settlers were primarily men, Massachusetts Bay Colony tended to attract families. The settlers in Massachusetts were eager to build permanent, cohesive communities, and they were willing to labor; they were not looking for quick riches. Massachusetts Bay Colony burgeoned with ten new towns in the first decade after 1630 and more than 130 by the end of the century.

GREAT MIGRATIONS 大迁徙

Avoid confusing the seventeenth-century "Great Migration" of the Puritans to New England with the twentieth-century "Great Migration" of African Americans from the rural South to the urban North and West.

New Hampshire 新罕布什尔

Some Puritans moved north to the area that would become New Hampshire. These settlers were predated by small fishing villages founded by the English in the 1620s. Massachusetts soon claimed the region, and a 1641 agreement gave it jurisdiction over New Hampshire. A royal decree separated the two colonies in 1679.

Roger Williams and the Founding of Rhode Island 罗杰·威廉姆斯与罗德岛的建立

Puritan society encouraged the intensive study of scripture. At the same time, the Puritan hierarchy enforced a rigid conformity to its own religious doctrine. This combination of a promotion of learning but insistence on conformity led to inevitable conflicts in New England. Roger Williams was a devout Puritan minister who became an important dissenter in Massachusetts. Williams was increasingly concerned about the mistreatment of American Indians by the Puritans (see page 71). He was also critical of the involvement of the church in matters of civil governance. He was worried that the concerns of civil government would distract ministers from godly matters. He fled to the Narragansett Bay area in 1636, and founded the colony of Rhode Island. One of the distinguishing characteristics of Rhode Island was the separation of church and state in its governance.

The Banishment of Anne Hutchinson 安妮·哈钦森的流放

Another important theological dispute in Puritan New England involved Anne Hutchinson. Hutchinson was a deeply religious thinker and had the temerity to hold meetings in her house to discuss theological matters with both men and women. In many ways, she took Puritan thought to its logical extreme, arguing that ministers were not needed to interpret and convey the teachings of the Bible; rather, God could communicate directly to true believers. Further, she accused Puritan leaders of backsliding on the idea that salvation was determined solely by God's divine plan, not by the actions of individuals. In 1638, John Winthrop and other Puritan leaders tried, excommunicated, and banished Hutchinson and her family.

The Founding of Connecticut 康涅狄格的建立

Some settlers to the growing Massachusetts Bay Colony sought to rid themselves of the heavy-handed rule of the colony's governor, John Winthrop. The Reverend Thomas Hooker disagreed with Winthrop over who should be admitted to church membership. Winthrop insisted that new members be able to demonstrate to church leaders that they had had a conversion experience. Hooker argued for a rigorous requirement; he asserted that living a godly life was sufficient to be considered for church membership. Hooker led a group to the Connecticut River Valley in 1636, where they founded the town of Hartford, well away from the reach of Winthrop. Other towns formed along the Connecticut River, combining with Hartford to form the colony of Connecticut. The Fundamental Orders of Connecticut were adopted in 1639. In 1662, the town of New Haven merged into the Connecticut colony.

The Splintering of Puritanism　清教主义的分裂

By the end of the seventeenth century, divisions were seen in the Puritan experiment. To some degree, the second and third generation of Puritans did not maintain the zeal and fire of the founding group. By the 1650s, Puritan leaders were noting a decline in church membership. Also, the economic vitality of the New England communities might have pulled some people away from the demands of Puritanism. The splintering of Puritanism can be seen in both the creation of the Halfway Covenant and in the Salem witch trials.

The Halfway Covenant (1662)　《妥协契约》（1662）

Potential new members of Puritan churches in New England—either children of original members or new arrivals—had to demonstrate to church elders that they had had a conversion experience. The candidate for membership in the Congregational Church (as the Puritan church came to be called) had to convince church elders that they had experienced the workings of God in their soul. Demonstrating a conversion experience was exceedingly difficult. In the face of declining membership, the idea of partial membership evolved. The Halfway Covenant (1662) was an initiative in the Congregational Church to allow for partial church membership for children of church members. Even if they could not demonstrate a conversion experience, they could be baptized and become partial, non-voting members of the church.

Salem Witch Trials (1692)　塞勒姆审巫案（1692）

The 1692 witch trials in Salem, Massachusetts, also demonstrate division in the once-cohesive Puritan community. In a global sense, the Salem witch trials are a mere footnote to the centuries of witch-hunts in Europe that led to perhaps a hundred thousand people being executed. Events in Salem in 1692 came at the tail end of this chapter in history.

The first to be accused of witchcraft in Salem were teenage girls. To be accused of witchcraft meant that the defendant was thought to be working in consort with Satan. In Puritan thinking, every event had some cosmic explanation. Misfortune in one's life (a stillborn child or a bad harvest) could be divine punishment for sinful behavior. It could also, however, be the work of an enemy who was channeling the power of Satan. This second explanation of misfortune pushed blame onto someone else—a witch. The epidemic of accusations in Salem tells us much about the Puritan community, three generations after John Winthrop urged his fellow Puritans on board the *Arbella,* to "be knit together in this work as one man." The fact that over a hundred members of the Salem community were accused of consorting with Satan speaks to the perceived lack of Godly piety in New England. Also, the fact that neighbors were so ready to turn on neighbors, that men were ready to turn on women (the majority of the accused were women), and that the poorer members were ready to turn on the wealthy members, all reflect a fractured community.

C. THE MIDDLE COLONIES　中部殖民地

The most diverse colonies in British North America—in regard to religion, ethnicity, and social class—were the middle colonies. The middle colonies developed a thriving export economy based on the cultivation of cereal crops.

Pennsylvania　宾夕法尼亚

In 1681, King Charles II granted an enormous piece of land (25,000 square miles) to William Penn to settle a debt that the king had owed to Penn's father. William Penn and the king were on friendly terms, despite the fact that Penn had become a devout Quaker and was often at odds with the official Church of England. Charles was no doubt pleased to see the establishment of a colony to draw the dissenting Quakers out of England. The king named the colony after William Penn's father, much to the embarrassment of Penn, the younger.

Quakerism and the "Holy Experiment"　贵格会与"神圣实验地"

Quakerism provided the guiding set of beliefs in the founding of Pennsylvania. Quakerism developed in the religious ferment of seventeenth-century England. Its approach to religion, and indeed to life, was radically non-hierarchical. In a society characterized by social titles and rules of deference, Quakers saw one another as equals in the eyes of God. They addressed one another as "friend" (hence, the formal name of Quakerism, the "Religious Society of Friends"). They avoided the practice of the "lower sorts" bowing or removing their hats to their "betters"; Quakers shook hands with one another. Quakers did not have sermons; they attended "meetings" in which each congregant could speak if moved. Penn wanted to establish a "holy experiment" in the New World to put Quakerism's egalitarian values into practice. He initiated friendly relations with local native groups. Pennsylvania's Quakers practiced religious toleration and frowned upon slavery (although it did exist in colonial Pennsylvania). Pennsylvania thrived in the seventeenth century, and its largest city, Philadelphia, surpassed New York as a commercial center.

DEFERENCE AND EGALITARIANISM
差异与平等主义

Deference—the ritualistic display of submission by common people toward those of a "superior" class—was standard social practice in the European and colonial American world of the seventeenth and eighteenth centuries. The egalitarian spirit of Quakerism would come to shape social norms in the early United States.

New Jersey and Delaware　新泽西与特拉华

New Jersey and Delaware were both initially established by the Dutch. After Dutch New Netherlands came into the hands of the British in 1664 (see page 54), the Duke of York gave the land adjacent to New York, between the Hudson and Delaware Rivers, to two friends, Sir George Carteret and Lord Berkeley of Stratton, who established the colony of New Jersey.

Delaware was first settled by the Dutch in 1631, but all the initial settlers were soon killed in a dispute with Native Americans. In 1638, Sweden established a trading post and colony in Delaware at Fort Christina (present-day Wilmington). In 1651, the Dutch established a fort in the Swedish colony; Holland took over the colony and incorporated it into its North American holdings, New Netherland, in 1655. When the Dutch were ousted by the British in 1664, the Duke of York granted Delaware to his friend William Penn, who incorporated it into his Pennsylvania land grant (see page 61). In 1704 Pennsylvania's Lower Counties, as Delaware was referred to, developed their own representative body and effectively became independent of Pennsylvania.

(see page 61)

> ## NEW AMSTERDAM AND NEW YORK
> ## 新阿姆斯特丹和纽约
>
> There are commonalities between colonial New Amsterdam and modern New York City. In both, commerce plays a more important role than religion. Also, both are incredibly diverse ethnically and racially.

New York 纽约

New Amsterdam came into English hands in 1664, and was renamed New York. New York continued to function as a commercial port, similar to Boston or Philadelphia. One factor that distinguished New York from similar northern port cities was the central position that slavery played in the local economy. By the mid 1800s, New York had a slave population greater than North Carolina's (but less than the other southern colonies). On the eve of the American Revolution, New York City's 3,000 slaves accounted for 14 percent of the city's population.

The "Negro Plot of 1741" "1741年黑奴阴谋"

The tensions in New York between whites and enslaved African Americans came to the surface in several events in 1741. A series of unexplained fires in the city led authorities to believe that a slave conspiracy was afoot. Over 150 African Americans were arrested, along with 20 whites. At least 20 people were executed, more than during the period of the Salem witch trials. Historians have debated the extent of the plot, or whether there even was a plot.

> ## SLAVERY IN THE NORTH 北方的奴隶制
>
> In an essay that addresses slavery in the colonial period, do not ignore slavery in the northern colonies. Slavery was legal in all 13 colonies at one time. Northern slaves worked as sailors, domestic servants, longshoremen, and artisans' assistants. New York, especially, had a large slave population. Slavery in the North was never as strong as it was in the South, but it did exist.

D. THE LOWER SOUTH AND THE COLONIES OF THE WEST INDIES
下南部与西印度群岛殖民地

The colonies of the Deep South—Carolina and Georgia—as well as British colonies in the West Indies, all shared certain characteristics that set them apart from the rest of British colonial America. These colonies had longer growing seasons and came to depend on exporting staple crops and on the slave-labor system. The population of the Deep South was considerably less than that of the upper South, and the ratio of blacks to whites was significantly different. In many cases, enslaved Africans made up the majority of a colony's population. In South Carolina by the mid-eighteenth century, there were approximately twice as many black slaves as there were whites.

Sugar and Slavery in the West Indies　西印度群岛的蔗糖与奴隶制

Barbados was the most profitable colony in Britain's New World empire. Barbados developed an economy based on agriculture and slavery, as did the colonies of the Chesapeake region. However, the Barbados model was significantly different.

Barbados was settled by English colonists in the 1630s and soon became very successful. The source of wealth for the planters of Barbados was sugarcane. Sugar produced from sugarcane received high prices in England. By the end of the seventeenth century, the English colonies of the Caribbean were exporting nearly 50 million pounds of sugar per year. Sugarcane favored wealthy planters, because only they could afford the initial investment needed in a sugar growing and processing operation. Unlike Virginia, there was no small-scale yeoman-farmer class in Barbados. The wealthy sugar planters of Barbados were, on average, four times as wealthy as the tobacco planters of Virginia. In addition, the slave population of Barbados was much larger than that of Virginia. By the end of the seventeenth century, slaves made up 75 percent of the population of Barbados, compared to less than 25 percent in Virginia. The average sugar grower in Barbados owned 115 slaves, far more than the average plantation in Virginia. Plantation work in Barbados was brutal—long hours of intense labor under the hot sun. Slaves in Barbados were much less likely to form families than slaves in Virginia, with men outnumbering women two to one in Barbados.

Carolina　卡罗莱纳

The initial settlers of the colony of Carolina were mostly planters who had migrated from Barbados. They brought with them the system of slavery that they had developed on the island, making the economy of Carolina resemble that of Barbados more than that of Virginia. Carolina was established in 1663 by King Charles II. Charles II was restored to the throne in 1660, and to reward eight noblemen who had helped him regain the crown, he granted them a charter for the lands south of Virginia. These proprietors recruited additional wealthy slave-owning English settlers in Barbados to resettle in Carolina. The early Carolinians looked to replicate the export-oriented plantation economy of Barbados, but they could not find a crop nearly as profitable as sugar. By the late 1600s, they began making money growing and exporting rice.

In the 1670s and 1680s, the economy of the northern part of Carolina began to diverge from that of the southern part (see page 56). The two regions were distinct economically and relatively remote from each other. This economic division led to political division; in 1691, a deputy governor was charged with administering the northern part of the colony. The split was made official in 1712. South Carolina, declared a royal colony in 1719, continued to operate an economic system like that of Barbados, with thousands of slaves controlled by a relatively small number of elite planters.

Georgia　佐治亚

The last of the original 13 colonies to be established was Georgia. Britain became increasingly concerned about competition from other European nations making New World land claims. Britain wanted to establish a buffer between South Carolina and Spanish-held Florida. Toward this end, Britain granted a charter to James Oglethorpe to establish the colony of Georgia in 1732. Oglethorpe was a philanthropist and hoped to establish a paternalistic colony for Britain's "deserving poor," including imprisoned debtors. Oglethorpe did not grant his charges any element of representative government. He mandated military service for all males. The royal plan seems to have been to enlist the poor colonists of Georgia to protect the wealthy planters of South Carolina from Spanish encroachment. Oglethorpe's plans did not come to fruition. Few "deserving poor" met Oglethorpe's requirements. Instead, Carolinians in search of new land moved into Georgia, and brought slavery with them. In 1752, Oglethorpe gave up on his project and ceded control of the colony to the Crown.

E. THE DEVELOPMENT OF SELF-GOVERNMENT IN BRITAIN'S NEW WORLD COLONIES 英国新世界殖民地自治的发展

By the eighteenth century, the British colonies of North America had developed institutions of self-government that were remarkably democratic for that era. These early attempts at representative democracy can be seen as laying the groundwork for eventual independence from Great Britain.

The Evolution of Governance in Colonial North America 北美殖民地的治理的发展

Institutions of self-government developed in a relative power vacuum—Great Britain did not create an extensive governing structure in its North American colonies (as it later would in India), in part because of their remoteness from the "mother country" as well as Great Britain's lax attention to its New World empire. Rather, most of the 13 colonies followed a different form of political development. Whether the colonies were first ruled by a corporation or a proprietor, they eventually all became royal colonies, under the supervision of the Crown. The king appointed a governor to rule over each colony (sometimes one governor ruled over two colonies). However, in all cases, some sort of colonial legislature existed. These legislatures dealt with local matters (not trade regulations, for example), including the power to tax the inhabitants of the colony. Governors came to depend on funding from this tax revenue to run the colony. In many instances, the colonial legislatures were able to exercise a good deal of leverage over the royal governors because of this "power of the purse," which instilled in many colonists a sense of their ability to govern themselves.

Town Meetings in New England 新英格兰的镇民大会

New England town meetings were face-to-face decision-making assemblies that were open to all free male residents of a town. These meetings, usually held annually, made important decisions about the town and selected a group of representatives, "selectmen," who carried out governing functions until the next town meeting. This form of direct democracy allowed for a high degree of citizen participation in decision-making.

The House of Burgesses in Virginia 弗吉尼亚州的殖民地议会

The House of Burgesses was created by the Virginia Company in 1619. The company had founded the colony of Virginia in 1607 as a profit-generating venture. The company saw the need for some sort of body to govern the inhabitants of the colony and created this representative assembly. Initially, all free adult men could vote for representatives; later, voting rights were limited to wealthy men. After the king transferred governance of Virginia from the Virginia Company to the crown in 1624, he allowed the House of Burgesses to continue. Over time, the House of Burgesses became less powerful and more exclusive, as smaller planters were barred from voting.

III. Trade, Competition Over Resources, and Conflict in Colonial North America 北美殖民时期的贸易、资源争夺与冲突

In the seventeenth and eighteenth centuries, conflict intensified in North America between rival European empires and between North American colonists and American Indians. A major source of conflict in colonial North America was competition over resources—notably land and furs.

A. THE ATLANTIC ECONOMY AND THE EVOLUTION OF COLONIAL ECONOMIES
大西洋经济与殖民经济的发展

The 1700s witnessed the growth of an Atlantic economy—one characterized by an increased exchange of goods. Colonial economies focused on selling commodities to Europe and in gaining new sources of labor. Ultimately, these interactions led to a tremendous growth in colonial economies, new forms of social interactions, and an increase in the use of slave labor.

Trade Networks 贸易网

Traditionally labeled the "triangle trade," this complex trading network developed in the 1700s brought manufactured items from England to both Africa and to the Americas. These items included firearms, shoes, furniture, ceramics, and many other items. In Africa, kidnapped people were sold by human traffickers who forced them into the international slave trade. Africans were taken from interior regions, usually by members of coastal African groups. In the port towns, European traders exchanged manufactured items for human cargo. Then, these captives had to endure the brutal Middle Passage to the New World.

New World colonies tended to focus on growing and obtaining foodstuffs that could be traded with Europeans. The colonies of the Americas produced a wide variety of raw materials. Caribbean sugar, for instance, was shipped both to New England and to Europe.

Tobacco, Indigo, Rice, Sugar, and Slavery in the South and the West Indies
南方与西印度群岛的烟草、靛蓝、稻米、蔗糖和奴隶制

By the eighteenth century, the economic status of most of the North American colonies improved, as the colonies focused on crops and economic activities that were suited for the local climate and geography, and that could be marketed to European nations. After several years of economic uncertainty, Virginians came to settle on the cultivation, processing, and export of tobacco (see page 55). The colonies of the lower South specialized in indigo and rice. These two crops made up nearly two-thirds of exports from the lower South by 1750. All told, the southern colonies supplied 90 percent of the exports from British North America. However, the most profitable of all the British New World colonies were the sugar-growing islands of the West Indies. Throughout the South and the West Indies, agricultural work was performed primarily by slave labor (see page 63).

The Fur Trade in the North American Interior 北美内陆的毛皮贸易

A lucrative fur trade drew French, Dutch, and English traders and colonists to the interiors of the North American continent—specifically the broad swath of land stretching north from the Ohio River toward the St. Lawrence River and Great Lakes. This fur trade led Europeans to reach accommodations with American Indian groups, in contrast to the agricultural settlements along the Atlantic Coast, where relations with American Indians were characterized by extermination and removal. The increased trade in furs often destabilized American Indian communities by pushing native peoples to extend their traditional territory in search of more furs. This territorial expansion inevitably brought on conflict with neighboring Indian groups. We see an increase in the intensity of warfare in the seventeenth and eighteenth centuries, as Indian groups, allied with and armed by competing European powers, fought for territory and trading privileges (see pages 67–70).

Wheat, Indentured Servants, and Redemptioners in the Middle Colonies
中部殖民地的小麦、契约佣工和偿债佣工

By the eighteenth century, settlers in the middle colonies of Pennsylvania and New York, many of them German and Scotch-Irish immigrants, developed the cultivation of wheat and other cereal crops for export to Europe. Whereas the southern colonies used the slave system to solve the problem of finding laborers in the New World, the middle colonies tended to rely on indentured servants (see page 56) and "redemptioners." Redemptioners were transported to the New World by sea captains; they promised to pay for their passage once they arrived in the New World by either borrowing money from a friend or relative already there, or by contracting for several years of servitude. Redemptioners were at a distinct disadvantage as compared to indentured servants. Indentured servants generally worked out the details of their indenture back in Europe; they could negotiate and refuse unreasonable offers. Redemptioners, on the other hand—tired, ill-fed, frequently sick, and stuck on an unsanitary ship in a New World harbor—were in no position to negotiate effectively with potential masters. Over time, however, the initial difficulties faced by the redemptioners usually paid off. Once freed from their service, they thrived, particularly in Pennsylvania. The standard of living for typical Pennsylvania farmers was higher than in any other comparable agricultural region in the eighteenth-century world.

Fish and Lumber in New England   新英格兰的鱼类与木材

The New England countryside did not lend itself to growing profitable export crops. New England farmers tended to grow a variety of crops for local consumption. Many New Englanders engaged in fishing in order to participate in the Atlantic trade. Salted fish made up a third of total exports from New England to Europe. Livestock and timber accounted for another third of New England exports. New Englanders acquired molasses from the sugar-growing British West Indies and distilled it into rum, which became an increasingly important export after 1700. These distillers also purchased French molasses, leading Parliament to pass the Molasses Act of 1733 (see page 71). The act, which was loosely enforced and routinely violated, placed a steep duty on foreign molasses.

New England towns grew into commercial centers engaged in an Atlantic exchange with Europe, the West Indies, and Africa. The population of New England was the most homogenously English of any of Great Britain's New World holdings. After the waves of Puritan migrations of the 1600s, few immigrants ended up in New England, favoring the middle colonies instead. In fact, many New Englanders left the region in the eighteenth century. The region grew through natural reproduction in the eighteenth century, but less rapidly than the middle colonies or the South.

B. CONTACT, TRADE, DISEASE, AND DEMOGRAPHIC CHANGES FOR AMERICAN INDIANS   美洲印第安人与外界的联系、贸易、疾病及人口变化

The expansion of European colonial effort in the New World dramatically altered the traditional cultures of American Indian peoples. Patterns of trade as well as the arrival of diseases reshaped their communities. Many American Indian tribes were devastated by disease, while others managed to maintain sustainable population levels. To some degree, the choices made by American Indians themselves played an important role in the outcome of increased contact with European colonists.

The Catawba—Contact, Trade, and Cultural Adaptation
卡托巴人——联系、贸易与文化适应

In the face of conquest and encroachment by European settlers, American Indian groups were often left with stark choices—work for the settlers, move inland, resist encroachment, or join other American Indian groups. The Catawba people of the American Southeast attempted to ensure their survival by making themselves useful to the advancing settlers. They had extensive contact with the towns of colonial South Carolina as traveling peddlers, selling goods such as pottery, baskets, and moccasins. Sustained contact with settlers altered Catawba culture in significant ways. The nature of basket-making and pottery changed, as Catawba artisans transformed ancient practices to meet heightened demand. By the 1750s, the introduction of alcohol as a form of payment for goods led to drunkenness and increased brawls and instability within the Catawba community. The Catawba had generally amicable relations with colonists, but prolonged contact slowly eroded traditional cultural ways.

Contact, Disease, Warfare, and the Collapse of the Huron
休伦人与外界的联系、经历的疾病、战争及其溃散

Early in the seventeenth century, the Huron people, who lived in Ontario, made contact with French explorer Samuel de Champlain. In 1609, the Huron made an alliance with the French. By the 1630s, increased contact with French settlers, including Jesuit priests, proved to be disastrous for the Huron. It is estimated that the Huron numbered between 20,000 and 40,000 at the time of European contact. As contact increased after 1634, a major epidemic of measles and smallpox afflicted the Huron people, resulting in the deaths of half to two-thirds of the population.

The Beaver Wars (see below) further devastated the Huron. In 1649, an Iroquois war party of about a thousand warriors, supplied with firearms by their Dutch allies, destroyed the Huron mission villages in Ontario, killing approximately 300 people. Iroquois warriors also killed several Jesuits. The Huron ended up fleeing from the Iroquois to an island in Georgian Bay, Ontario, where large numbers died due to harsh conditions and lack of food. Eventually, many Huron resettled to Quebec and others to the upper Lake Michigan region. The intensity of the new form of warfare unleashed by European contact completely upended traditional methods of resolving conflicts for many American Indian groups. In the end, entire communities were often destroyed or relocated.

C. IMPERIAL CONFLICTS AND NORTH AMERICAN POLITICAL INSTABILITY
帝国的冲突与北美的政治动荡

The political situation in North America grew increasingly unstable in the seventeenth and eighteenth centuries. Old rivalries in Europe among the French, Dutch, British, and Spanish spilled over to the New World, and in the process drew various American Indian groups into these conflicts. The introduction of European firearms into conflicts among American Indians altered the political and military landscape of North America.

The Beaver Wars (1640–1701) 海狸战争（1640—1701）

Traditional rivalries between American Indian groups took on new dimensions in the age of European colonization. Several European powers formed alliances with American Indian groups. Further, the introduction of European firearms, often obtained in the fur trade, intensified the impact of armed conflicts. The Beaver Wars, an especially brutal series of events in the middle and late seventeenth century, illustrate the destabilizing influence of trade and European firepower on American Indian relations.

Competition in the fur trade (as the name of the wars implies) led to violent conflict. Both the Dutch and the French had established trading posts to obtain furs from native groups in exchange for a variety of goods, including firearms. French traders established a series of trading posts along the St. Lawrence River in the early 1600s, aligning themselves with Algonquian-speaking tribes. The Dutch had established a trading post at present-day Albany in 1614, at the edge of territory controlled by the Iroquois, and had developed an alliance and profitable trade with the Iroquois Confederacy. The Iroquois hoped to expand their trading network, but the Huron stood in their way. By 1645 long-simmering tensions between the Dutch-allied Iroquois and the French-allied Algonquian-speaking tribes of the Great Lakes region, notably the Huron, exploded into open warfare.

Dutch rule was superseded by the British, who took control of New Netherland in 1664. The British allied themselves with the Iroquois Confederacy in its ongoing battles with the French and their American Indian allies until the Beaver Wars ended in 1701, with the Great Peace of Montreal. The Iroquois were able to expand their territory and influence; the Huron suffered disaster (see page 67). The Iroquois also realized that they held the balance of power between the British and the French. The wars, the pressures of the fur trade, and the introduction of European firearms all contributed to a realignment of American Indian alliances and a reorganization of their societies.

The French and Indian Wars and Control of North America (1688–1763)

法国对印第安人的战争与对北美的控制（1688—1763）

There were four significant conflicts for control of much of North America between 1688 and 1763. These wars, labelled the French and Indian Wars, include King William's War (1688–1697), Queen Anne's War (1702–1713), and King George's War (1744–1748). The fourth war, called the French and Indian War (1754–1763), was the most decisive, eliminating the French military and governmental presence in North America (see more on the French and Indian War in Period 3).

These wars followed similar patterns. For one, the first three (each named after the reigning British monarch) grew out of conflicts in Europe between Great Britain and France; the fourth war originated in North America and turned into a worldwide conflict between the two empires. Second, the wars involved, and intensified, ongoing rivalries between American Indian groups. Tribes formed alliances with the British or the French. They were able to maintain a degree of autonomy in North America through the first half of the century through these alliances. As long as neither of these two sides was able to achieve a decisive victory, American Indians were able to maintain some control of their territory. This changed, as we shall see in Period 3, with the complete withdrawal of the French colonial presence from North America following the French and Indian War. Finally, the wars tended to increase the bonds between the British colonists and the government of Great Britain. As long as enemies threatened colonial interests along disputed and ambiguous borderlands, the colonists felt the need of British military might. After the defeat of the French in 1763, colonists began to reevaluate their role within the British Empire.

King William's War (1688-1697) 威廉王之战（1688—1697）

King William's War was the New World manifestation of the Nine Years' War in Europe between France and an alliance of countries, including Great Britain. The war in the New World grew out of conflicts over the borders between British and French claims in North America as well as tensions and concerns of competing American Indian confederations.

In New York and the Great Lakes region, the Iroquois Confederacy, allied with British colonists, had come to dominate the fur trade since the 1680s, largely as a result of the Beaver Wars (see page 67). This domination was challenged by French colonists and their Indian allies farther to the west. In 1688, skirmishes occurred in New York and Canada between Indian groups, encouraged and supported by their European colonial allies. At the same time, farther east, violence erupted over the boundary between New England and New France. English settlements in Maine were encroaching upon the French colony of Acadia (which included present-day Nova Scotia, New Brunswick, and Maine north of the Kennebec River). These encroachments were challenged by the French, as well as by Indian groups in the area. These northern groups had formed the Wabanaki Confederacy in order to halt further encroachments by New Englanders after the defeat of native peoples in King Philip's War (see page 72).

Following the war, the Iroquois Confederacy, decimated and exhausted by war, skillfully negotiated the Grand Settlement of 1701 with France and other Indian nations. For the next fifty years, the Iroquois were primarily neutral in the conflicts over control of North America.

Queen Anne's War (1702-1713) 安妮女王之战（1702—1713）

Queen Anne's War occurred on the border with Canada and in the American South. In the North, French and British forces continued the struggle for territory as they had earlier in King William's War. British forces gained control of Newfoundland and Hudson Bay; the boundary between British Maine and French Acadia was left unresolved.

Again, the Wabanaki Confederacy joined the French in trying to stop the northern advance of British colonists. During the war, the Wabanaki, with French support, staged a bold raid on Deerfield, Massachusetts, and destroyed the town, killing 56 colonists and taking 112 as captives to Quebec. The captivity captured the imaginations of New Englanders. One of the captives, Deerfield's minister, Reverend John Williams, wrote a best-selling account of his capture and subsequent return to Massachusetts. Williams's daughter, Eunice, ended up choosing to stay in Quebec. She married a Kahnawake and lived out her life among them. Her decision to live among the Indians led to soul-searching among her family and fellow Puritans.

In the South, European powers and allied American Indian groups fought for control of territory. In the late 1600s, French fur traders pushed down the Mississippi River. France wanted to reinforce earlier claims to the lower Mississippi River basin made by French explorer Robert de La Salle in 1670. At the same time, British traders and slave raiders pushed west from Carolina. The Chickasaw people emerged as active participants in procuring slaves for British traders and formed an alliance with them. Meanwhile, the Choctaw, traditional enemies of the Chickasaw, formed an alliance with the French, who established forts at present-day Biloxi, Mississippi, and Mobile, Alabama. Meanwhile, tensions emerged between Great Britain and Spain over the boundary between Spanish Florida and British Carolina, south of the Savannah River (in present-day Georgia). The French and Spanish formed an alliance, also enlisting the Apalachee, to challenge the British presence in the South.

The ensuing war did not settle boundary issues, but it weakened the Spanish presence in Florida and devastated American Indians in Spanish Florida. The Apalachee and the Timucua were virtually destroyed in a massacre by the British in 1704. In terms of the Mississippi River basin, the Chickasaw (allied with the British) suffered huge losses but were able to hold their ground against continued attacks by the Choctaw and the Illini, with assistance from the French. The attacks drove the Chickasaw to become increasingly dependent on the British. Fighting between these groups continued into the 1730s, with major encounters in 1736 and 1739. The fighting did not cease until the defeat of the French in the French and Indian War in 1763.

King George's War (1744–1748)　乔治王之战（1744—1748）

The third conflict between the French and the British, King George's War (1744–1748), was fought in New York, Massachusetts, New Hampshire, and Nova Scotia. The war included a successful siege by Massachusetts soldiers on the newly built French fortress at Louisbourg in Nova Scotia. French and Indian forces destroyed Saratoga, New York. This war did not settle ongoing territorial disputes. In the peace treaty, the British agreed to return the fort at Louisbourg to the French (in exchange for France returning the city of Madras in India to the British). This decision angered the northern colonies, which had lost a large number of men to cold and disease while occupying the fort during the harsh winter after the siege.

D. DIVERGING INTERESTS—BRITISH POLICIES AND COLONIAL DISSATISFACTION　利益分歧——英国的政策与殖民地的不满

Mercantilist principles guided British policies in the New World. However, many colonists began to chafe at imperial policies and developed a set of priorities often at odds with the powers in Britain. Colonists grew increasingly dissatisfied over a number of issues.

Mercantilism　重商主义

Britain's ambitions in the New World were shaped by mercantilism—a set of economic and political ideas that shaped colonial policy for the major powers in the early modern world. Mercantilism holds that only a limited amount of wealth exists in the world. Nations increase their power by increasing their share of the world's wealth. Nations therefore try to maximize the amount of precious metals they hold. One way of acquiring precious metals is to maintain a favorable balance of trade, with the value of exports exceeding the value of imports. Mercantilist theory suggests that imperial governments should advance these goals by maintaining colonies so as to have a steady and inexpensive source for raw materials. The theory also holds that the colonies should not develop manufacturing but should purchase manufactured goods from the "mother country." The British government imposed several navigation laws (see below) on the American colonies to make sure they fulfilled their role. But some of these laws were difficult to enforce, and the 13 colonies began to develop an economy independent of Britain.

Navigation Acts and Mercantilism　航海条例与重商主义

From the 1650s until the American Revolution, Britain's Parliament passed a number of Navigation Acts. The goal of the acts, in conformity with mercantilist principles, was to define the colonies as suppliers of raw materials to Britain and as markets for British manufactured items. Toward this end, Parliament developed a list of "enumerated goods"—goods from the colonies that could only be shipped to Britain. These included goods that were essential for ship building, such as tar, pitch, and trees for masts. Also, Britain insisted that profitable staple crops from the southern slave colonies, such as rice, tobacco, sugar, and indigo, could be shipped only to England. These goods were sold both within England and at a considerable profit to other countries. The enumeration of these goods was a double-edged sword; the colonies could not always get the highest price for their goods, but they had a consistent market for them. Several of the acts—such as the Wool Act (1699), the Hat Act (1732), and the Iron Act (1750)—prohibited the colonies from exporting these items. In this way, Parliament gave an advantage to manufacturers in Britain.

MERCANTILISM VERSUS CAPITALISM
重商主义与资本主义

Be prepared to distinguish the economic ideas that shaped mercantilism from those that shaped capitalism. Mercantilism, for example, involved extensive government regulation of trade and economic activities; modern capitalism puts much more emphasis on free trade.

Lax Enforcement of Mercantilist Policies 重商主义政策执行不到位

The Navigation Acts existed on paper, but were difficult to enforce. The administrative costs of rigorous enforcement, combined with the distance between the colonies and Great Britain, contributed to lax enforcement of the Navigation Acts. In this setting, colonists routinely smuggled banned goods into and out of the 13 colonies. For example, the Molasses Act (1733) placed a prohibitive import tax on sugar and molasses from non-British colonies into North America. Boston merchants routinely flouted this law, importing illegal sugar to supply Massachusetts rum distilleries.

E. BRITISH COLONIAL EXPANSION AND CONFLICTS WITH AMERICAN INDIANS
英国的殖民扩张以及与美洲印第安人的冲突

As British colonial populations grew, colonists pushed inland, beyond their initial settlements. As they encroached upon land held by native peoples, a series of military confrontations occurred between colonists and Indians. Unlike the imperial struggles that occurred throughout North America (see pages 67–70), these conflicts were carried out by the colonists themselves. In many ways, these conflicts shaped the identity of the colonists in addition to transforming the lives of American Indian communities.

The Pequot War (1634–1638) 佩科特战争（1634—1638）

Contact between Native Americans and British colonists grew increasingly violent in New England, just as they had been in Virginia. The intensity of the clashes in New England led to major demographic changes in New England, as American Indians died in large numbers, with survivors moving farther into the interior of the region. The Puritan project of building an ideal community did not preclude them from forcing American Indian populations off land the Puritans intended to settle. The most violent episode in the first years of settlement was the Pequot War of 1634–1638. The colonies of Massachusetts Bay and Plymouth worked in alliance with each other and with the Narragansett and the Mohegan peoples to defeat the Pequots. Later, further warfare would virtually eliminate a cohesive native presence from New England.

King Philip's War (1675–1678) 菲利普国王战争（1675–1678）

Relations between New England colonists and Indians were relatively peaceful after the Pequot War of the 1630s (see page 71). However, brutal conflict occurred again in the 1670s. The Wampanoags, led by Chief Masassoit, had maintained peaceful relations with the Plymouth settlers. Masassoit had forged an alliance with the Pilgrims in 1621. Afterward, the Wampanoags and the Plymouth settlers maintained peaceful relations. However, by the 1670s, relations had deteriorated. New Englanders had steadily been pushing into the interior of New England, onto Wampanoag lands. The catalyst for combat was the 1675 execution of three Wampanoags who had been tried in a Plymouth court for killing a Christianized Wampanoag. The chief of the Wampanoag, Metacomet, the grandson of Masassoit, launched an attack on a string of Massachusetts towns. Several towns were destroyed, and over a thousand white people were killed. The counterattack by the New Englanders was fierce. The New Englanders received crucial support from the Mohawks, who were longtime foes of the Wampanoags. Metacomet, also known to whites as King Philip, was killed by a group of Mohawks, and several Wampanoag villages were destroyed by the colonists. By spring 1676, over 40 percent of the Wampanoag were killed. The war was catastrophic for both sides—the deadliest of the wars of European settlement in North America in regard to the percentage of the populations of each side killed.

"Praying Indians" in Puritan New England 清教新英格兰"祈祷的印第安人"

Whereas the Pueblo Indians managed to pressure Spanish colonizers to make some accommodations with Pueblo culture (see page 36), the native peoples of New England were less able to maintain traditional cultural patterns in the face of English colonization efforts. Some New England Indian groups mounted armed resistance to encroachments by the English; these efforts, the Pequot War (1637) and King Philip's War (1675–1678), ended tragically for the native peoples. Others made efforts to coexist with the Puritan settlers of New England. Some converted to Christianity and settled on farms. Puritan missionaries established "praying towns" for these "praying Indians." By the 1670s, there were 14 "praying towns" in New England. "Praying Indians" were still seen as second-class citizens by the Puritans. Puritans insisted that the converted Christian Indians wear European-style clothing and that they completely abandon their spiritual traditions (in contrast with French Jesuit missionaries in Canada, who accepted that native peoples might combine elements of Catholicism with their traditional beliefs). In the end, the "praying towns" tended to impose English practices on the Indians rather than allowing native peoples to retain some elements of their traditional ways.

Racial Hierarchy and American Indians 种族等级制度与美洲印第安人

The attitudes of English colonists toward American Indians changed over the course of the seventeenth century, as did their attitude toward enslaved Africans. Earlier in the century, the primary goal of the English settlers was to maintain peace with the native peoples. The early English settlements were precarious, and the importance of maintaining peace was acute. In this situation, English settlers made efforts to understand their neighbors and to figure out ways to coexist. As the century progressed, and as the settlements became growing colonies, the colonists' primary desire was no longer to maintain the peace, but was to acquire Indian land. As the English colonists expanded their land holdings, violent conflicts with American Indians inevitably ensued. This can be seen in King Philip's War in 1675. In the context of these clashes, the English colonists increasingly saw the American Indians as savages. "Savagery" became not just a description of American Indian behavior, but a trait of their race. As the seventeenth century progressed, this racial hierarchy hardened and, in the minds of the English, justified the continued exploitation of American Indian lands.

F. SPAIN AND AMERICAN INDIANS IN NORTH AMERICA 北美的西班牙与美洲印第安人

The Spanish pattern of colonization differed from the English pattern. To a large degree, these divergent patterns reflected the cultural norms of each colonizing power as well as the power dynamics that developed between the colonizers and the colonized. Spanish colonial efforts were more ready to make some accommodations to American Indian cultural ways, in contrast with English efforts, which often resulted in more complete destruction of American Indian communities.

Pueblo Revolt 普韦布洛叛乱

By the second half of the seventeenth century, Pueblo Indians in New Mexico had grown increasingly resentful of Spanish rule. The Spanish *encomienda* system undermined the traditional economy of the Pueblos, forcing them to labor in mines and fields. In addition, the Spanish outlawed traditional Pueblo religious practices. In 1680, these grievances came to the surface in the Pueblo Revolt, also known as Pope's Rebellion. The rebellion was centered in Santa Fe and resulted in attacks on Spanish Franciscan priests as well as ordinary Spaniards. More than 300 Spaniards were killed. Spanish residents fled, but returned later in the decade. As a result of the uprising, Spanish authorities appointed a public defender to protect native rights and agreed to allow the Pueblo to continue their cultural practices. Also, each Pueblo family was granted land. The outcome of this rebellion was markedly different from conflicts between English settlers and native peoples, whose clashes usually resulted in Indian removal or eradication.

> ## THE SPANISH COLONIAL EXPERIENCE
> ## 西班牙的殖民经历
>
> Students often ignore developments in New Spain. Be familiar with Spanish colonization, especially in the areas that would eventually become the United States. Contrary to traditional accounts, the American West was not an empty region before the period of "Manifest Destiny."

KEY CONCEPT 2.2 GREAT BRITAIN AND THE 13 COLONIES
核心概念2.2：大不列颠与13个殖民地

Great Britain and its 13 North American colonies participated in political, cultural, and economic exchanges. These exchanges led to stronger bonds between Great Britain and the colonies and among the 13 colonies themselves. Ultimately, the priorities and interests of the 13 colonies diverged from those of Great Britain, leading to tensions and to resistance on the part of the colonies.

I. The 13 Colonies and the Transatlantic World
13个殖民地与大西洋两岸的世界

Increasing cultural, political, and economic exchanges within the "Atlantic World" reshaped the worldviews and the prerogatives of New World colonists, as they became increasingly tied to Great Britain and to one another.

A. RELIGIOUS PLURALISM IN COLONIAL AMERICA   殖民地时期美国的宗教多元论

A variety of religious and spiritual movements flourished in colonial America. Many of these movements grew out of religious debates in Great Britain, while others reflected the religious sensibilities of immigrants from the Germanic states, Ireland, and elsewhere in Europe.

The "Great Awakening"   "大觉醒"

In the face of declining church membership and a lessening of religious zeal among New Englanders (see page 60), as well as the rise of Enlightenment philosophy and deism (see below), Protestant leaders sought to take action. By the 1730s, we see several charismatic ministers attempt to infuse a new passion into religious practice. These ministers and their followers were part of a religious resurgence known as the "Great Awakening." The origins of the Great Awakening can be traced to Great Britain. The most well-known Great Awakening preacher was the English minister, George Whitefield. Whitefield visited the North American colonies seven times, holding large revival meetings in dozens of locales in the 1740s, bringing huge audiences to a state of religious ecstasy. Other itinerant preachers brought an emotional religious message to thousands of colonists. The leaders of the movement took a more emotional, and less cerebral, approach to religion. In Massachusetts, the Puritan minister Jonathan Edwards delivered his most famous sermon, "Sinners in the Hands of an Angry God" to a mesmerized audience. The Great Awakening's core message was that anyone could be saved, and that people could make choices in their lives that would affect their afterlife. This was in stark contrast with traditional Puritan ideas of "original sin" and predestination. In this, the Great Awakening was more egalitarian and democratic.

Immigration and Dissenting Denominations   移民与不同的教派

In the seventeenth century, the great majority of churches in the British colonies were either Anglican or Congregational. These "established" churches were recognized and funded by the various colonial administrations (this was not the case in Rhode Island, New Jersey, and Pennsylvania, which separated government from religious institutions). Quakers continued to have a strong presence in Pennsylvania (see page 61).

However, by the mid-eighteenth century, acceptance of dissenting Protestant denominations became widespread throughout the colonies. Baptist and Methodist churches grew out of the Great Awakening. In addition, immigrants from Europe brought new denominations with them. The largest group of immigrants came from the Germanic states (over 100,000 in the colonial period). Most of these Germans settled in the backcountry areas of Pennsylvania, New York, and the South. Many were Lutheran and Calvinist; smaller sects of Mennonites, Moravians, and Dunkers were also established in Germanic areas of the colonies. Urban centers such as New York, with a great diversity of immigrant populations, including Sephardic Jews, added to the religious diversity of colonial America.

Deism and the Enlightenment   自然神论与启蒙运动

In the 1700s, many educated colonists moved away from the rigid doctrines of Puritanism and other faiths and adopted a form of worship known as *deism*. In a deist cosmology, God is as a distant entity. Deists did not see God intervening in the day-to-day affairs of humanity. God had created the world and had also created a series of natural laws to govern it. In their beliefs, deists were aligned with the Enlightenment ethos, including the aspiration to understand Earth's natural laws. Deists saw God as a great clockmaker—the Earth is like a clock, which God created, but it is the mechanisms of the clock, rather than God's interventions, that move the hour and the minute hands.

B. THE ANGLICIZATION OF BRITISH NORTH AMERICA 英属北美殖民地的英国化

The imprint of Great Britain on its North American colonies cannot be overstated. Many ideas and structures—from self-government to legal codes, from commerce to print culture, from religious toleration to Enlightenment thought—made their way from Great Britain and found fertile soil in the New World.

Emulating the British 效仿英国

Many residents of the British colonies—especially the more well-to-do—consciously attempted to model their lives in the New World on British patterns of culture. In many respects, each of the American colonies had more interactions with Great Britain—through trade and communication—than they had with the other colonies. Wealthy merchants and planters frequently sent their sons to Great Britain for schooling. Colonists of even modest means became increasingly interested in acquiring British-made goods. Colonists purchased British-made bedding, clocks, silver, china, wigs, books, and more. For many colonists, the pioneering ways of the seventeenth century, characterized by homemade goods, gave way to a more consumerist culture in the eighteenth century. For colonists of means, connections with British culture and goods allowed them to elevate their status; they did not want to be seen as provincial hicks on the edge of the civilized world.

Trans-Atlantic Print Culture 横跨大西洋的印刷文化

Residents of the 13 colonies had a high degree of literacy, which created a demand for printed materials. By the middle of the eighteenth century, Boston had eight printers, and New York and Philadelphia each had two. By the 1730s, newspapers existed in most colonial cities, including Charleston, South Carolina, and Williamsburg, Virginia. John Peter Zenger created the *New York Weekly Journal* in 1733. Benjamin Franklin took the reins of the *Pennsylvania Gazette* in 1729. These newspapers devoted a great deal of space to European affairs—at first, reprinting items from the British press, and later writing articles covering both European and local affairs. By the time of the American Revolution, over 40 weekly newspapers existed in colonial America.

Anglicanism and Enlightenment Thinking—from Great Britain to North America 英国国教与启蒙思想——从大不列颠到北美

The Anglican Church in Great Britain, and subsequently in colonial America, began to incorporate Enlightenment ideas. Anglicanism in the seventeenth century was beset with internal strife between High Church and Low Church factions. The more conservative and ritualistic High Church was embraced by the Archbishop of Canterbury, William Laud (1633–1640). His strict interpretation of dogma fueled the rise of Puritanism and the exodus of Puritans to the New World in the 1630s. Later, some Anglican theologians, influenced by Enlightenment thinking, embraced a more reform-minded, liberal approach to spirituality. These Low Churchmen tried to combine Enlightenment rationalism with broad-minded theology. Allowing for much latitude in matters of faith and practice, they are also known as Latitudinarians. These reformers, rejecting fanaticism, superstition, and rigidity, gained a foothold in England and in the colonies. Harvard University (founded in 1636) moved in this more liberal, independent direction under the leadership of John Leverett, Jr., who was installed as president in 1708.

Religious Toleration 宗教宽容

The idea of religious toleration—allowing religious groups outside of the official or established religion to practice freely—had European roots and New World manifestations. In both the Old World and the New World, the concept was the object of much debate and contestation. The concept has a long history in Europe. The Edict of Nantes (1598) allowed Calvinist Protestants (known as Huguenots) to practice their religion in predominantly Catholic France. Several Enlightenment thinkers advocated religious toleration. Baruch Spinoza, the Dutch philosopher from a Portuguese Jewish family, embraced the idea of religious toleration in the mid-1600s. In 1689, amid concerns of a Catholic ascendancy to the throne in England, John Locke wrote "A Letter Concerning Toleration," urging toleration of different Christian sects. Later, the French philosopher, Voltaire, wrote "A Treatise on Toleration" (1763) echoing Locke's sentiments but extending them to all faiths—including Islam and Judaism.

In colonial America, while religious orthodoxy shaped New England life, the idea of religious toleration emerged, haltingly, in several colonies. In 1649, Maryland passed the Act of Religious Toleration, guaranteeing rights to Christians of most denominations. The act did not apply to Jews or Muslims, nor to Christian sects that did not believe in the holy trinity. In Dutch New Amsterdam, several residents wrote the Flushing Remonstrance in 1657, requesting that Peter Stuyvesant lift his ban on Quaker worship in the colony. Both documents are seen as early expressions of religious tolerance—an idea that would later come to fruition in the First Amendment of the United States Constitution, guaranteeing freedom of religion.

C. BRITISH IMPERIAL POLICIES—FROM DOMINION TO SALUTARY NEGLECT
大英帝国的政策——从统治到有益忽视

From the late seventeenth century through the middle of the eighteenth century, the British approach to governing their North American colonies changed dramatically. In the 1680s, the British attempted to exert greater control over the colonies, enforce mercantilist rules and integrate many of them into a single administrative unit. Because of colonial resistance, these efforts failed. By the early 1700s, the British embarked on a policy of "salutary neglect" that allowed the colonies to develop without excessive oversight.

From Charter Colonies to Royal Colonies 从特许殖民地到皇家殖民地

Over the course of the seventeenth century, almost all the British colonies—charter colonies and proprietary colonies—were taken over directly by the Crown and became royal colonies, as the Crown attempted to tie the colonies more closely into the imperial system. In Virginia, this occurred early, after King James I revoked the charter of the Virginia Company in 1624 and made Virginia a royal colony under the control of a governor appointed by the king. James had become alarmed at the level of violence directed against American Indians, at the high mortality rate among the colonists, and at the general level of mismanagement in the colony.

The Dominion of New England 对新英格兰的统治

The shift toward greater imperial control in New England occurred in the late seventeenth century, in the wake of King Philip's War (see page 72). In the aftermath of the fighting, King

Charles II sent an agent to New England to investigate the practices of the New Englanders. Charles II became increasingly resentful of the New Englanders, especially in light of the fact that Puritans had executed his father, Charles I, during the English Civil War. The agent found ample evidence of New Englanders not living in conformity with English law. In 1686, royal officials revoked the charters of all the colonies north of Maryland and formed one massive colony called the Dominion of New England. This new colony was ruled directly by a royal appointee, Sir Edmund Andros. England's move to incorporate several of its North American colonies into a single administrative unit was met with resistance. New England Puritans were shocked at Andros's support for the Anglican Church and his refusal to enforce Sabbath laws. Throughout the affected colonies, his rigid tactics and stern demeanor aroused ire. Colonists insisted that he was rescinding their rights as Englishmen.

The Glorious Revolution and the Restoration of Colonial Charters
光荣革命与殖民特许的恢复

The Dominion of New England did not last long. Events in England again had a major impact on events in English North America. A crisis developed involving religion and succession to the throne. After King Charles II died, his brother James II became king (1685). James had previously converted to Catholicism. Many Protestants in England were troubled by this, but were calmed by the fact that James's daughter, Mary, the heir apparent, was Protestant, having married William of Orange, a Dutch prince and leader of the republic. However, in 1688, James's wife bore a male child—a new heir apparent and a Catholic. If James's son assumed the throne, England would have a Catholic king and perhaps additional Catholic monarchs in successive generations. Protestant parliamentarians would not stand for this. They rose up in the "Glorious Revolution" (1688), inviting William and Mary to become England's monarchs. King James was deposed in this bloodless uprising. The Glorious Revolution empowered Parliament and ended absolute monarchy in England. It also led to the establishment of the English Bill of Rights. The turmoil in the mother country inspired New Englanders in 1689 to arrest Andros and to do away with the Dominion of New England. In New York, rebels led by Jacob Leisler took power from royal authorities that same year. The rebel movement drove Andros's lieutenant governor in New York into exile, captured Fort James, in lower Manhattan, and established a new government. Also in 1689, Protestants in Maryland deposed the absentee proprietor of the colony, Lord Baltimore (a Catholic). They assumed (incorrectly) that Baltimore had sided with the Catholic King James against William and Mary. These rebellious governments were short-lived, however.

The Evolution of Governance in British North America
英属北美殖民地统治形式的演变

The end of the Dominion of New England and the ouster of Andros did not mean the end of imperial oversight. In some ways, the opposite occurred, as the new royal charters of the affected colonies affirmed royal control and bound the colonies closer into the imperial system. New royal governors were sent to the former Dominion colonies by 1691. In Massachusetts the Puritan-inspired charter of the pre-Dominion period was replaced with a standard-issue charter. Voting rights, for example, were now based on property qualifications, rather than church membership. To some degree, the colonists welcomed a resumption of imperial oversight. During the chaos of the Glorious Revolution (1688), French and Indian forces attacked villages in northern New York and New England (see King William's War, page 68). The colonists saw the dangers they faced on their frontiers if they did not have the protection of the English government.

"Salutary Neglect" "有益忽视"

Following the Glorious Revolution (1688) and the Dominion of New England (1686–1689), England attempted to incorporate the 13 colonies more closely to the empire with new charters and royal governors. However, the difficulties and costs of carrying out imperial laws in a sprawling empire, thousands of miles from the mother country, remained. In the eighteenth century, the policy of "salutary neglect" came to characterize Great Britain's relationship with the 13 colonies. The policy is often attributed to Prime Minister Robert Walpole (1721–1742) because he urged the Crown to not excessively interfere with the profitable trade generated by the North American colonies. The policy of "salutary neglect" allowed the North American colonies to thrive economically. However, "salutary neglect" also allowed the colonies to develop a unique set of cultural and political practices that later made independence from Britain a viable option.

D. THE BACKGROUND TO COLONIAL RESISTANCE TO IMPERIAL CONTROL
殖民地反抗帝国统治的背景

Tensions developed between Great Britain and its North American colonies in the first half of the eighteenth century. As Britain attempted to exert greater control, the colonies began to chafe at the erosion of the autonomy they had come to enjoy living on the edge of the British Empire. Many residents of the 13 colonies remained firmly loyal to British rule and thrived economically within the empire. Others, however, began to resist imperial control. These colonists drew on a long history of local self-government, new ideas about liberty, the growing influence of Enlightenment thinkers, greater religious diversity, and the growing perception that the imperial system was rife with corruption.

Enlightenment Thinking and Resistance to British Rule 启蒙思想与反抗英国统治

Many colonists who challenged imperial control drew on the political thought of the Enlightenment. John Locke, the British political theorist, was widely read in the colonies. He insisted that the primary role of government was to protect certain "natural rights"—including life, liberty, and property. Locke broke with an earlier Enlightenment thinker Thomas Hobbes. Hobbes emphasized the selfish, "nasty," and "brutish" nature of humanity, and concluded that humans need ironfisted rulers to keep them in line. Locke shared with Hobbes the notion of the self-interested nature of humans, but he was much more optimistic about the ability of humans to use reason and to make sound decisions about governance. His thinking deeply influenced the colonial idea of the legitimacy of self-government (see more on John Locke in Period 3).

Influence of the Country Party and "Cato's Letters" 乡村党的影响与 "加图信札"

Colonial resistance to British imperial control drew some of its inspiration from an unlikely source—British writers. In Great Britain, reformers and radicals developed a critique of the British government based on perceptions of corruption, wastefulness, and tyranny. These writers and reformers were labelled the "Country Party," because they were seen as representing the interest of the entire country. The opposite tendency was labelled by critics, the "Court Party," because its members operated within the inner sanctum of power in London. The Country Party was critical of Prime Minister Robert Walpole for amassing power and wealth at the expense of the elected members of Parliament. The Country Party, also labelled "Commonwealth men," accused overreaching political figures, notably Walpole, of upsetting the balanced constitution of Great Britain and endangering individual liberties. These ideas became popular among the North American colonists, providing an intellectual and political framework for grievances against the imperial system.

One of the more popular Country Party essayists in the American press was "Cato"—the pseudonym for the writing team of John Trenchard and Thomas Gordon. They borrowed the name from the foe of Julius Cesar who passionately defended republican values. The essays, labelled "Cato's Letters," were first published between 1720 and 1723 in British newspapers and were frequently reprinted in the colonies. "Cato's Letters," later collected in the volume *Essays on Liberty, Civil and Religious*, condemned corruption within the British political system and warned against tyrannical rule. The collection was a best-selling book in the colonies and was frequently cited by the Patriot cause during the American Revolution.

American Legal Procedures and Freedom of the Press 美国的法律程序与新闻自由

During the eighteenth century, the British colonies developed legal systems and procedures that differed in significant ways from the British system. This was partly due to the lack of British-trained lawyers in the New World and partly the result of local circumstances. Chronic labor shortages in the colonies, for example, led to less reliance on imprisonment as a punishment (removing potential workers from the labor force), and greater reliance on whipping, branding, and public shaming. In general, procedures were streamlined and simplified in the New World.

Further, colonial legal practices redefined crimes, such as libel. In Great Britain, any printed criticisms of public officials could be considered libelous. In the colonies, courts ruled that critical items could not be considered libelous if they were truthful. In 1735, New York City newspaper publisher, John Peter Zenger, was arrested and charged with seditious libel for printing articles critical of the royal governor. His lawyer successfully argued that he had the right to print such articles because they were truthful. The jury acquitted Zenger. In the wake of the case, more newspaper publishers and editors were willing to write articles critical of royal authorities. The verdict was indicative of the value placed on a free press in the colonies.

DEMOCRACY IN COLONIAL AMERICA
殖民时期美国的民主

It is tempting to argue in an essay that American democracy can be found in the history of the colonial period. Be cautious: One can easily find as many undemocratic features of colonial life, from theocracy in New England to slavery throughout the colonies.

II. The Development of Slavery in the British New World
英国新世界奴隶制的发展

Slavery developed in British North America in response to the economic, demographic, and geographic characteristics of the colonies. Slavery was part of English colonial North America from the earliest years. In 1619, 20 Africans arrived in Virginia, probably as slaves. However, slavery did not become central to the southern economy until later in the seventeenth century.

A. THE DEVELOPMENT OF BRITISH SLAVERY 英国奴隶制的发展

The persistent problem of the wealthy planters in the English New World was attracting enough settlers to do the difficult work of the cultivation and processing of staple crops. In the 1600s, the system of indentured servitude was used to facilitate the migration of workers to the New World. However, the system did not provide an adequate number of workers. As a result, slavery developed to meet this chronic need for additional workers. All the British colonies participated, to some degree, in the Atlantic slave trade. Few slaves were used by the small-scale farms of New England. Most prominent port cities had significant numbers of enslaved laborers. Large slave populations existed in the colonies of the Chesapeake region as well as in the deep South. Within the British colonial world, the great majority of enslaved Africans ended up in the West Indies.

Bacon's Rebellion and the Development of Slavery in Virginia
培根起义与弗吉尼亚奴隶制的发展

In the latter half of the seventeenth century, Virginia planters began to experience problems with the system of indentured servitude (see page 66). Upon the end of their indenture, these men and women were generally not integrated into Virginia society. Many moved from the fertile tidewater region of Virginia into the hilly piedmont region. This inland region was also where many American Indians had settled after being dislocated by the initial wave of English settlers. The former indentured servants grew resentful of the taxes they were required to pay the Virginia government and of their lack of representation in the House of Burgesses. Things grew worse for them, as violence intensified on the frontier between these hardscrabble farmers and the nearby American Indians.

In 1676, frontier tensions erupted into a full-scale rebellion, known as Bacon's Rebellion. Nathaniel Bacon, a lower-level planter, championed the cause of the frontier farmers and became their leader. Governor William Berkeley refused to offer help in fighting the American Indians. Many of the wealthier Virginians engaged in a profitable trade with Indians and, therefore, did not want war waged against them. When colonial authorities refused to aid the frontier farmers, Bacon led a group of them into Jamestown, burning the homes of the elite planters and even the capital building. During the rebellion, Bacon himself died of disease, and the rebellion was soon put down.

> ### THE SHIFT TO SLAVERY
> ### 从契约仆役制到奴隶制的转换
> Remember, historians view Bacon's Rebellion as a key event in the shift from indentured servitude to slavery as the main form of labor in the South.

The rebellion proved to be an important turning point in colonial history, as the elite planters turned increasingly to African slaves as their primary labor force. African slavery allowed the planters to emphasize a commonality of interests between themselves and the frontier farmers. Although the position of these frontier farmers did not appreciably improve, they could at least take solace in the fact that they were among the free Virginians and members of the race they were told was superior.

The African Slave Trade 非洲奴隶贸易

African slave trafficking in sub-Saharan Africa became a thriving business in the eighteenth century. European traders set up operations in African coastal towns and encouraged men to venture into the interior to kidnap members of other tribal groups. The slave trade not only resulted in kidnapping, but it also exacerbated ethnic and societal tensions and served to destabilize the region. The victims of the slave trade were from a variety of cultural and linguistic groups. These Africans—mostly young and male, with men outnumbering women two to one—were brought to coastal ports where they were sold to European slave traders. They were next transported to the New World in horrid conditions. This grueling, and often deadly, part of the journey was known as the "middle passage." The most famous account of the middle passage by an African is contained in the narrative of Olaudah Equiano. This African slave trade is one of the legs of the Atlantic trade (also known as the triangle trade) that evolved during the colonial period.

B. IDEAS ABOUT RACE AND THE DEVELOPMENT OF SLAVERY IN BRITISH NORTH AMERICA 种族观念与英属北美殖民地奴隶制的发展

Slavery in British North America differed from earlier slave systems in some fundamental ways. British notions of racial hierarchy reinforced the idea that slavery would be a permanent condition for both sub-Saharan Africans who were enslaved and their descendants.

The Origins of Racial Hierarchies 种族等级制度的起源

Spanish, French, and Dutch colonies, which had fewer female colonists, were relatively accepting of intermarriages with native peoples, and unions with Africans were fairly common in the Spanish colonies. In contrast, the British colonies attracted both male and female colonists and did not tolerate intermarriage. In this context, as in New Spain, a rigid hierarchy developed in the British colonies.

The racial hierarchy that developed within the British colonial world followed a long tradition in English thought of making divisions within humanity. These divisions—between civilized and barbaric, between Christian and heathen, between English and non-English— shaped English understandings of the world. Historians continue to debate whether racism toward Africans developed as a result of the enslavement of Africans, or whether racist notions predated and allowed for the enslavement of Africans (see "Subject to Debate," page 82).

The Nature of Slavery in British North America 英属北美殖民地奴隶制的本质

Historians note that slavery evolved in the British colonies during the seventeenth century. Some contend that the few slaves present in colonial Virginia in the early seventeenth century were treated in a manner similar to other "unfree" people, such as indentured servants. Over the course of the seventeenth century, rules about slavery hardened in colonial Virginia. In 1640, an indentured servant of African descent, John Casor, was declared by a civil court to be a slave for life. The case represents an important turning point in the shift toward permanent enslavement. Later, in 1662, the Virginia legislature passed a law stating that the child of a slave woman would inherit its mother's status—that is, would be a slave for life. This principle, called in Latin *partus sequitur ventrum*, broke with traditional English common law; previously, the child would inherit its father's status, meaning the child of a white man and an enslaved woman would be considered a free person. This principle had a major impact on the dynamics of slavery in the British colonial system. In effect, it sanctioned the rape of slave women by their white owners.

Even the language that English settlers used to describe Africans changed by the end of the century. Early in the seventeenth century, English accounts of African slaves in Virginia usually describe them as "Negroes." By the end of the century, they are more frequently referred to as "black," a color with negative overtones for English people at the time. Colonists began to identify themselves as "white"—a color that denoted purity and beauty. After 1660, laws in Virginia made it clear that slavery was a permanent and inherited status. By the end of the century, white Virginians came to see "blacks" and "slaves" as nearly synonymous terms.

D. RESISTANCE TO SLAVERY 对奴隶制的反抗

Slaves resisted brutality, humiliations, and grueling work in a number of ways. Resistance was both overt and covert.

The main fear of slave owners was overt resistance in the form of violent rebellion. Such rebellion was uncommon. Since slave owners and white authorities had the law behind them and a monopoly on weaponry, outright rebellion was tantamount to suicide. Yet, attempts at rebellion did occur. The most famous slave rebellion of the colonial period was the Stono, South Carolina, rebellion in 1739. The rebellion, initiated by 20 slaves who obtained weapons by attacking a country store, led to the deaths of 20 slave owners and the plundering of half a dozen plantations. But the rebellion was quickly put down, and the participants beheaded with their heads placed on mileposts along the road. Lesser forms of resistance, however, occurred on a daily basis, from working slowly to breaking tools. Also, slaves resisted by retaining cultural connections to Africa, maintaining traditional names and practices.

SUBJECT TO DEBATE 相关讨论

There are several important historiographical questions surrounding the English settlement of North America. Historians have questioned traditional accounts contrasting English and Spanish colonization. In such accounts, the Spanish are portrayed as brutal, almost to the point of being sadistic, in their treatment of the native populations of Central and South America. Traditional accounts of English settlement of North America have de-emphasized warfare with American Indians and focused more on theological issues among the Puritans and the economic development of the colonies. More recently, historians have questioned the veracity of some of the more graphic descriptions of Spanish actions in the Americas and have shed new light on the history of violence by the English against native peoples.

Another question that has engaged historians is the comparisons between the New England and the Chesapeake colonies in the seventeenth century. Historical accounts have looked for differences between the northern and southern regions—examining such differences almost from the first day of settlement. To some degree historians can be faulted for reading the more recent past (the Civil War) into the more distant past (the colonies in the 1600s) and concluding that the bloodshed of the 1860s was rooted in seventeenth-century patterns of development. It is open to interpretation whether the differences between the regions are more important than the commonalities.

Historians continue to debate several important issues about the development of slavery. Historical work has examined the relationship between racism and slavery. Did African slavery develop because of preconceived notions of racial hierarchies, or did these notions of superior and inferior races develop over time to justify the continued enslavement of hundreds of thousands and, ultimately, millions of black Americans?

In addition, historians have debated whether the 13 colonies' ties to Great Britain were beneficial or not to the colonies. On the one hand, mercantilist rules restricted colonial economic activity. The economic activity that was permitted was designed to benefit Great Britain more than the colonies. To support the argument that mercantilist rules hampered colonial economic development, historians have cited many colonists complaining of being "oppressed" and reduced to the status of "slaves." Other historians note that many of the mercantilist rules were simply ignored by the colonists.

PRACTICE MULTIPLE-CHOICE QUESTIONS 选择题练习

Directions: Pick the letter that best answers the following questions.

Questions 1–2 refer to the following passage: 根据以下段落，回答第1—2题

"There is little doubt that Puritanism was closer to medieval theory than the material goals and values of a growing middle class that was becoming prominent in England and western Europe after the fifteenth century. While the Puritan never thought of his religion in economic terms, he did emphasize the fact that man could serve God not by withdrawing from the world, but rather by following an occupation or calling that served the world.

"In spite of the proximity of certain Puritan values to the rising capitalistic ethic, Puritanism was more medieval than modern in its economic theory and practice. The idea of unrestrained economic individualism would have seemed a dangerous notion to any self-respecting Puritan. The statute books and court records of seventeenth-century Massachusetts abound in examples of price and wage controls instituted by the government of the colony. The Puritans, furthermore, always looked upon wealth as a gift from God given in the form of a trust; and they emphasized not only the benefits that accrued from work and wealth, but also their duties and responsibilities. In 1639, for example, one of the richest merchants in the colony was fined by the General Court (the highest legislative body) for excessive profiteering, despite the fact that there was no statute against the practice. The Puritans could never separate religion and business, and they often reiterated the medieval conception of the 'just price.'

"In the long run, however, the Puritan ethic, when divorced from its religious background, did serve to quicken and stimulate the spirit of capitalism. The limitations placed by the Puritans on the individual and the freedom of movement within society were subordinated as the time went on in favor of the enterprising and driving individual who possessed the ability and ambition to rise through his own exertions."

—Gerald N. Grob and Robert N. Beck, *American Ideas*, 1963, p. 63

1. In the second paragraph, the authors discuss the 1639 legal proceedings against "one of the richest merchants in the colony," in order to show that

   (A) impoverished New Englanders used the legal system to vent class frustrations against the wealthy.
   (B) political corruption was common in Puritan New England.
   (C) Puritan magistrates were evenhanded in that they prosecuted anyone—rich or poor—who expressed heretical religious views.
   (D) the Puritans attempted to enforce economic values that emphasized communal notions of fairness over free-market individualism.

2. Which of the following reflects the main point that Gerald N. Grob and Robert N. Beck are making in the passage?

   (A) Puritan restraints on economic activity prevented the economy of New England from growing, leading it to fall behind the South and the middle colonies during the colonial period.

   (B) The economy of Puritan New England came to resemble the feudal economy of medieval Europe, dominated by large estates passed on from father to son over several generations.

   (C) The economy of New England only began to thrive when non-Puritan immigrants began to move into New England after the 1640s.

   (D) As the seventeenth century progressed, the decline of Puritan orthodoxy, combined with Puritan patterns of work, allowed for the emergence of a market-oriented economy.

Questions 3–5 are based on the following passage: 根据以下段落，回答第3—5题

"Asked what causes or motives the said Indian rebels had for renouncing the law of God and obedience to his Majesty, and for committing so many kinds of crimes, [Josephe answered] the causes they have were alleged ill treatment and injuries received from [Spanish authorities], because they beat them, took away what they had, and made them work without pay. Thus he replies.

"Asked if he has learned if it has come to his notice during the time that he has been here the reason why the apostates burned the images, churches, and things pertaining to divine worship, making a mockery and a trophy of them, killing the priests and doing the other things they did, he said that he knows and had heard it generally stated that while they were besieging the villa the rebellious traitors burned the church and shouted in loud voices, 'Now the God of the Spaniards, who was their father, is dead, and Santa Maria, who was their mother, and the saints, who were pieces of rotten wood,' saying that only their own god lived. . . . The captains and the chiefs ordered that the names of Jesus and Mary should nowhere be uttered. . . . He has seen many houses of idolatry which they have built, dancing the dance of the cachina [part of a traditional Indian religious ceremony], which this declarant has also danced. Thus he replies to the question."

> —Account of questioning of Josephe, a Spanish-speaking Pueblo Indian, by Spanish authorities following the Pueblo Revolt of 1680 (1681)

3. The events described by Josephe in the account, above, reflect

   (A) adaptation by American Indians to European cultural practices.

   (B) conflict among American Indian groups as a result of displacement and relocation by Spanish colonial forces.

   (C) the high rate of intermarriage between American Indians and Spaniards in the New World.

   (D) resistance by American Indians to Spanish colonial practices.

4. The testimony of Josephe indicates that the Pueblo Indians

   (A) were thoroughly Christianized by 1680.
   (B) practiced nonviolent means of protest.
   (C) traded extensively with the Spanish, but resented heavy taxes imposed on trade.
   (D) targeted symbols of Spanish culture as well as the Spanish political and economic system.

5. Which of the following trends occurred in the aftermath of the events described in the account?

   (A) Spanish colonizing efforts in North America in the late 1600s and 1700s saw an accommodation with some aspects of American Indian culture.
   (B) Spanish military actions and disease wiped out the American Indian populations in Spanish North America.
   (C) Spanish forces, having been defeated by the Pueblo Indians, abandoned all land claims in North America by 1700.
   (D) Spain and Great Britain formed an alliance to establish European control over North America.

Answers and Explanations to Multiple-Choice Questions
选择题的答案与解析

1. **(D)** The mention of the arrest of "one of the richest merchants in the colony" by the authors of the secondary source is meant to illustrate Puritan attempts to enforce economic values that emphasized communal notions of fairness over free-market individualism. Puritan communities passed a series of laws enforcing "fair prices" and "fair wages." This notion of a moral economy precedes capitalist individualism, dating back to the Middle Ages. The existence of such laws not only helps us understand the Puritan notion of an ideal community, but these laws also demonstrate that some members of the community were moving away from the ideal. After all, why would such laws be needed if everyone observed the guidelines of a moral economy? The authors are pointing to a shift toward a more individualistic, market economy.

2. **(D)** The reading raises one of the interesting contradictions of Puritanism. The religion emphasized a rejection of worldly temptations and a rigid asceticism. Yet, its injunction to carry out one's calling—the work that God has intended you to do on Earth—with dedication and vigor often led to material success. The reading is arguing that once the white hot zeal of Puritanism declined in New England, the road toward economic success was wide open.

3. **(D)** The events described by Josephe in the account reflect resistance by American Indians to Spanish colonial practices. The events described are part of the Pueblo Revolt of 1680. Tensions between the Pueblo people and Spanish conquerors began almost a century before the rebellion. The Spanish conquistador, Juan de Onate, and his soldiers had, in the 1590s, occupied land held by the Acoma Pueblo people. In 1598, in response to Pueblo resistance, Onate responded by firing cannons from a mesa above the Acoma Pueblo people, killing over 800. Resentment of Spanish rule by the Pueblo people intensified by the late 1600s. The Spanish *encomienda* system had undermined the traditional economy of the Pueblo people. In addition, Spanish officials imposed Christianity on the

Pueblo people and outlawed traditional spiritual practices. This resentment led to the Pueblo Revolt, also known as Pope's Rebellion (1680). The rebellion included attacks on the Spanish clergy as well as on ordinary Spaniards. The Pueblo Revolt resulted in over 300 Spanish deaths and a temporary withdrawal of Spanish forces from the area.

4. **(D)** The testimony of Josephe indicates that the Pueblo Indians targeted symbols of Spanish culture as well as the Spanish political and economic system. Josephe notes that the Pueblo rebels burned churches and decided that the names of Jesus and Mary should never be uttered. These actions indicate that the rebellion was not only about harsh treatment; it was also an attempt to assert cultural autonomy in the face of Spanish efforts to Christianize the local people.

5. **(A)** After the Pueblo Revolt, Spanish authorities adjusted their approach to dealing with the Pueblo people. In the late 1600s and 1700s, Spanish authorities attempted to be more accommodating of some aspects of Pueblo culture. A public defender was appointed with the responsibility of protecting the rights of the Pueblo people. The Spanish reaction to the rebellion was markedly different from the response of British officials to conflicts between colonists and native peoples. The British response usually entailed removal or eradication rather than accommodation.

Period 3: 1754–1800 The Crisis of Empire, Revolution, and Nation Building

第三个时期（1754—1800）：帝国危机、革命与国家建设

5

TIMELINE 大事年表

1784	First Land Ordinance
	Treaty of Fort Stanwix
1785	Second Land Ordinance
1786	Shays' Rebellion
	Annapolis meeting to revise Articles of Confederation
1787	Northwest Ordinance
	Constitutional Convention in Philadelphia
1788	Publication of *The Federalist*
	Ratification of the Constitution
	First federal elections
1789	Inauguration of George Washington
	Judiciary Act
	Beginning of French Revolution
	Publication of *The Interesting Narrative of the Life of Olaudah Equiano*
1791	Ratification of the Bill of Rights
	Alexander Hamilton issues "Report on Manufacturers"
	The Bank of the United States approved
1793	War between Great Britain and France
	Washington's Neutrality Proclamation
1794	Whiskey Rebellion
	Jay's Treaty
1795	Pinckney's Treaty
1796	Washington's Farewell Address
1798	XYZ Affair
	"Quasi-war" with France
	Alien and Sedition Acts
	Kentucky and Virginia Resolutions
1800	Election of Thomas Jefferson

INTRODUCTION　简介

> The attempt by Great Britain to restructure its North American empire following the French and Indian War and to assert greater control over its colonies led to intense colonial resistance and finally to revolution. The American Revolution produced a new American republic. The first decades of the United States were marked by a struggle over the new nation's social, political, and economic identity.

The American Revolution was a monumental event in the history of the United States, as well as in world history. The American Revolution brought to the surface tensions that existed between the 13 American colonies and the government of Great Britain. It also brought into existence a democratic republic. The democratic spirit that imbued the founding of the United States inspired movements for change—both within the United States and abroad. The American Revolution did not give birth to a perfect democracy. Americans have struggled with the meaning and extent of democracy for the more than 230 years since winning independence.

The decade of the 1780s was a trying one for the new American nation. The newborn United States fought and won the final stages of the American Revolution and then was faced with a series of threats from within and from abroad that threatened its very existence. By the end of the "critical period," the nation had shifted directions in regard to governing structure—rejecting the Articles of Confederation and adopting the Constitution.

The first dozen years after the ratification of the Constitution were key in the shaping of the United States political system. The government reformed in conformity with the Constitution. The Bill of Rights established important civil liberties. It was in this period that many of the American political system's traditions and precedents—collectively known as the "unwritten Constitution"—were established. We see the development of political parties and of the two-party system during these years. Further, we see continuing struggles over the new nation's identity.

KEY CONCEPT 3.1 CRISIS OF EMPIRE—FROM THE FRENCH AND INDIAN WAR TO INDEPENDENCE
核心概念3.1：帝国危机——从法国与印第安战争到独立

The French and Indian War (1754–1763) proved to be a turning point in the relations between Great Britain and the 13 colonies. Before the war, a British policy of "salutary neglect" allowed both Great Britain and the colonies to benefit under loosely enforced mercantilist rules (see Period 2). After the war, the British government enacted a series of measures designed to assert greater control over its North American colonies. Many colonists objected, asserting the right to self-government. Colonial resistance to British authority resulted in the American Revolution.

I. The French and Indian War and Its Aftermath　法国与印第安战争及其后果

Competition among the British, French, and American Indian nations culminated in the French and Indian War. American Indians were forced to adjust alliances in the wake of the victory of Great Britain over France.

A. EXPANSION AND WAR　扩张与战争

In the 1740s and 1750s, British colonists began to venture from Virginia to settle beyond the Appalachian Mountains in the Ohio River valley, land claimed by France. France began building fortifications in the region, notably Fort Duquesne at present-day Pittsburgh. The British colonists built a makeshift fort of their own nearby, Fort Necessity. In 1754, skirmishes between the two groups led to the beginning of the French and Indian War, which brought on a shift in American Indian alliances.

Origins of the French and Indian War　法国与印第安战争的起源

The French and Indian War had complex origins. In part, it was a continuation of decades of conflict between Great Britain and France, both in the Old World and in the New World (see Period 2). Both Great Britain and France had extensive land claims in North America. France's land claims stretched from Quebec, Montreal, and Detroit in the north to New Orleans at the mouth of the Mississippi River in the south, and from the Appalachian Mountains in the east to the Rocky Mountains in the west. France claimed more land in the New World, but Great Britain had many more colonists.

British Victory in the French and Indian War　英国在法国与印第安战争中的胜利

There are three distinct phases of the French and Indian War. At first (1754–1756), the war was a local affair—a continuation of the skirmishes between British colonists and French forces. Most of the American Indian tribes sided with the French, who tended to be more accommodating than the British to native peoples. The scattered colonists attempted, unsuccessfully, to work with one another during this period. Colonial leaders met in Albany, New York (1754), in an attempt to organize an intercolonial government. Benjamin Franklin's proposed Albany Plan was rejected by the delegates. On the battlefield, the British colonists were in retreat.

> ## A GLOBAL WAR
> ## 全球战争
>
> The French and Indian War led to a worldwide conflict between France and Britain and their allies, known as the Seven Years' War. In North America it was fought from Nova Scotia in the north, to the Great Lakes region in the west and to the Caribbean in the South.

In the second phase (1756–1758), the British government, under Prime Minister William Pitt, took full charge of the war. Pitt alienated many colonists with his heavy-handed tactics, including forcing colonists into the army and seizing supplies from them. The colonists resisted these moves, putting the entire British effort at risk.

In the final phase (1758–1761), Pitt tried to work with colonial assemblies and also reinforced the war effort with more British troops. These moves proved successful. In 1761, French forces surrendered at Montreal. Two years later, a formal peace treaty was signed.

The Treaty of Paris (1763)　《巴黎和约》（1763）

In the Treaty of Paris, France surrendered virtually its entire North American empire. It ceded to Great Britain all French territory in Canada and east of the Mississippi River. France ceded to Spain all of its territory west of the Mississippi River. British North American colonists were pleased that the land beyond the Appalachians seemed ready for additional settlement. American Indians living in these lands were in an increasingly vulnerable position.

B. DEBT AND TAXATION FOLLOWING THE FRENCH AND INDIAN WAR
法国与印第安战争之后的债务与税收

If British colonists celebrated the removal of the French from North America, their celebration was short-lived. Almost immediately, the British government attempted to confront an ongoing problem—the large debt that had accumulated during almost half a century of constant warfare. The British government believed its victory in the French and Indian War had been especially beneficial to the colonists. In return, the British reasoned it was fair for the colonists to assume some of the costs of the war and of continued protection through increased taxation.

The Sugar Act 《糖进口条例》

The first significant post-war tax was enacted with the Sugar Act (1764). The act actually lowered the existing tax on molasses imported into North America from French colonies in the West Indies. However, along with lowering the tax, the act also sought to crack down on widespread smuggling. The act strengthened the admiralty courts system, shifting prosecutions of smuggling cases from local jury trials to British maritime courts. The British hoped to generate additional income through these measures.

The Stamp Act 《印花税法案》

The Stamp Act (1765) provoked the most intense colonial opposition of all measures enacted by the British following the French and Indian War. It represented a departure from previous British colonial policy. Previous tax acts were aimed at regulating trade; this act was purely designed to raise revenue. It was a direct tax on the colonists, rather than an indirect trade duty. The act imposed a tax on all sorts of printed matter in the colonies—court documents, books, almanacs, deeds (see more on opposition to the Stamp Act, page 94).

Quartering of British Troops 英国军队的驻扎

The Quartering Act of 1765 addressed the housing of British soldiers who were stationed in the colonies following the French and Indian War. The act stipulated that Great Britain would house soldiers in barracks, but if the number of soldiers exceeded available facilities, local inns, pubs, and even private residences could be used by British authorities to house them. Colonial assemblies were expected to shoulder the costs of housing and feeding these soldiers. Often these troops were given part-time wages, compelling them to supplement their wages by finding work in the community. The largest number of troops were stationed in Boston.

C. MIGRATIONS AND CONFLICT IN THE WAKE OF THE FRENCH AND INDIAN WAR
法国与印第安战争后的移民与冲突

In the aftermath of the French and Indian War, American Indians in the areas newly won by Great Britain found themselves in an increasingly precarious position—on the one hand they wanted to maintain the lucrative fur trade with Europeans, while on the other, they hoped to resist encroachment by British colonists.

Clashing Cultures in the Great Lakes Region 五大湖地区的文化冲突

As the British made their presence felt in the lands formerly held by the French, the difference between the British and the French in their approach to American Indians became more evident. The French, for practical and cultural reasons, worked at developing harmonious relations with American Indian tribes. For instance, they negotiated with Indian leaders and participated in ceremonial exchanges of gifts with the tribes. The British, on the other hand, had little patience for gift exchanges. General Jeffrey Amherst, commander-in-chief of British forces in North America, saw gift exchanges as demeaning. Why, he argued, should the British pay tribute to American Indians? American Indians, on the other hand, saw in generous gift-giving an expression of dominance and protection.

In the uncertain world created by the defeat of the French, some American Indians attempted to foster a greater sense of unity and cultural resistance among the often-fractious tribes of the Great Lakes and Ohio Valley regions. In 1760 and 1761, a Delaware leader named Neolin offered American Indians an apocalyptic vision of a future that could transpire if American Indians did not change their ways. He encouraged American Indians to curb their contact with European fur traders, reduce the presence of guns, alcohol, and other European goods, and lessen infighting. His efforts set the stage for unified, violent resistance.

Pontiac's Rebellion 庞蒂亚克战争

With the defeat of the French in the French and Indian War, American Indian groups that had been allied with the French found themselves in a precarious situation. The Ottawa tribe, for instance, in the northern Ohio region found itself without allies as the British colonists set their sights on traditional Ottawa lands. After the war, British troops had occupied the French-built forts. The Ottawa chief, Pontiac, and other Indian leaders organized resistance to British troops stationed around the Great Lakes and southward on several rivers. In the months after the 1763 signing of the Treaty of Paris, Indian warriors attacked British-held Fort Detroit. This attack was followed by strikes on six other forts and on colonial settlements along a swath of land from upstate New York to the area south of Lake Michigan, and along the Appalachian frontier, where settlers were entering Indian country. The attacks were initially successful; Pontiac and his allies captured several forts west of Detroit, with more than 400 British soldiers and 2,000 colonists killed or captured. Amherst was replaced by the more capable Thomas Gage in August 1763. Bloodshed continued into 1764. Pontiac's Rebellion was finally broken by Gage. Smaller skirmishes continued until the American Revolution, when many American Indian groups sided with the British.

The Proclamation Act (1763) 《宣告法案》（1763）

In response to the outbreak of Pontiac's Rebellion, Great Britain issued the Proclamation Act (1763), which drew a line through the Appalachian Mountains. Great Britain ordered the colonists not to settle beyond the line. After the French and Indian War, Americans were restless to push into the interior of the continent; they migrated toward the foothills of the Appalachians beyond existing settlements, and they made their way through the mountain passes. The Proclamation Act (1763) attempted to halt colonists from settling beyond the Appalachian Mountains. The British government did not want to provoke additional warfare with native peoples in the region, and incur the costs of additional campaigns in the West. Further, the British wanted to continue garnering profits from the valuable fur trade with Indians. Colonists were disgruntled; they felt that they had made sacrifices during the French and Indian War and they were now eager to settle in these newly claimed lands.

Conflict in the Interior of the Continent Following the French and Indian War
法国与印第安战争后大陆内部的冲突

Settlement of the interior of colonial America in the decades after the French and Indian War set the stage for ongoing tensions between the policies of ruling authorities—generally based in the cities along the Atlantic seaboard—and the poorer folk inland, remote from the commercial activity of the cosmopolitan centers. After the American Revolution, the flow of pioneers beyond the Appalachians increased dramatically. This movement frequently displaced Indians, setting the stage for a new series of battles over the vast interior of the United States. The movement was challenged by the continued presence of Spain and Great Britain along the borderlands of the newly formed United States.

The Scotch-Irish 苏格兰–爱尔兰人

The middle colonies—Pennsylvania, New York, New Jersey, and Delaware—experienced remarkable growth in the eighteenth century. German, Scotch-Irish, and other immigrants contributed to the growth of the colonies. The largest immigrant group in the eighteenth century was the Scotch-Irish, Presbyterians originally from Scotland, who generations earlier had settled in Ireland, where they got their name. Difficult economic conditions impelled thousands to migrate to America. Immigrants from the southwestern German states were the second biggest group. These immigrants tended to be good farmers and artisans, as well as laborers.

Economic Opportunity in Pennsylvania 宾夕法尼亚的经济机遇

The initial destination of the Scotch-Irish was Pennsylvania, where the availability of land and the need for workers attracted immigrants, especially to Philadelphia. Many soon moved westward into the mountainous interior. Farther south, slavery was the dominant form of labor; farther north, the legacy of Puritanism still enforced a cultural homogeneity. New York City attracted immigrants, but farmers found that the best land along the Hudson River was taken up by large estates.

The Paxton Boys 帕克顿青年

As early as the 1720s, some farmers were settling beyond the crest of the Appalachian Mountains, in the backcountry of Pennsylvania, Virginia (the area that would later become West Virginia), and North Carolina. Small-scale farmers in Pennsylvania specialized in growing wheat and experienced a higher standard of living than their counterparts in Europe. The Scotch-Irish farmers carried with them from Europe resentments toward British rule. In the aftermath of the French and Indian War and Pontiac's Rebellion, a vigilante group of these Scotch-Irish immigrants organized raids against American Indians on the Pennsylvania frontier. In 1763, these raids included an attack on peaceful Conestoga Indians (many of them Christians) that resulted in 20 deaths. After the attacks on the Conestoga, in January 1764, about 250 Paxton Boys marched to Philadelphia to present their grievances to the Pennsylvania legislature. Their "Apology" (or explanation), presented to the legislature, reflected bitterness at the American Indians on the frontier of Pennsylvania, as well as resentment of the Quaker elite of the colony for maintaining a more lenient policy toward American Indians.

> **A SHIFT IN COLONIAL POLICY**
> **殖民政策的转变**
> Note the shift in British policy from the "salutary neglect" approach prior to the French and Indian War to the close supervision of the postwar period.

II. From Resistance to Rebellion—Colonial Responses to British Policies

从抵抗到起义——殖民地对英国政策的反应

New taxes and more rigorous enforcement of existing taxes generated intense resentment and resistance among many colonists. This movement culminated in the independence movement and revolution against Great Britain.

A. COLONIAL RESISTANCE TO BRITISH POLICIES IN THE AFTERMATH OF THE FRENCH AND INDIAN WAR　法国与印第安战争后殖民地对英国政策的反抗

After the French and Indian War, the relationship between the British colonists and Great Britain changed, as the colonists began to unite and organize around a series of threats—actual and perceived—posed by changing British policies. This changing relationship fostered a resistance movement and finally an independence movement.

The Stamp Act Congress　印花税法案会议

The first significant, coordinated protests against British policies occurred in response to the Stamp Act (see page 91). In October 1765, delegates from nine colonies met in New York and drew up a document listing grievances, which went beyond the Stamp Act. The Declarations of the Stamp Act Congress asserted that only representatives elected by colonists could enact taxes on the colonies. "No taxation without representation" became a rallying cry of opponents of British policies. The declarations followed on the heels of a series of proposals, written by Patrick Henry, called the Virginia Resolves. Not all of the resolves were passed by the Virginia assembly, but they were all written up and circulated throughout the colonies. The resolves, debated in June 1765, called for a degree of colonial self-government that went beyond more moderate proposals.

> **PURPOSE OF TAXES**
> **税收的用途**
> The distinction between taxation to regulate trade and taxation to raise revenue was important to many colonists.

The British responded to the cry of "No taxation without representation!" with the theory of "virtual representation." The theory held that members of Parliament represented the entire British Empire. The colonists therefore were "virtually represented" by the members of Parliament.

Committees of Correspondence　通信委员会

In communities throughout the colonies, committees of correspondence were organized, starting in 1764. These committees of opponents of British policies initially spread information and coordinated resistance actions. By the 1770s, they had become virtual shadow governments in the colonies, assuming powers and challenging the legitimacy of the legislative assemblies and royal governors.

Crowd Actions　群体活动

The Stamp Act generated a variety of crowd actions in the colonies. In cities and towns throughout the colonies, "Sons of Liberty" groups harassed, and occasionally attacked, Stamp Act agents. There were several incidents of stores ransacked if the proprietor did not comply with boycotts of British goods. In Boston, the home of the lieutenant governor, Thomas Hutchinson, was ransacked. Finally, the Stamp Act itself was rescinded (1766), but a series of British moves and colonial responses in the coming years worsened the situation.

> **MOBS AND CROWDS　暴民与群众**
> Be aware of the different implications of "mob actions" and "crowd actions." "Mob actions" imply random acts of violence committed by angry groups of people, while "crowd actions" imply acts taken with a particular goal in mind by groups of people with an articulated agenda. Of late, social historians have tended to favor the term "crowd actions."

The Townshend Acts 《汤森法案》

The Townshend Acts (1767), passed in the wake of the Stamp Act fiasco, imposed additional taxes on the colonists. Britain's Chancellor of the Exchequer, Charles Townshend, made sure these new taxes—on paint, paper, lead, tea—were "external" taxes, on imports, not "internal" sales taxes on items. Although opposition to these import duties was slow to develop, by 1768 many colonial leaders renewed their calls for boycotts of British goods. The boycott movement gained strength throughout the 13 colonies. Patriotic women engaged in producing homespun clothing. Artisans benefitted from the boycott as Americans sought locally produced goods. These simple goods were seen as virtuous substitutes for extravagant British goods.

The Boston Massacre 波士顿惨案

In 1768, Great Britain redeployed royal troops to Boston following rioting that year. The presence of these troops angered many Bostonians. Many colonists associated "standing armies" as threats to liberty. This concern held that armies of citizens could be mobilized during times of war, but that they should then be disbanded during times of peace. Further, the British soldiers competed with colonists for waterfront jobs. During the winter of 1770 a deadly incident in Boston reverberated throughout the colonies. In March, a disagreement between an on-duty British sentry and a young wigmaker's apprentice escalated into a scuffle. Angry colonists heckled and threw stones at British sentries ordered out to restore calm. Finally, the troops fired on the colonists, resulting in five deaths, including an African American named Crispus Attucks. In years to come, the incident would be repeatedly used as colonial propaganda to illustrate the brutality of the British troops.

> ### STANDING ARMIES 常备军
>
> During the eighteenth and nineteenth centuries, suspicion of standing, professional armies was part of the British and American political tradition. In today's world, most people accept the presence of professional armies, even in peacetime.

Gaspee Affair "加斯皮号" 事件

After the Boston Massacre, the early 1770s seemed to offer a lessening of public acts of resistance. However, many colonists were growing increasingly resentful of British officials. The seeming calm broke in June 1772, when a British revenue schooner, the *Gaspee*, ran aground in shallow waters near Warwick, Rhode Island. The schooner was searching for smugglers who thrived in those waters. Local men boarded the ship, looted its contents, and finally torched it. The *Gaspee* affair represented a shift toward more militant tactics by colonial protestors.

The Tea Act and the Boston Tea Party 《茶叶条例》与 "波士顿倾茶事件"

Relations between British authorities and American colonists took a dramatic turn for the worse in 1773 with the passage of the Tea Act. The British East India Company was in crisis; its stock value had virtually collapsed. To bolster the company, the British passed the Tea Act, which eliminated British tariffs from tea sold in the colonies by the British East India Company. The act enabled the company to sell massive quantities of low-priced tea in the colonies, thus bypassing local merchants and undercutting smugglers. This act actually lowered tea prices in Boston, but it angered many colonists who accused the British of doing special favors for a large company. The colonists responded by dumping cases of tea into Boston harbor. The dumping of the tea was not just a symbolic act; its value, adjusted for inflation, would be more than $4 million.

The Coercive/Intolerable Acts 《不可容忍法案》

The British passed a series of acts in 1774, in the wake of the Boston Tea Party, called the Coercive Acts, or Intolerable Acts.

- The Massachusetts Government Act brought the governance of Massachusetts under direct British control. It limited the powers of town meetings and provided the royal governor with the power to directly appoint officials who had previously been elected.
- The Administration of Justice Act allowed British authorities to move trials from Massachusetts to Great Britain. British policy after the French and Indian War consistently sought to move trials away from local communities. This move struck colonists as an abridgement of a basic right of Englishmen—the right to a trial by a jury of one's peers.
- The Boston Port Act closed the port of Boston to trade until further notice.
- The Quartering Act expanded the scope of the 1765 Quartering Act and required Boston residents to house British troops upon their command.
- A fifth act, the Quebec Act, was passed around the same time but was unrelated to the Boston Tea Party. This act let Catholics in Quebec freely practice their religion. Protestant Bostonians assumed that this was an attack on their faith.

C. REVOLUTION FROM ABOVE AND FROM BELOW 全民参与的革命

Traditional accounts of the American Revolution stress the guidance of important colonial leaders, such as Benjamin Franklin, John Adams, and John Hancock. Their participation in the Committees of Correspondence and the Continental Congress, as well as their oratory and writing, played an important role in the effort for independence. However, the activism of groups of artisans, laborers, and women also pushed the revolutionary movement forward.

The Role of Women in the American Revolution 美国独立战争中妇女的角色

Many women participated in the effort for American independence. Women made clothing, both to honor boycotts of British goods and also to help supply the revolutionary forces. Women were also prominent in crowd actions against merchants who were thought to be holding back goods in order to profit from wartime shortages. Women helped on the actual battlefield as nurses and carrying water. At least one woman enlisted in the Continental Army. Deborah Sampson disguised herself as a man and participated courageously in several battles.

Artisans and Laborers and the American Revolution 匠人、工人与美国独立战争

Urban artisans had long been active in resistance to British policies. Artisans encouraged boycotts of British goods, knowing that such boycotts would lead to a greater demand for American-made goods. However, they were driven as much by ideology as self-interest. Artisans became increasingly radicalized in the years leading up to the American Revolution.

Anti-British street actions in Boston and Philadelphia needed the mobilization of artisans and workers to be effective. Colonial elites realized that these commoners were reliable allies in the struggle against the British. Boston shoemaker Ebenezer Macintosh was an important leader of crowd actions in the Stamp Act period. When the fighting began, craftsmen and laborers made up the bulk of both local militias and Continental Army units.

In Philadelphia, radicalized artisans were instrumental in the revolutionary struggle in 1776. The prewar Philadelphia political leadership, primarily members of the merchant class, opposed independence and cutting ties to British trade. Artisans and laborers, with Thomas Paine and Benjamin Rush participating in the leadership, formed extra-legal committees and militia groups in support of revolution. They ended up crafting the most democratic constitution among the new states (see more on the Pennsylvania constitution, page 104).

D. FUNDING THE WAR EFFORT　资助战争

Civilians attempted to provide financial and material support to the Patriot cause. However, these efforts were insufficient. The Continental Army faced economic shortages throughout the war.

Currency, Inflation, and Financial Difficulties　货币、通货膨胀与财政困难

The Continental Army was persistently underfunded and frequently was short of basic supplies. Congress lacked the power to levy taxes on the people; it had to request funds from the various states. The war was a massive undertaking in terms of organization and financing. The newly formed and disorganized Congress was not prepared for the task. Congress attempted to solve the financial problems of the war by printing money, but this currency soon lost its value amid runaway inflation. Merchants frequently sold goods to the British, who could pay in gold and silver rather than have to accept the worthless currency of the Continental Congress. This was starkly evident in the winter of 1777–1778, when Washington's troops at Valley Forge, Pennsylvania, suffered from food shortages. One cause of the shortages was that merchants simply would not sell to the army.

Congress turned to other measures to pay the soldiers. It began issuing certificates for frontier land in lieu of payment. These certificates were often used as currency, as soldiers had more immediate needs than frontier land and used the certificates to procure goods.

Men and women helped the Patriot cause in a variety of ways. Women, for instance, created homespun clothing for the army (see page 95). Local committees attempted to force merchants to sell products at fixed prices in order to stem inflation.

E. THE WAR FOR INDEPENDENCE—FACTORS IN THE VICTORY OF THE PATRIOT CAUSE　为独立而战——赢得爱国热情的因素

The American crisis reached a boiling point by 1775. Fighting between the British Army and rebellious colonists began at Lexington and Concord in that year and intensified after the Second Continental Congress declared independence in July 1776.

Lexington and Concord　莱克星顿与康科德战役

In April 1775, fighting began between colonists and British troops in the Massachusetts towns of Lexington and Concord. Americans often call the first shot of this clash, "the shot heard round the world." The event symbolized a marked shift in the colonial situation from resistance to rebellion.

Factors in the Outcome of the War　影响战争结果的因素

Both sides had important advantages and disadvantages in the American Revolution. The British had a highly trained, professional army; they had the strongest navy in the world; and they had substantial financial resources. The British could also count on the support of about a third of the colonial population, which remained loyal. Great Britain offered freedom to slaves who joined the British side. The British also could count on a majority of American Indian tribes for support.

However, the British troops were fighting far from home. It was difficult to maintain supply lines over the course of a long war and over a huge theater of war. Also, Great Britain had enemies, such as the French who wanted to see them defeated. The entry of France into the war on the American side tipped the scales decisively against the British.

> ## DEFENSIVE VERSUS OFFENSIVE WARS
> ## 防御战与进攻战
> It is easier to defend one's territory than it is to conquer another's territory. This is seen in the American Revolution, and it was one of the advantages of the Confederacy in the American Civil War (1861–1865).

The Patriots had excellent leadership in General George Washington, who counted on several key generals, especially Nathanael Greene and Henry Knox. In addition, Washington had support from talented European volunteer officers: the Marquis de Lafayette (French); Baron von Steuben (Prussian); and Thaddeus Kosciusko and Casimir Pulaski (Polish). The Patriots had the advantage of defending their home territory; they did not have to attack Great Britain to emerge victorious. Finally, many Patriot soldiers believed deeply in the cause of independence. Colonial disadvantages included lack of financing (see page 105) and a lack of a strong central governing authority.

The Phases of the American Revolution　美国独立战争的三个时期

Historians point to three distinct phases of the American Revolution. The first (1775–1776) took place primarily in New England. In this phase, Great Britain did not grasp the depth of Patriot sentiment among many colonists. The British thought that the conflict was essentially brought on by a few hotheads in New England. After the British suffered heavy losses in their victory at the Battle of Bunker Hill (March 1776), they abandoned Boston and reevaluated their strategy.

The second phase (1776–1778) occurred primarily in the middle colonies. The British thought that if they could maintain control of New York, they could isolate rebellious New England. A massive British force drove George Washington and his troops out of New York City in the summer of 1776. However, British forces coming south from Canada suffered a major defeat at the Battle of Saratoga in October 1777. The battle made it evident that the British might be able to hold urban centers, like New York City, but it would be very difficult to control the vast stretches of eastern and southern North America. Saratoga also showed France that the colonists could mount formidable forces for battle. Early in 1778, France formally recognized the United States and agreed to

> ## URBAN AND RURAL AREAS
> ## 城市地区和农村地区
> Later in American history, the United States also came to realize that urban centers are easier to hold on to than rural areas. This lesson was shown in the Vietnam War.

supply military assistance. France's motivation was its animosity toward Great Britain, not affinity with the ideals of the Declaration of Independence.

The third phase (1778–1783) took place in the South. Great Britain hoped to rally loyalist sentiment in the South, where it was strongest, and even tap into resentment among the slave population of the South. The southern strategy did not bear fruit despite British victories at Savannah, Georgia, and Charleston, South Carolina. In the North, fighting had reached a stalemate, despite the aid that turncoat Benedict Arnold supplied to the British (1780). By October 1781, a joint American–French campaign caught British General Cornwallis off guard, and he surrendered at Yorktown, Virginia. Skirmishes continued between the two sides until the 1783 Treaty of Paris formally ended the American Revolution.

TREATIES OF PARIS 《巴黎条约》

There are three important treaties called the "Treaty of Paris" in American history—following the French and Indian War (1763), the American Revolution (1783), and the Spanish-American War (1898). Look at contextual information to understand which treaty is being discussed in a document or a question.

KEY CONCEPT 3.2 EXPERIMENTS IN DEMOCRATIC AND REPUBLICAN FORMS OF GOVERNMENT
核心概念3.2：民主政府与共和政府的试验

The ideas that grew out of the American Revolution did not develop in a vacuum. Experiments in democratic and republican forms of government developed across the Atlantic world. These ideas were shaped by new religious, economic, and cultural ideas.

I. The Ideas of the American Revolution 美国独立战争的理念

The American Revolution occurred in the midst of a fertile period in the history of ideas. A variety of schools of thought put forth contending new ideas about society, politics, religion, and governance. The ideas of the American Revolution reverberated around the world. At home, an ongoing tension emerged between those who sought to expand democratic participation and those who sought to maintain traditional forms of inequality.

A. PROTESTANT EVANGELISM AND ENLIGHTENMENT PHILOSOPHY 新教福音与启蒙哲学

The rise of Protestant evangelical movements shaped the worldviews of many British colonists, inspiring them to see themselves as a chosen people, surrounded by the blessings of liberty. In addition, the ideas of the Enlightenment shaped American thinking about the ideal political system.

The Ideas of John Locke 约翰·洛克的思想

John Locke's ideas (introduced in Period 2) were profoundly influential in America during the time of the Revolution. Locke had written *Two Treatises on Government* in the early 1690s to defend England's Glorious Revolution (1688). He identified the basis of a legitimate government in his *Second Treatise of Government* (1689). Locke argued that a ruler gains legitimacy through the consent of the governed. The basic responsibility of government is to protect the natural rights of the people; Locke identified the most basic of these rights as life, liberty, and property. If a government should fail to protect these basic rights, it is the right of the citizens to overthrow that government. Locke's theory of natural rights states that power to govern belongs to the people. Locke was one of the main intellectual influences in the writing of the Declaration of Independence. Locke's writings challenged Thomas Hobbes's defense of an absolutist monarchy and Sir Robert Filmer's assertion of the divine right of kings.

B. *COMMON SENSE*, THE DECLARATION OF INDEPENDENCE, AND REPUBLICAN SELF-GOVERNMENT　《常识》、《独立宣言》与共和党自治

Theoretical debates about the proper form of government took on urgency in the North American colonies in the 1770s as the imperial crisis intensified. Enlightenment ideas informed the writings of Thomas Paine and shaped the content of the Declaration of Independence. American thinkers and revolutionaries embraced the ideas of republican self-government based on natural-rights theory.

Divided Loyalties　分裂的忠诚

By 1776, even though fighting had begun between colonists and British forces, independence was not a foregone conclusion. A third of the colonists, known as "Patriots," wanted independence; an equal number, known as "Loyalists," wanted to retain ties to Great Britain. (Another third did not choose either side in the conflict.) Both warring sides had good reasons for their stance—whether those reasons were economic or emotional.

The Olive Branch Petition　《橄榄枝请愿书》

Some members of the Continental Congress still hoped for reconciliation. Congress sent the "Olive Branch Petition" to the British king in July 1775, affirming loyalty to King George III and blaming the current problems on Parliament (George rejected the petition).

Common Sense　《常识》

As the debate over independence ensued, Thomas Paine published a best-selling pamphlet called *Common Sense*. He advocated that the American colonies declare independence from Great Britain. He wrote that he could not see a "single advantage" in "being connected with Great Britain." The revolution was well under way in January 1776, when Paine wrote *Common Sense*. He argued against the logic of the Olive Branch Petition, plainly and forcefully putting the blame on the king.

The Declaration of Independence　《独立宣言》

On July 4, 1776, the delegates to the Second Continental Congress formally ratified the Declaration of Independence. The body of the Declaration of Independence is a list of grievances against the king of Great Britain, but the eloquent preamble contains key elements of Locke's natural rights theory. It states that "all men are created equal" and "endowed by their Creator with certain unalienable Rights." The declaration goes on to assert that government gains its legitimacy from "the consent of the governed." If a government violates people's natural rights, the people have the right "to alter or abolish it." These ideas have shaped democratic practices in the United States and beyond.

Visions of Republicanism 共和主义的憧憬

When the United States declared, and eventually won, its independence from Great Britain, it was not immediately clear what type of government it would embrace. There was widespread agreement that America would become a republic—a country in which sovereignty, or power, ultimately rested with the people rather than a monarch. This was a radical move for the time; there had been virtually no republics in the world since the Roman republic, two thousand years earlier.

There was, however, disagreement about what was expected of citizens in a republic. For many Americans, republicanism implied a particular moral stance in the world. Republican citizens, in this formulation, were independent people who embodied civic virtue, putting the interests of the community above their own self-interest. Republican citizens led industrious, simple lives. This vision of republicanism looked back to the ancient Roman republic as an ideal, true or not. In this understanding of republicanism, virtuous citizens had to be on the watch for decadent and corrupt leaders who pursued luxury and power at the expense of the common good.

At the same time, other Americans were developing a different set of ideas about republicanism. They argued that individuals pursuing their own self-interest were the ideal republican citizens. This understanding of republicanism drew inspiration from the economic ideas of Adam Smith. It put more of a focus on ambition and economic freedom, while the earlier understanding put more of an emphasis on public virtue and civic-mindedness. These competing visions of republicanism shaped many of the debates during the first decades of the United States.

REPUBLICANISM 共和政治

The eighteenth-century ideology of republicanism is not synonymous with the ideas of the Democratic–Republicans (1790s–1820s), nor with the ideas of the later Republican Party (1850s–present).

C. THE CALL FOR EGALITARIANISM 呼吁平等主义

Although the primary goal of the American Revolution was independence from Great Britain for the 13 colonies, the rhetoric that was employed to justify the revolution inspired others to demand fundamental changes in society. Many called for the abolition of slavery and for greater political democracy in the new governing structures.

Moves to Abolish Slavery 废除奴隶制运动

Despite the language of equality in the Declaration of Independence and in many state constitutions, political leaders were reluctant to apply such language to enslaved African Americans. In several northern states, slaves petitioned state legislatures to grant them their "natural rights," namely freedom. In 1779, petitions for emancipation in New Hampshire and Connecticut were rejected. In Massachusetts, seven free African Americans, including the brothers Paul and John Cuffe, refused to pay taxes on the ground that they did not vote and were, therefore, not represented. Their actions led to the extension of voting rights to taxpaying African Americans in Massachusetts. Slaves in Massachusetts sued for their freedom, initiating several legal cases that cited the language of the Massachusetts constitution, "all men are born free and equal." Several such cases were decided in favor of the slaves, effectively ending slavery in Massachusetts through judicial decisions.

Several other states slowly began to take action against slavery. Vermont, which was a sovereign entity from 1777 to 1791 (when it was admitted as the fourteenth state), outlawed slavery in its 1777 constitution, citing the language of the Declaration of Independence. In 1780, political leaders in Pennsylvania voted to end slavery by gradual emancipation. The law was not immediately beneficial to enslaved people in Pennsylvania. It stated that infants born on or after March 1, 1780, would be free, but only after they reached the age of 28. However, many slaves in Pennsylvania simply ran away, sometimes aided by sympathetic whites.

D. EVOLVING IDEAS ON GENDER   性别观念的发展

The importance of women in the revolutionary struggle and the spread of Enlightenment ideas around equality set the stage for the evolution of ideas around gender. The ideal of "republican motherhood" emerged in the decades after the American Revolution.

"Republican Motherhood"   "共和母亲"

The arguments deployed by the Patriot cause in the American Revolution inspired many male and female writers to challenge traditional notions of gender and to put forth new ideas about the proper role of men and women in the new nation. The concept of "republican motherhood," drawing together a number of elements, asserted that women did indeed have civic responsibilities in the evolving culture of the new nation. The concept drew on Enlightenment thinkers, such as John Locke, who asserted, in his *Two Treatises on Government*, that women and men had more equal roles in marriage, challenging traditional notions of female subordination. Further, the experience of women participating in the struggle for independence, from organizing boycotts to aiding men on the battlefield, engendered a sense of egalitarianism among many women and men. Finally, the rhetoric of the revolutionary era railed against tyrannical rule. Many found analogies between the tyranny of king over subject and the tyranny of husband over wife.

The concept of "republican motherhood" did not put forth an agenda of political equality between men and women. It went only so far as to assert that women did have a role to play in civic life. The main feature of this role was to raise civic-minded republican sons and to reform the morals and manners of men. It asserted that women were active agents in maintaining public virtue—a realm traditionally associated with men. The ideas of "republican motherhood" still confined women to a largely domestic role, but they did expand the possibilities for women to gain an education; after all, it was important for women to gain the literacy and knowledge needed to raise the next generation of republican leaders.

E. THE IMPACT OF THE AMERICAN REVOLUTION ABROAD   美国独立战争对他国的影响

The ideas of the American Revolution reverberated among many different peoples struggling against oppressive regimes.

Revolution in France   法国革命

In 1789, a little over a decade after the 13 colonies declared independence, and a mere six years after the Treaty of Paris was signed, a revolution began in France. The French revolutionaries were inspired by some of the same Enlightenment ideas that had inspired revolutionaries in America and were inspired by the American model itself. This first phase of the French Revolution was begun by the national legislature against the absolutist power of the monarch. The first phase had widespread support in the United States. Soon, the revolution entered a more radical phrase. In 1793, the monarchy was completely abolished, the power of the church was limited, and, during a fever of revolutionary zeal, more than 40,000 suspected enemies of the revolution were publicly executed, among them the king and queen of France. This "reign of terror," carried out by the Jacobins' political club, peaked in 1793–1794. The leader of the Jacobins, Maximilien Robespierre, was himself executed in 1794 in the Thermidorian Reaction. The Directory, a body of five men, took power in 1795 and held that power until 1799, when the French Revolution came to an end. After that, Napoleon Bonaparte assumed power in a coup d'état. As the revolution took its turn into a more radical direction in 1793, Americans became increasingly divided about the events in France.

Rebellion in Haiti 海地革命

In 1791, a revolution broke out in the western part of the Caribbean island of Hispaniola. The revolution occurred in the French part of the island, called Saint Domingue. This French colony was primarily a sugar-producing slave society, made up of half a million African slaves, and 60,000 free people. Of the free people, about half were white and half were mixed-race (*gens de couleur*). The mixed race population of Saint Domingue owned about a third of the slaves on the island, but were barred from participation in the political system.

The revolution had three phases. First, the white colonists resisted French rule, inspired in part by the model of the American Revolution and in part by the recent French Revolution. Second, the mixed-race planters rebelled, challenging their second-class status. Finally, the slaves themselves rebelled. The slave rebellion, led by Toussaint L'Overture and aided by Spanish troops, occupied much of the country. The rebellion of slaves on Saint Domingue sent waves of fear among southern planters in the United States, especially after fleeing whites and mixed-race people brought stories of the rebellion to communities in the southern United States. Soon after L'Overture's death, Haiti established its independence (1804) as the first black republic in the Americas.

Independence Struggles in Latin America 拉丁美洲独立战争

Of all the revolutions that followed the American Revolution, those in Latin America are most similar. After all, in both the British North American colonies and the Spanish American colonies, colonists decided to break long-held ties with European powers. Also, both the North American and the South American struggles for independence involved deep divisions within the respective colonial societies; rebels and loyalists clashed on both continents. Both revolutionary struggles occurred in societies that included slavery. Starting in 1808, several nations in Spain's vast New World empire—which extended from Mexico in the north to Argentina in the south, Peru in the west to Venezuela in the east—rebelled against Spanish rule. The revolutionaries were inspired by a combination of ideology, geopolitics, and material interests—just as their North American predecessors were.

II. Creating Governance in the New Republic 在新共和国建立统治

After declaring independence, Americans experimented with different forms of government, both on the state level and the national level. As the limitations of the Articles of Confederation became more apparent, American political leaders drafted the Constitution, which was based on the principles of federalism and separation of powers. Debates over the Constitution led to the adoption of a Bill of Rights as Americans continued to debate the proper balance between liberty and order.

A. GOVERNANCE ON THE STATE LEVEL 州级统治

After the Second Continental Congress declared independence, the newly established states created constitutions that placed power in the hands of the legislative branch. State constitutions varied in their embrace of democratic participation.

State Constitutions 州宪法

In May 1776, even before independence had been declared, the Second Continental Congress urged the colonies to draft constitutions. By 1778, ten states had drawn up constitutions, and Connecticut, Massachusetts, and Rhode Island updated their colonial charters. All the state constitutions affirmed the republican notion that government ultimately rests on the consent of the governed. Most of these constitutions reflected the older view of republicanism (see page 101). That is, these constitutions tended to be based on the idea that governing units should be relatively small and that distant power could become tyrannical. Some states created some form of direct democracy. Many states strengthened the lower legislative house. The lower house would be more responsive to the will of the people, through more frequent elections. Some states established annual elections in the lower house. Pennsylvania and Georgia abolished the upper house altogether.

Pennsylvania created the most radical of the state constitutions. The older, elite leadership of the colony was marginalized after it came out strongly against independence in the summer of 1776. The power vacuum that resulted was filled by a pro-independence, democratic-minded group of activists, including Thomas Paine and Benjamin Rush. These activists gave voice to the artisan and lower-class communities of Philadelphia rather than to the merchant elite class. The constitution that was drafted abolished property qualifications for voting and also abolished the office of governor. This constitution was in effect until the 1790s. Although Pennsylvania created the most democratic constitution, many states included lists of individual liberties that government was not to abridge. Virginia's bill of rights inspired other states to follow suit.

B. THE ARTICLES OF CONFEDERATION AND THE CRITICAL PERIOD
《十三州联邦宪法》与关键时期

The framers of the Articles of Confederation created a "firm league of friendship" among the states, rather than a strong, centralized nation. Before 1776 they had lived under a powerful, distant authority and they did not want to repeat that experience. Also, many of these early leaders were fiercely loyal to their states and did not want to see state power taken away. The Articles of Confederation may have appealed to those who feared arbitrary and distant authority, but during the period of their operation, often called the "Critical Period," the United States faced a series of domestic and international problems that led some to call for a stronger central government.

CRITICAL CONDITION
临界情况
Think of a patient in critical condition when you see the label "critical period" to describe the decade of the 1780s. Just like a patient in critical condition, the continued existence of the United States was in question.

The Articles of Confederation 《十三州联邦宪法》

The Articles of Confederation was written in 1776, just as the Declaration of Independence was being written and debated. The Articles of Confederation, however, lacks any of the philosophical grandeur of Thomas Jefferson's document. The Articles essentially put down on paper what had come to exist organically over the previous year, as the First and Second Continental Congresses began to assume more powers and responsibilities. The main concern at the time was carrying out the war against Great Britain. The document was edited and sent to the states for ratification in 1777. It took, however, an additional four years for all the states to ratify it. The issue of western land claims caused several states to initially reject the document (see page 118).

Structure of Government Under the Articles 联邦宪法下的政府架构

The Articles called for a one-house, or unicameral, legislature, continuing the practice of the Second Continental Congress. This Congress would have delegations from each state. States could send anywhere from two to seven delegates, but each state delegation would get one vote. Decision-making in Congress was not easy. Routine decisions required just a simple majority, or seven votes. Major decisions, however, required nine votes, allowing five states to block major legislation. Changes and amendments to the document itself required a unanimous vote in Congress and ratification by all the state legislatures. In retrospect, these decision-making requirements seem to be a recipe for dysfunction. At the time, however, many Americans were wary of distant authority and wanted to keep decision-making close to home; they did not want to see a central government with a free hand to do as it pleased.

Raising Revenue 征税

Under the Articles of Confederation, the national government's lack of broad powers was especially problematic in regard to raising revenue. This was an acute problem during wartime. The central government did not have the power to tax the people directly. The idea of being taxed only by local representatives carried over from the days of the Stamp Act. The central government depended on voluntary contributions from the states. Congress agreed that states would contribute revenue in proportion to their population, but the states were often tardy or resistant.

Inflation, Debt, and the Rejection of the Impost 通货膨胀、债务与反关税

The United States faced serious economic problems during the 1780s. The Confederation government and the states printed millions of dollars in paper money, driving up inflation. In addition, the government borrowed millions of dollars during the war. After the war, the government had trouble paying off these debts.

Robert Morris, chosen by Congress to address these issues, proposed a 5 percent impost, or import tax, to raise revenues. Since this would require a change in the Articles themselves, all 13 states had to be on board. Rhode Island and New York, which both had thriving ports, did not want to give up the revenue stream from state duties, so they rejected the proposed impost. This rejection demonstrated the difficulties Congress faced in passing important reforms.

Shays' Rebellion (1786–1787) 谢司起义（1786—1787）

Tensions between coastal elites and struggling farmers in the interior can be seen most clearly in Massachusetts. Several of the problems associated with the "critical period" were evident in a farmers' rebellion in Massachusetts, called Shays' Rebellion (1786–1787). In the western part of the state, struggling farmers, many of whom were veterans of the Revolution, were troubled by several government actions. Taxes in Massachusetts were stiff, unlike some states, and had to be paid in hard currency (backed by gold or silver), not cheap paper currency. Unable to pay these taxes, many farmers were losing their farms to banks. The farmers petitioned the legislature to pass stay laws, which would have suspended a creditors' right to foreclose on

> ### SHAYS' REBELLION
> ### 谢司起义
> The incident is considered one of the catalysts for creating a completely new governing document rather than simply amending the Articles of Confederation.

farms. This, along with petitions to lower taxes, was rejected by the Massachusetts legislature.

After being frustrated by the legislature, hundreds of Massachusetts farmers, led by veteran Daniel Shays, protested and finally took up arms. They were responding to a perceived injustice as they had a decade earlier when under British rule. They closed down several courts and freed farmers from debtors' prison. Local militias did not try to stop the actions, which spread to more towns in Massachusetts. After several weeks, the governor and legislature took action, calling up nearly 4,000 armed men to suppress the rebellion. Concerns about the ability of the authorities to put down future uprisings were on the minds of the delegates to the Philadelphia convention, which convened just three months after Shays' Rebellion ended.

Toward a New Framework for Governance 新的统治框架

By 1786, many Americans, especially elite property owners, began to raise concerns about the stature of the United States on the world stage and the competency of a weak central government. With these concerns in mind, in 1786 a group of reformers received approval from Congress to meet in Annapolis, Maryland, to discuss possible changes in the Articles of Confederation. A follow-up meeting was scheduled in Philadelphia for May 1787. In between these meetings, from August 1786 until February 1787, Shays' Rebellion erupted in Massachusetts (see above). It was eventually put down, but it added fuel to the impetus to reform the governing structure. By the time of the Philadelphia meeting, the delegates were ready to scrap the entire Articles of Confederation and write something new.

C. THE FRAMING OF THE CONSTITUTION 宪法的制定

The delegates who had been chosen to work on changes to the Articles of Confederation quickly agreed at the 1787 Philadelphia meeting to get rid of the Articles altogether and to create a new framework for government. For four months, delegates met, argued, and wrote. These deliberations resulted in a series of compromises that formed the basis of the new Constitution.

The Great Compromise 大妥协

The delegates at the Constitutional Convention agreed that a central government with far greater powers was needed, but several contentious issues occupied much of their attention. A major source of debate was how the various states should be represented in the new government. Bigger states expressed dissatisfaction with the one-vote-per-state system that existed under the Articles; they argued that larger states should have a larger voice in government. The delegates from these states rallied around the Virginia Plan, which would have created a bicameral legislature that pegged the number of representatives from each state to the population of the state. The small states feared their voices would be drowned out in such a legislature. They countered with the New Jersey Plan, which called for a one-house legislature with each state getting one vote (similar to the existing Congress under the Articles of Confederation). After much wrangling, the delegates agreed on the Great Compromise, which created the basic structure of Congress as it now exists. The plan called for a House of Representatives, in which representation would be determined by the population of each state, and a Senate, in which each state would get two members.

The Three Branches of Government, Separation of Powers, and Checks and Balances 政府的三个分支，分权与制衡

The framers of the Constitution created three separate branches of government. The legislative branch creates laws, the executive branch carries out laws, and the judicial branch interprets laws. The Constitution spells out the powers of each branch. The powers of Congress are enumerated in Article I. These include the power to levy taxes, to regulate trade, to coin money, to establish post offices, to declare war, and to approve treaties. The framers of the Constitution wanted it to have the flexibility to deal with the needs of a changing society. Toward this goal they included the elastic clause, which stretched the powers of Congress by allowing it to "make all laws necessary and proper." However, the definition of "necessary and proper" soon became a matter of much debate. The powers of the president are included in Article II. These include the power to suggest legislation, to command the armed forces, and to nominate judges. The president is charged with carrying out the laws of the land. The powers of the judiciary, headed by the Supreme Court, are outlined in Article III.

The framers were very conscious of the problems of a government with limitless powers. After living under the British monarchy, they came to believe that a powerful government without checks was dangerous to liberty. Therefore, they created a governmental system with three separate branches, each with the ability to check the powers of the other two. The goal was to keep the three branches in balance. An example of this concept of checks and balances is the president's ability to veto (or reject) bills passed by Congress, or the Supreme Court's ability to strike down laws that it deems unconstitutional.

MADISON AND THE CONSTITUTION
麦迪逊和宪法

The basic structural elements of the Constitution—three branches of government, with a system of checks and balances—are explained and defended in James Madison's *Federalist Number 51*.

Federalism—the National Government and the States 联邦制——国家政府与州政府

Federalism refers to the evolving relationship between the national government and the states. The Constitution gave the national government considerably more power than had the Articles of Confederation. Under the Constitution, states still hold on to certain powers (reserved powers), but an expanded national government is given many new powers (delegated powers). These expanded national powers include the power to tax, borrow money, regulate commerce, and promote the "general welfare." At one point, Madison proposed granting Congress the power to strike down state laws, but this measure was rejected. The Constitution does make it clear that the national government is the "supreme law of the land."

D. THE CONSTITUTION AND SLAVERY—COMPROMISE AND POSTPONEMENT
宪法与奴隶制——妥协与延期

Though many voices noted the inconsistency of slavery and the ideals put forth in the nation's founding documents, slavery continued in the United States. The framers of the Constitution were, to some degree, uneasy with the "peculiar institution," as it would be termed. This uneasiness is reflected in the fact that the word "slavery" is not used once in the entire document. Slaves are often referred to as "other persons." Although the framers of the Constitution did not mention the word *slavery*, they were willing to compromise on the issue and postpone any final decision about it to the future. This postponement led to decades of debate and conflict over the issue.

The "Three-Fifths Compromise" "五分之三妥协"

Once it was established that representation in the House of Representatives would be based on population (see page 107), the question arose: Who would be counted in determining a state's population? Specifically, would a southern state be able to count its slave populations in the census? This was a major issue when one considered that for states such as South Carolina and Mississippi slaves comprised more than 50 percent of the populations. To count them in the census would more than double the size of their delegations in the House. Northern states objected on the grounds that slaves could not vote; in fact, they were considered property, not human beings. After much debate, a compromise was reached in which southern states could count three-fifths of their slave populations in the census. This "Three-Fifths Compromise" defied common sense, but it got the delegates through an impasse.

Tacit Approval of Slavery 默许的奴隶制

Other sections of the Constitution seem to give tacit approval of the institution of slavery. The delegates voted to protect the international slave trade for 20 years, guaranteeing the flow of slaves into the country from Africa and the Caribbean for another generation. (The international slave trade was ended by Congress in 1808, the earliest date that the Constitution allowed.) Finally, the Constitution provided for the return of fugitive slaves. (A mechanism for their return was contained in the Fugitive Slave Act of 1793; the process was strengthened with the Fugitive Slave Act of 1850.) Though slavery was not mentioned by name, the inclusion of regulations around slavery made clear that the Constitution recognized its existence.

E. FEDERALISTS, ANTI-FEDERALISTS, AND THE ADOPTION OF THE
BILL OF RIGHTS 联邦党人、反联邦党人与《权利法案》的通过

Once the Constitution was completed, it went to the states for ratification. Each state was to call a convention to vote for ratification, and only nine states were needed for approval. This was still not an easy process. Large numbers of Americans opposed the creation of a powerful central government. Public opinion in Virginia, Massachusetts, and New York was clearly against ratification. North Carolina and Rhode Island did not even hold conventions. Finally, all the states did vote to ratify the Constitution. Many opponents of the new Constitution came around to voting in the affirmative only after leading supporters of the document promised to add a bill of rights to the Constitution.

The Federalists 联邦党人

The supporters of the Constitution labeled themselves Federalists. Three important Federalist theorists were Alexander Hamilton, John Jay, and James Madison. As the New York convention was debating ratification, the three wrote a series of articles that were later published in book form—*The Federalist.* This highly influential political tract outlined the failures of the Articles of Confederation and the benefits of a power-ful government, with checks and balances. In *Federalist Number 10,* Madison argued that, for a large and diverse population, a complex government was the best guar-antee of liberty. With such a complex government, no one group could gain control and dominate others. This argument challenged the traditional republican notion that republics must be small in order to be democratic.

In *Federalist Number 51,* he argued for a separation of powers within the government and a system of checks and balances. In this essay, Madison asserted that "ambition must be made to counteract ambition."

Anti-Federalism 反联邦制度

Opponents of the new Constitution, Anti-Federalists, as they were called by their Federalist adversaries, worried that the new government would be controlled by members of the elite. They saw the document as favoring the creation of a powerful, aristocratic ruling class. Leading Anti-Federalists were Patrick Henry and George Mason. They argued that officials in the national government would be, almost by definition, removed from the concerns, and the control, of ordinary people. They were distrustful of distant authority. The 13 colonies had just emerged from under the thumb of the British Empire, so many colonists were eager to see power was exercised locally. One of the Anti-Federalists' primary concerns was that individual rights were not adequately protected by the Constitution. They noted that the document did not contain a bill of rights.

THE ANTI-FEDERALISTS 反联邦党人

The Anti-Federalists have been saddled with an unfortunate name. They sound like naysayers. However, you should take their ideas seriously. They had a comprehensive view of the world. Just because they lost the fight over ratification does not mean they should be dismissed. After all, their agitation led to the Bill of Rights.

Ratification 批准

Delaware ratified the Constitution almost immediately, in December 1787. By January 1788, four more states—Pennsylvania, New Jersey, Georgia, and Connecticut—voted for ratification. In January, supporters of the Constitution faced their first real test in Massachusetts. Prominent Massachusetts political leaders, including Samuel Adams and Governor John Hancock, opposed ratification. Also, many followers of Daniel Shays were active in the process and strongly opposed to the Constitution. Federalist leaders assured the ratifying convention that they would recommend the creation of a national bill of rights in order to address Anti-Federalist concerns. In February, Massachusetts voted to approve the Constitution. By May, Maryland and South

Carolina came on board. New Hampshire provided the ninth, and deciding, vote in June 1788. By May 1790, the final four states—Virginia (1788), New York (1788), North Carolina (1789), and Rhode Island (1790)—voted for ratification and joined the new union.

The Bill of Rights 《权利法案》

During the debate over ratification of the Constitution, seven of the states voted to ratify only on the condition that Congress would pass a list of rights of the people. Anti-Federalists in these states feared that a sprawling, powerful government would step on individual liberties. As promised, one of the first acts of Congress was passage of the Bill of Rights—the first ten amendments to the Constitution. Much of the language in the Bill of Rights, written by James Madison, comes from the various states' constitutions.

The First Through Fourth Amendments: Basic Rights of the People

第一至第四条修正案：基本人权

The First Amendment contains the "establishment clause" prohibiting the establishment of an official religion in the United States. The remainder of the First Amendment deals with various forms of freedom of expression. The Second Amendment guarantees the right to bear arms. Some have argued that the language of the Second Amendment seems to link the right to bear arms to participation in militias; others have argued that it is an absolute individual right. The Third Amendment addresses a much-hated British practice—forcing colonial residents to house soldiers. Americans would not be compelled to quarter soldiers. The Fourth Amendment guarantees a modicum of privacy from searches by government officials. People are protected in their "persons, houses, papers and effects" from "unreasonable searches and seizures." Authorities must first obtain a warrant, issued by a judge upon evidence of "probable cause."

The Fifth Through Eighth Amendments: Rights of the Accused

第五至第八条修正案：被告的权利

Several amendments in the Bill of Rights address protections people have when they are brought into the legal system. The logic of these amendments is that the legal system is powerful and well-funded, and should therefore have checks placed upon it to protect the individual. The Fifth Amendment calls for grand jury indictments, prohibits authorities from trying a suspect twice for the same crime ("double jeopardy") and from forcing a suspect to testify against him or herself. The Fifth Amendment also prohibits the government from seizing someone's property, unless it is for a "public use" and the owner receives "just compensation." This power of the government to seize private property under these stipulations is known as "eminent domain." The Sixth Amendment guarantees suspects the right to a "speedy and public" trial, with a jury, conducted in the district where the crime was committed. Also, the suspect has a right to be informed of the charges and has the right to question witnesses giving testimony. Finally, suspects have the right to call friendly witnesses to the stand and have a lawyer. The Seventh Amendment guarantees the accused the right to a trial by jury, even in civil cases (involving conflicts between two parties over monetary damages). The Eighth Amendment prevents the government from inflicting "cruel and unusual" punishments and prevents the setting of "excessive bail."

The Ninth and Tenth Amendments 第九和第十条修正案

The last two amendments of the Bill of Rights deal with limits and parameters of rights and powers inherent in the government. The Ninth Amendment guarantees that additional rights, not mentioned in the Bill of Rights, shall be protected from government infringement. The Tenth Amendment deals with governmental powers and the relationship between the federal government and the states. It puts forth that powers not delegated to the federal government, nor prohibited by the Constitution, shall be retained by the states and by the people.

The Right to Vote 选举权

The right to vote is absent from the Bill of Rights. The federal government left it to the states to formulate rules for voting. It was only later that voting would be seen as a fundamental right that needed the protection of constitutional amendments. The Fifteenth Amendment (1870) prohibited voting restrictions based on race, the Nineteenth Amendment (1920) prohibited restrictions based on gender, and the Twenty-sixth Amendment (1971) lowered the voting age to 18.

III. Politics and Culture in the New Nation 新生国家的政治与文化

After the United States achieved independence, two trends emerged simultaneously. First, the period from independence to the end of the eighteenth century witnessed the development of political institutions and cultural forms that united the new country. At the same time, the nation experienced regional variations and heated debates over economic, political, social, and foreign policy issues.

A. PUTTING THE CONSTITUTION INTO PRACTICE 宪法的实施

The Constitution, ratified in 1788, existed on paper. It took the first two presidential administrations, those of George Washington and John Adams, to put the principles of the Constitution into practice.

The Judiciary Act of 1789 《1789年司法条例》

The Constitution called for a federal judiciary, including a supreme court, but left it up to Congress to flesh out such a system. The Judiciary Act of 1789 created a federal district court in each state and three district courts that could hear appeals from the district courts. The Supreme Court could hear appeals from the circuits and would have the final say. In addition, the act stipulated that the Supreme Court could hear cases on appeal from state courts if the case involved federal law. The act made it clear that the Supreme Court would have the last word on constitutional interpretation.

Washington and the "Unwritten Constitution" 华盛顿与"不成文宪法"

President George Washington established several traditions and customs that have come to be known as the "unwritten constitution." The establishment of a presidential cabinet is one of these customs. Washington wisely chose capable and experienced men to run the new government's three departments—state, war, and the treasury. Washington chose Thomas Jefferson for the Department of State, General Henry Knox for the Department of War, and Alexander Hamilton for the Treasury. He also chose Edmund Randolph as the nation's first attorney general and John Jay for chief justice of the Supreme Court. Washington began meeting regularly with these men, seeking their input on important decisions. This practice of meeting regularly with a presidential cabinet was subsequently followed by all American presidents. Washington's decision to run for no more than two terms was also part of the "unwritten constitution," until Congress and the states ratified the 22nd Amendment (1951), following Franklin D. Roosevelt's four electoral victories, making the traditional two-term limitation part of the written Constitution.

B. POLICY DEBATES IN THE NEW NATION 新生国家的政策辩论

A series of policy conflicts and disagreements emerged during the presidential administrations of George Washington and John Adams, reflecting a growing divide among the public. Around these divides coalesced two political groups, Federalists and Republicans. These policy conflicts centered around economic policy, foreign policy, and the relationship between the federal government and the states.

Federalists and Republicans 联邦党人与共和党人

The first two political parties—the Federalists and the Republicans—were both able to articulate profound differences around public policy, while at the same time facilitating a national debate on these issues. Federalists tended to be more pro-British, more critical of the French Revolution, more friendly to urban, commercial interests, and more ready to use the power of the federal government to influence economic activity. The leading theorist of the Federalists was Alexander Hamilton. The Republicans tended to be more critical of the British, more supportive of the French Revolution, at least in its early stages, more critical of centralized authority, and more favorable to agricultural interests. Jefferson was a leading theorist of the Republicans.

Hamilton's Economic Program 汉密尔顿的经济计划

Washington's secretary of the Treasury, Alexander Hamilton, proposed a series of economic measures meant to put the United States on a sound economic footing. Central to his plans was a national bank, which would hold the government's tax revenues and act as a stabilizing force on the economy. Hamilton proposed a bank that would be 20 percent publicly controlled and 80 percent privately controlled. Hamilton thought it was important to have wealthy investors financially and psychologically invested in the new government. The proposal to create a national bank became a source of disagreement between Hamilton and Secretary of State Thomas Jefferson, who argued that the Constitution did not permit Congress to create a national bank. This was not among the powers listed in the Constitution. Hamilton countered that the elastic clause, which lets Congress do what it considered "necessary and proper" in carrying out its duties, implicitly allowed for the creation of a national bank. President Washington agreed and signed the bank law in 1791.

INTERPRETING THE CONSTITUTION 解释宪法

The debate over a national bank represents an ongoing debate in American history between strict and loose interpretations of the Constitution.

Dealing with Debt 解决债务问题

Hamilton's economic program included two other significant parts. He proposed an elaborate and controversial plan to deal with the new nation's substantial debt. He insisted that debts carried over from the war years be paid back, or funded, at full value. Many of the debt certificates had been sold by their holders. The original holders had little faith that the government would ever make good on the actual loans. The certificates were changing hands at a fraction of their original value. Full funding meant a financial windfall for speculators who bought up the certificates. In addition,

FUNDING AND ASSUMPTION
资金与假设
Be familiar with these two terms when thinking about Hamilton's approach to paying off war-related debt.

Hamilton insisted that the government assume, or agree to pay back, state debts incurred during the war. The proposal met with strenuous opposition from states that either did not have a large debt or had already paid back their debts. To accomplish the goals of "funding" and "assumption," Hamilton prodded the government to take out new loans by selling government bonds.

Encouragement to Manufacturing　鼓励制造业

The final piece of Hamilton's financial program was to encourage manufacturing by imposing tariffs on foreign-made goods and subsidizing American industry (Congress adopted Hamilton's "Report on Manufactures," except for his recommendation of subsidies to industry). He believed industrial development would be key to a balanced and self-reliant economy. The nation, however, was not yet ready for developing its manufacturing sector; the War of 1812 brought the importance of manufacturing to the fore.

The Excise Tax and the Whiskey Rebellion (1794)　消费税与威士忌之乱（1794）

A conflict between elites and western farmers occurred in rural Pennsylvania in 1794. To help raise revenues to pay for his ambitious plans, Hamilton proposed enacting new taxes. The most prominent of these taxes, and most controversial, was an excise (or sales) tax on whiskey. This tax hit grain farmers especially hard. These hardscrabble farmers in remote rural areas were barely making ends meet. Distilling grain into whiskey allowed them to increase their meager profit. Transporting bushels of grain over primitive roads to population centers was prohibitively expensive; distilling grain into whiskey made the crop much more valuable, and it was easier to transport.

RESPONSES TO REBELLIONS
对不同叛乱的反应
Be prepared to contrast the ineffective response to Shays' Rebellion, which lasted for months in 1786 and 1787, with the massive force of troops sent to put down the Whiskey Rebellion.

The grain farmers of western Pennsylvania felt they could not shoulder this substantial tax. In 1794, farmers took action. Fifty men marched to the home of the local tax collector. From there the gathering swelled to 7,000 men and marched to Pittsburgh. At this point, the federal government took action. Alexander Hamilton and George Washington had vivid memories of Shays' Rebellion of less than a decade earlier. Farmers in western Massachusetts had staged a violent rebellion for weeks before it was finally put down by a militia funded privately by merchants. In 1794 the government was determined that the current rebellion would not get out of control. Washington nationalized nearly 13,000 militiamen into the army and marched them himself to Pennsylvania to suppress the rebellion and ensure that the laws of the land would be followed. Washington's response to the rebellion had the desired effect. It established federal authority and made clear that a strong national government would not tolerate unlawful challenges to its authority.

The Alien and Sedition Acts (1798) 《外国人与煽动叛乱法案》（1798）

In an atmosphere of animosity and distrust between the Federalists and the Republicans, the Alien and Sedition Acts were passed by a Federalist-dominated Congress in order to limit criticism from the opposition Republican Party. The Alien and Sedition Acts actually comprised four acts. The main two acts were the Alien Act, which made it more difficult for foreigners to achieve American citizenship, and the Sedition Act, which made it a crime to defame the president or Congress. The broad wording of the Sedition Act was consistent with contemporary British sedition laws, but seemed to challenge the free-speech guarantees of the recently ratified First Amendment. Jeffersonians were especially troubled by the expansion of federal power that the acts represented.

The Kentucky and Virginia Resolutions 肯塔基与弗吉尼亚决议

Thomas Jefferson and James Madison were so opposed to the Alien and Sedition Acts that they proposed the idea of nullification in their Virginia and Kentucky Resolutions. These resolutions put forth the idea that a state had the right to nullify a law it found to be inconsistent with the Constitution. The idea of state nullification of a federal edict did not slow down the Alien and Sedition Acts, but it raised issues about the relationship between the federal government and the states. These issues emerged on several occasions in the first half of the nineteenth century and were part of the slavery debates that led to the Civil War.

> ## STATE VERSUS FEDERAL POWER
> ## 国家权力与联邦权力
> The Kentucky and Virginia Resolutions were part of an ongoing debate over the respective powers of the federal government and the states' governments. The issue appeared to have been largely settled by the Civil War, but it would persist into the twenty-first century.

C. DIVERGENT REGIONAL ATTITUDES TOWARD SLAVERY 各地区对待奴隶制的不同态度

After the American Revolution, attitudes around slavery became increasingly shaped by region, as slavery became more entrenched in the South and in adjacent western lands, while it began to disappear in the North.

The North Moves Toward a Free Labor System 北方为自由劳动力制度发起运动

Many northerners came to see unfree labor as inconsistent with the republican ideas of the American Revolution. Even indentured servitude disappeared from most states by 1800. In many northern states, slavery became less important to the economy. Vermont outlawed slavery altogether, Pennsylvania passed a gradual emancipation law, and other northern states began to follow suit. Gradual emancipation laws did not free existing slaves; they provided for the freedom of the future children of slave women (often after serving their master for a certain number of years). Such an approach respected contemporary understandings of property rights. In the years after the American Revolution, free-black communities developed in many northern states and in some states of the upper South, such as Virginia and Maryland.

The Growth of Slavery in the South 南方奴隶制的发展

In the decades after the American Revolution, slavery became increasingly important in the South. Eli Whitney's invention of the cotton gin in 1793 set the stage for a remarkable growth in the production of cotton, in the growth of the southern economy, and in the reliance on slavery (see Period 4). Despite gradual emancipation in the North, voluntary emancipation throughout the United States, and the escape of many slaves during the chaos of the American Revolution, the number of slaves in the United States grew from 500,000 in 1776 to 700,000 in 1790. With the ending of indentured servitude, the stark differences between the growing free-labor ideology of the North and the expanding slave-labor system of the South became more apparent. These diverging attitudes on slavery would come to shape many of the debates leading up to the Civil War.

D. CULTURE AND IDENTITY IN THE EARLY NATIONAL PERIOD 建国初期的文化与认同

In the decades following independence, a variety of cultural products were created that expressed a sense of national identity. For many Americans, political independence from Great Britain needed to be followed by cultural independence from European forms and traditions.

American Education 美国教育

Noah Webster, a noted author, political thinker, and educator, asserted that American culture was separate from, and superior to, British culture. He saw the United States as a tolerant, rational, democratic nation—distinct from the superstitions, ostentatious habits, and warring history of Europe. He published a three-volume set of textbooks that were intended for American schoolchildren—*A Grammatical Institute of the English Language*. The work consisted of a speller (1783), a grammar (1784), and a reader (1785). The speller, known as the *American Spelling Book*, put forth simplified Americanized spellings—*theater* instead of *theatre*, *color* instead of *colour*. After 1800, he expanded his speller into a comprehensive dictionary: *An American Dictionary of the English Language*, completed in 1828. American schoolchildren also used *Geography Made Easy*, by Jedidiah Morse, who insisted that American schoolchildren should use American textbooks.

American History 美国历史

Within decades of independence, several writers set out to frame American history in a heroic light. Mercy Otis Warren, a long-time writer, political activist, and Anti-Federalist agitator, wrote a three-volume *History of the Revolution* (published in 1805). Mason Weems wrote a best-selling glowing biography of the "Father of the Country," *The Life of Washington*, first published in 1800. A later edition of the book contained the imagined story of a young George Washington admitting to his father that he had damaged a cherry tree with his hatchet, prefacing the admission with the words, "I cannot tell a lie." These volumes were intended to instill a nationalist spirit in Americans.

American Architecture　美国建筑

During this period, the first true architects appeared on the American scene. Among them was Charles Bulfinch (1763–1844) who is credited with bringing the Federal style to the United States after his own European tour. Federalist architects were highly influenced by the Scottish architect Robert Adam (1728–1792). Simplicity and balance characterize Federal architecture, a style indebted to ancient Greek and Roman elements. Americans consciously wanted to draw connections between the United States and the democratic and republican models of the ancient world; this impulse is reflected in Federal architecture.

KEY CONCEPT 3.3 MIGRATIONS AND CONFLICT IN MULTIETHNIC NORTH AMERICA
核心概念3.3：多民族北美的移民与冲突

The closing decades of the eighteenth century witnessed increased migrations, competition for resources, and cooperative interactions. Intensified conflicts between peoples and nations led to shifting boundaries and changing policies.

I. Migrations, Government Policies, and Cultural Blending
移民、政府政策与文化融合

After the United States achieved its independence, interactions among different groups on the North American continent resulted in shifting alliances, competition for resources, and new forms of cultural blending.

A. MIGRATIONS, AMERICAN INDIANS, AND SHIFTING ALLIANCES
移民、美洲印第安人与变化的联盟

As more white settlers moved into the interior of North America in the decades after the American Revolution, various Indian groups were forced to evaluate and adjust their alliances—with other tribes, with European powers, and with the United States. These Indians wanted to both limit the movement of settlers into the interior of the continent and to safeguard tribal lands and natural resources.

The Status of American Indian Lands After the American Revolution
美国独立战争后美洲印第安人家园的状况

After the Revolution, land struggles between white settlers and American Indian groups continued. The 1783 Treaty of Paris between the United States and Great Britain ignored the status of Indians in the American West. The land between the Appalachian Mountains and the Mississippi River had been set aside as an Indian Reserve by the Proclamation of 1763 (see page 92). In the Treaty of Paris, the British agreed to withdraw their garrisons from this area, but the agreement did not make any accommodations for the Indians living there. As more Americans moved into this area after the Revolution, especially between the Ohio River and the Great Lakes, the status of the native peoples became more precarious.

Treaty of Fort Stanwix　《斯坦尼克斯堡条约》

In 1784, under the Articles of Confederation, the government tried to solve the problem of native land claims north of the Ohio River by working out the Treaty of Fort Stanwix. The negotiations occurred with the six-nation Iroquois Confederacy. The stated purpose of the negotiations was to formulate a peace treaty in the wake of the Revolution (in which two of the six Iroquois nations sided with the British). The negotiations included the Iroquois ceding control of land north of the Ohio River. However, the Iroquois did not, for the most part, occupy the land in question, and their claims to it—based on the outcome of the Beaver Wars of the previous century—were dubious. The main occupants of the region, the Shawnee, Delaware, and Miami, were not part of these negotiations and protested bitterly that their land had been ceded without their consent.

Additional treaties were negotiated in the 1780s. In the Treaty of Fort McIntosh (1785), representatives of Wyandotte, Delaware, Chippewa, and Ottawa ceded lands in the trans-Ohio River region, now known as the Northwest Territory. Another agreement, the Treaty of Fort Harmar (1789), addressed the issue of control of other lands north of the Ohio. None of these treaties provided a satisfactory solution to the issue of control of the region. First, the powerful Shawnee were not part of the negotiations. Also, the continued presence of the British, as well as disputes about the authority of negotiators, complicated the issue.

American Defeat at the Wabash River 美国沃巴什河战败

The situation between American Indians and white settlers grew increasingly tense after 1790. Settlers continued pushing into Indian territory. A series of military conflicts ensued in the 1790s in the region. Forces of Indians, led by the Miami warrior Little Turtle, engaged in major battles against U.S. troops in present-day Ohio. American troops led by General Arthur St. Clair suffered a massive defeat at the mouth of the Wabash River in 1791. More than 600 troops were killed in this encounter, making it the United States' single most costly battle in the entire history of wars with American Indians.

The Battle of Fallen Timbers and the Treaty of Greenville 落木战役与《格尼维尔和约》

In the aftermath of the defeat of U.S. troops at the Wabash River, President George Washington was determined to gain control of the region north of the Ohio. He doubled the U.S. presence in Ohio and appointed General Anthony ("Mad Anthony") Wayne to lead American forces. At the Battle of Fallen Timbers (1794), the Indians were soundly defeated by superior American firepower. The following year, 1795, native groups gave up claims to most of Ohio in the Treaty of Greenville. The treaty brought only a temporary peace. Within a generation, settlers would push farther into Ohio and Indiana; these incursions would become connected with the U.S. declaration of war against Britain in 1812.

B. INTERNAL MIGRATIONS, FRONTIER CULTURES, AND TENSIONS IN THE BACKCOUNTRY 国内迁移、边境文化与偏远地区的紧张局势

The United States pursued policies to encourage migration beyond the Appalachian Mountains. Many individuals needed no encouragement; land and economic opportunity beckoned to many struggling farmers to move westward. As more people began leaving settled coastal towns and moved inland, tensions increased between elites and backcountry farmers. These tensions evolved along cultural, political, and ethnic lines.

The Dynamics of Backcountry Settlements 偏远地区的殖民动态

From the seventeenth century, tensions have existed between backcountry settlers and elite policymakers in the more established urban centers of the East. This was evident in Bacon's Rebellion in 1676. Backcountry Virginia settlers grew resentful of the policies of Governor William Berkeley and the House of Burgesses. They argued that they paid a disproportionate share of taxes in the colony and were not represented in the House of Burgesses. Also, they believed that the colonial government was not taking sufficient action to push native tribes farther west (see more on Bacon's Rebellion in Period 2).

Similar tensions surfaced in the second half of the eighteenth century, during both the colonial period and the early national period. The Carolina Regulators movement, composed of backcountry farmers in North and South Carolina, challenged the policies and practices of merchants, bankers, local officials, and the colonial government. The tensions came to a fore between 1765 and 1771, when the movement took up arms against colonial authorities in the War of the Regulation. A catalyst for the uprising was the collection of debts in these backcountry areas. After several years of drought and poor harvests many farmers suffered income loss as well as shortages of basic supplies. They were forced to rely on local merchants and bankers to extend them credit and loans. The collection of debts was, the farmers contended, rife with corruption. The system of local court officials and sheriffs, and the political infrastructure that supported it, was perceived as an oppressive outside force. The uprising was an attempt to challenge this outside force. The uprising did not change the power structure in the Carolinas, but it did establish patterns of thought and action that became evident in the coming years in the rebellion against British rule.

Similar tensions were seen in the actions of the Paxton Boys in western Pennsylvania (1763–1764), as bitterness toward local Indian groups and objections to the policies of Pennsylvania's colonial government resulted in violence (see page 93). Such tensions did not subside with independence. During the Critical Period of the 1780s, farmers in western Massachusetts, experiencing the burdens of debt, taxation, and lack of access to currency, staged a months-long rebellion against local courts as well as the policies of the Massachusetts legislature (1786–1787). Shays' Rebellion was finally put down, but is seen as an important catalyst for the convening of the 1787 Constitutional Convention (see page 106). Several years later, the Whiskey Rebellion, culminating in 1794, staged by farmers in western Pennsylvania over the excise tax on whiskey, again demonstrated backcountry mistrust of the polices of elites (see pages 113–114).

C. ORGANIZING THE NORTHWEST TERRITORY　整顿西北地区

The Confederation Congress made important progress in incorporating the country's western lands by passing the Northwest Ordinance and establishing procedures and guidelines for the incorporation of new states.

The Northwest Territory　西北地区

The Treaty of Paris (1783) set the boundary of the United States at the Mississippi River. There was debate about the status of the vast swath of land between the Appalachian Mountains and the Mississippi River. Some states insisted that western land claims from the colonial period should be honored. Virginia, for instance, claimed all of the land north of the Ohio River. New York claimed a huge portion of the West, including land that overlapped with Virginia's claim. Some states, such as New Jersey and Maryland, had no claims. Maryland insisted that it would not ratify the Articles until all states gave up their land claims and the western lands became part of a national domain. Congress persuaded the states with claims to do just that.

Land Ordinances and the Northwest Ordinance　土地法令与西北法令

Once the western land came under the control of the national government, Congress set about passing a series of acts to clarify the status of these lands and to encourage their settlement. The Land Ordinance of 1784 divided the Northwest Territory into ten new states, with the guarantee of self-government. The following year, Congress passed the Land Ordinance of 1785, reducing the number of states from ten to five, and calling for the area to be surveyed and divided into lots. A lot in every town was set aside for education; the rest were to be sold. In 1787, Congress passed the Northwest Ordinance, setting up a process by which areas could become territories, and then states. Once the population of a territory reached 60,000, it could write a constitution and apply for statehood. These states would be on equal footing with the original 13 states; they would not have a second-class, colonial status. Also, the Northwest Ordinance banned slavery in the territory north of the Ohio River. These acts encouraged the steady and orderly flow of settlers into the West. This, however, proved disastrous for American Indians.

> ### SUCCESS IN THE WEST
> ### 西部的胜利
> The most significant accomplishments of the Articles of Confederation government involved dealing with the complex problems associated with the lands to the west of the Appalachian Mountains.

Moving into the Northwest Territory 移居西北地区

In the 1790s, a steady stream of migrants made their way into the southern portion of the Northwest Territory, settling along the Ohio and its tributary rivers. The process was made easier by further congressional action. Future president William Henry Harrison, who from 1799 to 1800 was a nonvoting congressional delegate from the Northwest Territory, successfully promoted the passage of legislation that made it easier for ordinary settlers to buy land there. The Harrison Land Law, which allowed for sales of smaller plots, facilitated the rapid population growth of the Northwest Territory. In 1803, the southeastern portion of the territory was incorporated as the State of Ohio. The remainder of the region was designated as the Indiana Territory in 1800. This territory later became the states of Indiana, Illinois, Michigan, and part of Wisconsin.

D. AMERICAN INDIAN POLICY IN THE NEW NATION 新生国家对美洲印第安人的政策

The ratification of the Constitution did not bode well for American Indians within the boundaries of the United States. The Constitution did not precisely define the relationship between the government and the American Indians. This shortcoming set the stage for further bloody conflicts on the frontier.

> ### ONGOING INDIAN WARS
> ### 对印第安的不间断的战争
> The "Indian Wars" of the 1790s are part of an ongoing pattern of the United States breaking treaties, expanding westward, and engaging in conflicts with American Indians. The pattern stretches from the seventeenth century to the late-nineteenth century.

American Indians and the Constitution 美洲印第安人与《宪法》

The U.S. Constitution did not clarify the status of Indian tribes and nations within its borders. The document did recognize the tribes as legal entities. For instance, it gave Congress the power to regulate commerce—among the states, with foreign nations, and "with the Indian tribes." However, in mentioning them separately from foreign nations, the Constitution made it clear that they did not have legal standing as foreign nations. Further, although the tribes are not foreign nations, most individual Indians were not fully citizens of the United States either. Members of the tribes were not entitled to representation in Congress. Finally, the central issue of control of land was not settled by the Constitution. Over time, a series of treaties, agreements, and court decisions attempted to clarify the legal status of American Indian lands. However, these measures proved to be provisional, leaving Indian lands vulnerable to incursions by white settlers.

E. SPANISH MISSIONS IN CALIFORNIA 西班牙向加利福尼亚的迁徙

Spain encouraged migration into the northern reaches of New Spain—present-day California—by expanding mission settlements. These missions offered opportunities to Spanish soldiers and settlers, while fostering a cultural blending of Spanish and Indian peoples.

The Expansion of the Mission System 传教体系的扩大

In the last decades of the eighteenth century and into the nineteenth century, Spanish Catholics of the Franciscan order established a series of missions in California with the goal of spreading their faith among local Indians. A Catholic priest, Junipero Serra, was instrumental in establishing the first missions in California; ultimately 21 missions were founded. These settlements were both religious missions and military outposts, and represented an attempt by Spain to maintain a presence along the northern borderlands. The goal of the missions was not only spiritual. The Spaniards extracted labor from the Indian peoples.

The missions had disastrous results for the natives of California. Disease ravaged their populations; in 1806, a measles epidemic wiped out a quarter of the mission Indians in the San Francisco area. Further, missionaries and their employees often treated the local populations brutally, subjecting local populations to beatings and slavery-like working conditions and raping women. An Indian revolt took place at the Mission San Diego de Alcala in 1775, but the mission system continued to exist into the early 1800s. By the 1830s, the Mexican government abandoned the mission project, selling mission lands to private individuals.

II. Forging a Foreign Policy in the Early Republic
共和国早期制定对外政策

The United States faced several foreign policy challenges in its first years of independence. The continued presence of European powers in North America challenged the government to find ways to safeguard the borders. At the same time, war and conflict in Europe made it difficult for the United States to pursue both free trade and neutrality.

A. SPAIN AND GREAT BRITAIN CHALLENGE AMERICAN GROWTH
西班牙与大不列颠质疑美国的发展

The United States continued to have difficulties with the presence of European powers in North America. The British were reluctant to abandon their claims and Spain persisted in challenging American use of the Mississippi River.

The British and the American Indians 英国人与美洲印第安人

Americans became increasingly frustrated that the British seemed intent on thwarting the westward movement of Americans from the towns of the eastern seaboard. British forces had not evacuated forts in the western territories following the signing of the Treaty of Paris (1783). The British maintained a thriving fur trade with Indian groups in the area above the Ohio

River. Further, the British provided the Shawnee, the Miami, and the Delaware with weapons that could be used in resisting American migration. The British insisted that they would not abandon their western presence until the United States repaid its war debts and allowed loyalists to recover property that had been confiscated during the war. The United States minister to Great Britain pressed for a resolution of these issues, but to no avail.

Conflicts with Spain and Pinckney's Treaty　与西班牙的冲突及《平克尼条约》

The United States had ongoing conflicts with Spain following the Treaty of Paris (1783). First, the borders with Spanish territory were in dispute. The Treaty of Paris, between the United States and Great Britain, stipulated that American territory extended south to the northern boundary of Spanish Florida. However, in a separate treaty between Great Britain and Spain, the extent of Spanish territory was not spelled out. An earlier treaty between the two countries gave Spain control of territory north of that boundary, in present-day Alabama and Mississippi. Second, although American territory abutted the Mississippi River, Spain repeatedly attempted to limit American shipping on the river. The United States was able to resolve these issues with Spain. Negotiations between the diplomats Thomas Pinckney of the United States and Don Manuel de Godoy of Spain resulted in Pinckney's Treaty (1795; ratified in 1796). Spain agreed to allow for American shipping on the Mississippi River. The treaty also defined the border between the United States and Spanish-held territory in western Florida. Spain's willingness to negotiate with the United States was motivated, in part, by the apparent friendship between the United States and Great Britain following Jay's Treaty (see below).

Conflicts with Great Britain and Jay's Treaty　与大不列颠的冲突及《杰伊条约》

There were several contentious issues between the United States and Great Britain in the 1790s. Once war broke out between France and Great Britain in 1793, U.S. ships maintained a brisk trade with both the French West Indies and with France itself. Great Britain was none too pleased with this development and began intercepting American ships (almost 300) in or near the West Indies. In addition, southern planters wanted reimbursement from the British for slaves that had fled to British lines during the American Revolution and were never returned. Also, western settlers were resentful of the continued presence of British forces in forts in the West. This last issue became significant in light of the increasingly bloody clashes between U.S. forces and the Indians. Americans accused the British of aiding the Indians in order to maintain their profitable fur trade.

Washington sent John Jay, the chief justice of the Supreme Court, to Great Britain to seek redress of these grievances. Jay returned in 1795 with a treaty that was perceived as especially favorable to the British, who did agree to withdraw from the West, but only after 18 months. The British would not compensate American shippers for lost cargoes, nor would they compensate American planters for lost slaves. In addition, American planters would be forced to repay debts to the British that dated from the colonial era. The one concession that Jay managed to wrest from the British was limited trading rights in the West Indies. Other issues would be addressed in the future by arbitration commissions.

> **LACK OF PROGRESS IN FOREIGN RELATIONS**
> **外交关系未取得重大进展**
> The United States failed to achieve important foreign policy goals during the Articles of Confederation period. This can be attributed to the weaknesses of the Articles or to the precarious position of a newly created nation.

Reactions to Jay's Treaty were decidedly mixed. Alexander Hamilton and his supporters saw the treaty as the best they could get at the moment. Supporters of Thomas Jefferson, especially from the South and the West, argued that their interests had been sold out to the mercantile interests in New England. They saw the treaty as evidence of the pro-British sympathies of the Hamiltonians. An opponent of the treaty scrawled on a wall: "Damn John Jay! Damn everyone who won't damn John Jay!"

B. ROLE OF THE UNITED STATES IN THE AFTERMATH OF THE FRENCH REVOLUTION 法国大革命后美国的角色

Despite America's intention to be independent of European affairs, events in Europe greatly impacted the newly formed United States. Just as Americans were ratifying the Constitution in 1789, the French Revolution was beginning. Americans were divided, and their debates about the French Revolution foreshadowed ongoing debates about the role of the United States in the world.

The Question of Alliances 联盟问题

The debates over the role of the United States in the world took on greater significance after France and Great Britain went to war in 1793. Many Americans felt the United States had an obligation to help France, in return for helping the United States in the American Revolution, and because a 1778 treaty committed the United States to help if France were under attack. Others argued that the United States should stay out of the war. After all, the treaty was made with a French government that no longer existed, and the French Revolution had devolved from a democratic movement into a bloodbath. King Louis XVI and thousands of his countrymen had been guillotined. Many of these neutrality-minded Americans also harbored warm feelings for the British system, despite the fact that the war with Great Britain had concluded a mere decade earlier. Already, the two nations had resumed commercial ties.

Conflict with France and the XYZ Affair 与法国的冲突及XYZ事件

Events during the administration of President John Adams challenged America's commitment to neutrality (see page 123). In 1797, in retaliation for America's favorable treaty with Great Britain (Jay's Treaty; see page 121), France rescinded the 1778 alliance with the United States and allowed French privateers to seize American ships. After more than 300 ships were seized, President Adams sent a delegation of negotiators to Paris to attempt a peaceful solution. The delegation was not initially allowed to discuss the matter with the French foreign affairs minister Charles Talleyrand. Rather, three agents approached the American delegation and informed them that they could begin negotiations if they paid $250,000 and promised a $12 million loan to France. The three French agents were never named. When word of this interchange made its way into American papers, the three agents were referred to simply as X, Y, and Z. The XYZ affair incensed President Adams and many Americans. Congress allocated money for a military engagement against France. Warships were dispatched to the Caribbean and fought French ships in America's first undeclared war,

> ## PARTIES AND FOREIGN POLICY
> ## 政党与外交政策
> Note that, during the presidential administration of the Federalist John Adams, U.S. relations with France were more strained; during the administrations of Democratic–Republican presidents in the early 1800s, U.S. relations with Great Britain were more strained.

labeled by historians the Quasi-War (1798–1800). Americans were deeply divided by this military action.

C. THE STRUGGLE FOR NEUTRALITY IN THE 1790s　18世纪90年代争取中立

Despite attempts by the United States to remain neutral in regard to European affairs in the 1790s, the country found itself drawn into foreign conflicts. President George Washington took the opportunity in his "Farewell Address" to caution against the formation of "permanent alliances."

Washington and Neutrality　华盛顿与中立

President Washington chose to remain neutral in the conflicts between Great Britain and France. He issued the 1793 Neutrality Act and he urged the United States to avoid permanent alliances with foreign powers. In his Farewell Address, he cautioned the newly independent nation against being drawn into the seemingly endless conflicts in Europe. His calls for neutrality have been invoked by isolationists throughout American history, including during debates about U.S. entrance into both twentieth-century world wars.

SUBJECT TO DEBATE　相关讨论

Along with the Civil War, the American Revolution is one of the most heatedly debated topics in the field of history. The Revolution gave birth to the United States, so the stakes involved in understanding and interpreting it seem especially high—one's understanding of the Revolution is shaped by, and shapes, one's understanding of the United States itself.

Historians for generations have debated the reasons the 13 colonies declared independence. Some historians have stressed economic grievances against the mother country—colonists declared independence to be free of British mercantilist rules. These historians have emphasized the colonial cry, "No taxation without representation," as central to the struggle. This theory assumes a basic continuity in terms of values from the colonial period to the national period; the values of the market shaped both periods.

Opposing historians argue that economic issues were only part of the equation. They see a real break with the past—socially, culturally, and ideologically. Bernard Bailyn's *The Ideological Origins of the American Revolution* (1967) points to the development of a new set of ideas about politics and democracy, shaped by radical British libertarian writers.

Historians influenced by the "New Left" look at class divisions within American society, not just divisions between the colonies and Great Britain. This approach sees a class conflict in colonial America. On one side of the conflict were the colonial elites, who tried to prevent the American Revolution from becoming truly revolutionary. They wanted to maintain the colonial social structure, but without the British overlords. On the other side were dockworkers, artisans, small-scale farmers, apprentices, slaves, free blacks, and other "lower sorts" who pushed for a real break with the hierarchies of the past. Their radical agenda was largely derailed by the delegates at the Constitutional Convention, who put a lid on these revolutionary impulses.

There are several important questions about the Critical Period that students should be aware of: The first important question examines the nature of the Articles of Confederation. Because the Articles lasted less than a decade, and because the Constitution has endured for more than 230 years, there is a tendency to elevate the historical standing of the Constitution and to denigrate the Articles of Confederation. This is to be expected, but we should be careful not to go too far. To admit to the effectiveness of the Constitution does not require us to ignore anything positive about the Articles. The 13 colonies won the American Revolution during the Articles of Confederation period. Also, the Articles did an excellent job in dealing with the newly acquired western lands. It is true that the national government was weak while under the Articles; but even this can be seen as a positive. The Articles, we can argue, effectively protected the traditional rights of the states. Historical debate should be fair to the much-maligned Articles.

The Constitutional Convention has been the subject of much debate through American history. Charles Beard, a Progressive-era historian, asserted that the men who wrote the Constitution were all men of means who made sure to protect their economic interests. This interpretation notes the undemocratic features of the Constitution (the electoral college and the method for selecting senators) and asserts that the document is essentially interested in protecting the economic interests of the propertied class at the expense of democracy. Some left-leaning historians see the ratification of the Constitution as a virtual coup d'état, checking the more revolutionary elements of the American Revolution. This view runs counter to mainstream thinking, which elevates the effectiveness of the Constitution, especially when contrasted with the (by comparison) ineffective Articles of Confederation.

PRACTICE MULTIPLE-CHOICE QUESTIONS　选择题练习

Directions: Pick the letter that best answers the following questions.

Questions 1–3 are based on the following passage: 根据以下段落，回答第1—3题

"And We do further declare it to be Our Royal Will and Pleasure, for the present as aforesaid, to reserve under our Sovereignty, Protection, and Dominion, for the use of the said Indians, . . . all the Lands and Territories lying to the Westward of the Sources of the Rivers which fall into the Sea from the West and North West as aforesaid.

"And We do hereby strictly forbid, on Pain of our Displeasure, all our loving Subjects from making any Purchases or Settlements whatever, or taking Possession of any of the Lands above reserved, without our especial leave and Licence for that Purpose first obtained."

—Royal Proclamation of 1763 (excerpt)

1. A primary impetus for the British king issuing the proclamation, excerpted above, was

   (A) a series of armed conflicts between colonists and an alliance of Native American tribes, known as the Covenant Chain, led by Chief Pontiac.
   (B) raids by Cherokee and the Creek warriors in the interior of Georgia and South Carolina following the "Trail of Tears."
   (C) a bloody conflict, known as King Philip's War, waged by the Narragansett against encroachments by colonists.
   (D) skirmishes between Virginia settlers and the Powhatan Confederation.

2. The Royal Proclamation of 1763 had the effect of

(A) uniting British colonists and American Indians in mutual distrust of British intentions.
(B) slowing down British immigration to North America.
(C) intensifying tensions between Great Britain and France.
(D) creating resentment by colonists toward British policies in North America.

3. The Royal Proclamation of 1763 could best be understood in the context of

(A) Great Britain shifting the structure of its empire and allowing colonies more direct control of internal affairs.
(B) Great Britain's attempting to consolidate imperial control over its North American colonies.
(C) Great Britain attempting to prevent the spread of revolutionary sentiment.
(D) Great Britain shifting its policies from a mercantilist model to a free-market capitalist model.

Questions 4–6 refer to the following image: 根据下图，回答第4—6题

—Benjamin Franklin, "Magna Britannia: Her Colonies Reduc'D," 1767

4. The main point of the cartoon above is that

(A) the 13 British North American colonies should unite in order to better advance their grievances against Great Britain.
(B) the North American colonists, in the aftermath of the French and Indian War, should develop a better system of defending themselves from attacks from Great Britain.
(C) British policies in North America, notably enacting taxes, could result in fatal effects on the British Empire.
(D) the presence of a British standing army in North America would have a detrimental effect on the liberties and rights of the British colonists.

5. The primary intended audience for this cartoon was

   (A) members of Parliament in Great Britain.
   (B) Boston merchants and traders.
   (C) backcountry settlers in Pennsylvania.
   (D) members of the Sons of Liberty.

6. The sentiment reflected in the image was also reflected in which of the following?

   (A) Paul Revere's engraving, "Boston Massacre," 1770.
   (B) The Treaty of Fort Stanwix, 1768.
   (C) The "Olive Branch Petition," adopted by the Continental Congress in 1775.
   (D) Thomas Paine's pamphlet, *Common Sense*, 1776.

Questions 7–9 are based on the following passage: 根据以下段落，回答第7—9题

"SECTION 1.

"Be it enacted by the Senate and the House of Representatives of the United States of America in Congress assembled, That it shall be lawful for the President of the United States at any time during the continuance of this act, to order all such aliens as he shall judge dangerous to the peace and safety of the United States, or shall have reasonable grounds to suspect are concerned in any treasonable or secret machinations against the government thereof, to depart out of the territory of the United Slates, within such time as shall be expressed in such order, which order shall be served on such alien by delivering him a copy thereof, or leaving the same at his usual abode, and returned to the office of the Secretary of State, by the marshal or other person to whom the same shall be directed."

—An Act Concerning Aliens (excerpt), 1798.

7. The legislative act, excerpted above, enjoyed widespread public support, despite opposition from Democratic–Republican leaders, because, in part,

   (A) President John Adams was extremely popular; any opposition to him was seen as treasonous.
   (B) Irish immigration was changing the composition of many American cities; many Americans wondered if the United States could retain its Anglo-Saxon heritage without limiting immigration.
   (C) federal authorities had uncovered and thwarted a plot by disgruntled North Carolina farmers to assassinate President John Adams; desperate times, it seemed, called for desperate measures.
   (D) large numbers of Americans had become intensely critical of the revolutionary French government during the Quasi-War with France; restricting the ability of French immigrants to participate in American politics seemed reasonable.

8. Leaders of the Democratic–Republican Party responded to legislative acts, such as the one excerpted, by

   (A) calling for the impeachment of President John Adams.
   (B) challenging the laws in the Supreme Court.
   (C) putting forth the theory of state nullification of federal legislation.
   (D) boycotting the elections of 1800.

9. The governmental action allowed for in the excerpt is similar to government actions taken

   (A) against Mexican-Americans during the Mexican-American War (1846–1848).
   (B) during the "Red Scare" following World War I.
   (C) in the aftermath of the sit-in strikes of the 1930s.
   (D) as part of the COINTELPRO program, initiated by the Federal Bureau of Investigation against protest movements in the 1960s.

Answers and Explanations to Multiple-Choice Questions
选择题的答案与解析

1. **(A)** A primary impetus for the British government issuing the Proclamation of 1763 was a series of armed conflicts between colonists and an alliance of Native American tribes, known as the Covenant Chain, led by Chief Pontiac. The act drew a line through the Appalachian Mountains. Great Britain ordered the colonists not to settle beyond the line. The British government did not want to provoke additional warfare with native peoples in the region in the wake of the French and Indian War.

2. **(D)** The Royal Proclamation of 1763 had the effect of creating resentment among colonists toward British policies in North America. Many colonists were disgruntled because they felt that they had made sacrifices during the French and Indian War and they were now eager to settle in these newly claimed lands.

3. **(B)** The Royal Proclamation of 1763 could best be understood in the context of Great Britain's attempting to consolidate imperial control over its North American colonies. If British colonists celebrated the removal of the French from North America following the French and Indian War, their celebration was short-lived. Almost immediately, the British government attempted to confront an ongoing problem—the large debt that had accumulated during almost half a century of constant warfare. The government believed its victory in war had been especially beneficial to the colonists. In return, the British reasoned it was fair for the colonists to assume some of the costs of the war and continued protection through increased taxation. New taxes and more rigorous enforcement of existing taxes generated intense resentment and resistance among many colonists.

4. **(C)** In this cartoon, Benjamin Franklin is warning of an unfortunate future. He is predicting that British taxation policies, notably the Stamp Act, could have fatal effects on the British Empire. A dismembered Britannia has fallen from the globe and sits surrounded by her scattered limbs, identified as different North American colonies. In the background of the cartoon we see British ships sitting idle—an allusion to the importance of Britain's trade with America. On the ground sits a rejected olive branch. The banner across Britannia's body reads "Date Obolum Bellisario," an allusion to a Roman military hero who was reduced to beggary after being accused of treason.

5. **(A)** The primary intended audience for this cartoon was members of Parliament in Great Britain. Franklin was living in Great Britain at the time and spent a great deal of effort trying to pressure Parliament to rescind the Stamp Act. The cartoon shows solidarity with Great Britain and reflects a hope that bridges could be mended between Great Britain and its North American colonies.

6. **(C)** The sentiment reflected in the image—that peace and reconciliation between Great Britain and the colonies was a desirable goal—was also reflected in the "Olive Branch Petition," adopted by the Continental Congress in 1775. Franklin himself had moved toward a more oppositional position by that point, but many colonists still held out hope that a peaceful solution could be reached.

7. **(D)** The Act Concerning Aliens, 1798, part of the set of laws known as the Alien and Sedition Acts, enjoyed widespread public support despite opposition from Democratic–Republican leaders because, in part, large numbers of Americans had become intensely critical of the revolutionary French government during the Quasi-War with France. At the time, restricting the ability of French immigrants to participate in American politics seemed reasonable to many Americans. Relations between the United States and France deteriorated in the late 1790s. The French Revolution took a violent turn and war broke out between France and Great Britain. France perceived that the United States was favoring Great Britain in the war, and French privateers began to seize American ships. After an American delegation to Paris was rebuffed (the "XYZ Affair"), Congress allocated money for a maritime conflict with France. Warships were dispatched to the Caribbean and fought French ships in America's first undeclared war, labeled the Quasi-War (1798–1800) by historians. It was in this context that the Alien and Sedition Acts were passed.

8. **(C)** Leaders of the Democratic–Republican Party, notably Thomas Jefferson and James Madison, responded to the Alien and Sedition Acts by putting forth the theory of state nullification of federal legislation. The theory of nullification held that states could declare objectionable laws invalid within their borders. The theory was articulated by Jefferson and Madison in the Virginia and Kentucky resolutions (drafted in 1798 and 1799). The theory was again put forward by John C. Calhoun and other opponents of the Tariff Act of 1828, labeled the "Tariff of Abominations."

9. **(B)** The governmental action allowed for in the excerpt is similar to government actions taken during the "Red Scare" following World War I. The Red Scare was also set in motion by a series of bombs detonated in several cities in 1919 and 1920 by radical groups. In January 1920, Attorney General A. Mitchell Palmer began a broad hunt for suspected radicals. Palmer's Justice Department carried out unwarranted raids, known as "Palmer raids," of suspected radicals' homes. While Palmer did not uncover the makings of an uprising, he did end up deporting over 500 noncitizens. In December 1919, the Russian-born anarchist activist Emma Goldman was deported by the Justice Department. In both cases the government was empowered to deport aliens.

Period 4: 1800–1848 The Meaning of Democracy in an Era of Economic and Territorial Expansion

第四个时期（1800—1848）：经济与领土扩张时代的民主

6

TIMELINE　大事年表

1800	Election of Thomas Jefferson
1803	Louisiana Purchase
	Marbury v. Madison
1804	Reelection of Jefferson
1807	*Chesapeake* affair
	Embargo Act
1808	Election of James Madison
1810	*Fletcher v. Peck*
1811	Battle of Tippecanoe
1812	Beginning of War of 1812
	Reelection of Madison
1814	Hartford Convention
	Treaty of Ghent
1815	Battle of New Orleans
1816	Election of James Monroe
	Chartering of the Second Bank of the United States
1817	Construction of Erie Canal begins
1819	Panic of 1819
	Dartmouth College v. Woodward
	McCulloch v. Maryland
1820	Missouri Compromise
	Reelection of Monroe
1821	Opening of the Lowell factories
	Cohens v. Virginia
1822	Stephen Austin establishes first American settlement in Texas
1824	*Gibbons v. Ogden*
	Election of John Quincy Adams
1825	Opening of the Erie Canal
1827	Public school movement begins in Boston

1828	Passage of the "Tariff of Abominations"
	Election of Andrew Jackson
1829	Publication of "David Walker's Appeal to the Coloured Citizens of the World"
1830	Opening of the Baltimore and Ohio Railroad
	Passage of the Indian Removal Act
	Founding of Mormonism
1831	William Lloyd Garrison begins publication of the *Liberator*
1832	Beginning of Nullification Crisis
	Jackson vetoes renewal of Second Bank of the United States
	Worcester v. Georgia
	Reelection of Jackson
1833	Founding of the American Anti-slavery Society
1834	Whig Party organized
	First strike by the "Lowell girls"
1835	Publication of Alexis de Tocqueville's *Democracy in America*
1836	Congress passes the "gag rule"
	Jackson issues Specie Circular
	Battle of the Alamo
	Texas independence
1837	Elijah Lovejoy murdered by proslavery mob
1838	"Trail of Tears"
1840	Election of William Henry Harrison
	Formation of the Liberty Party
1841	John Tyler assumes presidency upon Harrison's death
	Brook Farm founded
1843	Dorothea Dix organizes movement for asylum reform
1844	Samuel Morse invents the telegraph
	Election of James Polk
	Texas annexation
1846	Creation of the Independent Treasury
	Resolution of dispute with Great Britain over Oregon Territory
	Beginning of Mexican War
1848	Seneca Falls Convention
	Treaty of Guadalupe Hidalgo ends Mexican War
	Gold found in California
1851	Herman Melville writes *Moby Dick*

INTRODUCTION 简介

> The first half of the nineteenth century witnessed a series of economic, territorial, and demographic changes that led to struggles over the definition and limits of democratic control.

Growth and expansion were defining features of the United States in the decades between 1800 and the Civil War. The economy was rapidly changing and growing, as an older semi-subsistence economy was giving way to a market economy with a national, and even international, reach. The "market revolution" affected various parts of the country differently. Reformers and intellectuals tried to make sense of these changes and entered into debates about the meaning and shape of democracy. The boundaries of the United States grew several times during this period, as the country attempted to fulfill its professed "manifest destiny," and American Indians resisted and changed in the process. In the northern states the beginnings of industrialization appeared, while slavery grew dramatically in the South on the strength of cotton cultivation. In some ways, the regions of the United States became more interlinked as local economies were drawn into national markets, but at the same time, the issue of free labor versus slave labor pushed the country further apart.

KEY CONCEPT 4.1 DEMOCRACY, REFORM, AND THE FORMATION OF A NATIONAL CULTURE
核心概念4.1：民主、改革与国家文化的形成

The turn of the nineteenth century witnessed the unfolding of the world's first mass democracy and the beginning of a national culture. Americans debated the nature of its democracy, and many worked to reform social institutions to match the nation's democratic ideals.

I. Political Parties, Power, and Economic Policy in a Mass Democracy 大众民主的政党、权利与经济政策

In the first decades of the nineteenth century, states expanded suffrage by reducing or eliminating property qualifications for voting. This led to a growth in the importance of political parties. Also during this time, Supreme Court decisions asserted federal power over state power, while many political leaders asserted regional economic interests over national concerns.

A. THE RISE AND FALL OF THE FIRST TWO-PARTY SYSTEM 第一个两党制的兴起与没落

Although many of the founders of the United States did not anticipate them, political parties developed in the 1790s and have been a feature of American political life ever since. These parties are often large tents built around a variety of interest groups and constituencies. The first two-party system included the Democratic–Republicans and the Federalists.

The First Two-Party System: The Democratic–Republicans and the Federalists
第一个两党制：民主共和党与联邦党

Usually, two primary parties compete for votes. In a winner-take-all system of voting, it is difficult for a third party candidate to gain traction. The first two-party system developed in the 1790s and pitted the Democratic–Republicans against the Federalists (see Period 3). The Federalists, coalescing around the plans of Alexander Hamilton, embraced a broader national agenda, advocating the use of a national bank and import duties to promote commercial and manufacturing activities, while the Democratic–Republicans, following the lead of Thomas Jefferson, sought to limit the power of the national government and reserve greater authority at the state level. These two parties developed a strong dislike of each other, especially after the passage of the Alien and Sedition Acts in 1798, which seemed like thinly veiled attempts to silence and weaken the Democratic–Republicans. The passage of the acts seemed to backfire; the Democratic–Republicans gained strength and won the presidential election of 1800.

The Decline of the Federalist Party and the "Era of Good Feelings"
联邦党的没落与"善意的时代"

Despite fears of turmoil, power peacefully changed hands in 1800 from the Federalist Party to the Democratic–Republicans (commonly known at the time as the Republicans). Some of the political acrimony of the 1790s died down during the first decades of the nineteenth century. The Federalist Party lost support in this time as the agricultural areas of the country grew more rapidly than the commercial centers of the Northeast. The Federalists suffered a further blow because of their vigorous opposition to the popular War of 1812 (see page 155). The decline of the Federalist Party led to the "Era of Good Feelings" in the 1810s and 1820s—when only one major party competed for votes on the national level.

With the Federalist Party in its death throes, the Democratic–Republican Party candidate, James Monroe, easily won the election of 1816. Four years later, the Federalists made even less of a challenge to Madison, who was a throwback to the eighteenth-century presidents. He was the last president to consistently wear the silk stockings, knee breeches, and powdered wigs of the earlier era. He also adopted President George Washington's practice of bringing men of differing ideological bents into his administration. Many of Madison's policies, such as promoting "internal improvements," seemed like pages out of the Federalist playbook.

The Federalist agenda also lived on in the Supreme Court, which was not subject to the whims of the electorate and kept alive many elements of the Federalist agenda. Also, the nation began to adopt manufacturing, just as Alexander Hamilton had hoped. Henry Clay's "American System" kept alive much of Hamilton's program (see pages 152–153).

B. THE SUPREME COURT ASSERTS FEDERAL POWER AND THE POWER OF THE JUDICIARY 最高法院主张联邦权利与司法部门的权利

The Supreme Court, during the tenure of Chief Justice John Marshall (1801–1835), issued a series of decisions that extended the power of the federal government over state laws while establishing the primacy of the judiciary in interpreting the meaning of the Constitution.

Marbury v. Madison (1803) and the Principle of Judicial Review
马伯利诉麦迪逊案（1803）与司法审查原则

The most important decision of the Marshall Court was in the case of *Marbury v. Madison*. The important outcome of the case was that the principle of judicial review was established. The details of the decision have to do with the seating of judges who had been appointed in the last days of the John Adams administration. These judges had been appointed by Adams to fill slots created by an expanded judiciary that grew out of the Judiciary Act of 1801. The act was passed in the final weeks of the Adams administration, and he worked feverishly to fill these seats before his term expired, thereby solidifying Federalist power in the court system for years to come. When Thomas Jefferson assumed office, not all of the commissions had been formally delivered. Jefferson, angered at the eleventh-hour appointments, ordered his secretary of state, James Madison, to not deliver them. In this way, he could appoint his own judges.

One potential judge, William Marbury, sued to have his commission delivered. The Supreme Court ruled that Marbury was not entitled to his seat because the law he was basing his argument on—the Judiciary Act of 1789—was unconstitutional. Marshall established the Supreme Court's power to review laws and determine whether they are consistent with the Constitution. Laws declared unconstitutional by the court are immediately struck down. This power of judicial review has been the main function of the Supreme Court since then and has been instrumental in maintaining a balance among the three branches of the government.

The Marshal Court and Federal Power　马歇尔法庭与联邦权利

Several important Marshall Court decisions strengthened federal power over state power. *McCulloch v. Maryland* (1819) prohibited Maryland from taxing the Second Bank of the United States, a federal institution. *Gibbons v. Ogden* (1824) invalidated a monopoly on ferry transportation between New York and New Jersey that had been issued by New York, and asserted that only the federal government could regulate interstate trade. In the case of *Cohens v. Virginia* (1821), the Marshall Court affirmed the right of the Supreme Court to receive appeals from state courts. The case, which originated in the Virginia state court system, involved the ability of the state to prohibit the Cohen brothers from selling lottery tickets in Virginia. The court upheld Virginia's right to forbid the sale of the tickets.

The Supreme Court again revoked a state statute in the case of *Worcester v. Georgia* (1832). The case resulted in a judicial challenge to the national government's forced removal of the Cherokee people under the dictates of the Indian Removal Act (see page 159). Specifically, the decision struck down a Georgia statute that forbade non-American Indians from entering American Indian territory without first obtaining a license from the state. In a larger sense, the court upheld the autonomy of American Indian communities. The Cherokees were "a distinct community, occupying its own territory," the court asserted; "the laws of Georgia can have no force." The decision was largely ignored by the United States government as it pursued its Indian removal policy.

C. THE SECOND TWO-PARTY SYSTEM: THE DEMOCRATS AND THE WHIGS
第二个两党制：民主党与辉格党

A second two-party system developed in the 1830s out of the contentious issues of the era of President Andrew Jackson. The tense unity of the one-party "Era of Good Feelings" broke apart as the Jacksonian branch of the Democratic–Republicans became known simply as the Democratic Party, and Jackson's opponents, led by Henry Clay, organized the Whig Party (1833).

> ## THE TWO-PARTY SYSTEM　两党制
> The United States has always had two principle political parties vying for power, except during the "Era of Good Feelings," when there was only one viable party, the Democratic–Republicans.

Jacksonian Democracy　杰克逊式民主

Many of the political divisions that characterized this period emerged in force during the administration of President Andrew Jackson. The years of his presidency (1829–1837), as well as the immediate aftermath, bear the name the Age of Jackson, or the Age of Jacksonian Democracy. Jackson and his supporters were bitter at the results of the election of 1824; they held on to the accusations of a "corrupt bargain" made by President John Quincy Adams and Henry Clay. In the election of 1828, Jackson's supporters painted John Quincy Adams as out-of-touch and elitist, while Adams's supporters portrayed Jackson as ill-tempered. Jackson's backwoods, populist appeal helped him win the election.

The election of 1828 is considered by many historians to be the first modern election. First, the electorate was much broader than in previous elections. In the 1820s most states reduced or removed property qualifications for voting so that most free males had the right to vote. Consequently, candidates had to campaign more aggressively and tailor their appeal to reach a broader audience. Related to the democratization of the voting process was an increased focus on character and personality.

JACKSON AND STATES' RIGHTS
杰克逊与国家权利

Be careful about generalizing in regard to Jackson's attitude toward states' rights. He comes from a southern states' rights tradition, and he defended Georgia against the Supreme Court decision *Worcester v. Georgia*. But he *was* the president, and when John Calhoun challenged federal tariff policy, Jackson took the side of federal power. Read Jackson's Farewell Address for a good summary of his political thought.

The "Tariff of Abominations"　"厌恶关税法"

Tariff rates became an extremely contentious issue in the first half of the nineteenth century. A major controversy around tariff rates occurred during the administration of President Jackson and reflected the escalation of regional tensions. The controversy originated with the Tariff of 1828, which revised tariff rates on a variety of imports. The act, known by its critics as the "Tariff of Abominations," dramatically raised tariff rates on many items and led to a general reduction in trade between the United States and Europe. This decline in trade hit South Carolina, which depended on cotton exports, especially hard.

TARIFFS IN THE 1800S
19世纪初的关税

Though tariff rates do not stir passionate debate today, they were one of the most divisive issues throughout the nineteenth century and into the twentieth century.

John C. Calhoun and the Nullification Crisis
约翰·C.卡尔霍恩与拒行联邦法危机

In the 1830s, debates over tariff rates pitted many southern politicians against federal policy. The high tariff rates established by the Tariff Act of 1828 (see above) especially angered southern politicians. By 1832, South Carolina politicians, led by President Jackson's former vice president, John C. Calhoun, asserted the right of states to nullify federal legislation. Under this theory of nullification, a state could declare an objectionable federal law null and void within that state. In actuality, from the early nineteenth century until today, only the Supreme Court can strike down a law if it finds the law to be inconsistent with the Constitution. Jackson was alarmed at this flouting of federal authority and challenged the move. He pushed through Congress the Force Bill (quickly nullified by the South Carolina legislature), which authorized military force against South Carolina for committing treason. At the same time, Congress revised tariff rates, providing relief for South Carolina. The Force Bill and the new tariff rates, passed by Congress on the same day, amounted to a face-saving compromise. However, the issue of states' rights versus federal power would emerge again in the coming decades in relation to the issue of slavery.

Destruction of the Second Bank of the United States 美国第二银行的毁灭

One of the fiercest battles of the Andrew Jackson presidency was over the Second Bank of the United States. Jackson revived the criticism of a national bank that had been part of the national discourse since Alexander Hamilton had first proposed such an institution in 1791. Despite the fact that the bank was performing its function admirably, Jackson insisted that it put too much power into the hands of a small elite. Jackson's political opponents thought that his animosity to the bank would hand them a political victory. These opponents brought the issue of rechartering the bank to Congress in 1832, four years before the bank's charter was to expire. They thought that a Jackson veto would weaken his chances for reelection. But Jackson's opponents miscalculated. He did veto the rechartering of the bank. However, the angry class-based rhetoric in his veto message played well with the voters and he won reelection. Jackson, encouraged by his electoral success, was not satisfied to let the bank die its natural death upon its charter running out in 1836. He took actions to kill the "monster" bank immediately. He moved federal deposits from the Bank of the United States to state banks in Democratic-leaning states.

> ## FEDERAL AID 联邦援助
> The idea that the federal government should intervene to help the victims of economic downturns did not gain currency until the twentieth century. Politicians still debate the appropriate level of federal assistance.

The Specie Circular and the Panic of 1837 金属通货公告与1837年的恐慌

President Jackson's suspicion of bankers and credit led him to issue the Specie Circular (1836), mandating that government-held land be sold only for hard currency (gold or silver "specie"), not paper currency. The move resulted in a shortage of government funds. Both the destruction of the Second Bank of the United States and the Specie Circular contributed to the economic downturn known as the Panic of 1837.

Whigs and Democrats 辉格党与民主党

The opponents of President Andrew Jackson and the Democratic Party founded the Whig Party in 1833. It is difficult to generalize about the constituents of each party. Northerners and southerners, for example, could be found in both parties. Many Whigs supported government programs aimed at economic modernization (based on the thinking of both Alexander Hamilton and Henry Clay). The language of the Democratic Party was more populist, arguing that high tariffs would "fatten" urban commercial interests. Issues, in general, tended to be less important in this period than they had been in the formative years of the country or than they would become again during the lead-up to the Civil War. Both parties focused intently on winning elections and holding on to power.

> ## HAMILTON AND CLAY 汉密尔顿与克莱
> Note the marked similarities between Hamilton's economic program and Clay's "American System." Both support a tariff, a central bank, and government encouragement for manufacturing. Contemporary Republicans often are pro-business; however, current pro-business policies favor low tariffs and deregulation of the economy—not funding for "internal improvements."

D. THE PERSISTENCE OF REGIONAL PRIORITIES　持续的地区优先权

A growing schism between northern and southern political leaders can be seen in the first half of the nineteenth century. Regional economic interests often trumped national interests.

The Market Economy and Regional Loyalties　市场经济与地区忠诚

Although the growth of the national economy was evident in the first half of the nineteenth century, regional economic and political loyalties persisted. In the northern states, the beginnings of industrialization became apparent, while slavery grew dramatically in the South on the strength of the cultivation of cotton. In some ways, the regions of the United States became more interlinked as local economies were transformed into national markets, but at the same time, the issue of free versus slave labor steadily divided the country.

II. Cultural Ferment in the First Half of the Nineteenth Century
19世纪上半叶的文化融合

During the first decades of the nineteenth century, Americans participated in a variety of cultural movements. Many Americans contributed to the development of a national culture, combining European aspects with distinctly American aspects. At the same time, groups of people in the United States developed cultural forms that reflected the particularities of their own experiences and worldviews.

A. RELIGIOUS AND SPIRITUAL MOVEMENTS　宗教运动与信仰的发展

A variety of political, economic, cultural, and demographic issues led to the development of the "Second Great Awakening." This spiritual awakening inspired other religious movements as well as reform movements.

The "Second Great Awakening"　"第二次大觉醒"

In the first decades of the nineteenth century, American clergy members sought to revive religious sentiment among the American people. The situation was similar to the first "Great Awakening" of a century earlier. At the turn of the nineteenth century, many clergy members worried that Americans seemed more captivated by politics—forming and building a new nation—than by God and salvation. Many ordinary Americans also felt a yearning to get in touch with a more immediate religious experience. The result was the Second Great Awakening. The movement of large "camp meetings" began in Kentucky early in the 1800s, and soon spread to other states. It was especially strong in upstate New York and western Pennsylvania. The growing towns along the Erie Canal came to be known as the "burned-over district" because of the intensity of the religious revival there.

The movement spoke to many of the farmers, merchants, and businessmen and women who were brought into the larger U.S. society by the market revolution. The messages of the market and of the Second Great Awakening were similar. Market relations told the individual that success or failure was in his or her hands; hard work, dedication, and self-restraint would lead to economic success. The Second Great Awakening told the individual that salvation was also in his or her hands. Righteous living, self-control, and a strong moral compass would lead to salvation. This idea that one could determine his or her eternal life was very different from the old Puritan notion of predestination, which held that one's eternal life was planned out by God.

The Second Great Awakening not only encouraged individual redemption, but also societal reformation. Not only could one become perfect in the eyes of God, but one could work to perfect society as well. In this respect the Second Great Awakening acted as a springboard for a variety of reform movements.

Mormonism 摩门教

The Church of Jesus Christ of the Latter-Day Saints, known as the Mormons, was founded in 1830 by Joseph Smith, in upstate New York, growing out of the Second Great Awakening. It was one of many sects that developed during this period of spiritual ferment. Several of these sects, including Mormonism, separated themselves from the larger community, developing cohesive and insular communities of their own. As the Mormons gained more adherents, the group was met by hostility for its unorthodox teachings and practices. Some mainstream Protestants mocked Mormon beliefs that, to them, appeared to be superstitious or magical. Others dismissed Mormonism for rejecting the belief in the "holy trinity." The most controversial practice was polygamy—allowing men to have multiple wives (long since renounced by the Mormon church). The group journeyed from New York to Ohio, then to Missouri, and then to Illinois. In Illinois, Smith was killed by an anti-Mormon mob (1844), and a new leader named Brigham Young led the majority of the Mormons to Utah (1847).

Transcendentalism 超验主义

Transcendentalism was a spiritual and intellectual movement critical of the materialist direction the United States was taking in the first half of the nineteenth century. The movement put more stock in intuition than in empirical observation. Henry David Thoreau wrote about the importance of nature in finding meaning. He lived in relative isolation at Walden Pond for two years (1845–1847). He wrote a famous essay called "Resistance to Civil Government" (more commonly known as "Civil Disobedience"; 1849), urging individuals to not acquiesce to unfair and unjust government dictates. The other important figure in the movement was Ralph Waldo Emerson, who wrote a series of philosophical essays, including "On Self-Reliance" (1841). Although the transcendentalists were critical of the direction of mainstream society, they did not gravitate toward the reform movements of the day. Some transcendentalists separated themselves from mainstream society; several utopian communities were started by transcendentalist thinkers during this period.

> **THE IMPACT OF THOREAU**
> 梭罗的影响
> Thoreau's book, *Walden; or, Life in the Woods* (1854), was influential in the back-to-the-land movement of the 1960s and 1970s.

Utopian Communities 乌托邦公社

Utopian communities were experiments in communal living, usually in rural settings, and structured around a guiding principle. These communities shared with transcendentalism an aversion to the materialistic direction of mainstream society. However, whereas transcendentalists focused on the cultivation of the self, utopian communities sought a more collective alternative to society. The most well-known community was Brook Farm, established outside of Boston in 1841. Brook Farm, started by the transcendentalist George Ripley, was based on the idea that all the residents would share equally in the labor of the community and would partake equally in leisure. Contrary to much antebellum thought, the adherents at Brook Farm saw leisure in a positive light—as a means of becoming a fuller human being.

Writer Nathaniel Hawthorne (see below) was one of the original participants in the commune, but grew disillusioned with the experiment. Inspiration for utopian communities came from thinkers such as the French socialist Charles Fourier and the Scottish industrialist and philanthropist Robert Owen. The New Harmony community in Indiana was founded by Owen himself in 1825 around principles of total equality.

Spiritual Developments in American Indian Communities
美洲印第安社区信仰的发展

Many American Indians, in the face of warfare, disease, dispossession, and displacement, developed spiritual practices that both borrowed from their traditional religious beliefs and adapted elements from their contemporary experiences, including exposure to Christianity. In the wake of the defeat and dispossession of the Iroquois Confederacy, a Seneca named Handsome Lake developed a set of spiritual practices that came to be known as the "Longhouse Religion." Drawing on traditional native and Quaker motifs, he denounced the factionalism that undermined Indian resistance to white incursions, and he spoke out against alcohol consumption and the breakdown of the family. Although Handsome Lake met resistance from both Christian missionaries and native traditionalists, he offered many American Indians a sense of hope in the face of staggering setbacks.

B. THE EMERGENCE OF A NATIONAL CULTURE　民族文化的出现

The aftermath of the War of 1812 (see page 115) saw not only an increase in nationalist sentiment, but also the development of a uniquely American culture. This culture borrowed elements of European culture, but also sought to create something uniquely American. Noah Webster, for instance, sought to codify a specifically American dictionary, separate from British English, when he published his *American Dictionary of the English Language* in 1828 (see Period 3).

The American Renaissance　美国的文艺复兴

The antebellum period experienced a renaissance in literature. Some of the greatest literature in American history comes out of the decades before the Civil War. In the early 1850s, this literary spirit reached its peak. The literature of that period included Herman Melville's *Moby-Dick* (1851), the first edition of Walt Whitman's *Leaves of Grass* (1855), Nathaniel Hawthorne's *The Scarlet Letter* (1850) and *The House of the Seven Gables* (1851), and Thoreau's *Walden* (1854). This literature is uniquely American, grappling with religious and existential questions raised by the legacy of the Puritans and focusing on the promise and the contradictions of America's experiment in building a democratic nation in the New World.

C. EUROPEAN ROMANTICISM, HUMAN PERFECTIBILITY, AND AMERICAN CULTURE　欧洲浪漫主义、人类的可完善性与美国文化

Romanticism, which had its origins in Europe, deeply influenced art, literature, and thought in the United States. The movement was strongest, both in Europe and the United States, during the first half of the nineteenth century.

The Romantic Perspective　浪漫主义精神

In many ways, romanticism was a reaction to industrialization and to the market revolution—to work becoming more ordered around routines, to the increasing value attached to wealth accumulation, and to the rationalization of nature. Romantics often harkened back to a simpler, more authentic past—or at least to their perception of this idealized past. In some ways, romanticism represented a radical, even revolutionary, response to the modern world. In other ways, it was deeply nationalistic, and even reactionary, in its embrace of a pure, uncorrupted sense of national community.

Hudson River School 哈得孙河画派

The reverence for European cultural products combined with a desire to create a uniquely American form of expression can be seen in the landscape paintings that came to be known as the "Hudson River School" of painting. The Hudson River School, which flourished from the 1820s to the 1870s, is best represented by three artists—Thomas Cole, Asher Durand, and Frederic Church. These artists were inspired by the European tradition of romantic paintings of dramatic landscapes, often featuring the ruins of ancient castles or temples. The United States lacked such ancient ruins. In their place, these artists captured pristine wilderness. Many of the paintings hinted at the impending hand of civilization, about to spoil virgin landscapes. Many Hudson River painters shared transcendentalist ideas about the glory of nature. Many of the works focused, of course, on the Hudson River, a waterway that generated new interest in the aftermath of the opening of the Erie Canal (1825). These paintings often emphasized emotion and sentiment over accuracy.

Romanticism in American Literature 美国文学中的浪漫主义

In the early 1800s, many Americans were captivated by the novels of the British writer, Sir Walter Scott. His novels, with classical historical settings (*Ivanhoe* was set in twelfth-century England) and larger-than-life heroic figures, epitomized romanticism in literature. Soon, American authors began to create literature that drew on Scott's romanticism, but was distinctly American. James Fenimore Cooper was perhaps the most successful American romantic writer. His "Leatherstocking Tales," including *The Last of the Mohicans* (1826), captured the danger and fascination of the frontier experience. Washington Irving also captured the spirit of romanticism in literature. His humorous short stories, "Rip Van Winkle" (1819) and "The Legend of Sleepy Hollow" (1820), portrayed a fanciful version of America. Both writers were internationally popular and set the stage for the more serious-minded authors of the American renaissance (see page 138).

D. THE CULTURES OF AFRICAN-AMERICAN COMMUNITIES—FREE AND SLAVE
非裔美国人社区——自由社区与奴隶社区的发展

African Americans developed cultural forms that emphasized maintaining dignity and autonomy in the face of enslavement and oppression. Both free communities and slave communities developed strategies and cultural patterns that challenged their status and pointed toward a better future.

David Walker 大卫·沃克

An important early figure in the anti-slavery movement was the African American David Walker. In 1829, he issued a pamphlet entitled "David Walker's Appeal to the Coloured Citizens of the World." This radical tract called on people of African descent to resist slavery by any and every means. His praise of self-defense made southerners furious. Several southern legislatures declared the pamphlet seditious and enacted penalties against anyone caught distributing it.

Frederick Douglass 弗雷德里克·道格拉斯

Starting in the 1840s, the towering figure in the abolitionist movement was Frederick Douglass. Douglass was born into slavery (1818) and escaped to the North in 1838. He had learned to read and write and soon became a powerful speaker in the antislavery movement. Douglass's autobiography, *Narrative of the Life of Frederick Douglass,* written in 1845, was a bestseller. One of the most well-known and important anti-slavery speeches is Douglass's July 5, 1852 address to the Rochester Anti-Slavery Sewing Society, "What to the slave is the 4th of July?" The speech is critical of the United States for not abiding by its founding principles, He asserts that it is preposterous to expect enslaved African Americans to celebrate the birth of American freedom when they, themselves, are still oppressed. Douglass remained an important figure before, during, and after the Civil War, until his death in 1895.

The African Methodist Episcopal (AME) Church 非裔卫理公会主教派教会

Throughout American history, African Americans developed religious beliefs and practices that reflected their experiences in America. The African Methodist Episcopal Church reflected this tradition. The denomination was founded by Richard Allen in Philadelphia in 1816 from several African–American Methodist churches. The founding of the AME reflected a desire on the part of the free African-American community to have greater autonomy and to tailor religious services to the needs and experiences of the African-American community. The AME borrowed many elements from the mainstream Methodist church; the founder of the Methodist movement, John Wesley, was an outspoken critic of the slave trade. However, in contrast to mainstream Methodism, the AME developed a distinctively racial theology.

Cultural Resistance to Slavery 对奴隶制的文化抵制

Slaves were not passive as they endured their harsh lives. Certainly, they learned that outright rebellion would almost certainly end in failure and death. However, slaves developed cultural practices that constituted subtler forms of resistance—practices that sustained families and communities, and that attempted to carve out some degree of autonomy in the face of near total control. Slaves passed on fanciful stories from generation to generation, stories that often had a pointed message—in the Br'er Rabbit stories, the weak often got the better of the strong. Music sustained slave communities. Slaves, for instance, might make their own fiddles and banjos, using a large gourd for the body and horsehair for the strings. These hybrids of African and American instruments helped create music that combined African traditions with the traditions of the South and provided some relief from the unremitting drudgery of slavery.

III. Religious and Secular Reform 宗教改革与世俗化改革

Reform movements and voluntary organizations grew in number and importance in the first half of the nineteenth century. These movements were influenced by the Second Great Awakening religious revival, as well as by liberal European ideas. The Romantic notion of human perfectibility was central to these movements.

A. REFORM MOVEMENTS IN THE ANTEBELLUM PERIOD 内战前的改革运动

Although reform movements have existed throughout most of American history, the antebellum period saw a dramatic upswing in reform activity. Reform movements have attempted to improve different aspects of American society, and have had varying degrees of success.

PERIODS OF REFORM　改革时期

Be familiar with the three most prominent periods of reform in American history: The reform movements of the 1830s and 1840s, the progressive reform movement of the 1900s and 1910s, and the reform movements of the 1960s and 1970s inspired by the civil rights movement.

The Temperance Movement　禁酒运动

The goal of the temperance movement was to limit or even ban the production, sale, and consumption of alcoholic beverages. Many temperance activists focused on individual self-control; they encouraged people to voluntarily take an oath to abstain from alcohol. Others sought to use the power of government to limit or eliminate the consumption of alcoholic beverages. The temperance movement was the largest reform movement of the first half of the nineteenth century.

There were several reasons the temperance movement attracted a large following in the antebellum period. Temperance was especially popular among women. Many women were troubled by the large amount of alcohol their husbands and sons drank. Heavy alcohol consumption was part of the fabric of daily life for many men. By 1830, the average man drank almost 10 gallons per year of hard liquor and about 30 gallons per year of beer, wine, and hard cider. In an era when pure water was difficult to come by, especially for urban working-class people, it made sense to drink the lighter alcoholic beverages. The alcohol killed dangerous bacteria. In addition, tavern owners were more than happy to cash men's paychecks on pay-day evening, knowing that much of that money would stay in the tavern. Men not only came home with little money in their pockets, they came home drunk. Many men, in this drunken state, took out their frustrations with violence on their wives and children. This acting out could take the form of verbal and physical abuse. So it made sense for women to be active in the movement.

The largest temperance organization in the antebellum period was the American Temperance Society, founded in 1826. Lyman Beecher's *Six Sermons on the Nature, Occasions, Signs, Evils, and Remedy of Intemperance* (1827) was a guiding text of the movement, which was successful in gaining recruits. The American Temperance Society claimed 1.5 million members by 1835. Alcohol consumption per person in the United States dropped by about half from 1830 to 1840. The "prohibitionist" impulse within the movement had successes in the 1850s. Maine became a "dry" state in 1851, completely banning the sale or manufacture of all alcoholic beverages, followed by 12 other states. The 1840s and 1850s proved to be the high point of the movement in the nineteenth century. By the 1870s, the movement had lost some of its intensity; most of the "dry" states had repealed their prohibition laws.

REFORMING SELF AND SOCIETY
自我改革与社会改革

Many of the reform movements of the 1830s and 1840s were as much about reforming the self as reforming society. Reformers urged individual self-restraint—whether it be with alcohol or cruelty to slaves.

The Asylum and Penitentiary Movement　收容所与监狱运动

In early America, the mentally ill were often treated as common criminals, spending years behind bars. In the 1840s, activists, including many women, spearheaded a movement to improve treatment for the mentally ill. One of the main organizers was Dorothea Dix, whose efforts led to the creation of the first generation of mental asylums in the United States.

Public Education　公共教育

The campaign for free public education gained a large following in the 1840s. Horace Mann was among the most vocal advocates during this period. Mann was secretary of education in Massachusetts in the 1840s and 1850s, and served in the U.S. House of Representatives. The movement saw education as essential to democratic participation.

B. DEBATING THE FUTURE OF SLAVERY IN AMERICA　关于美国奴隶制的未来的讨论

Slavery became an increasingly contentious issue in the United States in the first half of the nineteenth century. After the outlawing of the international slave trade in 1808, many states restricted the citizenship possibilities of African Americans. The period witnessed a growing abolitionist movement as well as plans for emancipation, including sending freed or escaped slaves to colonize Africa.

Abolitionism　废奴主义

The reform spirit of the Second Great Awakening inspired the modern abolition movement. Abolitionism was a minority opinion among northern whites in the antebellum period, but it had a major impact on America, opening up sectional divisions that contributed to the Civil War.

William Lloyd Garrison and "Immediate Emancipation"
威廉·劳埃德·加里森与"立即解放"

In 1831, William Lloyd Garrison, a white abolitionist, began publication of *The Liberator*. Garrison quickly became the key figure in the movement for the immediate and uncompensated abolition of slavery. Antislavery sentiment had existed before that, but most antislavery groups advocated a more gradual approach to ending slavery. That is, slave owners could keep their current slaves, but would not be able to enslave additional people. Slavery would therefore gradually end as the current slaves died. Additionally, most antislavery activists before Garrison advocated African colonization (see below). Garrison broke with both of these approaches. He said all slaves should be immediately freed, that there should be no compensation to their owners, and that freed slaves were entitled to the same rights as white people.

American Colonization Society　美国殖民协会

The American Colonization Society was founded in 1817 with the goal of transporting African Americans to Africa. The motives of the founders of the organization varied. Some sympathized with African Americans and urged them to leave the United States to escape from the ingrained racism of many white Americans. Other founders thought of African Americans as an inferior caste and wanted to rid America of them. Advocates of colonization believed that slaves either could not or should not receive treatment as equals in the United States. The society purchased land in West Africa and began a colony they called Liberia. Between 1820 and the Civil War only about 12,000 African Americans went to Africa. About 7,000 were former slaves who were freed under the condition that they leave the United States; the rest were free African Americans who believed they had a better chance to succeed in Liberia. Most African Americans, free or slave, showed very little interest in leaving their country to live in Africa. Frederick Douglass, for example, was very critical of colonization proposals.

> ## SUPPORT FOR COLONIZATION 对殖民的支持
>
> The American Colonization Society was started by antislavery Quakers, but it also had the support of many southern slave-owners who wanted to rid the South of its free black population. Slave-owners saw this population as a threat.

C. THE WOMEN'S RIGHTS MOVEMENT 女权运动

A women's rights movement developed in the antebellum period, seeking to address gender inequalities and to improve opportunities for women. The movement expressed its ideals at the 1848 Seneca Falls Convention in Western New York.

Women in the Public Sphere 公共领域的女性

The dictates of the "cult of domesticity"—that woman confine their activities to the private sphere—exerted a powerful influence on middle-class society in the antebellum period (see more of the "cult of domesticity" page 148). However, many women challenged these dictates. Women followed the lead of Dorothea Dix, who was active in the movement for more humane treatment for the mentally ill (see page 142), to push for a variety of reforms in the 1820s and 1830s. Middle-class New York City women formed the Female Moral Reform Society (1834) to urge women not to engage in prostitution. The society targeted the men who frequented prostitutes, publishing lists of names of such men. These movements allowed women, who otherwise were excluded from politics and government, to participate in the public sphere.

Women also played an important role in the abolitionist movement. Two important orators and activists in the movement were the Grimke sisters, Angelina and Sarah. They were the daughters of a prominent South Carolina slave owner. Later in life, in the 1830s, they converted to Quakerism and to the abolitionist cause. Two other abolitionist activists, Elizabeth Cady Stanton and Lucretia Mott, were barred from attending the World Anti-Slavery Convention in London (1840) because of their gender. Mott and Stanton began thinking not only about the abolition of slavery but also about the conditions of women in the United States.

Seneca Falls Convention 塞尼卡·福尔斯会议

In 1848, Elizabeth Cady Stanton and Lucretia Mott led a group of women, including many veterans of the abolitionist movement, to challenge the cultural and legal restrictions on women in the antebellum period. Their initial meeting in upstate New York, the Seneca Falls Convention, is often considered the birth of the women's-rights movement. This was the first public gathering convened to raise the issue of women's suffrage. The convention went beyond obtaining voting rights for women. It called attention to the whole structure of gender inequality, including issues relating to property rights, education, wages, child custody, divorce, and the overall legal status of women. The convention issued a Declaration of

Sentiments modeled after the Declaration of Independence. The document declared, "all men *and women* are created equal."

> ## THE WOMEN'S RIGHTS MOVEMENT OVER TIME
> ## 各时期的女权运动
>
> Be aware of continuities and discontinuities between the women's rights movement of the period 1848–1920, and the movement of the 1960s and 1970s. Tactics and priorities shifted once the right to vote had been attained. The earlier movement grew out of the abolitionist movement; the later movement was inspired by the civil rights movement.

KEY CONCEPT 4.2 ECONOMIC TRANSFORMATIONS AND SOCIAL CHANGE IN ANTEBELLUM AMERICA
核心概念4.2：美国内战前的经济转型与社会变化

Innovations in technology, agriculture, and commerce brought about a series of transformations in American society. These changes affected patterns of settlement, family relations and gender norms, political power, regional identities, and the way Americans acquired goods.

I. Changes in Commerce, Manufacturing, Agriculture, and Transportation　商业、制造业、农业与运输业的变革

A series of technological innovations dramatically altered the American economy. These changes created regional, national, and international markets for goods. Old patterns of economic activity gave way to new patterns of production, distribution, and consumption, changing the nature of agriculture and manufacturing.

A. THE MARKET REVOLUTION　市场革命

The growth of the market economy, often labeled the "market revolution" by historians, dramatically altered many aspects of American society—drawing local economies into the national and international economies.

The Expansion of Banking　银行的扩张

Banking and credit began to play an increasingly important role in economic expansion, especially after the "Panic of 1819," which demonstrated the volatility of the new market economy. However, the remarkable growth afterward demonstrated the vitality of the new economy. The Second Bank of the United States, chartered in 1816, extended credit, as did many newly chartered state banks. These banks issued bank notes, which were the only paper currency in circulation at the time. The system of banknotes as currency was imperfect—values of notes from one state might be less in another state—but the ability of banks to put currency into the economy fueled economic growth.

The Incorporation of America　美国的公司

The market revolution was facilitated by the changes in laws that made it much easier to create and expand a corporate entity. In the late 1700s and early 1800s, corporate charters were granted to groups of individuals, but mainly on a temporary basis, and mainly for a public-oriented purpose, such as building a bridge or a road. However, by the 1830s and 1840s, states began rewriting corporate laws allowing for the chartering of businesses. These laws allowed for the establishment of an entity—a corporation—in which members of the public could invest their money. Incorporation laws provided investors with "limited liability." Investors could only lose the amount they had invested; they were not liable for any debts beyond their investments, nor could they be held liable in any civil suits. In the following decades, the number of corporations and investors grew dramatically.

The Supreme Court and the Market Economy 最高法院与市场经济

Supreme Court decisions in the first half of the nineteenth century tended to uphold and define the rules of the growing market economy, especially the sanctity of contracts. The Supreme Court, in the decision of *Trustees of Dartmouth College v. Woodward* (1819), defined the charter that Dartmouth College had received during the colonial period as a contract. When the state of New Hampshire attempted to rescind Dartmouth's charter and make it a state college, the court ruled that the original charter was valid and must stand. In *Fletcher v. Peck* (1810), the Supreme Court upheld a corrupt land deal between the state of Georgia and private individuals. The Court ruled that the deal, in effect a contract, might not have been in the public interest, but a contract should be upheld.

B. ADVANCES IN TECHNOLOGY 技术进步

A series of technological innovations extended the market economy and brought efficiency to the production of goods. These innovations included the steam engine, interchangeable parts, the telegraph, agricultural implements, and machinery to produce textiles.

Agricultural Efficiency 农业效率

Several new inventions improved the efficiency of agricultural work in the antebellum period. These were not yet the mechanized implements of the Gilded Age (see Period 6). Rather, this period was characterized by hand-operated tools or animal-assisted implements. The steel plow, developed by John Deere in 1847, proved to be more durable and efficient than the cast-iron plow. Manufacturers developed more efficient grain drills, mowers, hay rakes, and harrows. There were two significant inventions that allowed for greater efficiency in grain production. The first, the automatic reaper, developed by Cyrus McCormack in 1831, cut and stacked wheat and other grains. The machine, operated by one farmer and pulled by horses, could harvest as much wheat as five men. After harvesting, the grain must be threshed—the individual edible kernels of grain must be loosened from the inedible chaff (the dry husks that surround the grain). This was traditionally done by hand or by animals walking on the harvested stalks. The second, the thresher, could process wheat far more quickly than previous methods. These machines were used on farms of the "Old Northwest" (as the region between the Great Lakes and the Ohio and Mississippi Rivers came to be called). They pointed the way toward the mechanized agriculture of the post–Civil War period.

Eli Whitney and Interchangeable Parts 伊莱·惠特尼与可互换零件

By the 1850s, as mass-production techniques spread beyond the textile industry, many industrial processes came to rely on the use of interchangeable parts. The parts of a specific product were made to exact specifications and could be rapidly assembled into standardized finished products. This technique was developed by Eli Whitney (who had earlier developed the cotton gin) in the production of small firearms. Others before him had implemented the idea of interchangeability, but Whitney successfully promoted the idea. By the time of the Civil War, it had spread to a wide variety of manufacturing operations.

The Development of Steam Power 蒸汽的发展

One of the important technological developments in the first half of the nineteenth century was the harnessing of steam power. Developments in Great Britain in the late eighteenth century led to high-pressure steam engines that could be used for powering ships and locomotives. In the United States, Robert Fulton developed a functioning steamboat, the *Clermont*, that was demonstrated on New York's Hudson River in 1807. Within 20 years, steamboats came to dominate commercial shipping, swiftly plying the major rivers and canals of the United States, as well as the Great Lakes. Soon, similar technologies were used by steam-powered locomotives. In the years leading up to the Civil War, steam power was beginning to be used in factories—replacing the water wheels that had characterized factories since the turn of the nineteenth century.

Advances in Communication 通信的进步

The major advance in communications in the antebellum period was the telegraph. Samuel Morse developed and patented the telegraph, and sent the first message—"What hath God wrought?"—in 1844. The first telegraph line was from Washington, DC, to Baltimore. Telegraph messages were transmitted in long and short electrical impulses, called Morse Code. By 1850, telegraph lines, usually built alongside railroad tracks, connected the country. The telegraph greatly facilitated the development of a national market for products and services. Clothing manufacturers in Massachusetts could send their orders to southern cotton growers in a matter of minutes. Previously, it could take days to send information long distances.

C. IMPROVEMENTS IN TRANSPORTATION, AND REGIONAL INTERDEPENDENCE
交通的改善与地区之间的相互依赖

Improvements in transportation made production for faraway markets possible. By 1850, the eastern half of the United States was crisscrossed by a series of roads, canals, and railroads that, along with navigable rivers, moved goods from city to city and from the interior to the coast. These improvements allowed for regional specialization—western grain and southern cotton could be rapidly transported to eastern population centers to be consumed or processed.

Canals and Roads 运河与公路

The first set of improvements, which occurred between 1800 and 1830, included the expansion and improvement of roads and canals and the development of the steamboat. The construction of canals and roads, called at the time *internal improvements*, did much to expand trade, especially between the Midwest (then known as the West) and eastern cities. These projects were often encouraged by the government and at least partially funded by it. Most significant was the Erie Canal (completed in 1825), which connected the Hudson River to the Great Lakes, thus connecting New York City with the interior of the country. The cost of moving a ton of freight from Buffalo to New York City dropped by approximately 90 percent with the completion of the Erie Canal. The most important road project was the building of the National Road, also known as the Cumberland Road, stretching from Maryland into the Ohio

River Valley. Construction took place from 1811 to 1853. Soon, however, roads and even canals were overshadowed by a quicker and more powerful means of transportation, the railroad.

Railroads　铁路

The first railroad tracks were laid in 1829 by the Baltimore and Ohio Railroad. By 1860, railroads connected the far reaches of the country east of the Mississippi River and beyond. Railroads sped up the movement of goods and expanded markets. The cost of moving a ton of wheat 1 mile by wagon in 1800 was between 30 and 70 cents; it dropped to about 1.2 cents by railroad in 1860. Railroad construction dramatically increased in the post-Civil War era, connecting the far-reaches of the continent and increasing the nation's economic activity (see Period 6).

II. Impact of the Market Revolution　市场革命的影响

The market revolution dramatically changed American society, drawing more people into its orbit, altering class relations, and redefining gender and family roles.

A. WORKERS ARE DRAWN INTO NEW METHODS OF PRODUCTION
新的生产方式产生了工人

New methods of production attracted men and women into a growing market economy and away from small-scale agricultural work.

The "Putting-out System"　"散工制"

In the first decades of the nineteenth century, a system of manufacturing developed in which many workers performed piecework at home. In this "putting-out system," men and women would perform a task arranged by an agent and would be paid by the piece produced. Often, the task was a small part of a larger operation, such as repeatedly cutting leather forms to be sewn elsewhere into shoes. This system was suited to small-town and rural communities. Often, families might be simultaneously involved in semi-subsistence agriculture and in the putting-out system; the seasonal nature of farm work allowed for additional work to be taken in at various times of the year. This system was something of a bridge between the craftwork of the eighteenth century and the industrial revolution of the late nineteenth century.

Slater Mill and the Development of the Factory System　斯莱特纺织厂与工厂制的发展

Before the Civil War, America began to move toward the industrial mass production of goods. This trend continued with even greater energy after the Civil War. The first field to industrialize was the textile industry. As early as the 1790s, Samuel Slater built the first factory in the United States after smuggling machinery plans out of Great Britain. This factory in Pawtucket, Rhode Island, and dozens that were built in the following years, spun cotton and wool into yarn or thread. The spinning machines in Slater's mill were powered by the fast-flowing Blackstone River. Water, human, and animal power characterized industry in the pre–Civil War era.

AN INDUSTRIAL REVOLUTION?　工业革命？

Most historians reserve the term "industrial revolution" for the post-Civil War expansion of American industry. Some historians label the prewar steps toward industrialization "the first industrial revolution," and postwar developments, "the second industrial revolution."

The Lowell System 洛厄尔制

Early elements of industrialization emerged in rural New England in the 1820s and 1830s. Extensive water-powered textile factories opened along the Merrimack River in Lowell, Massachusetts, starting in 1821, and drew in young women from the New England country-side to operate the machines. It was thought that these women could be paid less and would only be temporary factory operatives. At some point, it was assumed, they would get married and be replaced by new women, who would be recruited to replace them. Also, the era of mass migration from Europe had not yet begun, so it was difficult to recruit male factory operatives, especially with farmland in the United States still reasonably priced. By 1830, eight Lowell mills employed more than 6,000 women.

The fathers of these young women were told by factory recruiters that their daughters would be working in a "factory in the garden"—a clean, bucolic setting, unlike the dirty and dangerous factory cities of Great Britain. The women tended to live in closely supervised boarding houses, and the work was also strictly monitored. Despite this scrutiny, both on the job and even at the boarding houses, the "Lowell girls" experienced a degree of freedom and autonomy unheard of for young women at the time. Many participated in producing a periodical called the *Lowell Offering*. They demonstrated their sense of solidarity and assertiveness by going on strike in 1834 and again in 1836, following announced wage cuts. The 1836 strike restored their original wages, but by the 1840s the young farm women were being replaced by Irish immigrants who were in dire straits and ready to work for lower wages.

B. THE MARKET REVOLUTION'S IMPACT ON ECONOMIC CLASS
市场革命对经济阶级的影响

The market revolution altered the nation's social fabric. The gap between the rich and the poor widened, while fostering the growth of an emerging middle class. Changes in the economy contributed to changed ideas about class, gender, and family. Society also experienced a widening separation between the private realm of the home and the public realm of work and politics.

Work and Power 工作与权力

The market revolution ushered in changes to American society that undermined older notions of a self-governing citizenry and perceptions of a public composed of autonomous individuals whose rise and fall is determined by their own actions. With the growth of larger-scale manufacturing operations and increasingly powerful incorporated businesses, the ability of the individual to rise and become "his own man" was compromised. In this context, we see some working people, men and women, turning to the idea of forming unions in order to advance their goals. A labor union allowed workers in a firm to bargain "collectively" with their employer. The rise of the union movement signaled a shift away from the face-to-face relationships that characterized work-place settings in the eighteenth century.

C. GENDER AND FAMILY ROLES IN THE AGE OF THE MARKET REVOLUTION
市场革命时代的性别与家庭角色

The market revolution affected gender and family roles. During this period, many Americans came to see separate spheres in society—a male-dominated public sphere and a female-oriented private sphere. A set of domestic ideals, that came to be called the "cult of domesticity," developed in the first decades of the nineteenth century.

Gentility, Domesticity, and the Middle-class Ideal
上流阶层、家庭生活与中产阶级理想

Many contemporary writers and historians note the emergence in the first half of the nineteenth century of a new set of cultural ideas centered around the middle-class. This culture was built around the home, nostalgia, sentimentality, and a watered-down (non-Calvinist) Christian piety. This middle-class cultural ideal assigned to women a dependent role as the "weaker sex." In an increasingly market-oriented society, women were seen as outside of this rough-and-tumble world of money and politics. The qualities that were assigned to women were timidity and disdain for competition. This culture was manifested in sermons by Protestant ministers, seeking to broaden their appeal, and by female authors of popular fiction.

The "Cult of Domesticity" and the "Proper" Role for Women
"主妇居家崇拜"与妇女的"适当"角色

Antebellum society underwent a redefinition of women's "proper" role in society. The ideas of "republican motherhood," current in the decades after the American Revolution, gave way to a less public-minded conception of a middle-class woman's "place." Commentators in the first half of the nineteenth century tended to see women as intellectually inferior and insisted that their proper role was maintaining the house and caring for children. This "cult of domesticity" insisted that women keep a proper Christian home—separate from the male sphere of politics, business, and competition. This ideal discouraged women from participating in public life. The laws of the country already relegated women to a second-class status. Women could not vote or sit on juries. Women were not entitled to protection against physical abuse by their husbands. When women married, any property they owned became the property of their husbands. Under the legal doctrine of *femme covert*, wives had no independent legal or political standing.

III. The Market Revolution, National Unification, and Regional Specialization 市场革命、国家统一与区域专业化

The market revolution led to new settlement patterns in the United States—encouraging both the movement of immigrants from abroad into the United States as well as the movement of people within the country. Economic plans meant to unify the country also led to regional differences.

A. MIGRATIONS AND NEW COMMUNITIES IN THE AGE OF THE MARKET REVOLUTION 市场革命时代的移民与新社区

A variety of social and economic factors contributed to native-born white citizens moving into the West and settling in new communities along the Ohio and Mississippi Rivers. At the same time, the growth of manufacturing in the United States drew immigrants from abroad into growing cities.

> ## THE DEVELOPMENT OF A NATIONAL ECONOMY
> ## 国家经济的发展
> The market revolution linked cities and regions. The local economies of the eighteenth century began giving way to a national, and even international, economic system.

Migrations from Europe 欧洲移民

Immigrants from Europe in the first half of the nineteenth century were attracted by the growing economy and the sense of opportunity in the United States. The majority of immigrants who arrived in the United States between 1800 and 1860 came from northern and western Europe. The two largest groups came from Ireland and from the German states. Many immigrants stayed in the cities of the Northeast, while some ventured into the interior of the country.

Irish Immigration 爱尔兰移民

The largest immigrant group into the United States during the antebellum period came from Ireland. Increased immigration from Ireland during the 1840s was primarily the result of crop failures at home that led to mass starvation. Blight afflicted the potato crop, which was a staple for Irish people. The potato blight was partly a natural phenomenon and partly the result of British policies. Great Britain controlled Ireland and used the best land to grow wheat and other crops for export, while potato farming was pushed to marginal land. The result was weak potato plants less able to withstand disease. It is estimated that a million Irish starved to death between 1845 and 1850, while another million left for America. Four-fifths of the Irish immigrants settled in port cities such as New York and Boston and in other cities and towns of the Northeast.

German Immigration 德国移民

The second-largest immigrant group during the antebellum period was German. German immigrants to the United States tended to be better off than the Irish immigrants. Many were skilled craftsmen and entrepreneurs who emigrated to the United States to escape the political repression following the failed revolution of 1848 in the German states. German immigrants were more likely to have the resources to continue their journeys beyond their initial city of disembarkation (usually New York City). Many settled in the "German triangle" of western cities—Cincinnati, St. Louis, and Milwaukee.

The Movement to the West 西进运动

The West grew rapidly in the antebellum period, especially after the War of 1812, as improvements in transportation—first roads and canals, and later railroads—opened new areas for settlement. More than 4 million Americans crossed the Appalachian Mountains between 1800 and 1840 to settle in the West. Most of these migrants to the West traveled in groups. New communities grew quickly, with migrants depending on one another to clear land, construct dwellings and barns, and create a sense of community on the frontier. Many southern planters moved into Alabama, Mississippi, Louisiana, Arkansas, and, later during this period, Texas (see pages 160–161). Many of these small-scale farmers hoped to recreate the Cotton Kingdom, complete with slave labor, on the less expensive lands of the West. From the upper South, many farmers moved into the southern portions of Ohio, Indiana, and Illinois. Finally, many New England and New York farm families settled in northern Ohio, Indiana, and Illinois, as well as Wisconsin and Michigan. Some migrants "squatted" on their new land, lacking legal title or deed. Others purchased land from either the federal government or from speculators. Over time, the regional distinctiveness of the original 13 states left its imprint on newly settled areas. The towns and churches of the Old Northwest (the current upper Midwest) began to resemble New England, while the plantations and slave-labor system of the new lower South resembled the Old South.

B. REGIONAL SPECIALIZATION　区域专业化

The North and the South developed in different directions in the antebellum period. The North developed banking, manufacturing, and shipping industries, while the South focused on increasing its cotton production. Both the North and South were growing economically in the first decades of the nineteenth century. In many ways, the growth of each region reinforced the growth of the other. However, this symbiotic relationship would not persist. Political and ideological differences would emerge as America moved toward the midway point in the century. These differences would come to overshadow commonalities and lead to the Civil War.

Commerce, Trade, and Manufacturing in the North　北方的商业、贸易与制造业

Manufacturing expanded throughout the North in the 1820s and 1830s. By the early 1830s, more than 40,000 women worked in textile mills in New England (see more on the origins of textile manufacturing, page 147). The Waltham-Lowell System—bringing all stages of textile production under one roof, with employees living in company housing—soon spread to other industries and to other parts of the country. Manufacturing operations emerged in some of the cities of the Old Northwest, including Cincinnati and Chicago. In addition, the use of interchangeable parts, a key component of mass-production popularized by Eli Whitney (see page 145), soon spread to other processes. Manufacturers of agricultural implements, tools, clocks, and ironware began to use interchangeable parts.

The Growth of Cotton Production in the South　南方棉花生产的发展

In the first half of the nineteenth century, cotton replaced other staple crops as the most profitable crop throughout the South. The profitability of southern cotton contributed to a dramatic growth in slavery in the first half of the nineteenth century and an expansion of the internal slave trade. Most of the cotton used in the mills in New England was grown by slave labor in the South. The invention of the cotton gin by Eli Whitney (1793) allowed for the rapid processing of cotton. That, combined with insatiable demand in the North and in Great Britain for cotton, led to more and more acres being put under cultivation. Cotton production connected the United States to the global economy. By 1860, 58 percent of American exports consisted of cotton. Cotton production increased from about 700,000 bales in 1830 to nearly 5 million bales on the eve of the Civil War. Cotton was justifiably called "King Cotton." As cotton production increased, the number of slaves in the South also increased (see page 115).

> ## KING COTTON, NORTH AND SOUTH
> ## 南北方的产品之王——棉花
> Cotton was not only king in the South. The increase in cotton production benefitted many elements in the North as well as in the South. Cotton was bought and sold in New York City and processed into cloth in New England.

C. THE SOUTHERN EXCEPTION　南方的独特性

In many ways the South remained distinct from the rest of the country. Ideologically, politically, and culturally, the South developed a regional identity markedly different from the other regions of the country. The South was also distinct in its dependence on exports to the international market—by 1850 supplying approximately half of the world's cotton; by 1860, three-fourths.

Cotton and Slavery　棉花与奴隶制

Slavery became dominant in the South just as it was becoming unpopular in the eyes of the world. In 1807, Great Britain outlawed the international slave trade. The following year, the United States took the same step (the international slave trade had been protected by the Constitution until 1808). All of the northern states had voted to abolish slavery outright or gradually. Some northerners, and even some white southerners, were critical of slavery, but slavery and cotton were the main engines behind American economic growth in the first half of the nineteenth century.

Slavery and the Culture of the South　奴隶制与南方文化

The main source of the distinctiveness of the South was, as Alexis de Tocqueville noted in *Democracy in America* (1831), slavery. Slavery grew rapidly in the decades leading up to the Civil War. By 1850, nearly a third of the southern population was African American. In 1790, there were approximately 700,000 slaves in the South. By 1830, that figure had climbed to 2 million and, by 1860, to 4 million. In Mississippi and South Carolina, African Americans were the majority of the population. In contrast, on the eve of the Civil War only one northerner in 76 was African American. The presence of such a large African-American population in the South played an important role in shaping southern culture. This can be seen in language, food, music, and dialect. However, the most important consequence of the presence of a large slave population in the South was the commitment of white southerners to white supremacy. A belief in the racial inferiority of blacks, mixed with fear and even hatred, shaped white southern views of African Americans. Although many white northerners also held racist notions of African Americans, the white supremacist outlook lacked the intensity it held in the South.

D. THE AMERICAN SYSTEM AND SECTIONALISM　美国制度与地方主义

Attempts by the federal government to create linkages between the regions of the country were of limited success. The market economy ended up creating stronger links between the North and the Midwest; the South became increasingly isolated from the rest of the country.

Henry Clay's "American System"　亨利·克莱的"美国制度"

In the nationalist mood that followed the War of 1812, Henry Clay, a leading member of the House of Representatives, put forward a series of proposals to promote economic growth that he later called the "American System." First, Clay realized that America needed "internal improvements" in transportation in order to grow economically. At the beginning of the century, the transportation system in the United States was woefully lacking. At the time of the War of 1812, the military had difficulty moving materials and men because of the nation's inadequate transportation system. Second, Clay proposed putting high tariffs on imported goods. He believed that high tariffs on incoming manufactured goods would promote American manufacturing. High tariffs would make foreign goods more expensive to the consumer, and

American-made goods would seem cheaper by comparison. Third, Clay proposed chartering the Second Bank of the United States in order to stabilize the economy and make credit more readily available. These proposals were important steps taken by the government to usher in the market revolution. By the end of the Monroe Administration, Congress had rechartered the Bank of the United States and passed a protective tariff (both in 1816).

The Growing Isolation of the South 南方日渐孤立

Despite Henry Clay's attempt to foster unity among the regions of the country, the South became increasingly isolated from both the North and the Midwest. Roads and railroads connected the North and the Midwest but tended to bypass the South. Further, patterns of migrations connected the North and the Midwest culturally. Farmers, artisans, and laborers living in New England, New York, or Pennsylvania were far more likely to venture toward Ohio or Illinois in the first half of the nineteenth century than they were to go to South Carolina or Mississippi. These connections isolated the South culturally from the rest of the nation and, over time, would isolate it politically.

KEY CONCEPT 4.3 EXPANDING BOUNDARIES, TRADE, AND FOREIGN-POLICY CONFLICTS
核心概念4.3：扩张边界、贸易与外交政策的冲突

The United States pursued a foreign policy around the goals of expanding its boundaries, increasing trade, and isolating itself from European conflicts. These goals were pursued both through government actions and private initiatives.

I. Trade and Dominance of the Western Hemisphere 西半球的贸易与优势

During the first half of the nineteenth century, United States foreign-policy makers aimed at promoting foreign trade, establishing the United States as a global presence, and dominating North America. However, gaining control of territory led to conflicts with American Indians.

A. NEW MARKETS AND NEW LANDS 新市场与新土地

The desire of many Americans to establish new patterns of trade and to acquire new lands and open them up to settlement led to numerous economic, diplomatic, and military initiatives in both the Western Hemisphere and in Asia.

Trade and Territory 贸易与领土

The desire of the United States to trade freely throughout the world, across both the Atlantic and Pacific Oceans, led to a series of foreign-policy actions in the first half of the century. Early on, the United States struggled to establish favorable trading relationships across the Atlantic; these efforts led to the War of 1812. Later during this period, the United States took actions to open trade with Asia. As the American economy grew between the War of 1812 and the Civil War, many Americans continued the push ever farther into the continent. This westward movement had ominous implications for Canada and Mexico as well as for American Indian nations within the borders of the growing United States. Finally, the acquisition of additional territory enflamed sectional tensions, as the debate over the expansion of slavery intensified in the decade before the Civil War.

The Barbary Wars, 1801–1805　巴巴里战争（1801—1805）

President Thomas Jefferson's first foreign policy crisis involved U.S. trade with the Middle East. Trade in the Mediterranean was controlled by four seafaring North African states—Morocco, Algiers, Tunis, and Tripoli, whose domain was known as the Barbary Coast. These states demanded large payments from trading nations as "tribute." Nations that did not comply found their shipping subject to seizure and plundering by Barbary Coast pirates. Merchants during the colonial era had enjoyed the protection of Great Britain. When the United States became independent, Presidents George Washington and John Adams agreed to the terms set by the Barbary states. In 1801, Tripoli demanded a steep increase in payment from the United States. When Jefferson refused, Tripoli declared war on the United States. Jefferson sent warships to the region to engage in fighting and to protect American shipping. The move proved popular. The slogan "Millions for defense, but not a cent for tribute" became widespread in America. In the end, the United States did not achieve a decisive victory, but it boosted America's profile on the world stage.

Continued Troubles with European Nations　与欧洲国家持续的矛盾

The conflicts between Great Britain and France that occupied the Washington and Adams administrations reemerged during the administrations of Thomas Jefferson and James Madison. Both presidents, Jefferson and Madison, attempted to continue the policy of neutrality that Washington had set forth while, at the same time, extending foreign trade, sometimes with nations at war with each other. In 1803, Napoleon declared war on Britain. At first, the United States benefited from trading with both warring partners. Soon, both countries tried to block American trade with the other. Great Britain was more aggressive in its efforts to stop American ships. British Navy warships routinely stopped and boarded American merchant ships, often seizing cargo. More irritating still for the Americans was the practice of seizing American seamen and "pressing" them into service in the British Navy. Britain claimed that these men were deserters from the British Navy, but most were not. This practice of impressment affected 6,000 American seamen between 1803 and 1812. The situation between the United States and Britain reached a crisis in 1807 when the 50-gun British warship HMS *Leopard* fired on the unprepared 38-gun American frigate USS *Chesapeake*. Three Americans were killed and four were abducted in the *Chesapeake–Leopard* Affair.

"Peaceful Coercion" and Free Trade　"和平压迫"与自由贸易

As Great Britain continued to interfere with American shipping, Presidents Jefferson and Madison initially chose "peaceful coercion" over war. Jefferson passed the Embargo Act (1807), which cut off U.S. trade to all foreign ports. Jefferson thought that this would pressure the belligerent nations to agree to leave U.S. ships alone. However, the main effect of the embargo was to cripple America's mercantile sector. The embargo proved to be very unpopular, especially in New England, which depended on trade, now nearly at a standstill.

In the waning days of President Jefferson's administration, Congress replaced the unpopular Embargo Act (1807) with the Non-Intercourse Act of 1809, opening trade with all nations except for Great Britain and France.

> ## ECONOMIC INDEPENDENCE
> ## 经济独立
>
> The Embargo Act (1807), the Non-intercourse Act (1809) and the War of 1812 (1812–1815) all had the effect of creating demand for American-made goods. The acts proved to be a catalyst for American manufacturing and contributed to the United States becoming more economically self-sufficient.

However, this act proved to be almost as unpopular, as Great Britain and France had been two of America's biggest trading partners.

Macon's Bill No. 2 (1810) 《梅肯第二法案》（1810）

In an attempt to revive trade, Congress passed Macon's Bill No. 2 in 1810. The bill stipulated that if either Great Britain or France agreed to respect America's rights as a neutral nation at sea, the United States would prohibit trade with that nation's enemy. Napoleon agreed to this arrangement, and consequently, the United States cut trade to Britain in 1811. However, Napoleon did not honor his commitment and France continued to seize American ships. The cutting off of trade with Britain worsened relations and pushed the two nations to the edge of war.

War of 1812 1812年战争

Trade conflicts and pressure from the "War Hawk" congressmen (see page 159) pushed Madison to declare war against Britain in 1812. The vote on the war in Congress was divided along sectional lines. New England and some Middle Atlantic states opposed it; the South and Midwest voted for it. The declaration of war occurred just as Britain was making assurances that it would stop interfering with American shipping.

The war lasted two and a half years. Britain achieved several early victories, defeating American forces at Forts Dearborn and Detroit. Madison managed to win reelection in the midst of the war, but the Federalists, who were critical of the war effort, made a strong showing. By 1813, the United States began to achieve key victories in battle. The United States burned the city of York (now Toronto), and won several battles at sea and on the northern lakes. At the Battle of the Thames in Canada, American forces defeated British and American Indian forces and killed the Indian leader, Tecumseh. In one of the stunning episodes of the war, British forces seized Washington, DC, in 1814 and burned public buildings, including the Executive Mansion. The United States achieved a major victory at New Orleans in early 1815, led by General Andrew Jackson. Jackson and his British adversaries had not realized that the United States had already signed a peace treaty, formally ending the war weeks before, in late 1814.

The Hartford Convention and Opposition to the War of 1812

《哈特福德公约》与对1812年战争的抗议

The first major challenges to federal policy in the nineteenth century came not from the South but from Federalist politicians in New England. The War of 1812 was unpopular among some Americans, especially among New England merchants, who saw their trade with Great Britain disappear. As diplomats were negotiating an end to the war in December 1814, Federalists from New England convened in Hartford, Connecticut, to express their displeasure with the conflict. Some of the more radical delegates suggested that New England secede from the union, but this proposal was rejected at the convention. The Hartford Convention did pass a resolution calling for a two-thirds vote in Congress for future declarations of war.

> **TALK OF SECESSION**
> **脱离联邦会谈**
> The Hartford Convention demonstrated that talk of secession was not restricted to southerners.

The Treaty of Ghent 《根特条约》

The Treaty of Ghent (1814) ended the War of 1812. Britain had grown weary of war after fighting Napoleon for more than a decade and the United States for two years. The United States realized that it could not achieve a decisive victory over Great Britain. The treaty ended the war where it had begun. The two sides agreed to stop fighting, give back any territory seized in the war, and recognize the boundary between the United States and Canada that had been established before the war. The treaty did not mention the specific grievances the United States had against Britain—aid to American Indians, interference with American shipping, or impressments of American seamen.

"Old China Trade"　"旧中国贸易"

United States merchants opened a lucrative trade with China following the American Revolution. The Treaty of Paris (1783) freed American trade from British control. This commerce with China, not officially sanctioned by the United States government, is known as the "Old China Trade." The trade, driven by the American demand for Chinese products, such as tea, porcelain, silk, and nankeen (a coarse cotton cloth), opened new markets to the United States, but also brought to the fore cultural differences between the United States and China. From the American perspective, trade was seen as a basic right and as a means to expand national and personal wealth; it was assumed that other countries also would want to expand their trade for similar reasons. In traditional Chinese thought, however, commerce was looked down upon. Of the four social classes that were described, in ascending order of importance, in Confucian thought—scholars, peasants, artisans, and merchants—merchants were the one class that was seen as superfluous, making profit without producing anything.

Chinese officials did allow trade with foreign countries, but they saw this trade through the lens of tradition—the trade existed by the largess of the emperor in return for tribute paid by states that acknowledged the superior position of China. Trade increased in the nineteenth century as the United States found that furs were in demand in China. These furs were obtained from American Indian groups along the Pacific Coast through the "maritime fur trade," from as far north as Alaska. This trade was carried in increasingly large clipper ships. This unofficial "Old China Trade" ended in 1844. Seeing the growing power of Great Britain in China, the United States worked out the Treaty of Wanghia, in which China extended to the United States the same trading privileges that had been extended to Great Britain.

Nationalist Sentiment and the Monroe Doctrine (1823)

民族主义情绪与门罗主义（1823）

America's newfound confidence on the international stage was evident in President James Monroe's foreign policy address to Congress in 1823. Monroe was alarmed at threats by the Holy Alliance of Russia, Prussia, and Austria to restore Spain's lost American colonies. He also opposed a decree by the Russian czar that claimed all the Pacific Northwest above the 51st parallel. Although both problems worked themselves out, Monroe issued a statement warning European nations to keep their hands off the Americas. The major purpose of the Monroe Doctrine was to limit European influence in the Western Hemisphere. The United States did not have the military might to enforce this pronouncement at the time, but it was an important statement of intent. The Monroe Doctrine and Washington's farewell address became cornerstones of America's isolationist foreign policy.

Acquiring New Territories　获得新领土

Between 1803 and 1853, the United States took a number of steps to establish the international boundaries of the future 48 states (the final two steps, acquisition of the Mexican Cession in

1848 and the Gadsden Purchase in 1853, are discussed in Period 5). The first major acquisition of territory after the defeat of the British in the American Revolution was the Louisiana Purchase.

The Louisiana Purchase 路易斯安那购地案

In 1803, the United States was given the opportunity to purchase the vast swath of land beyond the Mississippi River known as the Louisiana Territory. The Louisiana Territory was long held by France, which ceded it to Spain in 1762, at the close of the French and Indian War. France regained the territory in 1801, but the ambitious French leader, Napoleon Bonaparte, in need of cash to fund war with Great Britain, soon was ready to sell the Louisiana Territory. American negotiators quickly agreed to a price of $15 million (1803).

Jefferson was at first reluctant to approve the deal because the Constitution did not allow for the acquisition of additional lands. Jefferson had long held a strict constructionist view of the Constitution, asserting that the government's power was limited to what was explicitly allowed in the Constitution (see Period 3). However, if Jefferson waited for a constitutional amendment specifically allowing Congress to acquire new lands, Napoleon could rescind his offer. So Jefferson violated his stated principle and quickly presented the offer to Congress, which assented and appropriated the funds.

The purchase of the Louisiana Territory was arguably the most significant act of Jefferson's presidency. The purchase was important for two reasons. First, it doubled the size of the United States, adding the fertile Great Plains. This flat area west of the Mississippi would become the most important agricultural region in the United States. Second, the United States gained full control of the port of New Orleans. New Orleans is at the outlet of the mighty Mississippi River, which stretches from Minnesota down the spine of the United States. The impact of the Louisiana Purchase on economic growth was remarkable. Between the 1810s and the 1850s, the value of produce from the interior of the United States went up more than tenfold.

The Lewis and Clark Expedition 刘易斯与克拉克远征

The Lewis and Clark expedition (1804–1806) increased understanding of the region included in the Louisiana Purchase. President Jefferson commissioned Meriwether Lewis and William Clark, army officers, to explore the territory. They explored and mapped the region, seeking practical routes through the mountains, and established the presence of the United States in the West.

The Adams–Onis Treaty (1819) 《亚当斯–欧尼斯条约》（1819）

The United States gained control over Florida with the Adams–Onis Treaty in 1819. This treaty with Spain was negotiated by John Adams, who was then secretary of state under President James Madison. The treaty transferred control of Florida to the United States, accepted Spain's claims to Texas, and settled the boundary between the state of Louisiana (which had entered the United States in 1812) and Spanish-held territory. The status of Florida became a concern for the United States, as it had been a destination for escaped slaves. The Florida issue became more pronounced during the First Seminole War (1814–1819) (see page 160). Americans were troubled by the so-called Negro Fort, along the Apalachicola River. The fort had been British during the War of 1812; after the war, a British officer transferred control of the fort to fugitive slaves and Seminole Indians. General Andrew Jackson organized the capture of this fort during the First Seminole War; after the war, gaining control of Florida became a goal of United States diplomats.

The Webster-Ashburton Treaty 《韦伯斯特-阿什波顿条约》

The United States settled a dispute in 1842 with Great Britain over the border between Maine and British-ruled Canada. The treaty split the disputed territory and also settled a dispute over the border between the Minnesota territory and Canada.

Annexation of Texas and Tensions with Mexico 兼并德克萨斯及与墨西哥的紧张关系

After much debate and delay (see page 163), Texas was annexed by the United States in 1844. This move was an important catalyst for the Mexican-American War (1846–1848) between the United States and Mexico. The Mexican government was furious that Texas had become part of the United States. Meanwhile, President James Polk and American expansionists were eager to incorporate the remainder of Mexico's northern provinces into the United States (see Period 5).

"Fifty-four Forty or Fight": Negotiating the Oregon Border

"要么54度40分，要么战斗"：协商俄勒冈州边界

Both Great Britain and the United States laid claim to the lands of the Pacific Northwest. In 1818, the two nations agreed on a "joint occupation" of the Oregon Country. In the 1830s and 1840s, adventurous Americans began traveling west along the Oregon Trail and settling in the lush valley of the Willamette River. In 1844 politicians pushed for sole U.S. ownership of the entire Oregon Country, the northern boundary of which was the north latitude line at 54°40'. "Fifty-four forty or fight" was the rallying call of those who wanted the United States to own the entire territory. Great Britain balked at giving up all the territory. In 1846, the Polk administration reached a compromise with Britain, establishing the border at the 49th parallel. That line is the current boundary between the western United States and Canada.

B. CONTENTION BETWEEN WHITES AND AMERICAN INDIANS OVER WESTERN LANDS 白人与美洲印第安人争夺西部土地

White settlers and American Indians clashed on the frontier. The enthusiasm of land-hungry settlers was matched by the determination of native peoples to hold on to their traditional lands. These clashes led to wars and to federal efforts to control American Indian groups.

American Indians and the West 美洲印第安人与西部地区

Westward settlers were continuing in the footsteps of early colonists—pushing into the interior of the continent and antagonizing native peoples in the process. In the early 1800s, white settlers were pouring into the region of the Ohio River and its northern tributaries, which included the state of Ohio (1803) and the Indiana territory. Federal and state officials had extracted land agreements from the Indians for years. It was never clear if the Indian leaders who made the agreements had the authority to do so, nor was it clear that white settlers would live by these agreements. In 1809, the governor of the Indiana territory, William Henry Harrison, negotiated the Treaty of Fort Wayne. Indians agreed to cede three million acres at a nominal fee. The most important regional native leader at the time, Tecumseh, was not present for this agreement. He was on a trip recruiting followers to resist encroachments by white settlers. He and his brother, Tenskwatawa, "the Prophet," had been organizing a spiritual and political front, attempting to unite all the Indian nations east of the Mississippi River.

Battle of Tippecanoe and the War Hawks 蒂珀卡努战役与鹰派

Settlers in the Indiana territory persuaded Governor William Henry Harrison to wage war against Tecumseh's confederation. The Battle of Tippecanoe (1811) ousted members of the confederacy and was perceived as an American victory. Western congressmen, who became known as the War Hawks, became convinced that Britain was encouraging and funding Tecumseh's confederation. Just as relations with Britain were deteriorating over trade issues, War Hawks led by Henry Clay of Kentucky and John C. Calhoun from South Carolina, were pushing for military action against the British. Such action, it was thought, would allow the United States to elimi-

> ### WAR HAWKS 鹰派
> The War Hawks tended to hail from western and southern states.

nate the American Indian threat and, perhaps, even allow the United States to invade Canada. This pro-war sentiment in the West and South was one of the causes of the War of 1812 (see page 155).

Indian Removal Act (1830) 《印第安人迁移法案》（1830）

As the profitability of cotton production rose in the South in the first half of the nineteenth century, the value of land increased dramatically. Many whites wanted to push westward and acquire land in the interior of the South. Much of the southern territory was the traditional lands of the "Five Civilized Tribes"—Cherokee, Chickasaw, Choctaw, Muscogee-Creek, and Seminole. As far back as the Jefferson administration, federal policy had been to respect the rights of American Indians to inhabit this land. President Andrew Jackson, however, abandoned this policy and, in deference to market pressures and the call of white southerners to expand, adopted a policy of Indian removal. This policy applied to the American Indians of the South as well as the Old Northwest and, to a lesser degree, New England and New York. Jackson asserted that it was necessary for these peoples to be removed to the areas of the United States beyond the Mississippi River. He said, perhaps disingenuously, that this was in the best interests of the Indians themselves, who were being forced off their traditional lands by the encroachment of white settlers. He pushed for the Removal Act of 1830.

The "Trail of Tears" "洒泪之路"

The state of Georgia, with the support of President Jackson and then Jackson's successor, President Martin Van Buren, initiated the process of moving American Indians to the West despite the Supreme Court decision in *Worcester v. Georgia* (1832) declaring that American Indian tribes were subject to federal treaties, not to the actions of states (see page 133). The decision, in effect, voided Georgia's efforts to remove the Cherokee. President Jackson purportedly said, "John Marshall has made his decision. Now let him enforce it." By 1838, the Cherokee had exhausted their legal and political challenges to removal. Some cooperated with removal and ceded their lands. However, the majority, led by the Cherokee "principal chief," John Ross, adopted a policy of passive resistance to remain on their land. Federal troops were dispatched to enforce Georgia's removal policy. The resulting expulsion of 18,000 American Indians to the Oklahoma territory, their trek labeled the "Trail of Tears" (1838), resulted in the deaths of approximately a quarter of the people on the journey.

American Indians and Florida   美洲印第安人与佛罗里达

Americans, especially white southerners, had a long history of conflict with native peoples in Florida, which had long been Spanish territory. It was ceded to Great Britain in 1763 following the French and Indian War and given back to Spain in the Treaty of Paris (1783) ending the American Revolution. In the late 1700s and early 1800s, white southerners grew frustrated with the number of escaped slaves who made their way into Florida. These fugitives were often given protection by Indians in Florida. This concern led to raids by southern whites into Florida, followed by counterraids by the Seminole and other American Indians on communities in Georgia and Alabama.

These hostilities led to the first Seminole War, which began during the War of 1812 and continued to the end of the decade. A second Seminole War occurred in the 1830s. Florida had come into American hands as a result of the Adams–Onis Treaty (1819) (see page 157). By the 1830s, the Seminole were being pressured by the federal government to relocate to the West. In the Second Seminole War (1835–1842), native warriors fought U.S. troops to a standstill in the Everglades. Many Seminole remained defiant of government removal efforts even after the capture of the Seminole leader, Chief Osceola.

"Indian Territory"   "印第安保留区"

As part of the government's Indian-removal policy, many tribes from east of the Mississippi River were relocated to a designated "Indian Territory" that existed within the future boundaries of present-day Oklahoma. This establishment of an Indian Territory was part of the Indian Intercourse Act of 1834. Many Indian groups resisted relocation to the Indian Territory through legal channels and through armed resistance. Once in the territory, conflicts ensued between American Indian groups indigenous to the area and those relocated there. Eventually this territory was reduced in size and finally it ceased to exist and was folded into the Oklahoma Territory in 1907.

II. Debate over the Extension of Slavery   关于是否扩大奴隶制的争论

As the United States acquired new territories, Americans debated whether these new lands should allow slavery or not. Attempts at compromise were made in the first half of the nineteenth century, with mixed results.

A. COTTON, SLAVERY, AND EXPANSION   棉花、奴隶制与扩张

As cotton became increasingly profitable in the first half of the nineteenth century, growers often depleted the soil through over-cultivation. As a result, cotton growers sought new lands in the new Southwest.

Expansion into Texas—From Settlement to Independence
向德克萨斯扩张——从殖民到独立

As early as the 1820s, white Americans began moving into the Mexican territory of Texas. Many of these settlers were southern whites who hoped to duplicate the plantation model from the Old South. Initially, Mexico was eager to attract settlers to its northern frontier, in part to provide a buffer from incursions by Indian raiding parties. Led by Stephen Austin, settlers were attracted to Texas because there was an abundance of affordable land that could be used for cotton cultivation.

Mexico allowed these settlers a degree of self-government through the 1820s, but tensions began to develop in the 1830s. The Texas settlers routinely flouted Mexican law—most notably in practicing slavery, which was banned in Mexico. The new president of Mexico, General Antonio Lopez de Santa Anna, sought to bring the Texans into line with Mexican law and custom. In 1835, the Texans rebelled. Many rebels were Spanish-speaking "Tejanos," who objected to being ruled from Mexico City. At first they suffered major setbacks. Almost 200 died defending the Alamo in San Antonio, a former mission where they had taken refuge. Weeks later, almost 400 were killed by Mexican forces near the town of Goliad. Under the leadership of General Sam Houston, the rebels regrouped and emerged victorious. Texans won independence from Mexico, establishing the independent Lone Star Republic in 1836.

B. GROWING TENSIONS OVER SLAVERY 日益紧张的奴隶制

In the first half of the nineteenth century, antislavery efforts intensified in the North. At the same time, white southerners defended the institution of slavery vigorously. The defense of slavery became an element in the development of regional pride in the South.

Abolitionism and Electoral Politics 废奴主义与选举政治

A group of abolitionists formed the Liberty Party in 1840. This minor third party put forth the idea that the Constitution was essentially an antislavery document and that the United States should live up to the ideals contained in it. In this, the party differed from William Lloyd Garrison, who insisted that the Constitution protected slavery and, therefore, should be condemned (see page 142). The Liberty Party hoped to influence public opinion through the electoral arena. Garrison, on the other hand, rejected participating in electoral politics.

Racism and Resistance to the Antislavery Movement 种族主义与反对废奴运动

Slavery shaped southern views of race in distinct ways. Although many northerners subscribed to white supremacist views, white supremacist ideas were not central to the culture of the region because there were very few African Americans in the North (less than 1 percent of the population). In the South, however, white supremacy became central to southern white culture in the first half of the nineteenth century, especially after northern abolitionists began to press the cause of antislavery forcibly in the 1830s. Most white southerners held that African Americans were inferior beings. This view justified slavery, as an institution both necessary and proper. White supremacy and slavery allowed the main divide in the South to be race rather than class. It allowed even the poorest whites to believe they were part of the superior caste and to feel they had something in common with the wealthiest plantation owners.

The Lovejoy Incident 洛夫乔伊事件

The abolitionist movement faced opposition in the North as well as from white southerners. A violent incident in 1837 sent a chill over the abolitionist movement. Elijah Lovejoy, an abolitionist newspaper publisher in Illinois, was killed by a proslavery mob. He had been the subject of harassment. Mobs had destroyed his printing press three times before they killed him.

Southern Defense of Slavery 南方为奴隶制的辩护

As the abolitionist movement attacked the system of slavery (see page 142), southern public figures emerged to give a vigorous defense of the institution. Arguments took a variety of approaches. Some contrasted the factory system of the North with the slave system of the South, arguing that northern "wage-slaves" were not taken care of or fed and were fired when business was slow. The most well-known defender of slavery in the 1850s was George Fitzhugh. He was sharply critical of the pronouncements of northern defenders of the "free labor" ideology, insisting that the system masked a heartless approach to the world. Other southerners argued that slavery was sanctioned in the Bible. This movement went so far as to claim that slavery was a "positive good" for the slaves—that it provided them with skills, discipline, and "civilization."

Biblical Defense of Slavery　引用《圣经》为奴隶制辩护

The southern defense of slavery frequently invoked biblical passages. Some southern clergymen argued that the Bible demanded the submission of the inferior classes to the superior classes—especially slave to master. They cited passages, often out of context, such as, "[T]ell slaves to be submissive to their masters and to give satisfaction in every respect" (from *The Epistle of Paul to Titus* in the New Testament). Religious defenders of slavery most frequently invoked the so-called "curse of Ham" to justify the institution. Noah, angry at his son, Ham, cast out Ham's son Canaan, with the words "a slave of slaves shall he be to his brothers" (from *Genesis*). The story is open to many interpretations, but it remained central to the biblical defense of slavery.

The "Mudsill Theory"　"底梁理论"

Some southern defenders of slavery argued that civilization—in the ancient world as well as in the contemporary South—depended on slavery. For civilization to flourish, it was necessary for a lower class of people to do the menial work so that a higher class could engage in more elevated pursuits. This lower class—in the case of the antebellum South, slaves—was analogous to the mudsill of a grand house. The mudsill was the lowest threshold of a building, which supported the foundation. This theory was popularized by South Carolina senator James Henry Hammond in a speech in 1858. He cautioned that a class of poor landless people could threaten social harmony and undermine civilization.

> ## A DIVIDED CONGRESS　分裂的国会
>
> In the antebellum period, the Senate tended to be friendlier to the slave system than the House. The southern states had more power in the Senate than they did in the population-based House.

C. A TEMPORARY TRUCE ON THE SLAVERY QUESTION　在奴隶制问题上的暂时休战

The most divisive regional issue in the first half of the nineteenth century was slavery. The Missouri Compromise (1820) created a temporary, uneasy truce over slavery in new territories. As the United States gained additional territories, this truce broke down.

The Missouri Compromise　密苏里妥协案

The "Era of Good Feelings" (1816–1825) was not free of disagreements and sectional competition. The issue of slavery, which most politicians sought to avoid, emerged in 1820. Controversy arose between the slave-holding states and the free states in 1820 when Missouri applied for statehood as a slave state. At the time, there were 11 slave states and 11 free states. The admission of Missouri would have upset that balance. A compromise was reached to maintain the balance between free and slave states by allowing for the admission of two new states— Missouri as a slave state and Maine as a free state. The Missouri Compromise also divided the remaining area of the Louisiana Territory at 36°30' north latitude. Above that line, slavery was not permitted (except for in Missouri); below the line, it was permitted. Throughout the coming decades, as white Americans continued to expand into the territories of the West, debates over the slavery question would continue to roil the nation.

The "Gag Rule" in the House of Representatives   众议院的"标签规则"

The issue of slavery became especially divisive in the House of Representatives. Beginning in the 1830s, abolitionists agitated to have antislavery resolutions introduced and debated on the floor of the House. Representative John Quincy Adams (who was elected to the House after his tenure as president) was a key House figure in attempting to bring such resolutions to the floor. In response, southern politicians successfully pushed for a series of resolutions that would automatically "table" any such resolutions, preventing them from being read or debated. Such "gag rules" were in effect in the House from 1836 to 1844.

ADAMS'S POST-PRESIDENCY
卸任总统后的亚当斯

Most presidents have rather dull retirements. John Quincy Adams did not. He is the only former president to serve in the House of Representatives. He became an outspoken critic of slavery. Other presidents with meaningful careers after their terms in office are William Howard Taft, who became chief justice of the Supreme Court, and Jimmy Carter, who has been active in Habitat for Humanity and international issues of war and peace.

Annexation of Texas and the Politics of Slavery   兼并德克萨斯与奴隶制政治

Many Texans were eager for their "Lone Star Republic," as the Republic of Texas was known, to join the United States; one of the first official acts of the Texas president was to send a delegation to Washington to offer to join the United States. Democratic President Andrew Jackson, however, not wanting to add to sectional tensions by admitting a large slave state, blocked annexation. His successors likewise did not want to open the contentious debate that would accompany Texas annexation. Presidents Martin Van Buren (1837–1841), William Henry Harrison (1841), and John Tyler (1841–1845) all avoided the issue.

The Election of 1844 and the Annexation of Texas   1844年的选举与兼并德克萨斯

The election of 1844 put the issue of Texas annexation on the national agenda. Democratic candidate James K. Polk promised to push for Texas annexation as well as for a resolution to a border dispute with Great Britain over Oregon (see page 158), offering something to both southern and northern voters. By 1844, the Democrats were clearly emerging as more expansionistic and more proslavery than the Whigs. Polk defeated the incumbent president, John Tyler. Even before Polk took office, the outgoing President Tyler saw Polk's victory as a mandate for Texas annexation and pushed it through Congress. Texas joined the United States as the 15th slave state in 1844. The issues raised by the annexation of Texas would reemerge in the aftermath of the Mexican-American War and assume a prominent place in the political schisms of the 1850s.

COMPETING MOTIVATIONS 不同的动机

Be aware of the variety of motivations that drew people to the West: Some were small farmers inspired by the "free soil" ideal; some were drawn to Texas to find a place as slave-owning cotton growers; some were part of the Mormon exodus to Utah; some were gold seekers drawn to California.

SUBJECT TO DEBATE 相关讨论

Historians have debated the nature of the "Era of Good Feelings." Consensus historians—those who deemphasize divisions in American history and focus on national commonalities—look to the era as a golden age of cooperation and growth. Other historians have noted the beginnings of divisions over the issue of slavery. These divisions were evident in the debates over the Missouri Compromise. Some historians have focused on class divisions that began to emerge in the United States as the old master–apprentice system gave way to the wage-labor system that came to dominate the economy by the post–Civil War period.

President Andrew Jackson has been a frequent topic of essay questions on the AP exam; an understanding of how he has been remembered will be useful in discussions of the period. In the latter part of the nineteenth century, he was scoffed at in historical literature. Historians of the era came from the elite classes of New England. To them, Jackson seemed boorish, arrogant, ignorant, and authoritarian. By the early twentieth century, Progressive-era historians influenced by Frederick Jackson Turner's frontier thesis looked more favorably upon Jackson. Turner saw the experience of the frontier as central to the shaping of the American character. The image of frontier pioneers became part of popular culture just as Americans were becoming more urban and more settled. Americans developed a sense of nostalgia for the pioneers, as is evident in the popularity of Laura Ingalls Wilder's *Little House on the Prairie* novels. In this cultural moment, Jackson was rehabilitated. He was seen as a man of the pioneer era who brought that democratic, frontier spirit with him to the White House.

More recently, the historical memory of Jackson has again taken a turn for the worse. From the 1960s onward, historians have drawn unfavorable parallels between Jackson's expansionistic impulses and American foreign adventures abroad, from Vietnam to Iraq. Further, since the 1970s many Americans have become more attuned to the historical suffering of American Indians. In this context, the Indian Removal Act and the "Trail of Tears" began to loom large in the historical memory of the Jackson administration.

The economic and social transformations of the antebellum period have become important topics in historical work recently. Social historians have become more interested in the lives of workers, women, American Indians, families on the frontier, and slaves than in the policies and acts of presidents. These social historians, active in the field since the 1970s, have done much to topple the "great, white men" from their pedestals in the historical field. In place of laws, speeches, and treaties, social historians look at letters, diaries, census records, and court records to get a better sense of what life was like for ordinary Americans. This is not to say that political history is no longer relevant or important; it is, both in the history field at large and on the AP exam. However, do not ignore the advances made in the field of social history. Be aware of the important social groups of each era and the impact they had on history.

Historians have disagreed over the nature of the reform movements in the antebellum period. Some have focused on the democratic and egalitarian impulses of the movement. The women's-rights movement and the abolitionist movement certainly were attempts to push America in a more democratic direction. However, other historians have focused on the more judgmental, restrictive nature of reform movements. One can see some of the Puritan dogma still present in the antebellum period. The temperance movement reflects the more restrictive aspect of reform movements. The push for public education can be seen in both lights. On the one hand, it embodies the democratic spirit of providing free education to all—a prerequisite for meaningful participation in the democratic process. At the same time, the lessons and the rote learning were meant to reinforce a rigid set of middle-class Protestant values.

History textbooks implicitly grapple with a major issue of interpretation—how the expansion of the United States should be discussed. Territorial expansion at the expense of indigenous peoples and neighboring nations would, if carried out elsewhere, earn the disfavor of textbook writers. These books, for instance, might discuss the arrogance of Napoleon's actions or the brutality of Japanese expansion in Asia in the 1930s. By contrast, the era of Manifest Destiny is often shrouded in the language of idealism, democracy, adventure, and optimism. Perhaps this is understandable, but historical interpretation, to be taken seriously, should try to maintain fair and consistent criteria in evaluating parallel actions committed by different nations.

PRACTICE MULTIPLE-CHOICE QUESTIONS　选择题练习

> **Directions:** Pick the letter that best answers the following questions.

Questions 1–3 refer to the following passage: 根据以下段落，回答第1—3题

"From whence originated the idea, that it was derogatory to a lady's dignity, or a blot upon the female character, to labor? and who was the first to say, sneeringly, 'Oh, she works for a living'? Surely, such ideas and expressions ought not to grow on republican soil. The time has been, when ladies of the first rank were accustomed to busy themselves in domestic employment.

"Homer tells us of princesses who used to draw water from the springs, and wash with their own hands the finest of the linen of their respective families. The famous Lucretia used to spin in the midst of her attendants; and the wife of Ulysses, after the siege of Troy, employed herself in weaving, until her husband returned to Ithaca. And in later times, the wife of George the Third of England, has been represented as spending a whole evening in hemming pocket-handkerchiefs, while her daughter Mary sat in the corner, darning stockings.

"Few American fortunes will support a woman who is above the calls of her family; and a man of sense, in choosing a companion to jog with him through all the up-hills and down-hills of life, would sooner choose one who had to work for a living, than one who thought it beneath her to soil her pretty hands with manual labor, although she possessed her thousands. To be able to earn one's own living by laboring with the hands, should be reckoned among female accomplishments; and I hope the time is not far distant when none of my countrywomen will be ashamed to have it known that they are better versed in useful, than they are in ornamental accomplishments."

—"Dignity of Labor," *The Lowell* [Massachusetts] *Offering*, 1842

1. The essay from the *Lowell Offering*, quoted above, describes the physical labors performed by important women—princesses in the time of Homer, the Roman noblewoman Lucretia, the wife of Ulysses, and the daughter of King George III of Great Britain—in order to

   (A) demonstrate the long history of women being treated as second-class citizens.
   (B) assure poor women that hard work and dedication were the keys to advancement to a higher status.
   (C) differentiate the emerging American culture from the corrupt traditions of Europe.
   (D) convince middle-class men and women that they should not look down upon women performing physical work.

2. The contributors to the *Lowell Offering* were

   (A) New England abolitionists who participated in the Second Great Awakening.
   (B) "factory operatives" at the textile mills in Lowell, Massachusetts, during the early stages of American industrialization.
   (C) Transcendentalist writers who lived at the Brook Farm utopian community.
   (D) African-American women who gained their freedom following the gradual elimination of slavery in Massachusetts.

3. The reading from the *Lowell Offering* reflects which of the following historical developments?

   (A) The popularity of the "Arts and Crafts" movement, which sought to revive traditional artisan techniques.
   (B) The cultural shift that allowed for women to replace men in offices, as typists, accountants, and receptionists.
   (C) The increasing number of Americans who made their living producing goods for national and foreign markets rather than relying on semi-subsistence agriculture.
   (D) The movement to encourage society to see women's work in the home as actual labor that contributed to the social good.

Questions 4–6 are based on the following image: 根据下图，回答第4—6题

—Lithograph of the Cherokee tribal member George Guess (also known as Sequoyah), 1828

4. The image above of the Cherokee tribal member George Guess (also known as Sequoyah) demonstrates

   (A) the desire of the Cherokees to establish an independent nation in the southern portion of the United States.
   (B) the resistance of Cherokees to laws prohibiting the establishment of schools on Cherokee lands.
   (C) the revival of traditional spiritual practices among members of the Cherokee nation.
   (D) the push by many Cherokee leaders to embrace white culture and to become full members of the new American nation.

5. In the decade following the publication of the image, above, Cherokee Indians

   (A) were relocated to "Indian Territory" in the West.
   (B) established long-lasting reservations in Georgia.
   (C) were wiped out by disease and warfare.
   (D) lost their recognition as a federally protected tribe.

6. The Cherokee Indians received the strongest support in the 1830s from

   (A) President Andrew Jackson.
   (B) the United States Supreme Court.
   (C) the United States Congress.
   (D) the legislature of the state of Georgia.

"When the day of election approaches, visit your constituents far and wide. Treat liberally, and drink freely, in order to rise in their estimation, though you fall in your own. True, you may be called a drunken dog by some of the clean-shirt and silk-stocking gentry, but the real roughnecks will style you a jovial fellow. Their votes are certain, and frequently count double.

"Do all you can to appear to advantage in the eyes of the women. That's easily done. You have but to kiss and slabber their children, wipe their noses, and pat them on the head. This cannot fail to please their mothers, and you may rely on your business being done in that quarter.

"Promise all that is asked, said I, and more if you can think of anything. Offer to build a bridge or a church, to divide a county, create a batch of new offices, make a turnpike, or anything they like. Promises cost nothing; therefore, deny nobody who has a vote or sufficient influence to obtain one.

"Get up on all occasions, and sometimes on no occasion at all, and make long-winded speeches, though composed of nothing else than wind. Talk of your devotion to country, your modesty and disinterestedness, or any such fanciful subject. Rail against taxes of all kinds, officeholders, and bad harvest weather; and wind up with a flourish about the heroes who fought and bled for our liberties in the times that tried men's souls."

—Robert Penn Smith (writing as David Crockett),
Colonel Crockett's Exploits and Adventures in Texas, 1837

7. Which of the following developments from the 1820s and 1830s is illustrated by the reading, above?

   (A) Demographic shifts were giving middle-class, literate voters increased power in determining the direction of national politics.
   (B) As larger numbers of citizens participated in the electoral process, the nature of political campaigning changed.
   (C) Reform-minded political leaders played an increasingly important role in national political campaigns.
   (D) Military heroes played a larger role in politics, while lawyers and statesmen played a diminished role in electoral politics.

8. Which of the following describes an important reason for the trend illustrated by the above passage?

   (A) Naturalization laws were changed, reducing the amount of time it took for immigrants to attain citizenship.
   (B) Several important states extended voting rights to women.
   (C) Civil rights legislation paved the way for large numbers of free African Americans to vote.
   (D) Most states reduced or eliminated property qualifications for voting.

9. The political shifts, evident in the reading, were especially beneficial to

   (A) the Jacksonian Democrats.

   (B) temperance reformers.

   (C) women's suffragists.

   (D) New England Federalists.

Answers and Explanations to Multiple-Choice Questions
选择题的答案与解析

1. **(D)** The main point of the essay in the *Lowell Offering* is that there is dignity in productive work. The writer is citing the long history of important women performing physical tasks in order to convince middle-class men and women that there is nothing inappropriate about women working. Many members of the middle class subscribed to a set of cultural ideas known as the "cult of domesticity," which insisted that women keep a proper, Christian home—separate from the male sphere of politics, business, and competition. This ideal discouraged women from participating in public life.

2. **(B)** The contributors to the *Lowell Offering* were "factory operatives" at the textile mills in Lowell, Massachusetts, during the early stages of industry in the United States. Starting in 1821 a series of textiles mills were built in Lowell, drawing in young women from the New England countryside to operate the machines. It was thought that these women could be paid less and would only be temporary factory operatives. The era of mass migration from Europe had not yet begun, so it was difficult to recruit male factory operatives. By 1830, eight mills employed more than 6,000 women.

3. **(C)** The reading from the *Lowell Offering* reflects the increasing number of women, as well as men, who were making the transition from semi-subsistence agriculture to production for distant markets. This was a key aspect of the market revolution. Although much of this work was done in factories, many people performed piecework at home as part of the "putting-out system," in which men and women would perform a particular task as part of a larger operation—such as making shoes or small firearms.

4. **(D)** The image of the Cherokee tribal member George Guess (also known as Sequoyah) demonstrates the push by many Cherokee leaders to embrace white culture and to become full members of the new American nation. Guess was the inventor of the Cherokee alphabet. He was born in Taskigi, Tennessee, around 1760. He was the son of a white man and a Cherokee woman. Sequoyah is pictured in western-style dress, demonstrating the teaching of the Cherokee alphabet.

5. **(A)** Despite the efforts of the Cherokee to adapt to the cultural norms of white society, state and federal authorities took action in the 1830s to remove the Cherokee and other tribes from the South, relocating them to areas labeled "Indian Territory" in the West (primarily in the future Oklahoma). President Andrew Jackson pushed for passage of the Indian Removal Act (1830). It took several years of political and legal maneuvering, but the Indian Removal Act was eventually implemented during the presidency of Jackson's successor, Martin Van Buren. The Cherokee, unlike the other affected tribes, resisted the pressure to sign a treaty that would cede their ancestral lands. The result of their resistance was their forcible removal, leading to the deaths of thousands of Cherokee, in an episode known as the "Trail of Tears."

6. **(B)** The Cherokee received their strongest support in the 1830s from the United States Supreme Court. Before their forced removal to the West, the Cherokee won a short reprieve from the Supreme Court decision in *Worcester v. Georgia* (1832), which recognized the Cherokee people as a nation within the state of Georgia and ruled that they would not be subject to the Indian Removal Act. However, the state of Georgia, with the support of the federal government, began moving them to the West anyway.

7. **(B)** The reading illustrates the fact that as larger numbers of citizens participated in the electoral process, the nature of political campaigning changed. Politics became less about ideas and character and more about appearances and personality. "Crockett" humorously puts forth a formula for winning elections in this changed environment, from kissing babies to making empty promises.

8. **(D)** A primary reason for the increase in the electorate in the 1820s and 1830s was that most states reduced or eliminated property qualifications for voting. Previously, voting was restricted to property owners, effectively excluding poor and working-class men from the political process.

9. **(A)** The political shifts evident in the reading were especially beneficial to the Jacksonian Democrats. In the 1820s and 1830s, most states reduced or removed property qualifications for voting so that most free males had the right to vote. This change helped Jackson win the presidential election in 1828. His humble origins appealed to the newly enfranchised working man.

Period 5: 1844–1877 Slavery, Civil War, and the Transformation of American Society

第五个时期（1844—1877）：奴隶制、内战与美国社会的转变

7

INTRODUCTION 简介

As the United States expanded its borders, economy, and population, sectional tensions—most notably over slavery—led to a civil war. The war and its aftermath dramatically transformed American society.

The acquisition and settlement of new territories in the western half of the North American continent opened up a question that politicians had sought to avoid—should these new territories allow slavery? Most northern politicians were not abolitionists; indeed, abolitionism was a minority position in the North in 1850. However, the issue of the expansion of slavery became increasingly divisive in the 1850s. Some northerners adopted the free-soil ideology—the idea that lands out West should be open to small-scale farming, without competition from large-scale plantation agriculture using slave labor. By the end of the decade, more northerners were grappling with the moral issues around slavery. Positions became decidedly more entrenched on the eve of the Civil War.

The importance of the Civil War to American history cannot be overstated. This bloody war settled one of the most vexing issues in American history—the existence of slavery in an otherwise democratic country—and opened up space for broad debates about the substance of democracy in post–Civil War America.

KEY CONCEPT 5.1: THE UNITED STATES AND GLOBAL CONNECTIONS 核心概念5.1：美国与全球联系

The United States became more connected with the world during the period immediately before and after the Civil War. The country pursued an expansionistic foreign policy within the Western Hemisphere while also becoming a primary destination for immigrants from other countries.

I. Territorial Expansion Shapes the National Debate
领土扩张形成了民族争论

The drive for the United States to expand westward had several causes. Many Americans came to believe that the economic growth and security of the United States depended on expansion. In addition, the drive to expand was fueled by a set of beliefs around race and culture that saw nonwhites in an inferior light. The desire for more territory resulted in war, new markets, the acquisition of territory stretching to the Pacific Ocean, major migrations of people to the West, and new overseas initiatives.

A. WESTWARD MIGRATIONS 西进运动

Many Americans migrated to the West during the period leading up to the Civil War. These migrants were driven by a variety of factors including economic opportunities in the West, the desire for raw materials, and religious persecution in the East.

Americans Respond to the Call of "Manifest Destiny" 美国对"命定扩张论"的反应

Many Americans came to believe that it was the "manifest destiny" of the United States to expand westward and extend its power in the Western Hemisphere. Manifest destiny refers to the movement of individuals to the West, but it also alludes to the political extension of United States territory. The term *manifest destiny* was coined in an 1845 newspaper article by John O'Sullivan. It captured the fervor of the westward expansion movement, implying that it was God's plan that the United States take over and settle the entire continent. The idea of manifest destiny shaped many of the political debates of the era. Americans who did settle out West were probably driven more by economic factors, such as cheap land or precious metals, than they were by a desire to fulfill a divine plan.

Overland Trails 陆路轨迹

Migrants to the West traveled along one of several overland routes. The most famous was the Oregon Trail, a 2,000-mile route from Missouri to the Pacific Northwest (see more on the settlement of the Oregon Territory in Period 4). Other trails included the Santa Fe Trail, which followed a more southern route, from Missouri to New Mexico, and the California Trail, which branched off from the Oregon Trail. It is estimated that about 300,000 people traveled these trails, usually in wagon trains, between 1840 and the Civil War. While stories of death and desperation on these treks capture the public imagination, an accurate account of the risks involved is more difficult to come by. The story of the Donner Party (1846–1847) is frequently repeated. A wagon train of 87 California-bound migrants became snowbound in the Sierra-Nevada mountains over the winter. Only 48 were rescued, with some of the survivors having resorted to cannibalism. Historians note, however, that the death rate on these trails was only slightly higher than for Americans in general at the time. They explain that American Indians were far more likely to work for the migrants as guides and to engage in trade with them than they were to ambush them.

The California Gold Rush 加利福尼亚淘金热

Discoveries of mineral resources in the West were a powerful draw on westward migration. The various discoveries of gold and silver from 1848 until the 1880s led to a repeated pattern of rushes, boomtowns, and economic consolidation, as lone prospectors and crowds of fortune seekers gave way to industrial-mining operations (see more on the mining frontier in Period 6). The most significant strike of precious metals in the antebellum period was at Sutter's Mill in Coloma, California, in 1848. That year, California became a United States territory, acquired as a result of the Mexican War (see page 175). As word spread, thousands of people came to California to try to strike it rich in this first Gold Rush. A large percentage of the 300,000 people who migrated to California came in 1849, thus their nickname, "Forty-niners." A few people did strike it rich. However, very soon, the easily accessible gold was panned from riverbeds. To get access to gold beneath the surface, capital-intensive methods were required. This expensive machinery was beyond the reach of ordinary prospectors.

The Mormon Exodus 摩门教的大迁徙

In 1847, the Church of Jesus Christ of the Latter-Day Saints, the religious group known as the Mormons, settled along the banks of the Great Salt Lake in Utah (see more on the origins of Mormonism in Period 4). The land at the time was Mexican territory. When the Mormons arrived, the Mexican War had already begun. After the United States victory in the war (1848), Utah and the remainder of the Mexican Cession became United States territory. The Mormons ended up in Utah after suffering persecution in more populated areas.

B. THE IDEOLOGICAL FOUNDATIONS OF MANIFEST DESTINY 命定扩张论的思想基础

The spirit of manifest destiny grew out of several important beliefs that were held by many Americans in the antebellum period.

Manifest Destiny and Race 命定扩张论与种族

In many ways, the ideology of Manifest Destiny reinforced contemporary notions of race. Americans had come to believe that the variety of peoples who inhabited the North American continent—Mexicans, American Indians, African Americans—were incapable of establishing or participating in democratic, efficient governance. This racial justification for westward expansion, which developed in the decades after 1810, drew on several sources. European Romanticism, which became increasingly influential in these decades (see Period 4), put more emphasis on uniqueness and individual difference. This focus on difference represents a break from the Enlightenment thinking that animated many of the founding generation of Americans. Earlier Enlightenment thinking embodied a more benevolent outlook, stressing universal principles and a common humanity. In addition, there was a rise in scientific racialism in the early 1800s. This idea held that "races" were fundamentally different from one another and that the Anglo Saxon race was superior to non-whites. The movement westward was seen as proof of the superiority of the so-called Anglo-Saxon race over the "savage tribes" of the West.

The Spread of Democratic Civilization 民主文明的传播

In addition to using racial theories, many Americans justified manifest destiny by asserting the superiority of American institutions and practices. These Americans cited the strong tradition of democratic practices in the United States. The conquest of Mexico was seen as a victory by liberty-loving Protestants over tyrannical and anti-republican Catholics.

C. THE MEXICAN WAR AND WESTWARD EXPANSION 墨西哥战争与西进运动

The Mexican-American War resulted in the United States gaining a large part of northern Mexico. Debates over the status of slavery, American Indians, and Mexicans in these newly acquired lands became heated in the years following the war.

War with Mexico 与墨西哥的战争

The immediate cause of the Mexican-American War was a border dispute. Mexico and the United States disagreed over the southern border of the new United States territory of Texas. Texas had recently (1844) been annexed by the United States (see Period 4). Mexico said the border was at the Nueces River. The United States insisted it was at the Rio Grande, 150 miles to the south. In 1846, skirmishes in the disputed area led to war between Mexico and the United States.

Victory over Mexico on the Battlefield 战胜墨西哥

The United States won several early battles. One prong of the invasion, in the area of Mexico south of Texas, was led by General Zachary Taylor. U.S. forces also won victories in present-day California. However, Mexico was determined not to part with its northern provinces after having lost Texas. It took an all-out attack on the Mexican capital, Mexico City, led by General Winfield Scott, to force the Mexican government to capitulate.

The Treaty of Guadalupe Hidalgo 《瓜达卢佩·伊达尔戈条约》

In 1848, the Mexican government signed the Treaty of Guadalupe Hidalgo, giving up its claims to the disputed territory in Texas and agreeing to sell the provinces of California and New Mexico, known as the Mexican Cession, to the United States for $15 million. This territory includes present-day California, Nevada, Utah, and parts of Arizona, New Mexico, Colorado, and Wyoming.

Gadsden Purchase 加兹登购地案

The final land acquisition in what would become the continental United States was the Gadsden Purchase, acquired from Mexico in 1853, five years after the Mexican War. It added an additional area to the vast swath of land obtained by the United States following the war. The Gadsden Purchase was sought by the United States as a possible southern route for a transcontinental railroad.

The Acquisition of the Mexican Cession and the Slavery Question

墨西哥割让土地与奴隶制问题

The Treaty of Guadalupe Hidalgo (1848) granted the United States a huge portion of Mexico for a mere $15 million. Very soon after, gold was discovered in California, leading to a rapid and substantial growth in the population. The question of whether the newly acquired territories would be admitted as free or slave states became a pressing issue in the years following the war. The Wilmot Proviso (introduced in 1846), banning slavery from the Mexican Cession, never became law (see page 182). The question of whether slavery would exist in the newly acquired territories continued to generate national controversy in the 1850s (see page 183).

D. GOVERNMENT PROMOTION OF WESTERN EXPANSION　政府推进西进运动

Groups and individuals were migrating to the West before the Civil War with little encouragement from the government. During and after the Civil War, the government passed legislation to promote Western transportation and development. With the Democrats absent from Congress during the war, the Republicans had a free hand to implement legislation that would further their vision of the United States. Congress passed the Homestead Act, the Morrill Land Grant Act, and the Pacific Railroad Act, all in 1862. These acts helped implement the "free labor" ideology of the Republican Party.

The Morrill Land Grant Act　《莫里尔土地赠与法案》

The Morrill Land Grant Act (1862) promoted secondary public education, primarily in the West. Under the act, the federal government transferred substantial tracts of its lands to the states. The states could build public colleges on these lands or they could sell the land to fund the building of educational facilities. The land-grant colleges in the West were designed to train and educate the next generations of western residents.

The Pacific Railroad Act　《太平洋铁路法案》

The Pacific Railroad Act (1862) and supplementary acts passed in the 1860s extended government bonds and tracts of land to companies engaged in building transcontinental railroads. These acts ended up granting 130 million acres of federally held land to railroad companies. Individual states sweetened the pot for railroad construction by extending another 50 million acres to railroad companies.

The Homestead Act　《宅地法案》

The government encouraged development of the West by passing the Homestead Act (1862), which provided free land in the region to settlers who were willing to farm it. The Homestead Act reflected the "free labor" ideal of the Republicans. With the absence of Democrats from Congress during the Civil War, the Republican Party was able to pass several pieces of legislation that reflected their vision of America. Hundreds of thousands of people applied for and were granted homesteads. Many of these homesteaders did not have extensive farming skills and went bankrupt. Increasingly, by the late 1800s, it became difficult for small farmers, even competent ones, to compete with large-scale agricultural operations.

E. ECONOMIC EXPANSION BEYOND THE WESTERN HEMISPHERE: THE UNITED STATES AND ASIA　西半球外的经济扩张：美国与亚洲

American economic interests included opening up trade to Asia. The United States initiated economic, cultural, and diplomatic ventures toward this end.

Opening Trade with Japan　对日本开放贸易

With the growth of the economy and the development of West Coast ports, the United States became increasingly interested in trading with Japan. The Tokugawa shogunate (1600–1868) had virtually isolated Japan from Western countries since the seventeenth century. It had allowed for limited trade with the Netherlands and with China. The Tokugawa government repeatedly resisted, occasionally by force, attempts by Americans and Europeans to establish business and diplomatic ties. The United States was determined to alter this policy and open

Japan to American trade. With a letter from President Millard Fillmore, Commodore Matthew C. Perry led a naval expedition to Japan. The first journey was in 1852–1853, and a second was made in 1854. Perry, through vague threats and skillful diplomacy, was able to secure a treaty with Japan that opened Japan up to American trade.

II. Expansion, Migrations, and Citizenship in the 1840s and 1850s
19世纪40年代和50年代的扩张、移民与公民身份

The United States experienced profound transformations in the 1840s and 1850s as a result of westward expansion and new migration patterns. As the boundaries of the nation were reshaped, conflicts ensued over the cultural identity of the nation. Americans debated questions of citizenship and rights for various groups of U.S. inhabitants.

A. IMMIGRATION INTO THE UNITED STATES 向美国移民

Large numbers of immigrants, mainly Irish and German, entered the United States before the Civil War. Many of these groups lived in ethnic communities and retained the religions, languages, and customs of the Old World. In response, many Americans developed antagonistic feelings toward new immigrant groups and attempted to limit their rights and their cultural influence.

Irish Immigration and the Five Points 爱尔兰移民与五要点

Large-scale immigration from Ireland in the antebellum period transformed American cities and contributed to a strong nativist movement (see more on the Irish migration in Period 4). The largest destination for Irish immigrants in the United States was the Five Points neighborhood of New York City. It was one of the most desperate urban slums in the western world in the mid-nineteenth century, comparable to London's East End. The neighborhood was certainly the worst in the United States in terms of density, disease, infant and child mortality, unemployment, prostitution, and violent crime. At the same time, the Five Points could be seen as the original American melting pot, combining elements of the African-American community (especially as slavery gradually ended in New York in the period up to 1827) and the Irish community. Irish immigrants and African Americans, and smaller numbers of other immigrant groups, worked side-by-side, lived in the same boarding houses, intermarried, and danced and sang together at dancehalls and saloons. Intermarriages were prevalent enough that the census added the category "mulatto" to the 1850 census. At the same time, tensions existed between the two groups. These tensions came to the surface in the draft riots during the Civil War (see page 188). This cultural race-mixing, combined with bitter racism, became an important element of American identity into the twentieth century.

B. ANTI-IMMIGRANT SENTIMENT IN THE ANTEBELLUM PERIOD 内战前的反移民情绪

A strong anti-Catholic nativist movement developed in the United States. The main goal of this movement was to limit the power and influence of newly arrived immigrants.

Nativism 排外主义

The first half of the nineteenth century witnessed a dramatic increase in immigration from Europe, as well as a strong xenophobic nativist movement. Nativism was both an emotional impulse as well as an organized movement. Many Americans thought that the new immigrants, who were mostly non-Protestant, lacked the self-control of "proper," middle-class

Protestant Americans. For nativists, this lack of self-control was evident in the drinking habits of immigrants. Nativists tried to regulate and weaken the drinking culture of immigrant communities, which manifested itself in Irish pubs and German beer halls.

The "Know-Nothings" "无知党"

The defining issue of the Know-Nothing Party was opposition to immigration. The party was the political wing of a growing anti-Catholic, anti-Irish movement that gained traction in the wake of the large-scale Irish immigration of the late 1840s and 1850s. The Know-Nothing Party (formally known as the American Party) emerged in the 1840s and, by the 1850s, had achieved electoral success in several states, especially in the Northeast.

NATIVISM OVER TIME   不同时期的排外主义

Anti-immigrant sentiment has surfaced several times in American history, usually targeting the most recent immigrant group: Irish immigrants in the 1840s and 1850s; Chinese immigrants in the 1880s; the "new immigrants" of eastern and southern Europe at the turn of the twentieth century; and Latino immigrants in the twenty-first century.

C. EXPANSION AND CONFLICT ON THE FRONTIER   边界的扩张与冲突

Western expansion led to conflicts on the frontier with American Indians and with Hispanics. As the boundaries of the United States changed, and as migrants pushed west, conflicts ensued over the control of land. These conflicts played an important role in changing the cultures and lifeways of the groups involved. Finally, questions emerged about the legal status of these groups.

Expansion and Violence on the Frontier   边界的扩张与暴力

The period between the 1850s and the turn of the twentieth century saw the last large-scale military conflicts between the United States and American Indian groups. These wars resulted in defeat for the Indians, as the last autonomous native groups came under the control of the U.S. government. By the 1850s, settlers were pushing beyond the Mississippi River in large numbers. Many were headed to the West Coast, following the annexation of the lush agricultural lands of the Oregon territory (1848) and the discovery of gold in California (1848). However, the trails west went right through Indian lands, creating tension and conflict.

The Treaty of Fort Laramie   《拉勒米堡条约》

In 1851, the United States government and more than ten thousand Plains Indians convened in Fort Laramie, in Wyoming, and came to an agreement that called for the Indians to provide a corridor for the passage of wagon trains to the Far West. In exchange, the U.S. government promised that the remaining Indian lands in the West would not be encroached upon.

The Great Sioux Uprising (1862)   伟大的苏族起义（1862）

White settlers refused to honor the Treaty of Fort Laramie. In 1862, Sioux Indians, led by Chief Little Crow, challenged white encroachments onto their lands. The Sioux ended up killing more than a thousand settlers before being defeated by the military.

The Sand Creek Massacre (1864) 沙河大屠杀（1864）

In 1864, Colonel John M. Chivington led an attack by a Colorado militia company upon a peaceful Cheyenne village, killing 270, mostly women and children. Chivington ignored the villagers' surrender flags.

American Indians in the Mexican Cession 墨西哥割让地的美洲印第安人

In the aftermath of the Mexican-American War (1846–1848), the settlement of white Americans in California had devastating effects for Indian peoples. The Indian population of California dropped from about 150,000 in 1848, on the eve of the gold rush, to less than 30,000 by the beginning of the Civil War (see more on the gold rush, page 173). California Indians were often falsely portrayed as degenerate, primitive, and idle. Disease took the lives of thousands, but systematic campaigns of extermination by white settlers against the native peoples of California contributed to what many historians label a genocide. In 1853 the federal government greatly reduced the size of reservations set aside for Indians in California. In addition, farmers were eager to exploit the labor of Indians. When the framers of the California constitution prohibited slavery, they had black slavery, not Indian slavery, in mind. As the 1850s progressed, thousands of Indians were either murdered or enslaved. The Yuki people of Round Valley in northern California were viciously targeted; their population fell from over 5,000 in 1854 to approximately 300 a decade later. Several Indian groups simply ceased to exist, with their people either killed or dispersed.

KEY CONCEPT 5.2 EXPANSION, SECTIONAL DIVISIONS, AND CIVIL WAR 核心概念5.2：扩张、地区分化与内战

The debate over slavery intensified as America expanded its boundaries westward. This debate, coupled with sectional divisions over economic, political, and cultural issues, contributed to the onset of the Civil War.

I. Increased Sectional Divisions in the 1840s and 1850s
19世纪40年代和50年代日益加剧的地区分化

Sectional divisions between the North and the South intensified in the decade leading up to the Civil War. These divisions resulted from the ideological debates around slavery, along with regional economic and demographic changes. The status of slavery in new territories brought these debates to the surface.

A. ECONOMIC DIFFERENCES BETWEEN THE NORTH AND THE SOUTH
北方与南方的经济差异

The economies of the North and South were moving in different directions in the period leading up to the Civil War. The economy of the North was increasingly focused on a free-labor model, with manufacturing industries at its base; the economy of the South was increasingly dependent on a slave-labor, agricultural economy. The population of the North grew rapidly during this period while the South's population growth was slow.

B. ABOLITIONISM IN THE 1850S—STRATEGIES AND TACTICS
19世纪50年代的废奴主义——战略与策略

The abolitionist campaign became increasingly visible and vocal in the 1850s. Abolitionists debated the most effective strategies and tactics. Some relied on the written word and forceful arguments against the institution of slavery. Others helped fugitive slaves make their way north. A small minority advocated using violence to achieve their goals.

The Fugitive Slave Act and Personal Liberty Laws 《逃奴法案》与《人身自由法》

Many northerners grew alarmed at the enforcement of the Fugitive Slave Act. Previously, the majority of northerners could ignore the brutality of the slave system, but following 1850, slave catchers brought the system to the streets of northern cities. In response, many northern states passed "personal liberty laws" offering protection to fugitives. Many whites and free African Americans in northern cities even formed vigilance committees to prevent the slave catchers from carrying out their orders. The Supreme Court protected slave catchers from state restrictions on their activities. In *Prigg v. Pennsylvania*, the court overturned the abduction conviction of Edward Prigg, a slave-catcher, on the grounds that federal law—the Constitution itself and the Fugitive Slave Law of 1793—was superior to state law. This approach was reinforced by the decision in *Ableman v. Booth* (1859). In this case, the court overturned a Wisconsin Supreme Court ruling. The Wisconsin court had ruled that Sherman Booth, who had interfered with the carrying out of the 1850 Fugitive Slave Act, was not guilty; the court declared the act itself unconstitutional. The United States Supreme Court reversed this decision, asserting the supremacy of federal court decisions over state courts.

Uncle Tom's Cabin 《汤姆叔叔的小屋》

Sectional tensions were further enflamed by the publication in 1852 of the novel *Uncle Tom's Cabin*. The novel, written by Harriet Beecher Stowe of the antislavery Beecher family, depicted in graphic and sentimental detail, the brutality of slavery. For many northerners, slavery now had a human face. The novel outraged southern supporters of slavery, who attempted to ban it.

John Brown and the Raid on Harper's Ferry 约翰·布朗与对哈珀渡船的袭击

In the fall of 1859, John Brown carried out a raid to acquire weapons from a federal armory in Harper's Ferry, Virginia (now West Virginia)—an event that pushed North–South relations to the breaking point. Brown, with ties to many of the leading abolitionists of the day, including Frederick Douglass, recruited a small group of men to capture the armory's weapons, intending to distribute them to slaves. Brown believed this would initiate a massive slave rebellion that would cause the collapse of slavery. The men managed to capture the armory, but were soon overwhelmed by reinforcements led by future Confederate commander Robert E. Lee. Brown was tried and executed later in 1859.

Although the event did not accomplish its stated goal, its impact on history is undeniable. It convinced proslavery southerners that there was a conspiracy afoot among northerners to violently interfere with the institution of slavery. The truth of the matter was that Brown's raid was roundly condemned by most northern politicians, but the perception of a united front among northerners persisted in the South.

WAS JOHN BROWN INSANE?
约翰·布朗疯了吗?

Be careful about referring to John Brown as "crazy" or "wild" or "insane." There is no strong evidence to support such a claim. His lawyer claimed he was insane in court, but that was to prevent Brown from getting the death sentence. Brown protested his lawyer's tactics. It is safe to say that Brown was deeply religious and committed to the antislavery cause.

C. THE SOUTHERN RESPONSE TO THE SLAVERY QUESTION 南方对奴隶制问题的反应

In the decade before the Civil War, white southerners defended slavery as a "positive good." This defense of slavery was accompanied by racist stereotyping of African Americans. The defense of slavery went hand-in-hand with a defense of states' rights and the theory of nullification.

Racism and the Defense of Slavery 种族主义与对奴隶制的辩护

In the first half of the nineteenth century, the defense of slavery shifted. From the revolutionary era into the nineteenth century, white southerners often defended slavery as a "necessary evil." Thomas Jefferson likened the institution to holding "the wolf by the ear, and we can neither hold him, nor safely let him go"—acknowledging that slavery was an evil, but asserting that its end would have dire consequences. John C. Calhoun dismissed this older, negative description of slavery; he labeled such views as "folly and delusion." By the middle of the nineteenth century, southern whites, influenced by writers such as George Fitzhugh, asserted that slavery was actually a "positive good" (see Period 4). By the 1850s, these arguments proliferated and shaped cultural and religious practices in the South.

Racism and Culture 种族主义与文化

Racist ideas were also reflected in the popular culture of the time, notably in the growing popularity of minstrel shows. Minstrel shows have a long tradition in American history. They generally consisted of whites (and occasionally blacks) performing variety shows in "blackface." The shows included skits, jokes, music, singing, and dancing. Minstrel shows presented racist caricatures of African Americans as lazy, shiftless, dim-witted, and happy-go-lucky. By the 1850s, the culture of minstrelsy evolved and grew—many historians see this evolution as a conscious rebuttal to abolitionist agitation. Minstrelsy in the 1850s often featured the characters of homesick former slaves or ridiculous northern dandies. Representations of blacks became increasingly vicious—with black characters cooked or hunted or fished for. The shows were not restricted to the South—they reflected a broader sentiment among American whites when it came to race. Some white southerners actually objected to the shows because they brought the issues of race and slavery to the fore. The shows, however, remained popular throughout the country and reinforced political and social ideas about the position of African Americans in society.

By the 1840s and 1850s, southern slave-owners became increasingly interested in the religious practices of their slaves, often building churches on their plantations and mandating attendance. Christian views in the South evolved in this context. Ministers in the South might point out that the Hebrews owned slaves or that slavery was not condemned by Jesus. Further, these ministers often cited biblical passages about the importance of servants obeying their masters.

II. The Failure of Compromise and the Journey from Mistrust to Secession 妥协失败与从怀疑到分裂

Northern and southern politicians tried repeatedly to compromise on the issue of slavery in the new territories of the United States in the 1850s, but these attempts proved unsuccessful. Whatever trust existed between sectional leaders broke down by 1860. The rancorous election of 1860 resulted in the secession of the southern states.

A. WESTWARD EXPANSION AND THE SLAVE QUESTION　西进运动与奴隶制问题

As America expanded to the West, the question of whether new territories should allow slavery or not led to heated political controversies. These controversies intensified as the United States acquired additional territory in the Mexican War (see page 175).

The Wilmot Proviso　威尔莫特但书

The issue of slavery in the new territories was one of the most divisive controversies of the first half of the nineteenth century and was the catalyst that would eventually plunge the nation into civil war. Americans reached an uneasy truce on the issue with the passage of the Missouri Compromise in 1820 (see Period 4). However, the controversy came to the fore again as the United States gained additional territory following the Mexican-American War (1846–1848). Northern politicians tried, unsuccessfully, to ban slavery in territories that might be gained in the war by putting forth the Wilmot Proviso (1846). These politicians were not, for the most part, abolitionists, but they believed in the "free soil" ideal. They wanted additional land for white settlers to set up homesteads, without competition from the slave system. The proviso was passed by the House of Representatives, where politicians from the populous northern states dominated, but failed in the Senate.

The Election of 1848 and the Free-Soil Party　1848年选举与自由之土党

In the election of 1848, both the Whigs and the Democrats avoided taking strong stands on the issue of slavery. Senator Lewis Cass was the Democratic candidate, but he lost to Whig candidate Zachary Taylor, one of the heroes of the Mexican-American War. In response to the conspicuous silence on the part of the major parties on the slavery question, antislavery men in both parties founded the Free-Soil Party in 1848. The party ran candidates in the presidential elections of 1848 and 1852. It garnered only 10 percent of the vote in 1848, and only 5 percent in 1852. Many of its members later joined the Republican Party, which was founded in 1854 (see page 185).

Popular Sovereignty　人民主权论

Senator Lewis Cass proposed a compromise measure on the question of slavery in the newly acquired territories. He came up with the idea that the question of slavery should be left to the people of a particular territory. This idea became known as *popular sovereignty*, and though Congress failed to act on his idea, popular sovereignty became an important issue in the 1850s.

CUBA AND THE UNITED STATES
古巴与美国

Cuba, 90 miles off the coast of Florida, has loomed large in American diplomatic history, from the French and Indian War through the Ostend Manifesto, the Spanish-American War, and the era of Fidel Castro.

Cuba and the Ostend Manifesto　古巴与《奥斯坦德宣言》

Southern expansionists hoped to extend their slavery empire beyond the continental United States. Cuba, with its profitable sugar plantations, came into their sights in the 1850s. President James K. Polk offered to purchase the island from Spain. When Spain balked, some American adventurers unsuccessfully tried to take it by force. Later, American diplomats, sent to Belgium by pro-southern president Franklin Pierce, again tried to secretly buy Cuba. Their goals, written up as the Ostend Manifesto (1854), provoked anger from northern politicians when the document was released to the press.

B. ATTEMPTS AT COMPROMISE IN THE 1850s　19世纪50年代的妥协尝试

From 1850 until the eve of the Civil War, political leaders in the North and the South, as well as the Supreme Court, put forth a variety of proposals and plans for resolving the issue of slavery in the territories. These included the Compromise of 1850, the Kansas–Nebraska Act (1854), and the *Dred Scott* decision (1857). However, none of these moves proved to be successful in reducing sectional tensions.

California and the "Compromise" of 1850　加利福尼亚与1850年的"妥协"

In 1849, President Zachary Taylor urged California and New Mexico to apply for statehood. Both regions had antislavery majorities. California was soon ready to apply for statehood. The population of California quickly grew to more than 300,000 in the wake of the discovery of gold.

By 1850, California had enough people to form a state. Californians wrote up a constitution to submit to Congress in which slavery would be illegal. Southern senators objected to the admission of an additional free state. Senate negotiators, led by the aging Henry Clay, worked out a series of measures to resolve this extremely contentious problem. These measures became known as the Compromise of 1850. The most important elements of the compromise were the admittance of California as a free state, which pleased northern politicians, and a more stringent Fugitive Slave Law, which pleased southern politicians. Other measures included allowing New Mexico and Utah to decide the question of slavery based on popular sovereignty, accepting a new boundary between Texas and Mexico, and banning the slave trade (but not slavery) in Washington, DC. Senate negotiators put forth these measures as an omnibus bill, but it soon became clear that neither antislavery senators from the North nor proslavery "fire-eaters" from the South would vote "yes" on the Omnibus Bill. Stephen Douglas, a Democratic senator from Illinois, proposed "unbundling" the legislative package and voting each measure separately. The measures all passed, and President Millard Fillmore (who assumed the presidency in 1850 upon the death of President Zachary Taylor) signed them into law.

> ### DIVISIVENESS IN CONGRESS
> ### 国会分歧
> The lack of agreement on the 1850 "compromise" highlights the hardening of sectional tensions.

The Kansas–Nebraska Act　《堪萨斯–内布拉斯加法案》

In 1854, Senator Stephen Douglas of Illinois introduced the Kansas–Nebraska Act to the Senate. Douglas, who owned significant tracts of land in Chicago, hoped that the first transcontinental railroad would have a more northern route, using Chicago as a hub. Any railroad construction would have to be carried out in organized territory. The act called for dividing the northern section of the Louisiana Purchase territory into two organized territories, Kansas and Nebraska. The most contentious part of the act was allowing for the possibility of slavery in the territories of Kansas and Nebraska—areas that had been closed to slavery by the Missouri Compromise (1820). The act mandated that the question of slavery in these territories be decided by popular sovereignty. Many northerners were angry at the act and at Douglas.

"Bleeding Kansas"　"血溅堪萨斯"

Violence erupted in Kansas as pro-slavery and anti-slavery men fought for control of the state. In keeping with the dictates of the 1854 Kansas-Nebraska Act, elections were held for a territorial legislature in 1855. Even though only 1,500 settlers were recognized as legal voters, more than 6,000 votes were cast, as thousands of pro-slavery Missourians came over the border for the day to cast votes. In response to such a clearly fraudulent election, anti-slavery Kansans chose their own shadow legislature. Each side wrote up a constitution for Kansas. Anti-slavery men wrote up the Topeka Constitution; pro-slavery men created the Lecompton Constitution. President Franklin Pierce recognized the pro-slavery government, and called the anti-slavery government traitorous. A pro-slavery posse of Missourians, under the auspices of a federal marshal, attacked the anti-slavery town of Lawrence in May 1856.

Several days after the "sack of Lawrence," and just two days after the beating of Senator Charles Sumner in Congress (see below), John Brown a deeply religious anti-slavery activist, initiated the killing of pro-slavery men along the banks of the Pottawatomie Creek in Kansas. Brown, his sons, and several followers killed five men with swords.

Open violence continued in the Kansas Territory, on and off, for the next several years. In many respects, "Bleeding Kansas" can be seen as a dress rehearsal for the Civil War. The question of slavery in Kansas was unresolved when Lincoln was elected. After southern secession began, Kansas soon joined the Union as a free state in January, 1861.

The Beating of Senator Charles Sumner 打击参议员查尔斯·萨姆纳

The growing tensions between North and South were evident in a violent incident that occurred on the floor of the Senate in 1856. Senator Charles Sumner from Massachusetts had given a pointed antislavery speech, called "Crimes against Kansas," in which he singled out Senator Andrew P. Butler of South Carolina. Butler's nephew, a South Carolina representative named Preston Brooks, heard about the speech and attacked Sumner at his desk in the Senate chamber, beating him viciously with a heavy cane. The injuries left Sumner incapacitated for four years. Northerners saw the beating as a further sign of southern barbarity; southerners made Brooks a hero.

The *Dred Scott* Decision 德莱德·斯科特判决案

Northern and southern relations were further pushed apart by the Supreme Court decision in the case of *Dred Scott v. Sanford* (1857). The case involved the fate of a slave named Dred Scott, owned by a doctor serving in the U.S. Army. Scott and his wife, along with their owner, lived for a time in Illinois and in the Wisconsin Territories, areas where slavery had been banned by the Northwest Ordinance. Years after returning to Missouri, Scott sued for his and his wife's freedom on the grounds that they had lived for a time in free areas, and that made them free. The Supreme Court did not find Dred Scott's arguments persuasive. First, the court ruled that Scott was still a slave and did not even have the right to initiate a lawsuit. Next, the court ruled that Congress had overstepped its bounds in declaring the northern portion of the Louisiana Purchase territory off-limits to slavery. It therefore invalidated the Missouri Compromise of 1820. Finally, the decision declared that no African Americans, not even free men and women, were entitled to citizenship in the United States because, according to the court, they were "beings of an inferior order." Northerners were astounded at the sweep of the decision. *Dred Scott* seemed to

> ## WAS SLAVERY BECOMING "NATIONAL"?
> ## 奴隶制正在走向"全国"?
> Antislavery politicians wondered if slavery was becoming a "national" rather than a "sectional" institution. They worried that the Supreme Court would hamper any attempts to stop slavery's spread.

argue that slavery was a national, rather than a regional, institution and that Congress could do little to stop it.

C. THE DEATH OF THE SECOND TWO-PARTY SYSTEM 第二个两党制的灭亡

Controversies over slavery weakened the second two-party system. As the Whigs collapsed, and the Democratic Party became stronger in the South and more explicitly proslavery, sectional parties emerged, notably the Republican Party, with strength in the North and in the Midwest.

Party Realignment 政党重组

The Kansas-Nebraska Act became a lightning rod for sectional divisions. The Whigs were bitterly divided between proslavery "Cotton Whigs" and antislavery "Conscience Whigs." Meanwhile, the Democratic Party became increasingly a regional southern, proslavery party.

The Birth of the Republican Party 共和党的诞生

In 1854, the modern Republican Party was born. This party was composed of many different factions—former members of the Know-Nothing Party, "Conscience Whigs," free-soilers, abolitionists, and former Democrats, to name a few. Though the party was critical of slavery, it did not advocate abolition. Rather, it adopted the position that slavery should not be allowed to spread to the new territories.

> ## REPUBLICANS, THEN AND NOW
> ## 共和党的过去与现在
> The Republican Party, started in 1854, is the same party that exists today; however, its politics have changed considerably. The party that was born in opposition to the spread of slavery now gets less than 10 percent of the African-American vote. Since the 1920s, it has been more conservative and pro-business than the Democratic Party.

The Election of 1856 1856年选举

The election of 1856 made clear that the stability of the Democrat–Whig two-party system was over. With the Whig Party dissolved and the Know-Nothing Party divided over the slavery issue, the Republican Party emerged as a major party just two years after its birth. The Democratic Party won the election by shrewdly picking a northern candidate who had southern sympathies, James Buchanan. It was clear after the election that a new two-party system was emerging, with the Democrats and the Republicans. Though these two parties have changed dramatically in the last century and a half, they remain the two main parties.

D. THE ELECTION OF 1860 AND SECESSION 1860年选举与脱离

The presidential election of 1860, with the victory of Abraham Lincoln who espoused a free-soil platform, convinced many southern political leaders that they should take action to withdraw their states from the Union.

The Election of 1860　1860年选举

The election of 1860 demonstrated the fractured nature of the American political system on the eve of the Civil War. The Democratic Party was divided between a northern wing and a southern wing. The northern Democrats, rallying around the idea of popular sovereignty, nominated Stephen Douglas for president. Douglas carried only Missouri and part of New Jersey. The southern Democrats, who strongly endorsed slavery, carried the deep South. A third formation, the Constitutional Union, which endorsed maintaining the Union and avoided the slavery issue, won the upper South. The Republican Party chose Abraham Lincoln in 1860 as its standard bearer.

Lincoln's Electoral Victory in 1860　林肯在1860年选举中的胜利

Lincoln had served briefly as a Whig congressman from Illinois, speaking out against the war with Mexico. He ran for Senate in 1858, losing to Stephen Douglas, but impressing the public with his oratory skills. In seven debates in different parts of Illinois, Lincoln repeatedly asked Douglas whether he favored the spread of slavery. Douglas avoided the issue, putting forth popular sovereignty as a cure-all to the slavery question, and race-baiting Lincoln. Lincoln had been opposed to the institution of slavery his entire life, and had been an advocate of the American Colonization Society but, as he ran for president in 1860, he indicated that he would not nor could not tamper with slavery where it already existed. He promised, however, to block its expansion to new territories in the West. Lincoln won 40 percent of the popular vote, but carried the electoral vote, winning virtually all the states of the North, as well as California and Oregon.

Even if Lincoln kept his promise to not interfere with slavery in the slave states, many southern slaveholders still would not have been satisfied. In many ways, slavery needed to grow in order to remain economically viable. Abraham Lincoln's electoral victory in 1860 alarmed southern defenders of slavery to the point that leading political figures in the South were ready to secede. Even before Lincoln was inaugurated, seven southern states did secede.

The Onset of War　战争的爆发

Once inaugurated, Lincoln made it clear that he would not permit southern secession, but he did not want to initiate a war with the breakaway states. The presence of U.S. troops at Fort Sumter, in the harbor of Charleston, South Carolina, proved to be the spark that ignited the war. The leadership of the nearly formed Confederate States of America decided that they would not tolerate the presence of the U.S. flag over Fort Sumter. In April 1861 Confederate president Jefferson Davis ordered bombardment of the fort, which was forced to surrender. This constituted the opening shots of the American Civil War. Lincoln reacted resolutely to this challenge. That same month, he issued a proclamation calling for 75,000 troops to "cause the laws to be duly executed." Soon, the United States and the seceded southern states, calling themselves the Confederate States of America, were at war.

WHAT HAPPENED TO THE "UNITED STATES"?
"the United States" 意味着什么？

When textbooks discuss the Civil War, they often call the United States "the Union." This is fine, but it is also fine to continue to use "the United States" in your essays. The United States did not disappear. Perhaps historians use "the Union" for the sake of clarity; however, the decision also has political overtones.

KEY CONCEPT 5.3 CIVIL WAR, RECONSTRUCTION, AND ISSUES OF POWER AND CITIZENSHIP
核心概念5.3：内战、战后重建与权利、公民问题

The victory of the United States over the secessionist South in the Civil War and the implementation of federal reconstruction plans settled two major issues—slavery and secession. However, these events left other issues unsettled, including questions about the power of the federal government and the citizenship rights of different groups of Americans.

I. Union Victory in the Civil War 联邦军在内战中的胜利

There are several key factors in understanding the Union victory over the Confederacy. The states that stayed in the Union comprised a larger population and a larger industrial capacity than the secessionist states. The decision to shift the focus of the war from maintaining national unity to eradicating slavery also played a part in the Union victory in the Civil War.

A. MOBILIZING FOR WAR 战争动员

Both the Union and the Confederacy had to mobilize their entire societies and economies in order to wage war. Both sides also faced opposition on their home fronts.

Industrialization 工业化

The Civil War spurred rapid industrialization of the North. During the Civil War, the Union government required an enormous amount of war materials, from guns and bullets to boots and uniforms. Manufacturers rose to the occasion by rapidly modernizing production. These changes in production sped up the process of industrialization that was in its beginning stages before the war. Industrialization stimulated a long period of economic growth, turning the United States into a world economic power. The manufacturers themselves benefitted from the war effort. Many of the "captains of industry" who came to dominate the economy in the Gilded Age, such as Andrew Carnegie, John D. Rockefeller, Jay Gould, J. P. Morgan, and Phillip D. Armour, began their economic rise through supplying the Union war effort.

Funding the War 资助战争

The United States government funded the war effort in three ways—issuing currency, borrowing money, and levying new taxes. These economic and financial policies greatly expanded the scope and size of the federal government. Though the federal government reduced its budget when the war ended, it did not return to the barebones condition of the antebellum period.

Congress issued three Legal Tender Acts in 1862 and 1863, allowing the government to issue paper currency, or "greenbacks." Unlike currency backed by gold or silver, greenbacks were backed only by people's faith in the government. The value of greenbacks fluctuated as the war progressed. In order to standardize the issuing of bank notes, stabilize the banking system, and stimulate economic growth, the government passed a series of National Banks Acts (1863–1864). These acts created a national banking system—allowing existing banks to join the system and to issue U.S. Treasury notes as currency. The system attempted to provide a degree of stability to the banking and currency system in the United States during a period when there was no central bank. (The Second Bank of the United States had expired in 1836; the Federal Reserve Bank was not created until 1913.)

For the first time, the government appealed to the public to purchase bonds in order to fund the war. Individuals lent the government approximately $400 million during the war by purchasing bonds. Banks and other financial institutions ended up loaning the government the vast majority of the $2.6 billion borrowed during the war.

Finally, the government created a wide array of new taxes including, for the first time, an income tax. Tax rates remained modest during the war in the face of widespread public opposition. The wartime income tax expired in 1872, but the call for additional income taxes became popular among socialist and populist reformers during the Gilded Age. A new income tax was enacted in 1894, but was declared unconstitutional by the Supreme Court in *Pollock v. Farmers' Loan & Trust Company* (1895). Later, the Sixteenth Amendment to the Constitution (1913) allowed Congress to levy income taxes (see Period 7).

New York City "Draft Riots" 纽约市 "征兵暴乱"

President Lincoln had to deal with a great deal of resistance to the war within the borders of the loyal states. One of the most significant episodes of resistance to Union policies involved riots against the wartime draft in New York City in July 1863. Protests began initially against government draft offices. Protesters were particularly angry about a law that allowed those who were drafted to pay $300 to avoid serving. This substantial sum was well beyond most working-class men. In the subsequent days, the protests turned violent, and one target of the rioters was the city's African-American population, accused of taking jobs from whites. At least 120 people were killed in the New York City draft riots.

Civil Liberties and Home Front Opposition 公民自由与后方的反对

President Abraham Lincoln suspended the writ of habeas corpus in 1863, authorizing the arrest, without due process, of rebels and traitors. Lincoln was responding to riots and threats of militia action in the border state of Maryland. After the war, the Supreme Court, in *Ex Parte Milligan* (1866), ruled that the suspension of habeas corpus did not empower the president to try and convict citizens before military tribunals; civilians can be tried in military courts only if civilian courts are not operating.

> ## CIVIL LIBERTIES DURING WARTIME
> ## 战时的公民自由
> Before condemning Lincoln as being "authoritarian" or "heavy-handed" for suspending habeas corpus, keep the following in mind. In many civil wars in human history, it has been common for authorities to simply kill enemy sympathizers; arresting them without due process, it could be argued, is relatively humane for a civil war.

B. ISSUING THE EMANCIPATION PROCLAMATION 颁布《奴隶解放宣言》

The issuing of the Emancipation Proclamation expanded the focus of the Civil War from preserving the union to emancipating the slaves. This move proved to be decisive to northern victory; it opened up the possibility of large-scale enlistment of African Americans and it contributed to the Confederacy remaining isolated diplomatically on the international scene.

Lincoln and Slavery 林肯与奴隶制

Lincoln's greatest wartime achievement was playing the key role in the emancipation of the slaves. Lincoln was partly motivated by the desire to keep Great Britain at bay during the war. The British might decide to aid the Confederacy to ensure the steady flow of southern cotton, but its population would not condone joining the South to perpetuate slavery. However, Lincoln did not achieve this historic goal on his own—abolitionists, Radical Republicans, and, of course, free blacks and slaves themselves all contributed to the effort to put the issue of liberation on the wartime agenda. Lincoln ushered in this historic event of emancipation while guiding the country through a devastating civil war. He was able to convince a reluctant country that ending slavery was consistent with the most basic of American values.

The Confiscation Acts (1861) 《没收法案》（1861）

Initially, President Lincoln was reluctant to take action against slavery for fear of pushing the border states toward secession. When Congress passed the Confiscation Acts in 1861 and 1862, Lincoln was opposed (although he did not veto them). These acts were framed as military measures. The first declared that any slaves pressed into working for the Confederacy could be taken as "contraband of war," meaning "confiscated property." The second act allowed for the seizure of the slaves owned by Confederate officials.

The Emancipation Proclamation (1862) 《奴隶解放宣言》（1862）

By the summer of 1862, President Lincoln had come to believe that the time was right for moving forward on the issue of emancipation. He waited until the Union had achieved a victory on the battlefield. The Battle of Antietam in September 1862 repelled a Confederate invasion, which was enough of a Union victory to prompt the president to issue the Emancipation Proclamation on September 22. The edict ordered the freeing of all slaves in rebel-held territory as of January 1, 1863. The order significantly exempted slaves in the loyal border states, and even in Union-held areas of Confederate states. Of course, orders from the United States government did not hold any weight for Confederate leaders, so the Emancipation Proclamation did not initially free any slaves. However, the order clearly changed the goals and tenor of the war, and made clear that this was as much a war for the liberation of the slaves as it was a war to preserve the Union.

TOWARD EMANCIPATION
"奴隶解放"的形成

The evolution of Lincoln's thinking about emancipation is a complex process. Historians cite a variety of circumstances—military, ideological, political, ethical—that entered into the equation. Certainly a complete understanding of the process cannot leave out the role of the slaves themselves in advancing the process.

C. LINCOLN AND THE MEANING OF THE CIVIL WAR 林肯与内战的意义

President Abraham Lincoln used a series of speeches, notably the Gettysburg Address (1863), to put the Civil War into a larger context and portray the elimination of slavery as part of the fulfillment of America's founding principles. Further, the Civil War, and Lincoln's understanding of the significance of the war, represents an important step in the transition of the United States from a union of individual states to a modern unified nation.

The Gettysburg Address and the Transition Toward a Modern Nation
葛底斯堡演说与向现代国家的转变

The Battle of Gettysburg (1863) was a major turning point in the Civil War. Several months after the battle, President Lincoln went to Gettysburg to dedicate a military cemetery at the site. His address at the ceremony succinctly framed the Civil War in the larger context of fulfilling the democratic goals that were implicit in the founding documents of the United States. He invoked the Declaration of Independence, which had been ratified "four score and seven years" before his "Gettysburg Address" (1863). He stated that the United States was "conceived in Liberty," and that an important founding principle was that "all men are created equal." The Civil War was, in Lincoln's thinking, a test of whether a nation conceived around the principles of liberty and equality can last. The men who died trying to make these principles a reality had made the battlefield a sacred site. It was up to the living, Lincoln asserted, to bring those principles into fruition—to ensure that there shall be "a new birth of freedom."

The outcome of the Civil War, especially in light of Lincoln's understanding of the conflict, played an important role in the growth of the United States as a modern nation. First, the war made it clear that the states did not have the autonomy to secede—that the nation was indivisible, larger than the sum of its parts. From the time of the Civil War, the United States was increasingly referred to as a nation, rather than a union of states. Historians, such as Eric Foner, see this transition in the context of nation-building processes in different parts of the world in the nineteenth century (such as the Meiji Restoration in Japan in 1868 or the Risorgimento that resulted in the formation of Italy, completed in 1871). The unification that occurred in the United States, however, was built around a set of democratic principles rather than around a particular ethnicity.

D. TURNING THE TIDE: FACTORS IN THE UNION VICTORY
形势逆转：联邦军获胜的因素

The Confederacy demonstrated initiative and military skill early in the war, but a variety of factors contributed to the Union victory in a prolonged war. The Union eventually found skilled military leadership and developed effective battlefield strategies. The material advantages of the North began to play a more important role as the war progressed. The Union decision to wage "total war" on the South's infrastructure and environment also played a part in Union victory.

Strengths and Weaknesses of the Two Sides 双方的优势与劣势

The Union side had some key advantages in the war. It had a far greater population than that of the rebellious southern states (22 million versus 6 million). It also had a far greater military capacity than the Confederacy, a more diverse economy, and an extensive railroad network. All of these advantages would become especially significant as the war dragged on. The Union had the capability to resupply its troops and to recruit reinforcements for fallen soldiers.

The Confederacy's greatest advantage was that it could fight a defensive war. It did not have to invade and conquer the North in order to declare victory. The Union, on the other hand, had to fight an offensive war in southern territory in order to win. Another Confederate advantage was the South's rich military tradition. It had able generals and a cohort of military men to draw from.

Fighting the Civil War 进行内战

The Union had a three-part strategy. First, the navy would blockade southern ports. The intent of this strategy, labeled the Anaconda Plan, was to prevent supplies from reaching the South and southern products from being shipped abroad. The second part was to divide Confederate territory in half by taking control of the Mississippi River. Finally, a contingent of troops would march on the Confederate capital of Richmond, Virginia, and achieve victory.

President Lincoln and much of the northern populace expected that the war would be quick and victory would be easy. These illusions were shattered after the First Battle of Bull Run, in Virginia. Confederate troops routed advancing U.S. troops. The Confederacy continued to hold the advantage on the battlefield for the remainder of 1861 and throughout 1862. Lincoln went through several generals-in-chief to lead the Union army before settling on Ulysses S. Grant (1864). Union forces suffered defeats at the Second Battle of Bull Run, the Battle of Fredericksburg, and other encounters. The 1862 Battle of Antietam that repelled a Confederate invasion is considered a Union victory, although a more aggressive Union general might have inflicted heavier damage. The early years also saw the first encounter between two ironclad ships, the Confederacy's *Merrimac* and the United States' *Monitor*. The fighting between the two ships resulted in a draw, but it pointed the way toward the future of naval battles worldwide.

MILITARY HISTORY 军事历史

The material in this section about the military aspects of the war is, more or less, the extent of what you need to know. For this and other wars, there might be a question about strategy, diplomacy, or "turning points," but there is rarely a question about the inner workings of a specific battle. The AP exam does not usually test on purely military history.

The Union Navy managed to maintain a successful blockade of the South. A few fast, steam-powered "blockade runners" managed to evade the blockade—but transporting cotton on such ships was too expensive to be profitable on the world market. At first, the Confederacy initiated an embargo on selling cotton to Great Britain, with the idea of bringing British factories to a standstill until Great Britain agreed to recognize the Confederacy and aid its war effort. However, this effort at King Cotton diplomacy simply hurt the southern economy. The Union blockade prevented the Confederacy from changing direction and selling its surplus cotton on the world market. Successful negotiating with Great Britain in 1862—by United States Secretary of State William Seward and Minister to England Charles Francis Adams—assured the Union that Great Britain would stay on the sidelines unless it were virtually certain that the Confederacy would become an independent nation.

An important turning point in the war was the Battle of Gettysburg (1863). This battle, in Pennsylvania, was the high-water mark for the Confederacy. After Gettysburg, the Confederacy was in retreat. Another important Union victory was at Vicksburg, Mississippi (1863). With that victory, Union forces gained control of the Mississippi River, cutting the Confederacy in two. In 1864, General William Tecumseh Sherman's "March to the Sea," from Atlanta to Charleston, shattered the South's last hope for a negotiated peace. Confederate general Robert E. Lee finally surrendered to General Ulysses S. Grant at Appomattox Courthouse, Virginia (1865).

II. The Impact of the Civil War and Reconstruction on Government and Society 内战的影响以及政府与社会的重建

The impact of the Civil War and Reconstruction on American society was profound. Broadly speaking, the war changed the relationship between the states and the federal government. Specifically, the war made it clear that the United States was indivisible; secession would not be allowed. Perhaps most important, the Civil War ended the practice of slavery in the United States. The Civil War and Reconstruction initiated debates over redefining citizenship, especially when it came to women and African Americans.

A. CONSTITUTIONAL AMENDMENTS AND THE EXPANSION OF CITIZENSHIP
宪法修正案与公民权利的扩大

Three constitutional amendments were ratified during the Reconstruction period, immediately following the Civil War. The Thirteenth Amendment (1865) outlawed slavery, the Fourteenth Amendment (1868) provided citizenship and due process of law to African Americans, and the Fifteenth Amendment (1870) prevented discrimination in voting based on race. These amendments were all designed to extend legal and political rights to former slaves.

The Thirteenth Amendment 《第十三条修正案》

Slavery had been virtually destroyed as Union troops defeated the Confederacy. Yet, by the end of the Civil War, some slaves were still not freed, especially in Kentucky. The Thirteenth Amendment (1865) freed the remaining slaves but, more importantly, it enshrined in the United States Constitution that slavery was illegal in America.

The Fourteenth Amendment 《第十四条修正案》

The Fourteenth Amendment, adopted in 1868, made all natural-born or naturalized people American citizens. Further, it stated that the "privileges and immunities" of citizens shall not be abridged by states. Also, it stated that no citizens shall be deprived of "life, liberty, or property without due process of law." The amendment was bitterly opposed by southern states, which were forced to approve it before they could regain representation in Congress. The amendment undid long-held custom as well as the *Dred Scott* decision (1857) by putting AfricanAmericans on an equal footing with whites and providing a guarantee of equality before the law.

The Fifteenth Amendment 《第十五条修正案》

The Fifteenth Amendment, granting African Americans voting rights, was ratified in 1869. The Fifteenth Amendment states that the vote may not be denied to someone based on "race, color, or previous condition of servitude." African American women, of course, still could not vote. Women were not guaranteed the right to vote until ratification of the Nineteenth Amendment (1920). The guarantee of voting rights for African Americans was a key element of the Reconstruction program of the "radical Republicans."

B. THE WOMEN'S RIGHTS MOVEMENT AND THE CONSTITUTION 女权运动与《宪法》

Some participants in the women's rights movements welcomed the Reconstruction-era Constitutional amendments. However, other participants objected to their limited nature. Specifically, issues of gender equality were not addressed by these sweeping changes.

Debates over the Fifteenth Amendment 关于《第十五修正案》的争议

The proposal to ratify the Fifteenth Amendment generated a great deal of debate within the women's rights movement. Elizabeth Cady Stanton and Susan B. Anthony refused to support the Fifteenth Amendment because it did not extend the right to vote to women. Other feminists, led by Lucy Stone and her husband, Henry Blackwell, while disappointed with the wording of the Fifteenth Amendment, argued that it was important to support Reconstruction and the Republican Party. They asserted that women's suffrage could be accomplished on a state-by-state basis. These divisions led to the formation of rival organizations. Stanton and Anthony formed the National Woman Suffrage Association (NWSA) in 1869. Stone, Blackwell, and others established the American Woman Suffrage Association (AWSA), also in 1869. The AWSA and NWSA eventually reconciled and in 1890 merged to become the National American Woman Suffrage Association (NAWSA).

C. THE LIMITED SUCCESSES AND ULTIMATE UNDOING OF RECONSTRUCTION
重建的有限成功与最终失败

The Reconstruction period resulted in some short-term successes—bringing the Union back together, extending political and leadership opportunities to former slaves, and altering the relationship between the races in the South. The period also saw a shift in power from the early phase of Reconstruction, dominated by the executive branch, to the latter period, dominated by Congress. The successes of the Reconstruction period proved to be short-lived. The Republican Party failed to establish itself as a viable political party in the South. Further, efforts at changing the culture and racial attitudes of the South proved elusive. Finally, a combination of resistance by white southerners and a lack of resolve on the part of northerners led to the end of the Reconstruction period.

Approaches to Reconstruction 重建方式

As the Civil War was coming to an end, President Lincoln and the Republican Party began to address several questions regarding the postwar world. These questions included: What accommodations would be made for the freed men and women of the South? How would the secessionist South be reintegrated into the United States? What punishments, if any, would be meted out to those who had rebelled against the United States? Finally, who held responsibility for reuniting and reconstructing the country—the president or Congress? Did, as the president argued, the secessionist states still exist as political entities, simply awaiting new governing personnel, or had they committed "suicide." Many congressional Republicans argued that the states had ceased to exist, and therefore needed to be readmitted by Congress. The answers to these questions formed the basis of competing visions of what Reconstruction would entail.

Wartime Reconstruction 战时重建

President Lincoln was eager to quickly restore the Union. An initial goal of his was restoring southern representation in Congress. In 1863, he announced his "ten percent" plan. Under this plan, if 10 percent of the 1860 vote count in a southern state took an oath of allegiance to the United States and promised to abide by emancipation, then that state could establish a new government and send representatives to Congress. This was a low bar for these states to comply with. In 1864, he vetoed the Wade–Davis Bill, which would have established much stricter standards for the southern states to meet. The bill would have required half of the voters in a state to sign a loyalty oath to the United States before Reconstruction could begin, and would have guaranteed equal treatment before the law for former slaves. Finally, in 1865, in his Second Inaugural Address, Lincoln announced that he wanted to reunite the country "with malice toward none; with charity for all." This approach was consistent with Lincoln's broader goals of ending the war as soon as possible. Lincoln was assassinated less than a month after his second inauguration, so it is difficult to surmise how he would have negotiated the difficulties of the Reconstruction era.

Presidential Reconstruction 总统重建

After President Lincoln's assassination, his vice president, Andrew Johnson, assumed power. Johnson had been tapped for the vice presidency by Lincoln because he did not vacate his seat in the Senate when his native Tennessee declared secession in 1861. Although Johnson had broken with the planter class in the South, it became clear that he had no affinity for the Republican Party, nor for emancipation and equality for African Americans. He continued with the lenient and rapid approach to Reconstruction that Lincoln had mapped out. Johnson quickly recognized the new southern state governments as legitimate after they renounced secession and ratified the Thirteenth Amendment banning slavery. In the South, many members of the old slave-owning class were now back in power. These men tried to replicate the conditions of the Old South, including passing a series of restrictive laws known as the Black Codes. Southern postwar conditions were so similar to prewar conditions that many northerners wondered if they had "won the war, but lost the peace."

Congress and the President Clash over Reconstruction
国会和总统对战后重建意见的冲突

In 1866, tensions increased between President Andrew Johnson and congressional Republicans. Johnson vetoed two measures passed by Congress—an extension of the Freedman's Bureau and a Civil Rights Act that was designed to overturn the Black Codes the southern states had implemented.

The biggest fight, however, between Johnson and congressional Republicans was over the ratification of the Fourteenth Amendment. This amendment made citizens of all people born in the United States. In this, it undid the *Dred Scott* decision, which held that African Americans were not citizens of the United States. The amendment further guaranteed all citizens "equal protection of the laws," and prohibited states from denying any citizen "life, liberty, or property without due process of law." Although the amendment did not extend voting guarantees to African Americans, it did allow Congress to reduce the representation of states that withheld the vote from African American males. In this section, the Constitution mentions the word "males" for the first time, much to the consternation of women who had hopes that the amendment would also extend voting privileges to them.

Radical Reconstruction 激进重建

President Andrew Johnson tried to mobilize skeptical white voters against the Fourteenth Amendment in the 1866 mid-term elections. However, the strategy backfired. Republicans won a resounding victory in the 1866 elections and embarked on more sweeping measures. This phase of Reconstruction, known alternatively as "Radical Reconstruction" or "Congressional Reconstruction," showed the potential of a biracial democracy in the United States while also showing the limits of federal resolve and the strength of white southern opposition.

Reconstruction Acts of 1867 　《1867年重建法案》

Congressional Republicans were able to push through the Reconstruction Acts of 1867. These sweeping acts divided the South into five military districts. These areas could only rejoin the United States if they guaranteed basic rights to African Americans. The radicals were not able to fully carry out their program. Representative Thaddeus Stevens introduced a bill in the spring of 1867 to redistribute land so that each freedman could be granted 40 acres. The idea resonated with freedmen, some of the Radical Republicans in Congress, and many poor whites in the South who were eager to limit the economic clout of the large planters. However, the idea ran against the basic Republican value of protecting private property. The issue of land reform died in committee in the summer of 1867.

Impeachment of President Johnson 　弹劾约翰逊总统

The clash between President Johnson and the congressional Republicans degenerated to such an extent by 1868 that the Republicans voted to impeach Johnson. The House charged the president with violating the Tenure of Office Act, an act the Republicans had passed to protect their ally, Secretary of War Edwin Stanton. The act prohibited the president from firing cabinet members without Senate approval. The act itself was of questionable legality, but Johnson fired Stanton anyway, initiating the impeachment trial. The Senate narrowly found Johnson not guilty, but the whole procedure rendered Johnson powerless to stop Congress's Reconstruction plans.

Reconstruction in Practice 　实践中的重建

The record of the Reconstruction governments in the South is still a subject of controversy, almost a century and a half later. White southerners at the time, and afterward, complained bitterly about the burdens imposed by the Reconstruction governments, and about their corruption and ineptitude. More recently, however, historians have pointed out that corruption was less pronounced than it was in other parts of the country, and that these governments accomplished a great deal, against great odds.

The southern governments were composed of a variety of elements. Democrats still served in state legislatures, often in the minority, during the Reconstruction period. The Republicans were made up of several different groups. Southern whites who joined the Republicans were labeled "scalawags" by their Democratic opponents. Many southern white Republicans were former Whigs and sought to promote economic progress for the South. In addition, many northerners came to the South to participate in Reconstruction. Some of these northern Republicans sought personal advancement in coming South; many were motivated by a desire to assist the former slaves in their adjustment to life as freed men and women. Southern Democrats labeled these northerners "carpetbaggers," implying that they hurriedly threw some belongings in a carrying bag and traveled to the South to make a quick fortune. Finally, many of the Republican legislators were African Americans. Only in South Carolina, and only briefly (1873), did African Americans control the majority of seats in even one legislative chamber. They were consistently in the minority. However, that African Americans were elected to public office in the South at all was a major accomplishment. In the 1870s, two African Americans were elected to the United States Senate—Hiram Revels and Blanche K. Bruce—and more than a dozen representatives were elected to the House of Representatives.

The accomplishments of Reconstruction included the establishment of schools for African Americans. The attainment of an education was a burning desire for many of the freed African American men and women. Schools thrived in the period despite the costs involved and despite the personal risk incurred by participants. Important African American institutions, such as Howard University and Morehouse College, were established during the Reconstruction period. In addition, the Reconstruction governments established hospitals that served the African American community, rewrote constitutions, updated penal codes, and began the physical rebuilding of the war-torn South.

"SCALAWAGS" AND "CARPETBAGGERS"
"南方佬" 与 "投机政客"

If you use these terms in an essay, do so with caution. Remember, they are not neutral descriptions; they are disparaging terms to describe those who cooperated with Reconstruction. When you use them, at least use quotation marks. Or consider modifying them with the phrase "so-called."

The End of Reconstruction 重建末期

Several factors contributed to the end of the Reconstruction, after only a dozen years. Southern conservative Democrats, who called themselves "redeemers," aggressively sought to regain power, state by state. The "redeemers" were aided by networks of white terrorist organizations that used violence to silence African Americans and to intimidate them from participating in public life. Also, northern whites simply lost their zeal for reforming the South. By the 1870s, many whites in the North were more interested in the industrial development of the North than in the "race problem" in the South.

The Formal End of Reconstruction: The Election of 1876

重建正式结束：1876年选举

The final nail in the coffin of Reconstruction was the disputed presidential election of 1876. The Democratic candidate, Samuel J. Tilden, won the majority of the popular vote, but neither he nor his Republican opponent, Rutherford B. Hayes, were able to claim enough electoral votes to be declared the winner. In three states—South Carolina, Louisiana, and Florida—the Democrats and the Republicans both claimed victory. A special electoral commission, with a Republican majority, declared Hayes the winner in the three contested states. Democrats protested, with some threatening to block Hayes's inauguration. Party leaders reached an informal agreement, known as the Compromise of 1877, which allowed Hayes to win the presidency. In return, the Republicans agreed to end Reconstruction, paving the way for rule by the Democratic Party in the South.

THE ELECTORAL COLLEGE 总统选举团

A working knowledge of the electoral college is essential to understanding some of the close elections in American history, especially those in which the winner of the national popular vote did not end up winning the presidency. This occurred in 1824, 1876, 1888, and 2000.

D. FROM SLAVERY TO SHARECROPPING 从奴隶制到佃农制

Even though slavery ended with the Civil War, patterns of land ownership remained unchanged. New economic patterns emerged that would prove to be both exploitative and soil-intensive—notably, the sharecropping system.

The Development of the Sharecropping System 佃农制的发展

Economically, most African Americans were still engaged in agricultural work. Immediately following the Civil War, plantation owners sought to hire gangs of African American workers to labor under the supervision of a white overseer. These workers chafed at this arrangement, with its stark resemblance to the slavery system. They desired a plot of their own—"forty acres and a mule." Some Radical Republicans urged the government to divide up the former slave plantations and distribute the land to freedmen. This radical proposal did not gain sufficient support to become reality. Short of this, African Americans began to rent land. They would customarily pay "rent" with a portion of their yearly crop—usually half. This "sharecropping" system was somewhat of a compromise—African Americans did not have to work under the direct supervision of an overseer, and white plantation owners acquired cotton to be sold on the open market. After paying back loans for seed money and tools, sharecroppers were left with very little for basic necessities. The system created a cycle of debt, which prevented African Americans from acquiring money and owning land.

III. Conflicts over Notions of Citizenship and American Identity
关于公民与美国身份认识的冲突

During the Reconstruction period, amendments to the Constitution reflected a changing notion of national purpose and identity. These changes led to debates among Americans over rights for African Americans, women, and other groups.

E. THE PROMISE AND LIMITS OF CONSTITUTIONAL CHANGES 宪法改革的前景与限制

The Fourteenth and Fifteenth Amendments to the Constitution granted African Americans citizenship, equal protection of the laws, and voting rights. In the years that followed, these rights were systematically reduced by violence and political tactics. A system of segregation, with approval from the Supreme Court, became entrenched in the South. Although the Fourteenth and Fifteenth Amendments were largely sidestepped in the decades following Reconstruction, they established judicial principles that came to fruition in twentieth-century civil-rights decisions.

Segregation in the South 南方的种族隔离

A series of segregation laws were passed in the southern states in the years following Reconstruction came to an end. These laws were known as Jim Crow laws. The origins of the term can perhaps be attributed to a song-and-dance routine from the 1830s called "Jump Jim Crow," which included white actors in blackface caricaturing African Americans. Later in the century, "Jim Crow" became an insulting term for African Americans; the laws that applied to African Americans, therefore, became known as Jim Crow laws. These laws segregated public facilities, such as railroad cars, bathrooms, and schools. Furthermore, they relegated African Americans to second-class status in the South. These state and local laws first appeared in the South after Reconstruction ended (1877).

The *Slaughter-house* Cases and the Narrowing of the Fourteenth Amendment

"屠宰场组案"与《第十四条修正案》的狭隘之处

The passage of Jim Crow laws in the South after Reconstruction was aided in part by a narrow interpretation of the Fourteenth Amendment by the Supreme Court. Advocates of civil rights for African Africans hoped that the Fourteenth Amendment (ratified in 1868) would prevent the implementation of Jim Crow laws. The amendment prevents states from making laws that limit the "privileges or immunities" of any United States citizen. However, the Supreme Court interpreted this broad language in such a narrow way that it allowed for the implementation of Jim Crow laws. Earlier, in the *Slaughter-house* cases (1873), the court made a distinction between national citizenship and state citizenship. The case was not a civil-rights case: it involved a suit by several New Orleans slaughterhouses that had been closed down by the state. The slaughterhouses asserted that their due-process rights had been taken away in violation of the Fourteenth Amendment. The court ruled that the Fourteenth Amendment applied to national citizenship rights, such as the right to vote in national elections and the right to travel between states. The court said that the amendment did not apply to rights that derived from "state citizenship." As a result, the Fourteenth Amendment would not be of use in prohibiting state Jim Crow laws. Later, in the case of *Plessy v. Ferguson* (1896), the Supreme Court specifically asserted that racial segregation did not violate the equal protection provision of the Fourteenth Amendment (see Period 6).

The Exclusion of African Americans from the Political Process

政治进程中对非裔美国人的排斥

A series of actions effectively removed African Americans from the political process and relegated them to the status of second-class citizens. Literacy tests and poll taxes limited their ability to vote. Poor whites got around these rules with the "grandfather clause," guaranteeing a man the right to vote if he or his father or grandfather had the right to vote before the Civil War. In addition, the Democratic Party often held "whites only" primaries, thus legally excluding African Americans from the only election that really mattered in the solidly Democratic South. African Americans who spoke out against this were targets of violence and even murder. The Ku Klux Klan was first organized in 1866. Thousands of African Americans were killed by lynch mobs as the local authorities looked the other way.

A "Second Reconstruction"   "第二次重建"

Reconstruction lasted only a decade; its accomplishments were limited and short-lived. However, in many respects the failures of Reconstruction in the nineteenth century set the stage for a "second reconstruction" in the twentieth. The democratic spirit of the Reconstruction period inspired civil-rights activists throughout the twentieth century. Furthermore, the principles established in the Fourteenth Amendment were invoked in several important Supreme Court decisions in the twentieth century—most notably, *Brown v. Board of Education* (1954). In the Brown decision, the court specifically cited the amendment's assertion that "no State shall . . . deny to any person . . . the equal protection of the laws." It used this wording as the basis for declaring segregated schools unconstitutional (see more in Period 8).

SUBJECT TO DEBATE   相关讨论

The events of the 1850s have assumed a central place in one of the most contentious historiographical discussions about American history: How should the coming of the Civil War be understood? Central to that question is the role of slavery in the coming of the Civil

War. Partisan historians from the South and the North have tended to blame the other side. Southern partisans blame the North for interfering with their "domestic institutions." Northern partisans blame the extreme language of the *Dred Scott* decision, the violence done to Senator Charles Sumner, and the strident defense of slavery as indicators of rigidity on the part of the South.

For decades after the war, many historians held that the war was an "irrepressible conflict." The phrase was actually coined before the war by Senator William H. Seward, discussing the possibility of a future conflict between the sections—one he saw as inevitable. The war was inevitable, the theory held, because of slavery, which was both at the heart of the issue and beyond compromise. The "irrepressible conflict" school has received more recent backing from contemporary historian Eric Foner, who focuses less on northern moral concerns about slavery and more on the "free labor" ideology. This ideology, which was a central part of the culture of the North, held that the lands out West should be for small-scale farming, without competition from slave labor.

Several historical schools have questioned the centrality of slavery in the conflict. Progressive historians Mary and Charles Beard, writing in the 1920s, argued that the conflict was actually between a capitalist industrial North and an agrarian, almost feudal, South. Other historians have blamed the conflict on "blundering politicians"—asserting that the politicians could have compromised on slavery and other issues. This school of thought gained adherents from the 1920s onward but has been challenged more recently in the post–civil rights movement era.

For decades, the southern myth of the "lost cause" has influenced mainstream historical writing on the Civil War. The "lost cause" myth holds that the Confederate cause was a noble and honorable one, as the South had a rich tradition of military skill and chivalry. The only reason the South lost the Civil War was because of the overwhelming forces of the North. The North had greater industrial capacity and a larger population to draw from. However, this understanding completely ignores the centrality of the slavery question. Even among northerners in the first half of the twentieth century, the question of slavery was left out of discussions of the war. It is only in the last third of the twentieth century that the history field has fully rejected the "lost cause" myth.

Traditional historical accounts of the Reconstruction period criticize the Republican Party for imposing crushing burdens on the South, for occupying it with troops, and for saddling it with inept and corrupt government. Recent historical accounts have moved away from this grim representation by emphasizing the real progress made by African Americans under Reconstruction. The short-lived gains made under Reconstruction helped to inspire civil rights activists in the twentieth century.

PRACTICE MULTIPLE-CHOICE QUESTIONS 选择题练习

> **Directions:** Pick the letter that best answers the following questions.

Questions 1–2 refer to the following passage: 根据以下段落，回答第1—2题

"It is the sentiment around which all their actions, all their arguments, circle, from which all their propositions radiate. They look upon it as being a moral, social, and political wrong; and while they contemplate it as such, they nevertheless have due regard for its actual existence among us, and the difficulties of getting rid of it in any satisfactory way and to all the constitutional obligations thrown about it. Yet, having a due regard for these, they desire a policy in regard to it that looks to its not creating any more danger. They insist that it should, as far as may be, *be treated* as a wrong; and one of the methods of treating it as a wrong is to *make provision that it shall grow no larger.*"

—Abraham Lincoln, from debate with Stephen Douglas, October 1858

1. The position of Abraham Lincoln in the above passage emerged most directly in response to which of the following mid-nineteenth century trends?

   (A) Large-scale immigration from Ireland.
   (B) The spread of the ideas of Romanticism.
   (C) Violent slave rebellions in the South.
   (D) Territorial growth of the United States.

2. The logic of the quotation is most consistent with

   (A) George Fitzhugh's 1857 book, *Cannibals All!*
   (B) the Wilmot Proviso, introduced in Congress in 1846, 1847, and 1848.
   (C) Frederick Douglass's 1852 oration commonly known as, "What to the slave is the 4th of July?"
   (D) "John Brown's Last Speech," read in court in 1859.

Questions 3–5 refer to the following passage: 根据以下段落，回答第3—5题

Occupations of Gainfully Employed Irish Immigrants in New York, 1855	Occupation # Irish-born (and % of total)
SKILLED 技能类	
Bakers	861 (23)
Blacksmiths	1,339 (50)
Brewers/Distillers	52 (14)
Carpenters	2,230 (30)
Dressmaker/Seamstress	4,559 (46)
Ironworkers	150 (56)
Machinists	398 (23)
Mason/Bricklayer	2,203 (61)
Merchants	278 (4)
Policemen	292 (25)
Printers	519 (25)
Retail shopkeepers	916 (35)
Shoemakers	2,121 (31)
Tailors	4,171 (33)
Wine and liquor dealers	891 (55)

PROFESSIONALS 职业类	
Doctors	113 (8)
Lawyers	40 (4)

UNSKILLED 非技能类	
Domestic Servants	23,386 (74)
Laundresses	1,758 (69)
Laborers	17,426 (86)
Drivers/Hackmen/Coachmen	805 (46)

Source: Robert Ernst, *Immigrant Life in New York City, 1825–1863* and *NY State Census of 1855* (1994).

3. Which of the following factors was an important cause of the immigration trend reflected in the chart?

(A) Great Britain had recently begun using harsh tactics against Irish dissidents, leading to large numbers of dissidents fleeing Ireland.

(B) The Irish agriculture sector had recently undergone rapid mechanization, displacing a large percentage of the rural population of Ireland.

(C) A large-scale famine in Ireland, caused by the failure of the potato crop, had recently occurred, driving many Irish people to flee the country.

(D) New York State had recently passed a religious toleration act, creating a more welcoming atmosphere for Irish Catholic immigrants.

4. Which of the following conclusions is supported by the evidence in the chart?

(A) Irish immigrants were quickly able to climb the economic ladder of New York City and gain employment in middle-class professions.

(B) Irish immigration to New York City in the period before the Civil War did not significantly alter the economic structure of the city.

(C) Irish workers played a prominent role in the union movement in New York City in the 1850s.

(D) Irish immigrants comprised a majority of the workers in low-paying, unskilled occupations in New York City by the 1850s.

5. Which of the following describes a significant response to the development reflected in the chart?

(A) The federal government implemented the National Origins Act, establishing a quota system to stem the flow of Irish immigrants into the United States.

(B) Congress rewrote naturalization laws in order to expand the number of years immigrants must live in the United States before they can attain citizenship and voting rights.

(C) The United States and Ireland reached an understanding that President Franklin Pierce would pressure New York State to end discriminatory practices against Irish immigrants, and that Ireland would pass legislation limiting immigration into the United States.

(D) A new political party, commonly called the Know-Nothing Party, attracted large numbers of voters in the 1850s with a strong anti-immigrant, anti-Catholic message.

"I have directed Commodore Perry to assure your imperial majesty that I entertain the kindest feelings toward your majesty's person and government.

"The United States of America reach from ocean to ocean, and our Territory of Oregon and State of California lie directly opposite to the dominions of your imperial majesty. Our steamships can go from California to Japan in eighteen days.

"Our great State of California produces about sixty millions of dollars in gold every year… and many other valuable articles. Japan is also a rich and fertile country, and produces many very valuable articles.… I am desirous that our two countries should trade with each other, for the benefit both of Japan and the United States.

"We know that the ancient laws of your imperial majesty's government do not allow of foreign trade, except with the Chinese and the Dutch; but as the state of the world changes and new governments are formed, it seems to be wise, from time to time, to make new laws. . . .

"These are the only objects for which I have sent Commodore Perry, with a powerful squadron, to pay a visit to your imperial majesty's renowned city of Yedo: friendship, commerce, a supply of coal and provisions, and protection for our shipwrecked people."

—President Millard Fillmore, letter to the Emperor of Japan,
presented by Commodore Matthew Perry, 1853

6. A major goal of Commodore Matthew Perry's expedition was to

   (A) challenge the "spheres of influence" system in Japan that had been developed by the major European powers.
   (B) reduce tensions that had developed between Japan and the United States over competing colonial claims.
   (C) expand American trade into a country that had traditionally isolated itself from most foreign powers.
   (D) overthrow the militaristic regime of Japan and replace it with a democratic government.

7. The United States naval expeditions to Japan in the 1850s, led by Commodore Matthew Perry, resulted in

   (A) a long period of Japanese isolation from Western trade and influence.
   (B) war between the United States and Japan.
   (C) Japan becoming an American colony.
   (D) Japan opening its ports to trade with the West.

8. The expedition by Commodore Matthew Perry could best be understood in the context of

   (A) an expanding American economy.
   (B) shifting alliances among major world powers.
   (C) increased nativist sentiment in the United States.
   (D) debates over the expansion of slavery.

Answers and Explanations to Multiple-Choice Questions
选择题的答案与解析

1. **(D)** Abraham Lincoln is describing the Republican Party's position on slavery in 1858. It comes from one of several debates with Stephen Douglas during their run for Senate that year. Lincoln was a member of the Republican Party, even though he uses the word "they," rather than "we," to describe the Republicans. In this excerpt, Lincoln notes that the Republicans were against the institution of slavery and opposed to its spread to new territories. The party felt that slavery was constitutionally protected in the states where it already existed. The territorial growth of the United States—following the acquisition of the Mexican Cession (1848)—forced public figures to take a position on the question of slavery. The Kansas-Nebraska Act (1854) further intensified debate over slavery in the United States.

2. **(B)** The logic of the Republican position—opposition to the spread of slavery—was most consistent with the Wilmot Proviso. During the Mexican-American War (1846–1848), Congressman David Wilmot and other northern politicians tried, unsuccessfully, to ban slavery in territories that might be gained in the war by putting forth the Wilmot Proviso (1846). The proviso was passed by the House of Representatives three times (1846, 1847, and 1848), where politicians from the populous northern states dominated; however, it failed to garner enough votes for passage in the Senate, where southern and northern politicians were equally represented.

3. **(C)** The chart indicates a significant Irish presence in New York City by 1855; the majority of unskilled jobs in New York City were held by the Irish. The single biggest factor contributing to this migration of people was the large-scale failure of the potato crop in Ireland and the devastating famine that following in its wake. By the 1840s, Great Britain controlled Ireland and used the best land there to grow wheat and other crops for export, while potato farming was pushed to marginal land. The result was weak potato plants less able to withstand disease. It is estimated that a million Irish starved to death between 1845 and 1850, while another million left for America.

4. **(D)** The chart shows that the Irish comprised a majority of workers in unskilled fields in New York in the 1850s. The Irish were in desperate straits and took low-paying unskilled jobs. Many were involved in building the city's Central Park in the 1850s. Irish immigrants tended to enter the labor market on a lower rung than German immigrants. The Irish immigrants tended to come from rural backgrounds, and did not have the skills needed to rise in the workforce. By contrast, German immigrants tended to arrive with skills in particular trades, including carpentry, brewing, metal-work, and other crafts.

5. **(D)** The large-scale Irish immigration into the United States in the 1840s and 1850s resulted in a strong nativist movement. The most successful political manifestation of this movement was the Know-Nothing Party. The party emerged in the 1840s and, by the 1850s, achieved electoral success in several states, especially in the Northeast. Many members of the party eventually ended up joining the newly formed Republican Party.

6. **(C)** A major goal of Commodore Matthew Perry's expedition was to expand American trade into a country that had traditionally isolated itself from most foreign powers. With the growth of the economy and with the acquisition of West Coast ports, the United States became increasingly interested in trading with Japan. The Tokugawa shogunate

(1600–1868) had virtually isolated Japan from Western countries since the seventeenth century. The United States was determined to open Japan to American trade.

7. **(D)** The United States naval expedition in the 1850s, led by Commodore Matthew Perry, resulted in Japan opening its ports to trade with the West. The first journey was in 1852–1853 and a second occurred in 1854. Perry was able to secure a treaty with Japan that opened the country up to American trade.

8. **(A)** The expedition by Commodore Matthew Perry could best be understood in the context of an expanding American economy. Growth and expansion were defining features of the United States in the decades between 1800 and the Civil War. The economy was rapidly changing and growing, as an older semi-subsistence economy was giving way to a market economy with a national and even international reach.

Period 6: 1865–1898 The Challenges of the Era of Industrialization
第六个时期（1865—1898）：工业化时代的挑战

8

INTRODUCTION 简介

The transformation of the United States during the last decades of the nineteenth century from an essentially rural and agrarian society to an increasingly industrial and urban one brought about a host of economic, political, diplomatic, social, cultural, and environmental changes.

The United States economy expanded tremendously in the late 1800s as the country experienced an industrial revolution. Before the Civil War, businesses generally served local or regional markets. After the war, we see the development of businesses with a national, and even international, reach. The era of industrial expansion after the Reconstruction period is known as the "Gilded Age." Although the nation as a whole enjoyed an increase in its wealth, that wealth was not equally distributed. The owners of big businesses, labeled "robber barons" by their critics, enjoyed unparalleled wealth, whereas many of the workers lived in squalid conditions in working-class slums. The contrast between the mansions of Andrew Carnegie and Henry Frick along New York City's Fifth Avenue and the tenements depicted in Jacob Riis's *How the Other Half Lives* (1890) startled many Americans.

THE GILDED AGE 镀金时代

The term alludes to gold leaf gilding on statues. These statues might be shiny like gold, but beneath the surface is often just cheap plaster. The age had great wealth, but beneath the surface was desperate poverty. The term was coined by Mark Twain and Charles Dudley Warner in their book, *The Gilded Age: A Tale of Today* (1873).

The era of rapid industrial and economic expansion in the late nineteenth century dramatically transformed American culture and society. Americans experienced new cultural products, new patterns of work and leisure, and new class and ethnic divisions. These new aspects of American life were most evident in the growing cities. Cities became centers of industrial production and magnets for the large number of immigrants coming into the United States. At the same time, agriculture was becoming more mechanized, requiring fewer people in rural areas. New York retained its stature as the largest American city, with Chicago, Cleveland, Detroit, and other cities of the Midwest and the Northeast also growing rapidly.

In addition, during the decades between the end of the Civil War and the turn of the twentieth century, a series of important developments transformed the South and the West. White and African American southerners both shaped the "new" South, as it left behind plantation slavery. Ultimately, white southerners were able to create a series of laws and customs that relegated African Americans to a second-class status. At the same time, government policies and economic opportunity encouraged waves of settlers to make their way west. The Midwest became a major agricultural region, and the center of a politicized and determined farmers' movement. As settlers ventured farther west, clashes ensued with American Indian groups who lived on coveted lands. These clashes led to the demise of autonomous native peoples within the United States borders.

KEY CONCEPT 6.1 THE RISE OF INDUSTRIAL CAPITALISM
核心概念6.1：工业资本主义的兴起

The rise of industrial capitalism in the last decades of the nineteenth century was facilitated by technological advances, mass-production techniques, and the opening of new markets.

I. Industrialization in the "Gilded Age" "镀金时代" 的工业化

During the last decades of the nineteenth century, the United States experienced unprecedented changes in production as large-scale industry and business consolidation replaced older forms of production. These changes were accompanied by innovations in technology, expanding international communications networks, and pro-business government policies. The age was marked by new forms of consumption and marketing.

A. TRANSPORTATION, COMMUNICATION, AND THE OPENING OF NEW MARKETS
交通、通信与新兴市场的开放

The government subsidized new transportation and communication systems during the Gilded Age. These new systems opened new markets in North America.

Land Grants to Railroads 给铁路的政府赠地

In the second half of the nineteenth century, the federal government encouraged economic growth by subsidizing improvements in transportation and communications. Most importantly, the government encouraged the building of railroad lines. Railroads connected the far reaches of the country and sped up the movement of goods and expanded markets. The cost of goods came down and the standard of living of Americans rose. The government encouraged this expansion of the railroad network by giving railroad companies wide swaths of land through which new rail lines would be built. Most of these grants occurred between 1850 and 1871. The Pacific Railway Act of 1862 greatly accelerated the process. Under the act, land grants went directly to railroad corporations rather than to states. These generous land grants totaled more than 175 million acres—which represents an area larger than the state of Texas. These land grants generated huge profits for railroad companies. The presence of railroad lines made the land on either side of the tracks more accessible and more valuable, bringing about $435 million to the railroad companies.

The Telegraph and the Telephone 电报与电话

Advances in communication greatly facilitated the development of corporations with a national, and even international, reach. The telegraph network developed before the Civil War (see Period 4) continued to spread throughout the country. In 1876, Alexander Graham Bell was granted a patent for the telephone. As is the case with many innovations, a host of individuals were working simultaneously on developing the telephone. Within a year, the Bell Telephone Company was established. By the end of 1880, almost 50,000 telephones were in use in the United States.

B. THE ELEMENTS OF MASS PRODUCTION AND DISTRIBUTION 批量生产与分销的要素

A variety of factors contributed to a dramatic increase in the production of goods after the Civil War. Technological innovations, greater access to raw materials, new business and financial models, advances in marketing, and a growing labor force all contributed to the development of mass production.

Steel and the Bessemer Process 钢铁与贝塞麦炼钢法

Steel production was key to the industrialization of the United States. Iron production grew throughout the nineteenth century, and was used extensively as the railroad system developed in the United States. Steel, an alloy made through the chemical bonding of iron with carbon, was far more durable, versatile, and useful than iron. Steel had existed since antiquity, but before the middle of the nineteenth century, it was too expensive to be commercially useful. The development of the Bessemer process by the Englishman Henry Bessemer greatly reduced the cost of steel and made it available to a wide variety of industrial operations. The process, which involved blowing air into molten iron, was patented by Bessemer in 1856. By the late 1860s, a more efficient production method, called the open-hearth process, replaced the Bessemer process.

Coal and Oil 煤炭与石油

The new industrial processes of the Gilded Age required new forms of fuel. The most practical fuel was a hard form of coal called anthracite. It was readily available in western Pennsylvania. Later, softer coal, called bituminous, came into wide use in industrial processes.

In the 1850s, innovators demonstrated that oil could be refined and used for a variety of processes, such as illuminating lamps. Its most important industrial use in the nineteenth century was lubricating machinery. The first oil well was established in 1859 by Edwin Drake in Pennsylvania. Later in the century, the demand for oil increased as it came to be refined into gasoline, a fuel for automobiles.

The Evolution of the Corporation 公司的发展

Before the Civil War, many states made it significantly easier for an entity to incorporate (see more on incorporation laws in Period 4). An early entity to incorporate was the Pennsylvania Railroad, in 1846. Many companies followed suit in the period following the Civil War. Large corporations developed management systems that separated top executives from managers who were responsible for day-to-day operations. This managerial revolution included modern cost-accounting procedures and the division of responsibilities among departmental managers.

Advances in Marketing 市场的新发展

During the last three decades of the nineteenth century, industrial capitalism devised methods to distribute the large quantities of goods produced by the growing factory system. As the living standards of many working-class people began to show signs of growth (see page 211), patterns of consumption began to change. Many products, most notably clothing, went from home production to commercial production. Over the course of the nineteenth century, ready-made clothing replaced homemade clothing. Commercially prepared canned food made inroads with families who had been used to growing and processing their own foodstuffs.

In addition, new types of retail outlets began to supplement, and to some degree replace, traditional small-scale, locally owned stores. By the end of the nineteenth century, chains such as the Atlantic and Pacific (A & P) Tea Company (groceries) and F. W. Woolworth (manufactured dry goods) opened outlets in cities and towns throughout the United States. Opulent department stores, such as Wanamaker's in Philadelphia and Macy's in New York City, catered to middle-class residents. Companies such as Sears, Roebuck and Montgomery Ward printed mail-order catalogs of the products they sold and encouraged people to purchase items from the catalogs using installment plans. Being far from a metropolitan center and the actual stores was no longer an impediment to participating in the burgeoning consumer culture of the early twentieth century because of mail-order catalogs.

The Labor Force in the Industrial Era 工业时代的劳动力

The expansion of industry required a growing labor force. Migrants from within the United States and abroad were drawn to America's industrial cities during the Gilded Age. Before the Civil War, immigrants were primarily from northern and western Europe—Great Britain, Ireland, and the Germanic states. By the 1870s, new sources of immigration included southern and eastern Europe, Mexico, and China (until passage of the Chinese Exclusion Act in 1882) (see more on the "new immigration," page 213 and Period 7). Employers often hired recruiters to entice Europeans to emigrate to America. Recruiters paid for the passage of these immigrants, with the money later deducted from their wages. This practice was made illegal in 1885, but the flow of immigrants continued until the first decades of the twentieth century.

C. POVERTY AND WEALTH IN INDUSTRIALIZING AMERICA
美国工业化时期的贫穷与富足

As America became increasingly industrialized, communities became divided between the wealthy, living lives of opulence and "conspicuous consumption," and those living in poverty. However, despite long hours and low wages, the relative standard of living improved for many working-class Americans, as the prices of many goods and services decreased.

The Wealthy Class 富裕阶层

The decades after the Civil War saw the growth of a well-to-do class that greatly surpassed previous wealthy classes in terms of money, cohesiveness, and power. These wealthy businessmen built gaudy mansions in exclusive urban neighborhoods, and built equally sumptuous summer "cottages" in Newport, Rhode Island, and other exclusive spots. The social critic and economist Thorstein Veblen's book, *The Theory of the Leisure Class* (1899), coined the phrase "conspicuous consumption" to describe the lavish spending habits of the wealthy.

The Working Class 工人阶层

Wages for workers rose slightly in the decades after the Civil War, but were well below levels that economists consider necessary for a minimum degree of comfort. Further, wages could be cut during economic downturns, as is evident in the years following the panics of 1873 and 1893. Also, workers were vulnerable to the seasonal nature of work. However, individuals and families, recent arrivals to industrial cities and towns, had amounts of spending money that were unimaginable in their former homes—whether small farms in Kansas or rural villages in southern Italy. Further, although wage increases were meager, prices were falling for mass-produced goods during the Gilded Age. These trends made a world of new goods and services available to many working-class people.

D. ECONOMIC CONSOLIDATION 经济的巩固

Consolidation, monopolies, trusts, and holding companies became defining features of the business landscape during the Gilded Age. At the same time, new theories, such as Social Darwinism, which defended this new business landscape, gained currency.

The Rise of Major Industries 主要行业的兴起

During the Gilded Age of the late 1800s, the era of small, locally-oriented businesses began to give way to large corporations and trusts that came to dominate entire industries. The three most important industries of the era were railroads, the steel industry, and the oil industry. The corporate model spread to a wide variety of industrial processes, including the production of bicycles, clothing, shoes, and paper, as well as the processing of food products.

The "Robber Barons" "强盗式资本家"

The men who controlled the major industries in the United States came to be known as "robber barons," a scornful title meant to call attention to their cutthroat business activities and their attempts to control governments.

Andrew Carnegie and Vertical Integration (or Consolidation)
安德鲁·卡内基与垂直整合（或巩固）

Andrew Carnegie came to dominate the steel industry by investing in all aspects of steel production, from mining to transportation to processing and distribution. This type of organization is called vertical integration.

Rockefeller and Horizontal Integration (or Consolidation)
洛克菲勒与水平整合（或巩固）

Horizontal integration entails creating a monopoly, or near monopoly, in a particular industry. A common way that corporations gained monopoly control of an industry was by establishing trusts. A trust consisted of trustees from several companies involved in the same industry acting together rather than in competition with one another. John D. Rockefeller organized, in the oil-processing industry, the most well-known trust: Standard Oil.

Other "Robber Barons" 其他 "强盗式资本家"

Carnegie and Rockefeller were the most famous "robber barons." Others included Collis P. Huntington, a railroad magnate; Mark Hanna, a coal and iron merchant who became a leading senator from Ohio; Philip Armour, a meat-processing giant in Chicago; and Stephen Elkins, a magnate in mining, railroads, and politics. Financiers, such as J. P. Morgan, parlayed leverage attained through control of various industries, including several railroad companies, into dominance of the entire U.S. economy.

E. LOOKING ABROAD FOR NEW MARKETS AND RESOURCES
转向国外寻找新的市场和资源

Both political and business leaders began to look abroad—to the Pacific, Asia, and Latin America—to gain greater access to foreign markets and resources.

Industry and Empire 工业与帝国

Not long after the major European powers began carving up Africa and Asia, the United States entered the scramble for overseas possessions. Many Americans resisted the idea of the United States embarking on overseas expansion; after all, the country had been born in a war against a major imperial power. However, the growing industrial capacity of the United States and the desire for new markets led the country to look abroad. The American acquisition of Hawaii and the Spanish-American War (both 1898) set the United States on the path of having a global presence. (The role of the United States as an imperialist power is discussed in detail in Period 7.)

II. Schisms and Contestation in Industrializing America
美国工业化时期的分裂与争论

Although many Americans hoped to create a unified, industrialized nation, divisions opened up on a number of fronts, including government policy, ethnicity, region, and class.

A. LAISSEZ-FAIRE POLICIES IN THE GILDED AGE 镀金时代的自由放任政策

Critics of corporate power pushed the government to take steps to rein in the massive corporations of the Gilded Age. However, these efforts at regulation were vigorously opposed by industrial leaders. Opponents of regulation argued that laissez-faire policies promoted economic growth. The French phrase *laissez-faire* means "to let alone." It describes a government policy that would take a hands-off approach to regulating economic activities.

Resistance to Regulation 对管理的抵制

Reformers and critics of the new industrial capitalist order pushed for government measures designed to regulate economic activities. These efforts were strenuously opposed by defenders of laissez-faire policies. Efforts at regulation were often hampered by the courts and by lax enforcement. Take, for example, the case of railroad regulation: In 1886 the Supreme Court, in the *Wabash, St. Louis and Pacific Railway Company v. Illinois* case, limited the ability of states to regulate railroads, asserting that states could not impose "direct" burdens on interstate commerce. In response, the federal government created the Interstate Commerce Commission (1887) to regulate railroads. However, the ICC was chronically underfunded and was, therefore, ineffective. A similar pattern can be seen in antitrust legislation. In 1890 the Sherman Antitrust Act was passed to break up trusts. The act, however, had only limited usefulness. In the case of *United States v. E. C. Knight Company* (1895), the Supreme Court greatly limited the scope of the act by making a distinction between trade (which would be subject to the act) and manufacturing (which would not).

B. MIGRATIONS AND A DIVERSE WORKFORCE 移民与多元化的劳动力

Migrations from abroad and from within the United States created an expanded and more diverse industrial workforce. The growing labor force also resulted in lower wages and an increase in child labor.

Immigration and the Industrial Workforce 移民与工业劳动力

After 1880, immigration took on new importance in providing a steady stream of workers for American factories and in transforming American society. Immigrants, and internal migrants, flooded into the industrializing cities of the United States (and to a lesser degree of Europe).

Women and Children in the Labor Force 劳动力中的妇女和儿童

As the nature of work changed from skilled craftsmanship to unskilled tasks in a mass-production system, children and women began to enter the paid workforce in large numbers. Because wages for working-class men remained relatively low, families often had to supplement their incomes with children and women entering the labor force. In turn, the influx of women and children into the labor force depressed overall wages. From the 1870s until World War I, child labor grew each decade. By 1900, children, aged 10–15 years old, made up 18 percent of the industrial workforce. The number of women in working-class communities who worked in the industrial labor force also increased in the Gilded Age. By 1900, women made up 17 percent of the industrial workforce.

C. CONFLICT AT THE WORK SITE　工作地冲突

The post–Civil War period witnessed a marked increase in the number and intensity of workplace conflicts between labor and management. Workers organized local and national unions and engaged in battles with management over wages and working conditions.

The Declining Status of Work in the Age of Industrialization
工业化时代工作地位的下降

Workers saw their position and status erode during the Gilded Age period, as cutthroat competition and mechanization of the production processes worsened working conditions. Wages rose incrementally for workers during this period, but gains were precarious—often erased during cyclical downturns in the economy. In addition, the increased reliance on child labor and the growing number of immigrants further eroded wages. The wealth generated by the rapid expansion of industry in the post–Civil War period was certainly not evenly distributed.

In addition, marginal gains in income were offset by a countervailing trend—the loss of control over the processes of production. Mass-production techniques entailed the breakdown of processes, so that workers could perform a specific task that did not require a great deal of training or skill. The age of the autonomous craftsman, who determined the conditions and pace of work, went by the wayside in the age of industrial capitalism. This "de-skilling" of the work process led to a loss of any sense of pride in one's work, but also to an increase in unsafe and unsanitary conditions. The loss of control of the work process was often a root cause of worker grievances of the Gilded Age. Many workers responded by forming and joining labor organizations, or unions, to advance their cause through collective bargaining and, if all else failed, through striking.

An Era of Pitched Battles in the Workplace　工作地的激战时代

The fierce labor battles were almost exclusively won by management, with its near-monopoly on firepower, the support of the government and the courts, and vast numbers of poor, working-class men willing to serve as strike-breakers. These battles often occurred in the wake of announced pay cuts during the economic downturns of the 1870s and of the 1890s.

The Knights of Labor　劳动骑士

A significant early union was the Knights of Labor, founded in 1869. This union welcomed all members, regardless of race, gender, or level of skill. The Knights had a broad agenda that included not only improvements in wages and hours for their workers, but also social reforms such as better safety rules and an end to child labor. By 1886, the organization had approximately 800,000 members, but by the 1890s a series of circumstances, as well as organizational problems, caused a sharp decline in the Knights' membership and influence. Ethnic, linguistic, and racial barriers among members of the Knights of Labor made united action more difficult. In addition, a centralized and autocratic governing structure within the Knights of Labor prevented new leadership from expanding the organization. Finally, government repression in the wake of the Haymarket bombing in Chicago (see below) weakened the organization.

The Great Railroad Strike of 1877　1877年铁路大罢工

In 1877, The Baltimore and Ohio Railroad (B&O) announced a 10-percent pay cut for its workers. Wages had already been falling during the economic depression that followed the Panic of 1873. Railroad workers in West Virginia went on strike. Railroad workers down the line—in Pittsburgh, Chicago, and even San Francisco—followed suit. At its height, the Great Railroad Strike involved more than 100,000 railroad workers and more than half a million other workers. Violence erupted in nine states. President Rutherford B. Hayes called out federal troops, many recently withdrawn from enforcing Reconstruction policies in the South. Many observers thought a second civil war was unfolding.

> ## REASSIGNMENT OF TROOPS　军队重组
> Many of the soldiers assigned to put down the Great Railroad Strike of 1877 had just been released from duty in the South, as Reconstruction ended earlier that year.

The Haymarket Incident (1886)　甘草市场事件（1886）

In 1886, a strike at the McCormick Reaper Works in Chicago turned violent. Unskilled workers at the McCormick works struck and their jobs were quickly given to "scabs"—replacement workers. The striking workers attacked several of the "scabs" on May 3, two days after a large May Day rally in Chicago to demand an eight-hour day. The police and Pinkerton guards opened fire on the strikers, killing or injuring six men. The strikers called for a rally on May 4 in Haymarket Square. Toward the end of the rally a bomb exploded in the midst of the police ranks. Several police were killed. The police responded by opening fire on the rally. Eight strikers were tried and convicted on scanty evidence; four were executed. At the time, many Americans shied away from the perceived violence of the labor movement. The popularity of the Knights of Labor was especially hard hit.

The American Federation of Labor (1886)　美国劳工联合会（1886）

The American Federation of Labor, formed in 1886, differed from the Knights of Labor in that it included only skilled workers, the "aristocracy of labor." It did not permit unskilled workers to join, nor did it allow African Americans or women to join. It was known as a craft union, in distinction from the Knights, which was an industrial union. Further, the AFL did not engage in any sort of political activities. It was known as a "bread and butter" union, in that its one goal was getting higher wages and better conditions for its members. It did not work for broader social reform. The AFL maintained a growing membership into the twentieth century. One of its founders and its first leader was a cigar maker named Samuel Gompers

The Homestead Strike (1892)　霍姆斯特德大罢工（1892）

A momentous labor battle took place at Andrew Carnegie's steelworks in Homestead, Pennsylvania, in 1892. Though Carnegie had the reputation of being a friend of labor, he was determined to break the union—the Amalgamated Association of Iron and Steel Workers, a powerful craft union under the AFL umbrella. When the Amalgamated's contract expired in 1892, Carnegie announced that he would not renew it—in effect breaking the union. Carnegie traveled outside of the country in the summer of 1892 and left the plant under the charge of manager Henry Clay Frick, a notorious anti-union man. Frick built a fence around the plant, locked-out the workers, brought in "scabs," and hired Pinkerton guards to enforce his edicts. A battle ensued between the "Pinks" and the workers. The workers won a temporary victory, and took over the plant, but the governor then called in 8,000 National Guard troops to retake it. Frick was able to reopen the plant, without union workers, in a devastating blow for organized labor.

The Pullman Strike: Strife in a Company Town (1893)
普尔曼大罢工：工业城镇的冲突

The Pullman strike occurred during the economic downturn following the Panic of 1893. The Pullman Company, which built railroad cars, cut wages several times in 1893 and 1894. Pullman was also the name of the town in Illinois where the workers lived. The town was built by the Pullman Company in 1880 as a model company town. The housing was better than most working-class housing, but was also more costly. The town exemplified the two sides of company towns—on the one hand it provided decent housing, but on the other hand it allowed the company to have a great deal of control over its workers and to deny housing to "troublemakers" (such as pro-union workers). The company owned all the housing, and rent was taken directly out of wages. When wages were cut in 1893 and 1894, rents were not cut. Workers appealed to the American Railway Union (ARU), led by Eugene V. Debs, to come to their aid. In May 1894, three union organizers were fired. Soon, most of the 3,300 workers were on strike. ARU members across the nation voted to support the strike by refusing to handle trains that contained Pullman cars. Railroad traffic was brought to a standstill. Courts issued two injunctions against the strike. President Grover Cleveland eventually called out federal troops to put it down. Violence immediately ensued, leading to the death of 25 strikers. The strike ended in defeat for the union, with new workers hired by Pullman. In the wake of the episode, the Supreme Court, in *In re Debs* (1895), decided that the government was justified in stopping the strike.

> **THE COURTS AND STRIKERS**
> **法院与罢工**
>
> During the Gilded Age, the courts generally sided with management over labor. *In re Debs* and *United States v. E. C. Knight Company* are two examples of Supreme Court cases that went against labor.

> **"COMPANY TOWNS"** **"工业城镇"**
>
> Pullman, Illinois, was one of many company towns built during the industrialization of America in the late nineteenth and early twentieth centuries. Those towns shared certain features with Pullman: slightly better living conditions in exchange for being under the control and watch of the company.

D. THE LIMITED SUCCESS OF CALLS FOR A "NEW SOUTH"   呼唤"新南方"的有限成功

Promoters of a "New South" encouraged industrialization in the southern states. Although some segments of the southern economy experienced industrialization, overall the South remained predominantly agrarian, with sharecropping and tenant farming dominating the region.

The "New South" "新南方"

After the Civil War, several southern public figures argued for a "New South." The most prominent of these spokesmen was Henry Grady, an Atlanta journalist. He argued for a mixed economy in the South that would include industrialization. He wanted to move away from the single-crop plantation agriculture of the "Old South." It was hoped that southern industrialists could join forces with northern businessmen and bankers.

There were pockets of industrialization in the South, especially textile production. However, for the most part, the promise of a "New South" proved to be hollow. For the remainder of the nineteenth century, and well into the twentieth century, the South remained mired in poverty and underdevelopment. African Americans continued to toil in the sharecropping system or as tenant farmers (see Period 5). Both systems involved African Americans working land that they did not own. In the sharecropping system, farmers would pay "rent" with a portion—or share—of their yearly crop. Tenant farming was a slight step up the social ladder from sharecropping. Generally, tenant farmers rented land from a landowner, paying in cash. Often the tenant farmer owned his own tools and only had to rent the land itself at a fixed rate.

III. Farmers Respond to Mechanized Agriculture 农民对机械化农业的反应

Farmers in the last decades of the nineteenth century found themselves drawn into the world of mechanized agriculture. In many cases, these farmers formed local and regional organizations in order to resist the power of railroads (which controlled the price of shipping crops) and corporate interests.

A. MECHANIZATION AND THE TRANSFORMATION OF AMERICAN AGRICULTURE
机械化与美国农业的转变

By the late 1800s, mechanization was rapidly transforming American agriculture. Mechanization had both positive and negative effects for American farmers. It increased overall agricultural production, but it also led to lower prices for agricultural products.

The Impact of Mechanization 机械化的影响

During the decades following the Civil War, expensive machines, such as the mechanical reaper and the combine harvester, replaced hand-held tools to harvest field crops. This equipment greatly expanded agricultural output and reduced the man-hours needed for agricultural tasks such as mowing, baling, and threshing. Production of corn and wheat soared, more than doubling between 1870 and 1900. The mechanical combine and the mechanical reaper allowed a single farmer to tend hundreds of acres instead of just a few. At the same time, mechanization worked to undermine small-scale family farms. First, the overall increase in production lowered the prices that farmers received per bushel of corn or wheat. Second, most farmers could not afford the new equipment. By the late 1800s and into the 1900s, large-scale farms came to dominate agriculture in the United States. Agriculture changed from small-scale farms with laborers using hand tools into large-scale mechanized operations. Many smaller farmers went out of business because they could not compete with the large farms.

B. AGRARIAN RESISTANCE IN THE FACE OF STRUCTURAL CHANGE
农民对农业结构变化的抵制

Farmers created local and regional organizations in response to dramatic changes in agriculture in the late 1800s.

Debt and Dependence in the Gilded Age 镀金时代的债务与依赖

During the post–Civil War period, farmers felt they were being squeezed from all sides. Railroad companies were overcharging farmers for carrying their produce to Chicago and other destinations. Also, the tight supply of currency in the United States was making it difficult for farmers to pay off their debts and at the same time was driving down the commodity prices they received for their crops. Also, banks were foreclosing on farms. These problems led farmers to seek solutions through forming local and regional organizations to challenge corporate power. Some of their political agitation was carried out within the two-party system but, significantly, they decided to also work outside of mainstream politics.

The Greenback Party 绿背党

An early political formation that sought an expansion of the currency supply was the Greenback Party. Founded in 1878—during the economic downturn following the Panic of 1873—the party advocated issuing paper money that was not backed by gold or silver. This was done briefly during the Civil War, resulting in farmers receiving higher prices for their crops. The party received a million votes in the 1878 congressional elections. The party soon disbanded, but the call for expanding the money supply was taken up again following the panic of 1893.

THIRD PARTIES IN AMERICAN HISTORY
美国历史上的第三党

It is very difficult for a third-party candidate to win elections in the American political system, which favors the two main parties. So why join a third party? Third parties often put issues on the national agenda, even if they do not win the election. This has been true from abolitionism to environmentalism.

The Grange and Granger Laws 格兰奇与《格兰奇法》

The National Grange of the Patrons of Husbandry, more commonly known as the Grange, is a farmers' organization that pushed for state laws to protect farmers' interests. Founded in 1867, it led the fight in many Midwestern states to pass laws that regulated railroad freight rates and made certain abusive corporate practices illegal. These laws came to be known as Granger Laws. Initially, the Supreme Court, in *Munn v. Illinois* (1877), upheld these laws, asserting that it was within the government's permissible powers to regulate private industry. Later, the court reversed itself. In *Wabash v. Illinois* (1886), the court ruled that individual states could not regulate railroads because they cross state lines. This led to the federal government establishing the Interstate Commerce Commission to regulate railroads (1887).

Protecting Communal Lands of the Southwestern *Hispanos*

保护西南方西班牙人公有地

Clashes occurred in the 1880s and 1890s in the Southwest between recently arriving settlers from older states and long-time Mexican and American Indian occupants of the land. Much of the conflict occurred in northern New Mexico, which was federally administered land that the United States gained from Mexico following the Mexican-American War (1846–1848). For years newcomers had been migrating to this area and squatting on the land. The Homestead Act of 1862 gave these squatters a degree of legitimacy in the eyes of the federal government.

Large portions of these lands were used communally by the local *Hispano* population (the name given to people of colonial Spanish descent in what would become the United States). Hispanos lived in villages and used the surrounding lands for grass, timber, water, and other resources. By the 1890s, the local Hispanos and Indians had lost more than 90 percent of their traditional lands and began organizing resistance. Attempts by the local population to regain their lands from federal authorities fell on deaf ears. The Surveyor of General Claims Office generally demanded that documentation of ownership be in English, but titles held by the Hispanos were in Spanish. Finally, groups such as Las Gorras Blancas (named after the white caps they wore) and Las Manos Negras (The Black Hands) organized resistance. This included raids on settler-held land, often cutting fences and burning property.

C. FARMERS AND THE POPULIST PARTY 农民与平民党

The People's (Populist) Party was formed by activists to challenge the growth of corporate power over the agricultural sector. The party sought a radical redistribution of power in the United States and pushed for stronger government control of the economy.

Organizing the Populist Party 组建平民党

The Populist Party, which was born in 1892, was able to harness growing discontent following the Panic of 1893 and gave a voice to a radical program for change that included increased democracy, a graduated income tax, regulation of the railroads, and currency reform. The Populists insisted that the amount of currency in circulation was insufficient. It sought to undo the "crime of '73," referring to the 1873 act of Congress to put the United States on the gold standard (see page 236). The call for the "free and unlimited coinage" of silver became one of the main rallying cries of the Populists. Their program was included in the Omaha Platform, written at their founding convention in 1892. The party did remarkably well in the presidential election later that year, garnering more than a million votes and 22 electoral votes. The party made solid gains in the midterm election of 1894, electing six senators and seven representatives from the farming regions in the South and the West. The Populists were perhaps the most successful third party in the nineteenth century, but their popularity was short-lived.

> ## THE "HAYSEED" VERSUS THE "POPULIST"
> ## "乡巴佬" 与 "平民党"
>
> Farmers have been represented throughout history as slow and dim-witted. Their participation in the Grange, in farmer coops, and in the populist movement demonstrated a level of sophistication at odds with the image of the "hayseed." Avoid condescending stereotypes.

The Election of 1896 and the "Cross of Gold" Speech 1896年选举与"金十字架"演说

The election of 1896 was significant in several ways. It resulted in the demise of the Populist Party and helped establish the identity of the major political parties in the twentieth century. The most contentious issue in the election was the amount of currency in circulation. William Jennings Bryan ran for president in 1896 on the ticket of the Democratic Party. He broke with the more conservative elements in the party and endorsed the call for the "free and unlimited coinage of silver." In his famous "Cross of Gold" speech, he promised not to let the American people be crucified "upon a cross of gold." He was also endorsed by the farmer-oriented

THE "CROSS OF GOLD" SPEECH
"金十字架" 演说

Be familiar with Bryan's speech; it appears frequently on the AP exam.

Populist Party because of his support for the free coinage of silver. The Republican candidate, William McKinley, appealed to banking and business interests by promising to keep the country on the gold standard. McKinley's victory was devastating to the Populist Party, which had thrown its support to Bryan. The positions of the two parties shaped the political landscape well into the twentieth century. The Republican Party continued to be more aligned with pro-business interests, and the Democratic Party continued to present itself as the champion of the "little guy."

KEY CONCEPT 6.2 URBAN AND RURAL TRANSFORMATION IN THE AGE OF INDUSTRIAL CAPITALISM
核心概念6.2：工业资本主义时代城市与农村的转变

Industrialization dramatically transformed both urban and rural areas. Waves of migration—both into cities and the American West—caused dramatic social and cultural changes.

I. The Transformation of the City in the Gilded Age 镀金时代城市的转变

During the age of industrial expansion, the population of urban centers grew dramatically. Migrants from abroad and from within the United States flooded into American cities and created a new urban culture.

A. MIGRATIONS AND URBANIZATION 移民与城市化

In the last decades of the nineteenth century, cities drew immigrants from southern and eastern Europe as well as from Asia. In addition, African Americans began leaving the rural South to come to cities in the South and in the North. A number of factors propelled these migrations—religious persecution, poverty, and the lack of social mobility in the countries and regions of origin of the migrants.

The "New Immigration" "新移民"

The large wave of immigrants who came to the United States between 1880 and 1920 was essential to the industrialization of the United States. Immigration patterns changed during the years of the Gilded Age. The Irish and German immigrations of the pre–Civil War years were supplemented by waves of immigrants from southern and eastern Europe and from Asia. An estimated 20 million people—from Russia, Italy, Poland, the Balkan region, China, and elsewhere—immigrated to the United States, most settling in industrial cities such as New York, Pittsburgh, and Chicago. The label "new immigrants" was applied to these groups.

These immigrants tended to come from the areas just behind the industrial core of Europe and North America (an area bounded by Chicago, St. Louis, and Toronto in the West, and Berlin, Warsaw, and Milan in the East). The ring of agricultural areas beyond this core—primarily southern and eastern Europe, but also Scandinavia, Canada, the South and West of the United States, and northern Mexico—supplied the vast majority of immigrants as traditional economic patterns broke down in the face of capitalist development. Immigrants were drawn to the economic opportunities of the United States, although many Jews left Russia to avoid anti-Semitic massacres known as pogroms.

The "Exoduster" Movement "大迁徙" 运动

As Reconstruction came to an end (see Period 5), many African Americans in the South realized that they were losing the few white political allies they had in their home states. The withdrawal of federal oversight in the South, accompanied by a rise in Ku Klux Klan violence and the enactment of Jim Crow laws, solidified the status of African Americans as second-class citizens. In this atmosphere, some African Americans decided to abandon the South. Starting in the late 1870s, a movement of approximately 40,000 African Americans—labeled the "Exoduster" movement—departed from states along the western tier of the former Confederacy, crossing the Mississippi River to settle in Kansas. Smaller numbers settled in Oklahoma and Colorado. Some "Exodusters" made it only as far as Missouri. African American activists and white philanthropists established organizations, such as the Colored Relief Board and the Kansas Freedmen's Aid Society, to help "Exodusters" make the journey to Kansas. The most successful "Exodusters" settled in the growing towns of Kansas.

B. THE NEW CULTURE OF THE IMMIGRANT CITY 移民城市的新文化

The growing cities of the Gilded Age provided new cultural opportunities for their residents, but also began to show deep social and economic divides along lines of class, race, ethnicity, and culture.

A Divided City 分裂的城市

The Gilded Age is characterized by a bifurcation, or division, of the city between working class districts and wealthy enclaves. Before the Civil War, different classes lived in close proximity to one another. An owner of a printing shop, for example, might live on the second and third stories of a building, above his street-level shop. His apprentices might live in his attic—owner and workers under one roof. However, in the second half of the century, the middle class and the wealthy moved from the industrial zones, away from the noisy factories and docks and from the stench of the slaughterhouses. In New York City, the wealthy moved uptown; elsewhere, they moved away from the urban core. In the bifurcated city the working-class districts tended to become utterly squalid, while the wealthier areas had the nicest amenities—wider streets, large parks, and sunlight.

Living Conditions for the Working Class and the Poor

工人阶层与穷人的生活状况

Despite small increases in wages, the working class and the poor were often crowded into substandard tenement housing in squalid neighborhoods. The densest neighborhood in the world in the late 1800s was the Lower East Side of New York. Conditions there were typical of many similar districts in other cities—many people packed into small apartments in substandard tenement buildings, lack of ventilation and light, streets thick with horse dung, and a lack of basic municipal services—sewer lines, running water, garbage removal. The conditions of the poor were chronicled in photojournalist Jacob Riis's *How the Other Half Lives*. His grim photographs of tenement life drew many people's attention to the plight of the poor.

> ### WAS JACOB RIIS A RACIST?
> ### 雅各布·里斯是种族主义者吗?
> Jacob Riis's work certainly reflected contemporary middle-class perceptions of different ethnic groups. His depictions could be read as condescending and sentimental. His descriptions of "hot-headed" Italians, of "senseless idolatry" among Chinese people, and of "the Jew [who] runs to real estate as soon as he can save up enough for a deposit to clinch the bargain," strike many contemporary readers as insensitive and reductionist.

Working-Class Culture and Urban Life　工人阶层文化与城市生活

City life, modest increases in wages, and a slightly shorter workday provided more opportunities for leisure-time activities for the masses of urban residents. The large number of working-class people moving into cities transformed urban culture and changed the physical city itself. The most popular leisure-time activity for working-class men was drinking in saloons. Saloons were often part social hall, part political club, and part community hub. The reformist attacks on saloons, and on alcohol consumption in general, were seen as attacks on working-class immigrant culture as much as they were on drunkenness.

C. DEBATES OVER IDENTITY AND IMMIGRATION　关于身份与移民的争论

Immigrants often grappled with issues of assimilation—how much would they "Americanize" and how much would they seek to retain their native cultures. In addition, many Americans already living in the country expressed concerns about the identity of the United States in an era of mass immigration.

The Persistence of Ethnicity in the Gilded Age City　镀金时代城市种族观念的持续

The large number of immigrants pouring into the United States in the late 1800s dramatically altered the social geography of American cities (see Period 7). At the same time, the experience of moving to the United States remade the immigrants themselves. Immigrants from the small towns and rural areas of Europe had to adjust to life in urban America. They felt the pull of assimilation on one hand and the desire to maintain a sense of ethnic solidarity on the other. In New York, Chicago, and other large cities, foreign-language papers emerged, such as the Yiddish-language *Jewish Daily Forward* and the Italian-language *Il Progresso Italo-Americano*. Parts of New York, such as lower Manhattan's Little Italy and the Jewish neighborhoods of the Lower East Side, became increasingly defined by ethnicity. Immigrant groups established savings institutions, insurance programs, choruses, political organizations, and summer camps. The various ethnic enclaves of the Gilded Age city provided grocery stores so that immigrants could purchase foods reminiscent of their countries of origin. Some newcomers to the city did not intend to stay. Millions of immigrants, mostly young men, worked for part of the year in the United States and then spent part of the year in their home country. These young men were called "birds of passage" because of their seasonal migrations.

Immigration and Nativism　移民与排他主义

These new immigrant groups were seen by some as markedly different from the pre–Civil War groups, in terms of appearance, language, and customs. The "new immigrants" heightened fears among conservative, Protestant public figures, such as Henry Cabot Lodge and Madison Grant. These nativists feared that the Anglo-Saxon Americans were committing "race suicide" by allowing "inferior" races to enter America in large numbers.

D. POWER AND REFORM IN URBAN AMERICA　美国城市的权利与改革

The growing cities experienced changes in governance and movements for political reform. Political machines became increasingly powerful in urban America, sometimes providing social services to immigrant groups in exchange for political support. Settlement houses and self-help groups emerged in the last decades of the nineteenth century to help immigrants adapt to life in America.

Urban Politics and the Rise of Machine Politics 城市政治与机器政治的兴起

Politics in major cities came to be dominated by "political machines." In the aftermath of the Civil War, political parties on the local level created smooth-running organizations whose purpose was to achieve and maintain political power. Political ideology was barely a concern in these bare-knuckled electoral contests. New York City was dominated by the Democratic Party machine, run by party "bosses" and headquartered at Tammany Hall. The most famous Tammany chief was William Marcy Tweed. "Boss" Tweed and other political leaders earned a reputation for corruption. Tweed's complicated schemes included the building of a courthouse that involved millions of dollars in kickbacks to Tammany Hall. Tweed's nefarious doings were exposed by the press, most notably by editorial cartoonist Thomas Nast. The Tammany Hall political machine was popular with German and Irish immigrants; under the Democratic Party, the city initiated massive municipal projects that provided jobs to thousands of immigrants.

> **IMMIGRANTS AND POLITICAL MACHINES**
> **移民与政治机器**
> Do not be too quick to condemn political machines for exploiting immigrants. The relationship is complicated. Political machines were corrupt, but they provided real benefits to immigrant communities.

The Campaign Against Prostitution 打击卖淫

The issue of prostitution tapped into the concerns of a variety of constituencies. Religious-based activists saw it as sinful. Campaigners for gender equality saw a double standard in society's acceptance of male extramarital sexual activities (including with prostitutes). Public-health advocates saw prostitution as a means of spreading venereal disease. Anti-poverty activists saw prostitution as reinforcing a cycle of poverty for working-class women. These forces united in pressuring local authorities to close "red-light" districts. Later, in the early twentieth century, progressive reformers successfully lobbied for the Mann Act (1910), which cracked down on the transport of women across state lines to engage in prostitution.

The Temperance Campaign 禁酒运动

The movement to ban alcohol from American society was one of the largest reform movements in the nineteenth century. The Anti-Saloon League (founded in 1895) and the Women's Christian Temperance Union (founded in 1874) headed the temperance campaign in the early twentieth century. The temperance movement was especially popular among women. Many women, who had the responsibility of putting food on the table, were troubled by the fact that their husbands often drank away their paychecks. Another reason for the popularity of the temperance crusade was that it complemented the growing nativist, or anti-immigrant, movement. (See more on the temperance movement in Period 7.)

E. THE GROWTH OF THE URBAN MIDDLE CLASS AND THE EXPANSION OF CONSUMER CULTURE 城市中产阶级的壮大与消费文化的扩张

The spread of the corporate model and the consolidation of major businesses led to a managerial revolution (see page 210). This revolution required a host of managers, clerical workers, salespeople, and accountants. The new urban industrial economy also required a host of support services—such as health care, education, and legal services. The expansion of the middle class and the growing amount of leisure time led to a new consumer culture.

The Rise of the Middle Class 中产阶级的兴起

Traditional accounts of the Gilded Age have often focused on the great disparities between the nouveau riche and the struggling working class—between the mansions of Newport, Rhode Island, and the tenements of the Lower East Side. Another important element of the new economy was the dramatic rise of the middle class. A class of white-collar employees became essential to the successful functioning of industrial capitalism. White-collar employees saw their wages rise faster than working class (blue-collar) men and women, and their average work day was shorter than that of laborers and factory workers.

Women filled many of the lower-level white-collar jobs, as more office workers were hired in the large firms of the Gilded Age. Secretarial work had been seen as men's work in the pre-Civil War period, as is evident in Herman Melville's 1853 short-story, "Bartleby, the Scrivener: A Story of Wall Street" (The story of an office clerk who suddenly refuses to perform his duties). As the typewriter came into use, literate women learned the skill and were hired to perform office duties. Women were also hired as schoolteachers, a growing field in the late 1800s. On the eve of the Civil War, there were only 100 public high schools in the United States; by 1900, that figure had climbed to 6,000.

> ### THE ROMANTICIZING OF THE WEST
> ### 西部的浪漫化
> Be aware of the differences between the real history of the West and the romanticizing of that history. "Buffalo Bill" Cody was romanticizing the "Old West" when people still had memories of the real West.

The Commercialization of Leisure 休闲的商业化

The growth of the middle class went hand in hand with the commercialization of leisure-time activities. The community-sponsored town fairs and dances of rural America were replaced by for-profit ventures in the city. The most successful large-scale "amusement park" was Brooklyn's Coney Island. Coney Island consisted of three main amusement areas, as well as a boardwalk, vaudeville theaters, and other assorted attractions. Among the most successful entertainments was "Buffalo Bill" Cody's Wild West show (starting in 1883), which mythologized the "Old West," just as the "Indian Wars" of the actual West were ending. Circuses became popular in the Gilded Age. P. T. Barnum created the most popular circus of the era (1871), labeling it "the greatest show on earth."

Newspapers 报纸

As printing costs went down and literacy went up, newspaper circulation increased dramatically in the Gilded Age. In the latter decades of the nineteenth century, large-circulation papers, such as Joseph Pulitzer's *New York World* and William Randolph Hearst's *New York Journal*, gained readership through exaggerated, sensationalistic coverage of events. This "yellow journalism" (named for yellow ink used on some sections) played a role in pushing public opinion toward support for the 1898 Spanish-American War (see Period 7).

> ### "MUCKRAKING JOURNALISM" VERSUS "YELLOW JOURNALISM"
> ### 揭发丑闻的新闻与耸人听闻的新闻
> Do not confuse these two terms. Muckrakers were genuinely interested in exposing social ills. "Yellow journalism" was simply a technique using sensational headlines to sell newspapers.

The Health of the City and the Parks Movement 城市健康与公园运动

As cities became denser and more disease-ridden, reformers sought to provide more opportunities for city dwellers to enjoy outdoor recreation. Older notions of disease causation—that disease, for example, was divine punishment for sinful behavior—gave way to the idea that our environment plays a significant role in our health. Later, doctors adopted the germ theory of disease causation, put forth by German microbiologist Robert Koch (who was active from the 1870s to the 1900s). Public parks were part of a strategy to provide an alternative to dirty streets and alleyways (as well as saloons) for healthful recreation.

Frederick Law Olmsted and New York's Central Park
弗雷德里克·劳·奥姆斯特德与纽约中央公园

The most important park project of the nineteenth century was New York's Central Park (1858). The design competition was won by Frederick Law Olmsted and Calvert Vaux. The park embodies some of the contradictions of the parks movement. On the one hand, Olmsted sought to create a democratic meeting place where the city's different classes could congregate and enjoy the benefits of nature. On the other hand, working-class advocates wondered aloud why the park was built so far from the working-class districts of the city. Also, the rules and regulations made the park seem, to some people, more about social control than enjoyment.

Recreation and Spectator Sports 娱乐与观赏性体育

Park grounds soon became centers for a variety of recreation activities. Several of these activities went from being participatory activities to spectator sports. These include:

Baseball: Developed in 1845, baseball became the "national pastime" by the Gilded Age. The first truly professional team was the Cincinnati Red Stockings (1869).

Tennis: Lawn tennis was developed in Great Britain (1873) as mainly a women's sport. It gained popularity in America among men and women during the Gilded Age.

Croquet: Croquet was a popular activity in public parks during the last third of the nineteenth century. It was often played by mixed-gender groups.

Cycling: "Wheeling"—bicycle riding—became very popular in the Gilded Age. The difficult "penny-farthing" bicycles, with their enormous front wheel, gave way to the modern design of the "safety bicycle" in the 1880s. Wheeling was especially popular among women, who enjoyed the freedom from male supervision that bicycle riding offered.

Football: College football games became popular in the Gilded Age. The first contest was between Rutgers and the College of New Jersey (Princeton) in 1869.

II. Westward Migrations in the Gilded Age 镀金时代的西迁

As settlers moved westward, Native Americans were increasingly threatened. The reservation system, the destruction of the buffalo, military actions, and assimilationist policies worked to circumscribe Indian options and culture.

A. PROMOTING WESTWARD EXPANSION—GOVERNMENT POLICIES, RAILROADS, AND MINING OPERATIONS 推动西进运动——政府政策、铁路与采矿作业

A series of government policies encouraged settlement of the West. The building of transcontinental railroad lines and the discovery of mineral resources drew ever more people westward after the Civil War.

Government Policies and Westward Expansion 政府政策与西进运动

The federal government had long made it a priority to promote settlement of the West. After having expanded to the Pacific Ocean—the government took several steps to encourage westward settlement. The national government granted railroads swaths of land east to promote further construction of rail lines west of the Mississippi and to the Pacific Ocean (see page 209). In addition, the government continued the policy of extending land to individual farmers that it had begun with the Homestead Act of 1862 (see Period 5). The original Homestead Act had not proven to be as successful as its promoters had hoped. The size of the grants, 160 acres, were too small for the grazing and grain farming that characterized western agriculture. Also, although the land was free, homesteaders still needed to build homes and purchase the expensive equipment necessary for large-scale farming. The majority of land recipients sold their plots. Congress responded by increasing the size of plots granted to homesteaders. The Timber Culture Act (1873) allowed homesteaders to receive additional lands if they agreed to plant trees on a portion of it, and the Desert Land Act (1877) offered acreage for a discounted price if the recipients agreed to irrigate the land.

Government Support for Transcontinental Railroads 政府扶持横贯大陆的铁路

The Pacific Railroad Acts, passed in the 1860s, promoted government bonds and land grants to railroad companies to complete rail lines to the Pacific Ocean (see page 209). The completion of the transcontinental railroad at Promontory Summit, Utah, in 1869 was a milestone in the development of a network of railroad lines that connected the far reaches of the country. In the coming decades, four additional transcontinental lines were completed. Only the last of the five lines, the Great Northern Railway (completed in 1893), was privately built without benefit of federal land grants.

Railroad companies were anxious to sell the land they had been granted. The land in towns and cities along the transcontinental railway was valuable because of the new accessibility created by the rail lines. Western railroad companies relentlessly promoted land sales to the populations of the overcrowded cities of the East.

Mining Operations in the West 西部的采矿作业

The extraction of precious metals was hugely profitable in the nineteenth century and was a major motivation in the settlement of the West. The rush for riches began with the discovery of gold in California in 1849 (see Period 4) and continued for the next four decades throughout the West. In 1859, the extensive silver deposits of Nevada's Comstock Lode were discovered, leading to the creation of a major boomtown, Virginia City (see pages 227–228). Later, 1869, gold was discovered at Pike's Peak, which included land reserves in Kansas and Nebraska Territories. The influx of over 100,000 people into the region resulted in the establishment of boomtowns such as Denver City and Boulder City, and the rapid establishment of the Colorado Territory in 1861. Similar "rushes" occurred in the Dakotas, Montana, Arizona, Utah, and Idaho.

Most of the mining operations in the West went through similar stages. After word got out about the discovery of a precious metal, thousands of prospectors hurried to the area to attempt to be first to cash in. A few did; most did not. Soon, whatever deposits existed along the surface were quickly found by placer mining—using pans, sluice boxes, picks, and shovels along river beds. After that, a more industrial phase of mining occurred. To extract the vast deposits that lay beneath the surface required expensive hydraulic equipment. This equipment was beyond the reach of placer miners. Large mining firms invested in elaborate operations. Thus, mining had more in common with industrial operations in the East, with investors enjoying substantial profits, shares in operations being traded on international markets, and wage workers replacing prospectors.

B. SETTLING THE WEST　定居西部

A variety of economic opportunities drew people to the West, including building railroads, mining, timbering, farming, and ranching. Migrants to the West hoped to achieve a degree of self-sufficiency and independence.

Settling the West　定居西部

A variety of factors brought hundreds of thousands of settlers to the West in the period after the Civil War. In addition, the Homestead Act of 1862 (see Period 5) drew settlers to the West. By the late 1800s, a system of agricultural production and distribution developed, drawing western grain farmers into national and international markets. The populations of Minnesota, the Dakotas, Kansas, and Nebraska all grew dramatically between the end of the Civil War and 1900: from 300,000 to 5 million. Immigrants from Scandinavia, Germany, Canada, and Great Britain mingled with native-born whites and African-American "Exodusters" (see page 221) in this multicultural West.

Chinese Communities in the West　西部的华人社区

Chinese immigrants were initially drawn to North America by the gold rush in California (see Period 5). By 1852, 20,000 Chinese immigrants had moved to California; by 1870, over 63,000 lived in America, with nearly 80 percent in California. White Californians pushed for laws prohibiting Chinese people from being licensed to work in mining—mainly because they usually were laborers for large China-based companies. Chinese laborers ended up doing jobs that others avoided. Up to 12,000 Chinese workers helped complete the first transcontinental line in 1869, representing 90 percent of the workforce.

Chinese immigrants faced a great deal of discrimination and outright hostility. Federal naturalization laws, altered after the Civil War to accommodate African Americans, denied citizenship to Asian immigrants. When the economy suffered a major downturn in the 1870s, following the Panic of 1873, many Californians singled out the Chinese population as the cause of the crisis. Many labeled Chinese residents, "coolie labor," and insisted that their presence in California depressed wages. The Workingmen's Party was formed in 1876 to argue for legislation excluding Chinese immigrants from the United States. This activism, coming as Reconstruction was ending in the South, proved to be successful. The 1882 Chinese Exclusion Act represents the only instance in which a particular national group has been explicitly excluded by Congress from entrance into the United States.

Mining Boomtowns in the West　在西部开发新兴城市

Bustling towns seemed to grow overnight in parts of the West during the post-Civil War period. These towns were often populated by prospectors trying to strike it rich. As the towns grew, many women began to arrive, finding employment as boardinghouse owners, washerwomen, cooks, and maids. A typical boomtown was Virginia City, in present-day Nevada. The town was born in the wake of the discovery of the Comstock Lode, in 1859. By 1875, Virginia City had a population of over 25,000 people, making it one of the largest towns in the interior of the West. These boomtowns were very different from the "Wild West" towns portrayed in classic Western movies. For one, they were just as ethnically and racially diverse as typical cities in the East. Virginia City included Irish, Chinese, Germans, Italians, Mexicans, Scandinavians, French, and Canadians, immigrants from several South and Central American countries, African Americans, American Indians, and immigrants from as far away as Morocco and the Pacific Islands. Further, as mining operations became more elaborate and industrial, the towns more closely resembled the established industrial cities in the East—complete with schools, theaters, and churches.

Ranching and the Era of the Cowboy in the West 大牧场经营与西部牛仔时代

After the completion of transcontinental rail lines, cattle-ranching operations were established on the Great Plains. Ranching gave rise to the era of the cowboy, romanticized in "Western" literature and movies. From the mid-1860s to the mid-1880s, cowboys drove large herds of cattle across the open plains. These cowboys, many of whom were African American and Mexican, herded the cattle to seasonal grazing areas, and then, to railroad stops, where they would be shipped to Chicago for slaughter. By the mid-1880s, several factors ended the era of open-range grazing. Large ranchers began to enclose grazing areas with newly-invented barbed wire. These enclosures ended the era of driving herds across open plains. Further, severe blizzards in the late 1880s decimated the cattle population of the Great Plains. When the herds recovered, free-spirited cowboys were replaced by wage-earning hired-hands, working under managers on the giant ranches.

Farming on the Great Plains 大平原地区的农业

While the promise of gold and silver drew many people to the West in the years before and after the Civil War, the promise of owning land drew many more people West.

The Homestead Act (1862) and completion of the transcontinental railroad (1869) facilitated the movement of settlers and speculators. In the last three decades of the nineteenth century, millions of native-born whites, immigrants, and African Americans settled on farms West of the Mississippi River. From the last years of the Civil War until the turn of the twentieth century, nine new states joined the United States—starting with Nevada (1864) and Nebraska (1867) and ending with Wyoming (1890) and Utah (1896).

The first-generation pioneers drawn to the Great Plains were nicknamed "sodbusters" because they had to cut through the thick layer of sod to get to the topsoil needed for farming. Many of these settlers used the cut sod itself to build their houses (nicknamed "soddies").

About a fifth of the farmers who established farms in this era obtained land directly from the government through the Homestead Act and similar federal legislation. Most purchased land, either from railroads, which had substantial holdings as a result of land-grants from the government, or from speculators who obtained land from unsuccessful homesteaders. As the century progressed, the dream of land ownership proved to be beyond the means of many people. The family farms of the prairie gave way to large-scale agribusiness. The costs of mechanization and irrigation drove many farmers into debt, leading to bankruptcies and consolidation. Large-scale farming in the West followed a pattern similar to mining and ranching operations. By the end of the century, increasing numbers of residents of the West were migrant farmers, tenant farmers, sharecroppers, and hired employees as land ended up in fewer and fewer hands.

C. VIOLENCE ON THE FRONTIER   边疆的暴力

Increased migration to the West often led to violence on the frontier. White settlers increasingly clashed with American Indians and Mexican Americans.

Destruction of the Buffalo   水牛的灭绝

As railroads pushed westward, the herds of the American bison (commonly known as buffalo) were wiped out. Railroad workers and passengers went on a killing spree, shooting buffalo for food and (mostly) sport. Also, industrial uses for the hides of buffalo put pressure on their numbers. In a matter of decades, the buffalo herds on the Plains were virtually exterminated. This greatly weakened the Plains peoples, who depended on the buffalo for spiritual and physical sustenance.

The End of Autonomous American Indian Groups   美洲印第安人自治团体的终结

As more and more white settlers made their way into the West, American Indians felt their world constricting. By the 1880s, the last autonomous American Indians had been defeated in the "Indian Wars" and brought under U.S. control through a series of military conflicts. From the earliest encounters between white people and American Indians, white settlers had encroached upon tribal lands and, using superior firepower, pushed Indians farther into the interior of the continent. American attitudes and policies toward native peoples sometimes emphasized assimilation, sometimes removal, and sometimes extermination. All these approaches saw Indians as a problem that needed to be rectified.

D. GOVERNMENT POLICIES AND THE FATE OF AMERICAN INDIANS
政府政策与美洲印第安人的命运

The movement of people put additional pressures on land held by Native Americans and caused the federal government to violate treaties it had made with the tribes.

The Growth of the Reservation System   保留制度的发展

After the Civil War, starting in 1867, the government attempted to solve the "Indian problem" through peaceful means, rather than through more warfare. The center of this policy was pushing the tribes onto reservations—confined areas that were set aside by the government. This policy made Indians wards of the government until they learned "to walk on the white man's road." Often the lands set aside for reservations were incapable of sustaining crops, reducing the inhabitants to utter poverty. Many tribal groups resisted being put into reservations.

Treaty of Medicine Lodge (1867)   《梅迪辛洛奇条约》（1867）

Southern Plains Indians signed a treaty with the government at Medicine Lodge, Kansas, in 1867, agreeing to move to a reservation in exchange for government protection of their land from white encroachment.

Helen Hunt Jackson and the Call for Reform   海伦·亨特·杰克逊与改革呼吁

By the 1880s, white sympathizers of American Indians pushed for a change in government policy. A prominent reformer was Helen Hunt Jackson, whose 1882 book, *A Century of Dishonor*, chronicled the abuses the U.S. government committed against native peoples. She sent a copy of the book to each member of Congress. Historians have framed the activism of Jackson and other women within the context of gender norms in the Victorian era. It was seen as the duty of white middle-class women to civilize people. This duty was evident in the call for a reduction of cruelty toward the Indians by government forces. It can also be seen in the desire to "civilize" the native peoples; women, after all, were expected to provide a civilized home life as an antidote to the competition and greed of the market economy. These women were successful in lobbying for the 1887 Dawes Act.

The Dawes Act (1887) 《道斯法案》（1887）

Efforts at reform resulted in a shift in government policy toward American Indians. The Dawes Severalty Act (1887), also known as the General Allotment Act, abandoned the reservation system and divided tribal lands into individually owned plots ("severalty," in this case, refers to lands that are owned by individuals, not owned jointly). The goal of the policy was for American Indians to assimilate into white culture—specifically into the norms of white middle-class culture. The idea of forcing Indians to have private dwellings, with gardens and fences, reflected ideal middle-class living arrangements. This reform proved to be as damaging to American Indians as was the earlier reservation policy. The government eventually undid this destructive policy with the Indian Reorganization Act (1934), allowing autonomy for tribal lands.

Indian Boarding Schools 印第安寄宿学校

Beginning in the late 1870s, the Bureau of Indian Affairs established a series of Indian boarding schools that were designed to assimilate Indians into white culture by stripping them of their culture. The Carlisle Institute in Pennsylvania, established in 1879, was a model for other schools. Students were forced to cut their hair and to rid themselves of traditional clothing. They also had to practice Christianity and were trained in menial tasks. Col. Richard Henry Pratt, who was the headmaster at the Carlisle Institute for 25 years, neatly summed up the goal of the schools; his motto was, "Kill the Indian, save the man."

E. AMERICAN INDIAN RESISTANCE 美洲印第安人的反抗

American Indians developed different strategies to respond to threats to their land. The U.S. government responded to resistance with violence and with calls for assimilation.

The Ghost Dance Movement 鬼舞运动

In the midst of the apocalyptic losses suffered by American Indians in the 1870s and 1880s, some tribes adopted a spiritual practice known as the Ghost Dance. The Ghost Dance movement was developed by a Northern Paiute prophet named Wovoka. He drew on traditional American Indian rituals and emphasized cooperation among tribes and clean living and honesty. It was not successful in stopping white incursions, but it led to a spiritual revival that had a profound effect on Indian tribes into the twentieth century.

Massacre at Wounded Knee 伤膝河大屠杀

The last "battle" of the "Indian Wars" was a massacre at the Lakota reservation near Wounded Knee Creek in South Dakota, in 1890. U.S. forces attempted to disarm a group of Lakota

(Sioux) Indians camped there, but soon opened fire on them. More than two hundred Lakota men, women, and children were killed.

"INDIAN WARS" "印第安战争"

Historians discuss the "Indian Wars" as occurring during the post–Civil War years, but violence between whites and American Indians had been happening since the early days of the Jamestown colony. The fighting had moved farther west, generally on the frontier of white settlement.

KEY CONCEPT 6.3 THE CULTURE AND POLITICS OF THE GILDED AGE 核心概念6.3：镀金时代的文化与政治

New intellectual and cultural movements developed during the last decades of the nineteenth century. Americans also engaged in political debates over economic and social policies.

I. Cultural and Intellectual Movements of the Gilded Age
镀金时代的文化运动与思想运动

During this era, a variety of individuals and groups put forth ideas about the age they were living in. Some of these ideas justified the prevailing social structure of the day; others challenged it.

A. JUSTIFYING SUCCESS 为成功辩护

Writers and intellectuals put forth ideas justifying the socioeconomic structure of the Gilded Age—ideas that gained currency. Theories such as Social Darwinism saw the inequities of the era as both fitting and unavoidable.

The Waning of the "Free Labor" Ideal "自由劳动"理想的黯淡

In many ways, the rise of giant corporations ran counter to traditional American ideas about the economy and society. The "free labor" ideology of the pre-Civil War era put forth the idea that working for another person was a temporary condition; eventually each employee would accumulate enough money to start his own farm or shop. However, with the army of unskilled workers flooding into the massive firms of the late nineteenth century, it became increasingly clear that these people, and their offspring, were not going to rise to become independent entrepreneurs. As older ideas about the nature of the American economy became outmoded, new ones gained traction. Some of these ideas unabashedly embraced the new corporate order. Others challenged it (see pages 232–233).

Social Darwinism 社会达尔文主义

Social Darwinism was one attempt to defend the new social order. Social Darwinists sought to apply Charles Darwin's ideas about the natural world to social relations. The theory was popularized in the United States by William Graham Sumner. Sumner was attracted to Darwin's ideas about competition and "survival of the fittest." He argued against any attempt at government intervention into the economic and social spheres, a position that favored laissez-faire economic policies. Interference, he argued, would hinder the evolution of the human species. The inequalities of wealth that characterized the late 1800s were part of the process of "survival of the fittest."

> ## THE APPEAL OF SOCIAL DARWINISM
> ## 社会达尔文主义的呼吁
> Social Darwinism, with its call for a laissez-faire approach to the economy, appealed to owners of large corporations, because it both justified their wealth and power and warned against any type of regulation or reform.

Horatio Alger and the Myth of the Self-made Man 霍雷肖·阿尔杰与白手起家的故事

Horatio Alger wrote a series of "dime novels" (they cost 10 cents) that often featured a poor boy who achieves success in the world. The boy's success is usually the result of a bit of luck and a bit of pluck—fortunate circumstances as well as determination and perseverance. These "rags-to-riches" novels, such as *Ragged Dick*, put forth the idea that anyone could make it in Gilded Age America; the reality, of course, was quite different.

B. THE MORAL OBLIGATIONS OF THE WEALTHY CLASS 富裕阶级的道德义务

During the Gilded Age, some members of the business elite argued that the wealthy had a moral obligation to give something back to the community. These sentiments, most clearly articulated in Andrew Carnegie's essay "Wealth," led several rich business leaders to make major financial contributions that improved cities and enhanced educational opportunities.

Andrew Carnegie and "The Gospel of Wealth" 安德鲁·卡内基与《财富福音》

Andrew Carnegie asserted, in his essay "Wealth" (1899), that the rich have a duty to live responsible, modest lives and to give back to society. This "gospel of wealth" asserted that successful entrepreneurs should distribute their wealth so that it could be put to good use, rather than frivolously wasted. Carnegie ended up donating the majority of his fortune to charity and public-oriented projects. He believed in a *laissez-faire* approach to social problems. He did not want the government interfering in the social and economic spheres. That is, in part, why he urged his fellow millionaires to take action on behalf of the community. In this way, the government would not have to.

C. CHALLENGES TO THE DOMINANT CORPORATE ETHIC
占主导地位的企业伦理所面对的挑战

A variety of critics challenged the dominant corporate ethic of the day. Some of these critics offered utopian visions of the future, others questioned the logic of the capitalist system itself.

Henry George and the "Single Tax" on Land 亨利·乔治与土地"单一税制"

Henry George was a thinker, economist, and politician who was critical of the persistence of poverty in a nation of such technological and industrial progress. In his book, *Progress and Poverty* (1879), he criticized the vast resources, especially land, controlled by wealthy elite. He argued for a "single tax" on land values, which he believed would create a more equitable society.

Socialism and Anarchism 社会主义与无政府主义

Many Americans began to question the basic assumptions of capitalism and embraced alternative ideologies, such as anarchism and socialism. These radical ideas never gained the number of adherents in the United States that they did in Europe. Occasionally, conservative newspapers and politicians exaggerated the strength of these movements in the United States. Newspapers often conflated the labor movement in general with these "dangerous" movements in order to delegitimize or stigmatize the labor movement. Still, these movements had adherents in the United States. After the utter failure of the Pullman strike (see page 216), Eugene V. Debs moved away from the labor movement and toward socialism. He was one of the founders of the Socialist Party of America in 1901.

Edward Bellamy's *Looking Backward, 2000–1887*
爱德华·贝拉米的《回顾》（2000—1887）

The most famous American socialist tract of the nineteenth century was Edward Bellamy's *Looking Backward, 2000–1887* (1888). This novel imagined a man who falls asleep in 1887 and awakens in 2000 to find a socialist utopia in which the inequities and poverty of the Gilded Age have been eradicated.

Coxey's Army 科克西失业请愿军

In 1894, "Coxey's Army," a group of disgruntled workers, many of whom were recently laid-off by railroad companies, marched from Ohio, through Pennsylvania, and on to Washington, DC, to demand that the government take action to address the economic crisis. There were other similar "armies" of populist-inspired working-class men.

> ## WAS COXEY AHEAD OF HIS TIME?
> ## 科克西领先于他的时代吗？
>
> In 1894, the Coxeyites were ridiculed and ignored. However, a generation later, the New Deal consisted of exactly the types of programs Coxey and his men were pushing for. It shows that social movements influence government policies, but sometimes the process takes a while.

II. The Politics of the Gilded Age 镀金时代的政治

The profound economic and social changes of the Gilded Age generated political debates around corruption, citizenship, and the proper relationship between government and business.

A. GOVERNMENT CORRUPTION, BIG BUSINESS, AND THE CALL FOR REFORM
政府腐败、财团与改革呼吁

Close ties—and charges of corruption—came to define the relationship between government and business in the Gilded Age. In response to these charges, members of the public called for reform at the local, state, and national levels.

The Evolution of the Two-Party System 两党制的发展

Neither the Democrats nor the Republicans, the two main political parties from the Civil War to the present, were able to dominate national politics during the last decades of the nineteenth century. The Republicans controlled the White House for most of the period from 1869 to the turn of the century (the one exception was the two nonconsecutive terms of President Grover Cleveland). However, the elections were extremely close, with no presidential candidate receiving a clear majority of the popular vote in any election between 1872 and 1896. Control of Congress was split. The Republicans controlled the Senate for most of the period, and the Democrats controlled the House. Only briefly, for three different two-year periods, did one of the parties control the White House and both houses of Congress.

In many ways, the Gilded Age saw the two main political parties, the Democrats and the Republicans, become increasingly removed from the concerns of ordinary Americans. Both parties seemed more responsive to the priorities of the newly formed trusts and industrial giants than to the needs of farmers, workers, or the urban poor. Corruption permeated political life from the backrooms of local political clubhouses to the corridors of power in Washington, DC. A spate of reform movements developed to address this situation, most notably the People's Party, better known as the Populist Party, in the last decade of the nineteenth century.

Ideology Takes a Backseat 意识形态居次要地位

Neither of the two political parties took strong stands on most of the pressing issues of the day. Neither party showed a willingness to deal with any of the various problems associated with the industrial expansion of the age. Issues like child labor, the consolidation of industries, workplace safety, and abuses by railroad companies were either avoided or dealt with in a superficial fashion. Neither party did much to protect the rights of African Americans (especially after the end of Reconstruction) or of American Indians. Neither party addressed the call of many women for the right to vote. The one issue that consistently divided the parties was the tariff (Democrats wanted lower tariff rates and Republicans wanted higher tariff rates).

Both parties seemed aligned with the priorities of big business. Owners of major companies openly curried favor with congressmen with contributions, gifts, and outright bribery. Political leaders, even presidents, seemed to shrink in importance when compared with the towering industrial figures of the day. Cornelius Vanderbilt II, John D. Rockefeller, and Andrew Carnegie are far more clearly imprinted on the national collective memory than are the "forgotten presidents" of the Gilded Age.

Corruption and the Grant Administration 腐败与格兰特政府

American political life was rife with corruption during the post-Civil War period. This was true on the local level, as evidenced by the illegal schemes of "Boss" Tweed in New York, as well as on the national level. The administration of Ulysses S. Grant, former Union commanding general in the Civil War, was tainted by corruption. Historians assess Grant's ability as a president far below his abilities on the battlefield. The Republican president was not decisive on the issue of Reconstruction (see Period 5). In addition, he surrounded himself with incompetent and corrupt advisors and appointees. Grant rewarded friends, army contacts, and party loyalists with jobs that required political

CORRUPTION AND THE HISTORY OF RECONSTRUCTION
腐败与重建的历史

Corruption in American politics seemed everywhere during the Gilded Age. However, traditional histories of Reconstruction tended to single out the state Reconstruction governments for "extravagance" and corruption. More recent histories of the period look at such claims with a more critical eye.

experience, which his appointees sorely lacked. Though Grant was not directly charged with corruption, key members of his administration, including his vice president, were.

Corruption and Civil Service Reform 腐败与公务系统改革

Civil service reform became a major issue in the late nineteenth century. The civil service is the workforce of government employees. Attempts were made to remove nepotism and cronyism from government hiring practices. Reformers in the 1880s pushed for civil service jobs to be allocated to the most qualified people rather than to allies and relatives of powerful politicians.

Mugwumps, Stalwarts, and Half-Breeds 超然派、扈从派与混育派

The issue of civil-service reform divided the Republican Party in the wake of the scandals of the Grant administration. Reform-minded Republicans, mainly from Massachusetts and New York, were nicknamed "Mugwumps" by their critics, after the Algonquian word for "chief." They wanted to move away from the corruption of the Grant years and create a merit-based civil service. Those most resistant to abandoning the spoils system were nicknamed "Stalwarts." Those loyal to the Republican leadership, but wanting some degree of reform, were known as "Half-Breeds." Hayes, who won the disputed election of 1876, was not well liked by any of the factions and chose not to run for reelection in 1880.

The Pendleton Act 《彭德尔顿法案》

A series of events in the summer of 1881 made civil service reform a more pressing issue and led to passage of the Pendleton Act. The Republicans nominated James A. Garfield for president in 1880. He won the presidency, but was shot four months after his inauguration in 1881. Garfield died from the wound two months later. The assassin was no doubt unbalanced, but the reason he gave for his actions was that he was passed over when he sought a government job, despite his work on the Garfield campaign. Congress finally passed the Pendleton Act in 1883 to set up a merit-based federal civil service, a professional career service that allots government jobs on the basis of a competitive exam. This system still covers most of the bureaucratic jobs in the federal government. Upper-level, policy-oriented positions are still rotated when new presidential administrations come into office.

The Politics of Tariff Rates 关税税率政治

The rate of taxation on imported goods had long divided many Americans. Industrialists tended to encourage higher tariffs to keep out foreign competition. Farming interests tended to support a lower tariff rate. Their cotton and wheat sales to Europe benefitted from increased international trade; high tariffs impeded international trade. Republicans had pushed tariffs higher during the Civil War to fund the war effort. By the 1880s, the government was awash in money from the tariff, and tariff reformers argued that lowering the tariff would put more money into circulation and stimulate economic activity. President Chester Arthur also broke with Republican orthodoxy and looked into lowering the tariff. Tariff reform foundered in Congress; ultimately, a small decrease in tariff rates was passed.

The tariff issue remained contentious during Democratic president Grover Cleveland's first administration. Many Democrats, including Cleveland, began to push for lower rates. These tariff reformers became increasingly critical of the power of trusts and large corporations in dominating the economy. They saw high tariff rates as benefiting these big business interests at the expense of consumers and small producers. In 1888, the Republican Party nominated Benjamin Harrison, grandson of President William Henry Harrison. Business interests poured money into the Harrison campaign. In 1890, Harrison signed into law the highest tariff in the nation's history. The tariff became the most divisive issue in national elections in the post–Civil War period.

The Currency Issue 货币问题

The vibrant economic growth that characterized much of the last decades of the nineteenth century came to a screeching halt in 1893 (see more on the Panic of 1893 in Period 7). Many observers, both contemporaries and historians, cite the inadequate amount of currency in circulation as one of the underlying weaknesses in the economy. The money supply in the last decades of the nineteenth century did not have the possibility to grow as the economy expanded. For a decade the United States used metallic money, as stipulated in the Mint Act of 1792. The act allowed for the "free and unlimited coinage" of gold and silver. Individuals could coin gold or silver at a fixed ratio (the amount of silver in a silver dollar was to weigh fifteen times as much as the amount of gold in a gold dollar). However, in 1873, Congress changed this policy, allowing only for the coinage of gold. The amount of gold being coined in the 1870s and 1880s could not keep up with the growing economy. This was especially hard on farmers, as it depressed the prices they received for their goods, which made it difficult to repay loans. The situation was beneficial to bankers, who wanted a relatively stable currency so that money repaid on loans retained its value.

> ## CURRENCY AND INFLATION 货币与通胀
>
> Be familiar with basic economic concepts involving the currency supply. An expansion of the currency supply increases inflation. This would tend to benefit farmers, but would hurt consumers.

B. RETHINKING GENDER IN THE GILDED AGE: WOMEN'S PARTICIPATION IN THE POLITICAL SPHERE 镀金时代对性别的反思：妇女参政

Increasingly, women in this time challenged prevailing notions of gender by forming voluntary organizations, working in settlement houses to aid immigrants, attending college, and promoting social and political reform. These women, and their male allies, pushed for a greater degree of equality in the United States.

Challenging Notions of Domesticity 对家庭生活观念的质疑

As the economic dislocations wrought by industrialization touched more and more families, many women became more politically engaged. Many women began to challenge the rigid gender expectations embodied in the "cult of domesticity" (see Period 4). In the 1880s and 1890s, women's clubs began to emerge in many towns and cities. These clubs investigated and advocated around issues of poverty, working conditions, and pollution. In 1890, women organized an umbrella organization—the General Federation of Women's Clubs. These clubs often used the rhetoric of domesticity to justify their activism outside the home. The organization used the term "maternalism" to describe the dual role of women as mothers and as social activists. Many women put their energy into the temperance campaign to curb alcohol consumption in the United States. Founded in 1874, the Women's Christian Temperance Union (WCTU) became a mass organization, especially under the leadership of Frances Willard. Members of the WCTU later became involved in both the populist movement of the 1890s and the Progressive movement of the early twentieth century (see Period 7). Women continued to press for voting rights in the late 1800s. The National American Woman Suffrage Association was formed in 1890, merging two earlier suffrage groups (see Period 5).

Jane Addams and the Settlement House Movement 简·亚当斯与睦邻友好运动

The settlement house movement was the most visible example of an alliance between middle-class reformers and working-class men and women. Settlement houses were established to aid immigrants, especially immigrant women. By 1911, more than 400 settlement houses existed in the United States, usually run by women. Jane Addams founded and ran Hull House in Chicago; she is considered one of the founders of the field of social work in the United States. Addams wrote two autobiographical volumes, including *Twenty Years at Hull-House* (1910), and was awarded the Nobel Peace Prize in 1931.

C. THE POLITICS OF RACISM AND DISCRIMINATION 政治上的种族主义与歧视

Racist theories became prominent in the Gilded Age. These theories, along with the Supreme Court decision in the *Plessy v. Ferguson* case, justified discrimination, segregation, and even violence against African Americans. African American reformers challenged white supremacy and fought for political and social equality.

Segregation in the "New South" "新南方"的种族隔离

After Reconstruction ended (1877), African Americans saw the meager gains from this era—in terms of political and economic rights—steadily erode. Jim Crow laws segregated public facilities such as railroad cars, restrooms, and schools. These laws further relegated African Americans to second-class status in the South. Though the Fourteenth Amendment (1868) guaranteed all citizens equal protection of the laws, in the *Slaughterhouse* cases (1873), the Supreme Court had ruled that the Fourteenth Amendment applied only to national citizenship rights, such as the right to vote in national elections and the right to travel between states—not to rights derived from "state citizenship" (see Period 5). In this legal setting, Jim Crow laws proliferated throughout the South.

Plessy v. Ferguson and the "Separate but Equal" Doctrine
"普莱西诉弗格森案"与"隔离但平等"原则

In the case of *Plessy v. Ferguson* (1896), the Supreme Court decided that racial segregation did not violate the equal protection provision of the Fourteenth Amendment. The decision was a setback for those who sought an end to the Jim Crow system of racial segregation in the South. Jim Crow laws were state and local ordinances that first appeared after Reconstruction ended (1877). Typical laws called for separate schools or separate train cars for African Americans. Opponents of racial segregation argued that Jim Crow laws violated the Fourteenth Amendment (1868). This amendment, ratified during Reconstruction, stated that no person shall be denied "equal protection of the laws." Jim Crow laws, opponents argued, violated the Fourteenth Amendment because the laws relegated African Americans to inferior public accommodations and had the effect of making African Americans second-class citizens. However, the court disagreed. The decision stated that segregation was acceptable as long as the facilities for both races were of equal quality.

Challenging Jim Crow in the Gilded Age 镀金时代反对"黑人隔离法"

In the face of segregation and marginalization, African Americans did not remain passive. Ida B. Wells was one of the more radical black voices for social justice in the Gilded Age. As a young woman, she sued the Memphis and Charleston Railroad for denying her a seat in the ladies' car. At first she won the case, but the railroad ultimately won on appeal. After three friends of hers were lynched, Wells began to write and campaign against the practice of lynching. Her journalism deconstructed many of the myths around lynching—most important, that lynching was carried out in response to the crime of interracial rape. Another important Gilded Age activist was Booker T. Washington, who encouraged African Americans to gain training in vocational skills. Toward this end, he was selected to be the first leader of the Tuskegee Institute (1881). He argued that confrontation with whites would end badly for African Americans; he counseled cooperation with supportive whites and collective self-improvement. Later, his conciliatory approach was challenged by the more radical W. E. B. Du Bois (see Period 7).

SUBJECT TO DEBATE 相关讨论

There has been a major disconnect between the "Old West" of popular memory and the West of the historical record. Generations of Western movies have presented a morality play between virtuous pioneers and treacherous Indians. It is only in the last generation that the popular memory of the West has shifted. Movies such as *Dances with Wolves* (1990) have served as correctives. In your writing, try to avoid the stereotypes and clichés of the "Cowboy-and-Indian" genre.

A central point of contention in interpretations of the Gilded Age is the place of the owners of big business. The image that has stuck is that of the bloated "robber baron." This image was promoted by many contemporaries during the Gilded Age. The unprecedented accumulation of such wealth and power seemed at odds with the ideal of the yeoman farmer or the urban artisan. Further, the lavish spending habits of these wealthy men—illustrated by the gaudy mansions of New York's Fifth Avenue—also seemed outside of the American tradition of thrift and humility. This image of greed and excess was kept alive by Progressive-era historians and is still part of the collective memory of the era. Recently, some historians have begun to question this representation of the Gilded Age. For one, even in the late nineteenth century, most of the big companies were incorporated and run by boards of directors. The age of an arbitrary proprietor ordering his employees around was an anachronism even in the late Gilded Age. Second, recent historical interpretations have noted the tremendous wealth generated during this period. Eventually, this rising tide of wealth helped lift all boats. It is not by accident that so many "new immigrants" came to the United States—it truly was a land of opportunity at the turn of the twentieth century. In your essay writing, keep in mind the origins of the image of the "robber baron" and its usefulness in understanding the realities of the Gilded Age.

Historians have long debated the "revolt of the farmers" in the 1880s and 1890s. You should be familiar with the different poles in the debate. On the one hand, some historians have looked admiringly on the Populist movement. They note the dire situation farmers found themselves in and see the movement as a reasonable response. This approach also looks approvingly at the legacy of the movement; some of its goals were taken up by the Progressive movement in the early decades of the twentieth century, and even by the New Dealers in the 1930s. Other historians paint the Populist movement as an irrational, emotional rebellion against the modern world. These historians cite the racism, anti-Semitism, anti-urbanism, and anti-immigrant sentiment evident in certain corners of the movement. In this light, the Populist movement might be seen as a precursor of the Ku Klux Klan in the 1920s and McCarthyism in the 1950s.

Historians have debated the impact of "machine politics" in the nineteenth century. Starting in the Progressive era, historians wrote disparagingly about the corruption of the political bosses of the Gilded Age. In this narrative, these bosses undermined democracy until reformers rose up and cleaned up the political process. There is certainly truth to the narrative. However, reality is always more complicated. Social historians have recently examined the positive impact the political machines had on immigrant communities. The machines may have been corrupt, but they provided the only safety net and jobs program for recently arrived immigrants. In some ways, the attacks on the political machines were attacks on the structure of the immigrant community. In your essay writing, it would be wise to exercise caution when talking about the political "bosses" of the Gilded Age.

PRACTICE MULTIPLE-CHOICE QUESTIONS　选择题练习

Directions: Pick the letter that best answers the following questions.

Questions 1–3 refer to the following passage: 根据以下段落，回答第1—3题

"*Be it enacted by the Senate and House of Representatives of the United States of America in Congress assembled*, That in all cases where any tribe or band of Indians has been, or shall hereafter be, located upon any reservation created for their use, either by treaty stipulation or by virtue of an act of Congress or executive order . . . , the President of the United States [is] hereby . . . authorized, whenever in his opinion any reservation or any part thereof of such Indians is advantageous for agricultural and grazing purposes, to cause said reservation, or any part thereof, to be surveyed . . . , and to allot the lands in said reservation in severalty [separate plots of land, individually owned] to any Indian located thereon in quantities as follows: . . ."

—Dawes Severalty Act (excerpt), 1887

1. A primary goal of the Dawes Severalty Act (1887) was to

   (A) turn American Indians into property-owning, profit-oriented, individual farmers.
   (B) keep alive traditional practices and languages.
   (C) open up American Indian lands in Georgia, South Carolina, and Alabama to mining and cotton production.
   (D) compensate American Indian tribes for lands that had been taken through fraudulent treaties.

2. An important impetus for the passage of the Dawes Severalty Act was

(A) the Supreme Court decision in the case of *Worcester v. Georgia.*
(B) a nonviolent protest movement against existing policies led by Crazy Horse.
(C) the success of the Freedmen's Bureau in addressing the problems of African Americans in the South.
(D) the depiction of mistreatment of American Indians in Helen Hunt Jackson's book, *A Century of Dishonor.*

3. Which of the following developments was similar to the Dawes Severalty Act in that they both had the same goal for the future of American Indians?

(A) The formation of the Ghost Dance movement.
(B) The establishment of Indian Boarding Schools.
(C) The passage of the Indian Reorganization Act.
(D) The founding of the American Indian Movement.

Questions 4–7 refer to the following image: 根据以下图片，回答第4—7题

4. The 1873 political cartoon shown makes the point that

   (A) railroads have brought prosperity to previously isolated communities.
   (B) the safety of railroad workers was being ignored by the powerful railroad corporations.
   (C) the public needed to recognize the threat that large railroad companies posed to the economic and political system.
   (D) railroad lines were undermining rural culture by bringing the vices of urban life to small-town America.

5. The Grange, represented by the standing figure in the cartoon, received its strongest support from which of the following groups?

   (A) Western farmers.
   (B) Urban immigrants.
   (C) Wealthy industrialists.
   (D) Middle-class managers.

6. The Grange emerged most directly in response to which of the following nineteenth-century developments?

   (A) The influx of migrants from Ireland in the aftermath of the "potato famine" of the 1840s and 1850s.
   (B) The growing power of corporations over the economy and the political system.
   (C) The development of political machines.
   (D) The efforts of corporations to gain control over resources and markets in Asia and Latin America.

7. Which of the following later groups or movements most fully adopted the political and economic agenda of the Grange?

   (A) The Congress of Industrial Organizations.
   (B) The Populist Party.
   (C) The National Association for the Advancement of Colored People.
   (D) The New Left.

Questions 8–10 are based on the following passage: 根据以下段落，回答第8—10题

"I am but one of many victims of Rockefeller's colossal combination," said Mr. [George] Rice, "and my story is not essentially different from the rest. . . . I established what was known as the Ohio Oil Works. . . . I found to my surprise at first, though I afterward understood it perfectly, that the Standard Oil Company was offering the same quality of oil at much lower prices than I could do—from one to three cents a gallon less than I could possibly sell it for.

"I sought for the reason and found that the railroads were in league with the Standard Oil concern at every point, giving it discriminating rates and privileges of all kinds as against myself and all outside competitors."

—George Rice, "How I Was Ruined by Rockefeller," *New York World*, October 16, 1898.

8. The business model described by George Rice could best be described as

   (A) global distribution.
   (B) horizontal integration.
   (C) regional planning.
   (D) vertical consolidation.

9. Attempts to rein in the power of corporations, such as the Standard Oil Company, in the 1890s and 1900s

   (A) were frequently approved by Congress but were stymied by presidential vetoes.
   (B) were largely successful, as a coalition of reformers, political leaders, and labor leaders collaborated on realigning the American economy.
   (C) were discussed by radical groups but were rejected by the vast majority of Americans as communistic and "anti-American."
   (D) were often hindered by Supreme Court decisions that upheld the rights of business to operate without excessive government regulation.

10. Defenders of corporate actions, such as the ones described in the passage above, would find support in

    (A) Herbert Spencer and the ideas of social Darwinism.
    (B) Henry George's proposal for a "single tax" on land.
    (C) the Omaha Platform of the Populist Platform.
    (D) Upton Sinclair's novel, *The Jungle*.

Answers and Explanations to Multiple-Choice Questions
选择题的答案与解析

1. **(A)** A primary goal of the Dawes Severalty Act (1887) was to turn American Indians into property-owning, profit-oriented, individual farmers. This was part of a push toward assimilation as a policy for Native Americans. Some reformers had come to believe that the reservation system was destructive to Indians and that the best strategy forward was to encourage them to give up traditional ways. In addition, the seeming inability or unwillingness on the part of native peoples to adopt a mainstream American lifestyle was seen by many Americans as both unacceptable and uncivilized.

2. **(D)** An important impetus for the passage of the Dawes Severalty Act was the depiction of mistreatment of American Indians in Helen Hunt Jackson's 1881 book, *A Century of Dishonor*. Her book chronicled the abuses by the U.S. government against the tribes. She hoped to awaken the conscience of the American people, and their representatives, to the brutal mistreatment of Indians. She sent a copy of the book to each member of Congress.

3. **(B)** American Indian boarding schools were established in the late nineteenth and early twentieth centuries as a means of educating native children according to the standards of mainstream white American culture. In this regard, they were similar to the Dawes Act in that both promoted assimilation as the solution to the "Indian problem." Children were forbidden to speak their native languages, were given European-American style haircuts, and given new names to replace their traditional names.

4. **(C)** The cartoon shows people sleeping under railway tracks, which normally lay on crossbeams termed "sleepers." A Granger tries to warn them of the approaching dangers—a locomotive with coaches labelled, "Consolidation Train," "extortion," "bribery," and so forth. The Grange, formally known as the National Grange of the Order of Patrons of Husbandry, was born in 1867. It initially was started to foster mutual aid among farmers and promote more efficient agricultural techniques. However, the organization soon began to focus on state and national political reforms. The Granger movement was successful in many states in regulating the railroads and grain-storage warehouses. The cartoon is titled "The Grange Awakening the Sleepers."

5. **(A)** The Grange was primarily an organization of farmers. Its agenda of subjecting the railroads to government control grew out of the concerns of farmers. It also organized cooperative businesses to help farmers market their goods directly to the public and avoid middlemen. Urban immigrants (B) might share some of the Granger bitterness toward the wealthy class, but they would not be drawn to the Granger agenda. The wealthy (C) and the rising middle class (D) of the late 1800s would not necessarily find common cause with the Granger movement.

6. **(B)** The Grange emerged in response to the unprecedented accumulation of power in the hands of a few massive corporations. Corporate power, many observers believed, was undermining the democratic system. Corporate leaders exerted a great deal of sway in the political system. Efforts to check corporate power, such as passage of the Sherman Antitrust Act (1890), often proved to be fruitless. In *United States v. E. C. Knight Company* (1895) the Supreme Court undermined the act by narrowing its scope to only trade, not manufacturing. The court ruled that the American Sugar Refining Company, which con-

trolled approximately 98 percent of all sugar refining in the United States, was exempt from the antitrust law.

7. **(B)** The organization that most clearly followed in the footsteps of the Grange movement was the Populist Party, which became a formidable force in the 1890s. The movement was primarily a farmer's movement that resented the concentration of wealth and power among industrialists and bankers. It supported a national income tax so that those with higher incomes would pay more than the poor. It also supported free and unlimited coinage of silver in order to increase the amount of currency in circulation.

8. **(B)** The business model described by George Rice could best be described as horizontal integration. Horizontal integration entails creating a monopoly, or near monopoly, in a particular industry. A common way that corporations gained monopoly control of an industry was by establishing trusts. A trust consisted of trustees from several companies involved in the same industry acting together rather than in competition with one another. John D. Rockefeller organized the most well-known trust in the oil-processing industry.

9. **(D)** Attempts to rein in the power of corporations, such as the Standard Oil Company, in the 1890s and 1900s, were often hindered by Supreme Court decisions that upheld the rights of business to operate without excessive government regulation. In the case of *United States v. E. C. Knight Company* (1895), for example, the Supreme Court examined the constitutionality of government attempts to check the power of large trusts. The Sherman Antitrust Act was passed in 1890 in order to rein in the power of the trusts. In the Knight case, the court greatly limited the scope of the act by making a distinction between trade, which would be subject to the act under the Commerce Clause, and manufacturing, which would not.

10. **(A)** Defenders of corporate actions such as those described in the passage, would find support in Herbert Spencer and the ideas of social Darwinism. Social Darwinism was an attempt to apply Charles Darwin's ideas about the natural world to social relations. The ideas of social Darwinism were put forth by the English philosopher, Herbert Spencer, and were popularized in the United States by William Graham Sumner. Social Darwinists argued that the inequalities of the late 1800s reflected the process of "the survival of the fittest." Any attempt to intervene in the process would be counterproductive. This hands-off approach to economic activities is known by the French phrase *laissez-faire*. Social Darwinism appealed to owners of large corporations, because it both justified their wealth and power and warned against any type of regulation or reform.

Period 7: 1890–1945 Economic Dislocation and Reform in the Age of Empire and World War
第七个时期（1890—1945）：帝国时期的经济混乱和改革与世界大战

9

1914	Federal Reserve Act
	Federal Trade Commission
	Clayton Antitrust Act
	Beginning of World War I
1914–1917	United States intervention in Mexico
1915	Release of D.W. Griffith's film *Birth of a Nation*
1916	Reelection of Woodrow Wilson
1917	United States enters World War I
	Espionage Act
1918	Sedition Act
	Armistice ends World War I
1919	Eighteenth Amendment (prohibition) ratified
	Creation of the Comintern
1919–1920	Boston Police Strike
1920	Nineteenth Amendment (women's right to vote) ratified
	Deportation of Emma Goldman
	Schenck v. United States
	Seattle General Strike
	Height of the "Palmer raids"
	Election of Warren G. Harding
1921	Emergency Quota Act
	Beginning of Teapot Dome Scandal
1924	National Origins Act
	Election of Calvin Coolidge
1925	Scopes trial
1927	Execution of Sacco and Vanzetti
1928	Kellogg–Briand Pact
	Election of Herbert Hoover
1929	Stock market crash
	The Great Depression begins
1930	Hawley-Smoot Tariff
1931	The Marx Brothers' movie *Duck Soup* released
1932	Bonus March
	Reconstruction Finance Corporation established
	Election of Franklin D. Roosevelt
1933	The 100 Days
	"Bank holiday"
	Agricultural Adjustment Act (AAA)
	Glass–Steagall Act (Federal Depositors Insurance Corporation established)
	National Industrial Recovery Act (NIRA)
	Civilian Conservation Corps (CCC)

TIMELINE 大事年表

	Ratification of Twenty-first Amendment (repeal of prohibition)
1934	Share Our Wealth clubs started by Huey Long
	Securities and Exchange Commission
	Clifford Odets writes the play *Waiting for Lefty*
1935	National Labor Relations Act (Wagner Act)
	Social Security Act
	Schechter decision strikes down NIRA
	Works Progress Administration
	First Neutrality Act
1936	Butler decision strikes down AAA
	Roosevelt's "court packing" plan
	Roosevelt elected to a second term
	Charlie Chaplin's *Modern Times* released
1936–1939	Spanish Civil War
1937	"Roosevelt Recession"
	Farm Security Administration
	Panay incident
	Quarantine Speech
1939	Cash-and-Carry Policy
	Nazi–Soviet Pact
	The movie *Mr. Smith Goes to Washington* released
	John Steinbeck writes *The Grapes of Wrath*
1940	Selective Service Act
	Tripartite Pact
	Roosevelt elected to unprecedented third term
1941	Lend–Lease Act
	Japanese attack on Pearl Harbor
	United States enters World War II
1942	Battle of Midway
1943	Tehran Conference
1944	D-Day—allied invasion of Normandy
	Korematsu v. United States
	Bretton Woods Conference
1945	Battles of Iwo Jima and Okinawa
	Yalta Conference
	Potsdam Conference
	German surrender
	Dropping of the atomic bomb on Hiroshima and Nagasaki
	Japanese surrender

INTRODUCTION 简介

> The United States faced a series of profound domestic and international challenges during the period 1890 to 1945. As the country became increasingly pluralistic, Americans debated how best to meet these challenges. Debate centered on the role of the government in the economic and social life of the country and on the role of the United States on the global stage.

In response to the rapid industrialization, political corruption, and unplanned urbanization of the Gilded Age, the Progressive movement grew and developed an extensive slate of proposals for reform. The movement claimed many legislative victories and ultimately influenced both the New Deal and twentieth-century liberalism.

After 1890, the United States began to play a more aggressive role on the world stage, intervening in Hawaii, Cuba, Panama, Mexico, and beyond, as well as acquiring possessions from Puerto Rico to the Philippines. These ventures (including building a modern U.S. Navy battle fleet) raised the profile of the United States and established it as a rising major power. When the Great War, later known as World War I, began in Europe in August 1914, most Americans were not eager to join the conflict. The war seemed to be a continuation of the age-old rivalries of the European nations. As the conflict dragged on, a number of factors pushed America toward intervention. The United States did not play a major role in World War I until the final year of the conflict, but the war ushered in some important changes in the United States. Culturally, the country became more aggressively patriotic and conservative; the reform impulse of the Progressive era was pushed to the background. The war expanded the role of the federal government and contributed to the "Great Migration" of African Americans toward the North. America's participation in the war strengthened its position on the world stage, even though the country withdrew into isolationism in the years following the war.

During the 1920s, we see the development of the some of the cultural divisions that have roiled Americans ever since. Many historians note the resurgence of "traditional values" in the United States in response to the unfolding of a more modern America. This tension between tradition and modernity has shaped much of the historical work on the 1920s. Not all the elements of the 1920s fit neatly into this model of tradition versus modernity. For instance, the experiment in the prohibition of alcohol; its origins were both in the Progressive movement's push for government-sponsored social engineering as well as in the religious crusade to eradicate "immoral" habits. Still, the tradition-versus-modernity model is a useful lens through which to examine the 1920s. This decade ended with the stock market crash that ushered in the Great Depression (1929–1939).

The Great Depression was the most devastating economic downturn in American history. It is one of several such downturns, which include the panics of 1819, 1837, 1857, 1873, and 1893. However, in none of these panics did the country reach the depths of despair realized during the Great Depression. A basic understanding of introductory economic concepts, such as supply and demand, Keynesianism, and the business cycle, will come in handy in assessing the causes and responses to the Great Depression. The most significant response to the Depression, the New Deal, helped to redefine the relationship between the government and the economy and helped launch the modern welfare state.

This period ends with World War II, a cataclysmic war that profoundly transformed the nations that participated in it, including the United States. World War II set in motion a series of demographic, political, and social trends that would shape American history for the remainder of the twentieth century. A large percentage of the millions of returning soldiers soon settled down, married, and had the children who would comprise the "baby boom" generation. Moreover, the war brought the United States out of the Great Depression and set the country on a trajectory of sustained economic growth for a generation. Wartime experiences inspired both African Americans and women, setting the stage for the civil rights movement and the women's liberation movement. The United States did not retreat into an isolationist stance after the war, as it had after World War I. The wartime alliance of the United States and the Soviet Union would soon degenerate into the Cold War (1945–1991).

KEY CONCEPT 7.1 RESPONSES TO ECONOMIC DISLOCATION AND UNCERTAINTY
核心概念7.1：对经济混乱与不确定性的反应

The industrialization of the Gilded Age and the accompanying trends of migration and urbanization dramatically transformed American society. While the growth of the economy expanded opportunity, it also contributed to economic instability. The government, as well as social and political organizations, attempted to address the impact these changes brought to American society.

I. The Transition of the American Economy 美国经济的转变

The consolidation of large corporations that began in the Gilded Age continued into the twentieth century. The growth and power of corporations transformed the social and economic life of the United States. These changes favored economic growth and urbanization, while at the same time contributed to economic instability and increasingly severe fluctuations in the business cycle.

A. THE DEVELOPMENT OF A CORPORATE ECONOMY 公司经济的发展

Large corporations came to dominate the American economy. Improvements in technology and new manufacturing techniques led to increased production of consumer goods, greater mobility, and improved standards of living.

Toward Greater Consolidation 趋向更大程度的整合

The Gilded Age saw the advent of the modern corporate economy, as mergers, holding companies, and trusts led to fewer entities controlling larger segments of the economy (see Period 6). This trend continued into the twentieth century, as the assembly line, mass production, and new management techniques brought about a further consolidation of the economy. In addition, the production and consumption of consumer goods stimulated the American economy for much of the 1920s. New products, such as automobiles and radios, captured the public's imagination, and new production techniques increased industrial output.

Henry Ford and Mass Production 亨利·福特与批量生产

The most important figure in the development of new production techniques was automaker Henry Ford. In 1913 he opened a plant with a continuous conveyor belt. The belt moved the chassis of the car from worker to worker so that each did a small task in the process of assembling the final product. This mass-production technique reduced the price of his Model T car and dealt a blow to the skilled mechanics who had previously built automobiles. Unskilled assembly-line workers gradually replaced skilled craft workers in American industry.

The Impact of the Automobile 汽车的影响

Americans embraced the automobile more rapidly and more thoroughly than people in other nations. By the end of the 1920s, Americans owned 80 percent of the world's automobiles. Approximately 23 million cars were on the roads. Automobiles became more affordable. When the Model T was first introduced in 1908, an average American worker would have had to work approximately 20 months to earn enough money to purchase an automobile. By 1924, a Ford car cost about the equivalent of two to three months' salary.

The automobile changed American society in profound ways. The proliferation of the automobile industry—using mass-production techniques developed early in the twentieth century by Henry Ford (see page 249)—stimulated the growth of the steel, chemical, oil, and glass-production industries, employing nearly 4 million Americans. The automobile led to a reshaping of demographic patterns, as more Americans began to settle in suburban communities (see more on the rise of suburbs in Period 8). Although automobiles reduced rural isolation, they also contributed to "urban sprawl." The growing cities that developed in the twentieth century, such as Los Angeles and Houston, were designed to accommodate the automobile.

Scientific Management 科学管理

The scientific-management techniques developed by Frederick Winslow Taylor were key to mass production. Taylor carefully watched workers, noted the most efficient techniques, and wrote down in exacting detail how a particular task was to be done. Work became more efficient, but also more monotonous. Many workers, especially those with a degree of skill, resisted the loss of control and autonomy that scientific-management techniques entailed.

Advertising and Mass Consumption 广告与大众消费

If the quality of work deteriorated for factory workers in the 1920s, the availability of consumer goods to average families greatly increased. Cars, radios, toasters, health and beauty aids, and other consumer goods filled showrooms and stores. Easy credit and layaway plans helped move merchandise. The advertising industry also changed a great deal in the 1920s. Advertising and public relations men tapped into the ideas of Freudian psychology and emerging ideas around crowd psychology. Many ads in this period attempted to reach the public on a subconscious level, rather than just presenting products and services in a straightforward manner. Public relations pioneer Edward Bernays, a nephew of Sigmund Freud, was a key figure in the shift in marketing toward elaborate corporate advertising campaigns. The values of advertising and promotion seeped into the broader culture—even into religion. Bruce Barton wrote a best-selling book, *The Man Nobody Knows* (1925), portraying Jesus Christ as a "super-salesman" and the spread of Christianity as a marketing triumph.

B. THE TRANSITION TOWARD AN URBAN, INDUSTRIAL ECONOMY
向城市工业经济的转变

The forces of change that began in the Gilded Age continued to transform the United States in the twentieth century. America continued its transition from a rural, agrarian society to an urban, industrial one. The new society offered new opportunities to women and to migrants—both from abroad and from within the United States.

The Growth of the City 城市的发展

Immigrants from abroad poured into American cities in the first two decades of the twentieth century, continuing a trend that had begun during the Gilded Age (see Period 6). Between the turn of the century and the beginning of World War I in 1914, approximately 13 million European immigrants made their way to the United States. By 1920, immigrants and their children comprised 76 percent of the population of New York City, 71 percent of Chicago, and 64 percent of San Francisco. At the same time, the mechanization of agriculture lowered the demand for labor in rural areas of the United States, contributing to the internal migration of people into cities. By 1920, the majority (51 percent) of Americans lived in cities.

New Opportunities for Women 妇女的新机遇

From the late 1800s into the twentieth century, urbanization and industrialization provided new opportunities for women in the workforce. The most common occupation for women in the mid-nineteenth century was in the field of domestic service; in the late nineteenth century, more women were working in factories and, by the first decades of the twentieth century, office work became their primary occupation.

New opportunities for women were not confined to the workplace. The "new" woman of the 1920s was engaged in public issues. She often participated in the political struggles of the Progressive movement and gained a new sense of confidence in public issues, especially after women achieved the right to vote in 1920. These economic and political changes for women were reflected in changing ideas around gender. The new image of women during the 1920s was symbolized by the popularity of the "flappers" and their style of dress. Flappers were independent-minded young women of the 1920s who openly defied Victorian moral codes about "proper" lady-like behavior.

WOMEN AND PUBLIC LIFE 妇女与公众生活

When traditional history texts discuss women and gender, they often discuss fashion and appearance—such as "bobbed" hair and shorter dresses in the 1920s. While fashion and style are certainly legitimate topics for historical inquiry, try to avoid limiting your discussions of gender to such topics.

C. ECONOMIC INSTABILITY AND THE CALL FOR GREATER FEDERAL REGULATION 经济的不稳定性以及对联邦政府加大管理力度的呼吁

The United States economy continued to grow in the late 1800s and early 1900s. However, fluctuations in the business cycle became increasingly common and increasingly severe. From the Panic of 1893 to the Great Depression (1929–1939), these economic downturns led to calls for greater federal regulation of the economy.

The Panic of 1893 1893年的大恐慌

Throughout American history, business activity has moved in cycles. In the nineteenth century, the economy experienced several economic downturns, often resulting in "panics."

Notable panics had occurred earlier in 1819, 1837, 1857, and 1873. As the economy became more consolidated in the post–Civil War era, with only a handful of corporations controlling larger and larger segments of the economy, the potential for more severe downturns intensified. If a few large corporations experienced downturns, the potential for a large-scale disruption to the economy became increasingly likely. Such a scenario played out in 1893, and again in 1907.

The Panic of 1893 signaled the beginning of the worst economic depression in American history before the Great Depression of the 1930s. The crisis began when the Philadelphia and Reading Railroad went bankrupt; two months later the National Cordage Company also failed. These bankruptcies led to a major decline in stock prices. Because many leading banks had invested their assets in the stock market, a wave of bank failures soon followed. With over 500 bank collapses, credit became hard to come by. This contraction of credit led to the subsequent collapse of approximately 15,000 businesses. By 1894, the unemployment rate had reached 20 percent of the workforce and approximately a million workers had lost their jobs. The economy did not fully recover until 1901.

The Panic of 1907 1907年的大恐慌

The economy took a serious downturn following the Panic of 1907. This panic involved a major fall in stock prices, which was caused by a lack of confidence in major New York banks. Several banks had invested in a scheme to gain control of the United Copper Company. When the scheme unraveled, there were runs on several of the banks that had invested large sums of money. One major New York bank, Knickerbocker Trust Company, collapsed, sending ripples of fear through the banking world and leading to a withdrawal of reserves. The panic was partly calmed by the action of J. P. Morgan, who offered to have U.S. Steel take over a struggling steel-industry rival that a major New York bank had invested in. However, the deal could not proceed until Morgan got assurances from President Theodore Roosevelt that the government would not initiate antitrust action. The entire episode demonstrated the lack of control the U.S. government had over the industrial and financial worlds.

Causes of the Great Depression 大萧条的起因

The economic crises following the Panics of 1893 and 1907 paled in comparison to the economic downturn of the 1930s. On the surface, the economy of the 1920s seemed strong, but there were structural weaknesses that became more apparent as the decade progressed. The precise reasons for the Great Depression are still debated by historians; the following explanations are frequently cited.

Overproduction and Underconsumption 生产过剩与消费不足

Industrial production greatly expanded in the 1920s. New products, such as automobiles and radios, captured the public's imagination, and new production techniques, such as the assembly line and "scientific management," vastly increased industrial output. For much of the 1920s, the public was induced by easy credit and seductive advertising to absorb this increased output of consumer goods. However, by 1927 manufacturers noticed that warehouse inventories were on the rise. Consumption just could not keep up with production. A weak labor movement in the twenties led to stagnant wages. Since ordinary Americans did not share in the economic expansion of the 1920s, the gap between the wealthy and the poor grew. During the 1920s, income for the top 1 percent of the population increased by nearly 75 percent, while the bottom 90 percent of the population saw their income rise by less than 10 percent. By the late 1920s, manufacturers made the logical decision to begin laying off workers, worsening a bad situation.

Problems on the Farm 农业问题

Throughout the 1920s, the agricultural sector lagged behind the rest of the economy. Farmers had put more acres under cultivation during World War I to meet increased demand for agricultural production. By the twenties, Europe was back on its feet, yet American farmers did not cut back on production. Mechanization and expansion left the farmers of the 1920s in a cycle of debt, overproduction, and falling commodity prices. Increased tariff rates and an isolationist foreign policy further reduced the international market for American agricultural goods.

An Inflated Stock Market 膨胀的股市

Investing in the stock market is always something of a gamble, but in the 1920s people gambled recklessly with borrowed money. They increasingly bought stocks on margin, paying only 10 percent of the purchase price up front, with the promise of paying the remainder in the future. This practice worked as long as stock prices rose, which they did throughout most of the 1920s. By the late 1920s, however, serious investors began to see that stock prices were reaching new heights as the actual earnings of major corporations were declining. This discrepancy between the price per share and the actual earnings of corporations led investors to begin selling stocks, which stimulated panic selling. On October 29, 1929, "Black Tuesday," the stock market crashed, destroying many individuals' investments.

SPECULATION AND THE STOCK MARKET
投机与股市

Many accounts of the economy in the 1920s fault the speculative practices of the stock market. Try to avoid an overemphasis on the speculative nature of the 1920s stock market. Speculation was and is, of course, at the heart of the stock market.

II. Progressive Era Reform 进步时代的改革

The Progressive movement was a response to the economic instability, social inequality, and political corruption that had begun during the Gilded Age and continued into the twentieth century. Progressive reformers called for greater government intervention in the economy, as well as increased democratization of the political process, social justice, and conservation of natural resources.

A. THE PROGRESSIVE MOVEMENT 进步运动

The Progressive movement developed in the late 1890s and continued through the first decades of the twentieth century. Reformers and journalists addressed a host of issues associated with industrial society. Progressive-era reformers tended to be largely urban and middle class; many were women. They worked on reform at the local, state, and national levels.

The Making of the Progressive Movement 进步运动的形成

The Progressive movement was essentially a middle-class response to the excesses of rapid industrialization, political corruption, and unplanned urbanization. Not only were middle-class college graduates the primary activists in the movement, but the tone and tenor of the movement was decidedly middle class. Progressivism existed at the grass-roots level as well as in the corridors of power. Two influential presidents, Theodore Roosevelt and Woodrow Wilson, took on the progressive mantle. However, the movement was more an amalgam of interests, ideas, groups, and individuals, rather than a tight-knit cohort of activists with a cohesive ideology and a clearly articulated vision of the future. The movement was a bundle of contradictions. The leaders of the movement championed reforms to benefit the working class but looked at the actual working class with a mix of paternalism and suspicion. The movement challenged women's exclusion from the political process, but largely accepted the prevailing social views of African Americans. To some degree progressivism challenged the abuses of unbridled capitalism, yet many industrialists embraced progressive legislation in order to rationalize the freewheeling nature of the capitalist system.

Women and the Progressive Movement 妇女与进步运动

A large percentage of progressive activists were women. The Progressive movement provided a means for women to become engaged in public issues in an era when in most states the vote was still restricted to men. Women often framed their participation in the movement as "social housekeeping." In this way, it did not seem like such a radical break from the traditional domestic activities in which women were expected to find fulfillment. Prominent women in the Progressive movement included Florence Kelly, an activist for the reform of factories and chief factory inspector for Illinois (1893); Frances Perkins, head of the New York Consumers' League (1910) and, later, secretary of labor under President Franklin Roosevelt (1933–1945); and Jane Addams, founder of Hull House in Chicago (1897) (see Period 6).

Pragmatism 实用主义

Progressives gravitated toward the pragmatist philosophical ideas of William James and John Dewey. Pragmatists questioned the philosophical quest for eternal truths. They argued that the value of an idea lay in its ability to positively impact the world. Experimentation was central to the pragmatists' work. Dewey put this idea into practice in an experimental school he started in Chicago, which put much more of an emphasis on the process of learning and on student participation than on the content of the curriculum.

Reform Darwinism 改革达尔文主义

Progressive activists rejected the ethos of social Darwinism, which applied Charles Darwin's ideas about the natural world to the world of human interactions (see Period 6). Progressives embraced the Darwinian idea of evolution but thought that the evolution of human society to its highest ideals required active intervention and cooperation rather than a laissez-faire approach. This call to active intervention in the evolution of the social order is called reform Darwinism.

Muckrakers and the Birth of Investigative Journalism
黑幕揭发者与调查性新闻的诞生

Progressives believed in the power of the newly developed mass print media to shed light on social ills and to inspire action. The practitioners of a new "investigative" form of journalism were known as "muckrakers." *McClure's, Harper's, Cosmopolitan*, and several other magazines became staples in middle-class homes by the turn of the twentieth century, their readers increasingly drawn to articles detailing the corruption and scandals of the modern world. Many muckrakers saw themselves on a mission to shine a light on sordid business and political practices of the day. Important muckrakers included Upton Sinclair, Ida Tarbell, Lincoln Steffens, and Frank Norris (discussed below in the context of the topics they wrote about).

Progressives and Municipal Reform 进步派与市政改革

Progressive activists were alarmed at the inefficiency and corruption of municipal government. The political machines that developed in large American cities in the nineteenth century continued to dominate cities in the early twentieth century. The most famous nineteenth-century political machine was the Democratic Party machine in New York City—headquartered in Tammany Hall and dominated by "Boss" William Marcy Tweed (see Period 6). The inefficiencies of urban governance were also highlighted in Lincoln Steffens's 1904 muckraking book, *The Shame of the Cities*. This book is a collection of pieces he had written for *McClure's* magazine.

Progressivism and Moral Reform 进步主义与道德改革

The progressive zeal to attack social ills led many to campaign against "sin" and "vice." These middle-class reformers were more than ready to impose their notions of proper behavior on the society as a whole. Reformers tackled excessive drinking, prostitution, rowdy behavior, and bawdy entertainment in their attempt to "civilize" the urban environment (see more on Prohibition, page 259).

The Progressive Response to the Triangle Factory Fire
进步派对纽约三角内衣工厂火灾的反应

In 1911, the Progressive movement was spurred to take action after a tragic fire swept through the Triangle Shirtwaist Factory. The factory, which produced women's blouses (then known as "shirtwaists"), was located in the upper floors of a factory building in the Greenwich Village section of New York City. Most of the employees were young women, many of whom were recent Italian or Jewish immigrants. A fire began in one of the scrap bins and soon spread. Trying to flee, the workers discovered that one of the entrances was blocked by flames and another was locked (perhaps to keep the workers in, or to keep union organizers out). Some escaped by elevator, some by a fire escape before it collapsed. Ultimately, 146 workers died. The tragedy led to the creation of fire safety laws in New York and to the rapid growth of the International Ladies Garment Workers' Union.

B. PROGRESSIVE REFORM ON THE NATIONAL LEVEL 席卷全国的进步改革

The Progressive movement had a profound impact on national politics. Progressives pushed for federal legislation to expand democratic participation and to protect both the economy and the environment from abuses.

Progressivism and Industrial Capitalism 进步主义与工业资本主义

During the Gilded Age of the late nineteenth century, America's industrial output grew exponentially with virtually no government regulation. Industrialists and their allies championed laissez-faire economics—the idea that government should stay out of economic activities (see Period 6). By the early twentieth century, many Americans came to believe that unregulated industry could be harmful to individuals, communities, and even to the health of industrial capitalism itself. If people lost confidence in the products of the industrial system, sales would suffer.

The Jungle and the Meat-packing Industry 《屠场》与肉类加工工业

A public outcry about the conditions of the meat-processing industry was generated by Upton Sinclair's 1906 novel, *The Jungle*, which vividly depicts the horrible conditions in the meat-packing industry. The novel takes place in Chicago and follows a Lithuanian immigrant family through the stockyards of Chicago. Based on extensive research by Sinclair, the novel brought to light the unsanitary and dangerous conditions of the meat-packing industry. While the socialist message of the book was largely ignored by the public, the depiction of meat processing was not. The public uproar that followed publication led Congress to pass the Meat Inspection Act (1906) and the Pure Food and Drug Act (also 1906), which established the Food and Drug Administration.

The History of the Standard Oil Company 《标准石油公司的历史》

The Standard Oil Company, a giant trust assembled by John D. Rockefeller, had come to dominate the petroleum-processing industry by the end of the nineteenth century (see Period 6). Journalist and teacher Ida Tarbell detailed the rise of Standard Oil in a series of articles in *McClure's Magazine* and then in her book, *The History of the Standard Oil Company* (1904). Her research exposed the ruthlessness of Rockefeller's oil company and contributed to the government breaking up the Standard Oil Trust in 1911.

Regulating Workplace Practices—*Muller v. Oregon* and the "Brandeis Brief"
管理工作场所的实践——"穆勒诉俄勒冈州案"与"布兰代斯诉讼法"

Progressives tackled the dual issues of long working hours and child labor. In the late nineteenth century, workdays of 12 hours or more were not uncommon, and child labor had become a normal practice in large factories. The movement to reform the workplace suffered a setback in 1905, when the Supreme Court shot down a New York State law restricting hours for bakers in the case of *Lochner v. New York*. The court cited the sanctity of private contracts between employers and employees. However, the Progressive movement achieved a major boost in another Supreme Court decision just three years later, *Muller v. Oregon* (1908). That decision upheld an Oregon law limiting the number of hours women could work. This case cited the supposed physical limitations of women and the threat to their health that long workdays posed. The case specifically cited women's role as child bearers. The case is significant because of the brief written by future Supreme Court justice Louis Brandeis on behalf of the state of Oregon. Brandeis cited copious scientific, psychological, and sociological studies to bolster the case for limiting women's hours of work. This type of legal argument has come to be known as a "Brandeis brief." The use of non-legal information in legal matters would become

> ### *MULLER* AND THE PROGRESSIVE AGENDA
> ### 穆勒判决与进步日程
> The *Muller* decision represented a major victory for the Progressive movement. The decision also reflected differing attitudes about gender within the movement. Although many progressives challenged traditional understandings of gender, this decision reinforced traditional notions of female frailty.

increasingly common in the twentieth century, including in the *Brown v. Board of Education of Topeka* case (1954).

Challenging Child Labor 对童工的质疑

Troubling photographs of children in workplace settings by photographers such as Lewis Hine brought the issue of child labor to public attention. In 1916, the Progressive movement had a short-lived success with the issue of child labor, when Congress passed the Keating-Owen Child Labor Act. Realizing that local factory rules were under the domain of state law, Congress addressed the issue of child labor by prohibiting the sale, across state lines, of goods produced by factories that employed children under 14. Congress used its power to regulate interstate commerce. Less than a year later, in the case of *Hammer v. Dagenhart* (1917), the Supreme Court shot down the act. The court asserted that the goods being regulated were not inherently "immoral," as prostitution or liquor might be. Therefore, what was being addressed by the law was manufacturing practices, and manufacturing practices were subject to state, not federal, law. Child labor was not effectively addressed until federal fair-labor standards were established during the New Deal era of the 1930s.

Progressivism in the White House 白宫进步主义

The Progressive movement was primarily a grassroots movement of thousands of activists, but in the early twentieth century, progressivism entered the discourse of the national political parties. President Theodore Roosevelt, a Republican, embraced many progressive reforms, but his handpicked successor, President William H. Taft proved to be a disappointment to the Progressive movement. The divisions within the Republican Party over President Taft contributed to the electoral victory in 1912 of Democrat Woodrow Wilson. The pervasiveness of the Progressive ideology crossed party lines, and Wilson implemented some important Progressive reforms.

Theodore Roosevelt and the "Square Deal" 西奥多·罗斯福与"公平交易"原则

Theodore Roosevelt assumed the presidency following the assassination of William McKinley (1901) and quickly began to move the Republican Party and the nation itself in a progressive direction. His domestic agenda was known as the "Square Deal." Moreover, he championed the cause of conservation of natural resources and came to be known as "the trust-buster."

Roosevelt and the Regulation of Business 罗斯福与商业管理

President Roosevelt's "Square Deal" approach to public issues is reflected in his handling of the anthracite coal strike in 1902. He called representatives from both management and labor to the White House, threatening to take over the mines if owners did not negotiate in good faith. Ultimately, the miners received a 10 percent wage increase, but not union recognition. Roosevelt also pushed for important consumer protections in the wake of the publication of *The Jungle* (see page 256), and stronger measures to protect the environment (see pages 260–261). Also, Roosevelt wanted stronger regulation of the powerful railroad industry. The strength of the railroad industry was the subject of Frank Norris's novel, *The Octopus: A California Story* (1901). Roosevelt strengthened the Interstate Commerce Commission (ICC, created in 1887) with the Elkins Act (1903), which targeted the railroad practice of granting rebates to favored customers, and the Hepburn Act (1906), which gave the ICC greater latitude to set railroad rates.

Roosevelt as "Trust Buster" "反托拉斯能手" 罗斯福

President Roosevelt saw the concentration of economic power in a few hands as potentially dangerous to the economy as a whole. Although the Sherman Antitrust Act (1890) was passed to limit monopolistic practices, the act was not enforced with a great deal of enthusiasm. Roosevelt made a point of using the act to pursue "bad trusts"—ones that interfered with commerce—not necessarily the biggest trusts. One of his first targets was the Northern Securities Company, a railroad holding company. His efforts were challenged in court. In *Northern Securities Co. v. United States* (1904), the Supreme Court upheld the power of the government to break up Northern Securities under the Sherman Antitrust Act. The case was a victory for Roosevelt, whose efforts at challenging monopolies earned him the nickname "trust buster."

The Administration of William Howard Taft 威廉·霍华德·塔夫脱政府

After President Theodore Roosevelt's nearly two terms in office, he picked his secretary of war, William Howard Taft, to succeed him. Taft readily won the nomination of the Republican Party and defeated the Democratic candidate, William Jennings Bryan, in the 1908 election.

Progressives were repeatedly disappointed by Taft, who was not a skillful politician and failed to develop a base of support. He agreed to higher tariff rates by signing the Payne-Aldrich Tariff into law (1909), despite the progressive goal of lowering tariff rates to reduce consumer prices. In addition, he ended up firing Gifford Pinchot as chief of the United States Forest Service after Pinchot's clashes with Taft's development-minded secretary of the interior, Richard Ballinger. Taft did pursue antitrust suits, even though his public rhetoric did not emphasize this. He initiated 90 antitrust cases, including a major case against U.S. Steel.

Taft, Roosevelt, and the Election of 1912 塔夫脱、罗斯福与1912年选举

Theodore Roosevelt came to regret his decision to throw his support behind President William Howard Taft. After 1910, a wide rift developed within the Republican Party between Taft and Roosevelt. By 1912, this rift became a virtual civil war within the party. Roosevelt and his supporters walked out of the Republican Party nominating convention in 1912 after the party chose Taft to run for reelection. Roosevelt and his loyalists founded the Progressive Party (more commonly known by its nickname, the Bull Moose Party), and nominated Roosevelt to run as a third-party candidate in the general election. The election was further complicated by the candidacy of Eugene V. Debs of the Socialist Party (see page 233). The split within the Republican Party allowed the Democratic Party candidate, Woodrow Wilson, to win the presidency. He won the majority of the electoral votes, despite winning only 41 percent of the popular vote, to Roosevelt's 27 percent, Taft's 23 percent, and Debs's 6 percent.

Progressivism and Woodrow Wilson 进步主义与伍德罗·威尔逊

Woodrow Wilson was an anomaly in the White House. He was only the second Democrat to serve since Andrew Johnson (1865–1869). Republicans had repeatedly "waved the bloody shirt"—referring to the role of the Democratic Party in secession and the Civil War—and won several close presidential elections during the Gilded Age. Wilson was also the first southerner elected to the White House since 1844 (he was born in Virginia). Wilson, a historian and a scholar, had been governor of New Jersey and president of Princeton University before assuming the presidency. Wilson had established a track record as a progressive reformer when he entered the White House.

Wilson and the Federal Reserve Act 威尔逊与《联邦储备法案》

President Wilson grew increasingly suspicious of the banking industry. He argued that it was inflexible and in the service of the stock market more than in the service of the American public. To rectify this situation, he pushed for passage of the Federal Reserve Act, which created the Federal Reserve Bank in 1913. The Federal Reserve Bank is a partly privately controlled and partly publicly controlled national bank. One of its main functions is to regulate economic growth. Its policies can expand or contract the currency supply. If the economy is sluggish, the Fed attempts to stimulate economic growth by expanding the currency supply. If inflation occurs, the Fed attempts to slow down economic activity by reducing the currency supply. An important mechanism for regulating economic growth is raising or lowering the interest rate at which the Fed loans money to other banks. Other banks follow suit, raising or lowering the interest rates at which they loan money to the public. For example, by lowering interest rates, the Fed stimulates economic activity by making it more attractive for people to make major purchases.

Regulation of Business 商业管理

President Wilson was a strong supporter of small business and took a dim view of the growing power of big business. He readily took on the mantle of business regulation that had been central to the agenda of the Progressive movement from its inception. Progressives had become increasingly alarmed at the power of unregulated business during the era of rapid industrialization in the late nineteenth century. In 1890, the Sherman Antitrust had been passed, but was used with limited success. Wilson strengthened the antitrust powers of the federal government with the Clayton Antitrust Act (1914). A key difference in the new act was that it specifically exempted labor unions from being targeted by antitrust actions. The Sherman Act had often been used to break up strikes.

President Wilson also pushed for the creation of the Federal Trade Commission (FTC, 1914) to regulate business practices. One of the many regulatory responsibilities of the commission is reducing the power of trusts and guarding against "unfair trade practices."

The Prohibition Movement and the Eighteenth Amendment
禁酒运动与《第十八条修正案》

The movement to ban alcohol from American society had been one of the largest reform movements in the nineteenth century. It gained new enthusiasts among progressives who sought to harness the power of the government to change social behavior. (See more on the temperance movement in Period 6.)

The final victory for the prohibition movement came in 1919, the year after World War I drew to a close. The movement equated the prohibition of alcohol with the quest to bring democracy to the world. The United States would purify the world of undemocratic forces and purify its citizens of corrupting alcohol. Furthermore, the anti-German sentiment that developed during World War I also played a role because many American breweries had German names. All these factors led to the ratification of the Eighteenth Amendment, which banned the production, sales, and transportation of alcohol as of January 1, 1920.

C. ADDRESSING ENVIRONMENTAL ISSUES IN THE PROGRESSIVE ERA
进步时代应对环境问题

By the late nineteenth century, many observers began to note the toll that industrial processes began to take on the natural environment. Debates ensued during the Progressive Era over appropriate strategies to address environmental degradation.

Concern for Disappearing Wilderness 关注消失的荒野

By the last decades of the nineteenth century, some Americans were beginning to note the disappearance of wilderness and the toll that human activities were taking on the environment. Logging and mining operations were destroying forested areas starting in the late 1800s. Sportsmen were early advocates of environmental protection. In 1887, the sportsman, zoologist, and adventurer George Bird Grinnell and Theodore Roosevelt organized the Boone and Crockett Club—named after two prominent American backwoodsmen—to not only promote outdoor activities but also to lobby for environmental protection. In addition, romanticism, a dominant intellectual and artistic movement of the early to mid-nineteenth century, had generated interest in untouched natural environments. Romantics worried about the corrupting influences of civilization and championed the restorative powers of nature. Paintings of the West by Albert Bierstadt, depicting awe-inspiring landscapes and hinting at the storm clouds of modern civilization on the horizon, generated interest in "unspoiled" landscapes. Even though Romanticism had fallen out of favor by the early twentieth century, its influence continued.

Roosevelt and Conservation 罗斯福与保护区

As president, Theodore Roosevelt embraced the cause of environmental conservation. In keeping with the progressive reliance on expertise, he appointed the scientifically trained Gifford Pinchot to head the U.S. Forest Service and to lead the government's conservation efforts. The roots of the Forest Service date back to the 1870s, as concerns grew about clear-cutting of forests. In 1876, Congress appointed a special agent in the Department of Agriculture to assess the condition of forested land. This office became the Division of Forestry in 1881, renamed the Forest Service in 1905.

Expansion of the National Park System 国家公园体系的扩大

The federal government began the National Park System in 1872 when it created Yellowstone Park, primarily in Wyoming. In 1890, California's Yosemite Valley and the surrounding area were designated a national park (it had been granted federal protection in 1864). President Roosevelt expanded the system, creating five additional national parks. He also established 150 national forests, including Shoshone National Forest, the nation's first national forest. Ultimately, Roosevelt put over 200 million acres under public protection.

Conservationism and Preservationism 资源保护主义与保存主义

President Roosevelt endorsed the view that the nation's natural resources should be used in a responsible way so they would continue to exist for future generations. This view, labeled conservationism, can be contrasted with the views of environmental preservationists. Preservationists want society to have a hands-off approach to the remaining relatively untouched natural areas. An early preservationist was John Muir, one of the founders of the Sierra Club (1892), an organization dedicated to preserving wilderness and to monitoring the federal government's oversight of protected lands. Conservationism, by contrast, with its emphasis on regulation and responsible economic utilization of resources, tapped into major strands of progressive thinking—efficiency, expertise, scientific management, and government intervention.

The Controversy over the Hetch Hetchy Valley 围绕赫奇峡谷的争议

Both conservationists and preservationists were concerned about the rapid disappearance of natural areas in the United States and both endorsed the establishment of national parks. However, the two positions were often at odds. The destruction of the Hetch Hetchy Valley in California illustrates divergent approaches to the environment during the progressive era. The spectacular Hetch Hetchy valley, within the borders of Yosemite National Park, was targeted by San Francisco officials as a possible water source for the growing city. Officials sought to dam the Tuolumne River and turn Hetch Hetchy into a giant reservoir. Although federal officials initially balked at destroying the valley, they reversed themselves after a devastating earthquake and fire destroyed much of San Francisco in 1906. The plan was given final approval by the Woodrow Wilson administration in 1913 and was completed a decade later.

D. DIVISIONS WITHIN THE PROGRESSIVE MOVEMENT 进步运动中的分化

The Progressive movement consisted of a broad constellation of individuals and groups. While progressivism is associated with certain goals and principles, the individuals and groups involved often hold divergent views on particular issues—including race and segregation, popular participation in government, and immigration restrictions.

The Progressive Movement and Segregation 进步运动与种族隔离

White progressives generally accepted prevailing notions around race. As discussed in Period 5, a rigid system of segregation developed in the South following the end of Reconstruction (1877). Southern states had passed a series of Jim Crow laws, segregating African Americans from whites in public facilities. Further, voting laws and intimidation had virtually excluded African Americans from voting, despite passage of the Fifteenth Amendment (1870). Violence by the Ku Klux Klan and others had become the backdrop to life in the South for African Americans. By the beginning of the twentieth century, a new science of eugenics gave intellectual support to segregation by holding that different races had distinctly different mental characteristics and capabilities. This pseudo-scientific theory also contributed to the growing anti-immigrant sentiment in the United States (see more on nativism, page 277).

Many progressive activists and writers simply ignored the conditions of African Americans. Some endorsed the segregation system that had developed in the South. Progressive president Woodrow Wilson, for example, was an outspoken racist. He ordered the segregation of government offices, including post offices, throughout the country. His advocacy of white supremacy went even further than contemporary social attitudes. He praised the racist film, *Birth of a Nation* (1916) by D. W. Griffith, with its positive portrayal of the Ku Klux Klan during the Reconstruction period.

Fighting Segregation in the Progressive Era 进步时代的种族隔离斗争

A small number of white progressives challenged the Jim Crow system. Lillian Wald, the director of the Henry Street Settlement in New York City, was active in the fight for racial integration. However, the principal voices for social justice for African Americans came from African

American activists who attempted to put the issue of race and racism on the national agenda. W. E. B. Du Bois was a militant civil-rights activist who wrote about the injustices carried out against African Americans in the South. He was one of the founders of the National Association for the Advancement of Colored People (NAACP) in 1909. The leadership of the organization had first met in 1905 on the Canadian side of Niagara Falls, where they formed the Niagara movement. Du Bois's call for full political equality and civil rights for African Americans was in marked contrast to the more conciliatory approach of Booker T. Washington (see Period 6). A third important figure in the African American community was Marcus Garvey, best known for urging African Americans to return to their ancestral homelands in Africa. Not many African Americans made the journey, but Garvey was influential in instilling a sense of pride among many African Americans; in this he is seen as an important figure in the Black-nationalist movement.

Democracy Versus Expertise in Progressive Governance 进步派治理下的民主与专业

As discussed earlier in this chapter, progressive reformers were troubled by corruption and cronyism in government. Lincoln Steffens's book, *The Shame of Our Cities* (1904), turned a spotlight on municipal corruption, but corruption was rampant on all levels of government. Progressive reformers were of two minds when it came to challenging the power of corrupt political machines. One progressive impulse was to empower professional managers and planners, while the other impulse was to empower the citizenry through democratic reforms.

Expertise, Efficiency, and Mastery 专业、效率与控制

Many Progressive reformers embraced the goals of expertise and efficiency in terms of reforming governments. A system of expert managers would replace systems based on cronyism, nepotism, and favoritism. Many progressives looked favorably to the "scientific management" techniques developed by Frederick Winslow Taylor (see more on Taylor, page 250). The movement held the optimistic belief that experts in government could address a variety of social ills, using scientific and rational criteria. Many of these ideas are articulated in Walter Lippmann's book, *Drift and Mastery* (1914). Lippmann argued that governance based on rational scientific ideas could overcome forces contributing to societal drift. By "drift," he meant a society lacking direction and discipline.

Efficiency and Municipal Government in the Wake of the Galveston Flood
加尔维斯顿洪水后的市政效率与政府

The issue of municipal inefficiency and corruption came to the fore in the aftermath of a devastating hurricane and flood that struck Galveston, Texas, in 1900. Upwards of 8,000 people died in the disaster. Given the ineffective response by the city government, local leaders were convinced to create commissions to spearhead the cleanup and rebuilding of the city. This commission form of government soon spread from Galveston to other cities. Elected commissioners run the city and head various departments, such as public works, fire, and sanitation. The idea of the commission form of government is that city officials would not be under the sway of powerful political bosses. Other cities hired managers, with professional training, to administer municipal affairs.

The Push for Expanded Participation in Democracy 推动扩大民主参与

While many progressive reformers looked to experts and managers to counteract governmental corruption, a large segment of the movement pushed for democratic empowerment of the citizenry. This push did not address the most obvious impediment to democratic participation—laws and practices preventing the majority of African Americans from voting. However, a host of reforms were advocated to make local, state, and national government more responsive to the popular will.

Women's Suffrage 妇女选举权

Perhaps the most important reform to come out of the Progressive era was the ratification of the Nineteenth Amendment to the Constitution (1920), which gave women the right to vote. The push for women's suffrage dates back to at least the 1848 Seneca Falls Convention (see more on the origins of the women's suffrage movement in Period 5 and Period 6). The National American Woman Suffrage Association, which formed in 1890 out of two earlier organizations, grew to over two million members by 1917. A more radical National Woman's Party, founded by Alice Paul, was founded in 1916. Men and women in the movement organized hundreds of parades, raised millions of dollars, and engaged in hunger strikes and civil disobedience. President Woodrow Wilson came to support women's suffrage in 1918, recognizing the "suffering and sacrifice" that women had experienced during World War I.

The Referendum, the Recall, and the Initiative 公民投票权、罢免权与立法提案权

Reformers hoped that by expanding democracy, the power of political machines would be lessened. In states across the United States, progressives proposed, and often implemented, reforms to expand democracy. The referendum was a Progressive era reform that allowed people to vote directly on proposed legislation. A proposed referendum item would appear on the ballot on election day. Voters would either vote "yes" or "no" on the referendum. Several states still have the referendum. The recall empowered the people of a city or state to remove an elected official before his or her term ended. Several states still have the recall. In 2003, Californians recalled Governor Gray Davis and replaced him with Arnold Schwarzenegger. The initiative allowed citizens to introduce a bill to the local or state legislature by petition.

Direct Primaries 直接预选

In the nineteenth century, political party leaders usually picked the candidates who would run in the general election. This practice removed a key element of the electoral process from public participation. In some districts, where one political party dominated the general elections, the only meaningful input into the political process occurred at the primary stage. The Progressive movement, therefore, pushed for the adoption of direct primaries, which empowered voters to choose party candidates to run for elected public office. Minnesota was the first state to adopt a direct primary in 1899. Most other states had also adopted direct primaries by 1916.

Direct Election of Senators 直接选举参议员

Progressives pushed for the direct election of senators. Previously, senators were chosen by state legislatures. The framers to the Constitution had envisioned the Senate as an august body of even-tempered men, who would counterbalance the enthusiasms and rash decisions of the House of Representatives—the "people's

> ### PROGRESSIVE-ERA AMENDMENTS
> ### 进步时代产生的修正案
> Four important amendments to the Constitution came out of the Progressive era: the Sixteenth Amendment allowed for a federal income tax; the Seventeenth Amendment provided for the direct election of senators; the Eighteenth Amendment called for prohibition; and the Nineteenth Amendment extended the vote to women.

chamber." Such thinking was deemed elitist by many progressive activists. The Seventeenth Amendment was ratified in 1913.

The Australian Ballot 澳大利亚（秘密）投票表决法

In the nineteenth century, political machines routinely printed ballots with their candidates on them. Voters would then deposit these ballots in voting boxes, allowing anyone who was interested to see which ballot a voter deposited. This system allowed for voter intimidation. In 1888, Massachusetts adopted a secret ballot, which was already in use in Australia. These ballots, printed by the state instead of the parties and filled out by voters in curtained booths, became the norm in America by 1910.

III. The New Deal and Debates over a Limited Welfare State
（罗斯福）新政与有限福利国家的争议

A series of developments led to the creation of a limited welfare state in the 1930s. The most important development was the ongoing economic dislocation caused by the Great Depression. Reformers at all levels of government advocated moving beyond the dictates of laissez-faire capitalism.

A. THE CREATION OF THE "NEW DEAL" "新政"的创立

During the depths of the 1930s Great Depression, President Franklin Roosevelt pushed for a series of reforms to address both the causes and effects of the economic crisis. Roosevelt and his advisors drew on progressive ideas in the creation of the "New Deal." The focus of the New Deal was three-pronged—extend relief to the poor, stimulate economic recovery, and create long-term reform of the American economy.

From Hoover to Roosevelt 从胡佛到罗斯福

In the presidential election of 1932, Franklin Delano Roosevelt offered the public a marked contrast to President Herbert Hoover. Hoover had been very reluctant to harness the power of the central government to intervene in economic matters. He feared that government intervention into the Depression would stifle individual initiative. Rather, he invoked the idea of "rugged individualism"—the belief that the problems of the nation could best be solved by the determination and resolve of the American people. When people were unable to help themselves, Hoover encouraged voluntary cooperation and private charities to step in. Hoover's one major program designed to address the economic crisis was the Reconstruction Finance Corporation (1932). This government agency extended loans to struggling railroads, banks, insurance companies, and other firms. He refused, however, to extend direct relief to individuals.

> **HOOVER'S ECONOMIC POLICIES**
> **胡佛的经济政策**
> Hoover's approach to the economy and his rhetoric set a template for Republican economic policy for much of the twentieth century.

Hoover's limited response to the Great Depression, coupled with his handling of the Bonus March protest in 1932 (which resulted in the deaths of two World War I veterans who were demanding early payment of their government bonuses), set the stage for the election of Franklin D. Roosevelt. Roosevelt, a distant cousin of Theodore Roosevelt, was from a wealthy New York family. In 1928, Roosevelt won the governorship in New York and introduced a number of innovative programs to help New Yorkers as the Great Depression deepened. Though Roosevelt was from an affluent background, he was able to convey to the public a sense of empathy and personal warmth. Further, his openness to experimentation allowed for a more flexible response to the Depression than Hoover's more ideological approach. Roosevelt won the election of 1932 easily, garnering 57 percent of the popular vote and 472 out of 529 electoral votes.

Roosevelt moved the federal government in a new direction by asserting that it should take some responsibility for the welfare of the people. The Roosevelt administration developed a series of programs known collectively as the New Deal. Previously, people received assistance in times of need from churches, settlement houses, and other private charities. However, the levels of poverty and unemployment during the Great Depression were unprecedented. Roosevelt believed that the government needed to take action. The New Deal provided relief to individuals through a variety of agencies.

TARIFFS IN THE 1920S
20世纪20年代的关税

Tariffs in the 1920s were at their highest rate in American history other than in the period following the "Tariff of Abominations." Raising tariff rates during the 1920s was exactly what the country did not need. The United States needed to trade more with Europe in order to sell excess goods. Tariffs closed off trade with Europe.

The First New Deal 第一次新政

The Roosevelt administration developed a remarkable array of programs during its first hundred days in 1933 and in the months immediately following. These programs, which comprised the first New Deal, reflected both Roosevelt's willingness to experiment and the scope of problems that faced the nation. Below are some of the more important programs.

THE NEWNESS OF THE NEW DEAL
新政的创新之处

The extension of the federal government into the economic lives of individuals represented a marked departure from the traditional role of the government.

Glass-Steagall Act (1933) 《格拉斯–斯蒂格法案》（1933）

One of the most pressing problems President Roosevelt faced was the instability of the banking industry. Many people had lost confidence in the banking system and withdrew their money in fear that their banks might fold. With thousands of people withdrawing their money at the same time, many banks actually did close, turning collective fears into a self-fulfilling prophecy. The Federal Deposit Insurance Corporation, created by the Glass-Steagall Act, insures deposits so that if a bank does fold, people do not lose their savings.

National Industrial Recovery Act (1933) 《国家工业复兴法案》（1933）

The National Industrial Recovery Act called for representatives from labor and competing corporations to draw up a set of codes. These codes were designed to shorten hours for workers, guarantee trade union rights, establish minimum wage levels, regulate the price of certain petroleum products, and promote fair business practices. The idea was that cutthroat competition hurt the economy and pushed workers' wages down and limited their ability to purchase goods.

Agricultural Adjustment Act (1933)　《农业调整法案》（1933）

The Roosevelt administration took the counterintuitive measure of paying farmers *not* to grow crops. An important goal of the Agricultural Adjustment Act was to reduce production in order to bolster sagging commodity prices and strengthen the agricultural sector. Commodity prices did increase, but the AAA had an unintended negative effect. Landowners often evicted tenant farmers and sharecroppers in order to take land out of cultivation. This hurt many of the nation's poorest farmers, including numerous African American farmers.

Tennessee Valley Authority (1933)　田纳西河流域管理局（1933）

The Tennessee Valley Authority (TVA), still in existence, was the federal government's first experiment in regional planning. The TVA built dams, generated electricity, manufactured fertilizer, provided technical assistance to farmers, and fostered economic development in the Tennessee Valley.

Federal Emergency Relief Act (1933)　《联邦紧急救济法》（1933）

The Federal Emergency Relief Act was created to distribute more than $500 million to state and local governments, which would, in turn, distribute aid to the poor. FERA was intended to provide temporary relief for people in need.

Civilian Conservation Corps (1933)　民间资源保护队（1933）

Roosevelt created the Civilian Conservation Corps (CCC) to provide outdoor work for young men between the ages of 18 and 24. Projects initiated by the CCC included soil conservation, flood control, trail and road building, bridges, and forest projects. During the 1930s, approximately 2.75 million men worked on CCC projects.

Securities and Exchange Commission (1934)　证券交易委员会（1934）

Many individuals had lost confidence in the stock market after the 1929 crash, which was partly caused by unsound practices. The Securities and Exchange Commission was created to oversee stock market operations by monitoring transactions, licensing brokers, limiting buying on margin, and prohibiting insider trading.

B. CRITICS OF THE NEW DEAL AND THE SECOND NEW DEAL
对新政的评论与第二次新政

President Franklin D. Roosevelt had to negotiate the New Deal through the tumultuous political currents of the 1930s. A variety of social and political movements emerged, each offering different solutions to the economic crisis. To some degree, these movements hindered the New Deal, and to some degree, they influenced it. From the left, union activists, radicals, and populist leaders pushed for more extensive reforms. From the right, conservatives—in the media, in Congress, and on the Supreme Court—attempted to limit the scope and influence of the New Deal. The left critique of the New Deal ultimately led to a second set of reforms, which went beyond the scope of the programs of Roosevelt's first year in office.

The Growth of the Communist Party　共产党的壮大

Although the Communist Party never attracted a large following in the United States, it did gain new members and exerted influence beyond its numbers in the 1930s. Some Americans were impressed with the achievements of the Soviet Union, and some simply felt that the capitalist system was not working. The Communist Party attracted members by adopting the "Popular Front" strategy (1934–1939); the strategy called for the Party to drop talk of an impending revolution and to cooperate with a spectrum of anti-fascist groups and governments, including Roosevelt's New Deal administration.

Populist Opposition to the New Deal　平民党反对新政

Although President Roosevelt could count on tacit support from the Communist Party, other voices on the left criticized the New Deal as being overly cautious. Upton Sinclair (author of *The Jungle*) ran for governor of California in 1934 under the banner "End Poverty in California," proposing sweeping, somewhat socialistic solutions. Francis Townsend, also from California, proposed a tax to generate enough money to give everyone over 60 a monthly stipend. The most serious threat to Roosevelt from the left came from Huey Long, the flamboyant populist governor, then senator, from Louisiana. Beginning in 1934, he organized a national network of clubs under the "Share Our Wealth Society" banner; the movement proposed breaking up the fortunes of the rich and distributing them to everyone else. His slogan was "Every Man a King." He talked of running against Roosevelt in 1936, but was assassinated in 1935.

The Growth of Organized Labor　劳工组织的壮大

President Roosevelt encouraged union membership in order to increase the purchasing power of workers. Organized labor, in turn, pushed Roosevelt to adopt more extensive reform measures. The National Industrial Recovery Act (1933) and the Wagner Act (1935) legalized union membership in the United States. Union membership, which had been falling in the 1920s and early 1930s, rose from 3 million in 1933 to 10.5 million by 1941. By the end of World War II, 36 percent of nonagricultural American workers were in unions.

The Congress of Industrial Organizations　产业工会联合会

The drive to organize workers in the 1930s led to tensions within the labor movement. The 50-year-old American Federation of Labor (AFL), a coalition of craft unions, had never shown much interest in organizing unskilled assembly-line workers. Labor leaders such as John L. Lewis of the United Mine Workers wanted the AFL to do more organizing in this growing sector of the labor force. In 1935, he and other leaders from primarily unskilled unions organized the Committee for Industrial Organization within the AFL. The committee's task of organizing basic industries met the ire of AFL leadership,

> ### THE CIO AND THE AFL
> ### CIO与AFL
> The CIO started out as the Committee for Industrial Organization within the AFL in 1935. In 1938 it became the independent Congress of Industrial Organizations. In 1955, it merged with the AFL to form the AFL-CIO.

which ordered the committee to disband in 1936, and when it refused, expelled the committee's unions in 1937. In 1938, the committee reconstituted itself as the independent Congress of Industrial Organizations (CIO). It grew rapidly, surpassing the AFL by 1941—the CIO had about 5 million members compared to the AFL's 4.6 million.

The Sit-down Strike　静坐罢工

Although unions were legal in America, employers were still under no compulsion to accept union demands. In the late 1930s, a wave of strikes ensued. A new, militant tactic of CIO unions was the sit-down strike, in which employees stopped work and refused to leave the shop floor, thus preventing the employer from reopening with replacement workers (or "scabs"). The most famous sit-down strike took place at the General Motors plant in Flint, Michigan, in the winter of 1936–1937.

Conservative Critics Denounce "Creeping Socialism"

保守派批评人士谴责"温和社会主义"

Some conservative critics saw the New Deal as socialism in disguise. The New Deal, they argued, had pushed the government too far into new realms. Roosevelt's "court-packing" scheme (see page 269) seemed especially heavy-handed to many Americans. The most prominent group on the right was the American Liberty League (founded in 1934), which consisted primarily of conservative businessmen. This group supported conservative politicians of both parties, and promoted the "open shop"—a business in which the employees are not required to join a union. Catholic priest Father Charles Coughlin, using his popular national radio show, attacked Roosevelt as being a communist and a dictator. Coughlin had initially supported Roosevelt in 1932, but grew increasingly critical of the New Deal, adding anti-Semitic and even fascistic elements to his broadcast.

The Second New Deal　第二次新政

By 1935, President Roosevelt was facing several problems, although the economy had improved slightly between 1933, when Roosevelt took office, and 1935. Average weekly earnings had increased for workers and unemployment had dropped from about 25 percent to 20 percent. But with more than 10 million people out of work, Roosevelt could not claim that the New Deal had resolved the nation's economic woes. In addition, the Supreme Court had declared key New Deal legislation unconstitutional. In *A.L.A. Schechter Poultry Corp. v. United States* (1935), the court declared the National Industrial Recovery Act unconstitutional because it violated the constitutional separation of powers by delegating legislative powers to the executive branch. Several months later, the court declared the Agricultural Adjustment Act unconstitutional in the *United States v. Butler* decision (1936). The court held that taxes enacted by the AAA amounted to statutory regulations; such actions, therefore, fell under state powers, not federal powers.

With mounting pressure from a variety of populist and leftwing forces, and with a presidential election looming in 1936, Roosevelt introduced a second set of programs known as the Second New Deal. This second phase of the New Deal was less about involvement with the different sectors of the economy and more about providing assistance and support to the working class.

Works Progress Administration (1935)　公共事业振兴署（1935）

The Works Progress Administration (WPA) was a massive initiative that created jobs for millions of unemployed men and women. The jobs ranged from construction work to theatrical productions to writing guidebooks about each of the states. Earlier jobs programs, such as the Civilian Conservation Corps, were piecemeal compared with the immense WPA. At its peak in 1938, over 3 million people worked for the WPA; over 8 million people in total worked for it by the time it was shuttered in 1943.

Social Security Act (1935)　《社会安全法案》（1935）

Social Security is perhaps the initiative that has had the largest long-term impact on American society. The Social Security Act was designed to help the unemployed, the elderly, and the disabled. The most important element of the plan was retirement benefits, funded by taxes on workers and employers, which workers collected after they turned 65. The Social Security Agency is still in existence and has remained popular with large segments of the public.

The Wagner Act (1935)　《瓦格纳法案》（1935）

The Wagner Act encouraged the formation of unions. The act established the National Labor Relations Board, which is still in existence, to oversee union elections and to arbitrate conflicts between workers and owners. It also prohibited owners from taking punitive actions against workers who sought to organize unions. As a result, the act led to a tremendous increase in union activity.

The Second New Deal and the Supreme Court　第二次新政与最高法院

President Roosevelt feared that the Supreme Court would invalidate key elements of this second New Deal, as it had earlier New Deal acts. In 1937, he proposed a bill to alter the composition of the Supreme Court by allowing him to appoint six additional justices. This "court-packing" bill generated a great deal of opposition. Congress rejected this plan, but the court became friendlier to the president anyway. Over the next few years, some of the more conservative justices retired, and Roosevelt was able to appoint seven new justices, including the liberal Hugo Black.

THE SUPREME COURT AND POLITICS
最高法院与政治

Throughout history, note the connections between Supreme Court decisions and contemporary political currents. The justices are products of their society; they do not make their decisions in a vacuum.

The Rollback of the New Deal　新政的反转

In late 1937 and 1938, President Roosevelt took the New Deal in a new direction that, many historians believe, hurt the economy. By 1937, the economy was showing signs of improvement. Unemployment was going down and banks and businesses were showing signs of stability. Roosevelt took the advice of some of the more conservative members of his cabinet and cut back on spending with the goal of balancing the budget.

The "Roosevelt Recession"　"罗斯福衰退"

President Roosevelt's move to cut spending on New Deal programs contributed in 1938 to a further downturn in economic activity, known as the "Roosevelt Recession." Later in 1938, Roosevelt shifted direction again and increased government spending. The economy did show signs of growth, but the real boost came in 1939 as the United States began producing armaments and supplies in the looming shadow of World War II.

Keynesian Economics 凯恩斯主义经济学

When President Roosevelt cut back spending to balance the budget in the middle of the Great Depression (see page 269), he was rejecting the advice of the economist John Maynard Keynes. Keynes's most important book, *General Theory of Employment, Interest and Money* (1936), argued that deficit spending by the government was acceptable, even desirable, as a means of increasing overall demand and stimulating economic activity. This idea of using the tools of the government—the Federal Reserve Bank, and spending and taxation polices—to influence economic activity is known as Keynesian economics.

> ## KEYNES AND GOVERNMENT POLICY
> ## 凯恩斯与政府政策
> Be familiar with Keynesian economics. His theories have influenced government policy in the twentieth century, especially during Democratic administrations. Republicans have focused on cutting government spending.

C. THE LEGACY OF THE NEW DEAL 新政的遗产

The New Deal did not solve the economic crisis of the 1930s, but it did profoundly change the United States. It left a legacy of agencies and laws aimed at economic security, and it ushered in a major political realignment, as a new coalition of ethnic groups, African Americans, and working-class communities identified with the goals of the Democratic Party.

Political Realignment 政治重组

The 1930s witnessed the emergence of the political and ideological alignment that has existed, to some extent, to the present. President Herbert Hoover's generally conservative laissez-faire approach has been echoed in the policies of Republican presidents Ronald Reagan, George H. W. Bush, and George W. Bush, while President Roosevelt's generally liberal interventionist approach inspired Democratic president Lyndon Johnson's "Great Society." Today, Democratic leaders debate how closely their party should be associated with New Deal liberalism, while Republicans brand their opponents "tax and spend" liberals. The debates of the 1930s are still part of the political culture.

The Depression and Affected Groups 大萧条与受影响的群体

The various sectors of society were affected differently by the Great Depression and the New Deal. Although the 1930s was certainly a dismal time economically, some groups in the United States were better able to put forth agendas for change and to achieve gains than others.

African Americans 非裔美国人

African Americans, already in a vulnerable position in U.S. society before the Great Depression, were especially hard hit by the economic difficulties of the 1930s. Many New Deal programs ignored African Americans—such as the Agricultural Adjustment Act, which did not help tenant farmers. Roosevelt was wary of losing the support of the southern wing of the Democratic Party, so he did not push for civil rights legislation. Neither did he endorse federal anti-lynching legislation (which Congress never passed).

Despite President Roosevelt's reluctance to take the lead in civil-rights legislation, African Americans switched their allegiance from the party of Lincoln (the Republicans) to the Democratic Party. There are several reasons for this historic shift. First Lady Eleanor Roosevelt and Interior Secretary Harold Ickes did champion civil rights causes. The most dramatic gesture by Eleanor Roosevelt was organizing a concert by Marian Anderson in 1935 on the steps of the Lincoln Memorial after Anderson was blocked by the Daughters of the American Revolution from performing at their concert hall. Also, the president met periodically with a group of African American advisors to the president, called the "Black Cabinet." In 1941, Roosevelt issued an executive order banning discrimination in the defense industry (see page 298). Finally, African Americans believed that Roosevelt, despite his shortcomings, was attempting to improve conditions for poor and working-class people.

SLOW STEPS TOWARD CIVIL RIGHTS
走向民权的缓慢步伐

We can see Roosevelt and the Democratic Party just beginning to shift toward support for civil rights in the 1930s. This was a major shift for a party that in the 1860s pushed the southern states to secede in order to defend slavery.

The "Scottsboro Boys" Case　"斯科茨伯勒男孩"案

The racial biases of the justice system were demonstrated in the highly publicized "Scottsboro Boys" case (1931–1935). Nine African American youths were convicted of rape in Alabama on flimsy evidence. In 1932, the Supreme Court reversed most of the convictions on the grounds that the defendants' due process rights had been violated because they were denied effective counsel. The cases were then sent back to state court for retrial. The defendants were again found guilty, even after one of the alleged victims admitted fabricating her story. Charges were later dropped for four out of the nine defendants.

Women　妇女

Women suffered a double burden during the Depression: on the one hand, they were responsible for putting food on the table during difficult times, while on the other hand, they were frequently scorned if they "took a job away from a man" by working outside the home. Further, New Deal programs tended to slight women; the Civilian Conservation Corps (1933), a New Deal program that sent young men from urban areas to work on federal lands, excluded women, and the National Industrial Recovery Act (1933) set lower wage levels for women than for men. Nonetheless, individual women such as Frances Perkins, the first female cabinet member (secretary of labor) and Eleanor Roosevelt, one of the most active and public first ladies in American history, opened doors for women. Despite criticism, more women were working outside the home in 1940 than in 1930.

American Indians　美洲印第安人

New Deal legislation profoundly affected American Indians. The Indian Reorganization Act (1934) largely undid the Dawes Severalty Act (1887), which had attempted to assimilate American Indians into mainstream society by breaking up reservations and dividing the land into small plots for individual Indians. The Indian Reorganization Act reversed this policy by restoring tribal ownership of reservation lands and recognizing the legitimacy of tribal governments. The act also extended loans to American Indian groups for economic development.

KEY CONCEPT 7.2 THE STRESSES OF MODERNITY
核心概念7.2：现代化的重压

In many ways, the first decades of the twentieth century ushered in key elements of the modern world. New forms of communication and travel helped create a modern mass culture. As the reach of this new culture extended to more and more Americans, a series of culture clashes ensued. These culture clashes were exacerbated by large-scale migrations, world wars, and economic crises.

I. Popular Culture and the Making of Modernity 流行文化与现代性的形成

New technologies and new forms of media were a double-edged sword for American society in the early twentieth century. Although standards of living improved, divergent reactions to these changes resulted in political and cultural conflict.

A. NEW MEDIA AND NATIONAL AND REGIONAL CULTURES 新媒体与国家文化和地区文化

New technologies, such as radio and cinema, emerged during the first decades of the twentieth century. On the one hand, these new technologies helped usher in a national, mass-media oriented culture. On the other hand, the experiences of particular groups—based around race, ethnicity, and region—produced a variety of other cultural expressions.

Radio and the Development of Mass Culture 无线电广播与大众文化的发展

Radio grew from being virtually nonexistent at the beginning of the 1920s to becoming an extremely popular medium by the end of the decade. Radio programming was initiated by amateurs who sent out music or sermons to the few scattered people who had "wireless receivers." Soon, Westinghouse and other corporations saw the potential to reach the masses with radio. By 1923, there were almost 600 licensed radio stations. Early successful programs included *The Amos 'n' Andy Show* (1928), a holdover from "blackface" minstrel shows of the nineteenth and early twentieth centuries.

Radio continued its popularity in the 1930s. Americans listened to weekly serials such as *The Shadow* and *The Lone Ranger*, to comedians such as Jack Benny and George Burns, and to soap operas. In addition, big-band swing music became very popular. Americans listened to orchestras led by Duke Ellington, Tommy Dorsey, and Glenn Miller. Radio and movies tended to create a more homogenous culture in the United States in the 1930s.

Movies and the Development of Mass Media 电影与大众媒体的发展

Movie attendance achieved staggering levels in the 1920s. By the end of the decade, three-fourths of the American people (roughly 90 million) were going to the movies every week. The first "talkie," *The Jazz Singer*, came out in 1927.

The movie industry continued to thrive during the Great Depression. Escapist musicals such as *Gold Diggers of 1933* and *42nd Street* (1933), with lavish sets and spectacular numbers, proved popular. In *The Wizard of Oz* (1939), Dorothy, played by Judy Garland, escapes a Kansas farm, shown in black-and-white, and is transported, along with the audience, to the magical land of Oz, shot in Technicolor. The Marx Brothers produced and starred in anarchic comedies, such as *Monkey Business* (1931) and *Duck Soup* (1933), which mocked authority figures and the pretensions of the wealthy. Charlie Chaplin's comedy *Modern Times* (1936) satirized the entire capitalist system, from the drudgery of assembly-line work to the corruption of the law enforcement system. Some movies attempted to grapple with the wrenching public issues of the time. *The Grapes of Wrath* (1940), the film version of John Steinbeck's novel, chronicled the conditions of "Dust Bowl" farmers migrating to California, while Frank Capra's *Mr. Smith Goes to Washington* (1939) depicted the triumph of a decent, "everyman" politician.

> ## MOVIES IN THE PRE-TELEVISION ERA
> ## 电视出现之前的电影
> Movies would never again draw as large a percentage of the public as they did in the 1930s and 1940s. Some thought that television would destroy the movie industry. The predictions did not come true, but television certainly made deep cuts into the movie industry's audience.

B. ART AND LITERATURE   艺术与文学

Migration patterns and urbanization contributed to the emergence of new forms of art and literature. Some of these cultural products can be seen as responses to the advent of the modern world. Much of this art and literature reflects ethnic and regional identities.

The Harlem Renaissance   哈莱姆文艺复兴

The Great Migration of African Americans from the rural South to the urban North (see page 278) contributed to the Harlem Renaissance, a literary, artistic, and intellectual movement centered in the primarily Black neighborhood of Harlem, in New York City. A key goal of the movement was to increase pride in Black culture by celebrating African American life and forging a new cultural identity among African American people. Contributions included the poetry of Langston Hughes, Claude McKay, and Countee Cullen and the jazz music of Louis Armstrong, Duke Ellington, and Bessie Smith. Langston Hughes's poems include "Harlem," "The Negro Speaks of Rivers," and "I, Too, Sing America." He wrote an essay that became a manifesto for Harlem Renaissance writers and artists, entitled "The Negro Artist and the Racial Mountain." Duke Ellington is perhaps the most important figure in twentieth-century jazz. Some of his most important compositions are "Mood Indigo," "Don't Get Around Much Anymore," and "Take the A Train."

The "Lost Generation" Writers of the 1920s   20世纪20年代 "迷惘的一代"

The "Lost Generation" literary movement expressed a general disillusionment with society, commenting on everything from the narrowness of small-town life to the rampant materialism of American society. Several writers were troubled by the destruction and seeming meaningless of World War I. *The Great Gatsby* (1925) by F. Scott Fitzgerald exposed the shallowness of the lives of the wealthy and privileged of the era. Sinclair Lewis's novels, such as *Main Street* (1920) and *Babbitt* (1924), mocked the narrowness of the middle class. Ernest Hemingway's *A Farewell to Arms* (1929) critiqued the glorification of war.

Literature of the 1930s   20世纪30年代的文学

Pearl Buck's *The Good Earth* (1931), a story of peasants in China, John Steinbeck's tale of "Dust Bowl" migrants, *The Grapes of Wrath* (1939), and Margaret Mitchell's account of the Old

South, *Gone With the Wind* (1936), have endured as classics of 1930s literature. Several novels of the 1930s reflected the influence of the Communist Party on American culture. Anti-fascist novels included *It Can't Happen Here* (1935) by Sinclair Lewis. Proletarian literature included the novel *The Disinherited* (1933) by Jack Conroy and the play *Waiting for Lefty* (1935) by Clifford Odets.

C. THE CONSERVATIVE BACKLASH OF THE 1910s AND 1920s
20世纪前20年保守派的强烈抵制

The years during and immediately following World War I saw a backlash against the experimentation of the Progressive era and a rise in patriotism and xenophobia. Government restrictions on freedom of speech during World War I were followed by a "Red Scare" after the war.

Civil Liberties During Wartime　战时的公民自由

Despite the hopes of many progressives, World War I ushered in a repressive atmosphere that stymied progressive reform and led to the curtailment of civil liberties. The Espionage and Sedition Acts were passed during World War I to put limits on public expressions of antiwar sentiment. The Espionage Act (1917), along with the Sedition Act (1918), made it a crime to interfere with the draft or with the sale of war bonds, or to say anything "disloyal" about the war effort.

The Espionage Act was upheld by the Supreme Court in the decision in *Schenck v. United States* (1919). Charles Schenck and other members of the Socialist Party had been arrested for printing and distributing flyers opposing the war and urging young men to resist the draft. The Supreme Court argued that freedom of speech is not absolute and that the government is justified in limiting certain forms of speech during wartime. The court argued that certain utterances pose a "clear and present danger." By analogy, the court reasoned that one is not allowed to falsely shout "Fire!" in a crowded theater.

CIVIL LIBERTIES IN COMPARISON
对比公民自由权

The debate over civil liberties during wartime is an ongoing issue. Be prepared to compare restrictions on civil liberties in the context of the "Quasi-war" with France, the Civil War, World War I, World War II, and even the current war on terrorism.

The Crusade Against Organized Labor and Dissent　对劳工组织的讨伐与不信教者

Attacks on organized labor occurred amidst a dramatic increase in union activism in the immediate aftermath of World War I. Labor conflict and the increased visibility of radical movements led to an atmosphere of repression against radicals and immigrants.

When World War I ended, the government disbanded the agencies that it had created to regulate economic activity during the war. Workers, for instance, no longer had the protections of the National War Labor Policies Board. In addition, inflation was no longer kept in check by the government. In 1919, prices rose nearly 75 percent. In these conditions, workers across America organized and fought to protect wartime gains. The year 1919 saw the second biggest strike wave in American history. There were more than 4,500 strikes, involving 4 million workers. The biggest strike was the Seattle General Strike in February. The radical

Industrial Workers of the World and the more moderate American Federation of Labor worked together to virtually close down Seattle. In September, more than 340,000 steelworkers went on strike. Late in 1919 and into 1920, the police force in Boston went on strike. In all three of the strikes, and in countless others, the workers were soundly defeated.

Management used a variety of techniques to maintain the upper hand in dealing with organized labor. First, management was able to paint striking workers as subversives and would-be Bolsheviks. Second, corporate leaders strenuously pushed for open shops—workplaces in which the union could not require workers to join the union. Finally, the government intervened on behalf of management. The Supreme Court, for instance, held that picketing was not protected by the First Amendment. It was not until the New Deal era of the 1930s that the labor movement was able to regain momentum.

The "Red Scare" "红色恐怖"

The backlash against the strike wave of 1919, combined with the virulent strain of patriotism unleashed by World War I, set the groundwork for the "Red Scare" of the late 1910s and early 1920s, a campaign against communists, anarchists, and other radicals. The "Red Scare" also targeted labor leaders, attempting to portray the labor movement as a front for communist organizing. The Red Scare was a grassroots response of ordinary Americans as well as a government-orchestrated campaign. The scare can be traced to the successful Bolshevik revolution in Russia that brought the Communist Party to power and led to the establishment of the Soviet Union. In 1919, the Bolsheviks created the Comintern, an international organization of Communist Party leaders determined to duplicate the success of the Bolsheviks in other countries. Conservative Americans took the pronouncements of the Comintern at face value, even though the communist movement in the United States was extremely small.

In December 1919, the Russian-born anarchist and activist Emma Goldman was deported by the Justice Department. Later, in January 1920, Attorney General A. Mitchell Palmer began a broad hunt for suspected radicals. Palmer's Justice Department carried out unwarranted raids, known as "Palmer Raids," of suspected radicals' homes. Six thousand alleged radicals were identified by Palmer's men. Although Palmer did not uncover the makings of an uprising, he did end up deporting more than 500 noncitizens. The movement spread to the local level as radical newspapers were shut down, libraries were purged of allegedly radical books, and accused elected officials were removed from office. The Supreme Court decision in *Schenck v. United States*, which established the "clear and present danger" guideline for limiting free speech, gave cover to such excesses (see page 274). Soon, Americans began to question Palmer's aggressive tactics, but suspicion of "reds" persisted throughout the 1920s.

The Trial of Sacco and Vanzetti 萨柯和范泽蒂死刑案

The repressive atmosphere of the Red Scare era can be seen in the trial of Nicola Sacco and Bartolomeo Vanzetti. Their trial for robbery and murder illustrated the intolerance that many Americans had toward immigrants and toward alleged radicals in the 1920s. The two men were accused of robbing and killing a payroll clerk in Massachusetts in 1920. The evidence against them was sketchy, but the judge was openly hostile to the men, who were not only immigrants but also anarchists. After they were found guilty, many Americans protested the verdict and wondered if an immigrant, especially with radical ideas, could get a fair trial in the United States. Despite protests, the two men were executed in 1927.

D. CULTURE CLASHES IN THE 1920s　20世纪20年代的文化冲突

The advent of modernity—embodied in new technologies, mass culture, and changing demographics—gave rise to a culturally conservative backlash. A host of conflicts—rural versus urban, Christian fundamentalism versus scientific modernism, native-born versus immigrant—pitted Americans against one another. These included conflicts around race, immigration reform, control of the workplace, and morality.

The Resurgence of the Ku Klux Klan　三K党的复苏

The original Ku Klux Klan, a violent, racist group with its roots in the immediate aftermath of the Civil War, had died out by the 1870s. By the 1920s, however, the organization was a genuine mass movement. By 1925, it grew to 3 million members, according to its own estimate. The Klan was devoted to white supremacy and "100 percent Americanism." The white supremacist ideology of the Ku Klux Klan was evident in a number of race riots in the United States in the late 1910s and 1920s (see page 278).

The Bible Versus Science　《圣经》与科学

During the 1920s, a large number of Americans, especially in the South, adopted a fundamentalist, literalist approach to the Bible and to religion. The Scopes trial of 1925 illustrated the conflict between Protestant fundamentalism and modern science. The Scopes trial involved the teaching of evolution in public schools. John Scopes, a Tennessee biology teacher, was arrested for violating the Butler Act, a state law forbidding the teaching of evolution. The case turned into a national spectacle, with the famous lawyer Clarence Darrow representing Scopes and William Jennings Bryan representing the state. Scopes was found guilty and fined $100. This trial is one of several important events that highlighted cultural divisions in the 1920s.

> ## A THIRD GREAT AWAKENING
> ## 第三次大觉醒
> Some historians refer to the rise of fundamentalism in the 1920s as a "third great awakening."

Rural and Urban Responses to Prohibition　乡村与城市对禁酒令的反应

The movement to ban alcohol from American society was one of the largest movements in the nineteenth and early twentieth centuries. It finally achieved success in 1919 when prohibition became national policy with the ratification of the Eighteenth Amendment to the Constitution (see page 259). The amendment called for a ban on the manufacture, sale, and transportation of alcoholic beverages. However, the victory of the movement proved to be hollow. Although per capita consumption of alcohol dropped dramatically in the early 1920s, it increased as the decade progressed, approaching pre-Prohibition levels by 1925. Further, the amount of lawlessness in America went up as bootleggers, speakeasies, and organized crime filled the gap left by the death of the legitimate alcoholic beverage industry. Criminal activity became so widespread that Congress ratified the Twenty-first Amendment (1933), which repealed Prohibition.

II. Migrations During the World Wars and in the Interwar Years
世界大战时与两次大战间的移民

There were great variations in migration patterns from the 1910s to the 1940s. These variations were caused by economic pressures as well as by global conflicts. Political developments in the United States led to a dramatic reduction in international immigration, while internal migrations persisted.

A. IMMIGRATION RESTRICTIONS IN THE 1920S　20世纪20年代对移民的限制

Congress passed restrictive immigration quota acts in the 1920s, responding to a rise in xenophobia in America in the late 1910s and 1920s.

Anti-Immigrant Sentiment　反移民情绪

Nativism, or opposition to immigration, rose sharply in the years after World War I. A large wave of immigrants from southern and eastern Europe had arrived in the United States between 1880 and 1920 (see page 220). There are several reasons nativists resented this new wave of immigration. Some nativists focused on the fact that most of the new immigrants were not Protestant. Poles and Italians tended to be Catholic, Russians and Greeks tended to be Eastern Orthodox, and Jews came from several countries in Eastern Europe. The cacophony of languages heard on the streets of New York or Chicago repelled many nativists. Some Americans were anti-European after the trauma of World War I. Many nativists associated immigrants with either radical movements or drunkenness. Finally, working-class people feared that low-wage immigrant laborers would take jobs from native-born American workers.

The Quota System　定额分配制

The nativist sentiment that characterized the postwar period (see above) led to passage of legislation that greatly reduced the number of immigrants allowed into the United States. The Emergency Quota Act (1921) and the National Origins Act (1924) set quotas for new immigrants based on nationality. The first act set the quota for each nationality at 3 percent of the total number of that nationality that was present in the United States in 1910. The second act reduced the percentage to 2 percent and moved the year back to 1890. This had the effect of setting very low quotas for many of the "new immigrants"—from eastern and southern Europe. The acts did not set any limits on immigrants from within the Western Hemisphere.

B. DEPRESSION, WAR, AND INTERNAL MIGRATIONS　萧条、战争与国内迁徙

Large numbers of people moved within the United States because of the economic dislocation caused by the Great Depression. In addition, wartime job opportunities also led to migrations during both of the world wars.

The Migration from the Dust Bowl to California　从干旱尘暴区向加利福尼亚迁移

From 1934 to 1937, parts of Texas, Oklahoma, and surrounding areas of the Great Plains suffered from a major drought. The area was so dry that it became known as the "Dust Bowl." The Dust Bowl was caused by unsustainable over-farming coupled with a devastating drought. The natural grass cover of the region had been removed in the years leading up to the Dust Bowl, as wheat farmers increased the number of acres under cultivation. With this natural root system gone, the fertile topsoil simply blew away when drought struck from 1934 to 1937. The government, through the Soil Conservation Service, encouraged farmers to replant trees and grass and purchased land to be kept out of cultivation.

The Dust Bowl prompted some significant cultural responses, such as the album *Dust Bowl Ballads* by the folk singer Woody Guthrie (1940) and the novel *The Grapes of Wrath* (1939) by John Steinbeck. These cultural responses chronicled the plight of Dust Bowl refugees, including the "Okies" who fled from Oklahoma.

C. WAR, OPPORTUNITY, AND THE AFRICAN AMERICAN COMMUNITY
战争、机遇与非裔美国人社区

Economic opportunities brought about by industrialization and World War I caused many African Americans to embark on the "Great Migration" out of the rural South. Segregation and racial violence also contributed to this migration. In many cases, white residents of cities reacted to the arrival of African Americans with hostility and violence.

The Great Migration 大迁徙

The needs of industry for labor during World War I led to the migration of African Americans out of the South, which lasted until the onset of the Great Depression (a second wave of the migration occurred during and after World War II). There are several important reasons for the migration of African Americans from the rural South to the urban North. A basic factor was the mistreatment African Americans received in the South. White southerners created a series of Jim Crow laws that separated African Americans from whites in schools, busses, trains, and other facilities. A rigid system of segregation persisted in the South well into the twentieth century and constantly reminded African Americans of their second-class citizenship. In addition, African Americans were excluded from the political system in the South. A series of obstacles, such as literacy tests and poll taxes, limited their ability to vote.

The main factor that drew African Americans to the North was jobs. By the turn of the twentieth century the industrial revolution was in full swing in northern cities such as New York and Chicago. Factories using new mass production techniques were able, at first, to fill the jobs with local people and European immigrants. But World War I created a labor crisis for these factories, which were producing goods around the clock. Even before the United States entered the war in 1917, American factories were turning out war materials for Great Britain. After the United States entered the war, demand for these goods increased. In addition, European immigration to the United States dropped significantly because of the war. Also, almost 3 million potential factory hands were drafted into the U.S. military. Factory agents from the North frequently made recruiting trips to the South, offering immediate employment and free passage to the North.

Racial Violence—Chicago, Washington, DC, Tulsa, and Beyond
种族暴力——芝加哥、华盛顿特区、塔尔萨以及其他地区

As the Great Migration led to many African Americans making the journey from the rural South to the urban North, racial violence ensued in many cities. There were at least 25 significant race riots in 1919 alone. This racial antagonism was, in part, an offshoot of the reactionary political backlash against progressivism following World War I and in part a reaction to the demographic changes brought about by the Great Migration. The rise of the Ku Klux Klan in the 1920s (see page 276) was fueled by these political and demographic changes and, in turn, provided ideological ballast to the racial violence of the era. In July 1919, a riot against African Americans occurred in Washington, DC, and an even more violent riot in Chicago left 38 people dead and more than 500 injured. Racial violence also occurred in the South, including at Longview, Texas, and Elaine, Arkansas.

The deadliest race riot in American history occurred in Tulsa, Oklahoma, in 1921. The immediate cause of the rioting was an encounter in an elevator between a young white female elevator operator and a young African American male shoe-shiner. The details of the encounter are murky—evidence suggests that the young man tripped or fell on the young woman. Rumors of rape quickly spread, and a white mob attempted to lynch the young man. A group of African American veterans intervened to try to prevent the lynching. A maelstrom of violence ensued, as white residents, including police and National Guardsmen, rioted through the Greenwood District of Tulsa, which was the center of the African American community. Greenwood was known as the "Black Wall Street," and was considered the wealthiest African American community in the United States at the time. The district was destroyed by the rioting, over 10,000 people left homeless, and more than 300 African Americans were killed.

D. MEXICO AND MIGRATIONS 墨西哥与移民

The United States put forth ambivalent policies in regard to Mexican migration in the 1930s and 1940s. During this period, many Mexicans migrated into the United States, drawn by economic opportunities.

Mexican Americans and the Great Depression 墨西哥裔美国人与大萧条

Many Mexicans had moved to the southwest United States in the 1920s to work in agriculture. These workers saw their wages plummet in the 1930s, and New Deal programs did little to help. For instance, the CCC and the WPA excluded migrant farm workers by requiring a permanent address. Many Mexicans returned to their homeland. The Mexican American population decreased by almost 40 percent during the Great Depression.

Mexicans and World War II 墨西哥人与第二次世界大战

The administration of Franklin Roosevelt initiated the *bracero* program in 1942 to bring into the United States temporary contract workers from Mexico. The Mexican government pushed the United States to guarantee that these temporary workers would not be drafted. More than 200,000 Mexicans participated in the program, and it is estimated that at least that number came into the United States as undocumented workers.

Mexicans and Mexican Americans were the object of discrimination, harassment, and violence during World War II. In California, whites frequently targeted Mexican Americans for violent attacks. These white teenagers and servicemen especially targeted Latinos wearing colorful "zoot-suits," then in style among Latinos and African Americans. A serious "zoot-suit riot" occurred in Los Angeles in 1943.

KEY CONCEPT 7.3 THE UNITED STATES ON THE WORLD STAGE
核心概念7.3：世界舞台上的美国

A series of conflicts from the 1890s to the 1940s forced the United States to reconsider its values and priorities. These conflicts revolved around resources, power, territories, and ideologies. During this period, the United States emerged as a dominant player on the world stage in terms of its military, political, cultural, and economic position.

I. The United States in the Age of Imperialism 帝国主义时代的美国

Many Americans pushed for the United States to become part of the imperialist effort to acquire overseas possessions. These territorial ambitions led the United States to acquire new territories in the Western Hemisphere and the Pacific.

A. THE MOTIVE OF AMERICAN IMPERIALISM 美国帝国主义的动机

A variety of motivations led America to pursue overseas possessions. These factors included economic motives, competition with the imperialist nations of Europe, and racial theories.

America began to reach beyond the North American continent as the perception grew that the western frontier was closed.

IMPERIALISM VERSUS COLONIALISM
帝国主义与殖民主义

The two terms are not always interchangeable. Colonialism usually implies the effort of one country to establish a settlement in another land; imperialism usually implies the effort to rule territory that is already occupied and organized.

Reasons for Overseas Imperialism 对海外进行帝国主义扩张的原因

The United States entered the overseas imperialism scramble a little after the major European powers began carving up Africa and Asia. Many Americans resisted the idea of the United States embarking on overseas expansion; after all, the United States was born in a war against a major imperial power. However, several factors led United States political leaders to engage in overseas expansion.

INTERROGATE SOURCES 询问来源

In a DBQ about the causes of American imperialism, be careful to note the source of a document. The pronouncements of a president or a senator might not explain actual motivation. Often a public rationale for an event is different from the actual rationale. Look carefully, for instance, at President McKinley's assertion that the war in the Philippines was motivated by a desire to "civilize" the Filipino people.

Alfred Thayer Mahan and the Importance of Naval Power

阿尔弗雷德·塞耶·马汉与制海权的重要性

Historian Alfred Thayer Mahan, a retired admiral, stressed the importance of naval power and colonies in achieving and maintaining influence on the world stage. This idea might seem commonplace, but the United States throughout the nineteenth century was more focused on domestic issues and expansion over the American continent. He pushed for the United States to develop a strong navy, maintain military bases and coaling stations throughout the world, and administer an overseas empire. These ideas were central to his book, *The Influence of Sea Power Upon History, 1660–1783* (1890).

Industrialization and the Depression of 1893 工业化与1893年的萧条

Contributing to the push for imperialism was the unprecedented growth of American industry. Some policymakers thought imperialism would become necessary if the United States were to become the world's predominant industrial power. Imperial holdings would provide American industry with important raw materials. Also, the people in these new American possessions could provide a market for the growing output of consumer products American industry was turning out. The desire for new markets intensified with the onset of the depression of 1893 (see page 251). This economic downturn left Americans unable to absorb additional consumer items. The economy did not fully recover until 1901.

"The White Man's Burden" "白种人的负担"

Imperialist ventures were motivated by a particular cultural set of ideas that created a racial hierarchy. Mainstream thinking in the United States in the late 1800s posited the superiority of the descendants of the Anglo-Saxon people, as well as the inferiority of the nonwhite peoples of the world. This racist notion was widely held, but it led to divergent impulses. Some white Americans felt it was the duty of the "civilized" peoples of the world to uplift the less fortunate; others felt that the inferior races would simply disappear in a struggle for the "survival of the fittest." The urge to uplift the peoples of the world was made clear in British writer Rudyard Kipling's famous poem, "The White Man's Burden" (1899). Josiah Strong, a Protestant clergyman, went further, arguing that the "Anglo-Saxon race" had a responsibility to "civilize and Christianize" the world.

The notion of racial hierarchy accepted by most white Americans was starkly displayed at the World's Fair in Chicago in 1893, as a sideshow of the "exotic" peoples of the world was presented to fairgoers. These displays of "natives" were contrasted with the industry and progress of the advanced civilizations. The obvious implication was that the advances of civilization must be made available to the rest of the world. Frederick Douglass attended the fair and, with Ida B. Wells, wrote a scathing critique of its racist assumptions.

CONSENSUS AND CONFLICT IN THE PAST
对过去的共识与冲突

Students often assume that the unpleasant ideas of earlier eras—such as slavery or racism—were simply accepted by all of society. However, it is important to recognize that these ideas were not universally accepted. In regard to both slavery and to notions of white supremacy, important voices challenged the mainstream thinking of the day.

Christian Missionaries 基督教传教士

Christian missionary work went hand in hand with American expansion. Missionaries were eager to spread the gospel and introduce new populations to Christianity. Many of these missionaries targeted China's large population.

Hawaii 夏威夷

American missionaries arrived in Hawaii as early as the 1820s. Later in the century, American businessmen established massive sugar plantations, undermining the local economy. Discord between the businessmen and the ruler of the island, Queen Liliuokalani, emerged after 1891. The pineapple grower Sanford Dole urged the United States to intervene. The Americans staged a coup in 1893, deposing Queen Liliuokalani. U.S. forces immediately protected the new provisional government, led by Dole. The provisional government hoped for U.S. annexation of the islands, but that did not occur until 1898.

B. DEBATE OVER THE ROLE OF THE UNITED STATES IN THE WORLD
关于美国在世界中的角色的争论

As America became increasingly involved in world affairs, debates ensued in the United States about the country's proper role. These debates pitted imperialists against anti-imperialists and, later, interventionists against isolationists.

Imperialism and National Identity 帝国主义与民族特性

The shift in United States foreign policy toward imperialism raised fundamental questions about America's place in the world. The United States annexed Hawaii in 1898 (see page 281) and that same year gained additional holdings as a result of the Spanish-American War (see below). To many Americans, these acquisitions were markedly different from earlier acquisitions; these islands were densely populated and far away from the settled parts of the United States, unlike the Louisiana Purchase (1803) or the Mexican Cession (1848). Perhaps the distinction amounted to splitting hairs, but critics did surmise one additional key difference. The earlier territorial gains of the United States were intended to absorb American citizens and to eventually achieve statehood and equal footing with the existing states. There was no expectation, on the other hand, that the Philippines, for example, would absorb large numbers of American citizens. The United States would, indefinitely, rule *over* a foreign population, much as Great Britain had ruled over its 13 American colonies.

The American Anti-Imperialist League 美国的反帝国主义联盟

In 1898, as the Treaty of Paris was debated in the Senate, a group of critics of American imperialism formed the American Anti-Imperialist League. The league was a coalition of conservative Democrats (known at the time as "Bourbon Democrats") as well as more progressive elements. The league included author Mark Twain, who became increasingly radical as he grew older. He was the vice president of the league from 1901 to 1910, and wrote some of the league's more scathing condemnations of imperialism.

The league suffered a major schism in 1900, as the more conservative members rejected the candidacy of Democrat William Jennings Bryan, while the more progressive elements embraced it. Jennings was an anti-imperialist, but many of his other positions, especially his criticism of the gold standard, alienated many of the conservative "Bourbon Democrats." The Republican William McKinley won reelection, continuing an aggressive foreign policy.

The imperialism debate—over whether the United States Constitution permitted the American government to make rules for peoples who were not represented by lawmakers—nearly imperiled ratification of the Treaty of Paris. Democratic opponents of imperialism rallied against the treaty, which barely achieved the necessary two-thirds majority in 1899.

Does the Constitution Follow the Flag? 《宪法》是否遵循了旗帜？

The question of whether constitutional provisions applied to people in the new American territories continued in the courts after the ratification of the Treaty of Paris. Expansionists argued that the Constitution did not necessarily follow the flag; anti-imperialists insisted that it should. The Supreme Court settled this issue in a series of cases in 1901 that have come to be known as the Insular Cases ("insular" means island-related). The court agreed with expansionists that democracy and imperialism are not incompatible, and that the imperial power need not grant its colonial subjects constitutional rights. The decisions were based on the racist assumption that the colonial subjects were of an inferior race, and the colonial power had the responsibility to uplift these peoples before granting them autonomy.

C. THE SPANISH-AMERICAN WAR AND ITS AFTERMATH 美西战争及其结果

The Spanish-American War was a turning point in terms of America's role in the world beyond North America. As a result of the war, the United States acquired island territories, became more involved in the Caribbean and Latin America, acquired the Philippines—after a protracted struggle that cost many thousands of Filipino lives—and became increasingly involved in Asia.

United States Interest in Cuba 美国对古巴的兴趣

In the 1890s, Spain was in control of Cuba, but an independence movement was trying to end Spanish rule. Spain's governor of Cuba, Valeriano Weyler, used brutal tactics to suppress the rebellion. Thousands of Cubans were crowded into concentration camps. By 1898, a quarter of Cuba's rural population (approximately 300,000 people) had died as a result of starvation and disease.

Many Americans wanted the United States to intervene on Cuba's side in its struggle against Spanish rule. Some Americans saw parallels between the Cuban struggle for independence from Spain and America's struggle for independence from Great Britain. Also, some American businessmen were angered by the interruption of the sugar harvest by the fighting between Cuban rebels and Spanish forces.

"Yellow Journalism" and the Call to War "耸人听闻的新闻"与对战争的呼唤

Events in Cuba were brought to the attention of ordinary Americans through mass-produced newspapers. Industrialization and increased literacy set the groundwork for America's first mass media. To attract customers, newspapers began printing bold, sensational headlines, often disregarding journalistic objectivity and even the truth. This sensationalist journalism came to be known as "yellow journalism." News organizations used these techniques of exaggeration and innuendo to build support for war with Spain. These newspapers breathlessly followed events in Cuba, with lurid accounts of Spanish wrongdoing and condemnations of "Butcher" Weyler, the Spanish governor.

The Sinking of the *Maine* "缅因号"战舰的沉没

The event that led directly to the Spanish-American War was the destruction of an American battleship, the USS *Maine*, which blew up in the harbor of Havana, Cuba's capital. Many in the United States thought the sinking was the work of Spain, especially after American newspapers bluntly accused Spain of the crime, despite the scarcity of evidence.

The Spanish-American War 美西战争

The Spanish-American War was brief. American forces landed in Cuba on June 22, 1898, and Spain surrendered on July 17. Fighting in the Philippines, also a Spanish possession, lasted just days, as Admiral George Dewey led American naval forces in an alliance with Filipino rebels to take the capital, Manila. Theodore Roosevelt led a charge up San Juan Hill in a key battle for Cuba. The colorful Roosevelt and his men—known as "Rough Riders"—made headlines in American papers, elevating Roosevelt's status in the political realm.

The Treaty of Paris 《巴黎和约》

The United States and Spain negotiated the Treaty of Paris (1898) following the war. In the treaty, Spain agreed to cede the Philippines, Puerto Rico, and Guam to the United States; the United States agreed to pay Spain $20 million for these possessions.

Cuba and the Platt Amendment 古巴与《普拉特修正案》

Cuba gained its independence following the Spanish American War. However, in many ways, Cuba became independent in name only. The United States wanted to ensure that American economic interests would not be challenged by a future Cuban administration. The United States, therefore, insisted that the Platt Amendment be inserted into the Cuban Constitution. This amendment allowed the United States to militarily intervene in Cuban affairs if it deemed it necessary. The amendment limited the Cuban government's ability to conduct its own foreign policy and to manage its debts. Also, the amendment allowed the United States to lease a naval base at Guantanamo Bay. American troops intervened in Cuba three times between 1902 and 1920.

War in the Philippines 美国在菲律宾的战争

Many Filipinos were surprised and disappointed to learn that the United States decided to hold on to the Philippines as a colony after the Spanish-American War. They had seen the United States as a liberating force that would help rid the nation of Spanish rule and usher in independence. However, this was not the intent of the United States. Following the ratification of the Treaty of Paris, a bitter, three-year long war ensued. The Philippine-American War was far more lengthy and deadly than the Spanish-American War itself (Filipino forces continued to resist American control for another decade). Filipino forces were led by Emilio Aguinaldo. The war cost American forces 4,000 lives. Estimates vary in regard to the number of Filipino casualties; historians estimate 20,000 to 30,000 Filipinos died fighting in the conflict and perhaps another 200,000 (and possibly more) civilians died. The United States held on to the Philippines until after World War II (1946).

A TALE OF TWO WARS 两次战争的故事

In writing about American imperialism, do not forget about the war in the Philippines. It lasted longer (three years) and resulted in more casualties (more than 4,000 American deaths; possibly 200,000 or more Filipino deaths) than the better-known Spanish-American War (four months; fewer than 400 American deaths; fewer than 15,000 combined Cuban and Spanish deaths).

China and the Open Door Policy 中国与门户开放政策

The bitter conflict in the Philippines was in many ways designed to provide the United States with a stepping-stone to an even greater prize—trade with China. Its large population and natural resources made China a target for the imperialist nations. The major powers of Europe had begun carving up China earlier in the nineteenth century. Britain, Japan, Germany, Russia, and France each proclaimed a "sphere of influence"—a port city and surrounding territory—from which other nations would be excluded. The United States asserted that all of China should be open to trade with all nations. U.S. secretary of state, John Hay, wrote to the major powers, asserting an "open door" policy for China. The United States claimed to be concerned for the territorial integrity of China, but actually was more interested in gaining a foothold in trade with China. The "open door" policy was begrudgingly accepted by the major powers.

The Boxer Rebellion 义和团运动

Christian missionaries came to China in large numbers, but met with little success there. The number of converts was small, and the presence of the missionaries inspired militant anti-foreign secret societies. The most well-known of these societies was the "Boxers," or the Society of Righteous and Harmonious Fists. The Boxers led a rebellion that resulted in the death of more than 30,000 Chinese converts as well as 250 foreign nuns. The United States participated in a multination force to rescue Westerners held hostage by the Boxers (1900).

Theodore Roosevelt and the "Big Stick" 西奥多·罗斯福与"大棒"政策

In September 1901, just six months into his second term as president, William McKinley was fatally shot while attending the Pan-American Exposition in Buffalo, New York, by the anarchist Leon Czolgosz. McKinley's vice president, Theodore Roosevelt, became president. (See more on President Roosevelt's domestic agenda, pages 257–258, and 260.) Roosevelt was an adventurer, an expansionist, and a hero of the Spanish-American War. His foreign-policy approach is neatly summed up in his famous adage that the United States should "speak softly, but carry a big stick" when dealing with other nations (Roosevelt borrowed the phrase from an African proverb). The "big stick" implied the threat of military force. He envisioned the United States acting as the world's policeman, punishing wrongdoers. He asserted that the "civilized nations" had a duty to police the "backward" countries of the world. He claimed that the United States had the right to militarily intervene in the nations of Latin America. This assertion of American might is known as the Roosevelt Corollary to the Monroe Doctrine. In 1902, he sternly warned Germany to stay out of the Americas after Venezuela failed to repay a loan to Germany and Germany threatened military intervention.

Panama and the Panama Canal 巴拿巴与巴拿马运河

President Theodore Roosevelt's aggressive approach to Latin America is clearly evident in regard to Panama. With the acquisition of overseas Pacific territories, and with increased interest in trade with China, American policymakers wanted a shortcut to Asia. Merchant ships and naval vessels had to travel around the southern tip of South America to reach the Pacific Ocean. The building of a canal through Panama, therefore, became a major goal for Roosevelt.

Before 1903, Panama was a region of Colombia. American investors picked this narrow piece of land as an ideal location for a canal to facilitate shipping between the Atlantic and Pacific Oceans. When Colombia refused the U.S. offer of $10 million to build a canal, American investors, with the backing of President Roosevelt and the U.S. military, instigated a "rebellion" in Panama against Colombia. Panama became an independent country and immediately reached a deal with the United States to build the canal. Roosevelt later boasted that he "took Panama."

FOREIGN POLICY AND ECONOMIC PRIORITIES
外交政策与经济工作的重点

Often, in American history, economic priorities drive foreign-policy decisions. A Central American canal was a major priority for American commercial and industrial interests at the beginning of the twentieth century.

Roosevelt, Diplomacy, and the Nobel Peace Prize　罗斯福、外交才能与诺贝尔和平奖

President Theodore Roosevelt was interested in establishing the United States as a major player in world diplomacy. Toward this end, he acted as mediator between France and Germany in their conflict over Morocco (1905). Roosevelt was also interested in maintaining a balance of power among the other world powers. That same year, Roosevelt offered to mediate an end to the Russo-Japanese War (1904–1905). A peace conference was held in Portsmouth, New Hampshire, with Roosevelt presiding. Despite Roosevelt's aggressive actions in Latin America, he was granted the Nobel Peace Prize (1906) for his other diplomatic efforts.

> ## THE NOBEL PRIZE　诺贝尔奖
>
> Three other United States presidents have won the Nobel Peace Prize: Woodrow Wilson in 1919; Jimmy Carter in 2002; and Barack Obama in 2009.

The "Gentleman's Agreement"　"君子协定"

In 1907, the diplomatic gains President Theodore Roosevelt had achieved with Japan were threatened by discriminatory legislation passed in California, restricting the rights of "Orientals." In 1906, San Francisco Board of Education decided that the small number of Japanese American students in the system would no longer be able to attend school with white students. They would be segregated and sent to racially specific schools, similar to segregated schools established for Chinese American students. The move reflected a strong nativist sentiment in California at the time. Roosevelt quietly worked out a "Gentleman's Agreement" in which Japan agreed to limit immigration to the United States and Roosevelt agreed to pressure California authorities to end discriminatory practices.

President Taft and "Dollar Diplomacy"　塔夫脱总统与"金元外交"

President William Howard Taft (1909–1913) continued to pursue an aggressive foreign policy, but he put more emphasis on expanding and securing American commercial interests than on pursuing the global strategic goals that Roosevelt had championed. Taft's foreign policy has come to be known as "dollar diplomacy." He sent troops to Nicaragua and the Dominican Republic to coerce them into signing commercial treaties with the United States. In general, he tried to substitute "dollars for bullets" in pursuing American interests. However, he failed to stem revolution in Mexico in 1911.

President Wilson's Foreign Policy　威尔逊总统的外交政策

President Wilson's initial focus as president was on domestic concerns (see pages 258–259). However, his administration became increasingly drawn into foreign policy matters, from problems in the Americas to war in Europe (see pages 287–290). Wilson was driven by both a desire to secure American economic interests abroad and by a strong moral compass; often these impulses clashed with each other.

Wilson immediately signaled a break with his Republican predecessors by appointing the anti-imperialist William Jennings Bryan to be secretary of state. Bryan sought peaceful accommodations with many nations, but he and Wilson were not above flexing America's military muscle in the Americas. Wilson authorized the occupation of Nicaragua by American marines to suppress a rebellion against the American-backed president of the country. He sent troops to Haiti in 1915 and to the Dominican Republic in 1916 to ensure that American business interests were not challenged.

Wilson and the Mexican Revolution 威尔逊与墨西哥革命

President Wilson became enmeshed in the twists and turns of the Mexican Revolution, which lasted through the 1910s. The revolution began with the ousting of an autocratic leader in 1910. The revolution soon degenerated into a civil war that left nearly a million Mexicans dead. In 1914, Wilson challenged the legitimacy of the new Mexican leader, General Victoriano Huerta. He sent 800 marines to Mexico to overthrow the regime. Huerta fled the country, and a new more pro-American government came to power. This new government was challenged by an uprising led by the rebel leader Francisco "Pancho" Villa. Villa successfully intercepted a train carrying American gold and led a raid into American territory that left 18 Americans dead. Wilson authorized more than 12,000 troops to invade Mexico to capture Villa, who eluded the American forces. By early 1917, the United States turned its attention away from Mexico as it began preparations for World War I.

II. The United States and World War I 美国与第一次世界大战

As World War I began in Europe, Americans began to debate the proper role of the United States in the world. The aftermath of the war led to debates about how the United States could best pursue its international interests.

A. THE UNITED STATES ENTERS WORLD WAR I 美国参加第一次世界大战

The United States initially proclaimed neutrality in World War I. A variety of factors, including President Woodrow Wilson's call to make the world "safe for democracy," led the United States to enter the conflict.

The Onset of War 战争的爆发

Historians cite several factors that created an unstable, even dangerous, situation in prewar Europe. History teachers often graphically represent these factors as sticks of dynamite; the sticks, in such a drawing, are labeled "nationalism," "imperialism," "militarism," and "the alliance system." By the end of the nineteenth century, one can certainly see a rise in nationalism among the European powers. The nations of Europe began to see themselves as actors in a Darwinian struggle to be the "fittest." Inexpensive newspapers and rising literacy rates allowed for the dissemination of patriotic sentiments to an entire nation. This sense of nationalism was fueled by a competition to imperialize the remaining independent areas of Asia and Africa. A scramble occurred among the major powers, setting the stage for tensions and conflict. The situation was made more dangerous by an ominous arms build-up among the European nations, especially the rival maritime nations of Great Britain and Germany. The two nations built larger and larger warships, typified by Great Britain's HMS *Dreadnought*, which ushered in an era of similarly massive Dreadnought-class battleships. Finally, the situation was made more volatile by a dangerous series of alliances. Essentially, a conflict between any two belligerents would soon degenerate into a broad European-wide war as mutual-defense treaties would drag more nations into the conflict.

If the long-term causes of World War I are presented as sticks of dynamite, then the spark that ignited them was the assassination of the heir to the throne of the Austro-Hungarian empire, Archduke Franz Ferdinand. While visiting the city of Sarajevo in Bosnia and Herzegovina, part of Austria-Hungary, the archduke was assassinated by a pan-Slavic nationalist. The assassination resulted in Austria-Hungary declaring war on Serbia. The alliance system brought Germany into the conflict on the side of Austria-Hungary, while Russia, and then France and Great Britain, were brought into the conflict on the opposing side. As the war began, Russia, France, and Great Britain comprised the Triple Entente (later known as the Allied Powers); Austria-Hungary, Germany, and Italy were known as the Triple Alliance, later as the Central Powers (Italy switched sides in 1915). The conflict would last four years and result in the deaths of an astounding 8.5 million soldiers.

United States Neutrality 美国的中立

The United States initially assumed that it could stay neutral during World War I. Several factors kept the United States neutral in the war for the first three years. The United States, from the time of Washington's farewell address, had attempted to stay aloof from the ongoing conflicts of Europe. That had not always been easy. The United States went to war with Great Britain at the beginning of the nineteenth century (1812) and with Spain at the end of the century (1898). These wars, however, were not fought in Europe. Isolationism when it came to European affairs remained strong. Neutrality also allowed the United States to trade with both sides in the conflict.

> ## UNDERSTANDING NEUTRALITY 理解中立
>
> Be familiar with the variety of social, economic, political, and historical factors that contributed to U.S. neutrality during the first years of World War I.

Immigration Patterns and Public Opinion Around World War I
移民模式与第一次世界大战的公众舆论

Immigration patterns did not immediately predispose the United States toward support for either side in World War I. The United States was home to millions of people from belligerent nations on both sides of the conflict. On the one hand, German and Irish immigrants tended to favor the Central Powers. Germans favored their fatherland, while the Irish had a long-standing resentment of Great Britain. On the other hand, America had ties to Great Britain. Despite the two wars that they had fought (the American Revolution and the War of 1812), the United States and Great Britain shared a language and strong cultural ties.

From Neutrality to Intervention 从中立到干预

Although several factors initially kept America out of World War I, important developments propelled the United States toward intervention. President Wilson emphasized the principle of freedom of the seas. He indicated that the United States would trade and sell weaponry to either side in the conflict, but Great Britain had effectively blockaded Germany. Trade, therefore, shifted to Great Britain as the war progressed. Between 1914 (when the war began) and 1917, U.S. trade with Britain increased by 300 percent, while trade with Germany shrank to almost nothing.

Germany responded by warning that U.S. ships in the waters off Great Britain would be subject to attack by U-boats (submarines). The sinking of the British ocean liner, *Lusitania*, in May 1915 infuriated many Americans (128 Americans were among the dead). Another British passenger ship, the *Arabic*, was sunk by a German U-boat attack in August 1915 (two Americans were among the dead). Germany, however, wanted to keep the United States out of the war and, in response to American protests, agreed in the *Arabic* Pledge (1915) to make no attacks on passenger ships without prior warning. The following year, after a French ferry named the *Sussex* was torpedoed, President Wilson threatened to break off relations with Germany. In response, Germany issued the *Sussex* Pledge (1916) to appease the United States, extending the promise of the *Arabic* Pledge to include merchant ships (unless the presence of war materials had been established). The United States took advantage of this pledge and traded extensively with Great Britain, much to the consternation of Germany.

Progressives and the War   进步派与战争

Progressives were initially divided about American participation in World War I. At the beginning of the war, many Progressives were leery about American involvement. They predicted that participation in a major war would distract the nation from domestic reform. However, many Progressives saw great possibilities in American participation in the war. John Dewey, in an essay in the *New Republic*, encouraged Progressives to see the "social possibilities of war." These possibilities included an expansion of the state, a sense of unity and national purpose, and a renewed focus on issues of social justice.

President Woodrow Wilson and the War   伍德罗·威尔逊总统与战争

As the war dragged on in Europe, public opinion began to shift toward the Allied Powers of Great Britain, France, and Russia. This was partly brought about by wartime news coverage, which tended to present Germany and the Central Powers as aggressive, and even barbaric, in their prosecution of the war. Also, the Allied Powers seemed to be more clearly the democratic side of the war after czarist Russia was no longer part of the alliance. (The czar was toppled in February 1917 and Russia later withdrew from the war.) President Wilson's approach to the conflict changed rapidly. During his bid for reelection in 1916, Wilson's campaign repeatedly reminded voters that "he kept us out of war." However, after his reelection, Wilson became increasingly convinced that U.S. participation in World War I was necessary to make the world "safe for democracy."

Wilson's shift to a pro-war stance divided Americans. Some joined Wilson on his intellectual journey; they too began to think of participation in the war as an idealistic crusade to create a new world order based on peace and autonomy. However, many opposed the drive for war. The government went to great lengths to alter public opinion (see page 290), and the United States finally entered the war in 1917.

The Zimmerman Note and Unrestricted German Submarine Warfare
齐默尔曼电报与德国无限制潜艇战

Many Americans moved toward a pro-war position after the secret "Zimmerman Note" became public. The intercepted telegram from German foreign secretary Arthur Zimmerman indicated that Germany would help Mexico regain territory it had lost to the United States if Mexico joined the war on Germany's side. Americans took this as a threat to their territory.

Finally, in early 1917, Germany announced it would rescind the *Sussex* Pledge and would resume unrestricted submarine warfare against Great Britain and its allies, including the United States. In February and March of 1917, hundreds of American ships had been sunk by German submarine attacks. This proved to be the final straw for the United States. In April 1917, the United States declared war on Germany.

Shaping Public Opinion 引导公众舆论

In the aftermath of the United States declaration of war, the government worked hard to shape public opinion. President Wilson established the Committee on Public Information in 1917 to organize pro-war propaganda. It was led by George Creel, a former muckraking journalist. The CPI sent "Four-Minute Men" around the country to give brief, impassioned speeches in favor of the war effort to schools, civic groups, churches, and any gathering that would have them. The CPI also produced a series of evocative posters to convince Americans to support the war. Several of these posters specifically targeted the supposed brutal actions of German soldiers, often labeled the "Huns," a derogatory term that alludes to the Germanic tribes of the ancient world that attacked Rome. One of the posters, created by the American artist and illustrator James Montgomery Flagg, featured the image of Uncle Sam, pointing directly at the viewer of the poster, with the famous tag line "I Want You for U.S. Army."

WORLD WAR I AND MODERN ADVERTISING
第一次世界大战与现代广告

The campaign organized by the Committee on Public Information could be considered one of the first major national advertising campaigns in United States history.

Federal Agencies and War Production 联邦机构与军工生产

Several government agencies were created during World War I to ensure a smooth transition to a war economy. The War Industries Board was created by the government to direct industrial production. The agency was led by Bernard Baruch. He sought to bring together labor and management in order to ensure uninterrupted production of armaments, uniforms, and other needed items. The Food Administration, with future president Herbert Hoover at the helm, was created to ensure sufficient food production to feed the troops as well as the civilian population. The National War Labor Policies board dealt with labor disputes. This constellation of government agencies was exactly what progressive reformers hoped to create on a permanent basis.

WORLD WAR I AND THE NEW DEAL
第一次世界大战与新政

Although the wartime agencies were disbanded after the war, a similar set of agencies was created by President Franklin Roosevelt, as part of his New Deal during the Great Depression.

B. THE ROLE OF THE UNITED STATES IN WORLD WAR I 美国在第一次世界大战中的角色

The United States played an important role during the final year of World War I. American troops, organized as the American Expeditionary Forces, was relatively limited. However, the infusion of fresh American troops helped tip the balance of World War I in favor of the Allies.

American Participation in World War I 美国参加第一次世界大战

The United States entered the war late in the game. It did provide the Allies—Great Britain and France—with much needed reinforcement. France and Great Britain had been at war for nearly three years when the United States joined the conflict. The 2 million soldiers of the American Expeditionary Force proved to be crucial in Allied offensives that led to victory.

By the time the United States entered, the war had bogged down into a brutal stalemate. Both sides had dug into trenches separated by a strip of "no-man's land." One side might attempt a frontal attack on the other, but as soon as the soldiers were ordered out of their trenches they were subjected to machine gun fire, barbed wire, and poison gas. Perhaps one side would capture a few hundred yards of desolate land, but usually only to be pushed back again. The five-month-long Battle of the Somme (1916), for example, resulted in more than a million casualties and no substantial gains for either side.

In June and July, 1918, American troops joined French troops in repelling German advances, fighting at Chateau-Thierry and Rheims. In September, American troops began to participate in assaults on German-held territory. By October, allied advances toward the German border led German military leaders to seek a cease-fire. An armistice was signed on November 11, 1918, bringing World War I to a close. American troops suffered over 300,000 casualties, including over 50,000 battlefield deaths, and over 60,000 non-combat deaths (many from a deadly influenza epidemic that soon raged around the world).

C. THE UNITED STATES AND THE POSTWAR WORLD 美国与战后世界

Following World War I, President Woodrow Wilson was active in the negotiations for a peace treaty. His involvement was important in proposals to create the League of Nations, an institution formed to maintain world peace. However, American participation in the League caused strenuous debates in the United States. Ultimately, the U.S. Senate refused to ratify the Treaty of Versailles and rejected American involvement in the League of Nations.

Wilson's Fourteen Points 威尔逊的十四点计划

President Wilson was determined to shape the structure of the postwar world. He felt strongly that the causes of the war should be identified, addressed, and alleviated. Wilson put forth a document, known as the Fourteen Points (1918), which emphasized international cooperation. He envisioned a world order based on freedom of the seas, removal of barriers to trade, self-determination for European peoples, and an international organization to resolve conflicts. These ideas were rejected by the victorious European powers, with the exception of the creation of the League of Nations.

United States Rejection of the Treaty of Versailles 美国反对《凡尔赛条约》

Ironically, the United States did not join the League of Nations. This international body was the one component of President Wilson's Fourteen Points document that was embraced by the victorious European nations. The United States would have had to approve the Treaty of

Versailles in order to join the League. Despite Wilson's enthusiasm for passage of the treaty, some senators wanted to isolate the United States from world affairs and opposed membership in the League. These isolationists announced that they would vote to reject the treaty. Other senators took a middle position: they would agree to vote to approve the treaty if the Senate put certain conditions on American participation in the League of Nations. Wilson refused to compromise in this and urged his allies in the Senate to reject any conditions. Without the senators in the middle, the Treaty of Versailles was rejected by the Senate. In many ways, the debates around the Treaty of Versailles and the victory of isolationist sentiment shaped American foreign policy for the next decade.

D. AMERICAN FOREIGN POLICY IN THE INTERWAR YEARS
两次大战间美国的外交政策

America largely maintained a position of neutrality in the interwar years. It did, however, play an increasingly large role in international treaties and investment. The United States engaged in military interventions, mostly in the Western Hemisphere, with the goal of advancing its vision of international order.

The Politics of Isolationism in the 1920s 20世纪20年代的政治孤立主义

Isolationist sentiment ran high in the United States. Many Americans were disillusioned by World War I, while others had grown resentful of the wave of "new immigrants" who had come to America (see page 220). The United States remained outside the League of Nations (see page 291 for the rejection of the Treaty of Versailles).

Higher Tariff Rates—From Fordney-McCumber to Smoot-Hawley

更高的关税税率——从佛德尼–马克昆柏到斯姆特–霍利

The isolationist Republican presidents of the 1920s enacted higher tariffs to keep out foreign goods. The 1922 Fordney-McCumber Act dramatically raised tariff rates. In 1930, in the midst of the Great Depression, isolationist legislators pushed through the Smoot-Hawley Tariff Act, which increased tariffs to their second-highest rate in United States history; only the 1828 "Tariff of Abominations" enacted higher tariff rates.

> ## TARIFF RATES IN HISTORY 历史关税税率
>
> Debates about tariff rates have existed throughout American history, from Alexander Hamilton's "Report on Manufactures" (1791) to the passage of the North America Free Trade Agreement (1994). Tariff rates were passionately debated in the nineteenth century.

The Washington Disarmament Conference 华盛顿裁军会议

The presidents of the 1920s attempted to isolate the United States from world affairs and reduce spending on war munitions. President Warren Harding successfully pressed for a reduction of naval power among Britain, France, Japan, Italy, and the United States at the Washington Disarmament Conference in 1921.

The Kellogg-Briand Pact 《凯洛格–白里安条约》

The United States was one of 63 nations to sign the Kellogg-Briand Pact, renouncing war in principle. Because the pact was negotiated outside of the League of Nations, it was unenforceable, rendering it meaningless.

E. FROM ISOLATIONISM TO INTERVENTION 从孤立主义到干预

The United States existed in an increasingly dangerous world in the 1930s, creating new debates around the isolationist stance that had shaped foreign policy in the 1920s. These debates ended with the Japanese attack on Pearl Harbor, which drew the United States into World War II.

The Challenges of Isolationism in the 1930s 20世纪30年代孤立主义遭遇的挑战

The traditional isolationism of the United States was severely tested by developments in Europe in the 1930s. The Fascist Party, led by Benito Mussolini, had taken power in Italy in 1922. Adolf Hitler and his Nazi followers came to power in Germany in 1933. A civil war in Spain led to the rise of a government run by the fascist dictator Francisco Franco in 1939. In Japan, militaristic leaders set Japan on an aggressive course. These dictatorial governments all took aggressive actions in the 1930s: Japan attacked China in 1931; Germany occupied the demilitarized Rhineland in 1936, annexed Austria in 1937, and occupied Czechoslovakia in 1939; and Italy conquered Ethiopia in 1936. The League of Nations protested, and Great Britain and France objected, but it was not until Germany attacked Poland in September 1939, that Hitler met decisive opposition. Great Britain and France declared war on Germany, beginning World War II. Germany, Italy, and Japan formed the Axis Powers with the signing of the Tripartite Pact (1940).

> ### EUROPE IN THE 1930s
> ### 20世纪30年代的欧洲
>
> Even though it is not American history, the events in Europe in the 1930s should be familiar to you. Often, events abroad have an impact on the United States—war between France and Britain at the turn of the nineteenth century; European imperialism in the late nineteenth century; the two world wars; and the Cold War, to name just a few.

The Continued Pull of Isolationism 孤立主义的继续拉动

As events degenerated into war in Europe, a debate occurred in the United States about America's role. Isolationists argued strongly that the United States should stay out of world affairs. Many isolationists looked back to World War I as a lesson in the futility of getting involved in European affairs. The United States had lost over 100,000 men in World War I for no apparent reason, they argued. World War I had not made the world safe for democracy. Almost as soon as the war ended, antidemocratic forces emerged and set Europe once again on the path toward war. In addition, the Senate's Nye Committee (1934–1937) uncovered evidence that certain American corporations had profited greatly from U.S. participation in World War I. Americans wondered if the so-called merchants of death had pushed the country into the war.

The Argument for Intervention　干预争论

While the pull of isolationism remained strong in the 1930s, many Americans believed it would be a mistake for the United States to isolate itself from world affairs on the eve of World War II. They mocked the idea that the Atlantic Ocean would indefinitely protect the United States from dangerous trends in Europe. Interventionists believed that the United States could no longer stand apart. Airplanes and submarines could bring the war to the United States very quickly. If Britain were defeated, there would be nothing standing between Hitler and America. Interventionists believed the Atlantic Ocean would be a means for Hitler to bring his war machine to the United States. Also, many interventionists believed the war in Europe was different from earlier European quarrels over territory or national pride. They believed that if Hitler was successful, civilization itself would be threatened. They were convinced that the Axis Powers were determined to defeat democratic forces all over the world.

President Franklin Roosevelt Proceeds with Caution
富兰克林·罗斯福总统谨慎行事

President Franklin Roosevelt was cautious in his responses to the conflict in Europe. He was sympathetic to the countries defending themselves against fascism, but he knew he could not commit the United States to an interventionist position without the support of the public. Early on, in 1937, Roosevelt recognized that a European war could engulf countries far from Europe. He was not ready to commit to intervention, but he did not pretend that the United States could isolate itself from the affairs of Europe.

The Onset of World War II—from "Cash-and-Carry" to Pearl Harbor
第二次世界大战的爆发——从"现购自运"到珍珠港

The question of the role of the United States grew more intense in 1939 as World War II formally began. The war started after Hitler attacked Poland. Britain and France quickly declared war on Germany. Soon after, Roosevelt pushed for legislation allowing the United States to send armaments to Britain with the condition that Britain pay for the weapons first and transport them in their own ships. This "cash-and-carry" policy allowed the United States to support Britain without the risk of U.S. ships being destroyed.

By mid-1940, the American public began to shift toward a more interventionist stance. The situation in Europe grew dire. Americans were shaken by the defeat of France at the hands of the Nazis in mid-1940. They saw how one of the great democratic powers was easily defeated by the Nazi war machine. Would Britain fall next? Would the United States be Hitler's next target? In 1940, the United States ratified the Selective Service Act, requiring compulsory military service for males between 21 and 35. By 1941, 70 percent of the American people were ready to help Britain directly, even if it risked getting involved in World War II. With this shift in public opinion and with his victory in the presidential election of 1940, Roosevelt was ready to take more direct action. In March 1941, Congress approved his Lend-Lease Act, which allowed the United States to send armaments to Britain in American ships. The Lend-Lease Act was extended to the Soviet Union after Hitler broke the Nazi-Soviet Pact (1939) and launched an invasion of the Soviet Union in June 1941. In July of that year, Roosevelt and British prime minister Winston Churchill solidified the alliance between their two countries by releasing a statement of "common principles" known as the Atlantic Charter. Though officially neutral, the United States was moving steadily toward intervening on the side of Great Britain.

The public was not unified in its support of intervention. Isolationists such as the renowned aviator Charles Lindbergh continued to argue against any U.S. steps toward helping Britain. Lindbergh was a leader of the America First Committee and, historians argue, a Nazi sympathizer. Even late in 1941, it was clear that many Americans still had major reservations about America entering World War II. Debates about intervention ended abruptly on December 7, 1941, when Japanese warplanes attacked Pearl Harbor, the U.S. naval base in Hawaii. Almost immediately, the United States entered World War II. With American involvement in the war, the isolationist position was largely silenced.

III. The United States and World War II 美国与第二次世界大战

Americans engaged in vigorous debate about involvement in global conflicts before and until the beginning of World War II. Ultimately, World War II had a major impact on the United States, both domestically and internationally. Domestically, the mobilization for the war transformed American society. Internationally, the war led to America playing a preeminent role in the world.

A. THE STAKES INVOLVED IN WORLD WAR II 参加第二次世界大战的利益得失

Americans came to see World War II as more than a conventional military conflict. As details of Japanese wartime atrocities and of the Holocaust began to emerge, many Americans came to see the war as a desperate fight for freedom and democracy against powerful militarist and fascist forces.

The Holocaust （第二次世界大战中纳粹对犹太人的）大屠杀

The Holocaust was the systematic murder of 6 million European Jews and millions of other "undesirables" by the Nazis. The roots of the Holocaust pre-date World War II, with Nazi persecution of the Jews in Germany and in territories it took over in the 1930s. In 1939, Hitler and other leading Nazis developed plans for a "final solution of the Jewish question," with the object of eliminating Europe's Jewish populations. After the Germans took over most of Continental Europe, this plan went from being the scheming of a madman to a horrible, deadly reality. The plan also included other groups such as Slavic people, gypsies (Romani), the disabled, and homosexuals. Nazis first ordered Jews into crowded urban areas called ghettos, then moved them to concentration or labor camps, and finally to death camps, where gas chambers and incineration ovens were built to carry out Hitler's "final solution." Reports of Nazi death camps began to trickle out of German-occupied Europe by 1942. As the war in Europe was ending, the Allies found these camps, revealing the full extent of the barbaric crimes against civilians committed by the Nazis during the war.

While news of the Holocaust put the nature of the Nazi regime into sharp focus, Americans were of different minds about what actions, beyond pursing military victory, the United States might take in response. American officials, for instance, had resisted pleas to admit large numbers of Jewish refugees fleeing Europe. In 1939, the German passenger ship *St. Louis*, carrying nearly a thousand escaped German Jews, was turned away when it was off the coast of Florida, after having been turned away by Cuban authorities. Such resistance to admitting refugees continued during the war. In addition, American leaders resisted calls to bomb the railroad lines leading to the death camps or even the death camps themselves, arguing that such actions would either not be feasible or effective.

Japanese Wartime Atrocities 日军在战争期间的暴行

Many Americans also saw Japanese wartime actions as representative of a militarist ideology that threatened to undermine democratic traditions. The most notorious episode of Japanese atrocities occurred before the beginning of World War II in Europe. In 1937, Japan widened its military campaign against China, overrunning most of China's port cities. In the city of Nanjing, Japanese troops killed thousands of civilians. While the exact number of people killed is in dispute, the Nanjing Massacre resulted in at least 80,000 deaths and perhaps as many as 300,000.

B. MOBILIZING FOR WORLD WAR II 为第二次世界大战做动员

The massive effort by the United States to mobilize for war led to the end of the Great Depression. In many ways, World War II required the participation of the entire American public, not simply members of the military. These efforts created a sense of unity and common cause in the country.

Rationing and Recycling 分配与回收

During the war, there were shortages of key items because of the needs of the military. Starting in 1942, the Office of Price Administration began rationing key commodities to civilians, such as gasoline and tires. Next, the government began rationing food—sugar, meat, coffee, lard, butter, and many other items. Families received ration books and used their ration stamps, along with cash, when they purchased these items. In addition, children organized Tin Can Clubs to collect scrap metal to be melted down for use in weapons and ammunition production.

Funding the War Effort 资助战争活动

The Roosevelt administration paid for the war effort through the sale of war bonds and increases in taxes. The government went into massive debt during the war, with the debt rising by a factor of six between 1940 and 1949. The experience of World War II demonstrates that massive government spending, and ensuing deficits, can play a significant role in stimulating a sluggish economy.

War Production—Becoming the "Arsenal for Democracy"
军工生产——成为"民主兵工厂"

If the United States were to become the "arsenal for democracy," as President Roosevelt promised in a speech in 1940, it would have to dramatically and rapidly step up the production of war-related materials. In 1942, Roosevelt created the War Production Board, and later the Office of War Mobilization, to oversee the conversion from civilian industry to war production. Almost overnight, the persistent unemployment of the 1930s ended. After the United States entered the war in December 1941, the country faced the opposite problem—labor shortages. With millions of men and women in the armed forces, the Roosevelt administration took several important steps to ensure a sufficient supply of factory workers. Women were heavily recruited to work in industry (see "Rosie the Riveter" below). To ensure uninterrupted production, labor unions agreed to refrain from striking during the war. This promise was kept, with the exception of a few strikes in the coal industry.

Staffing the Military 征兵

The Roosevelt administration began a push to enlarge the size of the army even before the attack on Pearl Harbor brought the United States into the war. The Selective Service Act, passed in September 1940, created the first peacetime draft in American history. By the summer of 1941, almost a million and a half men were in the armed forces. In the course of the war, more than 15 million men and women would serve in the military. Many women served as nurses. In addition, more than 150,000 women joined the Women's Army Auxiliary Corps (WAAC) later designated the Women's Army Corps (WAC), and in the Women Accepted for Volunteer Emergency Service (WAVES), the women's branch of the Navy.

C. WORLD WAR II AND AMERICAN VALUES 第二次世界大战与美国价值观

The efforts to supply troops for the armed forces and to produce war-related materials led to opportunities for women and minorities to improve their positions in society. At the same time, a series of debates and decisions during World War II—including the decision related to the internment of Japanese Americans and debates over race and segregation—raised fundamental questions about American values.

The Japanese Relocation 日裔美国人拘留案

In 1942, President Roosevelt issued Executive Order 9066 authorizing the government to remove more than 100,000 Japanese Americans from West Coast states and relocate them to distant camps in more than a dozen western states. The order applied to both Issei (Japanese Americans who had emigrated from Japan) and Nisei (native-born Japanese Americans). Most of their property was confiscated by the government. In *Korematsu v. United States* (1944), the Supreme Court ruled that the relocation was acceptable on the grounds of national security. Much later, in 1988, the U.S. government publicly apologized to the surviving victims and extended $20,000 in reparations to each one. The Korematsu decision is one of several rulings by the Supreme Court that have curtailed civil liberties in times of war. The court upheld restrictions on free speech during World War I in the *Schenck v. United States* decision (1919) (see page 274).

> ## CIVIL LIBERTIES DURING WARTIME
> ## 战时的公民自由
> The *Korematsu* case is often on the AP exam. Be prepared to discuss it in the context of the broader question of civil liberties during wartime.

"Rosie the Riveter" "铆工露斯"

The government made a concerted effort to recruit women to participate in the war effort. Women were needed because factories were working around the clock producing military goods, and much of the male workforce was in the military. Many recruiting posters were produced by the government, usually through the Office of War Information, showing women in industrial settings. The fictional "Rosie the Riveter" character was often featured in this public relations campaign. Female workers were presented in a positive light—helping the nation as well as supporting the men in combat abroad. Such a campaign was needed because prewar societal mores discouraged women from doing industrial work. During the Great Depression of the 1930s, women were encouraged to leave the job market so that there would be enough jobs available for male "breadwinners." The World War II recruiting campaign was successful. By 1945, a third of the workforce was female.

World War II and the Status of African Americans in American Society
第二次世界大战与非裔美国人在美国社会中的地位

During World War II, a series of changes occurred that led to a reevaluation of attitudes and practices around race. African Americans mounted a frontal challenge to the system of Jim Crow segregation, both through their participation in the armed forces and in war-related industries. In many ways, this challenge continued into the postwar world. It also put the issues of race and segregation on the national agenda.

African Americans in the Armed Forces—The "Double-V Campaign"
武装部队中的非裔美国人——"双重胜利运动"

African Americans participated in the war effort, in part with the expectation of raising their status at home. The National Association for the Advancement of Colored People encouraged African Americans to take part in the "Double V" campaign—promoting victory against fascism abroad and victory against racism in their home country. Ultimately, 125,000 African Americans served overseas during World War II. The most famous segregated African American units were the Tuskegee Airmen and the 761st Tank Battalion. African American effectiveness on the battlefield encouraged President Truman to later (1948) desegregate the armed services with Executive Order 9981.

African Americans and War Production 非裔美国人与军工生产

Initially, many war industries were reluctant to hire African Americans. An important African American labor leader, A. Phillip Randolph, the president of the Brotherhood of Sleeping Car Porters, planned a public demonstration in Washington, DC, in 1941 to protest discrimination in war-related industries. When the Roosevelt administration heard of these plans, it worked out a bargain. Roosevelt issued Executive Order 8802, banning discrimination in war-related industries, and Randolph called off the march.

African Americans joined millions of other Americans in moving toward industrial centers. The Great Migration that began in World War I continued, with African Americans moving to the West Coast in addition to moving to northern industrial cities.

D. THE ALLIED VICTORY OVER THE AXIS POWERS IN WORLD WAR II
第二次世界大战中同盟国对轴心国的胜利

The United States played an important role in the Allied victory over the Axis powers. American leaders participated in joint political and military efforts with the other Allied countries. In addition, American industrial production and advances in technology and science played important parts in the war effort. Finally, the commitment of large sections of the American public to victory and to the advancement of democratic ideals helped the overall war effort.

War in the Pacific Theater 太平洋战场的战争

Through the first year of the war, the United States sent more of its troops to the Pacific theater than to Europe. Even though the defeat of Hitler was a top priority for the United States, it was Japan that had directly attacked the United States. The United States suffered several setbacks at the hands of the Japanese military in the first few months of the war. Japan took over the Philippines at the end of December 1941. By May 1942, Japan controlled a massive Pacific empire and had Australia in its sights.

The Battles of Coral Sea and Midway 珊瑚海海战与中途岛海战

The United States turned the tide of the war in the Pacific in two naval battles in 1942. In May, in the Battle of the Coral Sea, the U.S. Navy stopped a Japanese fleet headed to New Guinea. In June, the United States achieved a victory over the Japanese fleet in the Battle of Midway. After Midway, the United States steadily began to push Japanese forces back toward the Japanese home islands.

> ## TURNING POINTS IN WAR 战争转折点
>
> Although extensive knowledge of battles is not required for the AP exam, be aware of key turning points in wars, such as the Battle of Saratoga in the American Revolution and the capture of Vicksburg and the Battle of Gettysburg in the Civil War.

"Island Hopping" "越岛作战"

By the end of 1943, the United States began employing a strategy called "island hopping" (also known as "leapfrogging") to capture key Japanese-held islands in the Pacific. The basic idea of island hopping was that the United States and its allies would avoid attacking some of the most heavily fortified islands. Instead, it would focus on islands that were most important—perhaps as airfields or as key positions to block or attack enemy naval movements. The United States cut off the Japanese-held islands it had "hopped" over, by blockading supply ships. Japanese forces on these islands would then "wither on the vine."

War in Europe 欧洲的战争

Before June 1944, most of the fighting against Germany was carried out by the Soviet Union in Eastern Europe. Joseph Stalin, the Soviet dictator, had been urging the United States and Britain to open a second front in Western Europe against Germany. At a top-secret meeting in Tehran, Iran (see more on the Tehran Conference, page 301), in November 1943, President Franklin Roosevelt and Prime Minister Winston Churchill assured Stalin that they would open up a second European front.

The Washington and Casablanca Conferences 华盛顿会谈与卡萨布兰卡会议

In June 1942, Roosevelt and Churchill met in Washington, DC, to discuss strategy. In January 1943, they met again in Casablanca, Morocco. Stalin did not attend either meeting, but he let it be known that he hoped the other Allies would soon open up a major second front in Europe. Although there was warfare in North Africa, the brunt of the fighting against Hitler's forces had been carried out by the Red Army. Nearly 90 percent of German casualties came at the hands of Soviet troops. At both meetings, Churchill opposed the idea of immediately invading France; the British did not want to prematurely initiate a repeat of the trench warfare of World War I. Churchill and Roosevelt agreed to open a front in North Africa, followed by an attack on "the soft under-belly" of the Axis—Italy.

Fighting in North Africa 对北非作战

The first offensive involving American troops against Nazi-occupied areas occurred in North Africa in November 1942. American forces, led by General Dwight D. Eisenhower, landed in Morocco and Algeria and pushed back the forces of France's Vichy government, which collaborated with the Nazis. Americans moved eastward to attack German troops in Tunisia and Libya, while British forces drove westward to trap the enemy. By May 1943, North Africa was in Allied hands, with some of Hitler's best troops defeated.

The "Soft-Underbelly" of the Axis 轴心国的 "软肋"

Approximately a quarter of a million Allied forces landed in Sicily in June 1943. The Allies captured Sicily by August, which led to the Italian king dismissing Mussolini as prime minister. A new Italian government left the Axis and eventually joined the Allies. Germany, however, was not ready to accept an Allied-occupation of Italy. Hitler sent reinforcements into Italy. After ferocious fighting, the Allies finally marched into Rome in June 1944, but the rest of the advance up the Italian peninsula was defended by German troops every step of the way. Italy was no soft underbelly at all.

"D-Day" and the Allied Assault on Europe "诺曼底登陆日" 与同盟军袭击欧洲

In June 1944, the Allies stormed the beaches of Normandy, France, and began pushing Hitler's forces back toward Germany. On "D-Day" itself, June 4, nearly 200,000 Allied troops landed. Over the next several weeks, more than a million additional troops arrived. By August 1944, after heavy fighting and great loss, Allied forces under the command of General Dwight D. Eisenhower had liberated Paris from Nazi occupation.

V-E Day 第二次世界大战欧战胜利纪念日

Hitler made a last attempt to stop the Allied assault in the winter of 1944–1945. German forces counterattacked Allied lines in Belgium in the Battle of the Bulge, but eventually were stopped and forced back. American and British troops approached Germany from the west as Soviet troops approached from the east. By April 1945, the Soviets were on the outskirts of Hitler's capital, Berlin, which was under brutal bombardment. On April 30, Hitler committed suicide; on May 7, Germany surrendered: "Victory in Europe Day."

Victory in the Pacific 太平洋战场的胜利

By February 1945, American forces had taken control of most of Japan's Pacific empire. Iwo Jima and Okinawa, two small, heavily fortified islands stood between American forces and the Japanese homeland. Capturing these two islands proved to be an onerous task for American forces. The battle for Iwo Jima lasted six weeks in February and March 1945. Approximately 7,000 Americans died in the battle. The struggle for Okinawa was even more deadly. The island of Okinawa was to be a staging area for an attack on the Japanese home islands. Fighting there lasted from early April until mid-June 1945. The United States mobilized 300,000 troops for the battle. Approximately 12,000 Americans died, while Japan lost approximately 140,000. After these bloody battles, Japan's sphere of control was reduced to its home islands.

The Decision to Drop the Atomic Bomb, and the Japanese Surrender
决定投放原子弹与日本的投降

In April 1945, President Roosevelt died suddenly. He was succeed by his vice president, Harry S. Truman. In July, just as preparations were under way for a final offensive against Japan, President Truman learned the United States (in collaboration with Britain and Canada) had successfully tested an atomic bomb and that more bombs were ready for use. Since 1942, scientists in the top-secret Manhattan Project had been working on this terrifying and deadly weapon. The project involved several research labs at different sites. The facility at Los Alamos, New Mexico, headed by physicist J. Robert Oppenheimer, was charged with construction of the bomb.

The United States used this new weapon twice on Japan. On August 6, 1945, the United States dropped an atomic bomb on Hiroshima; on August 9, a second bomb was dropped on Nagasaki. More than 129,000 people died. Soon after, on September 2, Japan officially surrendered, ending World War II. At the time, the decision to drop the atomic bomb did not generate much public debate. The atomic bombing swiftly ended a bloody conflict that had consumed 50 million lives. But in the decades since the war, some Americans have raised questions about the decision. Critics argue that it was morally wrong for the United States to have targeted civilian populations and that the Japanese were ready to surrender. Others stand by the decision to drop the bomb. They claim it was not clear that the Japanese were on the verge of surrendering. Some of the Japanese military had argued against surrender, even after the second bomb was dropped.

E. THE UNITED STATES AND THE POSTWAR WORLD 美国与战后世界

After World War II the United States played a lead role in shaping the postwar world through conferences and peace settlements. With Europe and Asia ravaged from the war, the United States emerged as the dominant power in the world.

> **AMERICAN ENGAGEMENT**
> **美国参战**
> Note the marked difference between American disengagement following World War I and American engagement following World War II.

Tehran Conference 德黑兰会议

Stalin, Churchill, and Roosevelt, met in Tehran, Iran, in November 1943. The Allies agreed that the D-Day invasion would coincide with a major Soviet offensive. Also, Stalin pledged that the Soviet Union would join the war in Asia following the defeat of Germany. The Allies agreed in theory to forming an international peacekeeping organization.

Bretton Woods Conference 布雷顿森林会议

In July 1944, 44 nations met at Bretton Woods, New Hampshire, to discuss the basis of the global economy following the war. The International Monetary Fund was established at this meeting.

Yalta Conference　雅尔塔会议

The Yalta Conference, held in February 1945, was the most significant, and last, meeting of Churchill, Stalin, and Roosevelt. At Yalta, a coastal city in Crimea, the "big three" agreed to divide Germany into four military zones of occupation (the fourth zone would be occupied by France). Also, Stalin agreed to allow free elections in Poland in the future, with a Soviet-dominated interim government immediately following the war. Also at the meeting, secret agreements were made allowing for Soviet control of Outer Mongolia, the Kurile Islands, and part of Sakhalin Island, as well as Soviet railroad rights in Manchuria. Critics later faulted Roosevelt and Churchill for "abandoning" Poland and the rest of Eastern Europe to communist forces. But there was little the United States and Britain could do to dislodge the Red Army from Eastern Europe, short of starting a third world war.

Potsdam Conference　波茨坦会议

In the summer of 1945, the final meeting of the United States, the Soviet Union, and Great Britain took place. The meeting was attended by President Harry S. Truman, Josef Stalin, and British prime minister Clement Atlee (successor to Churchill). These leaders hammered out the details of the administration of occupied Germany. The details included the process of "denazification" of Germany, which led to the Nuremburg War Crimes Trials. The victorious nations set up this international tribunal to try leading Nazis for waging aggressive war and for crimes against humanity. At these trials, about 30 American judges participated. The chief justice of the U.S. Supreme Court was a chief lawyer for the prosecution. Many of the Nazis defended themselves by claiming that they were merely following orders.

SUBJECT TO DEBATE　相关讨论

History textbooks can take one of several approaches to discussions of American imperialism. You should be familiar with these approaches in order to write about events and documents from this period within a broader intellectual framework.

James Loewen, in his survey of American history textbooks, identifies three approaches to talking about American imperialism. Critics of American imperialism often discuss the United States as if it were a "colossus," imposing its will on the world. This "American colossus" approach asserts that any talk of spreading democracy around the world is cynical window-dressing to hide the actual motives of American imperialism: economic exploitation. A competing view acknowledges that economic motives drive foreign policy, but is not troubled by that fact. This hard-nosed "realpolitik" approach holds that America must expand if it wants to maintain the standard of living that Americans have come to appreciate. A third view, which Loewen calls the "international good guy" approach, ignores economic motives altogether. It asserts that American motives in the world are altruistic and noble. This view takes the words of public figures at face value.[1]

These approaches are useful when confronted with a document such as President Woodrow Wilson's 1917 "War Message to Congress" calling for intervention in World War I. You should be able to interrogate Wilson's claims that we are entering the war to make "the world . . . safe for democracy." You should be able to discuss the intent of such a document, rather than simply recounting information contained within it as fact.

---

[1]James Loewen, *Lies My Teacher Told Me: Everything Your American History Textbook Got Wrong* (New York: New Press, 1995).

For much of the twentieth century, the Progressive movement was treated quite favorably by historians. Historians generally accepted the self-descriptions of the Progressive movement—that it was devoted to eliminating corruption, inefficiencies, inequalities of wealth, and unhealthy working and living conditions. It would be hard to find fault with such a movement, especially because a large percentage of historians would probably consider themselves progressive and would probably share many of the same ideas about society that members of the Progressive movement did. However, by the 1960s, we begin to see questions being raised about the movement.

Some historians argued that the Progressive movement did not pose a serious challenge to the profitability of business. They contend that much of the impetus to reform business either originated with the business community or was shaped by it. Members of the business community were interested in reining in the worst elements of the business world. The example of the meat-packing industry demonstrates this point well. After the publication of *The Jungle*, the public's confidence in the entire industry declined. Industry leaders wanted to reform their world—rationalize and standardize it—so that people would continue to buy meat. Rather than resisting reform, industry leaders initiated it in order to restore confidence in their industry.

A second avenue of criticism of the movement had to do with the attitude of the Progressive movement toward the poor. This critique painted the Progressive movement as elitist and condescending toward the working class it was trying to help. The movement was ready to impose its idea of proper behavior on others. This is most evident in the prohibition movement—in which middle-class activists told working-class people that they should not drink. The crusade against "immoral" behavior—gambling, prostitution, smoking—also raises this issue of elitism. The nature of reform movements in general continues to divide historians.

World War I is often relegated to a backseat in standard history curricula—with World War II much more prominent. Perception of World War II is of a war imbued with a sense of mission—it was a "good fight" carried out by the "greatest generation." On the mall in Washington, DC, a large World War II memorial occupies a prominent place between the Washington Monument and the Lincoln Memorial. The World War I monument, by contrast, is a modest gazebo tucked away to the side of the mall. It is not even a national monument—it commemorates local residents who perished in the conflict. One reason World War I has been largely ignored is that there is no clearly identifiable "evil" that the United States was trying to defeat. The history of World War I does not read like a morality play.

That said, it would be unwise for a student preparing for the AP exam to ignore World War I. There are several crucial questions to consider. For instance, how do we account for the fact that the American political landscape changed completely from the beginning of the war to the end of the war? In 1914, on the eve of the war, the Progressive movement was enjoying its heyday; in 1919, as the war ended, America had become violently conservative. The "Red Scare" was paving the way for the resurgence of the Ku Klux Klan, restrictions on immigration and attacks on secularism. Students should be aware of the role war plays in changing the political climate.

The decade of the 1920s poses problems for historians in the "consensus" tradition. Consensus history asserts that there is a broad agreement among Americans around basic ideas and feelings. According to consensus historians, Americans share a belief in democracy and individual liberties; they believe that hard work leads to advancement; they believe in God, but do not try to impose their beliefs on others or on society as a whole; and they are a tolerant, welcoming people. Consensus history gained traction in the 1950s; this broad set of ideas set America apart from the Soviet Union—an essentially different system developed by people from an essentially different background. True, as consensus historians acknowledge, there have been conflicts, but they have not been over essential values. Take the labor battles of the Gilded Age. Consensus historians would argue that these disagreements do not represent fundamental differences. The strikers were not revolutionaries; they simply wanted a fair share of the pie, just like all Americans.

Consensus historians have a great deal of difficulty explaining the 1920s. Here is a decade in which the Ku Klux Klan claimed to have 3 million members in a country of 100 million people. Even if the membership figures are inflated, the Ku Klux Klan was a huge organization. Up to 3 million Americans joined a violent, racist, intolerant, anti-Semitic organization. In addition, there were many cases of German American residents being beaten in their homes by mobs of Americans in the early 1920s. These violent episodes challenge the assumptions of the consensus historians. Some historians have tried to minimize the importance of these facts or stress the fun of the "jazz age." Others have seen the reactionary impulses of the decade as responses to rapid social change. However, the undercurrent of intolerance and violence in the 1920s is difficult to fit into the traditional consensus model of American history.

Historians have debated the legacy of President Herbert Hoover in recent years. History textbooks tend to give Hoover a bad name. He is presented as aloof and rigid in the face of economic disaster. Hoover is remembered for what he did not do (provide direct relief to the poor) rather than what he did do.

Hoover's legacy in historical work tells us a great deal about historical writing. Many historians have come to lionize Hoover's successor, President Franklin D. Roosevelt. Roosevelt both saved the country from the worst ravages of the Great Depression at home and from the fascist menace abroad. In the process, he created the modern liberal welfare state. This adoration of Roosevelt has influenced historical writing about Hoover. Hoover, in this context, has become the anti-Roosevelt, representing the negative side of the coin. Hoover is lumped in with the other two Republican presidents of the 1920s, Warren Harding and Calvin Coolidge. However, a brief look at the record would indicate that Hoover was not as incompetent as he is often portrayed. He was an exceptionally competent administrator, running the successful Food Administration during World War I. When the Depression hit, he did not sit idly by. He implemented the far-reaching Reconstruction Finance Corporation, which provided needed funds to key sectors of the economy. Later he implemented public works programs. Even his handling of the Bonus March is not as heavy-handed as usually portrayed; the most aggressive acts against the protestors were carried out by General Douglas MacArthur, against the orders of President Hoover.

The nature of the New Deal has been a subject of much debate among historians, as it was among contemporaries. Conservative critics in the 1930s railed against "creeping socialism." Liberals championed the expansion of the state to help society cope with economic dislocation. Radicals asserted that the New Deal was essentially a conservative scheme to prop up capitalism. Historians often have in mind contemporary debates about government intervention in the economy when they are looking at the New Deal.

Historians have tried to understand the intellectual and political origins of the New Deal. Some look to the Populist and Progressive movements of the late 1800s and early 1900s. They see continuities between the reform programs of Presidents Theodore Roosevelt and Woodrow Wilson and the reform impulses of the New Deal. They note that many New Dealers were active in the Progressive era. Some historians see more of a break between earlier reform efforts and the New Deal. The progressives were mostly middle-class men and women, imposing their values on society. The New Deal, some argue, was driven more by working-class concerns.

Was the New Deal successful or not? Some historians have noted that the New Deal did not solve the problems of the Depression. They see the creation of a bloated government bureaucracy that was too large and impersonal to address the concerns of ordinary people. These historians note that the Depression ended only when the United States began producing materials for World War II. Other historians, more sympathetic to Roosevelt and the New Deal, argue that the New Deal restored hope among the American people and prevented more widespread suffering. Defenders of the New Deal also note that organized labor made great strides because of New Deal legislation. These debates parallel contemporary debates about the efficacy of government efforts at solving social and economic problems.

Two of the most heated historical questions involving the World War II era both have to do with issues of morality, justice, and war. Historians have recently had heated debates over both the Holocaust and the dropping of the atomic bombs on Japan. Some historians have insisted that the United States could have done more to save European Jews. These historians cite prewar immigration restrictions that prevented Jewish refugees from coming into the United States. In 1939, the State Department had not allowed the passenger ship *St. Louis*, with nearly a thousand Jewish refugees seeking asylum, to dock in Florida (see pages 295–296). The ship was forced to return to Antwerp, where most of the Jews aboard were arrested and ended up dying in concentration camps. The question as to why this happened has resonated in the contemporary world, as Americans have debated how much their country should intervene in human rights crises abroad, such as in Kosovo or Darfur or Syria.

The debate over the use of the atomic bomb has also generated a great deal of controversy in the historical world. In 1994, the Smithsonian Museum announced plans for an exhibit to open the following year to commemorate the 50th anniversary of the dropping of the atom bomb on Hiroshima and Nagasaki. When the floor plans and the text of the proposed exhibit were released to the public, there was a firestorm of controversy. Veterans groups and conservative historians accused the Smithsonian of "revisionism" by portraying the United States in a bad light. The plans revealed a balanced exhibit, but it was not the heroic exhibit that critics had hoped for. The text asked troubling questions, such as whether Japan was actually ready to surrender. The exhibit also showed scenes of death and destruction, which one would expect at an exhibit about a nuclear explosion. Ultimately, the entire exhibit was scrapped. The museum ended up displaying the Enola Gay (the plane that dropped the bomb on Hiroshima), but it left out any context or thought-provoking questions.

PRACTICE MULTIPLE-CHOICE QUESTIONS　选择题练习

> **Directions:** Pick the letter that best answers the following questions.

Questions 1–2 refer to the following image:　根据以下图像，回答第1—2题

1. The point of view of the cartoon above is that

   (A) Christian missionaries were overly concerned with gaining converts in other lands while they ignored poverty at home.
   (B) open immigration policies were undermining the economic stability of the United States.
   (C) the United States should look beyond its borders and become an imperialist power.
   (D) the widening gap between the wealthy and the poor was creating a potentially revolutionary situation in the United States.

2. A reader who supported the sentiment of the cartoon above would most likely have been in support of which of the following?

   (A) The Chinese Exclusion Act.
   (B) The Spanish-American War.
   (C) The Supreme Court decision in the Insular Cases.
   (D) The settlement house movement.

"This book tells the story of how industrial workers in one American city made sense of an era in our recent history [the 1930s] when the nation moved from a commitment to welfare capitalism to a welfare state [and] from a determination to resist the organization of its industrial work force to tolerating it."

—Lizabeth Cohen, *Making a New Deal: Industrial Workers in Chicago, 1919–1939*, 1990

3. The changes described in the excerpt could best be attributed to

    (A) changes in the composition of the Supreme Court.
    (B) an increase in the power of local and state governments.
    (C) a renewed commitment to a laissez-faire approach to economic policy.
    (D) an expansion to the powers of the federal government.

4. Which of the following most strongly sought to limit or reverse the changes described in the excerpt?

    (A) Political radicals, such as members of the Communist Party.
    (B) Organizations advocating on behalf of senior citizens.
    (C) Civil rights organizations such as the Congress of Racial Equality.
    (D) Conservatives in Congress and on the Supreme Court.

5. The changes described in the excerpt were later reinforced by initiatives associated with

    (A) Senator Joseph McCarthy and the anti-communist crusade of the 1950s.
    (B) the "Great Society" agenda of President Lyndon Johnson in the 1960s.
    (C) the domestic agenda of President Ronald Reagan in the 1980s.
    (D) Representative Newt Gingrich and the "Contract with America" in the 1990s.

Questions 6–7 refer to the excerpt below. 根据以下选段，回答第6—7题

"To cast this case into outlines of racial prejudice, without reference to the real military dangers which were presented, merely confuses the issue. Korematsu was not excluded from the Military Area because of hostility to him or his race. He was excluded because we are at war with the Japanese Empire, because the properly constituted military authorities feared an invasion of our West Coast and felt constrained to take proper security measures, because they decided that the military urgency of the situation demanded that all citizens of Japanese ancestry be segregated from the West Coast temporarily, and, finally, because Congress, reposing its confidence in this time of war in our military leaders—as inevitably it must—determined that they should have the power to do just this."

—Justice Hugo Black, writing for the majority opinion of the
United States Supreme Court in *Korematsu v. United States*, 1944

6. The idea expressed in the excerpt demonstrates continuity with which of the following earlier Supreme Court decisions?

   (A) Decisions allowing for "separate but equal" public facilities, such as *Plessy v. Ferguson.*

   (B) Decisions limiting the powers of the executive branch, such as *Schechter Poultry Corp. v. United States.*

   (C) Decisions limiting the citizenship rights of certain groups, such as *Dred Scott v. Sanford.*

   (D) Decisions limiting civil liberties during times of national emergency, such as *Schenck v. United States.*

7. Which of the following was the most immediate result of the decision excerpted?

   (A) The United States military was forced to compensate Japanese Americans for land they had lost during World War II.

   (B) The United States military was forced to close detention centers for Italian Americans and German Americans who had been living in east coast cities and towns.

   (C) The United States military was permitted to keep over 100,000 Japanese Americans in internment centers for the duration of World War II.

   (D) President Franklin D. Roosevelt introduced a proposal to add additional members to the Supreme Court.

Answers and Explanations to Multiple-Choice Questions
选择题的答案与解析

1. **(A)** The central figure, with the telescope, represents a Protestant missionary worker. In the cartoon, the missionary worker is looking abroad to see which lands would be fruitful for missionary work. He seems to be ignoring the people in need right at his feet. The cartoon is not critical of immigration policies (B); the people at his feet are not shown to be recent immigrants. In any case, they are presented in a sympathetic light. The cartoon does not allude to imperialist ventures (C), nor to the constitutional rights of people in American colonies (D).

2. **(D)** Supporters of the point of view of the cartoon would also support the work of the settlement house movement, because the movement was addressing the issue that the cartoonist asserted was being ignored by Protestant missionaries—poverty at home. Settlement houses were established to aid immigrants, especially immigrant women. By the 1910s more than 400 settlement houses existed in the United States, usually run by women. Jane Addams ran Hull House in Chicago.

3. **(D)** The excerpt is describing the impact of the New Deal, a series of programs and agencies that sought to address the Great Depression. President Franklin D. Roosevelt took the federal government in a new direction by asserting that it should take some responsibility for the welfare of the people. Previously, churches, settlement houses, and other private charities helped people in times of need.

4. **(D)** The New Deal was most strongly challenged by a series of Supreme Court decisions. Roosevelt grew increasingly frustrated with the Supreme Court after it shot down the National Industrial Recovery Act in *Schechter v. United States* (1935) and the Agricultural Adjustment Act in *Butler v. United States* (1936). In 1936, he announced a plan to increase the number of justices on the Supreme Court, to as many as 15. He said that some of the older justices had difficulty keeping up with the heavy workload. But it was clear that he was trying to create a Supreme Court friendlier to his New Deal programs. Roosevelt's "court packing" scheme was widely criticized and ultimately abandoned.

5. **(B)** The general thrust of the New Deal was later reinforced by the "Great Society" agenda of President Lyndon Johnson in the 1960s. The main components of Johnson's Great Society were landmark civil rights acts as well as a comprehensive "war on poverty." An important program was Medicare, which provides health care for every American once reaching the age of 65. Many aspects of Johnson's Great Society were underfunded as the federal government spent more and more on the war in Vietnam.

6. **(D)** The *Korematsu* decision demonstrates continuity with several other Supreme Court decisions that allowed for the limiting of civil liberties during times of national emergency. The *Korematsu* decision upheld Executive Order 9066, issued by President Franklin Roosevelt during World War II, authorizing the government to remove over 100,000 Japanese Americans from west coast cities and relocate them to camps in the western United States. The *Schenck* decision (1919) upheld the Espionage Act, passed (along with the Sedition Act) during World War I to put limits on public expressions of antiwar sentiment. The Supreme Court argued that freedom of speech is not absolute and that the government is justified in limiting certain forms of speech during wartime.

7. **(C)** The *Korematsu* decision allowed the government to keep over 100,000 Japanese Americans in internment centers for the remainder of World War II. Of these individuals, two-thirds of them were citizens. After they were sent to the centers, most of their property was confiscated by the government. The Supreme Court ruled that the relocation was acceptable on the grounds of national security. Much later, in 1988, the United States government publicly apologized to the surviving victims and extended $20,000 in reparations to each one.

Period 8: 1945–1980 Redefining Democracy in the Era of Cold War and Liberal Ascendancy

第八个时期（1945—1980）：重新定义冷战时期的民主政治与自由崛起

10

TIMELINE 大事年表

1944	G.I. Bill passed
1946	*Baby and Child Care* by Dr. Benjamin Spock published
	Largest strike wave in U.S. history
1947	Publication of the "X Article" ("Sources of Soviet Conduct") by George Kennan
	Truman Doctrine (communist containment) announced
	$400 million in military aid to Greece and Turkey
	House Un-American Activities Committee begins Hollywood investigations
	Taft-Hartley Act
1948	Beginning of the Berlin Blockade
	President Truman issues executive order desegregating the military
	Election of Harry S. Truman
1949	Formation of North Atlantic Treaty Organization (NATO)
1950	Senator Joseph McCarthy gains public spotlight on issue of anticommunism
	NSC–68 adopted
	Korean War begins
	Passage of McCarran Internal Security Act
1951	Truman fires General Douglas MacArthur
	United States tests world's first hydrogen bomb
1952	Execution of Julius and Ethel Rosenberg
	Army–McCarthy hearings
	Election of Dwight D. Eisenhower
1954	Interstate Highway Act
	Brown v. Board of Education of Topeka
1955	Creation of Warsaw Pact

TIMELINE 大事年表

1956	Rosa Parks arrested for not giving up her seat; Montgomery Bus Boycott
	Reelection of Eisenhower
1957	Soviet launch of the *Sputnik* satellite
	Crisis in Little Rock, Arkansas, over school desegregation
	On the Road by Jack Kerouac published
1960	Soviet Union shoots down U-2 spy plane
	Lunch counter sit-in movement begins
	Election of John F. Kennedy
1961	Bay of Pigs invasion in Cuba
1961	The Freedom Rides begin
1962	Cuban Missile Crisis
1963	Campaign to desegregate Birmingham, Alabama
	President John F. Kennedy assassinated
	March on Washington, DC; Martin Luther King, Jr., delivers "I Have a Dream" speech
1964	Civil Rights Acts passed
	"Freedom Summer" voter-registration drive in Mississippi; murder of Michael Schwerner, James Chaney, and Andrew Goodman
	Gulf of Tonkin Resolution
	Election of Lyndon Johnson
1965	Voting Rights Act
	Malcolm X assassinated
	March from Selma, Alabama, to Montgomery, Alabama
1966	Founding of the Black Panthers
1967	"Summer of Love"
	Rioting in Detroit, Newark, and other cities
1968	Assassination of Martin Luther King, Jr.
	Assassination of Robert F. Kennedy
	Violence at Democratic Convention in Chicago
	Election of Richard Nixon
	Founding of American Indian Movement
1969	Woodstock Festival
	Stonewall Riot in New York City; birth of the gay liberation movement
	Apollo 11 lands on the moon

1970	President Nixon widens Vietnam War to Cambodia
	Four students killed by Ohio National Guard at Kent State protest
1971	Publication of Pentagon Papers in *The New York Times*
1972	Arrest of burglars at the Watergate Complex
	Reelection of Richard Nixon
1973	Congressional hearings on Watergate
1974	Nixon resigns presidency; Gerald Ford assumes presidency
	Ford grants Nixon complete pardon
1976	Election of Jimmy Carter
1977	Supreme Court decision in *Bakke v. University of California*
1978	Panama Canal Treaty
	Camp David Accords
1979	Three Mile Island nuclear accident

INTRODUCTION 简介

> In the post–World War II period, the United States assumed a position of global leadership and experienced unprecedented prosperity. At the same time, the country grappled with domestic and international issues as it sought to define itself and struggled with living up to its stated values.

The Cold War began after World War II, when two former allies, the United States and the Soviet Union, emerged as rival superpowers. The perceived threat of communist aggression presented several challenges to the United States. The country changed in many ways as a result of the Cold War. The country became much more engaged in the affairs of the world and assumed a leading role in the opposition to communism. In addition, the nation changed domestically. New governmental initiatives—from loyalty oaths to civil defense programs—were initiated during the Cold War. Some of these programs helped allay people's concerns about the threat of communism, while some initiatives might have added to people's fears.

In many ways, World War II was a turning point for American society. The postwar world was almost indistinguishable from the prewar world. A more modern, more affluent society emerged in the postwar era—one unimaginable in the depths of the Great Depression.

This period also witnessed the high tide of American liberalism, with the election of the youthful John F. Kennedy, a series of progressive decisions by the Warren Court, the implementation of President Johnson's "Great Society" programs, and the successful passage of landmark civil-rights legislation.

LIBERALISM 自由主义

Note that liberalism has meant different things at different times. In the nineteenth century, liberalism implied unfettered individual rights; since the New Deal, liberalism has meant support for government programs to rectify social ills.

Finally, the 1960s and 1970s saw the unraveling of the liberal agenda as the war in Vietnam sucked valuable resources from social programs, and urban rioting highlighted the limits of the federal government's ability to address the problems of the African American underclass. These years saw violence in the streets of American cities, a widening and eventual abandonment of the war in Vietnam, assassinations of major public figures, a nationwide energy crisis, and a major political scandal that brought down a sitting president. The roots of a resurgent conservative movement can be seen toward the end of this period.

KEY CONCEPT 8.1 THE UNITED STATES AND THE COLD WAR
核心概念8.1：美国与冷战

Emerging as the pre-eminent international power after World War II, the United States now engaged in the Cold War with the Soviet Union. The United States attempted to maintain a leadership position in an increasingly uncertain and unstable world. This new role for the country had profound domestic and international consequences.

I. Containment, Economic Stability, and Collective Security
遏制政策、经济稳定与集体安全体系

After World War II, the United States adopted a policy of containment, attempting to limit the influence of the Soviet Union and communism internationally. Toward this end, the United States sought to build a system of international security as well as a stable global economy.

A. FORGING A NEW FOREIGN POLICY IN THE POSTWAR WORLD
打造战后新外交政策

After World War II, the United States pursued a foreign policy that emphasized collective security and the establishment of a multinational economic framework. The goal of this new foreign policy was to bolster non-communist states in the Cold War era.

Origins of the Cold War   冷战的由来

Tensions existed between the United States and the Soviet Union from the time of the Russian Revolution (1917), when America opposed the communists. The U.S.–Soviet World War II alliance against the Nazis brought them briefly together. Historians date the beginning of the Cold War from the close of World War II. The United States believed the Soviets were intent upon extending their control over Europe. As the war ended, the Soviet Union left its Red Army troops occupying Eastern Europe, where the countries became Soviet satellites. The Soviets indicated they would allow free elections in Poland, but instead they installed a puppet regime. The United States worried the Soviets would try to push into Western Europe. The leader of the Soviet Union, Joseph Stalin, insisted that he only wanted to have friendly nations on his borders. After numerous attacks from Western powers on Russia and the Soviet Union, from Napoleon to Hitler, Stalin was wary of the West.

Containment and the Truman Doctrine   遏制政策与杜鲁门主义

In order to block any further aggression by the Soviet Union, Truman issued the Truman Doctrine (1947), in which he said that the goal of the United States would be to contain communism. The containment approach to the Soviet Union had been spelled out in an article entitled "Sources of Soviet Conduct," published in *Foreign Affairs* (1947). The article was also known as "X Article" because it was published using the pseudonym "X." Later it was learned that the author was George Kennan, a diplomat who had served in the U.S. embassy in Moscow (1944–1946). Although Kennan soon reversed himself and recommended dialogue with the Soviets,.the Cold War had begun. Military containment of communism remained the cornerstone of American foreign policy for decades to come.

CONTAINMENT　遏制政策

A sophisticated essay might draw comparisons between Truman's policy of containment of communism in the 1940s and 1950s and Lincoln's policy of containment of slavery in the 1860s. The position of the Republican Party, starting in 1854, was to contain slavery within its existing borders.

Military Aid to Greece and Turkey　对希腊和土耳其的军事援助

As part of the policy of containment, the United States extended military aid to Greece and Turkey in 1947. The aid helped the Greek monarchy put down a communist-influenced rebel movement. Further, the move quieted Republican criticism of Truman and improved the president's standing in public-opinion polls; he won reelection the following year. The United States demonstrated that it was committed to a policy of containment.

POSTWAR POLICIES　战后政治

Be prepared to compare U.S. foreign policy following each of the two world wars. After World War I, the United States retreated into isolationism; after World War II, the United States maintained its involvement in world affairs with the containment policy.

The Marshall Plan　马歇尔计划

The United States further demonstrated its global commitment with the massive Marshall Plan. Developed by Secretary of State George Marshall, the plan allocated almost $13 billion for war-torn Europe to rebuild. A total of 17 nations received aid between 1948 and 1951, with West Germany, France, and Britain receiving the bulk of it. The plan stabilized the capitalist economies of Western Europe and contributed to remarkable growth, as the standard of living there improved. The goal was to provide a viable alternative to Soviet-style communism; ultimately, the plan was successful in creating a strong Western Europe, allied with American interests.

The Berlin Blockade and the Berlin Airlift　柏林封锁与柏林空运

In 1948, the United States decided to challenge the Soviet blockade of the western-occupied section of Berlin, a free enclave deep within Soviet-occupied East Germany. This enclave, occupied by Allied troops after World War II was cut off within communist-controlled East Germany. In 1948, the Soviet Union decided to prevent food and other supplies from entering the western section of Berlin. The goal was for the Soviet Union to take over western Berlin and make it part of East Germany. The United States did not stand by idly in the face of the Berlin blockade. Over the next year, President Truman sent 200,000 flights (American and allied aircraft) carrying supplies into western Berlin. This action, known as the "Berlin Airlift," prevented the Soviet Union from taking over the city. Afterward, the city was formally divided and western Berlin became part of West Germany.

The Formation of NATO (1949)　北大西洋公约组织的成立（1949）

The United States demonstrated its commitment to protect Western Europe when it led in the founding of the North Atlantic Treaty Organization (NATO) in 1949. The members of NATO vowed to collectively resist any aggressive actions by the Soviet Union. This marked the first time that the United States joined a peacetime alliance.

B. CARRYING OUT THE POLICY OF CONTAINMENT　推行遏制政策

In the 1950s and 1960s, the United States pursued containment in several different ways, including direct military engagements in Korea and Vietnam, a robust nuclear weapons program, and the pursuit of a space race with the Soviet Union.

NSC–68 (1950)　国家安全委员会第68号文件（1950）

A National Security Council Paper, known as NSC–68, called for a more aggressive defense policy for the United States. It recommended raising taxes and devoting more funds to military spending. This document largely shaped U.S. foreign policy during the Cold War through the 1960s.

The Cold War in Asia　亚洲的冷战

The initial conflicts of the Cold War occurred in Europe, but by the late 1940s, American policymakers became increasingly concerned about events in Asia. America's Cold War policies had mixed results in Asia. The United States successfully ushered Japan toward democracy and economic self-sufficiency. The United States also granted independence to the Philippines in 1946. But the communist-ruled People's Republic of China proved to be a difficult problem for President Harry S. Truman.

Communism in China　中国的共产主义

In the 1930s, China had been roiled by an ongoing civil war. The conflict abated during the Japanese invasion of World War II, but began again after the war. The United States allied with the Nationalist side, led by Jiang Jieshi (Chiang Kai-shek). However, the Communist Party, led by Mao Zedong (Mao Tse-tung), amassed a huge following among the poor rural population of China. Mao's forces won in 1949 and the People's Republic of China was established. The news that China, the most populous nation in the world, had become communist shocked many Americans. Republicans accused Truman of "losing" China, although in reality there was not much that could have been done to prevent the eventual outcome.

> ### "SOFT ON COMMUNISM"
> ### "对共产主义采取温和政策"
> In your essays, try to make connections between foreign policy issues and domestic politics. After communism triumphed in China, Republicans accused Truman of being "soft on communism." This hurt the Democrats and helped Joseph McCarthy gain an audience.

The Korean War (1950–1953)　朝鲜战争（1950–1953）

The next hotspot in the Cold War was Korea. Korea had been divided at the 38th parallel after World War II, with the United States administering the southern half and the Soviet Union administering the northern half (similar to the division of Germany). In 1948, this arrangement was formalized with the creation of two nations, North Korea, a communist country, and South Korea, an American ally. In June 1950, North Korean troops, using Soviet equipment, invaded South Korea. President Truman decided to commit troops to support South Korea and managed to secure United Nations sponsorship. United Nations forces, led by U.S. General Douglas MacArthur, pushed the North Korean troops back to the 38th parallel and then marched into North Korea. When the UN forces got within 40 miles of the border between North Korea and China, China sent 150,000 troops over the Yalu River to push them back. After intense fighting, the two sides settled into defensive positions on either side of the 38th parallel.

The Firing of General MacArthur　麦克阿瑟将军的解职

During the Korean War, General Douglas MacArthur made it clear that he thought the United States could successfully invade China and roll back communism there. Truman was convinced that initiating a wider war, so soon after World War II, would be disastrous. MacArthur made public pronouncements about strategy, arguing that, "There is no substitute for victory." Truman fired MacArthur for insubordination and other unauthorized activities.

Armistice in Korea　朝鲜半岛停战

The Korean War ended as it began—with North Korea and South Korea divided at the 38th parallel. By 1953, an armistice was reached, although a formal treaty ending the war was never signed.

President Eisenhower, the "New Look" in Foreign Policy, and "Massive Retaliation"　艾森豪威尔总统、外交政策的"新气象"与"大规模报复战略"

Faced with the competing priorities of balancing the federal budget on the one hand and continuing the policy of containment on the other, President Dwight D. Eisenhower pursued a policy labeled the "New Look." The policy emphasized the development of strategic nuclear weapons as a deterrent to potential threats from the Soviet Union. The increased reliance on nuclear weaponry was accompanied by a shift away from maintaining costly ground forces. A strong nuclear arsenal, Defense Secretary Charles Wilson argued, would provide the United States with a "bigger bang for the buck."

Central to the strategy of increasing the American nuclear arsenal was the policy of "massive retaliation." The idea was put forth by Secretary of State John Foster Dulles in a 1954 speech. The idea of "massive retaliation" is that the United States would maintain a nuclear arsenal capable of retaliating with overwhelming force against aggressive moves by any enemy. The threat of massive retaliation was designed to deter conventional as well as nuclear strikes by the Soviet Union. Dulles also put forth the idea of "brinksmanship"—the Soviet Union needed to be aware that the United States was willing to "go to the brink" of war with its nuclear arsenal. As the Soviet Union developed a similarly powerful nuclear force, the ensuing nuclear standoff between the Soviet Union and the United States came to be known as "mutually assured destruction."

The Launching of *Sputnik*   "伴侣号"人造卫星的发射

Starting in the late 1950s, the Cold War expanded to a race for supremacy in terms of exploration of outer space. The space race began in earnest with the 1957 launching of the unmanned Soviet satellite, *Sputnik,* into space. The launch caught many Americans off guard and led to several important domestic developments. *Sputnik* alarmed U.S. government officials because the same type of rocket that launched the satellite could also be used to quickly deliver atomic weapons to any location on Earth.

The Space Race   太空竞争

After the launch of Sputnik, the United States created the National Aeronautics and Space Administration (NASA) in 1958 to carry out the nation's space program. In 1961, President John F. Kennedy announced the goal of landing a man on the moon before the close of the 1960s. The budget for NASA grew under Kennedy. The goal was accomplished in 1969, when the United States was the first nation to successfully land a spacecraft and men on the moon.

UNDERSTANDING NASA
了解美国国家航空航天局

Be aware of the different, and often competing, goals of NASA. On the one hand, it was created to engage in scientific research for the benefit of humanity; on the other hand, it helped further the military goals of the United States during the Cold War.

Espionage and the U-2 Incident   间谍活动及U-2事件

The United States maintained an extensive program of spying on the military capabilities of the Soviet Union. At first, the government denied the program existed, but in 1960 a U-2 high-altitude "spy plane" was shot down over Soviet territory. Eisenhower admitted the program existed and defended its goals. These actions all demonstrated that the United States would take a more active role in challenging the Soviet Union.

Cuban Missile Crisis   古巴导弹危机

The Cuban Missile Crisis occurred in 1962 when a U-2 spy plane discovered that Cuba was preparing bases for installing Soviet nuclear missiles. President Kennedy declared these missiles, in such close proximity to the United States, amounted to an unacceptable provocation and demanded that the Soviet premier, Nikita Khrushchev, halt the operation and withdraw the missiles. Khrushchev insisted on the right of the Soviet Union to install the missiles. For days, the world stood on the brink of nuclear war. Finally, a deal was reached in which the Soviet Union would abandon its Cuban missile program and the United States would agree to honor the sovereignty of Cuba. Quietly, the United States also agreed to remove missiles from Turkey.

The War in Vietnam   越南战争

Vietnam is a small country along the eastern edge of the Indochina peninsula in Southeast Asia. From the mid-nineteenth century to the mid-twentieth century Indochina, including what would become Vietnam, was a French possession. French Indochina was occupied by Japan during World War II, and when the war ended many Vietnamese hoped to finally be free of foreign control. But France reoccupied the peninsula when the Japanese left. A resistance movement, led by Ho Chi Minh, intensified in the 1950s. In 1954, French forces were defeated at the northern town of Dien Bien Phu, and France withdrew. Vietnam soon was divided at the 17th parallel between a communist-controlled North Vietnam, led by Ho Chi Minh, and a Western-allied South Vietnam. Rebel fighters, known as the Vietcong, fought to defeat a corrupt and dictatorial South Vietnamese government. American observers concluded that, without outside help, the government of South Vietnam could very likely fall to the communists.

The "Domino Theory" "多米诺理论"

American involvement in Vietnam was influenced by a belief in the "domino theory." This theory asserts that when a nation adopts a communist form of government, its neighbors are likely to become communist as well. The theory presumes that communism is imposed on a country from the outside—that it does not develop as a result of internal conditions.

The United States Sends Advisors to Vietnam 美国向越南派遣军事顾问

United States interest in Vietnam began during World War II, when it sent military advisors and assistance to support anti-Japanese fighters. After the country was divided in 1954, U.S. aid went to South Vietnam to fight anti-government rebels. The United States feared that South Vietnam would become a communist nation like North Vietnam.

The Gulf of Tonkin Resolution 东京湾决议

The United States became heavily involved in the Vietnam War after Congress passed the Gulf of Tonkin Resolution (1964), which gave President Lyndon Johnson broad latitude to pursue "conventional" military actions in Southeast Asia. In August 1964, Johnson announced that American destroyers had been fired upon by North Vietnamese gunboats in the Gulf of Tonkin, off the coast of North Vietnam. Later, reports questioned the accuracy of the announcement, but the incident led Congress to give Johnson a "blank check" to engage in military operations in Southeast Asia without a formal declaration of war. The Gulf of Tonkin Resolution can be considered the beginning of the Vietnam War.

The Tet Offensive 新年攻势

In January 1968 the Vietcong and North Vietnamese forces launched the Tet Offensive, a major attack on South Vietnamese, U.S., and allied bases and towns. This offensive left over 9,000 U.S., South Vietnamese, and allied troops dead (1,600 Americans), while the North Vietnamese and Vietcong suffered more than 40,000 deaths. The offensive was defeated, but it demonstrated the ability of the Vietnamese to organize a coordinated strike throughout South Vietnamese territory.

The My Lai Massacre 美莱村大屠杀

In 1968, a company of American troops killed nearly every inhabitant of the Vietnamese village of My Lai, despite finding no enemy forces there. The U.S. Army covered up the massacre for more than a year. In 1971, a U.S. military court found the commander of the company, Lieutenant William Calley, guilty of the massacre. The incident led many Americans to further question the morality of the war in Vietnam.

"Vietnamization" of the Vietnam War 越南战争的"越南化"

Nixon assured the American people that he had a plan for "peace with honor" in the Vietnam War when he ran for president in 1968. However, victory proved elusive for the United States in Vietnam. Instead of seeking peace, Nixon widened the war to Cambodia. Starting in 1969 Nixon began the policy known as "Vietnamization." This involved replacing American troops with South Vietnamese troops. However, all the measures that Nixon took would not lead to American victory. The United States pulled out of Vietnam in 1973. By 1975, South Vietnam was defeated. Vietnam was then reunited as a communist country.

C. THE COLD WAR—FROM CONFRONTATION TO DÉTENTE 冷战——从对抗到缓和

At times the Cold War involved military confrontations—both direct and indirect—while at other times it involved mutual coexistence or détente.

Eisenhower and Khrushchev Pursue Coexistence 艾森豪威尔与赫鲁晓夫寻求共存

After the death in 1953 of Soviet leader Joseph Stalin and the emergence of the more moderate Nikita Khrushchev, President Dwight D. Eisenhower held out hope for a warming of relations with the Soviet Union and a reduction in the threat of nuclear war. Eisenhower and Khrushchev held a "summit"—a meeting of top leaders—in Geneva, but no substantive agreements came out of it. The launching of *Sputnik* (see page 318) and the first Soviet test of an intercontinental ballistic missile (ICBM), both in 1957, pushed the two nations further apart. However, a new round of meetings, between Khrushchev and Vice President Richard Nixon occurred in 1959. Nixon's trip to the Soviet Union included the famous "kitchen debate" with Khrushchev while they toured an American model-home display at an international exhibition in Moscow. The two were photographed next to modern kitchen appliances as they debated the merits of communism versus capitalism. The following year, the two countries were on the verge of signing a nuclear test ban. Khrushchev and Eisenhower had scheduled a summit in Paris to finalize the treaty, but just before they met, the American U-2 spy plane was shot down (see page 318), scuttling any potential agreement.

U.S.–Soviet Relations Under Kennedy 肯尼迪时期的美苏关系

John F. Kennedy made attempts to ease tensions between the Soviet Union and the United States. In the wake of the Cuban Missile Crisis, the Partial Test Ban Treaty was signed by the United States, the Soviet Union, and Britain in 1963. The ban exempted underground nuclear tests.

THE LEGACY OF PRESIDENT NIXON
尼克松总统的遗产

Although Nixon is most vividly remembered for the Watergate scandal, there is no consensus among historians about Nixon's legacy. Many cite his foreign policy accomplishments alongside his scandalous downfall.

Détente with China and the Soviet Union
与中苏关系的缓和

President Richard Nixon's policy of détente represented a thawing in the Cold War and an improvement of relations with the Soviet Union. In 1971, Nixon initiated an agreement with the Soviets whereby they accepted the independence of West Berlin and the United States recognized East Germany. Also, the 1972 Strategic Arms Limitation Talks (SALT) led to two arms-control agreements. Tensions still existed, but détente led to discussions between the two sides, to limited arms-control agreements, and to cultural exchanges. In 1972, Nixon visited China, making it the first time an American president visited the People's Republic of China. The visit was an important step in normalizing relations with the communist government of China.

D. DECOLONIZATION, NATIONALISM, AND ALLEGIANCES IN THE COLD WAR ERA
冷战时期的非殖民地化、民族主义与寻求拥护

In the post–World War II period, nationalist movements developed in many colonized countries in Asia, Africa, and the Middle East, setting off a wave of decolonization struggles. Both of the major powers in the Cold War struggle attempted to gain the allegiance of these newly independent countries. However, many of these countries remained nonaligned.

Decolonization and U.S. Foreign Policy　非殖民地化与美国外交政策

In the two decades after World War II, many of the colonies of the European powers struggled to gain independence. A wave of nationalist movements developed throughout Asia and Africa. India, for example, gained independence from British rule in 1947 after a prolonged struggle led by Mohandas Gandhi; in Algeria an eight-year brutal war preceded independence from France in 1962. U.S. foreign policy evolved in the face of these movements. On the one hand, the United States professed support for the concept of self-determination—granting the Philippines independence in 1946—and on the other hand, it had strong ties with many of the European powers.

As the Cold War intensified, the Truman and Eisenhower administrations became increasingly concerned that the newly independent countries would end up in the orbit of the Soviet Union. The United States encouraged the European powers to negotiate with their colonies to insure peaceful paths to independence. It also took a number of measures to keep these newly independent countries from aligning with the Soviet Union. The United States extended aid packages and technical assistance to many of these countries. The Peace Corps, established in 1961, served this goal. The United States also resorted to military force and covert operations to install regimes favorable to U.S. interests.

Iran and the CIA　伊朗与中央情报局

During the Cold War, the United States engaged in a number of covert operations designed to oust regimes (often democratically elected) that were deemed insufficiently friendly to American interests. An early covert operation occurred in Iran in 1953. Earlier, in 1951, the left-leaning, reform-minded Mohammad Mosaddegh was elected prime minister of Iran. Mosaddegh nationalized oil fields and refineries, angering Western oil interests. In addition, he challenged the power of Iran's hereditary ruler, Shah Mohammed Reza Pahlavi, who was close to the Iranian elite and to Western oil interests. President Eisenhower, stressing the importance of having regimes friendly to American interests in the oil-rich Middle East, authorized the CIA, with the support of British M16 agents, to instigate a coup against Mosaddegh. The Iranian army took Mosaddegh prisoner and restored the Shah's power. Although the United States accomplished its goal of establishing a friendly regime in Iran, the events of 1953 came back to haunt the United States a generation later in the aftermath of the 1979 Iranian Revolution (see Period 9).

The Eisenhower Doctrine　艾森豪威尔主义

President Dwight D. Eisenhower became increasingly concerned about events in the Middle East after Colonel Gamal Abdel Nasser took power in Egypt in 1954, ousting a corrupt king who had maintained close ties with Great Britain. Nasser established close relations with the Soviets. The situation deteriorated after Nasser seized control of the Suez Canal, jointly owned by French and British shareholders. When France, Great Britain, and Israel invaded Egypt to retake control of the canal, Eisenhower and the leaders of the UN and the Soviet Union pressured them to withdraw. Afterward, Eisenhower took a more active role in the Middle East. In a 1957 speech, he pledged the United States would support any Middle Eastern countries threatened by "any nation controlled by international communism." The Eisenhower Doctrine was invoked in 1958 when a rebel movement friendly to Nasser emerged in Lebanon; U.S. Marines were quickly dispatched to support the Lebanese president.

E. THE COLD WAR IN LATIN AMERICA　冷战时期的拉丁美洲

During the Cold War, the United States supported a variety of non-communist regimes in Latin America. These regimes had varying levels of commitment to democratic practices.

Regime Change in Guatemala　危地马拉的政权更替

In Guatemala, the United States orchestrated the ouster of the democratically elected government of Jacobo Arbenz (1954). Arbenz, who had been elected president in 1951, was a reform-minded leader who began a land reform program. He moved to nationalize some of the vast landholdings of the American-owned United Fruit Company, growers of Chiquita Bananas. He intended to nationalize lands that were not under cultivation and distribute them to poverty-stricken peasants. He offered to buy the land from United Fruit Company at the value the company had declared the land for tax purposes, but the company refused. The CIA then organized a plan to overthrow the Arbenz government. It trained and armed an opposition army that ousted Arbenz and installed a military dictatorship in his place. The bitter feelings left in the wake of the coup contributed to civil war in Guatemala that lasted into the 1990s.

Hostilities with Cuba　对古巴的敌意

Events in Cuba occupied much of President John F. Kennedy's brief tenure as president, as Cuba became a hotspot in the Cold War in 1959. Cuba had been run as a military dictatorship with close ties with the United States from 1933 to 1959. In 1959, Fidel Castro led a successful guerrilla movement to overthrow the dictatorship. By 1960, the relationship between the United States and Cuba was hostile, while the relationship between the Soviet Union and Cuba grew friendly. In the final months of the Eisenhower administration, advisors planned for the United States to train, arm, and aid a group of Cuban exiles opposed to the communist government of Fidel Castro.

Kennedy adopted the plan and green-lighted its implementation in 1961. The exiles landed at the Bay of Pigs in Cuba in April 1961 but were quickly captured by Cuban forces. The Bay of Pigs incident was the first of several attempts to oust the communist regime from Cuba.

> ## CUBA AND FLORIDA　古巴与佛罗里达
>
> Hostile relations toward Cuba persisted from the 1960s until 2015. For years, U.S. presidents refused to normalize relations with Cuba for fear of alienating Cuban Americans in Florida, and losing Florida in the presidential election. In 2015, President Barack Obama announced that formal relations between the U.S. and Cuba would resume. He visited the country in 2016.

Intervention in the Dominican Republic 对多米尼加共和国的干涉

Just before the United States became heavily engaged in the conflict in Vietnam in 1965, President Lyndon Johnson intervened in the affairs of the Dominican Republic. Earlier, in 1961, the repressive military ruler, General Rafael Trujillo, was assassinated and his regime collapsed. For four years, different groups struggled for control of the country. In 1965, it appeared that the left-of-center nationalist leader, Juan Bosch, might ascend to power in a revolt against the government. Johnson dispatched 30,000 Marines to the Dominican Republic, claiming, without evidence, that Bosch was a communist in the mold of Cuba's Fidel Castro (see page 322).

II. Debates over Carrying Out the Cold War 关于推行冷战的争论

There were major debates and disagreements in the United States about appropriate activities in terms of pursuing international and domestic goals during the Cold War. Americans continued to debate the proper balance between liberty and order. In addition, some Americans questioned the growing power of the federal government.

A. CONTAINMENT AND THE DOMESTIC RED SCARE 遏制政策与国内的红色恐怖

Though there was consensus between the major parties in regard to the policy of communist containment, Americans debated the increasingly aggressive methods of the federal and state governments in terms of identifying and applying sanctions to suspected communists in the United States.

The Strike Wave of 1946 and the Taft-Hartley Act (1947)
1946年的罢工潮与《哈特莱法案》（1947）

Immediately following World War II, the United States experienced the largest strike wave in its history, as 5 million workers walked off their jobs. Unions, which had refrained from striking during the war, feared that the gains they had made during the war would be taken away. The strike wave was largely successful, boosting wages for factory workers and allowing them to partake in the consumer culture of the era.

The Taft-Hartley Act (1947), passed over President Truman's veto, was designed to monitor and restrict the activities of organized labor. The law was passed by a conservative, Republican-dominated Congress that had been elected in 1946. The law imposed restrictions on unions that made it more difficult to strike. It allowed states to pass "right to work" laws, banning union shops (a union shop is a workplace in which all the workers are

> **AN ASSAULT ON ORGANIZED LABOR**
> **殴打工会工人**
> Organized labor saw the Taft-Hartley Act as an unreasonable attack on the union movement. Labor unions labeled the act a "slave labor" law and the "Tuff-Heartless" Act.

required to join the union after a majority had voted to do so). The law also required union leaders to pledge that they were not members of the Communist Party.

Federal Employee Loyalty and Security Program (1947) 联邦雇员忠诚于安全计划（1947）

This loyalty program barred communists and fascists from serving in federal government positions. Created by President Truman with Executive Order 9835, it also allowed for investigations into the political affiliations of current employees. Employees had to promise to uphold the Constitution and swear they were not members of the Communist Party or other "subversive" organizations.

The McCarran Internal Security Act (1950) 《麦卡伦网络安全法案》（1950）

This restrictive act mandated that communist groups in the United States register with the government. It also allowed for the arrest of suspected security risks during national emergencies. Truman saw this act as a grave threat to civil liberties and vetoed it. However, Congress passed it over his veto.

Senator Joseph McCarthy 参议员约瑟夫·麦卡锡

The most prominent elected figure in the anticommunist movement of the 1950s was Senator Joseph McCarthy, a Republican from Wisconsin. McCarthy rose to national prominence in 1950 when he announced that he had a list of 205 "known communists" who were working in the State Department. He later reduced that figure to 57, but he encouraged a mindset whereby people began to suspect those around them of being secret communists. This and similar claims, mostly baseless, created a name for McCarthy and set the stage for a host of measures to halt this perceived threat. The anticommunist movement of the 1950s is often referred to as McCarthyism because Senator McCarthy was so closely identified with it.

The Attack on Hollywood 好莱坞袭击案

Senate and House anticommunists put a great deal of effort into investigating the film and broadcast (radio and the brand-new television) industries, fearing that communists would subtly get their messages out via radio, television, and movies. In 1947, several prominent directors and writers, later known as the "Hollywood 10" were summoned to testify in Washington. They refused, citing their First Amendment rights to freedom of speech and assembly. These ten and others who refused to cooperate were "blacklisted" in the 1950s, preventing them from finding work in Hollywood.

The Threat of Nuclear War 核战威胁

Although the fear of communist plots was overstated, the threat of nuclear war was a constant presence in American life during the Cold War. Both nations invested large sums of money in nuclear weapons programs. Americans were never sure whether a conventional conflict, such as the Korean War, would turn into a nuclear war. Many Americans built bomb shelters in their basements or backyards. Local authorities established civil defense programs to build bomb shelters in public buildings and prepare the population for a nuclear emergency.

"Duck and Cover" "卧倒并掩护"

The government took a series of actions in regard to the threat of nuclear war. One action taken by the government was air-raid drills in public schools. When an alarm sounded, students would either be ushered to a fallout shelter in the basement of the school or would be ordered to "duck and cover" under their desks.

The Rosenberg Case 卢森堡事件

When the United States learned that the Soviet Union had built and tested a nuclear bomb, many Americans were convinced that communists in the United States, loyal to the Soviets, had provided them with essential information about the bomb. Ethel and Julius Rosenberg were an American couple accused of passing secrets of the nuclear bomb to the Soviet Union. The

Rosenbergs, who were members of the Communist Party, insisted on their innocence but were sent to the electric chair in 1953. Evidence has emerged since the end of the Cold War that suggests that Julius had been involved in some sort of espionage on behalf of the Soviet Union.

The Smith Act and the Communist Party 《史密斯法案》和共产党

Government prosecutors used the World War II–era Smith Act to arrest leading members of the Communist Party in several states on the grounds that they "conspired" to "organize" and "advocate" the overthrow of the government by force. Between 1949 and 1957, more than 140 communists were arrested, including the leader of the party, Eugene Dennis.

The Fall of McCarthyism 麦卡锡主义的倒台

Eventually, critics began to assert that some of the harshest anticommunist measures violated people's constitutional right to freedom of speech. Criticism became more common after the conclusion of hostilities in the Korean War (1953). Finally, Senator McCarthy himself went too far, accusing members of the military establishment of being members of the Communist Party. The Senate voted to censure him in 1954, ending the worst excesses of what many people referred to as a witch-hunt. In the case of *Yates v. United States* (1957), the Supreme Court overturned the convictions of members of the Communist Party under the Smith Act.

B. DEBATE OVER THE VIETNAM WAR 关于对越战争的争论

Americans generally supported the containment policy as it was deployed in the Korean War. However, the Vietnam War generated a sizable antiwar movement. The movement used a variety of tactics as the war escalated.

Erosion of Support for the Vietnam War 对越作战受质疑

As the Vietnam War dragged on through the latter half of the 1960s, many Americans began to see that the war was unwinnable—a quagmire from which the United States could not extricate itself. Americans began to grow impatient with the war effort and many questioned the wisdom and morality of the war. Several factors led to this questioning of the Vietnam War.

The Draft 草案

In 1964, the Selective Service System began increasing the number of young men drafted to serve in the armed forces. In 1965, the monthly totals of draftees doubled. The draft made the Vietnam War an immediate concern for millions of young men and contributed to the number of young people participating in the antiwar movement.

A "LIVING ROOM WAR" "生存空间战"

> ### A LACK OF CONSENSUS
> ### 未达成共识
> Note the evolution of popular opinion about Vietnam and the factors that contributed to antiwar sentiment among many Americans.

The Vietnam War was the first American war to occur in an era when the vast majority of Americans owned television sets (90 percent by 1960). Americans were able to see brutal images of warfare in their living rooms for the first time. Many were shocked at what they saw. A report by Morley Safer in 1965 showed Marines evacuating Vietnamese civilians from their homes in the village of Cam Ne and then setting the village on fire. More disturbing images followed and contributed to public opinion questioning the wisdom and justness of the war.

A Working-Class War 工人阶级战争

In many ways, the war in Vietnam was a working-class war. Eighty percent of the troops in Vietnam were working class and poor. Middle-class youths often managed to get college deferments or had connections to get a stateside (in the United States) position in the National Guard. In 1967, Martin Luther King, Jr., gave a speech entitled "Beyond Vietnam," condemning the war and its impact on American society.

The Unraveling of the Vietnam War 越南战争的土崩瓦解

By 1968, the war in Vietnam increasingly seemed unwinnable. The Vietcong and North Vietnamese forces launched the Tet Offensive in January (see page 319), shocking the American public with their suicidal determination. Further, extensive media coverage of the war had left many Americans questioning its morality and purpose. By 1969, the horrific 1968 My Lai Massacre (see page 319) became known to the American public, further eroding faith in the war effort. Opponents of the war became increasingly vocal as the decade wore on.

The Antiwar Movement 反战运动

The antiwar movement can be traced back to the early 1960s as small peace groups questioned the purpose of the armed advisors who were sent to Vietnam. An important antiwar group on college campuses was Students for a Democratic Society, founded in 1960 (see more on page 342). By the late 1960s, several important antiwar groups had emerged out of the growing protest movement. The National Mobilization Committee to End the War in Vietnam was formed in 1967 to organize large national protests against the war. The movement organized several large demonstrations against the war in Washington, D.C., including two massive gatherings—in November 1969 and in April 1971—that each brought approximately half a million people to the nation's capital.

Vietnam Veterans Against the War 越南老兵反战

Another significant antiwar group was the Vietnam Veterans Against the War. Born in 1967, the organization harnessed the frustrations of returning veterans of the conflict. Many front-line soldiers grew to question the tactics, and even the purpose, of the war. There were several incidents of soldiers attacking commanding officers, including "fragging"—tossing live grenades at them during action in the field.

The Shootings at Kent State and Jackson State
肯特州立大学和杰克逊州立大学的枪击事件

The antiwar movement was stunned when four students were killed at Kent State University in Ohio in May 1970, during a demonstration against President Nixon's decision to invade Cambodia. Ohio National Guardsmen opened fire on the demonstrators, killing four and wounding ten—several of them just students walking to class. Eleven days later, two African American student demonstrators were shot and killed by state police at Jackson State University in Mississippi.

Publication of the Pentagon Papers 五角大楼文件的发表

Many of the suspicions of the antiwar movement were borne out with the publication of the *Pentagon Papers*, a secret study of the Vietnam War written by the Pentagon. The study revealed official deception and secrecy. It was leaked to the press by Daniel Ellsberg, a Pentagon official critical of the direction the Vietnam War was taking. The Nixon administration tried to block *The New York Times* and the *Washington Post* from publishing the papers. Initially, the Nixon administration obtained an injunction against publication, but the Supreme Court, in the case of *New York Times v. United States* (1971), overruled the injunction and upheld the right of the newspapers to publish the information.

THE GOVERNMENT AND A FREE PRESS
政府与自由媒体

The publication of the Pentagon Papers helped to clarify free-speech issues related to the government's ability to squelch embarrassing information. The Supreme Court upheld the rights of the press.

C. THE "MILITARY–INDUSTRIAL COMPLEX," THE ARMS RACE, AND THE POWER OF THE EXECUTIVE "军工联合体"、军备竞赛与行政首长的权力

A series of debates occurred during the Cold War about the power of the president to carry out foreign and military policies. In addition, many Americans became increasingly concerned about the power of what Eisenhower termed the "military–industrial complex." Finally, debates occurred around the expansion of America's nuclear arsenal.

The "Military–Industrial Complex" "军工联合体"

The term "military–industrial complex" was popularized after President Eisenhower used it in his televised farewell address. The term implies a close-knit relationship between government officials, leaders of the military, and corporate interests, especially those involved in the production of military material and services. The implication is that important decisions about policy—including decisions about military interventions—are made, in part, to advance the interests of the military–industrial complex.

Challenging America's Nuclear Policy 对美国核政策的质疑

Starting in the 1950s and 1960s, many American began challenging the country's military priorities. In the 1960s, many protested military involvement in Vietnam (see page 326). Even before that, there were those who were critical of America's nuclear weapons policy. It became evident the United States had produced enough nuclear weapons to destroy the world several times over. The policy of "massive retaliation" implied, to many people, a dangerous readiness to use nuclear weapons (see page 317). With both the United States and Soviet Union possessing such powerful nuclear arsenals, policymakers accepted the policy of mutually assured destruction, or MAD. For some policymakers, MAD created a powerful deterrent to the use of nuclear weapons; to critics, it represented a dangerous precipice on which the world was perched. The 1964 dark comedy, *Dr. Strangelove or: How I Learned to Stop Worrying and Love the Bomb*, directed by Stanley Kubrick, depicted MAD policy gone terribly wrong. Critics of nuclear proliferation formed the Committee for a SANE Nuclear Policy in 1957 to challenge the ongoing nuclear tests being conducted by the Eisenhower administration. In 1961, the newly formed Women's Strike for Peace resonated broadly and inspired more than 50,000 women in 60 cities to march for peace.

The War Powers Act 《战争权力法案》

During the Vietnam War (see pages 318–320), many members of Congress grew increasingly frustrated with the actions of both of the presidents who carried out the war—Lyndon Johnson and Richard Nixon. When Nixon expanded the war into Cambodia and Laos, many congressional critics believed the president was abusing his powers and taking away Congress's authority to make war. The War Powers Act (1973), which passed over President Nixon's veto just after the United States had withdrawn from Vietnam, was an attempt to check presidential power and strengthen the legislative branch in matters of war. The act requires the president to report any troop deployments to Congress within 48 hours and it gave Congress the ability to force the withdrawal of U.S. troops after 60 days.

D. CONFLICTING PRIORITIES IN MIDDLE EAST POLICY 对中东的冲突政策

United States policy in the Middle East during the Cold War was driven by several, sometimes conflicting, priorities. Ideological, military, and economic concerns shaped American policy in the Middle East. After several oil crises, the United States attempted to create a policy for its energy future.

The United States, Israel, and the Arab World 美国、以色列与阿拉伯世界

Since the founding of Israel in 1948, tensions have existed in the Middle East. The Arab nations refused to recognize Israel's right to exist. Four wars occurred between Israel and its neighbors between 1948 and 1973. The United States has remained a strong ally of Israel.

In 1973, the Arab oil-producing nations—the Organization of Petroleum Exporting Countries (OPEC)—cut off exports to the United States and increased the price of oil. These moves were largely in retaliation for U.S. support of Israel in the 1973 Yom Kippur War between Israel and its Arab neighbors.

The Camp David Accords (1978) 《戴维营协议》（1978）

President Jimmy Carter succeeded in providing a foundation for a peace treaty between Egypt and Israel. The Camp David Accords are considered one of the few triumphs for President Carter's troubled presidency. In 1977 Egyptian president Anwar Sadat broke with the other leaders of the Arab world and flew to Israel to meet with Israeli prime minister Menachem Begin. Negotiations ensued between the two leaders but they were unable to come up with a peace treaty. President Carter invited them to the Camp David presidential retreat in Maryland. The three men met for 13 days and emerged with the basis for a peace treaty. The treaty resulted in an end to hostilities between Israel and Egypt, but tensions continued to exist between Israel and its other neighbors.

The Energy Crisis and the Limits of Growth 能源危机与发展局限

In the wake of the OPEC oil embargo in 1973 (see page 328), fuel prices rose dramatically through the 1970s. America had to confront a stark reality—there were limits to the amount of fossil fuels, particularly petroleum, available in the world, and much of it came from the volatile Middle East. Until the 1970s, Americans assumed petroleum was a cheap, inexhaustible commodity. The 1970s saw a dramatic spike in petroleum prices and higher prices at gas pumps.

The Iranian Revolution and the Iran Hostage Crisis 伊朗革命和伊朗人质危机

In 1979, the U.S. supported leader of Iran, Mohammad Reza Shah Pahlavi, was ousted by a revolution led by the Muslim religious leader, the Ayatollah Khomeini. The United States supported the Shah to the end. Later that year, when the United States admitted the deposed Shah to the United States for medical treatment, angry Iranian students took over the U.S. embassy and kept the personnel there hostage. President Jimmy Carter finally secured their release after the U.S. presidential election in late 1980, but they were not actually released until 33 minutes into the administration of President Reagan in January 1981.

The Carter Doctrine 卡特主义

President Jimmy Carter asserted a more active role for the United States in the Middle East in 1980. The Carter Doctrine stated that the United States would repel any outside force that attempted to gain control of the Persian Gulf region. The doctrine reflects concerns about protecting United States oil interests, with an eye on halting any steps by the Soviet Union toward expanding its influence in the region. The more aggressive stance in the Middle East was brought about by the Iranian Revolution (1979) (see above) and Soviet intervention of Afghanistan, which also began in 1979. The Soviets had sent troops into Afghanistan to initially prop up a pro-Soviet government in the face of a concerted rebellion led by the Afghani Mujahideen rebel group. Soviet forces initiated a coup, installed a new government, and remained in the country for a decade. Carter saw the presence of Soviet forces near the Middle East as a threat to American interests in the region.

Toward a National Energy Policy 国家能源政策

While many policymakers were trying to find alternative sources of power to Middle East petroleum, some were looking for ways the United States could reduce its consumption of energy. Americans are by far the largest consumers of energy, consuming nearly twice the amount as the average resident of the United Kingdom or France. Starting as early as the 1950s, the United States increased reliance on nuclear power (see below). A National Maximum Speed Law was enacted in 1974 (since repealed). President Jimmy Carter, through the newly created Department of Energy (1977), encouraged conservation measures, such as turning down thermostats and turning off lights when not in use. He also encouraged investment in renewable sources of energy, such as solar power. Americans, however, were remarkably resistant to adopting conservation measures.

Nuclear Energy 核能源

As the availability of petroleum from the Middle East came into question in the 1970s, some Americans put faith in nuclear energy as an alternative to fossil fuels. In a nuclear power plant, a nuclear reaction produces heat to drive steam turbines that, in turn, run electric generators—rather than using water power or burning coal or oil to run the turbines. The material needed for nuclear power, such as uranium, is relatively cheap and plentiful, and the reaction does not produce the greenhouse gas, carbon dioxide. However, there are problems associated with nuclear power. The waste product of a nuclear reaction is radioactive and must be safely disposed of. Further, nuclear power brings with it the possibility of catastrophic accidents (see more on the accident at Three Mile Island, Pennsylvania, page 338). Nuclear power did not achieve the level of energy generation that planners had hoped for. Amid concerns about cost overruns and the safety of nuclear energy, only about half of the planned 253 generators in the United States were ever built. Currently, nearly 20 percent of U.S. electricity is generated by nuclear power.

KEY CONCEPT 8.2 THE HIGH TIDE OF LIBERALISM
核心概念8.2：自由主义高潮

Liberalism—an approach to politics that embraced anticommunism abroad and an activist federal government at home—reached its high point in the mid-1960s. Liberalism generated a wide variety of political and cultural responses in the United States.

I. The Civil Rights Movement 民权运动

An influential civil rights movement emerged in the years following World War II. Civil rights activists sought to press America to fulfill the promises of the Reconstruction era. The movement achieved some marked political and legal successes in ending legal segregation. However, progress toward achieving full racial equality in the United States proved to be a more daunting task.

A. STRATEGIES AND TACTICS OF THE CIVIL RIGHTS MOVEMENT
民权运动的战略与战术

After World War II, civil rights activists used a variety of strategies and tactics, including legal challenges, civil disobedience, nonviolent protests, and direct action, to press for an end to racial discrimination.

The Civil Rights Movement in the 1950s 20世纪50年代的民权运动

One of the most significant reform movements in American history blossomed in the 1950s—the civil rights movement. The movement challenged the legal basis of the segregation of African Americans in the United States, but it also challenged the pervasive racism of American society. This racism had justified the existence of slavery and the persistence of Jim

Crow segregation. The movement forced America to examine its most cherished institutions and also to reevaluate its patterns of thought.

World War II and the Origins of the Civil Rights Movement
第二次世界大战与民权运动的起源

World War II was a transformative experience for many African American men and women. Many returning soldiers felt a sense of empowerment and engagement they had not previously felt. These veterans had taken part in the NAACP's "Double V" campaign during the war—victory against fascism abroad and victory against racism at home. The injustices of American life seemed especially reprehensible to men who had just risked their lives serving their country. In addition, the migration of many African American men and women from the familiar patterns of rural southern life to the new challenges of urban, industrial America whetted their appetite for change and justice. This was the generation that would become the leaders of the civil rights movement in the decades after the war.

Rosa Parks and the Montgomery Bus Boycott (1955–1956)
罗莎·帕克斯与蒙哥马利巴士抵制运动（1955—1956）

Rosa Parks was a civil rights activist who refused to give up her seat to a white person on a Montgomery, Alabama, city bus in 1955. She was arrested for this action. Her arrest led to the Montgomery bus boycott, which lasted about a year (1955–1956). The boycott led to the bus company ending its policy of making African Americans give up their seats to whites.

Martin Luther King, Jr., and Nonviolent Civil Disobedience
马丁·路德·金与非暴力不合作

The Montgomery bus boycott was led by a young reverend, Martin Luther King, Jr., from Atlanta. King's leadership during the boycott made him a well-known figure. He soon became the central figure in the civil rights movement of the 1950s and 1960s. King advocated the tactic of civil disobedience to directly challenge unjust practices.

The Civil Rights Movement in the 1960s 20世纪60年代的民权运动

The civil rights movement continued into the 1960s. As the 1960s began, a younger generation of activists began to play a prominent role in the movement. Over time, rifts developed between the older, church-based leadership of the movement and a younger cadre of activists.

The Lunch Counter Sit-ins (1960) 午餐台静坐运动（1960）

In 1960, students in Tennessee and North Carolina began a campaign of "sit-ins" at lunch counters to protest segregation. The sit-ins occurred as some members of the movement grew frustrated with simply protesting and pushed the movement to take direct action to challenge and defy racist practices. The lunch counter sit-ins began in Greensboro, North Carolina, when four African American students challenged the "whites only" policy of a Woolworth's lunch counter and sat at the counter. The lunch counter sit-ins spread to other cities, including Nashville. They put segregation on the front pages of newspapers and eventually pressured companies to end the practice.

The Freedom Rides (1961) 自由之行（1961）

The Freedom Rides occurred in 1961, the year after the Supreme Court ruled that state laws separating the races on interstate transportation facilities were unconstitutional. Still, states maintained Jim Crow segregation codes that separated African American passengers from white passengers. In 1961, the Congress on Racial Equality (CORE) organized a series of bus rides through the South, with African-American passengers riding alongside white passengers, to challenge these local codes. These "Freedom Rides" met a great deal of resistance in the South. In Alabama, a mob slashed the tires of one bus and then firebombed it. President Kennedy finally sent federal marshals to Alabama to protect the Freedom Riders and to enforce federal law.

"Bull" Connor and the Birmingham Campaign (1963)
"公牛"康纳与伯明翰运动（1963）

Martin Luther King, Jr., and the Southern Christian Leadership Conference decided to launch a major campaign in Birmingham, Alabama, to protest racial segregation in the spring of 1963. The campaign proved to be a turning point in the push for federal legislation. The public safety commissioner of Birmingham, Eugene "Bull" Connor, would not tolerate public demonstrations. He used fire hoses, police dogs, and brutal force to put down the campaign. The campaign included a children's march, sometimes called the "children's crusade," in May 1963. Connor used violent tactics to break up the children's march. Images of police brutality brought the Birmingham campaign to the attention of the nation and helped to bring public sympathy to the side of the civil rights movement. During the Birmingham campaign, King was arrested and wrote his famous "Letter from Birmingham Jail." This letter was written in response to a call by white clergy members to allow the legal system to address the issue of racial injustice. King insisted that the black community had waited long enough for change to happen. The Birmingham campaign paved the way for the passage of the Civil Rights Act, a year later.

The March on Washington (1963) 华盛顿大游行（1963）

In 1963, the civil rights movement held one of the biggest demonstrations in American history, in Washington, DC. More than 200,000 people gathered to march, sing, and hear speeches, including Martin Luther King, Jr.'s, "I Have a Dream." Some of the tensions that divided the civil rights movement in the years to come were evident at the March on Washington. The leader of the Student Nonviolent Coordinating Committee, John Lewis, was told by some of the older organizers of the event to tone down his fiery rhetoric. The original draft of his speech, which urged the movement to march "through the heart of Dixie the way Sherman did . . . and burn Jim Crow to the ground," anticipated the growth of a more militant, direct-action oriented tendency within the civil rights movement in the coming years.

The Selma to Montgomery March (1965) 赛尔玛—蒙哥马利游行（1965）

With passage of the Civil Rights Act, the movement focused on voting rights. A major march in Alabama, from Selma to Montgomery, took place in March 1965. As the marchers crossed a bridge over the Alabama River, county and state police blocked their path and, after ordering them to turn back, attacked them with clubs and tear gas. The incident, known as "Bloody Sunday," was broadcast on national television and aroused indignation among many Americans. The march was finally held later in the month. "Bloody Sunday" and the Selma to Montgomery march raised awareness of the issue of voting rights.

B. GOVERNMENT RESPONSES TO CIVIL RIGHTS ACTIVISM 政府对民权运动的反应

The three branches of the federal government made several important policy shifts on race from the 1940s through the 1960s. These shifts included the 1948 desegregation of the armed forces, the Supreme Court's 1954 decision in the case of *Brown v. Board of Education*, and the passage of the Civil Rights Act of 1964. These measures, prompted in large part by civil rights activism, were intended to promote greater racial justice.

Truman and Civil Rights 杜鲁门与民权

President Truman, the Democratic president from Missouri who took office when President Franklin Roosevelt died in 1945, was an early supporter of civil rights. He created the Committee on Civil Rights in 1946 and pushed Congress to enact the committee's recommendations in 1948. That year, Truman issued Executive Order 9981 to ban segregation in the military, but he failed to implement it until the Korean War (when the military was in need of additional personnel). Truman was motivated to take these steps, both out of personal conviction and in response to actions by civil rights activists. Truman felt that he could not go too far because he would lose the support of southern Democrats.

A Favorable Supreme Court 受赞许的最高法院

Early civil rights activists pressed their cause in a number of ways, and many longed to bring the issue of segregation before the Supreme Court. The Supreme Court in 1954 was far more liberal than the 1896 Supreme Court, which had issued the infamous *Plessy v. Ferguson* decision. In 1953, President Eisenhower appointed a new, more liberal, chief justice: Earl Warren. The NAACP and its lead lawyer, Thurgood Marshall, thought the time was right to bring a key civil rights case to the court.

The Case of *Brown v. Board of Education of Topeka* (1954)
布朗诉托皮卡教育局案（1954）

The case of *Brown v. Board of Education of Topeka* was actually several cases looked at simultaneously by the Supreme Court. The Brown in the case was the Reverend Oliver Brown, whose eight-year-old daughter had to go to an African American school more than a mile from her house rather than attend a white school nearby. The court heard a variety of types of evidence, including studies on the psychological impact of segregation on young people. The court ruled unanimously that segregation in public schools was unfair and had to end. The Brown decision set in motion a major upheaval in American society. It gave great encouragement to the civil rights movement, which believed that the federal government was in favor of civil rights.

Kennedy, Johnson, and the Politics of Civil Rights 肯尼迪、约翰逊与民权政治

For years the Democratic Party had walked a fine line when it came to civil rights for African Americans. On the one hand, many Democratic leaders since the Franklin Roosevelt administration believed that extending civil rights to African Americans was the correct and just thing to do, but on the other hand, the party did not want to alienate its southern wing. As the civil rights movement put the issue on the national agenda and violence by white southerners put the issue on the nightly news, Democratic leaders had to react. In June 1963, the same month that civil rights leader Medgar Evers was murdered in front of his house in Jackson, Mississippi, President Kennedy gave a national address in which he called civil rights a "moral issue" and pledged to support civil rights legislation. After Kennedy's assassination in November 1963, President Lyndon Johnson, himself a southerner from Texas, took up the cause of civil rights legislation with vigor, pressuring reluctant Democratic legislators to support it.

Civil Rights Act (1964) 《民权法案》（1964）

The Civil Rights Act was passed by Congress and signed by President Lyndon Johnson in the summer of 1964. The act was intended to end discrimination based on race and gender. The Civil Rights Act guaranteed all Americans equal access to public accommodations, public education, and voting. Another section banned discrimination in employment based on race or gender.

The Voting Rights Act (1965) 《投票权法案》（1965）

The Voting Rights Act, passed in August 1965, authorized the federal government to oversee voter registration in counties with low African American registration. The act also outlawed literacy tests and poll taxes—means of preventing African Americans from voting. By 1968, the number of southern African American voters jumped from one million to more than three million. In many ways, the Civil Rights Act and the Voting Rights Act represented the culmination of the civil rights movement.

C. CHALLENGES FOR THE CIVIL RIGHTS MOVEMENT 民权运动面临的挑战

A series of challenges confronted the civil rights movement as the 1960s progressed. White resistance to desegregation grew more intense and slowed the progress of the movement. In addition, a series of debates occurred within the movement in the mid-1960s over philosophy and tactics.

"Massive Resistance"—in Little Rock Crisis and Beyond
"巨大阻力"——小石城危机与其他事件

The civil rights movement unleashed a violent backlash by many southern whites. These people vowed to engage in "massive resistance" against efforts toward integration. An example of the backlash was evident in the reaction of white southerners to segregation in Little Rock, Arkansas, in 1957 and 1958. The conflict in Little Rock began in 1957 when local authorities decided to allow nine African American students to enroll in Central High School at the beginning of the school year. Governor Orville Faubus refused to cooperate with the plan, leading to mob action and violence outside the high school. Faubus initially mobilized the National Guard to block the African American students from entering the school; later he removed all state authorities, leaving local police to deal with a combustible situation. The violence and the national news coverage of the flouting of federal authority convinced Eisenhower to send federal troops. Although he was decisive in Little Rock, his administration was otherwise very reluctant to take action in regard to civil rights for African Americans.

From "Freedom Now!" to "Black Power!" 从"现在就要自由"到"黑人需要权力"

As the civil rights movement achieved success in ending legal segregation (*de jure* segregation) and removing barriers to voting, pervasive problems continued to plague the African American community. Patterns of segregation enforced by custom, rather than law (*de facto* segregation) persisted. Also, the bitter realities of poverty, substandard housing, and lack of decent jobs continued to plague large sections of the African American community. A younger generation of activists continued to push the movement in a more militant direction and to demand power, not just rights. After 1964, a central rallying cry of the movement, "Freedom now," was, often replaced by the call for "Black Power!"

In 1966, the Black Panthers Party took up the call for a "Black Power" movement, embracing self-defense and militant rhetoric. Initially, the Back Panthers focused on community organizing; however, their activities grew increasingly confrontational.

Malcolm X 马尔柯姆·艾克斯

By the mid-1960s, many African American activists were attempting to push civil rights activism in a more militant, confrontational direction. Malcolm X was a central figure in the more militant turn the civil rights movement took. Between 1952 and 1964 he was a member and then a leader of the Nation of Islam, an African American group that shares certain practices with mainstream Islam, but differs in several important respects. The organization advocated that African Americans organize among themselves, separate from whites. After making a pilgrimage to Mecca in 1964 and seeing Muslims of different races interacting as equals, Malcolm X revised his views about black separatism. He also left the Nation of Islam. In 1965, he was killed by assassins from the Nation of Islam, but his words continued to inspire the civil rights movement.

The Assassination of King (1968) 马丁·路德·金被暗杀（1968）

Martin Luther King, Jr., was killed by an assassin on April 4, 1968, in Memphis, Tennessee. King's assassination was both a source of national mourning and an indicator of the end of the African American civil rights movement of the era. The movement had accomplished much, but was unable to provide a solution for many of the problems facing the African American community. As the 1960s wound down, rioting engulfed many African American neighborhoods, highlighting the continued frustrations of the black community.

II. The Civil Rights Movement Inspires Other Movements to Challenge Inequalities 民权运动激发了其他反抗不平等待遇的运动

The visibility and successes of the civil rights movement inspired other movements for social change. These movements, focused on gender, sexuality, and ethnicity, addressed a host of inequalities and issues of identity.

A. MOVEMENTS FOR WOMEN'S RIGHTS AND GAY LIBERATION
女权运动与同性恋解放运动

Activists began to challenge ingrained assumptions around gender. Movements developed in the 1960s to push for greater social and economic equality for women and for gays and lesbians.

The Women's Liberation Movement　妇女解放运动

In the 1960s, a women's liberation movement developed, challenging inequities in the job market, representations of women in the media, violence against women, and an ingrained set of social values. Women joined with others through consciousness-raising groups and realized that their contributions to society historically and within their own families were deemed less important than men. They saw connections to the larger society, giving rise to the motto, "the personal is political." Many women were inspired by Betty Friedan's 1963 book, *The Feminine Mystique*, which challenged the traditional options in life offered to middle-class women. Friedan was one of several women to found the National Organization for Women (1966), the leading liberal organization supporting women's rights. The movement gave birth to the nationally circulated magazine, *Ms.*, founded by Gloria Steinem, Letty Cottin Pogrebin, and others. Many women in the movement had come out of New Left activist organizations (see pages 342–343), empowered to fight for a better world, but frustrated at the treatment women received in these organizations.

Protest at the Miss America Pageant　美国小姐选美比赛的抗议

Many Americans heard about the women's liberation movement for the first time from news reports of a protest at the 1968 Miss America pageant. The pageant exemplified, to the protesters, society's attitude toward women in which women were valued for their looks above all else. Women were expected to parade in bathing suits and give vacuous answers to questions, in order to win male approval.

Title IX (1972)　《教育法修正案第九条》（1972）

An important success of the women's liberation movement was Congress's passage of Title IX of the Educational Amendments of 1972. Title IX banned gender discrimination in all aspects of education, such as faculty hiring and admissions. It has had a major impact on funding for female sports activities at the high school and college level.

The Gay Liberation Movement　同性恋解放运动

The gay liberation movement was born in 1969 when patrons at the Stonewall Inn, a gay bar in New York's Greenwich Village, resisted a raid by the police and fought back. The event brought a series of grievances into the open. Gay men and women had suffered discrimination in many walks of life, including in government civil-service jobs. Many gays attempted to avoid such discrimination by concealing their sexual identity and remaining "in the closet."

B. LATINOS, AMERICAN INDIANS, AND ASIAN AMERICANS PRESS FOR JUSTICE
拉丁美洲人、美洲印第安人和亚裔美国人迫切要求公正待遇

In the wake of the African American civil rights movement, various ethnic groups, including Latinos, American Indians, and Asian Americans, pushed for a redress of past injustices as well as economic and social equality.

The American Indian Movement　美洲印第安人运动

The example set by the civil rights movement also inspired a movement to fight for justice for American Indians. The American Indian Movement was founded in 1968. The following year, the movement made headlines when several dozen activists seized control of Alcatraz Island, in the San Francisco Bay, claiming the former prison belonged to the first inhabitants of the area—American Indians. The movement eventually won greater autonomy over tribal lands and affairs.

Cesar Chavez and the United Farm Workers 恺撒·查维斯和农场工人联合会

Cesar Chavez and Delores Huerta founded the United Farm Workers in 1962 to protect the interests of migrant farmers, including many Mexican Americans. The UFW organized a nationwide boycott of grapes to pressure farm owners to pay their workers a decent wage. The boycott did result in a wage increase in 1970.

C. POVERTY AMID AFFLUENCE 富足中的贫穷

The post–World War II period was marked by a growing middle class and the perception of overall affluence. However, writers and activists raised awareness of the persistence of poverty among large sectors of the population, which resulted in efforts to address the issue of poverty in America.

Abundance in Postwar America 战后美国的富足

Perhaps the most remarkable development of the postwar years was the unprecedented growth of the economy and the rising living standard for millions of Americans. The gross domestic product of the country—the total value of goods and services produced in the United States in a year—rose dramatically between 1945 and 1960, from $200 billion to $500 billion. Such growth is unprecedented in American society. In this period we see a dramatic rise in the middle class, as millions of Americans from working-class backgrounds were able to achieve many of the markers of middle-class life—home and car ownership, a college education, and a comfortable income.

The Other America 《美国的另一面》

Large pockets of poverty persisted despite the growth of the postwar economy. Many Americans, including President John F. Kennedy, were made aware of the existence of pervasive poverty alongside the affluence of American society by Michael Harrington's book, *The Other America: Poverty in the United States* (1962). Harrington, a writer and socialist activist, noted that 40 to 50 million Americans lived in poverty, many in decaying urban slums and many in isolated rural towns. He noted that many of the technological developments associated with economic growth, such as mechanization of agriculture and automation of factory work, resulted in job displacement and bitter poverty. Harrington's work helped shape the domestic agendas of President John F. Kennedy and President Lyndon Johnson.

D. THE GROWTH OF THE ENVIRONMENTAL MOVEMENT 环境运动的发展

As the American economy expanded dramatically in the postwar period, critics began to question the growing exploitation of the country's natural resources. In the 1960s, writers and activists began to call attention to the abuse of the natural environment. They spearheaded an environmental movement that was able to successfully push for measures intended to address these problems.

The Environmental Movement 环境运动

Another important movement for change in the 1960s and 1970s was the environmental movement. The movement became a national phenomenon and led to some important changes in laws and consciousness. Environmental issues were brought to the public's attention by Rachel Carson's 1962 book *Silent Spring*, which vividly described how modern society was poisoning the earth. Carson described the impact on the environment of the agricultural pesticide DDT. Many participants in the environmental movement were veterans of the New Left and of the movement to end the Vietnam War. Many of these New Left activists criticized corporate power and undue influence. Finally, the environmental movement was connected to the counterculture of the 1960s. The so-called hippies of the 1960s encouraged people to rid themselves of material possessions and live a more simple life. The environmental movement gained national exposure when the first Earth Day was celebrated in April 1970. That same year, the Nixon Administration created the Environmental Protection Agency (EPA) to oversee regulatory and clean-up efforts and approved the Clean Air Act to set standards for air quality.

The Dangers of Nuclear Energy and Three Mile Island 核能源的危险和三里岛事件

The environmental movement focused increasingly on the dangers of nuclear energy as the decade of the 1970s progressed (see more on the growth of nuclear energy, page 330). Groups such as the Clamshell Alliance in New England and the Abalone Alliance in California attracted thousands of activists. The movement gained strength in the wake of the worst nuclear-industry accident in U.S. history. In 1979, a partial meltdown of the core in one of the reactors at the Three Mile Island power plant in Pennsylvania resulted in the release of radioactive gases and radioactive materials into the environment. The accident was one of several that have dampened enthusiasm for nuclear energy. In 1986, a catastrophic accident occurred at a nuclear plant in Chernobyl, Ukraine (part of the Soviet Union). An explosion led to the release of large quantities of radioactive material into the environment over much of the western portion of the Soviet Union and parts of Europe. More recently, in 2011, an earthquake and tsunami led to three nuclear meltdowns at the Fukushima nuclear plant in Japan. The Chernobyl and Fukushima disasters are the first and second worst of almost one hundred accidents at nuclear power plants.

III. Liberal Gains and Challenges from the Left and the Right
左右两派对自由主义的收获与面临的挑战

Liberal ideals shaped federal policies and several key Supreme Court decisions in the 1960s and 1970s. This liberal agenda came under attack from groups and individuals on the left who insisted that the steps being taken were insufficient to create a truly just and equitable world. The gains of liberalism would also come under attack from a resurgent conservative movement that showed signs of life in the 1960s and 1970s, but did not come to fruition until the last decades of the twentieth century.

A. THE LIBERAL AGENDA IN THE 1960S 20世纪60年代的自由主义议程

Liberalism reached a high point in the mid-1960s, with its focus on an interventionist government at home and an anticommunist foreign policy.

The Elements of 1960s Liberalism 20世纪60年代的自由主义要素

The high point of 1960s liberalism was the domestic agenda of President Lyndon Johnson, called the "Great Society" (see below). However, 1960s liberalism has deep roots and drew its inspiration and strength from a number of sources.

At home, a key element of 1960s liberalism was the belief in the efficacy of government initiatives in addressing a series of social problems. This belief can be traced back to the Progressive agenda of the 1900s and 1910s, as well as to the New Deal of the 1930s. Liberals looked favorably upon the thinking of the economist John Maynard Keynes, who encouraged government expenditures both to stimulate economic activity as well as to address broader social and economic goals. The liberal coalition that coalesced in mid-century also included moderates within the labor movement, such as Walter Reuther of the United Automobile Workers. These moderate labor leaders had purged the labor movement of communists and radicals in the years after World War II. The coalition also included civil-society groups, such as the American Civil Liberties Union, the National Association for the Advancement of Colored People, and Americans for Democratic Action.

In terms of foreign policy, mid-century liberalism was decidedly anticommunist. Although liberals condemned the excesses of the anticommunist "witch-hunt" of the 1950s, it nonetheless embraced the cause of containing international communism. Some of the liberal intellectuals of the 1950s and 1960s had earlier allied themselves with the communist movement of the 1930s. Over time, however, the brutality and deceitfulness of Stalinism pushed them toward an anticommunist position. Liberal anticommunism was articulated in a book by Harvard historian Arthur Schlesinger, *The Vital Center: The Politics of Freedom* (1949).

Liberalism in the White House—From Kennedy to Johnson
白宫的自由主义——从肯尼迪到约翰逊

In many ways, John F. Kennedy's election in 1960 symbolized a break with the conservatism of the 1950s and an embrace of liberalism. Kennedy's domestic agenda was called the "New Frontier." Kennedy's presidency was cut short by an assassin's bullet, less than three years into his presidency.

President Kennedy's sense of idealism and his commitment to service are embodied in the Peace Corps. The program was established by Kennedy in 1961 to assist underdeveloped countries in Africa, Latin America, and Asia. Under the program, American volunteers work for two years at a particular site, serving as teachers, health workers, or agricultural advisors. The program still exists.

To mend frayed relations with the developing world, Kennedy created the Agency for International Development to coordinate aid to foreign countries, and the Alliance for Progress, a series of development projects in Latin America.

Lyndon Johnson took office upon the assassination of President Kennedy in November 1963. Johnson, a Texas Democrat, proved to be a remarkably effective president, passing a host of domestic programs that rivaled the New Deal in scope. However, his administration took a tragic turn, as Johnson's hopes for a "Great Society" were damaged by a costly and unpopular war in Vietnam (see pages 318–320 and 325–327).

B. THE GREAT SOCIETY AND THE SUPREME COURT ADVANCE OF THE LIBERAL AGENDA 伟大的社会计划与最高法院推进自由主义议程

President Lyndon Johnson's Great Society programs represented the high point of the liberal agenda. Johnson spearheaded a series of programs that sought to end racial discrimination, alleviate poverty, and address other social issues. A series of important Supreme Court decisions from the 1950s to the 1970s expanded democracy and individual freedoms.

The Great Society　伟大的社会计划

A major goal of President Johnson's Great Society program was to end poverty in the United States. Great Society programs included the development of Medicare and Medicaid, welfare programs, and public housing. Johnson created the Office of Economic Opportunity, which oversaw many of the Great Society initiatives. These programs have had limited success. The cycle of poverty proved to be too difficult to break in a short period of time. Further, the war in Vietnam became increasingly costly, diverting hundreds of billions of dollars that could have been used for antipoverty programs. Part of the Great Society included reforming the restrictive immigration policies that had been put in effect in the 1920s. The Immigration Act of 1965 continued to limit the number of immigrants in the United States, but it eliminated the quota system based on national origins (see more on immigration reform, page 347).

> ### FEDERAL PROGRAMS
> ### 联邦政府计划
>
> Note the continuities between the New Deal of the 1930s and the Great Society of the 1960s. Both expanded the role of the federal government in the lives of ordinary Americans. Both met with only limited success.

The Warren Court　沃伦法院

Earl Warren was chief justice of the Supreme Court from 1953 to 1969. The Court under his leadership moved in a decidedly liberal direction. The first case Warren dealt with as chief justice was the landmark *Brown* case (see page 333). Through the 1960s, the Warren court continued to protect the rights of minorities, reinforced the separation of church and state, established an individual's right to privacy, and protected the rights of those accused of crimes. Liberals have generally welcomed Warren Court decisions, while conservatives have accused him of practicing judicial activism.

> ### CHIEF JUSTICES　首席大法官
>
> The AP exam does not require you to know all the chief justices of the Supreme Court, but you should be familiar with John Marshall (1801–1835) and Earl Warren (1953–1969). Both courts maintained a consistent ideological approach that is evident in the respective decisions of each.

Expanding the Rights of the Accused　扩大被告的权利

Two important decisions expanded the rights of those accused of crimes. In *Gideon v. Wainwright* (1963), the Supreme Court ruled that the states must provide impoverished defendants with court-appointed attorneys. Previously, this stipulation only applied to federal court procedures. In *Miranda v. Arizona* (1966) the court ruled that arrested people must be read basic rights, now known as *Miranda Rights*, including the right to remain silent and the right to have a lawyer.

The Right to Privacy　隐私权

Although the right to privacy is not specifically mentioned in the Constitution, the Warren Court asserted that this right is implicit in it. In *Griswold v. Connecticut* (1965) the court ruled that laws forbidding the use of birth-control devices were unconstitutional. The right to privacy would become important in the case of *Roe v. Wade* (1973), which insisted that states allow abortions during the first two trimesters of pregnancy.

Free Speech　言论自由权

In *Tinker v. Des Moines* (1969), the Supreme Court ruled that a school board prohibition against students wearing black armbands in protest of the war in Vietnam was unconstitutional. The court ruled that students in school had the right to free speech, including symbolic speech, as long as their actions did not interfere with the educational process.

In *Brandenberg v. Ohio* (1969), the court ruled that the government cannot restrict inflammatory speech unless that speech is likely to directly incite imminent unlawful action. The case revolved around an incendiary interview with a Ku Klux Klan leader. Local authorities arrested him under a criminal syndicalism statute. The decision set the precedent of protecting anti-government and provocative speech.

Freedom of the Press　出版自由

In *New York Times v. Sullivan* (1964), the Supreme Court overturned a lower court libel award of $500,000 to L. B. Sullivan, a public safety commissioner in Montgomery, Alabama. Sullivan had sued *The New York Times* for running an ad calling attention to the violence being committed in the South against civil-rights demonstrators. Sullivan contended that the ad libeled him, even if it did not mention him by name. White southern officials frequently used plaintiff-friendly libel laws to curb reporting of civil rights issues. The court found such laws were detrimental to a free press. The court set a higher standard for libel—insisting that in order to prove libel public officials must show that a publication exhibited "actual malice." Specifically, a public official filing suit must show that a publication knew a statement was false and or recklessly disregarded the truth. The *Sullivan* decision has been the court's most forceful defense of press freedom.

Reapportionment and "One person, One vote"　连任与 "一人一票"

In *Baker v. Carr* (1966), the Supreme Court ruled that states must periodically redraw legislative districts so they have roughly equal numbers of people. At the time, Tennessee had not redrawn its legislative districts for more than 60 years. Urban areas such as Memphis had grown much faster than rural districts. Without reapportionment, urban areas would be underrepresented, violating the principle of "one-person, one-vote."

Prayer in Public Schools and the Separation of Church and State
公立学校的祈祷与政教分离

In *Engel v. Vitale* (1962), the Supreme Court ruled that the Regents' Prayer, a state-mandated prayer that was recited by public school children in New York State, was unconstitutional because it violated the doctrine of separation of church and state.

CHURCH AND STATE IN AMERICAN HISTORY
美国历史上的教会与国家

The relationship between church and state has been an issue throughout American history, from Roger Williams and the founding of Rhode Island in the 1630s to recent controversies about the teaching of evolution in public schools.

C. THE CONSERVATIVE RESPONSE TO RAPID SOCIAL AND ECONOMIC CHANGE
保守派对迅速变化的社会与经济的反应

Conservatives perceived that society was under threat from many of the transformations that occurred in the postwar period. They challenged many of the trends they saw: urban unrest, a perceived increase in juvenile delinquency, and new ideas about family structures.

The Origins of the Conservative Movement 保守主义运动的起源

The modern conservative movement came of age and became a powerful force with the victory of Ronald Reagan in the presidential election of 1980 (see more on the modern conservative movement in Period 9). However, the origins of this movement can be seen in the 1960s. Many Americans were dismayed by the street protests against the Vietnam War and the permissive attitudes of the counterculture. They also reacted negatively to the changing nature of the American family and the rise in divorce rates. In addition, many white southerners grew hostile toward the tactics and the gains of the civil rights movement.

As early as the 1960s, we begin to see divisions within the conservative movement that have persisted within the movement down to the present. On the one hand, we see the growth of an angry, paranoid conservatism, evident in the "massive resistance" movement in the South, the John Birch Society, and the 1968 candidacy of George Wallace for president. On the other hand, we see the growth of a more mainstream conservatism, evident in the influential magazine, *National Review*, edited by William F. Buckley and the candidacy of Barry Goldwater for president in 1964.

Young Americans for Freedom 美国青年争取自由组织

Conservatives founded Young Americans for Freedom in the 1960s. The YAF developed their founding document, the Sharon Statement, at a meeting at the estate of the conservative intellectual, William F. Buckley, in Sharon, Connecticut (1960). The organization brought together several strands of conservative thought—connections between free markets and "personal freedom," an emphasis on a muscular anticommunism, and a push toward limiting the size and scope of government.

Barry Goldwater and the Origins of the "New Right"
巴里·戈德华特和"新右派"的起源

Activists associated with Young Americans for Freedom became active in the campaign of Republican Senator Barry Goldwater for president in 1964. President Lyndon Johnson won reelection, capturing 61 percent of the popular vote. However, despite losing, the Goldwater campaign generated a great deal of grassroots enthusiasm. In many ways, Goldwater's campaign represented the beginning of the ascendency of a conservative movement that would become a force to reckon with later in the twentieth century (see Period 9).

D. THE NEW LEFT 新左派

Individuals and groups on the left criticized the liberal agenda of the 1960s for doing too little to significantly challenge the economic and racial inequalities at home and for pursuing an immoral foreign policy.

Students for a Democratic Society and the Rise of the New Left
学生争取民主社会组织和新左派的兴起

One of the most significant organizations in the antiwar movement of the 1960s was Students for a Democratic Society (SDS), with chapters at major college campuses across the country.

The name was coined in 1960, with SDS developing out of an earlier organization. SDS held its first national convention at Port Huron, Michigan. At this convention the organization adopted a guiding manifesto, known as the Port Huron Statement, which became an important document in the development of the New Left. The document, written by Tom Hayden, stressed participatory democracy and direct action. The label "New Left" applies to activist organizations of the 1960s that broke with the worker-oriented, top-down movement that developed in the 1930s. SDS continued to grow throughout the 1960s, but disbanded in 1969 amid intense factional infighting.

E. THE DECLINE OF PUBLIC TRUST IN THE 1970s 20世纪70年代公众信任的降低

A series of events and trends in the 1970s—economic decline and dislocation, major political scandals, a sense of moral decay, and a perception of misguided foreign policy priorities—contributed to a decline in public trust and confidence in the government.

"Stagflation" "滞胀"

The economy of the United States had remained strong throughout the 1960s, despite the costs of the war in Vietnam. As the 1970s began, however, the economy began to contract. By the early 1970s, economists noted an unusual set of phenomena—both unemployment and inflation were at high levels (both over 6 percent). High unemployment is a sign of a stagnant economy; but high inflation is usually a sign of an active economy. After all, it is consumer demand that pushes prices up. The incidence of both occurring simultaneously was dubbed "stagflation." Stagflation continued throughout the 1970s.

"Whip Inflation Now" "立刻制止通货膨胀"运动

President Gerald Ford attempted to address the economic malaise of the 1970s, but his solutions struck the public as inadequate. Ford's most public initiative was the promotion of the Whip Inflation Now (WIN) campaign. The campaign encouraged people to be more disciplined with their money. Supporters were encouraged to wear "WIN" buttons.

Foreign Policy "Failures" of the 1970s 20世纪70年代外交政策的"失败"

President Jimmy Carter (1977–1981) faced a number of foreign policy challenges with mixed results. In one area, pursuing peace in the Middle East, Carter achieved a major victory (see page 329). When it came to the Panama Canal Zone and the Iran hostage crisis (1979–1981) (see page 329), the results of Carter's foreign policy were more mixed, and they provided an opening for Republicans to assert that Carter had left the United States in a weaker position.

The Panama Canal (1977) 巴拿马运河（1977）

President Jimmy Carter negotiated two treaties with Panama in 1977, the Torrijos-Carter Treaties, which turned the Panama Canal Zone over to Panama. One agreement, known as the Panama Canal Treaty, called for the United States to turn over control of the canal to Panama by December 31, 1999. The other agreement asserted that the canal shall remain neutral and open to shipping of all nations; if any country challenged this neutrality, the United States reserved the right to intervene. The treaties were ratified by the Senate in 1978. Many conservatives, notably Senators Strom Thurmond and Jesse Helms, were harshly critical of the treaties for surrendering direct control of a major strategic asset.

F. CLASHING POLITICAL VALUES　冲突的政治价值观

The postwar period was marked by a number of political and social clashes between conservatives and liberals about the power of the presidency and the federal government, and about movements that sought to expand individual rights.

Watergate, the Undoing of President Nixon, and the Limits of Presidential Power　水门事件、尼克松总统的垮台与对总统权力的限制

A major effect of the Watergate scandal was that it reduced people's trust in government. The scandal began in June 1972, when five men were caught breaking into the headquarters of the Democratic Party at the Watergate Hotel in Washington, DC. Persistent reporting by Carl Bernstein and Bob Woodward of the *Washington Post* drew connections between the burglars and Nixon's reelection committee and ultimately the White House. When it became known that Nixon secretly taped his conversations in the White House Oval Office, investigators demanded that the tapes be turned over. Nixon argued that executive privilege allowed him to keep the tapes. In *United States v. Nixon*, the Supreme Court ordered Nixon to turn over the tapes. Also in 1974, the House Judiciary Committee voted in favor of articles of impeachment against President Nixon. Before the question of impeachment could be addressed by the entire House of Representatives, Nixon resigned. Since the 1970s, the percentage of people voting has declined and opinion polls have shown an erosion of trust in the government.

Clashes over Equal Rights　均权冲突

The culture clashes that would come to epitomize the last decades of the twentieth century could be seen in the push to add an Equal Rights Amendment to the Constitution in 1972. The Equal Rights Amendment would have prohibited the abridgement of "equality of rights under the law . . . on account of sex" either by the federal government or by the state governments. The movement galvanized the women's liberation movement (see page 336). It also led to a conservative backlash against the proposal. Conservatives argued that passage of the amendment would destroy the American family. The movement against the proposal was led by conservative activist Phyllis Schlafly. She organized a strong coalition, urging "positive women" to embrace femininity. The amendment was approved by both the House and the Senate in 1972 but failed to get the required 38 states to ratify it, even after the deadline for ratification had been moved forward to 1982. It therefore did not become part of the Constitution.

Clashing Views of Affirmative Action　关于平权法案的矛盾观点

The movement for affirmative action was part of the civil rights movement. Activists hoped not only to end segregation, but to take affirmative action to rectify past discrimination by taking race into consideration in hiring, college admissions, and other areas. In 1961, President Kennedy issued an executive order mandating that projects using federal funds take "affirmative action" to make sure that employers do not discriminate based on race. In 1965, President Johnson went further, mandating that federal contractors and subcontractors make efforts to hire "protected class, underutilized" candidates. Many public universities began taking race into consideration when looking at applicants. Some schools set aside a certain number of seats for underrepresented groups.

Affirmative action policies generated a great deal of resentment among some white applicants for university admission and for jobs. They felt they were being punished for wrongs done by others. The issue came to a head when an applicant to the University of California, Davis School of Medicine, Allan Bakke, a white student, was denied admission. The Davis School of Medicine had set aside 16 percent of the places in each entering class for minority applicants. Bakke, arguing that he was discriminated against, sued and took the case to the Supreme Court. In *Bakke v. University of California* (1978), the court decided that specific quotas for underrepresented minorities violated the equal protection clause of the Fourteenth Amendment. However, Justice Lewis Powell's decision asserted that race could be one of the many factors that universities may look at in the admissions process, since diversity in higher education was a "compelling interest."

KEY CONCEPT 8.3 THE TRANSFORMATION OF AMERICAN SOCIETY IN THE POST-WORLD WAR II ERA
核心概念8.3： "二战"后时代美国社会的转型

The United States experienced a series of demographic, economic, and technological changes in the decades following World War II. These changes profoundly impacted American society, politics, and the environment.

I. The Promise and Perils of Postwar Society 战后社会的希望和危机

Many Americans were optimistic about the rapid economic and social changes that were occurring in society in the period after World War II. At the same time, some Americans challenged many of the assumptions of postwar society.

A. THE GROWTH OF THE MIDDLE CLASS 中产阶级的壮大

The postwar period witnessed the growth of the middle class and demographic shifts toward the suburbs and toward the "sun belt." A variety of factors stimulated these trends, including strong economic growth, federal spending, a "baby boom," the expansion of higher education, and new technological developments.

The G.I. Bill 《退伍军人权利法案》

The federal government helped returning veterans adjust to the peacetime economy with the Servicemen's Readjustment Act (1944), more commonly known as the G.I. Bill. The act provided low-interest loans for veterans to purchase homes and attend college.

The Baby Boom 生育高峰

For several years before 1946, birthrates in the United States had remained relatively low. Couples tended to have fewer children during the lean years of the Great Depression; further, the dislocation and physical separation caused by World War II kept the birthrate low. However, when the war ended, returning veterans quickly got down to the business of starting families. The spike in birthrates from 1946 through the early 1960s produced a baby boom that would have lasting repercussions in American society. The baby boom required states to spend more money on public education in the 1950s and 1960s and on expanded college enrollment in the 1960s and 1970s.

Childrearing in the 1950s 20世纪50年代的儿童抚养

The parents of the baby-boom generation were enthusiastic readers of child-rearing guides. The most influential was Benjamin Spock's *Baby and Child Care* (1946). Spock urged parents to treat their children as individuals, to let them develop at their own pace, and to focus less on discipline and more on affection. When baby boomers joined the counterculture in the 1960s, conservative critics cited Spock's book as part of the problem.

B. SUBURBAN GROWTH AND THE RISE OF THE SUN BELT
郊区的发展与阳光地带的崛起

A series of demographic shifts occurred in the post–World War II period. Many middle-class Americans abandoned urban centers and moved to newly built suburbs. At the same time, large numbers of Americans moved to the Sun Belt states of the South and the West. These changes were facilitated by technological developments, expanded higher education opportunities, and an increased degree of social mobility in the United States.

The Growth of Suburbia   郊区的发展

An important postwar trend was the growth of suburbs. Suburbs were not a new phenomenon in the postwar period—indeed, the earliest residential suburbs were built around commuter railroad stations in the late nineteenth century. But a series of factors contributed to the unprecedented growth of these communities. New suburban communities were built just outside major American cities to meet the housing crunch created by all the returning World War II soldiers. Huge numbers of these soldiers quickly married, had children, and looked for affordable housing. Race also played a factor in the development of suburbia. Many white people did not want to live in the urban neighborhoods that had become integrated after many southern, rural African Americans had moved north to work in war industries.

Levittown and Suburban Development   利维镇与郊区的发展

Real estate developers facilitated the move to the suburbs. An innovative developer was William Levitt, who took large tracts of land outside major cities (often farmland) and built huge developments of nearly identical, modest houses. He applied the techniques of mass production to these houses, building them rapidly and cheaply. Levittown, on Long Island, New York, became synonymous with these mass-produced communities. These developments were not without their critics. Songwriter Malvina Reynolds skewered the monotony of life in these developments in the song "Little Boxes" (1962).

The Interstate Highway Act   《州际高速公路法》

Federal and local highway initiatives also made suburbia attractive. One could now drive into cities from the suburbs quickly and easily. With the National Interstate and Defense Highways Act (1956), the federal government initiated a massive highway-building project that resulted in the interstate highway system. The act was also promoted as a defense measure, allowing for the rapid movement of military equipment and personnel. Americans could now feasibly leave cities and enjoy a small piece of land to call their own.

"White Flight" and the Decline of Older Cities   "白人大迁移"与老城市的衰落

Not everyone shared equally in the abundance of the 1950s. As middle-class families left urban centers to move to the suburbs, they took with them their ability to pay local taxes. Cities saw their tax bases shrink dramatically. With funds scarce, cities had to cut back on basic services like policing and education. Crime became an unavoidable urban reality and city schools deteriorated. This decline in city services put more pressure on middle-class people to make the move to the suburbs. By the 1960s, entire sections of cities had become slums.

Urban Renewal 城区改造

To address the decline of older cities, the federal government developed a set of initiatives known as the urban renewal program. A central piece of the program was the Housing Act of 1949, which represented a dramatic expansion of federal money and power in the area of urban housing. Title I of the act provided federal financing for slum clearance programs, encouraging city administrations to declare areas blighted and then to demolish vast swaths of inner cities. The program displaced thousands of urban residents. In Boston, almost a third of the old city was demolished. Frequently, nothing was built to replace the demolished neighborhoods. Low-income urban housing projects, built with funds from the federal government, often proved to be soulless structures that bred crime and unsanitary conditions. Title I was often used to clear land to build highways rather than additional housing. Urban renewal programs often left cities in worse shape than before the programs were initiated.

C. IMMIGRATION AND ECONOMIC GROWTH 移民与经济增长

In the period following World War II, large numbers of immigrants were drawn to the political, economic, and social opportunities offered by the United States. Migrations from abroad increased dramatically after the passage of the Immigration Reform Act of 1965.

Immigration and Nationality Act of 1965 《1965年移民与国籍法》

The Immigration and Nationality Act of 1965 (also known as the Hart-Celler Act) changed American immigration policy that had been in place since the 1920s. It abolished the national quota system and replaced it with overall limits on immigration into the United States. There was, for the first time, a limitation of 120,000 per year placed on Western Hemisphere immigration; the limit for immigration from the Eastern Hemisphere was set at 170,000. Exemptions were set for those who had family members already in the United States, allowing for "chain immigration," outside the limits established by the act. Preference was also given to immigrants with particular skills that were needed in the United States. The act opened the door to increased immigration and has altered the demographic composition of the United States (see more on the impact of the act in Section 9).

II. A Nation Divided 分裂的国家

A variety of demographic and social developments, along with anxieties about the Cold War and the threat of nuclear war, led to bitter debates in the 1960s and 1970s that divided many Americans. These debates revolved around culture, social and political values, family structure and sexual norms, and religion.

A. CULTURAL CONFORMITY AND ITS DISCONTENTS 文化整合及其不满

American culture moved in distinctly different directions in the postwar period. On the one hand, an increasingly homogenous mass culture developed; on the other hand, many artists, intellectuals, and rebellious young people challenged the pressure toward conformity that marked postwar culture.

Conformity in a Conservative Decade 十年保守时期的整合

Several commentators noted the societal pressures toward conformity in the 1950s. Part of this push toward conformity can be attributed to the domestic Cold War and the dictates of McCarthyism (see page 324). Many Americans felt intimidated and were reluctant to appear to be nonconformist in the 1950s. Sociologists David Riesman, Nathan Glazer, and Reuel Denney, in their book *The Lonely Crowd* (1950), noted that Americans were more eager to mold their ideas to societal standards than they were to think independently. William H. Whyte's book, *The Organization Man* (1956), described the stultifying atmosphere of the modern corporation in which employees were expected to think like the group. The novel, *The Man in the Gray Flannel Suit* (1955), by Sloan Wilson, depicted a businessman trapped in the materialistic commercial world of the 1950s. J. D. Salinger's bestselling novel, *The Catcher in the Rye* (1951), railed at the "phonies" who had achieved success in mainstream 1950s society.

Television 电视

Widely available for the first time in the postwar period, television became an extremely popular medium. By the end of the 1950s nearly 90 percent of American homes owned a television set. After an initial burst of creativity in the late 1940s and early 1950s, television programming settled into safe, predictable genres. The most emblematic genre of the 1950s was the suburban situation comedy (sitcom), complete with a stay-at-home mother, as in *Leave It to Beaver* and *Father Knows Best*. Westerns, such as *Bonanza* and *Gunsmoke*, and daytime dramas (labeled "soap operas" because of sponsorship by soap manufacturers), such as *The Guiding Light* and *Search for Tomorrow*, dominated the airwaves. Many of these genres were carryovers from radio. The *Ed Sullivan Show*, a variety show, was extremely popular, airing from 1948 to 1971.

Rock 'n' roll Music 摇滚乐

Rock 'n' roll music became extremely popular among young people in the 1950s. Rock 'n' roll developed primarily in the African American community. It was dubbed "race music" and was deemed dangerous by mainstream white commentators. Elvis Presley, a white singer from Memphis, Tennessee, became a huge cultural force in America. He followed in the footsteps of numerous African American performers, some famous (Chuck Berry) and some largely forgotten ("Big Mama" Thornton). Rock 'n' roll music was part of a distinct youth culture ushering in a generational divide in American society.

Beat Generation Literature "垮掉的一代" 文学

The beat literary movement represented a subversive undercurrent in the 1950s. The beats represented a rejection of mainstream social values—the suburban lifestyle, the consumer society, patriotism. The most important text of the beat movement is *On the Road*, by Jack Kerouac (1957). Initially typed on paper taped together in a scroll, the book is a stream-of-consciousness screed. It depicts a life of spontaneity and freedom. Also important is Allen Ginsberg's book of poems, *Howl* (1956), which ripped apart the foundations of Cold War, materialistic American society.

> **COUNTERCULTURES**
> **反主流文化**
> Do not confuse the timeframe for countercultural movements. The Beats were in the 1950s; hippies were in the 1960s; and punks were in the 1970s.

Abstract Expressionism 抽象表现主义

An important artistic movement of the 1950s came to be called "abstract expressionism." Centered in New York City, the movement elevated the "process" of painting—emphasizing spontaneity, emotion, and intensity over studied, realistic reproductions of the visible world. The most well-known practitioner of abstract expressionism was Jackson Pollock, who splattered, poured, and dripped paint on his canvasses.

B. COUNTERCULTURAL VALUES AND AMERICAN CULTURE
反主流文化价值观与美国文化

A vibrant counterculture developed among young people in the 1960s. Feminists and participants in the counterculture rejected many of the mainstream values that characterized their parents' generation. As the baby-boom generation came of age in the 1960s, a large portion grew increasingly weary of the cultural products of the previous generation. Mainstream culture seemed inauthentic, shallow, and corporate-controlled. This counterculture initiated a sexual revolution in American society, greater informality in everyday life, and a rethinking of the traditional family structure in America. Although popular culture continued to portray idealized nuclear families, the increase in the number of working women and new social attitudes eroded the reality of this image.

The Sexual Revolution 性革命

The 1960s witnessed the development of more tolerant attitudes toward sexual behavior. In 1960, the birth control "pill" was introduced to the market, allowing women more control over reproduction and over their sexual lives. Many states impeded the distribution of information and products related to birth control. The Supreme Court invalidated such repressive laws in the case of *Griswold v. Connecticut* (1965), in which the court ruled that laws forbidding the use of birth control devices were unconstitutional because they violated the privacy rights of individuals.

Roe v. Wade (1973) 罗伊诉韦德案（1973）

One of the major issues of the women's rights movement was a woman's right to control reproduction, including the choice of whether to have an abortion. One of the major successes of the women's liberation movement was the Supreme Court decision in the case of *Roe v. Wade* (1973). The court declared that states shall not prohibit women from having an abortion during the first two trimesters of pregnancy. Previously the decision had been left to the states, and many states forbade abortions. The Supreme Court reasoned that the Constitution guaranteed people the right to privacy. Abortion, they argued, was a decision that should be left to the woman with the advice of her physician. This decision echoed the reasoning of the earlier decision, *Griswold v. Connecticut* (1965) (see page 341), in affirming an individual's right to privacy. The issue of abortion proved to be one of the most contentious issues in America in the late-twentieth and early twenty-first centuries.

The "Quiet Revolution" "无声的革命"

From the 1970s to the present, the percentage of women engaged in the workforce has grown. There are several reasons for this. The women's liberation movement (see page 336) challenged traditional gender expectations—many women felt less pressure to marry at a young age, have children, and work at home. Also, the availability of the birth control pill and of abortions allowed women to have greater control over their reproductive lives (see page 349). Many women made the decision to focus on a career first, putting off decisions about whether to have children. Historians note a "quiet revolution" of women entering the workplace from the late 1970s until the present. The percentage of households in which women are the sole or the primary breadwinner rose from 15 percent in 1970 to over 40 percent by 2011.

Bob Dylan and the Folk Revival   鲍勃·迪伦与民谣复兴运动

Despite his protests to the contrary, Bob Dylan was able to verbalize many of the fears and hopes of the younger generation in the 1960s. Even his initial musical choices—simple, acoustic instrumentation—seemed a welcome break from the bland, overproduced "pop" products of the record industry. Dylan soon "went electric"—to the dismay of folk purists—finding an enormous worldwide following. He cultivated a vocal approach that paid homage to the untrained, indigenous music of rural America, rather than to the smooth crooners of his parents' generation.

The British Invasion   英伦入侵

In the 1960s, a series of British bands, most notably the Beatles and the Rolling Stones, transformed American culture. These bands took inspiration from the rich tradition of African American music—from rhythm and blues to rock 'n' roll—and infused it with a youthful energy. The Beatles inspired a manic following in the United States, known as "Beatlemania." If one event symbolized the beginning of the British invasion it was the first appearance by the Beatles on the *Ed Sullivan Show* in February 1964. The Beatles also generated a backlash in the United States. Conservative Americans were troubled by their long hair, veiled allusions to drug use, interest in Eastern religions, and challenges to traditional notions of propriety. A comment by one of the Beatles, that the band had become more popular than Jesus Christ, added to the backlash.

The "Hippie Movement" and Haight-Ashbury   "嬉皮运动"与海德-艾斯布利

The "hippie" movement became visible in the late 1960s in neighborhoods such as San Francisco's Haight-Ashbury and New York's Greenwich Village. In many ways, this counterculture represented a complete rejection of the materialistic conformity that many young people grew up with in the 1950s (see page 348). A variety of activities came to be associated with the hippie movement—urban and rural communal living, a "do-it-yourself" approach to the varied tasks of life, mystic spiritual experiences, drug use, experimental music, and avant-garde art. Taking inspiration from sit-ins of the civil rights movement, the counterculture organized "be-ins"—gatherings of young people in San Francisco's Golden Gate Park or New York's Central Park.

Woodstock and Altamont   伍德斯托克与阿尔塔芒特

The counterculture reached its peak and showed its limits in two important events, months apart from each other, in 1969. The Woodstock Festival, in August, attracted half a million attendees to a massive weekend concert at a farm in upstate New York, and for many young people seemed to provide a glimpse of a utopian future. In December, promoters tried to duplicate the success of Woodstock with a giant music festival at the Altamont Speedway in California. However, the Altamont event was marred by incidents of violence; one concertgoer, armed and apparently crazed, was stopped and stabbed to death by a member of the Hell's Angels Motorcycle Club (the concert's security detail) as the Rolling Stones performed.

C. CHRISTIAN FUNDAMENTALISM AND THE RELIGIOUS RIGHT
基督教基要主义与宗教权利

The rapid growth of the Christian fundamentalist movement fueled a resurgence of the New Right. This fundamentalist movement started in churches but soon entered the political sphere, organizing opposition to liberal and progressive social trends.

Opposition to *Roe v. Wade* 对罗伊诉韦德案的抗议

The issue that propelled the cultural conservatives from the margins to prominence was abortion. In the wake of the 1973 *Roe v. Wade* decision, religious conservatives found their voice. The issue convinced evangelical Protestants to put aside their long-held suspicions of Catholicism and create a broad Christian conservative movement.

The "Moral Majority" and Focus on the Family "道德多数派"与爱家协会

The religious and cultural wing of the New Right found voice in several grassroots organizations. The "Moral Majority" was founded by the Reverend Jerry Falwell, a Southern Baptist pastor, in 1979. In the mid-1970s adherents embarked on a series of "I Love America" rallies. These rallies broke a traditional Baptist principle of separating religion from politics. Falwell asserted that this separation was at the heart of the moral decay that was afflicting America.

Focus on the Family was founded in 1977 by psychologist James Dobson. The organization is interdenominational, bridging the traditional divide between Catholics and Protestants. It promotes an abstinence-only approach to sex education, the reintroduction of prayer into the schools, and reinforcement of traditional gender roles. The organization has stood against the expansion of rights for gay, lesbian, bisexual, and transgendered people; it has been vocal in its opposition to same-sex marriage. Focus on the Family is one of the leading voices in the movement against abortion.

SUBJECT TO DEBATE 相关讨论

Many of our understandings of the Cold War were developed by American historians during its height in the 1950s and 1960s. As might be expected, these historians saw American actions in a positive light and Soviet actions in a negative light. "Our" side stood for democracy, freedom, and progress; "their" side stood for repression, aggression, and coercion. Since the fall of the Soviet Union in 1991, historians have reevaluated this standard narrative. Some historians have put renewed emphasis on covert operations by the United States during the Cold War, such as the 1954 CIA-backed coup in Iraq that deposed Mohammed Mosaddegh and installed the Shah. These covert operations complicate the story. In addition, historians have also looked at Soviet moves in a slightly different light. Stalin's occupation of Eastern Europe following World War II is still seen as an unfortunate move, but some historians have begun to put his actions in a larger historical context. After all, perhaps the moves are less reprehensible when looked at in the context of the history of attacks on Russia that had come through Eastern Europe.

On the other side of the political spectrum, historians of the Cold War period have revisited debates about the nature of the American communist movement in the 1940s and 1950s. For many years, historians looked at Communist Party members as victims of an irrational witch hunt. More recently, since the fall of the Soviet Union, a group of historians, led by Harvey Klehr and John Earl Haynes, have scoured old Soviet archives and found some damning evidence against the Communist Party in the United States. Klehr and Haynes have found, for instance, transcriptions that seem to implicate Julius Rosenberg in spying for the Soviet Union. Their findings have forced a reevaluation of the assumption that members of the Communist Party were innocent victims.

When writing history, beware of clichés. Mainstream media and popular memory often reduce a complex time period to a phrase or an image. When many of us hear the "Roaring Twenties," the first thing that pops into our heads might be "the jazz age." We think of *The Great Gatsby*, martinis, flappers, and speakeasies. But this image has become a cliché, obscuring the complex societal tensions of the 1920s. Yes, people went to speakeasies, but they also joined Ku Klux Klan rallies. The more we read about the 1920s, the harder it becomes to reduce it to a catchphrase.

The same is true of the 1950s. For many Americans, the image of the 1950s can be reduced to the word "conformity." We look condescendingly at the naïve suburbanites of the decade, blithely watching bland television programs. However, as students of history, we should be wary of such easy clichés. As in the 1920s, complex social factors were at work. Many trends in the 1950s flew in the face of conformity—the most obvious being the civil rights movement. The 1950s also saw the birth of the beat movement, the popularity of rock 'n' roll, and the beginnings of the "folk music revival."

On a related note, be careful about identifying the decade too closely with one individual—Joseph McCarthy. Yes, he was a powerful figure. However, his power was brief; by 1954, he was largely discredited. Also, even at his height, he was not the entire anticommunist movement. By focusing on McCarthy we forget there was a liberal anticommunist movement, one that was critical of the excesses of McCarthy. Historians are moving away from using the term "McCarthyism" to describe the entire anticommunist movement.

There has been much historical discussion about the origins of the civil rights movement. One key division in the discussion is between those who stress grassroots activism and those who focus on the actions of the government. Historians who take a more "top-down" approach elevate the importance of powerful institutions—the courts, the police, elected officials—in shaping events. This is the more traditional approach. Revisionist historians, many of whom come out of a New Left tradition, focus on the agency of ordinary people in shaping historical change. Of late, historians have looked at the interaction between the grassroots level and the halls of power. We see this at play with the Birmingham civil rights campaign in 1963. The campaign, which ignited a violent reaction from police (broadcast on the evening news), prompted the Kennedy and Johnson administrations to take action and to push for the 1964 Civil Rights Act. This act might not have been passed were it not for the violent events in Birmingham.

The legacy of the war in Vietnam has been hotly debated. Historians have argued about whether the conflict in Vietnam was essentially a civil war or an international Cold War struggle. Should the focus be on the rebellion by the indigenous Vietcong and its peasant supporters against an oppressive regime? Or should the focus be on North Vietnam and China fomenting chaos in South Vietnam? If we accept the first scenario, then American intervention seems misguided and bound for failure. If we accept the second scenario, then American intervention seems entirely reasonable. A related question is whether the war was winnable. To some, the United States was fighting a hopeless war—additional years of extensive bombing would simply steel the resolve of the populace to resist the American occupation. To others, victory was both possible and within sight, but President Nixon abandoned the fight at just the wrong moment. Domestic political considerations and the Watergate scandal caused Nixon to make a hasty exit from Southeast Asia.

Historians have also debated the overall legacy of the Nixon presidency. In the popular imagination, the Watergate scandal looms large. However, historians point out, the scandal should not overshadow some of Nixon's real accomplishments, including promoting détente with China and the Soviet Union. Historians have also praised Nixon for avoiding the divisive social and religious issues that characterized subsequent Republican administrations. Other historians insist that Nixon's legacy is irreparably tarnished by the bombing of civilians in Southeast Asia.

PRACTICE MULTIPLE-CHOICE QUESTIONS 选择题练习

> **Directions:** Pick the letter that best answers the following questions.

Questions 1–3 refer to the following cartoon 根据下列卡通漫画，回答第1—3题
(Note: In the cartoon, the figure on the left is intended to be Senator Joseph McCarthy; the figure on the right is intended to be President Dwight D. Eisenhower):

"HAVE A CARE, SIR"

—Herblock, *Washington Post*, 1954

1. The 1954 cartoon shown above makes the point that

   (A) Senator Joseph McCarthy and President Dwight D. Eisenhower successfully worked in tandem in the 1950s to slow the spread of communism in the United States.

   (B) Senator Joseph McCarthy went too far when he accused President Dwight D. Eisenhower of sympathizing with the communist movement.

   (C) Senator Joseph McCarthy had the foresight to guard America's borders from communist aggression, but President Dwight D. Eisenhower failed to perceive threats to national security.

   (D) President Dwight D. Eisenhower's criticisms of Senator Joseph McCarthy's anticommunist crusade were weak and ineffective.

2. The height of Senator Joseph McCarthy's power and influence coincided with

(A) the wave of labor strikes immediately following World War II.
(B) the Korean War.
(C) the "massive resistance" campaign among white southerners.
(D) the Cuban missile crisis.

3. The ideas expressed in the cartoon most directly reflect which of the following continuities in twentieth-century United States history?

(A) Debates about the proper role of political parties.
(B) Debates about acceptable means for pursing domestic goals.
(C) Debates about the relationship between the executive branch and the legislative branch.
(D) Debates about the role of the federal government in economic regulation.

Questions 4–5 refer to the following excerpt. 根据下列节选，回答第4—5题

"The pursuit of this widened war has narrowed domestic welfare programs, making the poor, white and Negro, bear the heaviest burdens both at the front and at home. . . . It is estimated that we spend $322,000 for each enemy we kill, while we spend in the so-called war on poverty in America only about $53.00 for each person classified as 'poor.' . . . We have escalated the war in Viet Nam and deescalated the skirmish against poverty. It challenges the imagination to contemplate what lives we could transform if we were to cease killing."

—Martin Luther King, Jr., speech, "The Casualties of War in Vietnam," 1967

4. The speech was written most directly in response to which of the following?

(A) The refusal of the federal government to desegregate the military.
(B) The failure of the Great Society to significantly reduce poverty in the United States.
(C) The focus of the Republican Party on international issues at the expense of domestic issues.
(D) Frustrations over the inability of the civil rights movement to persuade Congress to pass meaningful civil rights legislation.

5. The excerpt reflects which of the following trends?

(A) The growth of the antiwar movement in the 1960s as the Vietnam War escalated.
(B) The refusal of protest movements in the 1960s to draw connections between economic and foreign policy issues.
(C) The success of anticommunist propaganda in silencing opposition to government policies.
(D) The shift in tactics of the civil rights movement from civil disobedience to violent resistance.

Answers and Explanations Multiple-Choice Questions
选择题的答案与解析

1. **(D)** The cartoon is suggesting that President Eisenhower did not take a strong enough stand in opposition to the tactics of Senator Joseph McCarthy. "McCarthyism" is the name given to the extreme anticommunist movement in the early 1950s. Senator McCarthy became the central figure in this movement. In 1950 he announced that he had a list of "known communists" who had infiltrated the State Department. This and similar claims, mostly baseless, created a name for McCarthy and set the stage for a host of measures to halt this perceived threat. Congress established committees to investigate Communist Party infiltration in different sectors of society. Eisenhower walked a fine line in regard to McCarthy. On the one hand, he found McCarthy's tactics reprehensible. He once said of McCarthy, "I just won't get down in the gutter with that man." However, he also welcomed the benefits that McCarthyism brought to the Republican Party. The cartoon notes Eisenhower's reluctance to challenge McCarthy publicly.

2. **(B)** Senator Joseph McCarthy had the greatest influence during the period of the Korean War. Often, in American history, periods of war opened up political space for more extreme, jingoistic political movements. This can be seen in the anti-German sentiment that accompanied World War I. In 1950, the year the Korean War began, McCarthy gained a great deal of publicity for himself by announcing that he had a list of employees in the State Department who were also members of the Communist Party. The war ended in 1953; by 1954, political leaders were publicly challenging Senator McCarthy.

3. **(B)** The differences between McCarthy and Eisenhower reflect an ongoing debate about the acceptable means of pursing domestic goals. These debates can be seen in differences over the tactics of the "Red Scare" of the 1920s, in debates over President Franklin Roosevelt's "court packing scheme" in the 1930s, and in debates about the Patriot Act in the 2000s. In many cases, political leaders might agree about broad goals—challenging the influence of radical groups, advancing the New Deal agenda, eliminating domestic terrorism—but might disagree on whether specific means are acceptable.

4. **(B)** By 1967, Martin Luther King and members of the civil rights movement were growing increasingly frustrated by the lack of progress being made by the government in regard to reducing poverty in America. King came to make explicit connections between the war in Vietnam and the failures of domestic social programs. In 1967, he said in a speech: "The promises of the Great Society have been shot down on the battlefields of Vietnam." King's antiwar stance created a major rift between him and President Johnson.

5. **(A)** Martin Luther King was certainly not alone in his opposition to the war in Vietnam. By the late 1960s, a vocal and active antiwar movement developed in the United States. As the war dragged on, and as the United States suffered more casualties, many Americans began to question the wisdom of American policies in Vietnam. The fact that images from the war were transmitted into people's living rooms also contributed to antiwar sentiment. United States involvement in Vietnam continued until 1973, when President Richard Nixon withdrew the last American troops. In 1975, the government of South Vietnam was defeated and, in 1976, it united with North Vietnam as the Socialist Republic of Vietnam.

Period 9: 1980–Present Political and Foreign Policy Adjustments in a Globalized World
第九个时期（1980—）：全球化世界中的政治与外交政策调整

11

1998	Impeachment of President Clinton
1999	NATO Bombing of Serbia in response to violence in Kosovo
2000	Election of George W. Bush
2001	Terrorist attacks on the World Trade Center and the Pentagon
	Passage of the Patriot Act
	United States overthrow of the Taliban in Afghanistan
2003	Creation of the Department of Homeland Security
	Operation Iraqi Freedom
2008	Election of Barack Obama
2010	Passage of Affordable Care Act
2011	Raid and killing of Osama bin Laden
	Repeal of "Don't Ask, Don't Tell" policy
2012	Reelection of Barack Obama
2015	*Obergefell v. Hodges* decision establishes marriage equality
	Joint Comprehensive Plan of Action (Iran nuclear deal)

INTRODUCTION 简介

> The United States has had to adapt to a changing world in the late twentieth and early twenty-first centuries. The world of the recent past has been filled with challenges and possibilities. The United States faces divisions at home along ideological and cultural lines and has been compelled to adjust its foreign policy to meet changing global dynamics. The United States has also had to adapt to new technological and scientific advances and to economic globalization.

The late twentieth century saw the growth of a powerful conservative movement. There had been signs of a growing conservative movement in the United States since the 1964 campaign of Barry Goldwater. This movement celebrated the election of Ronald Reagan in 1980 and has been successful in redefining the terms of political debate in the late twentieth and early twenty-first centuries. Recent decades have seen an intensification of partisan divisions—from the "Contract with America" in the 1990s to the Tea Party Movement in the wake of the election of the nation's first African-American president, Barack Obama. The era has also seen a series of adjustments, in both domestic and foreign policy, in the aftermath of the terrorist attacks of 2001.

KEY CONCEPT 9.1 THE RESURGENCE OF CONSERVATISM
核心概念9.1：保守主义的复苏

During the 1980s, a renewed conservative movement rose in importance and achieved several political goals. This movement rejected liberal views on the role of the government and embraced "traditional" social values. It continued to exert influence over public discourse over the following decades.

I. The Achievements and Limits of the Conservative Domestic Agenda 保守的国内议程的成就与局限

The conservative movement achieved electoral successes in the 1980s, 1990s, and 2000s and witnessed the implementation of some of its policy and political goals. However, this period also made evident the limits of conservative reform—many of the government programs it sought to curtail or eliminate enjoyed broad public support.

A. THE ASCENDANCY OF THE NEW RIGHT 新右派的优势

The election of President Ronald Reagan in 1980 represented a dramatic achievement for the New Right. The growth of the New Right reflected a variety if economic, political, and social concerns. The movement achieved notable victories in terms of lowering taxes and deregulating business. In the decades following the Reagan administration, the New Right has continued to exert influence over the political process.

Anatomy of the New Right 新右派的剖析

The conservative movement has always had three distinct tendencies that sometimes have worked in unison and sometimes have been in conflict. First, there are Cold War conservatives, focused on containing or rolling back communist regimes abroad. In the post–Cold War era, interventionists have argued for continued U.S. actions abroad, notably in the Middle East. The second is comprised of the pro-business economic conservatives. These conservatives argue for lower corporate taxes, deregulation, and an economic atmosphere friendly to the priorities of big business. Economic conservatives might use the language of laissez-faire economics in regard to rolling back environmental regulations, but they are ready to use the power of the government to, say, extend military contracts to large corporations.

The third tendency within the conservative movement is the religious and cultural wing. It is this group that has had the greatest grassroots support, fueling electoral victories for Ronald Reagan (twice), George H. W. Bush (once), and George W. Bush (twice). This movement gained steam as tradition-minded people grew frustrated with what they saw as the excesses of the counterculture of the 1960s. They railed against the women's liberation movement for challenging traditional gender roles, and against the gay liberation movement. Many were troubled by the assertiveness of African Americans in the 1960s and pined for an earlier time, in which everyone "knew their place." The public nature of illegal drug use in the 1960s also angered cultural conservatives.

The New Right and the Election of Ronald Reagan 新右派与罗纳德·里根总统的选举

The New Right achieved a remarkable victory in the election of Ronald Reagan in 1980. Reagan had been a well-known actor in B-movies from the 1930s to the 1960s and was president of the Screen Actors Guild in the 1940s and 1950s. He became increasingly interested in politics, first as a New Deal Democrat. By the 1950s, he was increasingly anticommunist and became an active Republican in the 1960s. He served as governor of California from 1967 to 1975.

The election of the conservative Ronald Reagan in 1980 has been seen by many historians as a repudiation of the political and social movements of the 1960s. Reagan's victory can, in part, be attributed to more immediate causes. President Jimmy Carter was seen as ineffective in not securing the quick release of hostages held at the American embassy in Tehran by Iranian militants (see page 329). However, Reagan projected a sense of hope and optimism that promised to move the United States beyond the scandals and doubts of the 1970s. He promised a new "morning in America," and Americans listened. Reagan's tenure as president saw a tremendous military build-up and the beginning of the end for the Soviet Union and the communist bloc. He also gave voice to the rising New Right movement.

Reaganomics 里根经济政策

President Ronald Reagan advanced a series of economic initiatives that bear the name "Reaganomics." He was not the first conservative politician to advance such policies—Reaganomics bears striking similarities to Herbert Hoover's approach to the Great Depression. Reagan supported economic policies that favored big business. He based this on a belief in the effectiveness of supply-side economics. This approach to the economy stressed stimulating the supply side of the economy—manufacturers, banks, insurance corporations. The idea is that if there is growth in the supply side, there will be general economic growth, and the benefits of that growth will reach everyone. The alternative approach is to stimulate the demand side—consumers. Demand-side economics would emphasize government policies designed to increase workers' wages and would expand social programs such as welfare and unemployment benefits. As a believer in supply-side economics, Reagan implemented policies he thought would stimulate business. He cut taxes for corporations and greatly reduced regulations on industry. Reagan was a staunch proponent of deregulation. He and his secretary of the interior James Watt were criticized by environmental advocates for dismantling or weakening much of the environmental legislation of the 1970s.

> ### HOOVER AND REAGAN
> ### 胡佛与里根
> Be familiar with the similarities between Presidents Reagan and Hoover in regard to economics. Both promoted a supply-side approach to economic policy.

"Contract with America" (1994) 《美利坚契约》（1994）

During the administration of President Bill Clinton (1993-2001), the Republican Party, energized by conservative activists, made significant gains in both the House of Representatives and the Senate. The opposition party traditionally does well in the congressional elections that occur between presidential elections. In 1994, the Republican Party gained control of both the House and the Senate. The Republicans had not controlled the House since 1954. House Republicans, led by minority leader Newt Gingrich, had signed and publicly issued the "Contract with America" six weeks before the 1994 election. It was a call to arms for Republicans and a specific blueprint for legislative action. The document called for action on a number of fronts, such as tougher anti-crime measures, tort reform, and welfare reform. Many of the House's initiatives died in the Senate, some were vetoed by President Clinton, some were implemented, and some were reworked by both parties before being implemented. The success of the Republican Party in 1994 put President Clinton on the defensive in his dealings with Congress.

Impeachment Proceedings 弹劾程序

The impeachment proceedings against President Clinton constituted an important turning point in the deterioration of relations between the two main political parties. The proceedings demonstrated the growing strength of the more conservative elements within the Republican Party. Those elements doggedly pursued evidence of scandal relating to President Clinton.

During Clinton's first term, Senate Republicans appointed Kenneth Starr as an independent council to investigate the Clintons' participation in a failed and fraudulent real estate project in Arkansas that dated back to 1978, when Bill Clinton was governor. Starr pursued the so-named Whitewater Case relentlessly, but never tied the Clintons to the fraud.

President Clinton, however, was not able to avoid implication in a more salacious scandal. Clinton was publicly accused of having an affair with a White House intern named Monica Lewinsky. Clinton denied the accusations publicly and also before a federal grand jury. When Clinton was later forced to admit the affair, Congressional Republicans felt they had evidence of impeachable crimes—lying to a grand jury and obstructing justice. Clinton was impeached by the House of Representatives in 1998. Clinton was found "not guilty" by the Senate (two-thirds are needed for conviction). The entire incident reflected the tense relationship between the two major political parties. Clinton emerged from the affair largely unscathed. Many Americans disapproved of his personal misconduct, but resented the attempt by Republicans to remove him from office.

IMPEACHMENT 弹劾

Impeachment is not synonymous with removal from office. Impeachment is the act of bringing charges against the president (or other federal official). It is parallel to indictment in the criminal court system. After impeachment by the House, the Senate conducts a trial, based on the charges listed in the "articles of impeachment." If found guilty of these charges, the president is removed from office.

The Election of 2000　2000年总统大选

The 2000 election for president reflected political divisions in the United States and was one of the most contentious in American history. The voting in Florida was split almost evenly between the Democratic candidate, Vice President Al Gore, and Republican candidate George W. Bush. This would not have been such a problem beyond Florida but, based on the electoral votes of the other 49 states, neither candidate had 270 electoral votes, the number needed to be declared the winner. After several weeks of legal wrangling in Florida, the U.S. Supreme Court reversed an order by the Florida Supreme Court to do a hand recount of several counties in Florida. The decision in *Bush v. Gore* was five to four. By overturning a state decision, the court broke with its tendency in the 1990s to assert the power of states within the federal system. Critics contend that the partisan concerns of the justices might have shaped the decision. The decision by the Supreme Court in *Bush v. Gore* ended the dispute with Bush slightly ahead of Gore in Florida, securing the presidency for Bush.

The Presidency of George W. Bush　乔治·W.布什的总统任期

The New Right achieved a major victory with the election of George W. Bush in 2000. Bush, the son of the forty-first president, George H. W. Bush, was governor of Texas and had little national exposure. He ushered the country through the aftermath of one of the most tumultuous events on American soil since the Civil War—the terrorist attacks on 2001 (see page 376). By the end of Bush's second term, public approval of his presidency was at a historic low, hampering the chances of the Republicans to hold on to the White House.

"No Child Left Behind" 《"不让一个孩子掉队"法案》

The No Child Left Behind Act was signed into law in 2002 by President George W. Bush to institute reform of public education. The law extended the reach of the federal government into education—traditionally a state responsibility. The law mandated that states set learning standards, that students attain "proficiency" in reading and math by 2014, and that teachers be "highly qualified" in the subject area. The law allowed students to transfer to other schools if they were attending a school that fell short of meeting new guidelines. The law also allowed the state to take over schools and school districts that did not meet new guidelines. The program was criticized by many states for its lack of funding to help schools reach these new goals. Also, many educators questioned the increased reliance on standardized tests in judging schools and school districts.

The Tea Party Movement and the Reaction to the Election of President Obama
茶党运动与奥巴马当选总统的各方反应

The election of 2008 resulted in a profound milestone in American history—the election of the first African American to the presidency. Such an event was virtually unthinkable a generation earlier. As late as the 1960s, Jim Crow segregation was still the law of the land throughout the South and informal, de facto, segregation existed throughout the nation. The civil rights movement challenged and altered many of these practices, but racist attitudes persisted among large segments of the population.

Barack Obama's victory was the result of a series of factors. First, his campaign successfully held off a strong challenge for the Democratic nomination by Senator Hillary Clinton. Clinton's bid for the nomination, if successful, could have resulted in a different historic milestone—the first female president in the United States. The Obama campaign was able to harness the power of the Internet, as well as the candidate's abundant charisma, to build a large base. Clinton subsequently threw her support behind the Obama campaign in the general election. She was later named secretary of state.

In the general election, the Democratic Party was aided by an unpopular sitting Republican president, George W. Bush, and by an unfocused campaign by Republican Senator John McCain. The McCain campaign failed to articulate a consistent message. McCain's selection of the relatively unknown candidate, Sarah Palin, for vice president failed to propel the campaign forward. The outspoken Palin energized the more conservative elements of the Republican Party, but failed to broaden the party's appeal.

The election of Barack Obama to the presidency in 2008 and his reelection in 2012 have generated a vocal opposition movement known as the Tea Party, harkening back to the American colonists' action against perceived British tyranny. To some extent the movement is a creation of the media, heavily promoted by the Fox News channel, and to some extent it represents a grassroots sense of discontent with big government. However, the movement often exhibits hyperbolic language, predicting the onset of "tyranny," "fascism," and "communism."

B. REDUCING "BIG GOVERNMENT": RHETORIC AND REALITY
缩小"大政府"：华词与现实

Republicans repeatedly declared the era of "big government" was coming to an end. However, Republican administrations witnessed an increase in the size and scope of the government, as it became evident that eliminating or reducing popular programs would be politically dangerous.

The Expansion of Medicare and Medicaid 医疗保险与医疗补助计划的扩大

Since the creation of Medicare and Medicaid in 1965, as part of President Lyndon Johnson's "Great Society" (see Period 8), both programs have expanded. Medicare provides health insurance to those over 65, who have worked and paid into the system, and to those with disabilities. Medicaid is a government insurance program for low-income people. Both programs have, over the years, added conditions and situations that would qualify for coverage. In addition, as people live longer—the "graying of America"—the costs to the Medicare program increase. Despite Reagan's promise's to end "big government," he led the effort to pass a Social Security reform bill designed to ensure the long-term solvency of the program and supported the expansion of the Medicare program to protect the elderly and disabled against "catastrophic" health costs.

Growth of the Federal Deficit 联邦政府赤字的增长

President Reagan's pro-business economic policies had mixed results. By cutting corporate taxes and taxes on wealthy individuals he cut government revenues. But, at the same time, he increased spending on armaments. This combination of increased spending and decreased revenues led to a doubling of the national debt from around $900 billion in 1980 to over $2 trillion in 1986. A large debt is a problem because it requires large interest payments. By 1988, the interest on the national debt had reached 14 percent of total annual government expenditures. This huge debt has hindered economic growth to some degree since and forced future administrations to make difficult decisions about keeping the debt under control.

C. DEBATES OVER THE SCOPE OF GOVERNMENT AND INTERNATIONAL TRADE
围绕政府工作的范围与国际贸易的争论

A number of heated policy debates have occurred during the period from 1980 to the present about the role of the government social safety net, regulation of the financial system, and international trade.

NAFTA and the Push Toward Free Trade 《北美自由贸易协定》与推近自由贸易

A heated debate occurred in the 1990s over free trade and the globalization of the world economy. President Bill Clinton broke with organized labor and environmental groups by embracing the North American Free Trade Agreement (NAFTA). NAFTA was ratified by Congress in 1993. The agreement eliminated all trade barriers and tariffs among the United States, Canada, and Mexico. NAFTA was the subject of much controversy when it was promoted by President Clinton. Free-trade supporters promised global prosperity as more nations participated in the global

> ### CLINTON MOVES RIGHT
> ### 克林顿的右倾化
> Bill Clinton frustrated Republicans, especially his opponent in the 1996 election, Bob Dole, by moving in a rightward direction. His embrace of NAFTA and welfare reform stole Republican thunder and assured his reelection.

economy. Opponents worried that nations would no longer be able to implement environmental regulations, ensure workers' rights, or protect fledgling industries from foreign competition. Clinton's championing of NAFTA represents his conscious decision to try to move the Democratic Party away from its liberal traditions and toward a more centrist approach.

The General Agreement on Trade and Tariffs (GATT) 《关税暨贸易总协定》

The North American Free Trade Agreement and the General Agreement of Trade and Tariffs are international trade agreements that have sought to encourage countries to participate in the global economy by reducing barriers to trade. GATT has existed since 1948, but the 1994 agreement was far-reaching in its commitment to free trade. The 1994 GATT agreement called into being the World Trade Organization (1995), which has served as a global trade referee committed to reducing barriers to trade. Issues of globalization and free trade have inspired vocal protests. The legacy of GATT and other free-trade agreements continues to shape political debates in the twenty-first century. Some political leaders blame the decline of industrial jobs in the Midwest on these agreements; others cite the ready availability of inexpensive consumer products as evidence of the success of the free-trade ethos (see more on the deindustrialization of America, page 368).

Challenges to Globalization 全球化挑战

President Bill Clinton's embrace of NAFTA was part of a broader push toward the removal of trade barriers. Proponents of globalization argue that the elimination of trade barriers will lower prices of products and stimulate the global economy. However, the movement toward free trade has generated much debate. Labor organizations argue that eliminating trade barriers will lead to the loss of American manufacturing jobs as businesses gravitate to countries where the going wages are the lowest. Also, environmentalists worry that free trade treaties will prevent the participating countries from enacting strong environmental protections. These opponents came together in Seattle, Washington, in November 1999 to protest at a meeting of the World Trade Organization, an international body charged with reducing trade barriers.

Changes in the Welfare System 福利体系的变化

In 1996, Bill Clinton adopted one of the planks of the Republican "Contract with America" by ending welfare as a federal program and shifting its administration to the state level. Clinton's embrace of welfare reform shocked many liberal Democrats. The Democratic Party had pushed for federal entitlement programs since the New Deal of President Roosevelt in the 1930s. Clinton perceived that many Americans were growing weary of programs that cost taxpayers money and did not seem to lessen poverty. Some Americans argued that welfare fostered a sense of dependency among recipients of welfare payments and stifled individual initiative. The reform required welfare recipients to begin work after two years—a stipulation known as "workfare."

Toward Health-Care Reform 走向医疗改革

One of President Bill Clinton's first major domestic policy initiatives was reform of the country's health-care system. Clinton put forth the idea of a federal health insurance plan that would provide subsidized insurance to many of the 39 million uncovered Americans, and would, according to the plan, bring down health insurance costs for everyone. The president's wife, Hillary Clinton, chaired a taskforce on the issue. The idea of a federal health insurance plan had been proposed as early as the 1930s. It came to the fore again in the late-twentieth century as health-care costs spiraled out of control and more and more people could not afford insurance. The plan was vigorously opposed by the pharmaceutical and insurance industries, and was ultimately shot down by a Republican filibuster in the Senate.

President Obama and Health-Care Reform 奥巴马总统与医疗改革

Like President Clinton, President Barack Obama chose health-care reform as one of his first major domestic initiatives. The issues that motivated Clinton in 1993—spiraling health-care costs, large numbers of uninsured Americans—had become more pronounced in the ensuing years. Proposals for creating a "public option" in regard to health insurance generated enthusiasm among many Democrats but met fierce opposition from the pharmaceutical and insurance industries, and from the Republican Party. Many Republicans likened such a proposal to "socialism." In 2009, both houses of Congress passed versions of health-care reform. In early 2010, a special election to fill the late Senator Edward Kennedy's seat was won by a Republican, ending the Democrats' sixty-seat filibuster-proof majority in the Senate. Democrats were able to pass a watered-down version of healthcare reform in March 2010.

The Patient Protection and Affordable Care Act was challenged in several federal courts. Three upheld the act; two deemed provisions of it unconstitutional. Finally, in 2012, the Supreme Court upheld the major aspects of the Affordable Care Act; specifically, it upheld the constitutionality of the act's individual mandate as an exercise of Congress's taxing power. In 2015, the act withstood another Supreme Court challenge. Critics of the law challenged the Constitutionality of federal health insurance exchanges, citing one passage of the act which mentions exchanges "established by the state." The court decided that, even though the wording of the act was problematic, the intent of Congress was to establish federal exchanges as well as state exchanges. Still, the act has generated opposition from Republicans, even as more Americans have begun participating in the health insurance exchanges established by the act.

Debates over Social Security Reform 关于社会安全改革的争论

With the percentage of Americans over the age of 65 growing, by 2030 there will be a substantial increase in the number of people receiving Social Security. The "graying of America," and its impact on the Social Security system, have been concerns of politicians recently. One reason for the growing percentage of senior citizens is the large number of "baby boomers," born in the period after World War II, reaching retirement age. Many people worry that when such a large percentage of the American public is retired, programs extending benefits to the elderly, notably Medicare and Social Security, will be unable to stay financially solvent. The issue of reforming the Social Security system has divided Democrats and Republicans, with Republicans pushing for some degree of privatization of the system, and Democrats pushing for increased funding streams to ensure its viability in the future. President George W. Bush, for example, pushed unsuccessfully for a combination of a government-funded program and personal accounts.

Reform of the Financial Sector 金融部门的改革

Heated debates have occurred from the 1980s to the present about the role of the government in regard to regulating the United States financial system. Republicans have generally argued for deregulation of major industries, including financial firms, and have resisted calls for increased government oversight. Republicans have argued that excessive regulation impedes risk-taking, competition, and economic growth. Democrats, on the other hand, argue that regulation is necessary to check reckless behavior on the part of the financial industry and to protect the economy from rapid fluctuations that can result from crises in the financial sector.

The Savings and Loan Crisis and Bailout 储贷危机与紧急救助

The issue of deregulation of the financial sector came into stark relief in the 1980s with the near collapse of the savings and loan industry. In the 1980s, the nation's savings and loan associations (S&Ls) suffered from a spate of irresponsible and risky investments and a downturn in the housing market. Their situation was made worse by the deregulation of the industry in 1980. Legislation widened the options for S&Ls to invest their financial holdings, paving the way for riskier speculative investments. By 1989, more than 700 S&Ls had become insolvent. In response to this crisis, President George H. W. Bush signed a bailout bill that extended billions of dollars to the industry. Taxpayers ultimately paid more than $120 billion for the bailout. Some economists believe that the bailout of the S&L industry created a moral hazard for other lenders—that is, it created a situation in which actors are more willing to take risks knowing that the potential costs of such risks will be borne by others. Thus, these economists see a connection between the S&L crisis and the subprime mortgage crisis of 2007.

KEY CONCEPT 9.2 CHALLENGES FACING THE UNITED STATES AT THE TURN OF THE CENTURY
核心概念9.2：世纪之交美国面临的挑战

As the United States moved into the twenty-first century, it faced a series of challenges related to a variety of social, economic, and demographic changes.

I. Technological Advances and the Transformation of the Economy 技术进步与经济转型

Scientific and technological developments have transformed American society. While new technologies have transformed daily life, they have had mixed results on the American economy. On the one hand, productivity in many sectors has increased as the United States has become more enmeshed in the global economy. On the other hand, the country has seen the gap between the wealthy and the poor dramatically widen as wages have stagnated in many sectors.

A. THE ECONOMY IN THE DIGITAL AGE 数字时代的经济

The American economy adapted to the age of digital communications. Economic productivity growth has risen in the United States as participation in the global economy has grown.

The Digital Revolution 数字革命

The use of computers has transformed the American workplace. The principles behind modern computing developed in the 1930s, and the first general-purpose computer is considered to be the ENIAC, developed in the United States in 1946. Two years later, transistors were developed, allowing for the replacement of bulky vacuum tubes. An important breakthrough in computing occurred 25 years later, with the microprocessor (1971), allowing for the development of smaller computers that had formidable processing powers. Apple launched a personal computer in 1977, and IBM followed a few years later. In the early 1980s, Microsoft developed operating systems for IBM "PCs" (and, later, for the PCs of rival companies). Through the course of the 1980s, personal computers became ubiquitous in workplaces.

Economic Productivity in the Digital Age 数字时代的经济生产率

The impact of the digital revolution on the American economy has been the subject of a great deal of debate. Generally, economists cite an increase in productivity growth—a useful measure of an economy's overall health and efficiency—starting in 1995, after years of slow growth from 1973 to 1995. This increase in productivity is generally attributed to the widespread use of information technologies. This increase might be attributed to the ability to perform many work-related functions with computers and to the increase in the speed of communications across the globe. However, economists have noted that the increase in overall economic productivity has not led to the expected increases in standards of living. Some economists cite the costs of replacing outdated equipment as a countervailing factor. Others cite the changing nature of work in the digital age and the growing income gap as factors that prevent many ordinary Americans from enjoying the fruits of the digital revolution.

B. NEW TECHNOLOGIES, NEW BEHAVIORS 新技术、新行为

The late twentieth and early twenty-first centuries have witnessed the spread of computer technology. The Internet has dramatically altered daily life, increasing access to information and fostering new social behaviors.

The Development and Spread of the Internet 互联网的发展与传播

The origins of the Internet date from the 1960s as the Department of Defense sought to create a computer system that would allow far-flung military installations to exchange computer information. In the late 1980s, universities in the United States created a computer network to facilitate the sharing of research while, in Switzerland, engineers developed the World Wide Web—a system of interlinked hypertext documents that organizes electronic information transmitted and accessed via the Internet.

Internet use grew rapidly in the 1990s, and has reshaped many aspects of daily life in the twenty-first century. E-mail communications quickly rendered letter writing obsolete. File sharing of music and video have forced the entertainment industry to rethink its business model. Traditional news outlets—newspapers, magazines, and even television—have been forced to compete with the instantaneous information available on the Internet. The Internet has changed practices in the workplace, allowing for virtual business meetings and telecommuting (working from home or a cafe). The Internet has also altered the world of commerce, allowing users to browse merchandise on their personal computer and purchase items with a few clicks of a "pointing device" called a "mouse." This has made shopping easier in many ways, but has driven many brick-and-mortar stores out of business. Bookstores have been hard hit by online booksellers and by the increased use of electronic books.

Although the Internet had become a popular fixture in American life by the mid-1990s, it was not fully utilized by political campaigns until the 2000s. In 2004, the unsuccessful campaign of Howard Dean demonstrated the potential of the Internet to raise money through donations. The 2008 campaign of Barack Obama fully embraced the Internet, building a grassroots system of activists and contributors that helped carry Obama to victory. Today, websites and social media are central to political campaigns.

The Internet became more mobile with the introduction of smart phones in the early 2000s. Critics note the tendency of smart phones to distract users from tasks (such as driving) and social interactions in front of them, while enthusiasts marvel that the world of information on the Internet is now accessible in the palm of the hand.

C. ECONOMIC SHIFTS: THE DECLINE OF MANUFACTURING AND
THE RISE OF THE SERVICE SECTOR 经济转轨：制造业的衰退与服务业的兴起

The United States has undergone profound economic changes in the period of 1980 to the present. Most significantly, manufacturing jobs have dramatically declined, while the service sector has grown.

The Deindustrialization of America 美国的非工业化

From the 1960s onward, large numbers of factories have closed in northeastern cities such as New York and Philadelphia, as well as in Midwestern "rust belt" cities such as Pittsburgh, Cleveland, Detroit, and Chicago. Some firms have relocated to the South and other areas within the United States where they can take advantage of lower-wage expectations and a weak labor movement. Since the 1980s, there has been a rapid shift of the manufacturing sector out of the United States and other developed countries and to the less-developed parts of the world. Free-trade agreements have accelerated this trend (see page 364). The rise of the private manufacturing sector in communist China has also played a major role. Because firms in China are able to produce goods at lower costs—a result of considerably lower labor costs and an exchange rate that is favorable to China—American imports from China grew dramatically in the late twentieth and early twenty-first century. In 2012, the U.S. trade deficit with China was $315 billion.

Decline of Union Membership 工会成员的减少

The decline of manufacturing jobs in the United States has contributed to a drop in union membership. In 1954, union membership (as a percentage of the total workforce) peaked in the United States at 35 percent; currently, it is about 12 percent. Another contributing factor in the decline of unionized workers was the ability of the New Right to press an agenda that values deregulation and free-market economics. A major turning point in government policy toward unionized workers came in 1981 under President Reagan. When air traffic controllers went on strike in 1981, he had them all fired. This action broke their union, the Professional Air Traffic Controllers' Organization (PATCO), and was consistent with helping the supply side (the airline industry), rather than the demand side (the unionized air traffic controllers). The destruction of PATCO was a major blow to organized labor in the late twentieth century. In such an environment, and with a falling membership, there has been a marked decline in the militancy of the union movement. In 1970, there were more than 380 major strikes or lockouts in the United States; by 1980, that figure dropped to under 200. In 2010, there were 11 major strikes or lockouts.

The Growth of the Service Sector 服务业的壮大

The service sector grew significantly in the period of 1980 to the present. The service sector of the economy is also called the tertiary sector. The primary sector includes the extraction and production of raw materials—such as mining, lumber operations, agriculture, and fishing. The secondary sector is generally considered manufacturing—the process involved in transforming raw materials into finished products available to the public. The tertiary, or service, sector involves the production of services, rather than end products. Such services enable and enhance other sectors of the economy. The service sector includes shipping and trucking, banking services, information technology, waste disposal, education, government, health care, legal services, and a whole host of retail and food-service operations. Throughout the Western world, service-sector employment, as a percentage of overall employment, has grown over the last century, with the pace of growth accelerating since 1980. Currently, 70 percent of jobs in the United States are in the service sector. The growth of the service sector illustrates a profound shift in the American economy from the production of things to the providing of services.

While the service sector includes a wide variety of jobs, the growth of low-wage jobs in the retail and fast-food fields has contributed to the stagnation of wages and to a growing income gap (see page 00). The three largest employers in the United States are currently Wal-Mart, Yum! Brands (which includes Taco Bell, KFC, and other fast food outlets), and McDonald's. Efforts to unionize workers in these fields have almost all failed due to vigorous anti-union activities by the corporations and to structural difficulties in organizing a decentralized work-force. Unions and worker-advocacy groups have pushed state legislatures to raise the minimum hourly wage allowed by law. The goal of a $15 minimum hourly wage has been a rallying cry of this movement.

D. THE PERSISTENCE OF ECONOMIC INEQUALITY 经济不平等的持续

At the close of the twentieth century, the gap between the wealthy and the rest of the population widened in the United States. Workers experienced stagnation in terms of real wages.

The Growth of the Income Gap 收入差距的扩大

Since the 1970s, economists have noted that the income gap between the wealthy and the middle class has grown increasingly wide. The incomes for the top-earning 1 percent of households increased by about 275 percent between 1979 and 2007, while the middle 60 percent of wage-earners saw their incomes rise by just under 40 percent during the same period. The flattening of wages for the middle class and the poor has meant an increase in debt for many Americans and, for many population groups, a decrease in consumer spending. A variety of political and economic factors can help explain this growing gap. Many economists cite factors mentioned above—the disappearance of higher-paying manufacturing jobs and the growth of low-wage service-sector jobs. Other factors include the decline of the union movement and changes in the tax code, including the massive tax cuts initiated by President George W. Bush (implemented in 2001 and 2003).

II. Demographic and Social Changes 人口与社会变化

The United States experienced major demographic shifts in the late twentieth and early twenty-first centuries, contributing to significant cultural and political consequences.

A. IMMIGRATION AND THE GROWTH OF THE "SUN BELT" 移民与"阳光地带"的发展

Since 1980, there has been a significant shift in the population toward the states of the South and the West. The growth of these regions was partly the result of increased immigration from Latin America and Asia.

Growth of the "Sun Belt" "阳光地带"的发展

The states of the "sun belt"—notably California, Texas, Arizona, Nevada, and Florida—have seen remarkable growth. This trend was seen as early as World War II when defense-related industries there attracted large numbers of workers. Affordable air conditioning also played a role in attracting migrants from within the United States to the sun belt. Florida has become a prime destination for retirees from colder parts of the country. Immigration from Latin America accounts for much of the growth of the region. Many immigrants have been drawn to agricultural work in California and to the cities of the sun belt. The political power of the South and the West has grown significantly since 1980. This has generally augured well for the Republican Party as national politics have come to reflect the more conservative views of those in the West and South. As a result of the most recent census (2010), Arizona, Nevada, South Carolina, Georgia, and Utah each gained one member of Congress; Texas added four seats; and Florida added two. By contrast, some of the more liberal states of the Midwest and Northeast lost power in Congress. Pennsylvania, Illinois, Michigan, Massachusetts, and New Jersey, each lost a House seat; New York and Ohio each lost two seats.

B. ASIAN AND LATIN AMERICAN IMMIGRATION　亚洲与拉丁美洲的移民

One of the most significant demographic changes in the late twentieth and early twenty-first centuries is the influx of Asian and Latin American immigrants into the United States.

Post-1965 Immigration Patterns　1965年后的移民模式

After passage of the Immigration and Nationality Act of 1965, immigration increased significantly—especially from Asia, Latin America, Africa, and the Middle East. Although the act added limits for migration from the Western Hemisphere for the first time, overall the impact of the act and of illegal immigration into the United States from within the Western Hemisphere, have dramatically altered the demographics of the United States. Before the act, immigration accounted for less than 10 percent of population growth into the United States. Currently it accounts for approximately a third of population growth. In the 35 years before the act was passed, approximately 5 million immigrants came into the United States; in the 1970s alone, that number was 4.5 million, rising to more than 7 million in the 1980s, and more than 9 million in the 1990s. This has been an important factor in the growth of the Southwestern states (see page 369).

The Changing Ethnic Makeup of the United States　不断变化的美国种族构成

As the percentage of the American population composed of Asian, African, Middle Eastern, and Latin American immigrants and their children has grown, the percentage of the American population composed of non-Hispanic whites has declined—from 75 percent of the overall U.S. population in 1990 to just over 63 percent in 2011. It is estimated that by the year 2042, non-Hispanic whites will no longer constitute a majority of the population of the United States.

C. DEBATES AROUND IMMIGRATION POLICY AND IDENTITY
围绕移民政策与美国身份的争论

In the late twentieth and early twenty-first centuries a number of social and political issues have divided Americans and led to debates around American identity. Specifically, debates have occurred around immigration policy, the status of gays and lesbians, and gender roles and family structures.

Debates Around Immigration 围绕移民的争论

From the 1970s to the present, immigration into the United States has increased dramatically, supplying workers to the workforce, while also leading to intense political, economic, and social debates. The changing profile of the population has raised concern among some Americans and has generated a broad debate around immigration policy. Many Americans argue that immigration should be restricted because it hurts the country economically; others focus on stopping illegal immigration. Members of the New Right expressed concern about the cultural impact of large-scale immigration. Will America, they wonder, fragment into ethnic enclaves? The Republican Party has generally embraced and courted the anti-immigrant sentiment. Republican politicians have argued for a more secure border with Mexico and for deportations of immigrants without proper immigration papers. The Immigration Reform and Control Act of 1986 reflected some of these concerns. Although the act enabled some immigrants without proper papers to achieve legal status, it also forced employers to ensure that their workforce was composed only of legal immigrants.

Further reform of immigration policy has been a priority of the Obama administration in the 2010s. Republican opposition in the House of Representatives has blocked a bipartisan immigration reform act, introduced in 2013, that would have provided a path to citizenship for some undocumented immigrants. In 2014, President Obama took executive action on the issue of immigration reform. By executive order, he expanded the scope of the Deferred Action for Childhood Arrivals (DACA) program. The action is currently held up in the courts, but if implemented, it would allow as many as 5 million illegal immigrants who are the parents of citizens or of lawful permanent residents to apply for a program that would spare them from deportation and would provide them with work permits.

Redefining Family Structures 重新定义家庭结构

The last decades of the twentieth century witnessed major changes in family structures in the United States. These changes, in turn, generated intense debate about the identity of the American family. An important trend was the growth of nontraditional families. In 1972, non-married households (either with or without children) stood at 26 percent of all families; that figure rose to 47 percent by 1998. This trend has divided liberals and conservatives, with liberals pushing for measures to extend rights and services to such households, and conservatives calling for a return to traditional family values.

Women in Professions 各行各业的女性

The "quiet revolution," beginning in the 1970s, of women entering the workplace in larger numbers continued through the end of the twentieth century (see Period 8). Though women have made advances in the workplace, many note that disparities still exist. In the 1970s, women earned on average 59 cents for each dollar that men earned doing comparable work. That gap has closed somewhat (to approximately 70 cents for each dollar earned by men) but still exists. In addition, women argued that they were often barred from higher positions in the corporate world. They claimed a "glass ceiling" existed that prevented them from climbing higher. The women's movement has also pushed for government-funded day care and greater participation by men in childcare.

The Gay Rights Movement and Changing Public Perceptions
同性恋权利运动与不断变化的公众认知

The gay rights movement grew in intensity after the Stonewall riots of 1969 (see Period 8). The growth and development of the movement, coupled with a strong conservative backlash against gay rights and against public acceptance of homosexuality, has shaped debates around gay, lesbian, bisexual, and transgender identity, acceptance, and rights.

The AIDS Crisis 艾滋病危机

In the 1980s, the gay community faced a major health crisis that brought the public divide around homosexuality into stark relief. Starting in 1981, news reports began to appear about a mysterious disease that seemed to disproportionately affect gay men, causing anxiety and sorrow in the gay community, but also resolve and action. The Centers for Disease Control and Prevention (CDC) identified the disease that would become known as acquired immunodeficiency syndrome (AIDS) in 1981. Soon, it also found that the cause of the disease was infection by the human immunodeficiency virus (HIV), present in bodily fluids such as semen and blood. The National Institutes of Health (NIH), a government body within the U.S. Department of Health and Human Services, was slow to acknowledge and address the crisis. It was not until 1987 that NIH established a committee to research the impact of HIV.

AIDS swept through gay communities in New York, San Francisco, Los Angeles, and elsewhere. On the one hand, AIDS became a lightning rod in the culture wars of the 1980s and beyond. Many Christian fundamentalists saw AIDS as God's punishment for sinful behavior. On the other hand, the crisis galvanized the gay community and led to an outpouring of both grief and activism. The group ACT-UP popularized the slogan "silence = death," and staged militant protests in New York and San Francisco. In 1987, ACT-UP staged a "funeral" on Wall Street in New York, with participants lying in the street, symbolizing those who had died from AIDS—suggesting that this would be the rapid fate of millions of people if more resources were not devoted to research and treatment.

"Don't Ask, Don't Tell" "不问，不说"政策

The armed forces of the United States has historically discriminated against gays serving in the military. In 1982, the Department of Defense issued a policy in which it stated, "Homosexuality is incompatible with military service." In the following years, gay and lesbian members of the military, and those excluded from the military, began a campaign to change the policy. The Gay and Lesbian Military Freedom Project was founded in 1988. Finally, in 1994, the military implemented a policy that allowed gay and lesbian members of the military to serve, as long as they remained "closeted," keeping their sexual identity hidden from public view. Advocates for gays and lesbians insisted that the policy, called "Don't Ask, Don't Tell," was discriminatory and that it limited the freedom of speech and expression of gays and lesbians in the service. The policy was repealed by an act of Congress, signed by President Obama in 2011.

Same-Sex Marriage 同性婚姻

Perhaps the clearest indicator of the rapid changes in societal attitudes toward homosexuality can be seen in the changing legal status of marriage between same-sex couples. Although gay rights proponents have long demanded that the right to legally marry be extended to same-sex couples, the issue became part of the national dialogue in 1993, when the Hawaii Supreme Court, in the case of *Baehr v. Lewin*, ruled that the state ban on same-sex marriage was discriminatory under the state constitution. Although the court did not mandate that the state begin issuing marriage licenses to gay couples, it had the effect of galvanizing social conservatives to mobilize against same-sex marriage and to defend "traditional" marriage. Hawaii ratified an amendment to its constitution, allowing the state legislature to ban same-sex marriage. Many states followed in Hawaii's footsteps by amending their constitutions so as to prevent the legalization of same-sex marriage. These amendments usually limited the definition of marriage as an act between a man and a woman. Further, Congress passed the Defense of Marriage Act in 1996, which allowed states to not recognize same-sex marriages performed in other states and also defined, for federal purposes, marriage as an act between one man and one woman.

The tide against same-sex marriage began to turn in 2003, when the Massachusetts Supreme Judicial Court ruled that the state may not forbid same-sex couples from legally marrying; it asserted that "the Massachusetts Constitution affirms the dignity and equality of all individuals. It forbids the creation of second-class citizens." Several other state high courts followed suit in the 2000s. In 2009, Vermont became the first state in the United States to legalize same-sex marriage through legislative means rather than through the court system. In 2013, the Supreme Court, in *United States v. Windsor*, struck down the section of DOMA that defined marriage, for federal purposes, as an act between a man and a woman. Public opinion moved rapidly on this issue. According to the Gallup organization, the aggregate of polls taken in 1996 showed 68 percent of Americans opposed extending legal recognition to same-sex couples, with only 27 percent supporting such a move. By 2015, the aggregate of polls showed that nearly 60 percent of Americans favored legalized same-sex marriage. The Supreme Court took heed. In 2015, in the case of *Obergefell v. Hodges*, the court ruled that marriage is a fundamental right that must be guaranteed to same-sex couples. The decision cited the due-process clause and the equal-protection clause of the Fourteenth Amendment to the Constitution.

KEY CONCEPT 9.3 THE END OF THE COLD WAR AND THE REDEFINITION OF FOREIGN POLICY GOALS
核心概念9.3：冷战的结束与外交政策目标的重新定义

The United States redefined its role in the world in the 1990s and 2000s and had to redefine its foreign policy as well. This change was a response to the ending of the Cold War and growing importance of global terrorism.

I. The End of the Cold War 冷战的结束

President Reagan had gained prominence earlier in his career as a strong anticommunist. He brought this rhetoric to the White House, and pursued an aggressive anticommunist agenda. His interventionist approach to foreign policy set the tone for the following administrations.

A. THE UNITED STATES AND THE WORLD DURING THE REAGAN ADMINISTRATION 里根政府时期的美国与世界

In the post–Vietnam War years, debates ensued about the proper role of the United States in the world. President Ronald Reagan (1981–1988) asserted opposition to communism through diplomatic efforts, military interventions, and a buildup of nuclear and conventional weapons.

Soviet-American Relations from Détente to Confrontation 美苏关系由缓和到对立

Relations between the Soviet Union and the United States, which had been improving since Nixon's détente overtures in the 1970s, soured after the Soviet Union invaded Afghanistan (1979). President Jimmy Carter suspended grain sales to the Soviets in protest of the invasion. He also pushed for a U.S. boycott of the 1980 Summer Olympics in Moscow.

President Reagan continued to confront the Soviet Union. He roundly denounced the Soviet Union, using pointedly ideological language. In a 1982 speech to the British Parliament, Reagan said, "[T]he forward march of freedom and democracy will leave Marxism–Leninism on the ash heap of history." In 1983, he predicted the collapse of the Soviet system. Later that year, in another speech, he labeled the Soviet Union "an evil empire" (1983).

Increased Military Spending 军费支出的增加

President Reagan was determined to challenge the Soviet "evil empire." He initiated several weapons programs, vowing to close what he called a "window of vulnerability"—the ability of Soviet missiles to attack and decimate American missile locations before the United States could adequately respond. He began research on the Strategic Defense Initiative, dubbed "Star Wars" by critics, and initiated the costly MX missile program.

The Reagan Doctrine 里根主义

The Reagan administration supported regimes that were anticommunist, no matter if they were undemocratic, or even repressive. This foreign policy came to be known as the Reagan Doctrine. Reagan sent troops to the island of Grenada in 1983 to topple the Marxist leaders of the country. He continued to support the dictatorial regime of the Philippines led by Ferdinand Marcos despite reports of electoral fraud. The regime was finally ousted in 1986, with Corazon Aquino replacing Marcos.

Central America and the Iran-Contra Scandal 中美洲与伊朗门丑闻

As part of the Reagan Doctrine, his administration consistently tried to undermine the left-wing Sandinista government in Nicaragua. The Sandinistas took power in 1979, after overthrowing the U.S.-backed dictatorship of Anastasio Somoza. The United States funded and trained an anti-Sandinista military group known as the Contras. In 1982, Congress, alarmed at reports of human rights abuses by the Contras, passed the Boland Amendment, to halt U.S. aid to the group.

Congressional action did not deter members of the Reagan administration from covertly funding the Contras. An elaborate scheme was developed to secretly sell weapons to Iran and use funds from these sales to support the Contras. In 1986, details of the Iran-Contra affair became public. Ultimately 14 members of the Reagan administration were tried for violating U.S. law, and 11 were convicted. Among the convicted was Secretary of Defense Caspar Weinberger. Oliver North, of the National Security Council, an architect of the program, was also initially convicted. The convictions were overturned on appeal. Reagan himself claimed to have had no direct knowledge of the program. Critics labeled him the "Teflon president," because accusations of wrongdoing did not stick to him.

B. THE FALL OF THE SOVIET UNION AND THE COLLAPSE OF COMMUNISM
苏联的解体与共产主义的瓦解

President Reagan is often given credit for helping precipitate the fall of the communist governments of the Eastern Bloc. By 1989, mass public protests had begun to weaken the governments in Poland and East Germany. It was clear that Soviet leader Mikhail Gorbachev would not intervene militarily to halt this development (as previous Soviet leaders had). The iconic image of the movement was the November 1989 demolition of the Berlin Wall by the Berliners from both sides. The wall, separating West Berlin from East Berlin, was a symbol of the rift between the Communist bloc countries and the Western countries. By 1991, the Soviet Union itself had collapsed, ending communism in Europe. It is true that an accelerated arms race taxed the Soviet economy more than it did the American economy, but one must also look at the internal dynamics of Soviet society to understand this major development.

C. THE UNITED STATES IN THE POST–COLD WAR WORLD 冷战后的美国

Debates continued about the U.S. role in the world after the end of the Cold War, as the United States engaged in a number of military and peacekeeping interventions, including the Persian Gulf War of 1990–1991.

President George Bush and the Persian Gulf War 乔治·布什总统与海湾战争

President George H. W. Bush's main accomplishments were in the field of foreign affairs. It was during Bush's presidency (1989–1993) that the Berlin Wall came down, and the Soviet Union collapsed. After Iraq, under the leadership of Saddam Hussein, invaded neighboring Kuwait in 1990 in an attempt to gain more control over the region's oil reserves, Bush organized a 34-nation coalition to challenge the move. In late 1990, after fruitless negotiations, President Bush gave Hussein approximately six weeks (until January 15, 1991) to withdraw from Kuwait. When Hussein did not act, the coalition initiated "Operation Desert Storm," defeating Iraqi forces and driving them from Kuwait by February 1991. During the Persian Gulf War significant numbers of women served in combat roles for the first time.

Chaos in Somalia 索马里混乱

The administration of President Bill Clinton, like previous Democratic administrations, set out broad domestic reform goals but became enmeshed in foreign-policy matters. Clinton deployed U.S. forces to aid a United Nations humanitarian mission in Somalia in 1993. Troubles in Somalia had begun earlier, in 1991, after the government was overthrown and fighting broke out between competing factions. The civil war in Somalia resulted in widespread famine, with more than half a million people dying. The UN took the initiative to deliver food to Somalia, but much of it was stolen by the warring factions and sold for weapons. In December 1992, President Bush had approved the use of U.S. troops to aid UN relief activities. By 1993, these troops were under attack, resulting in intense fighting in the capital, Mogadishu. American forces suffered 19 deaths. The mission soon ended with a U.S. withdrawal.

Democracy in Haiti 海地的民主政治

President Clinton took the lead in insuring a transition to democracy in Haiti in 1994. After decades of dictatorship, a democratic election had brought Jean-Bertrand Aristide to power in 1990. Subsequently, a Haitian general ousted him. Clinton announced American intentions to use force, if necessary, to return Aristide to power. The United Nations authorized such a move, but former President Jimmy Carter was dispatched to Haiti to try to negotiate an end to military rule. He was successful, and Aristide returned to power in 1995.

Intervention in the Former Yugoslavia　对前南斯拉夫的干预

President Clinton became increasingly concerned about violence in the former Yugoslavia. Under communism, Yugoslavia had been a patchwork of different ethnicities. After communism fell in 1989, the country split into several smaller nations. Ethnic violence developed as Serbian forces attempted to gain control of areas of Bosnia with large Serbian populations. In the process, Serbian forces initiated a campaign to remove Bosnians, by force if necessary, from these areas. This "ethnic cleansing" campaign resulted in atrocities against the civilian population and became a focus of concern in the media and among foreign countries. The United States and other countries decided to take action as reports of Serbian brutality became known. President Clinton brought leaders from Bosnia, Serbia, and Croatia together in 1995 in Dayton, Ohio. A peace treaty was signed, known as the Dayton Agreement, and 60,000 NATO troops were dispatched to enforce it.

The United States again became concerned about violence in the region in 1998 when reports emerged of Serbian attacks against ethnic Albanians in the Serbian province of Kosovo. President Clinton approved the use of U.S. forces, under NATO auspices, to engage in a bombing campaign against Serbia in 1999.

Clinton and the Conflict in the Middle East　克林顿与中东冲突

Toward the end of his second term, Clinton put a great deal of effort in attempting to broker a peace agreement between Israel and the Palestinians (see more on the conflict between Israel and the Palestinians in Period 8). Since the Six-Day War in 1967, Israel has occupied adjacent lands where large numbers of Palestinians live. These lands currently include the West Bank of the Jordan River, the Gaza Strip, and Eastern Jerusalem. Palestinians have insisted these lands should comprise a Palestinian state. Israel has resisted agreeing to the formation of a Palestinian state as long as Palestinians launch attacks on Israel. The continued growth of Jewish settlements in the West Bank complicates the situation. In 2000, President Bill Clinton invited Palestinian leader Yasser Arafat and Israeli prime minister Ehud Barak to Camp David. The goal was to work out a "final status settlement" to the Israeli-Palestinian conflict. The discussions at Camp David in 2000 did not find an agreement to the conflict, which still remains unresolved.

II. The United States in the Age of Global Terrorism
全球恐怖主义时代的美国

The terrorist attacks on the United States in 2001 caused the United States to focus its foreign policy on the war on terrorism. The actions taken by the United States, both at home and abroad, have generated debate about security and civil liberties.

A. THE TERRORIST ATTACKS OF 2001 AND THE U.S. RESPONSE
2001年的恐怖袭击与美国的反应

Following the terrorist attacks on the World Trade Center and the Pentagon, a series of foreign policy and military initiatives aimed at preventive future terrorist attacks got under way. These initiatives included prolonged and controversial military campaigns in Afghanistan and Iraq.

Terrorist Attacks Against the United States 针对美国的恐怖袭击

On the morning of September 11, 2001, 19 terrorists affiliated with the al-Qaeda network hijacked four domestic airplanes. The plan was to turn the airplanes into missiles that would destroy symbols of American power. One plane was flown into the Pentagon, inflicting heavy damage, and one plane crashed in a field after the hijackers were overwhelmed by passengers. The other two airplanes did the most damage, crashing into the two towers of the World Trade Center in New York City. The damage inflicted on each building weakened their structures so that both collapsed within two hours. Approximately 3,000 people died in the four incidents, the vast majority of the deaths occurring at the World Trade Center.

War in Afghanistan 阿富汗战争

The terrorist attacks of 2001 were soon followed by President George W. Bush initiating military action on two fronts—Afghanistan and Iraq. The United States initiated military actions in Afghanistan in 2001, less than a month after the September 11 terrorist attacks. American forces overthrew the Taliban, the government that had given refuge to al-Qaeda. The United States hoped to find the leader of al-Qaeda, Osama bin Laden, who was still at large at the end of President Bush's presidency.

War with Iraq 伊拉克战争

"Operation Iraqi Freedom," begun in 2003, was the U.S. military campaign to remove Iraq's president, Saddam Hussein, from power and create a less belligerent and more democratic government in Iraq. President Bush insisted that Hussein was developing weapons of mass destruction that could be used against the United States and its allies. (U.S. forces failed to find evidence of such weapons.) The administration also asserted that there was a connection between Hussein and the terrorist attacks of 2001. No evidence of such a link has been uncovered, and the administration moved away from that rationale. This operation proved to be more difficult and costly than "Operation Desert Storm." Defeating the Iraqi army and overthrowing Saddam Hussein was relatively easy. After these goals were accomplished, President Bush declared "mission accomplished" in May 2003. However, creating stability in Iraq proved to be an elusive goal for the Bush administration. Attacks by insurgents continued, both against U.S. forces and between various factions within Iraq. Operation Iraqi Freedom hurt President Bush's approval ratings in the United States and created tension between the United States and some European nations.

B. LIBERTY, SECURITY, AND HUMAN RIGHTS IN THE WAR ON TERRORISM
反恐战争中的自由、安全与人权

The war on terrorism has fostered a series of intense debates among the American people about the proper methods of carrying out a global war on terrorism. Many Americans became increasingly concerned about issues of human rights and civil liberties in this campaign against terrorism.

The Patriot Act 《爱国者法案》

The Patriot Act was passed in 2001, six weeks after the September 11 terrorist attacks. It greatly expanded the government's authority in the fight against terrorism. Some critics have said that it impinges on people's civil liberties. Perhaps one of the biggest controversies around the Patriot Act is the use of National Security Letters, or NSLs, by the FBI. These NSLs allow the

FBI to search telephone, e-mail, and financial records without a court order, raising constitutional concerns for many people.

Department of Homeland Security 国土安全部

The creation of the Department of Homeland Security was a result of the September 11, 2001, terrorist attacks. It was created in 2003, absorbing the Immigration and Naturalization Service. It is a cabinet level department, with the responsibility of protecting the United States from terrorist attacks and natural disasters.

Tactics in the War on Terrorism 反恐战争的策略

In 2004, the release of photographs of United States Army personnel humiliating and, apparently, abusing prisoners at the Abu Ghraib prison in Iraq cast light on new tactics used by the United States in its handling of prisoners in the aftermath of the 2001 terrorist attacks. Army personnel at detention camps in Iraq, Afghanistan, and Guantanamo Bay, Cuba, were given permission to use "enhanced interrogation" techniques. Critics said these techniques, which include "waterboarding," amounted to torture. The government also began to hold suspects at these facilities indefinitely, denying them due process rights. The Supreme Court, in *Hamdan v. Rumsfeld* (2006), ruled that the Bush administration could not hold detainees indefinitely without due process and without the protection of the Geneva Accords.

President Obama and the War on Terrorism 奥巴马总统与反恐战争

Some of the concerns about the way the war on terrorism was being carried out under the administration of President George W. Bush helped elevate Barack Obama to the White House in 2008 over Republican John McCain. In 2011, the Obama administration was able to report that a Navy "SEAL Team Six" had killed Osama bin Laden. However, to the disappointment of many of Obama's supporters in 2008, the president has continued many of the controversial antiterrorism policies begun during the Bush administration and has pursued some new programs. The Patriot Act, for instance, is still in effect. In 2011, Obama allowed for the extension of three controversial measures within the Patriot Act that were set to expire. During the election campaign in 2008, he called the reports of prisoner abuse at the Guantanamo Bay detention camp "a sad chapter in American history" and promised to close it down by 2009. As of 2015, he has not closed it down.

In addition, President Obama has generated a great deal of debate over the increased use of unmanned drone attacks on suspected terrorist targets. The program, begun under President George W. Bush, has been greatly expanded under the Obama administration, despite it being criticized by the United Nations as "extrajudicial killings," and "summary justice." Finally, President Obama renewed a clandestine program known as PRISM, which allows the National Security Agency to conduct mass data mining of phone, Internet, and other communications—including, under certain circumstances, those of United States citizens. The clandestine program was exposed by computer specialist and former NSA contractor, Edward Snowden, in 2013. The revelations revived the ongoing debate among Americans around the protection of civil liberties in the age of global terrorism.

C. ENERGY POLICY, CONSUMPTION, AND THE LIMITS TO GROWTH
能源政策、消费与发展的局限

A series of developments have generated debates in the United States around energy use and policy. Ongoing conflicts in the Middle East and overwhelming evidence of long-term climate change have generated concern about continued reliance on fossil fuels. In addition, many Americans have become increasingly concerned about the overall impact of mass consumption on the environment.

Climate Change and Energy Policy 气候变化与能源政策

Americans are by far the world's largest consumers of energy. In the aftermath of the Arab oil embargo of 1973 and the energy crisis that followed the 1979 Iranian Revolution, some American policymakers began to look for ways for the United States to reduce its consumption of energy (see Period 8). This push toward a reduction in energy consumption has been augmented in recent decades by growing concerns over climate change.

Since the early 1980s, scientists have become aware of a trend toward warmer global temperatures. Some became convinced that this warming trend was caused by trapped greenhouse gasses, which, in turn, were caused by human activities, primarily the burning of fossil fuels. In the 1990s and 2000s, a virtual consensus emerged in the scientific community around the connection between global warming and the emissions generated by the burning of fossil fuels. Calls were made to limit the human activities linked to global warming. The 1992 "Earth Summit" in Brazil led to the adoption by most of the countries in the world of the United Nations Framework Convention on Climate Change. The 1997 Kyoto Protocols sets binding obligations on industrialized countries to reduce the emission of greenhouse gasses. The United States signed, but did not ratify, the protocol. More recently, the United States played in important role in the negotiations that led to the Paris Agreement (2015). The framework was negotiated through the United Nations Framework Convention on Climate Change (UNFCCC). The agreement, calling for broad carbon dioxide reduction measures, will be open for formal ratification in 2016. Global climate change has generated debate in the United States between those who would like to see limits placed on greenhouse-gas emissions and those who emphasize economic growth.

To some degree, American society is making changes. California passed legislation in 2006 that would reduce greenhouse-gas emissions from all sources, including automobiles. Other communities are taking steps that include encouraging bicycling and mass transit. Scientists and many observers wonder if the small steps being taken in the United States and elsewhere will be able to slow down the process of global warming.

D. UNITED STATES FOREIGN POLICY IN THE TWENTY-FIRST CENTURY
21世纪美国的外交政策

The United States remains the world's leading superpower in the twenty-first century. Debates have continued about U.S. goals and actions on the global stage.

President George W. Bush and the Withdrawal from the International Community 乔治·W. 布什总统与从国际社会的退出

The debate over the role of the United States in the world continued during the administration of President George W. Bush. Although President Bush worked with a coalition of nations in the invasion of Iraq in the aftermath of the terrorist attacks of 2001 (see page 376), he distrusted many of the multilateral entities in which the United States had previously participated. Bush withdrew the United States from the Kyoto Protocol, an international agreement on environmental goals. Also, the administration violated international guidelines about the treatment of military prisoners. Bush withdrew from the Anti-ballistic Missile Treaty, in effect since 1972, in late 2001 so that the United States could develop a space-based missile-defense system. In 2002, the United States withdrew from the treaty creating the United Nation's International Criminal Court, which went into effect later that year.

The Bush Doctrine 布什主义

Debates about military interventions continued during the presidency of George W. Bush. These debates took on added urgency in the aftermath of the terrorist attacks of 2001. Bush shifted American foreign policy away from its traditional reliance on deterrence and containment. He put forth a more aggressive approach in the fall of 2002 that called for pre-emptive strikes against nations perceived as threats to the United States. In a speech at West Point, Bush identified an "axis of evil" consisting of Iraq, Iran, and North Korea. This reliance on pre-emptive warfare is known as the Bush Doctrine.

President Obama and the Middle East 奥巴马总统与中东

President Obama has taken a variety of steps in regard to the Muslim world. Soon after coming into office, he made a major speech in Cairo, Egypt, pledging to mend relations with the Muslim world. He has committed additional forces to Afghanistan while beginning a withdrawal of troops from Iraq. In 2011, Obama spoke favorably of the changes brought about by the "Arab Spring" protests in the Middle East and North Africa. He committed United States forces, working with European allies, to challenge forces loyal to Libyan leader Muhammar Qadaffi. During the 2008 campaign, Obama repeatedly pledged to commit United States forces to finding and killing Osama Bin Laden. That pledge was fulfilled in the spring of 2011.

President Obama has also focused on preventing Iran from acquiring nuclear weapons. Negotiations between the United States and Iran began in 2013 and, after several setbacks, resulted in a deal entitled the Joint Comprehensive Plan of Action (2015). The main components of the deal involve removing sanctions against Iran in exchange for measures to insure that country would not produce a bomb. The deal was endorsed by 90 nations that applauded the move toward bringing Iran into the broader community of nations. Many saw the deal as an important step toward making the world safer and toward opening up economic opportunities with Iran. The deal was roundly condemned by Republican and conservative observers and by Israeli prime minister Benjamin Netanyahu. Many conservatives saw the deal as capitulation to a dangerous regime with ties to terrorist organizations.

SUBJECT TO DEBATE 相关讨论

With Ronald Reagan's passing away (in 2004), his legacy has increasingly been the subject of historical work. Much of that work is highly partisan. On the one side, critics cite Reagan's background in B-movies, such as *Bedtime for Bonzo*, and his seeming disinterest in matters of intellect, as evidence of incompetency as president. These critics note that Reagan napped during meetings while important policy matters were discussed. He seemed aloof from issues, and claimed ignorance of the complicated schemes that comprised the Iran-Contra scandal. Reagan's defenders focus on one of the major events of the Reagan-Bush years—the fall of communism in Europe. Reagan initiated a massive military buildup that the Soviet Union could not keep up with. The Soviets' attempt to keep pace broke their bank and led to the opening of the floodgates of change. In much of the recent work on Reagan's legacy, these poles dominate discussion.

Historians of social movements have tried to understand the rise of the New Right. Some historians have drawn comparisons to previous conservative movements—the "Red Scare" of the 1920s or McCarthyism in the 1950s. Others have connected it to religious movements of the past, such as the Second Great Awakening of the early nineteenth century. Historians have also looked at the movement in the context of a backlash against the social movements and protest culture of the 1960s. If the legacy of the 1960s is "free love," protest, and multiculturalism, the New Right stands for its opposites—conservative approaches to sexuality, respect for authority and discipline, and a unifying patriotism. The persistence of this movement into the age of President Barack Obama ensures that it will remain a topic of debate.

It is very difficult to debate the legacy of the very recent past. One topic that historians have begun to wrestle with is the origins of the toxic partisan atmosphere in Washington, DC. Some historians look to the impeachment process against President Clinton as a turning point in recent political history. The Republican-initiated inquest went beyond the usual jockeying between parties and made compromise between the parties increasingly difficult. Historians also note the unusual closeness in public appeal of the two major parties in recent elections and in opinion polls. Both parties always feel as if victory is within reach and seek to press any advantage they can to win points with the electorate. Future historians will have to put the election of the nation's first African-American president in a larger context.

PRACTICE MULTIPLE-CHOICE QUESTIONS 选择题练习

> **Directions:** Pick the letter that best answers the following questions.

Questions 1–2 refer to the following passage: 根据以下段落，回答第1—2题

"[As] Members of the House of Representatives and as citizens seeking to join that body we propose not just to change its policies, but even more important, to restore the bonds of trust between the people and their elected representatives.

"That is why in this era of official evasion and posturing, we offer instead a detailed agenda for national renewal, a written commitment with no fine print.

"This year's election offers the chance, after four decades of one-party control, to bring to the House a new majority that will transform the way Congress works. That historic change would be the end of government that is too big, too intrusive, and too easy with the public's money. It can be the beginning of a Congress that respects the values and shares the faith of the American family.

"To restore accountability to Congress. To end its cycle of scandal and disgrace. To make us all proud again of the way free people govern themselves."

—"Contract with America" (excerpt), 1994

1. The writing of the "Contract with America," excerpted, demonstrates which of the following?

    (A) The growth and influence of the conservative movement in the United States in the 1980s and 1990s.

    (B) The ability of the Democratic Party and the Republican Party to forge alliances in the 1980s and 1990s.

    (C) The importance of "third-party" movements in terms of shaping political debate in the United States in the 1980s and 1990s.

    (D) The growing importance of social and religious issues, such as gay marriage and abortion, in public discourse.

2. Which of the following generalizations is illustrated by the impact of the Contract with America?

    (A) The Republican Party experienced electoral setbacks, being shut out from control of the House of Representatives, the Senate, and the White House for the decade after the Contract with America appeared.

    (B) The Republican Party was able to roll back or eliminate key elements of the Great Society agenda of President Lyndon Johnson.

    (C) Although Republicans continued to denounce "big government," the size and scope of the federal government continued to grow in the 1990s, as many programs remained popular with voters and difficult to reform or eliminate.

    (D) Many Congressional Republicans quit the Republican Party and joined the Democratic Party in protest of the divisive tone of the Contract with America.

Questions 3–4 are based on the following passage: 根据以下段落，回答第3—4题

"As citizens of global society, recognizing that the World Trade Organization is unjustly dominated by corporate interests and run for the enrichment of the few at the expense of all others, we demand:

"Representatives from all sectors of society must be included in all levels of trade policy formulations. All global citizens must be democratically represented in the formulation, implementation, and evaluation of all global social and economic policies.

"Global trade and investment must not be ends in themselves, but rather the instruments for achieving equitable and sustainable development including protection for workers and the environment.

"Global trade agreements must not undermine the ability of each nation-state or local community to meet its citizens' social, environmental, cultural or economic needs.

"The World Trade Organization must be replaced by a democratic and transparent body accountable to citizens—not to corporations.

—Global Exchange (Seattle), "Declaration for Global Democracy" (1999)

3. The "Declaration for Global Democracy," excerpted, reflects

    (A) opposition to free trade agreements in the late twentieth century.
    (B) concerns about punitive steps taken by the United States government as part of the war on international terrorism.
    (C) the desire of Congressional leaders to expand global trade and to reduce trade barriers.
    (D) fears that environmental regulations will impinge upon economic growth.

4. The political sentiments reflected in the "Declaration for Global Democracy," are most similar to which of the following?

    (A) President Woodrow Wilson's "Fourteen Points" document (1918).
    (B) Agreements at the Bretton Woods (New Hampshire) Conference (1944) that led to the formation of the International Monetary Fund.
    (C) New Left critiques of the Vietnam War in the 1960s.
    (D) The Republican Party's "Contract for America" (1994).

Answers and Explanations to Multiple-Choice Questions
选择题的答案与解析

1. **(A)** The "Contract with America" demonstrates the growth and influence of the conservative movement in the United States in the 1980s and 1990s. By 1994, the Republicans had not controlled the House in more than four decades. In an effort to create a national campaign in the congressional elections of 1994, House Republicans, led by minority leader Newt Gingrich, had signed and publicly issued the Contract with America six weeks before the election. The document called for action on a number of fronts, such as tougher anti-crime measures, tort reform, and welfare reform. The Republican Party made significant gains in the Senate and gained control of the House of Representatives. Many of the House's initiatives died in the Senate, some were vetoed by President Bill Clinton, some were implemented, and some were reworked by both parties before being implemented.

2. **(C)** Although Republicans gained control of the House in 1994, Republican legislative successes were limited. The party continued to denounce "big government," but the size and scope of the federal government continued to grow in the 1990s and even grew in the first decade of the twenty-first century, with a Republican president, George W. Bush, in the White House.

3. **(A)** The "Declaration for Global Democracy" reflects opposition to free trade agreements in the late twentieth century. The major powers of the world have taken measures to reduce tariffs on imports, thus making the movement of goods and companies across the globe easier. The United States approved the North American Free Trade Agreement (NAFTA) in 1993 and joined the new World Trade Organization in 1994 with the goal of reducing or eliminating tariffs. Free trade and economic globalization is defended by many, such as columnist Thomas Friedman, as a positive development that will create greater understanding in the world and will raise living standards in developing countries. Others, such as protestors at the 1999 meeting of the World Trade Organization in Seattle, condemn globalization as reducing environmental protections and shifting manufacturing jobs to sweatshops in poor countries.

4. **(C)** The political sentiments reflected in the "Declaration for Global Democracy" are most similar to New Left critiques of the Vietnam War in the 1960s. Both the anti-globalization movement and the antiwar movement made connections between foreign-policy decisions and corporate domination. Both movements also focused on increasing democratic participation in decision-making. Also, both movements used street demonstrations to put forth their agendas.

PART THREE
Practice Exams
第三部分
模拟考试

ANSWER SHEET
Practice Test 1
答题纸
模拟测试一

SECTION I: PART A—MULTIPLE-CHOICE 第一部分：A——选择题

1. Ⓐ Ⓑ Ⓒ Ⓓ
2. Ⓐ Ⓑ Ⓒ Ⓓ
3. Ⓐ Ⓑ Ⓒ Ⓓ
4. Ⓐ Ⓑ Ⓒ Ⓓ
5. Ⓐ Ⓑ Ⓒ Ⓓ
6. Ⓐ Ⓑ Ⓒ Ⓓ
7. Ⓐ Ⓑ Ⓒ Ⓓ
8. Ⓐ Ⓑ Ⓒ Ⓓ
9. Ⓐ Ⓑ Ⓒ Ⓓ
10. Ⓐ Ⓑ Ⓒ Ⓓ
11. Ⓐ Ⓑ Ⓒ Ⓓ
12. Ⓐ Ⓑ Ⓒ Ⓓ
13. Ⓐ Ⓑ Ⓒ Ⓓ
14. Ⓐ Ⓑ Ⓒ Ⓓ
15. Ⓐ Ⓑ Ⓒ Ⓓ
16. Ⓐ Ⓑ Ⓒ Ⓓ
17. Ⓐ Ⓑ Ⓒ Ⓓ
18. Ⓐ Ⓑ Ⓒ Ⓓ
19. Ⓐ Ⓑ Ⓒ Ⓓ
20. Ⓐ Ⓑ Ⓒ Ⓓ
21. Ⓐ Ⓑ Ⓒ Ⓓ
22. Ⓐ Ⓑ Ⓒ Ⓓ
23. Ⓐ Ⓑ Ⓒ Ⓓ
24. Ⓐ Ⓑ Ⓒ Ⓓ
25. Ⓐ Ⓑ Ⓒ Ⓓ
26. Ⓐ Ⓑ Ⓒ Ⓓ
27. Ⓐ Ⓑ Ⓒ Ⓓ
28. Ⓐ Ⓑ Ⓒ Ⓓ
29. Ⓐ Ⓑ Ⓒ Ⓓ
30. Ⓐ Ⓑ Ⓒ Ⓓ
31. Ⓐ Ⓑ Ⓒ Ⓓ
32. Ⓐ Ⓑ Ⓒ Ⓓ
33. Ⓐ Ⓑ Ⓒ Ⓓ
34. Ⓐ Ⓑ Ⓒ Ⓓ
35. Ⓐ Ⓑ Ⓒ Ⓓ
36. Ⓐ Ⓑ Ⓒ Ⓓ
37. Ⓐ Ⓑ Ⓒ Ⓓ
38. Ⓐ Ⓑ Ⓒ Ⓓ
39. Ⓐ Ⓑ Ⓒ Ⓓ
40. Ⓐ Ⓑ Ⓒ Ⓓ
41. Ⓐ Ⓑ Ⓒ Ⓓ
42. Ⓐ Ⓑ Ⓒ Ⓓ
43. Ⓐ Ⓑ Ⓒ Ⓓ
44. Ⓐ Ⓑ Ⓒ Ⓓ
45. Ⓐ Ⓑ Ⓒ Ⓓ
46. Ⓐ Ⓑ Ⓒ Ⓓ
47. Ⓐ Ⓑ Ⓒ Ⓓ
48. Ⓐ Ⓑ Ⓒ Ⓓ
49. Ⓐ Ⓑ Ⓒ Ⓓ
50. Ⓐ Ⓑ Ⓒ Ⓓ
51. Ⓐ Ⓑ Ⓒ Ⓓ
52. Ⓐ Ⓑ Ⓒ Ⓓ
53. Ⓐ Ⓑ Ⓒ Ⓓ
54. Ⓐ Ⓑ Ⓒ Ⓓ
55. Ⓐ Ⓑ Ⓒ Ⓓ

SECTION I: PART B—SHORT ANSWER　第一部分：B——简答题
Use dark blue or black ink only for the short-answer questions. Do not write outside of the box.

Question 1　问题1

SECTION I: PART B—SHORT ANSWER　第一部分：B——简答题
Use dark blue or black ink only for the short-answer questions. Do not write outside of the box.

Question 2　问题2

SECTION I: PART B—SHORT ANSWER 第一部分：B——简答题
Use dark blue or black ink only for the short-answer questions. Do not write outside of the box.

Question 3 问题3

Use dark blue or black ink only for the short-answer questions. Do not write outside of the box.

Question 4　问题4

SECTION II: PART A—DOCUMENT-BASED QUESTION 第二部分：A——材料分析题

SECTION II: PART B—LONG ESSAY 第二部分：B——论述题

Circle the number of the Essay that you are answering on this page.	Mandatory: 1	Circle one: 2 or 3

Practice Test 1　模拟测试一

SECTION I　第一部分

Part A: Multiple-Choice Questions　选择题

> **Directions:** The questions in this section are grouped in sets of 2–4. Each set is organized around a primary source, secondary source, or historical issue. Select the best answer for each of the questions in this section. (55 minutes)

Questions 1–3 refer to the following passage:

"The question, therefore, should be quickly settled, whether free colored persons, born and naturalized in this country, are not American citizens, and justly entitled to all the rights, privileges and immunities of citizens of the several states; and whether the Constitution of the United States makes or authorizes any invidious distinction with regard to the color or condition of free inhabitants.

"For myself, I have not the shadow of doubt on the subject. I believe that the rights of the free colored persons need only to be vindicated before the U.S. Supreme Court, to be obtained; that no prejudice or sophistry . . . can prevent their acknowledgement . . . and that the present laws, affecting your condition, are clearly unconstitutional. The fact that you have been treated, by common consent and common usage, as aliens and brutes, is not proof that such treatment is legal, but only shows the strength, the bitterness, and the blindness of prejudice."

—William Lloyd Garrison, "To the Free People of Color
of the United States," *The Liberator*, January 15, 1831

1. The approach of William Lloyd Garrison and *The Liberator* can best be seen as

   (A) an outgrowth of the Second Great Awakening.

   (B) an expression of Transcendentalist individualism.

   (C) a reflection of literary romanticism.

   (D) a rejection of the idea of "Republican motherhood."

2. The argument put forth by William Lloyd Garrison in the passage was later contradicted in which of the following Supreme Court decisions?

(A) *Dred Scott v. Sanford* (1857)

(B) *Ex parte Milligan* (1866)

(C) *Plessy v. Ferguson* (1896)

(D) *Brown v. Board of Education of Topeka* (1954)

3. The reform that William Lloyd Garrison is advocating in the passage was later enacted as a result of the

(A) issuing of the Emancipation Proclamation (1863).

(B) passage of the Reconstruction Act of 1867.

(C) ratification of the Fourteenth Amendment (1868).

(D) passage of the Civil Rights Act of 1875.

Questions 4–5 refer to the following images:

4. The differences in the two maps shown above illustrate which of the following?

(A) The result of the Articles of Confederation government successfully handling the question of western lands.

(B) Territorial transfers that were brought about by the treaty ending the French and Indian War.

(C) The evolving status of slavery in the newly acquired territories of the United States.

(D) The impact of the "Quasi-War" with France on competing land claims in the American West.

5. The establishment of the Northwest Territory (visible in the second map) by the Northwest Ordinance of 1787 contributed to problems in the subsequent decades of American history because the ordinance

(A) ignored the earlier designation of that land as an "Indian Reserve" by the British, setting the stage for violent conflict in the region.

(B) failed to address the issue of slavery in the Northwest Territory, leading to violence between pro-slavery and anti-slavery forces.

(C) called for any political entities carved out of the Northwest Territory to be treated as inferior bodies to the original 13 states, leading to a constitutional conflict that was eventually resolved by the Supreme Court.

(D) made no provisions for individuals to gain title to land in the Northwest Territory, setting off a series of violent skirmishes among people with competing land claims.

Questions 6–8 refer to the following image:

UNCLE SAM'S NEW CLASS IN THE ART OF SELF-GOVERNMENT.

6. The circumstances depicted in the cartoon suggest that the cartoon was published in the immediate aftermath of

(A) the War of 1812.

(B) the Mexican-American War.

(C) the Spanish-American War.

(D) World War I.

7. Which of the following reflects a main point of the political cartoon?

   (A) The United States used excessive violence in suppressing independence movements in its recently acquired territories.
   (B) The inhabitants of America's newly acquired colonial holdings might not initially be able to handle self-government and would require some degree of long-term American control.
   (C) American expansionistic efforts were misguided and costly; the United States would be well-advised to abandon its experiment in imperialism.
   (D) The United States should extend citizenship rights to inhabitants of its newly acquired colonies; the Constitution should follow the flag.

8. In the period following the events depicted in the cartoon, the United States

   (A) formed multilateral agreements and regional alliances with developing nations.
   (B) withdrew from global affairs in the face of opposition at home and abroad to imperialistic ventures.
   (C) expanded its economic and military presence in the Caribbean, Latin America, and Asia.
   (D) insisted that the countries referred to in the cartoon improve their human rights records or suffer a reduction of foreign aid.

Questions 9–10 refer to the following passage:

"The power . . . given to the commanding officer over all the people of each district is that of an absolute monarch. His mere will is to take the place of all law. . . . It reduces the whole population of the ten states—all persons, of every color, sex, and condition, and every stranger within their limits—to the most abject and degrading slavery."

9. The excerpt from the presidential veto message above is from

   (A) President Thomas Jefferson's veto of the Alien and Sedition Acts.
   (B) President James Monroe's veto of an act for the preservation and repair of the Cumberland Road.
   (C) President Andrew Jackson's veto of the bill rechartering the Second Bank of the United States.
   (D) President Andrew Johnson's veto of one of the Reconstruction Acts of 1867.

10. The political sentiment of the veto message above is most similar to which of the following political positions taken in the twentieth century?

   (A) Justice Frank Murphy's dissent in the Supreme Court case, *Korematsu v. United States* in 1944.
   (B) U.S. Army lawyer Joseph Welsh's opposition to Senator Joseph McCarthy in the Army-McCarthy hearings in 1954.
   (C) Governor Orval Faubus's response to the steps taken by President Dwight Eisenhower to resolve the Little Rock crisis in 1957.
   (D) John Lewis's endorsement of the Voting Rights Act in 1965.

Questions 11–12 refer to the following image:

11. The 1883 cartoon above makes the point that

(A) the "new" immigrants from eastern and southern Europe, with their different customs and religious beliefs, were just as dangerous to the American way of life as the American Indians were to the Pilgrims in the seventeenth century.

(B) the United States was filling up with people; additional immigrants would displace native-born Americans, just as the seventeenth-century Pilgrims displaced the American Indians.

(C) among the "new immigrants" were many hard-working men and women, but also many radicals, anarchists, revolutionaries, criminals, and other "dangerous" elements.

(D) incoming immigrants faced a gauntlet of dangers when they arrived in America, just as the Pilgrims did when they arrived in the seventeenth century.

12. Which of the following best represents a continuity with the political sentiments expressed in the cartoon above?

(A) Jane Addams and Ellen Gates Starr founding Hull House in 1889.

(B) The platform of the "Know-Nothing" Party (1854).

(C) Attorney General A. Mitchell Palmer carrying out deportation hearings during the "Red Scare" of the 1920s.

(D) Congressmen Albert Johnson and David Reed proposing the Immigration Act of 1924.

13. The 1936 cartoon above, from the *New York Daily News*, is making the point that

    (A) although European individuals and countries might be seduced into waging another major war, the United States would be wise to avoid participating.
    (B) the policy of appeasement is a bankrupt policy that can only lead to more death and destruction.
    (C) munitions manufacturers, the so-called merchants of death, were pushing the world toward war in the name of profits.
    (D) the weaponry of modern warfare had advanced to such a degree that future military engagements would result in unprecedented carnage.

14. Which of the following political positions most closely parallels the political position reflected in the cartoon?

    (A) Newspaper publisher William Randolph Hearst's position on declaring war on Spain in 1898.
    (B) The Abraham Lincoln Brigade position on American intervention in the Spanish Civil War in 1937.
    (C) Secretary of State Dean Acheson's position on U.S. intervention in the Korean War in 1950.
    (D) Martin Luther King, Jr.'s position on the Vietnam War in 1967.

Questions 15–17 refer to the following passage:

"The seeds of totalitarian regimes are nurtured by misery and want. They spread and grow in the evil soil of poverty and strife. They reach their full growth when the hope of a people for a better life has died. We must keep that hope alive. . . . Great responsibilities have been placed upon us by the swift movement of events. . . . I am confident that the Congress will face these responsibilities squarely."

—President Harry S. Truman, 1947

15. The passage above is part of President Truman's argument to Congress in favor of

    (A) the Servicemen's Readjustment Act (G.I. Bill).
    (B) development of the hydrogen bomb.
    (C) the McCarran Internal Security Act.
    (D) an extension of aid to Greece and Turkey.

16. The passage above can best be seen as providing a rationale for

    (A) the policy of containment.
    (B) the principle of "massive retaliation."
    (C) participation in the Atlantic Charter.
    (D) embarking on a "roll-back" of communism.

17. The ideas expressed in the passage above most directly reflect which of the following continuities in U.S. history?

    (A) Debates about the relationship between Congress and the president.
    (B) Debates about the use of military force in volatile situations.
    (C) Debates about the role of the United States in world affairs.
    (D) Debates about the proper role of political parties.

—"Your Honor, this woman gave birth to a naked child" (the figure speaking is
Anthony Comstock, United States Postal Inspector), *The Masses*, September 1915

18. The political cartoon above is making the point that

   (A) government officials were taking their crusade against immoral behavior to
   extreme lengths.
   (B) unregulated immigration was leading to an increase in crime among men and
   women in urban centers.
   (C) "flappers" were imposing their standards of moral behavior on an unsuspecting
   public.
   (D) the court system was bogged down with insignificant complaints while
   perpetrators of major crimes were left untouched by the law.

19. The cartoon reflects a point of view about which of the following continuities in
    U.S. history?

   (A) Debates about immigration policy.
   (B) Debates about the role of the federal government in regulating morality.
   (C) Debates about access to health care for working-class women.
   (D) Debates about the rights of the individuals accused of crimes.

Questions 20–22 refer to the following passage:

"If it be conceded, as it must be by every one who is the least conversant with our institutions, that the sovereign powers delegated are divided between the General and State Governments, and that the latter hold their portion by the same tenure as the former, it would seem impossible to deny to the States the right of deciding on the infractions of their powers, and the proper remedy to be applied for their correction. The right of judging, in such cases, is an essential attribute of sovereignty, of which the States cannot be divested without losing their sovereignty itself, and being reduced to a subordinate corporate condition. In fact, to divide power, and to give to one of the parties the exclusive right of judging of the portion allotted to each, is, in reality, not to divide it at all; and to reserve such exclusive right to the General Government (it matters not by what department to be exercised), is to convert it, in fact, into a great consolidated government, with unlimited powers, and to divest the States, in reality, of all their rights, It is impossible to understand the force of terms, and to deny so plain a conclusion."

—John C. Calhoun, "South Carolina Exposition and Protest," 1828

20. The issue that precipitated the passage excerpted above was

    (A) the removal of American Indians from the South.
    (B) the rechartering of the Second Bank of the United States.
    (C) the passage of an act creating higher tariff rates.
    (D) the funding of "internal improvements."

21. The argument put forth by John C. Calhoun in the passage above states a position in a debate that is most similar to which of the following debates from earlier in U.S. history?

    (A) The debate over whether to count slaves in the census for purposes of representation.
    (B) The debate over the Constitutionality of acquiring the Louisiana Purchase.
    (C) The debate over disestablishment of the Episcopal Church in several states.
    (D) The debate over replacing the Articles of Confederation with the Constitution.

22. The language of "protest" that Calhoun used in his "Exposition and Protest" was similar to the language of which of the following political positions?

    (A) The response of supporters of Andrew Jackson to the "corrupt bargain" of 1824.
    (B) The response of New England Federalists to the War of 1812.
    (C) The response of the Jefferson administration to the actions of the "Barbary pirates."
    (D) The response of Daniel Shays to fiscal policies of the Massachusetts legislature in the 1780s.

23. The 1933 political cartoon shown above makes the point that

    (A) the New Deal's proposals for open immigration would threaten American democracy.
    (B) the New Deal would be ineffective in addressing the problems of the Great Depression.
    (C) the Supreme Court acted in a tyrannical way in declaring certain New Deal measures unconstitutional.
    (D) New Deal programs would usher in unconstitutional restrictions on American freedoms and liberties.

24. The sentiment expressed in the cartoon above most directly reflects which of the following continuities in U.S. history?

    (A) Debates about the proper role of the federal government in the economy.
    (B) Debates about the power of the Supreme Court to "legislate from the bench."
    (C) Debates about the proper relationship between the federal government and the states.
    (D) Debates about individual liberties during time of war.

25. The sentiment reflected in the cartoon was similar to which of the following political expressions?

(A) Support by the feminists for the Equal Rights Amendment in 1972.
(B) Opposition by the Republican Party to the creation of Great Society programs in the 1960s.
(C) Opposition by environmentalists to passage of the North American Free Trade Agreement in 1994.
(D) Opposition by Korean War veterans to the firing of General Douglas MacArthur by President Eisenhower in 1951.

Questions 26–27 refer to the following passage:

"A drunkard in the gutter is just where he ought to be. . . . The law of survival of the fittest was not made by man, and it cannot be abrogated by man. We can only, by interfering with it, produce the survival of the unfittest. . . . The millionaires are a product of natural selection, acting on the whole body of men to pick out those who can meet the requirement of certain work to be done. In this respect they are just like the great statesmen, or scientific men, or military men. It is because they are thus selected that wealth—both their own and that entrusted to them—aggregates under their hands. Let one of them make a mistake and see how quickly the concentration gives way to dispersion."

—William Graham Sumner, *What Social Classes Owe to Each Other*, 1883

26. During the late 1800s, those who followed the ideas of William Graham Sumner in his book, *What Social Classes Owe to Each Other* (excerpted above), would most likely have advocated

(A) government ownership of major banks and railroad companies.
(B) a social welfare "safety net" to help people get through difficult economic times.
(C) government efforts to curb alcohol consumption.
(D) a laissez-faire approach to the economy.

27. The sociological ideas of William Graham Sumner reflect the idea that during the late 1800s

(A) cultural and intellectual arguments justified the success of those at the top of the socioeconomic structure as both appropriate and inevitable.
(B) popular writers rejected ideas from the sciences, and based their arguments on faith.
(C) intellectuals were critical of the cut-throat competition of the ages, and proposed radical alternatives based on creating a cooperative economy.
(D) cultural products of the era tended to ignore the economic direction of society and looked back wistfully to the past.

Questions 28–30 refer to the following passage:

"If any person or persons shall, from and after the passing of this act, by force and violence, take and carry away, or cause to be taken or carried away, and shall, by fraud or false pretense, seduce, or cause to be seduced, or shall attempt so to take, carry away or seduce, any negro or mulatto, from any part or parts of this commonwealth, to any other place or places whatsoever, out of this commonwealth, with a design and intention of selling and disposing of, or of causing to be sold, or of keeping and detaining, or of causing to be kept and detained, such negro or mulatto, as a slave or servant for life, or for any term whatsoever, every such person or persons, his or their aiders or abettors, shall on conviction thereof, in any court of this commonwealth having competent jurisdiction, be deemed guilty of a felony."

—Excerpt from Pennsylvania law, 1826

28. Critics challenged the constitutionality of this 1826 law in the Supreme Court on the grounds that it

    (A) violated the Constitutional injunction against bills of attainder.
    (B) undermined the intent of the fugitive slave clause of the Constitution.
    (C) circumvented the three-fifths clause of the Constitution.
    (D) was inconsistent with the "eminent domain" clause of the Fifth Amendment of the Constitution.

29. The passage and implementation of this Pennsylvania law reflected an ongoing conflict between

    (A) rural and urban interests.
    (B) federal law and state law.
    (C) those who favored gradual emancipation and those who favored immediate emancipation.
    (D) supporters and opponents of government regulation of commerce.

30. Debate and conflict over the Pennsylvania law, excerpted above, reflected the fact that the framers of the Constitution

    (A) specifically declared that the institution of slavery would be protected "in perpetuity" in the original 13 states.
    (B) allowed for a state to be exempt from federal laws that went against that state's constitution.
    (C) postponed a solution to the problems of slavery.
    (D) declared that slaves could be both citizens and property.

Questions 31–32 refer to the following passage:

"I come to present the strong claims of suffering humanity. I come to place before the Legislature of Massachusetts the condition of the miserable, the desolate, the outcast. I come as the advocate of helpless, forgotten, insane and idiotic men and women; of beings, sunk to a condition from which the most unconcerned would start with real horror; of beings wretched in our Prisons, and more wretched in our Alms-Houses. . . .

"If my pictures are displeasing, coarse, and severe, my subjects, it must be recollected, offer no tranquil, refined, or composing features. The condition of human beings, reduced to the extremest states of degradation and misery, cannot be exhibited in softened language, or adorn a polished page.

"I proceed, Gentlemen, briefly to call your attention to the present state of Insane Persons confined within this Commonwealth, *in cages, closets, cellars, stalls, pens! Chained, naked, beaten with rods,* and *lashed* into obedience!"

—Dorothea Dix, "Memorial to the Massachusetts Legislature" (1843)

31. Dorothea Dix's testimony to the Massachusetts legislature reflects the influence of which of the following?

   (A) Social Darwinism.
   (B) The Second Great Awakening.
   (C) Second-wave feminism.
   (D) The Christian Science movement.

32. Dorothea Dix's research and testimony is best understood in the context of

   (A) women gaining the right to vote in many states.
   (B) an economic downturn that was responsible for the closure of many state institutions.
   (C) an evolving relationship between the federal government and issues of health and poverty.
   (D) the rise of voluntary organizations to promote religious and secular reforms.

"I was once a tool of oppression
And as green as a sucker could be
And monopolies banded together
To beat a poor hayseed like me.

"The railroads and old party bosses
Together did sweetly agree;
And they thought there would be little trouble
In working a hayseed like me. . . ."

—"The Hayseed"

33. The song lyrics above would most likely have appeared in

(A) an abolitionist newspaper in the 1830s.
(B) a Republican leaflet in the 1870s.
(C) a populist newspaper in the 1890s.
(D) a civil rights pamphlet in the 1950s.

34. Which of the following is an accomplishment of the political movement that was organized around sentiments similar to the one in the song lyrics above?

(A) Establishment of the minimum wage law.
(B) Enactment of laws regulating railroads.
(C) Shift in U.S. currency from the gold standard to the silver standard.
(D) Creation of a price-support system for small-scale farmers.

35. The song, and the movement that it was connected to, highlight which of the following developments in the broader society in the late 1800s?

(A) Corruption in government—especially as it related to big business—energized the public to demand increased popular control and reform of local, state, and national governments.
(B) A large-scale movement of struggling African American and white farmers, as well as urban factory workers, was able to exert a great deal of leverage over federal legislation.
(C) The two-party system of the era broke down and led to the emergence of an additional major party that was able to win control of Congress within ten years of its founding.
(D) Continued skirmishes on the frontier in the 1890s with American Indians created a sense of fear and bitterness among western farmers.

Questions 36–37 refer to the following passage:

"We are men; we have souls, we have passions, we have feelings, we have hopes, we have desires, like any other race in the world. The cry is raised all over the world today of Canada for the Canadians, of America for the Americans, of England for the English, of France for the French, of Germany for the Germans—do you think it is unreasonable that we, the Blacks of the world, should raise the cry of Africa for the Africans?"

—Marcus Garvey, 1920

36. The passage could best be understood as

(A) an argument in favor of restrictions on immigration into the United States.
(B) an attempt to unite working-class African American and white men and women.
(C) an expression of black nationalism.
(D) a pamphlet designed to promote the advancement of African Americans in industry.

37. The passage above presents a position in which of the following ongoing debates in American history?

(A) The debate between interventionism and isolationism in foreign policy.
(B) The debate between separatism and integration when it came to the place of African Americans in American society.
(C) The debate between exclusion and inclusion when it came to immigration policy.
(D) The debate between laissez-faire policies and government intervention in economic affairs.

PRACTICE TEST 1

PRACTICE TEST 1   411

Questions 38–39 refer to the following passage:

"But even if southern progressivism included women, was it reserved for whites? The answer is that whites intended for it to be, and it would have been even more racist, more exclusive, and more oppressive if there had been no black women progressives. . . . As much as southern whites plotted to reserve progressivism for themselves, and as much as they schemed to alter the ill-fitting northern version accordingly, they failed. African-American women embraced southern white progressivism, reshaped it, and sent back a new model that included black power brokers and grass roots activists. Evidence of southern African-American progressivism is not to be found in public laws, electoral politics, or the establishment of mothers' aid programs at the state level. It rarely appears in documents that white progressives, male or female, left behind. Since black men could not speak out in politics and black women did not want to be seen, it has remained invisible in virtually every discussion of southern progressivism. Nonetheless, southern black women initiated every progressive reform that southern white women initiated, a feat they accomplished without financial resources, without the civic protection of their husbands, and without publicity."

—Glenda Elizabeth Gilmore, "Diplomatic Women," from *Gender and Jim Crow: Women and the Politics of White Supremacy in North Carolina, 1896–1920* (Chapel Hill: University of North Carolina Press, 1996)

38. The excerpt above, from the essay by Glenda Elizabeth Gilmore, implies that historians of the Progressive movement have

    (A) failed to adequately explain why the agenda and goals of the Progressive movement never resonated with the African American community.
    (B) ignored the latent racism and white supremacy inherent in the Progressive movement.
    (C) not written extensively on the contributions of black women to progressivism in the South because of a scarcity of documentary evidence.
    (D) overemphasized the extent of African American participation in the Progressive movement in order to improve the public perception of the movement.

39. The efforts described in the reading above occurred in the context of

    (A) increased federal support for civil rights measures in the United States, as American political leaders sought to bolster the democratic image of the United States on a global stage.
    (B) rapid industrialization in the South, which brought African American working-class activists in closer contact with whites.
    (C) successful efforts by the U.S. military to segregate units fighting in the Spanish-American War and World War I, but resistance by state governments to follow the lead of the military.
    (D) a nadir in race relations in the United States as "scientific" ideas about race, inaction by the federal government, and rigid segregation in the South relegated African Americans to a second-class status in the United States.

Questions 40–42 refer to the following passage:

"Your sentiments, that our affairs are drawing rapidly to a crisis, accord with my own. What the event will be is also beyond the reach of my foresight. We have errors to correct. We have probably had too good an opinion of human nature in forming our confederation. Experience has taught us that men will not adopt and carry into execution measures the best calculated for their own good without the intervention of a coercive power. I do not conceive that we can exist long as a nation without having lodged somewhere a power which will pervade the whole Union in as energetic a manner as the authority of the state governments extends over the several states. . . .

"What astonishing changes a few years are capable of producing. I am told that even respectable characters speak of a monarchical form of government without horror. . . . What a triumph for our enemies to verify their predictions! What a triumph for the advocates of despotism to find that we are incapable of governing ourselves, and that systems founded on the basis of equal liberty are merely ideal and fallacious. . . ."

—George Washington, letter to John Jay, August 1, 1786

40. The sentiments in the letter by George Washington, above, reflect which of the following continuities in American history?

(A) Debates about the proper balance between liberty and order.
(B) Debates about reconciling republicanism with the institution of slavery.
(C) Debates about the relationship among the three branches of government.
(D) Debates about the use of the military in subduing domestic disturbances.

41. Based on the context of the letter, which of the following most closely describes the meaning of Washington's phrase, "We have probably had too good an opinion of human nature"?

(A) Contemporary Deist spiritual beliefs were misguided in that they abandoned the Calvinist notions of "original sin."
(B) The United States had overestimated the good will and honor of Great Britain in terms of following the stipulations of the Treaty of Paris (1783).
(C) The U.S. Army misread the willingness of American Indians in the Ohio Valley and Great Lakes regions to live side-by-side with white settlers.
(D) The framers of the Articles of Confederation made a mistake in allowing for too great a degree of democracy in the new republic.

42. In subsequent U.S. history, those who shared the sentiments George Washington expressed in the letter, above, would most likely have taken which of the following positions?

(A) Support for joining France in its war with Great Britain in 1793 in honor of the 1778 Treaty of Alliance with France.
(B) Opposition to the chartering of a national bank in 1791.
(C) Support for ratification of the Constitution in 1789.
(D) Opposition to the Alien and Sedition Acts of 1798.

Questions 43–44 refer to the following passage:

"As our late Conduct at the Conestoga Manor and Lancaster have occasioned much Speculation & a great diversity of Sentiments in this and neighboring Governments; some vindicating & others condemning it; some charitably alleviating the Crime, & others maliciously painting it in the most odious & detestable Colours, we think it our duty to lay before the Publick, the whole Matter as it appeared, & still appears, to us. . . .

"If these things are not sufficient to prove an unjustifiable Attachment in the Quakers to the Indians Savages, a fixed Resolution to befriend them & an utter insensibility to human Distresses, let us consider a few more recent Facts. When we found the last Summer that we were likely to get no Assistance from the Government, some Volunteers went out at our own Expense, determined to drive our Enemies from our Borders; & when we came near to the great Island, we understood that a Number of their Warriors had gone out against our Frontiers. Upon this we returned and came up with them and fought with them at the Munfey Hill where we lost some of our Men & killed some of their Warriors & thereby saved our Frontiers from this Story in another Expedition. But no sooner had we destroyed their Provisions on the great Island, & ruined their trade with the good People at Bethlehem, but these very Indians, who were justly suspected of having murdered our Friends in Northampton County, were by the Influence of some Quakers taken under the Protection of the Government to screen them from the Resentments of the Friends and Relations of the Murdered, & to support them thro the Winter."

—"Apology of the Paxton Boys" (pamphlet), 1764 (Note: "apology" in this context should be read as an explanation, not an admission of guilt or regret.)

43. The sentiments expressed in the explanation above reflect which of the ongoing tensions during the colonial period of American history?

   (A) Tensions between British policies and the aspirations of North American colonists.
   (B) Tensions between American Indians allied with the French and those allied with the British.
   (C) Tensions between freed African Americans and white planters.
   (D) Tensions between backcountry settlers and elites within colonial America.

44. Which of the following events from either earlier or later in the colonial period can best be seen as being part of a continuity with the events described in the passage above?

   (A) The expulsion of Anne Hutchinson from Massachusetts Bay Colony.
   (B) Bacon's Rebellion in colonial Virginia.
   (C) The Boston Tea Party.
   (D) The trial of John Peter Zenger.

Questions 45–48 refer to the following passage:

"When we were kids the United States was the wealthiest and strongest country in the world; the only one with the atom bomb, the least scarred by modern war, an initiator of the United Nations that we thought would distribute Western influence throughout the world. Freedom and equality for each individual, government of, by, and for the people—these American values we found good, principles by which we could live as men. Many of us began maturing in complacency.

"As we grew, however, our comfort was penetrated by events too troubling to dismiss. First, the permeating and victimizing fact of human degradation, symbolized by the Southern struggle against racial bigotry, compelled most of us from silence to activism. Second, the enclosing fact of the Cold War, symbolized by the presence of the Bomb, brought awareness that we ourselves, and our friends, and millions of abstract 'others' we knew more directly because of our common peril, might die at any time. . . ."

—Port Huron Statement, 1962

45. The Port Huron Statement, excerpted above, can most clearly be seen as an important document in which of the following movements?

   (A) The labor union movement.
   (B) The civil rights movement.
   (C) The New Right.
   (D) The New Left.

46. The language of this document can be seen as a repudiation of which of the following policies or actions from the Eisenhower years?

   (A) The "New Look" foreign policy.
   (B) Increases in funding for the United Nations.
   (C) Intervention in the Little Rock, Arkansas crisis.
   (D) Renewed focus on education.

47. The primary intended audience for the Port Huron Statement was

   (A) African Americans in the South.
   (B) government officials.
   (C) middle-class college students.
   (D) factory workers.

48. Through the remainder of the 1960s, the growth of the organization that published the Port Huron Statement can best be understood in the context of

   (A) rapid industrialization, urban growth and congestion, and corporate consolidation.
   (B) the baby boom, economic growth, and a rapid expansion of higher education.
   (C) economic polarization, supply-side economic policies, and the disappearance of the middle class.
   (D) the proliferation of personal computer technologies, the rise of Christian fundamentalism, and an increase in student apathy.

"An act for the more effectual protection of the property of married women:

"§1. The real property of any female who may hereafter marry, and which she shall own at the time of marriage, and the rents, issues, and profits thereof, shall not be subject to the sole disposal of her husband, nor be liable for his debts, and shall continue her sole and separate property, as if she were a single female.

"§2. The real and personal property, and the rents, issues, and profits thereof, of any female now married, shall not be subject to the disposal of her husband; but shall be her sole and separate property, as if she were a single female, except so far as the same may be liable for the debts of her husband heretofore contracted.

"§3. Any married female may take by inheritance, or by gift, grant, devise, or bequest, from any person other than her husband, and hold to her sole and separate use, and convey and devise real and personal property, and any interest or estate therein, and the rents, issues, and profits thereof, in the same manner and with like effect as if she were unmarried, and the same shall not be subject to the disposal of her husband nor be liable for his debts."

—Married Women's Property Act, New York State (1848)

49. The Married Women's Property Act was significant in that it

    (A) expanded women's participation in the political sphere.
    (B) challenged traditional understandings of women and property embodied in the legal concept of *femme covert*.
    (C) codified the cultural assumptions implicit in the concept of "Republican motherhood."
    (D) relegated women to a second-class status in regard to citizenship.

50. Which of the following groups would be most likely to support the perspective of the Married Women's Property Act?

    (A) Participants in the Seneca Falls Convention.
    (B) Southern supporters of the concept of "female virtue."
    (C) Proponents of the "cult of domesticity" value system.
    (D) Congregational ministers.

51. The ideas expressed in the passage above most directly reflect which of the following continuities in U.S. history?

    (A) Debates about access to voting rights.
    (B) Debates about the role of federal government in marriage law.
    (C) Debates about discrimination in employment.
    (D) Debates about the legal status of women.

"The law of love, peace and liberty in the states extending to Jews, Turks and Egyptians, as they are considered sonnes of Adam, which is the glory of the outward state of Holland, soe love, peace and liberty, extending to all in Christ Jesus, condemns hatred, war and bondage. And because our Saviour sayeth it is impossible but that offences will come, but woe unto him by whom they cometh, our desire is not to offend one of his little ones, in whatsoever form, name or title hee appears in, whether Presbyterian, Independent, Baptist or Quaker, but shall be glad to see anything of God in any of them, desiring to doe unto all men as we desire all men should doe unto us, which is the true law both of Church and State; for our Saviour sayeth this is the law and the prophets.

"Therefore if any of these said persons come in love unto us, we cannot in conscience lay violent hands upon them, but give them free egresse and regresse unto our Town, and houses, as God shall persuade our consciences, for we are bounde by the law of God and man to doe good unto all men and evil to noe man. And this is according to the patent and charter of our Towne, given unto us in the name of the States General, which we are not willing to infringe, and violate, but shall houlde to our patent and shall remaine, your humble subjects, the inhabitants of Vlishing (Flushing, part of the colony of New Netherlands)."

—The Flushing Remonstrance, 1657

52. Which of the following most accurately describes the context in which the above document was written?

(A) The Dutch West India Company had sought to establish a model community in the New World, based on Enlightenment principles; the document grew out of this mandate.

(B) The policies of the Dutch West Indian company had discouraged non-Dutch immigrants from settling in New Netherlands; the document was an attempt to diversify the colony.

(C) Religious toleration had become the norm in the neighboring New England colonies in the seventeenth century; the document was an attempt to bring New Amsterdam to the same levels of toleration.

(D) The director-general of the colony of New Netherlands, Peter Stuyvesant, was attempting to enforce conformity in New Netherlands despite the multi-ethnic makeup of the colony; the document was an attempt to accommodate the diverse population.

53. Which of the following was most significant in enshrining into the U.S. legal structure the ideas contained in the Flushing Remonstrance?

(A) The preamble of the Declaration of Independence.
(B) The enumeration of congressional powers in the Constitution.
(C) The "Free Exercise Clause" of the First Amendment.
(D) The "Establishment Clause" of the First Amendment.

Questions 54–55 refer to the following passage:

"The petition of several poor negroes and mulattoes, who are inhabitants of the town of Dartmouth, humbly showeth,—

"That we being chiefly of the African extract, and by reason of long bondage and hard slavery, we have been deprived of enjoying the profits of our labor or the advantage of inheriting estates from our parents, as our neighbors the white people do, having some of us not long enjoyed our own freedom; yet of late, contrary to the invariable custom and practice of the country, we have been, and now are, taxed both in our polls and that small pittance of estate which, through much hard labor and industry, we have got together to sustain ourselves and families withall. We apprehend it, therefore, to be hard usage, and will doubtless (if continued) reduce us to a state of beggary, whereby we shall become a burthen to others, if not timely prevented by the interposition of your justice and your power.

"Your petitioners further show, that we apprehend ourselves to be aggrieved, in that, while we are not allowed the privilege of freemen of the State, having no vote or influence in the election of those that tax us, yet many of our colour (as is well known) have cheerfully entered the field of battle in the defence of the common cause, and that (as we conceive) against a similar exertion of power (in regard to taxation), too well known to need a recital in this place."

—Paul Cuffe's Petition, Massachusetts, 1780

54. The main purpose of the petition by Paul Cuffe, excerpted above, was to demand

(A) that the petitioners be released from slavery because slavery was incompatible with the Massachusetts constitution.
(B) that the Massachusetts legislature extend reparations to the petitioners as compensation for their time in slavery.
(C) that the petitioners receive land that had been expropriated from loyalists in order to reward them for their service to the Continental Army during the American Revolution.
(D) that the Massachusetts legislature either grant the petitioners the right to vote or that it excuse them from paying taxes.

55. The petition by Paul Cuffe, above, best illustrates which of the following developments?

(A) The rhetoric of the American Revolution raised awareness of social inequalities and inspired groups and individuals to call for greater political democracy.
(B) Slave rebellions, such as the Stono Rebellion, inspired enslaved Americans throughout North America to engage in similar behavior.
(C) African Americans who had fought alongside the British during the American Revolution felt doubly vulnerable—as African Americans and as traitors to the patriot cause—after the British defeat.
(D) African Americans received worse treatment under the state government of Massachusetts than they had under British law during the colonial period.

STOP

If there is still time remaining, you may review your answers.

Part B: Short-Answer Questions 简答题

> **Directions:** The following section contains four questions. Answer each of the questions, using the source material and your knowledge of American history. Note: students are not required to develop and support a thesis statement in responding to these questions. (50 minutes)

Question 1 is based on the following passage:

"DECLARATION OF RIGHTS

"The members of this congress, sincerely devoted, with the warmest sentiments of affection and duty to His Majesty's person and government . . ., and with minds deeply impressed by a sense of the present and impending misfortunes of the British colonies on this continent; having considered as maturely as time would permit, the circumstances of said colonies, esteem it our indispensable duty to make the following declarations, of our humble opinions, respecting the most essential rights and liberties of the colonists, and of the grievances under which they labor, by reason of several late acts of Parliament.

"1st. That His Majesty's subjects in these colonies owe the same allegiance to the crown of Great Britain that is owing from his subjects born within the realm, and all due subordination to that august body, the Parliament of Great Britain.

"2d. That His Majesty's liege subjects in these colonies are entitled to all the inherent rights and privileges of his natural born subjects within the kingdom of Great Britain.

"3d. That it is inseparably essential to the freedom of a people, and the undoubted rights of Englishmen, that no taxes should be imposed on them, but with their own consent, given personally, or by their representatives.

"4th. That the people of these colonies are not, and from their local circumstances cannot be, represented in the House of Commons in Great Britain.

"5th. That the only representatives of the people of these colonies are persons chosen therein, by themselves; and that no taxes ever have been or can be constitutionally imposed on them but by their respective legislatures.

"6th. That all supplies to the crown, being free gifts of the people, it is unreasonable and Inconsistent With The Principles And Spirit Of The British Constitution For The People Of Great Britain To Grant To His Majesty The Property Of The Colonists. . . ."

—*The Declaration of Rights of the Stamp Act Congress*, 1765

1. Use the document above and your knowledge of U.S. history to answer parts A, B, and C.

   (A) How did British political leaders, most notably Prime Minister George Grenville, respond to the arguments put forward by the Stamp Act Congress in the labelled points "3rd," "4th," and "5th"?

   (B) How does the tone of this declaration differ from Thomas Paine's pamphlet, *Common Sense*, published in January 1776? Use evidence from this declaration to support your answer.

   (C) Describe the context of the meeting of the Stamp Act Declaration in terms of relations between Great Britain and its 13 North American colonies.

"The Tournament of To-Day.—A Set-To Between Labor and Monopoly," *Puck*, 1883

2. Use the image above and your knowledge of U.S. history to answer parts A, B, and C.

   (A) Explain the point of view of the above cartoon, published in 1883.

   (B) Discuss a specific event from the era in which the cartoon was published that would support the point of view of the cartoon (1865–1900).

   (C) Discuss the continuities and changes between the period in which the cartoon was published and the period of the 1930s New Deal with regard to the position of labor in society.

Question 3 is based on the following two passages:

"It is too true that there are public journals who try to dignify this mob by some respectable appellation. The Herald characterizes it as the people, and the World as the laboring men of the City. These are libels that ought to have paralyzed the fingers that penned them. It is ineffably infamous to attribute to the people, or to the laboring men of this metropolis, such hideous barbarism as this horde has been displaying. The people of New-York and the laboring men of New-York are not incendiaries, nor robbers, nor assassins. They do not hunt down men whose only offence is the color God gave them; they do not chase, and insult; and beat women; they do not pillage an asylum for orphan children, and burn the very roof over those orphans' heads. They are civilized beings, valuing law and respecting decency; and they regard with unqualified abhorrence the doings of the tribe of savages that have sought to bear rule in their midst."

—Editorial, *The New York Times,* July 15, 1863

"To the Editor of the New-York Times:

"You will, no doubt, be hard on us rioters tomorrow morning, but that 300-dollar law has made us nobodies, vagabonds and cast-outs of society, for whom nobody cares when we must go to war and be shot down. We are the poor rabble, and the rich rabble is our enemy by this law. Therefore we will give our enemy battle right here, and ask no quarter. Although we got hard fists, and are dirty without, we have soft hearts, and have clean consciences within, and that's the reason we love our wives and children more than the rich, because we got not much besides them, and we will not go and leave them at home for to starve. Until that draft law is repealed, I for one am willing to knock down more such rum-hole politicians as Kennedy. Why don't they let the nigger kill the slave-driving race and take possession of the South, as it belongs to them."

—Letter to the editor of *The New York Times*, signed,
"A poor man, but a man for all that," July 15, 1863

3. Use the two documents above and your knowledge of U.S. history to answer parts A, B, and C.

   (A) Explain the source of the anger of the participants of the riot described in both documents.

   (B) Explain how the point of view of the letter to the editor of *The New York Times* differs from the point of view of the paper's editorial?

   (C) Compare the event described in the documents with one of the three following events in U.S. history:

   Shays' Rebellion (1786–1787)
   March of Coxey's Army (1894)
   Tulsa race riot (1921)

Question 4 is based on the following images:

—Josiah Priest, 1852

4. Use the images above and your knowledge of U.S. history to answer parts A, B, and C.

(A) Explain the point of view, reflected in the images above, regarding slavery.

(B) Explain how the point of view reflected in the images represents a shift in thinking among southern planters about slavery from earlier (pre-1830) ideas about slavery.

(C) Explain how the point of view in the images above reflects the context in which the images were produced (with attention to the period 1830–1852).

SECTION II 第二部分

Part A: Document-Based Question 材料分析题

> **Directions:** The following question is based on the accompanying Documents 1–7. This question is designed to test your ability to apply the historical thinking skills of **causation**, in conjunction with **argumentation, analyzing evidence, contextualization,** and **synthesis.** Your response should be based on your analysis of the documents and your knowledge of the topic. **(55 minutes)**

Write a well-integrated essay that does the following:

- States an appropriate thesis that directly addresses all parts of the question.
- Supports the thesis or an appropriate argument with evidence from all or all but one of the documents AND your knowledge of U.S. history beyond/outside the documents.
- Analyzes a majority of the documents in terms of such features as their intended audience, purpose, point of view, format, argumentation, and/or social context as appropriate to the argument.
- Places the argument in the context of broader regional, national, or global processes.

Question 1

What were the economic, political, and social causes of the conflict between congressional Republicans and President Andrew Johnson over plans for Reconstruction in the South? In your answer, use the documents and your knowledge of the years 1864–1877.

DOCUMENT 1

Source: Abraham Lincoln, "Second Inaugural Address," March 4, 1865.

With malice toward none, with charity for all, with firmness in the right as God gives us to see the right, let us strive on to finish the work we are in, to bind up the nation's wounds, to care for him who shall have borne the battle and for his widow and his orphan, to do all which may achieve and cherish a just and lasting peace among ourselves and with all nations.

Source: Mississippi legal codes, "An Act to Confer Civil Rights on Freedmen, and for other Purposes," 1865.

An Act to Amend the Vagrant Laws of the State

Section 1. All rogues and vagabonds, idle and dissipated persons, beggars, jugglers, or persons practicing unlawful games or plays, runaways, common drunkards, common night—walkers, pilferers, lewd, wanton, or lascivious persons, in speech or behavior, common railers and brawlers, persons who neglect their calling or employment, misspend what they earn, or do not provide for the support of themselves or their families, or dependents, and all other idle and disorderly persons, including all who neglect all lawful business, habitually misspend their time by frequenting houses of ill-fame, gaming-houses, or tippling shops, shall be deemed and considered vagrants, under the provisions of this act, and upon conviction thereof shall be fined not exceeding one hundred dollars, with all accruing costs, and be imprisoned, at the discretion of the court, not exceeding ten days.

Section 2. All freedmen, free negroes and mulattoes in this State, over the age of eighteen years, found on the second Monday in January, 1866, or thereafter, with no lawful employment or business, or found unlawful assembling themselves together, either in the day or night time, and all white persons assembling themselves with freedmen, Free negroes or mulattoes, or usually associating with freedmen, free negroes or mulattoes, on terms of equality, or living in adultery or fornication with a freed woman, freed negro or mulatto, shall be deemed vagrants, and on conviction thereof shall be fined in a sum not exceeding, in the case of a freedman, free negro or mulatto, fifty dollars, and a white man two hundred dollars, and imprisonment at the discretion of the court, the free negro not exceeding ten days, and the white man not exceeding six months.

Source: "Acts of the General Assembly of Louisiana Regulating Labor, Extra Session," 1865.

[Each laborer] shall not be allowed to leave his place of employment, until the fulfillment of his contract, unless be consent of his employer, or on account of harsh treatment, or breach of contraction the part of the employer; and if they do so leave, without cause of permission, they shall forfeit all wages earned to the time of abandonment. . . .

In cases of sickness of the laborer, wages for the time lost shall be deducted, and where the sickness is feigned for purpose of idleness, . . . and also should refusal to work be continued beyond three days, the offender shall be reported to a justice of the peace, and shall be forced to labor on roads, levee, and other public works, without pay, until the offender consents to return to his labor.

When in health, the laborer shall work ten hours during the day in the summer, and nine hours during the day in winter, unless otherwise stipulated in the labor contract; he shall obey all proper orders of his employer or his agent. . . . Failure to obey reasonable orders, neglect of duty, and leaving home without permission will be deemed disobedience; impudence, swearing, or indecent language to or in the presence of the employer, his family or agent . . . shall be deemed disobedience. . . . For all absence from home without leave, the laborer will be fined at the rate of two dollars per day.

Source: "Selling a Freeman to Pay His Fine at Monticello, Florida," *Frank Leslie's Illustrated Newspaper*, January 19, 1867.

DOCUMENT 5

Source: "Petition to U.S. Congress, South Carolina Colored People's Convention," November 1865.

We simply desire that we shall be recognized as men; that we have no obstructions placed in our way; that the same laws which govern white men shall direct colored men; that we have the right of trial by a jury of our peers, that schools be opened or established for our children; that we be permitted to acquire homesteads for ourselves and children; that we be dealt with as others, in equity and justice.

We claim the confidence and good-will of all classes of men; we ask that the same chances be extended to us that freemen should demand at the hands of their fellow-citizens. We desire the prosperity and growth of this State and the well-being of all men, and shall be found ever struggling to elevate ourselves and add to the national character; and we trust the day will not be distant when you will acknowledge that by our rapid progress in moral, social, religious and intellectual development that you will cheerfully accord to us the high commendation that we are worthy, with you, to enjoy all political emoluments—when we shall realize the truth that "all men are endowed by their Creator with inalienable rights," and that on the American continent this is the right of all, whether he come from east, west, north or south; and, although complexions may differ, "a man's a man for that."

DOCUMENT 6

Source: Speech, Samuel J. Tilden, leader of the Democratic Party, New York, 1868.

[The Republican Party] resolved to make the black race the governing power in those States, and by means of them to bring into Congress twenty senators and fifty representatives practically appointed by itself in Washington. . . .

The effect of a gain to the Republican party of twenty senators and fifty representatives is to strengthen its hold on the Federal Government. . . . Nor is there the slightest doubt that the paramount object and motive of the Republican party is by these means to secure itself against a reaction of opinion adverse to it in our great populous Northern commonwealths. The effect of its system and its own real purpose is to establish a domination over us of the Northern states.

DOCUMENT 7

Source: Thaddeus Stevens, speech in Congress, January 3, 1867.

Since the surrender of the armies of the confederate States of America a little has been done toward establishing this Government upon the true principles of liberty and justice; and but a little if we stop here. We have broken the material shackles of four million slaves. We have unchained them from the stake so as to allow them locomotion, provided they do not walk in paths which are trod by white men. We have allowed them the privilege of attending church, if they can do so without offending the sight of their former masters. We have imposed on them the privilege of fighting our battles, of dying in defense of freedom, and of bearing their equal portion of taxes; but where have we given them the privilege of ever participating in the formation of the laws for the government of their native land?

What is negro equality, about which so much is said by knaves and some of which is believed by men who are not fools? It means, as understood by honest Republicans, just this much, and no more: every man, no matter what his race or colour; every earthly being who has an immortal soul, has an equal right to justice, honesty, and fair play with every other man; and the law should secure him those rights. The same law, which condemns or acquits an African, should condemn or acquit a white man.

Part B: Long Essay Questions 论述题

Choose ONE of the following questions and write an analytical essay that uses specific, relevant evidence to support your thesis and to demonstrate the specified historical thinking skills. *Historical Thinking Skills: **Historical Causation**, used in conjunction with **Argumentation**, **Use of Evidence**, and **Synthesis**. Thematic Learning Objective: **America in the World**, #2—Analyze the reason for and results of U.S. diplomatic, economic, and military initiative in North America and Overseas.* (35 minutes)

1. Historians debate the long-term and short-term causes of the Mexican-American War. Analyze the relative importance of the different causes of the war.

2. Historians debate the long-term and short-term causes of the Spanish-American War. Analyze the relative importance of the different causes of the war.

SCORING THE TEST 估分

The AP United States History test is composed of four parts grouped into two sections. The multiple-choice test is scored with one point given for each correct answer.

- *There is no penalty for guessing,* so you should answer every question on the test.
- The DBQ is given a score from 0–7.
- The long essay is given a score from 0 to 6.

To attain your final AP score, the following method should be used:

Multiple-Choice Score × 1.31 = _____

+

Short-Answer Score × 3.0 = _____

+

DBQ Score × 6.43 = _____

+

Long Essay Score × 4.5 = _____

Total of all above scores is composite score = _____(round it)

Score Range	AP Score
111-180	5
91-110	4
76-90	3
57-75	2
>56	1

To get a final score for the test, compare your composite score to the chart directly above.

Following are four separate guides to scoring each section of this test. Once you have scored each piece of the test, place the score on the appropriate line above. When you are done, do the computations to get your final score. Remember that this test is designed to mimic the AP exam, but you will not take it in the same conditions that you will during the real test, and it is not scored by professionals who are reading 1,000 or more essays daily. While this test is a good predictor of success, it is only as good as the student using it, so do not stop studying just because you got a good score here.

ANSWER KEY 答案
Practice Test 1 模拟测试一

1. **(A)**	11. **(D)**	21. **(D)**	31. **(B)**	41. **(D)**	51. **(D)**
2. **(A)**	12. **(A)**	22. **(B)**	32. **(D)**	42. **(C)**	52. **(D)**
3. **(C)**	13. **(A)**	23. **(D)**	33. **(C)**	43. **(D)**	53. **(C)**
4. **(A)**	14. **(D)**	24. **(A)**	34. **(B)**	44. **(B)**	54. **(D)**
5. **(A)**	15. **(D)**	25. **(B)**	35. **(A)**	45. **(D)**	55. **(A)**
6. **(C)**	16. **(A)**	26. **(D)**	36. **(C)**	46. **(A)**	
7. **(B)**	17. **(C)**	27. **(C)**	37. **(C)**	47. **(C)**	
8. **(C)**	18. **(A)**	28. **(B)**	38. **(C)**	48. **(B)**	
9. **(D)**	19. **(B)**	29. **(B)**	39. **(D)**	49. **(B)**	
10. **(C)**	20. **(D)**	30. **(C)**	40. **(A)**	50. **(A)**	

ANSWERS AND EXPLANATIONS 答案与解析

Section I 第一部分

PART A: MULTIPLE-CHOICE QUESTIONS 选择题

1. **(A)** William Lloyd Garrison was a central figure in the abolitionist movement that developed in the 1830s. The movement, and other reform movements, grew out of the Second Great Awakening. This spiritual movement conveyed the message that salvation was also in each individual's hands. If one lived a moral life and practiced self-control, one could feel confident about going to heaven. In this respect the Second Great Awakening acted as a springboard for a variety of reform movements, such as abolitionism.

2. **(A)** Garrison is specifically calling for equality and citizenship for free African Americans in the United States. The decision in the *Dred Scott* case asserted the exact opposite; it stipulated that African Americans, whether slave or free, could not be American citizens and therefore had no standing to sue in federal court. *Ex parte Milligan* (1866) (B) held that military tribunals, used on occasion during the Civil War, were unconstitutional when civilian courts were functioning. *Pace v. Alabama* (1883) ruled that Alabama's anti-miscegenation statute was constitutional. *Plessy v. Ferguson* (1896) (C) allowed for segregated facilities, using the principle, "separate but equal."

3. **(C)** With ratification of the Fourteenth Amendment (1868), African Americans were granted citizenship in the United States. This amendment, ratified during Reconstruction, also stated that no person shall be denied "equal protection of the laws." This was a vindication of the position that Garrison took a generation earlier. "Garrisonians" would have endorsed the developments in the other three choices, but those choices did not specifically bestow citizenship on African Americans.

4. **(A)** The differences in the two maps illustrate the result of the Articles of Confederation government successfully handling the question of western lands. After the American victory in the Revolution, there was a great deal of debate about the status of the area between the Appalachian Mountains and the Mississippi River. Some states insisted that their western land claims from the colonial period should be honored, while other states

had no claims on this land. Maryland, a state with no western land claims, insisted that it would not ratify the Articles until all states gave up their land claims and the western lands became part of a national domain. Congress persuaded the states with claims to do just that. The handling of western lands was considered one of the major successes of the Articles of Confederation government. The maps do not indicate any French land claims (B), nor do they refer to slavery (C). By the time of the "Quasi-War" (1798–1800) (D), western land claims by the various states had long been settled.

5. **(A)** The Northwest Ordinance did not recognize the land claims of the American Indians in the region that dated from the period of British rule. The act encouraged fair treatment of native peoples, but it did not recognize their earlier claims to the land, setting the stage for a series of clashes between whites and American Indians during the 1780s and 1790s in the Ohio River Valley and Great Lakes region. In general, the Northwest Ordinance is considered an important piece of legislation from the "critical period." It divided up the land and provided a plot in every town for public schools. The Northwest Ordinance spelled out the steps that these areas would have to go through in order to become states, on equal footing with the original 13 states (C). In addition, the Northwest Ordinance banned slavery in the Northwest Territory (B).

6. **(C)** In many ways, the Spanish-American War can be seen as a turning point in American history. After the war, the United States became a colonial power like Britain, the nation America had defeated in order to establish its own independence. The United States and Spain negotiated the Treaty of Paris (1898) following the war. In the treaty, Spain agreed to cede the Philippines, Puerto Rico, and Guam to the United States; the United States agreed to pay Spain $20 million for these possessions. The political cartoon is depicting problems that ensued in these newly acquired lands. However, the cartoon does not question the wisdom of American policy, nor does it display empathy for residents of the newly acquired lands. Rather, it portrays them as unruly children that the United States needs to discipline.

7. **(B)** Following the Spanish-American War in 1898, the United States gained control of the Philippines, Puerto Rico, and Cuba. The acquisition of new territories generated a great deal of debate in the United States. The cartoon reflects contemporary racist notions about the inhabitants of the Philippines, Puerto Rico, and Cuba—asserting that they are childlike, unruly, and violent. The cartoon suggests that only the strong hand of the United States could steady these peoples and prepare them for self-government at some point in the future

8. **(C)** In the period following the Spanish-American War (1898), the United States expanded its economic and military presence in the Caribbean and Latin America, and increased its involvement in Asia. America's more active role in the world was due, in large part, to the aggressive foreign policy of President Theodore Roosevelt (1901–1909). Roosevelt's aggressive approach to Latin America is clearly evident in regard to Panama, where Roosevelt engineered a coup and quickly made a deal with the new Panamanian government to build a canal.

9. **(D)** The excerpt from the presidential veto message is from President Andrew Johnson's veto of one of the Reconstruction Acts of 1867. The message alludes to treating the former Confederate states (Tennessee was excluded) as military districts. This was a central aspect of the acts. These sweeping acts divided the South into five military districts.

These areas could only rejoin the United States if they guaranteed basic rights to African Americans. The radicals were not able to fully carry out their program. They were not able to extend land ownership to African Americans, nor did they carry out mass arrests of former Confederates.

10. **(C)** Governor Orval Faubus's response to the steps taken by President Dwight Eisenhower to resolve the Little Rock crisis in 1957 echoes the sentiment of President Andrew Johnson in 1867. Faubus knew that alluding to the Reconstruction period would resonate among white southerners; bitterness over that period was still present in the collective memory of white southerners almost a hundred years later. The conflict began when local authorities had decided to allow nine African American students to enroll in Central High School at the beginning of the school year in 1957. Governor Orval Faubus refused to cooperate with the plan, leading to mob action and violence outside of the high school. The violence and the national news coverage of the flouting of federal authority convinced Eisenhower to send federal troops. The use of federal troops in a southern state provided Faubus with a metaphor that aroused bitterness almost a century after Reconstruction.

11. **(D)** The 1883 cartoon makes the point that incoming immigrants faced myriad dangers when they arrived in America, just as the Pilgrims did when they arrived in the seventeenth century. The dangers immigrants faced in the late nineteenth century included crooked money-changers, baggage handlers who stole all of the immigrant's worldly possessions, landlords renting out substandard housing, and employers looking to exploit cheap labor. This is a rare pro-immigrant cartoon. Most cartoons of the period saw immigrants as a threat to the United States in one way or another (A), (B), and (C).

12. **(A)** The founding of Hull House in Chicago (1889) by Jane Addams and Ellen Gates Starr represents a continuity with the political sentiments expressed in the cartoon. Both the cartoon and the settlement house movement demonstrate empathy for the predicament that recent immigrants often found themselves in. Settlement houses, such as Hull House, were established to aid immigrants, especially immigrant women. By 1911 more than 400 settlement houses existed in the United States, usually run by women. The other choices all reflect aspects of the nativist, or anti-immigrant, movement.

13. **(A)** The 1936 cartoon is making the point that although European individuals and countries might be seduced into waging another major war, the United States would be wise to avoid participating. The cartoon is an expression of isolationism, which became a common sentiment among many Americans between the two world wars. The cartoon is implying that war may be seductive, but it is also brutal and deadly. Many Americans had vivid memories of World War I, and many had lost friends and loved ones. Ultimately, many asked, was it worth it? In addition, the Senate's Nye committee (1934–1937) uncovered evidence that certain American corporations greatly profited from World War I. Americans wondered if the so-called merchants of death had pushed the country into World War I.

14. **(D)** In many ways, the position of Martin Luther King, Jr., in 1967 paralleled the sentiment of the cartoon. Both argued against military involvement in foreign conflicts, and both held that the conflicts in question—World War I and the Vietnam War—did not have the potential to significantly advance American interests in the world. Initially, King did not take a position on the Vietnam War, focusing instead on domestic civil rights issues. However, King began to see the disproportionate role that African Americans played on

the front lines of Vietnam, and he began to see the war as a question of morality and justice. In 1965 King began to publicly express doubts about the Vietnam War. In a 1967 appearance at the Riverside Church in New York City, King delivered a speech titled "Beyond Vietnam: A Time to Break Silence."

15. **(D)** The passage is part of President Truman's argument to Congress in favor of an extension of aid to Greece and Turkey. As part of the policy of containment, the United States extended military aid to Greece and Turkey in 1947. The aid was successful. It helped the Greek monarchy put down a communist-influenced rebel movement. Further, the move quieted Republican criticism of Truman and improved the president's standing in public opinion polls; he won reelection the following year.

16. **(A)** The passage can best be seen as providing a rationale for the policy of containment. In order to block any further aggression by the Soviet Union, Truman issued the Truman Doctrine (1947), in which he said that the goal of the United States would be to contain communism. The containment approach to the Soviet Union had been spelled out in an article entitled "Sources of Soviet Conduct," published in *Foreign Affairs* (1947). Containment remained the cornerstone of American foreign policy for decades to come.

17. **(C)** The ideas expressed in the passage most directly reflect a continuity with debates about the role of the United States in world affairs. This debate emerged as early as President George Washington's "Proclamation of Neutrality" (1793), as war broke out between France and Great Britain. It can be seen in the aftermath of the American victory in the Spanish-American War (1898) and in the lead-up to both world wars.

18. **(A)** The political cartoon is making the point that government officials were taking their crusade against immoral behavior to extreme lengths. The cartoon is depicting Anthony Comstock, a former U.S. postal inspector and the public face of the moral reform movement, dragging a woman into court and, absurdly, accusing her of giving birth to a "naked child." Although the cartoon is satirical, Comstock's actual actions were only slightly less outrageous. For example, he prohibited certain anatomy textbooks from being sent to medical students. The 1873 Comstock Law outlawed the distribution of information or devices related to contraception. Comstock repeatedly clashed with birth-control advocate Margaret Sanger.

19. **(B)** The cartoon reflects a point of view in the ongoing debate about the role of the federal government in regulating morality. This debate can be seen in the lead-up to the ratification of the Eighteenth Amendment in 1919. This amendment called for a ban on the manufacture, sale, and transportation of alcoholic beverages. The movement to ban alcohol from American society was one of the largest movements in the nineteenth and early twentieth centuries. The debate can also be seen in the 1960s in discussions of various forms of birth control, including "the pill," as well as in recent debates around gay marriage and marijuana policy.

20. **(C)** The issue that precipitated the speech was the passage of an act creating higher tariff rates. The act, known by its critics as the "Tariff of Abominations," dramatically raised tariff rates on many items, and led to a general reduction in trade between the United States and Europe. This decline in trade hit South Carolina's cotton plantations especially hard. By 1832, John C. Calhoun and other South Carolina political leaders asserted the right of states to nullify federal legislation. Under the theory of nullification, a state

could declare an objectionable law null and void within that state. President Jackson, a defender of states' rights, was, nonetheless, alarmed at this blatant flouting of federal authority. He pushed for passage of the Force Bill, which authorized military force against South Carolina for committing treason. At the same time, Congress revised tariff rates, providing relief for South Carolina. The Force Bill and the new tariff rates, passed by Congress on the same day, amounted to a face-saving compromise.

21. **(D)** The debate over nullification and the debate over ratifying the Constitution are similar in that in both, the issue of the power of the states was at stake. Under the Articles of Confederation, the states had a great deal more power. Those who defended the Articles—the Anti-Federalists—used language strikingly similar to Calhoun's. In the excerpt, Calhoun argues, "to reserve such exclusive right to the General Government . . . is to convert it, in fact, into a great consolidated government, with unlimited powers, and to divest the States, in reality, of all their rights. . . ." Such an argument echoes the arguments of the Anti-Federalists against the Constitution.

22. **(B)** Calhoun's protest included the threat of state nullification of federal decisions. He even threatened to consider secession if other measures did not work. This form of protest can also be seen in the response of New England Federalists to the War of 1812. The Hartford Convention (1814) raised the very real possibility that New England would secede from the United States in order to protect their economic and maritime trade interests. Although talk of nullification and secession is more associated with southern political leaders, these issues were also brought up in the intense debates about the War of 1812. The war ended before the Federalists could follow through on their threat.

23. **(D)** The main purpose of the cartoon is to point out that President Franklin D. Roosevelt had a secret agenda. In this view, Roosevelt claimed he was creating programs to help people, but secretly he was attempting to create some sort of dictatorship that would take away people's freedom. The cartoon reflects conservative criticisms of the New Deal. Note that the presence of a "Trojan horse" in a political cartoon implies that someone has a sinister agenda different from a stated agenda.

24. **(A)** This cartoon is taking a position in the debate about the proper role of the federal government in the economy. This debate first become part of the national agenda during the Progressive era of the early decades of the twentieth century, when reformers insisted that the federal government should play a greater role in regulating economic activity in the United States. The debate continued through the New Deal, the Great Society, and into the debates in recent decades about the federal government playing a role in reforming the health care system. Some conservatives accused the Supreme Court of legislating from the bench in the 1950s and 1960s, under Chief Justice Earl Warren (B). Conservative opposition to the New Deal did not center on issues of states' rights or the power of the states (C). The country was not at war in 1933 (D).

25. **(B)** The sentiment reflected in the cartoon is similar to opposition by the Republican Party to the creation of Great Society programs in the 1960s. Johnson's Great Society programs included Medicare and Medicaid. The Medicare program provides health care for every American once each reaches the age of 65. The main components of Johnson's Great Society were landmark civil rights acts as well as a comprehensive "war on poverty." Many aspects of Johnson's Great Society were underfunded as the federal government spent more and more on the Vietnam War. In both the 1930s and the 1960s, conservatives

argued that the federal government's reach was extending beyond its traditional limits and threatening individual liberty and the Constitution.

26. **(D)** William Graham Sumner is associated with the intellectual movement, social Darwinism. Followers of Sumner and his book, *What Social Classes Owe to Each Other*, would most likely have advocated a laissez-faire approach to the economy. The French phrase *laissez-faire* means "to let alone." It describes a government policy that would take a hands-off approach when it comes to economic activities. Social Darwinism was an attempt to apply Charles Darwin's ideas about the natural world to social relations. Sumner was attracted to Darwin's ideas about competition and Herbert Spencer's term, "survival of the fittest." He argued against any attempt at government intervention into the economic and social spheres. Interference, he argued, would hinder the evolution of the human species. The inequalities of wealth that characterized the late 1800s were part of the process of "survival of the fittest." Social Darwinism appealed to owners of large corporations, because it both justified their wealth and power and warned against any type of regulation or reform.

27. **(A)** The ideas of social Darwinism justified the success of those at the top of the socio-economic structure as both appropriate and inevitable. Sumner argues that we should let nature run its course; to do otherwise could lead to disaster. He argues, "We can only, by interfering with [the natural order], produce the survival of the unfittest. . . ." He therefore was against government regulations of economic activity.

28. **(B)** The law, excerpted in the question, mandated that citizens in Pennsylvania do not cooperate with slave-catchers, seeking to capture fugitive slaves. The fugitive slave clause of the Constitution was present from the drafting of the Constitution, but it was given teeth later in history, with the passage of the Fugitive Slave Act, as part of the Compromise of 1850. Even before that act was passed, states were not allowed to pass laws that went directly against returning slaves to their owners. In the case of *Prigg v. Pennsylvania* (1842), the Supreme Court declared the Pennsylvania law invalid.

29. **(B)** The existence of the Pennsylvania law, excerpted in the question, demonstrates an ongoing tension between federal and state law. The Supremacy Clause of the Constitution states that the Constitution and federal laws and treaties are the "supreme law of the land." Therefore, state laws must operate within the bounds of the Constitution, as defined by the Supreme Court. However, states repeatedly asserted their right to do as they pleased in the antebellum period, hoping the federal government would not try to enforce the Constitution. This tension persisted into the twentieth century, with many white southerners vowing "massive resistance" to federal edicts against segregation.

30. **(C)** The conflict around the Pennsylvania law reflected the ambiguous nature of slavery in the Constitution. The framers of the Constitution were, to some degree, uneasy with the institution. This uneasiness is reflected in the fact that the word "slavery" is not mentioned in the entire document. Slaves are often referred to as "other persons." Although the framers of the Constitution did not mention the word slavery, they were willing to compromise on the issue and postpone any final decision about slavery to the future. This postponement led to decades of debate and conflict over the issue.

31. **(B)** Dorothea Dix's testimony to the Massachusetts legislature reflects the influence of the Second Great Awakening. The movement spoke to many of the men and women

who were brought into the larger society by the "market revolution." The Second Great Awakening told the individual that salvation was also in his or her hands. Righteous living, self-control, and a strong moral compass would lead to salvation. This idea that one could determine his or her eternal life was very different from the old Calvinist notion of predestination, which held that one's eternal life was planned out by God. The Second Great Awakening not only encouraged individual redemption, but also societal reformation. Not only could one become perfect in the eyes of God, but one could work to perfect society as well. In this respect the Second Great Awakening acted as a springboard for a variety of reform movements.

32. **(D)** Dorothea Dix's research and testimony is best understood in the context of the rise of voluntary organizations to promote religious and secular reforms. This activism was inspired in part by the Second Great Awakening. The era also saw the rise of the abolitionist movement, the women's rights movement, and the temperance movement. Women did gain the right to vote in state and local elections in several states, but that was not until the late 1800s; women were guaranteed the right to vote in all elections with the passage of the Nineteenth Amendment (1920) (A). Dix's activism was not motivated by an economic downturn (B); on the contrary, many historians note that the Second Great Awakening and the market revolution went hand in hand, suggesting such activism occurred in an expanding economy. Dix was making her argument to the Massachusetts state government, not the federal government (C). It is not until the twentieth century that the federal government begins to play a role in issues of health and poverty.

33. **(C)** The song lyrics appeared in a populist newspaper in the 1890s. The allusions to monopolies, railroads, and party bosses indicate that this song was meant to publicize the plight of farmers in the late 1800s. The populist movement tapped into growing discontent among farmers in the West about the economic bind they found themselves in, and became a formidable force in the 1890s. The populists grew angry at the concentration of wealth and power by eastern industrialists. They supported a national income tax so that those with higher incomes would pay more than the poor. They also supported free and unlimited coinage of silver. Populists wanted the United States to get off the gold standard and to issue money backed by silver as well. This would increase the amount of money in circulation and would lead to inflation. Farmers supported inflationary policies so that the prices they received for their produce would increase.

34. **(B)** The farmers' movement pushed state governments to pass laws regulating railroad rates and practices. These laws, known as Granger Laws, had limited effectiveness. In the 1886 Wabash case, the Supreme Court limited the ability of states to regulate railroads. In response, the federal government created the Interstate Commerce Commission (1887) to regulate railroads. However, the ICC was chronically underfunded and was, therefore, ineffective.

35. **(A)** The era saw widespread corruption in government; this is hinted at in the allusion to old party bosses. As the extent of corruption in government became more widely known, from the Grant Administration in Washington to Tammany Hall in New York City, activists demanded reform of local, state, and national governments. Some activists hoped for the formation of the broad coalition described in choice (B), but differences in race, ethnicity, and location made such a coalition untenable. The farmers did create a third party, the Populist Party, but it remained just that—a third party; it did not rise in promi-

nence on a national level to compete with the two main political parties (C). The "Indian Wars" of the West were over by the 1890s (D).

36. **(C)** The passage from Marcus Garvey is best understood as an expression of black nationalism. Garvey is best known for urging African Americans to return to their ancestral homelands in Africa. Not many African Americans made the journey, but Garvey instilled a sense of pride among many African Americans; in this he is seen as an important figure in the movement for black nationalism.

37. **(B)** Marcus Garvey argued for African Americans to build separate institutions to demand greater power. His activism highlights the ongoing debate between separatism and integration as to the place of African Americans in American society. There are echoes of this tension in the 1960s between King's call for integration and the rise of the "Black Power" movement.

38. **(C)** The excerpt from the essay by Glenda Elizabeth Gilmore implies that historians of the Progressive movement have not written extensively on the contributions of black women to progressivism in the South because of a scarcity of documentary evidence. She argues that African American women "remained invisible in virtually every discussion of southern progressivism" because they did not have access to the public expressions of activism that white women did. She implies that it is the job of the historian to recognize this limitation, and to figure out other ways of studying the activities of black women in the Progressive movement.

39. **(D)** The efforts by black women to participate in the southern Progressive movement occurred in the context of a nadir in race relations in the United States as "scientific" ideas about race, inaction by the federal government, and rigid segregation in the South relegated African Americans to a second-class status in the United States. The year 1896, the beginning of Gilmore's study, was also the year the Supreme Court issued the *Plessy v. Ferguson* decision, giving sanction to segregation, on a "separate but equal" basis.

40. **(A)** The letter by Washington reflects his position in the ongoing debate about the proper balance between liberty and order. This same debate also occurred around President Abraham Lincoln's suspension of habeas corpus during the Civil War, around the Espionage and Sedition Acts during World War I, around the Japanese internment during World War II, and around the McCarran Internal Security Act of 1950. It is occurring today around the 2001 Patriot Act.

41. **(D)** George Washington came to believe that the Articles of Confederation government erred in allowing for too great a degree of democracy. There was a heated debate in the 1780s about the appropriate degree of democratic participation in society and about the nature of the public. Many of the political leaders who coalesced around the Federalist point of view on the Constitution came to believe that too much democracy was dangerous. Their fears would be borne out in the coming weeks when Shays' Rebellion began in Massachusetts. This was a central reason that Washington, Hamilton, and other Federalists wanted to replace the Articles of Confederation with the Constitution.

42. **(C)** George Washington is expressing great unease with the ability of the government, under the Articles of Confederation, to maintain order in the United States. He was worried about the lack of strong authority in the United States. People who shared this view would have supported the ratification of the Constitution, as Washington himself

did. People who favored order over democracy would certainly not have supported the revolutionary French government in 1793 (A). Supporters of increasing the power and authority of the central government generally supported the chartering of a national government (B). The Alien and Sedition Acts imposed greater order and restraints on the people (D); therefore, someone who shared Washington's sentiments would have supported it, not opposed it.

43. **(D)** The actions of the Paxton Boys represent ongoing tensions between backcountry settlers and elites within colonial America. In the aftermath of the French and Indian War, during Pontiac's Rebellion, a vigilante group of these Scotch-Irish settlers organized raids against American Indians on the Pennsylvania frontier. These raids included an attack on Conestoga Indians in 1763 that resulted in 20 deaths. After the attacks on the Conestoga, in January 1764, about 250 Paxton Boys marched to Philadelphia to present their grievances to the Pennsylvania legislature. Tensions began to develop around this time between colonists and British authorities (A), but the Paxton Boys are citing resentment at local elites, not British authorities. Tensions did exist among Indian groups allied with different European powers (B); this was evident in the Beaver Wars of the 1600s. Tensions existed in colonial America between freed African Americans and white planters (C), as evidenced in court proceedings, changing attitudes of whites, and legislative acts, but this was not central to the grievances of the Paxton Boys.

44. **(B)** Bacon's Rebellion and the march of the Paxton Boys form a clear continuity in colonial American history in that both events were precipitated by tensions on the frontier between backcountry settlers and American Indians; both events reflected resentment by the western backcountry settlers against the eastern colonial elites; both events reflected differing opinions around policies in regard to American Indians: and both involved extralegal violence. The other events reflected tensions in colonial America, but do not represent as clear a continuity as does Bacon's Rebellion.

45. **(D)** The Port Huron Statement, written by Students for a Democratic Society, was an important foundational document of the emerging New Left of the 1960s. It raises a host of concerns that shaped the New Left of the 1960s—poverty, racism, the misguided priorities of an affluent society, the proliferation of nuclear bombs, the paranoia of the anticommunist crusade. The New Left was supportive of the civil rights movement (B); however, this document reflects the concerns of middle-class students, "bred in at least modest comfort." The New Left was generally supportive of workers' rights and just wages for working-class people, but it was often at odds with some of the more conservative political positions of large unions—including anticommunism and support for the war in Vietnam (A). The concerns in the Port Huron Statement are far different from the agenda of the New Right (D). In some ways, the New Right can be seen as a reaction to the rise of the New Left.

46. **(A)** The "New Look" foreign policy shifted American military priorities away from conventional forces and toward increased reliance on nuclear weapons. The Port Huron Statement expressed concern about the proliferation of nuclear weapons that occurred, in part as a result of the "New Look" foreign policy. U.S. funding for the United Nations increased in the 1950s (B); however, the sentiments in the Port Huron Statement are not critical of the United Nations. The Port Huron Statement expressly embraces the "southern struggle" for racial justice; as such, it would have supported Eisenhower's inter-

vention in the Little Rock crisis (C). The United States devoted additional resources to education, especially in math and science, in the wake of the *Sputnik* launch (D); the Port Huron Statement contains no repudiation of funding for education.

47. **(C)** The primary intended audience for the Port Huron Statement was middle-class college students. The statement was written at the founding convention of Students for a Democratic Society, and was intended to be a recruiting tool as SDS tried to attract support on college campuses. The statement refers to having grown up in "comfort," not poverty. The statement expressed solidarity with African Americans in the South, but it was not meant as a recruiting tool for African Americans (A). SDS made many appeals and petitions to government officials (B), but this is not one of them. The "Old Left" of the 1930s attempted to recruit factory workers (D); the "New Left" focused more on recruiting college students.

48. **(B)** The growth of Students for a Democratic Society—the organization that published the Port Huron Statement—can best be understood in the context of the baby boom, economic growth, and a rapid expansion of higher education. The campus-based organization thrived at a time when the size of the college-aged demographic ballooned as baby boomers reached their upper teens. In addition, the growth of the middle class contributed to a large increase in the number of students enrolled in four-year universities in the 1960s.

49. **(B)** The New York law, cited in the question, allowed married women to own their own property and to keep money they might inherit. This challenged traditional understandings of women and property embodied in the legal concept of *femme covert*. Under the legal doctrine of *femme covert*, wives had no independent legal or political standing.

50. **(A)** Participants in the Seneca Falls Convention, which occurred in New York State, just weeks after the New York legislature passed the Married Women's Property Act (1848), would certainly have supported the act as a step forward for the women's rights movement. The Seneca Falls Declaration, written at the Convention, specifically cites unequal property rights as an injustice to be rectified.

51. **(D)** The passage of the Married Women's Property Act directly reflects the ongoing debate around the legal status of women. From the colonial period until the contemporary period, the legal status of women has changed so that women currently enjoy the same legal rights and responsibilities as men. These debates have involved divorce, custody, property, voting, serving on juries, serving in the military, and other issues.

52. **(D)** The Flushing Remonstrance (1657) was written by English residents of the village of Flushing in the Dutch colony of New Netherland. The director-general of the colony, Peter Stuyvesant, was attempting to enforce conformity in New Netherland despite its multiethnic makeup. The authors were protesting a ban on Quaker worship in New Netherland, even though the authors themselves were not Quaker.

53. **(C)** The main idea of the Flushing Remonstrance—that government should not interfere or limit different religious practices—was enshrined into the U.S. legal structure by the "Free Exercise Clause" of the First Amendment. The First Amendment mentions religion in two contexts. The "Establishment Clause" (D) prohibits the establishment of an

official religion in the United States. The "Free Exercise Clause" asserts that Congress shall make no laws limiting the right to worship freely.

54. **(D)** The main purpose of the petition by Paul Cuffe was to demand that the Massachusetts legislature either grant the petitioners the right to vote or excuse them from paying taxes. Cuffe and his brother were free African Americans. They paid taxes, but they were not permitted to vote. The petition was based on the oft-repeated principle of the Patriot cause—no taxation without representation.

55. **(A)** The petition by Paul Cuffe illustrates the fact that the rhetoric of the American Revolution raised awareness of social inequalities and inspired groups and individuals to call for greater political democracy. The documents and publications of the Revolutionary era are filled with the language of inequality, injustice, and enslavement. The Declaration of Independence contains the idea that all men have certain basic rights, expressed in the phrase, "life, liberty, and the pursuit of happiness." Many groups—African Americans (free and enslaved), indentured servants, women, American Indians—were inspired by this language and insisted that the new government abide by its principles.

PART B: SHORT-ANSWER QUESTIONS   简答题

Good responses to question #1

A. A good response would present a description of the British theory of "virtual representation."

. . . British political leaders responded to the colonial demand of "No taxation without representation" by arguing that the colonists *were* represented in Parliament. Members of Parliament represented their home district, but they also represented the interests of the entire British empire, including residents of the colonies.

B. A good response would mention a specific difference between the tone of the "The Declaration of Rights of the Stamp Act Congress" and that of Thomas Paine's pamphlet, *Common Sense*, and would provide evidence from this declaration to support the contention of the response.

. . . The Stamp Act Congress document is very careful to express loyalty to the monarch, using words such as "sincerely devoted" and "with the warmest sentiments" to describe the colonists' feelings about the king and the British government, whereas Paine's *Common Sense* urges colonists to reject the king as a tyrant.

. . . The Stamp Act Congress declarations are intended to reform British policies, whereas Paine's *Common Sense* is urging people to endorse the movement for independence from Great Britain. The Stamp Act Congress expresses a sense of "duty and affection" to the king, while reserving criticism for specific acts of Parliament.

C. A good response would describe the context of the meeting of the Stamp Act Declaration in terms of relations between Great Britain and its 13 North American colonies.

. . . The Stamp Act Congress met in response to recent acts by Parliament to raise revenues from the 13 North American colonies. There was widespread opposition to these taxes, which were direct taxes on the colonists—not import duties. The taxes were passed in the aftermath of the French and Indian War.

. . . The Stamp Act Congress met at a time of increased tensions between the 13 colonies and Great Britain. In the aftermath of the French and Indian War Parliament set about reorganizing the administration of Britain's North American empire. The war had left the government in debt, and both the king and legislature believed the American colonies should help pay it off.

Good responses to question #2

A. A good response would explain the point of view of the cartoon.

. . . The cartoonist is expressing sympathy for working people in the Gilded Age. It represents the working class with a scrawny man on a feeble horse (with "Labor" on his cap). The owners are represented by the medieval jouster, clad in a suit of armor, sitting on a steam engine. Labor does not stand a chance in workplace conflicts; the deck, according to the point of view of the cartoonist, is stacked in favor of the owners of the era.

. . . The cartoon is commenting on the power of the "robber barons" of the late nineteenth century. That power is represented by the jouster. He has the power of a locomotive beneath him. He is engaged in a contest with laborers, represented by a weak man on a horse. The jouster, labeled "monopoly," has the power and money on his side. The worker, presented empathetically, has no way to defend his interests.

B. A good response would mention one specific event from 1865 to 1900 that would support the point of view of the cartoon, such as:

. . . The rise of monopolies, trusts, and other large corporate entities, such as U.S. Steel, that exercised monopoly control over particular industries.

. . . The defeat of unionized workers in some of the major labor battles of the late nineteenth century, such as the Great Railroad Strike of 1877, the Homestead Strike of 1892, and the Pullman Strike of 1894.

. . . The power of the "robber barons" of the era—Cornelius Vanderbilt, Andrew Carnegie, John D. Rockefeller—to dominate the workers and exert great influence over society.

C. A good response would mention continuities and changes in the position of workers in the Gilded Age of the late 1800s and the New Deal era of the 1930s.

. . . A key change that occurred between the Gilded Age of the late 1800s and the New Deal era of the 1930s was that workers had more power in the latter period. The New Deal made it clear that the government would protect the rights of unions to organize workers and fight for higher wages. The passage of the Wagner Act (1935), which then created the National Labor Relations Board, ensured that the right of collective bargaining would be protected by the government. The government was generally hostile to organized labor in the Gilded Age.

Good responses to question #3

A. A good response would explain the source of anger of the participants in the riot described in both documents.

. . . The rioters mentioned in both documents were angry at the U.S. government's draft policy during the Civil War. The riots, which occurred in New York City in 1863, reflected discontent among members of the working-class with the Enrollment Act, passed by Congress earlier that year to draft men to fight in the Civil War. Many of the rioters were especially incensed that the Union draft law allowed men to be exempt from the draft if they could either furnish a suitable substitute to take their place, or pay $300.

. . . The New York City draft riots in the summer of 1863 had an immediate cause and an underlying cause. The immediate cause was the Enrollment Act, passed earlier in 1863 to draft men into the army to fight in the Civil War. The law allowed wealthy people to pay $300 to avoid service. The underlying cause of the riot was racist resentment of African Americans among the city's Irish population. Many of these working-class men feared that if slavery ended, thousands of freed African Americans would come north to compete with them for jobs.

B. A good response would explain how the two documents differ in their point of view.

. . . The first document, an editorial in *The New York Times*, is highly critical of the draft rioters, while the second document, a letter to *The New York Times*, asks the public to sympathize with the rioters. The editorial states that the rioters are uncivilized, citing their burning of an orphanage for African American children, and their wanton violence. The letter presents the riot in class terms. It asserts that the rioters, the working-class poor of New York City, have no other means of challenging the wealthy class in the city. The draft law, they contend, was written by and for the wealthy. The rioters are simply trying to protect their rights and their families.

C. A good response would select one of the three options and provide a brief explanation of how the New York City draft riots can be compared to the event chosen. Explanations might include:

Shays' Rebellion (1786–1787)

. . . Shays' Rebellion also represents a popular uprising against policies deemed by the rebels as unfair. In this case farmers in Western Massachusetts challenged the policies of the state government. Unpopular policies included high rates of taxation and the lack of government support to prevent bank foreclosures. Also, the government insisted that all back taxes be paid for in hard currency, not cheap paper currency.

. . . Shays' Rebellion also represents a resort to violence in protest of policies deemed unfair by the participants. In the case of Shays' Rebellion, armed rebels closed court-houses and engaged with a private militia sent to defeat them.

. . . Shays' Rebellion was primarily a rural uprising, whereas the New York City draft riots were urban. Race was not a factor in Shays' Rebellion, and individual civilians were not targeted by the Shaysites as they were by the New York City rioters.

Coxey's Army (1894)

. . . The march of Coxey's Army was also a working class action against government poli-cies that were perceived to be unfair. In the case of Coxey's march, which occurred during the severe economic downturn following the Panic of 1893, the protestors objected to the lack of action to help the unemployed. They insisted on a government public works program.

. . . Both protests, the march of Coxey's Army and the New York City draft riots, repre-sented working-class resentment of policies that seemed to favor the wealthy.

. . . Coxey's marchers did not resort to violence, as the draft riots had.

Tulsa race riot (1922)

. . . The Tulsa race riot was similar to the New York City draft riots in that both events targeted African American civilians in random and brutal acts of violence. The Tulsa race riot was the deadliest riot against African Americans in U.S. history. Over 300 African Americans were killed. In both case, white mobs targeted African Americans. The Tulsa race riot was different from the New York City draft riots in that there was no political grievance that set the rioters in motion—it was simply a vicious attack on the African American community.

Good responses to question #4

A. A good response would explain the point of view of the two-paneled image in the question.

. . . The two-paneled image is a defense of slavery. It is contrasting the life of an African in "in his own country" with the life of an enslaved African American in the South. The artist is implying that the African is uncivilized—he is carrying a spear and there are no signs of refinement around him. In fact, there is an unburied skeleton on the ground. The alternative to this savage, violent world is, according to the artist, the refinement of southern plantation life. Southern slaves are depicted in the panel as gaining the benefits of Christianity and education from their benevolent master.

B. A good response would explain the shift in thinking among southern planters about slavery from the early decades of the country (before 1830) to the period of the images.

... In the early decades of U.S. history, defenders of slavery frequently described slavery as a "necessary evil." Slave owners, such as Thomas Jefferson, asserted that slavery was not ideal, but it was essential for the economy of the South, and for the health of the country. After around 1830, southern defenders of slavery, such as George Fitzhugh and John C. Calhoun, began to endorse slavery as a "positive good"—that is, it was actually beneficial to the slaves themselves. From this perspective, slavery would uplift slaves; Fitzhugh argued that slaves were the freest and happiest people on Earth.

C. A good response would mention events and developments from 1830 onward that help explain the development of the point of view of the images. These developments and events could include:

... The growth of the abolitionist movement and the increasing focus of antislavery activists on the immorality of slavery.
... The activism of Elijah Lovejoy, William Lloyd Garrison, Frederick Douglass, and others.
... The growing critique that industrialization in the North was treating workers as "wage slaves"; actual slaves, so the argument went, were treated decently by comparison.
... Heightened sectional tensions between northerners and southerners over the spread of slavery to new territories.
... The abolition of slavery in many countries, including most of Latin America, in the first half of the nineteenth century.

Section II 第二部分

PART A: DOCUMENT-BASED QUESTION 材料分析题

What good responses will include:

A good response would draw on six or seven documents (that is, all or all but one of the documents provided) to present an analysis of each of the elements mentioned in the question: the economic, political, and social context of the conflict between congressional Republicans and President Andrew Johnson in regard to plans for Reconstruction in the South in the years 1864 to 1877.

Thesis and Argument Development—Targeted Skills: Argumentation and (in this case) Historical Causation (2 points)
论点及论证发展——目标技能：论证与历史起因（2分）

Given the nature of the question, the thesis should focus on the historical thinking skill of **historical causation**. It should address the economic, social, and political factors that contributed to the tensions between the legislative and executive branches and assess the most important causes. The thesis should make a claim about the cause of the tension—the lenient attitude of the president in regard to the freedmen and women in the South; the aggressiveness of the former slave-owning class following the war; the persistent mistreatment of African Americans in the immediate aftermath of the war; or the insistence of African Americans that a more sweeping restructuring of the South take place. A simple claim would earn one point. For the second point, the thesis should recognize and account for historical complexity by explicitly noting contradiction, corroboration, and qualification, as illustrated by historical evidence. Such a thesis might note the idealism of radical Republicans in challenging the president, but would also acknowledge the desire of Republicans to limit the power of their Democratic rival in the White House. Or a thesis could focus on the interplay between the agency of ordinary individuals (in this case, the activism of African Americans in the South to create a just society) and the actions of powerful politicians (the Republicans in Congress).

Document Analysis—Targeted Skills: Analyzing Evidence: Content and Sourcing, and Argumentation (2 points)

材料分析——目标技能：分析史料的内容、来源并进行论证（2分）

In order to receive credit for the first point, the essay should use the content of at least six of the documents to support the stated thesis or a relevant argument. For the second point the student must explain one of the following for at least four of the documents: author's point of view, author's purpose, historical context, or audience. A good essay should not simply describe the contents of the documents, one after another. Rather, a good essay should make connections between documents or sections of documents in crafting the documents into a convincing argument.

The attitude of President Abraham Lincoln toward Reconstruction is illustrated in Document 1. Lincoln is urging the nation to "bind up" its wounds, and to do this "with charity to all." This can be interpreted as a call for a quick and lenient approach to Reconstruction. Such an approach was evident in Lincoln's "10 percent plan," and was evident in President Andrew Johnson's Proclamation of Amnesty and Reconstruction. The audience of the address is the American people; the context is the period at the very end of the Civil War, as the nation is contemplating what the post-Civil War will look like. Students can contrast this attitude with the more sweeping approach of Thaddeus Stevens, who notes how little has been done in the South in terms of creating new governments "based on principles of liberty and justice" (Document 7). Documents 2 and 3 show different aspects of life in the South in the immediate aftermath of the Civil War, specifically the nature of the "black codes" implemented throughout the South. Restrictions were put on African Americans with laws on "vagrancy," "idleness," and "labor contracts." Document 4 depicts the punishment for a freeman who cannot pay a fine. Students should see the resemblance to a slave auction. The student should be able to note comparisons between life under the black codes and life under slavery for African Americans. Document 5 illustrates action taken by African Americans to challenge the injustices that were rampant under presidential Reconstruction. The fact that the image appeared in a national newspaper can be used to note the political agenda of the cartoon, convincing people of the unjust nature of Southern black codes and their resemblance to the system of slavery. The South Carolina Colored People's Convention sets forth many of the elements of a more sweeping plan—one that is embodied in Thaddeus Stevens's speech (Document 7). The audience for this document was, as the title indicates, the U.S. Congress, but such petitions were also meant to be published and circulated in order to convince the public of a particular point of view. Document 6, a speech by a Democratic leader of Congress, can be used to complicate the motivations of congressional Republicans, asserting that their goal was political "domination."

Using Evidence Beyond the Documents—Targeted Skills: Contextualization and Argumentation (2 points)

使用给定资料之外的材料——目标技能：联系有关背景进行论证（2分）

Essays should situate the argument in its historical context by explaining broader historical events, developments, or processes immediately relevant to the question. Such contextualization will earn the student one point; an additional point can be earned by providing specific examples and evidence beyond what is contained within the documents. In this case, students could establish a broader context by discussing the heated political controversies between the Democrats and the Republicans in the years leading up to the Civil War. This point can be illustrated with mention of one or more of the following: the lack of compromise evident in the Compromise of 1850, the caning of Senator Charles Sumner, the fiery rhetoric of John C. Calhoun, or the events of "Bleeding Kansas." Students could also place the events of the era into the larger context of the treatment of African Americans from before the Civil War through the end of the nineteenth century. Such contextualization could discuss slave codes and the lack of autonomy implicit in the slave system. Looking beyond the period of the question, students could discuss the elements of the Jim Crow system, the Supreme Court decision in *Plessy v. Ferguson* (1896), violence against African Americans, and the exclusion of African Americans from the political process.

Synthesis—Targeted Skill: Synthesis (1 point)   整合——目标技能：信息整合（1分）

The final point of the document-based question requires the student to extend the argument of the essay, by explaining connections between the argument and one of the following: a development in a different historical period, situation, or geographical area; or a theme and/or approach to history that is not the focus of the essay (such as political, economic, social, cultural, or intellectual history). In this case, students might want to extend the argument of the essay to other clashes between Congress and the president in U.S. history, such as clashes between Congress and President Nixon over the Vietnam War and the Watergate scandal in the early 1970s. Students could also choose to explore the interplay between actions on the grassroots level and initiative on the governmental level. In this case, on the local level we see violence by white Southerners and activism by African Africans for social change; on the national level, we see implementation of a sweeping Reconstruction plan. The student could point to similar dynamics in the Progressive era, with activism on the local level and reform legislation on the national level. Also, this dynamic is at play in regard to the civil rights movement of the 1950s and 1960s.

PART B: LONG-ESSAY QUESTIONS   论述题

Question 1

What good responses will include:

A good response to long-essay question #1 will discuss the long-term and short-term causes of the Mexican War and analyze the relative importance of the different causes of the war.

Thesis—Targeted Skill: Argumentation (1 point)   论点——目标技能：论证（1分）

Students will earn one point for presenting a thesis that makes a historically defensible claim and responds to all parts of the question. The thesis, which must consist of one or more sentences and must be located in either the introduction or the conclusion, must also make a convincing claim about the relative importance of the causes of the Mexican War (1846–1848). A convincing thesis can, for example, argue that one cause is more important than others or that two causes worked in tandem to set the stage for war. In addition, the student should explain why the cause or causes he or she chose were most significant in understanding the war.

Argument Development: Using the Targeted Historical Thinking Skill— Targeted Skills: Argumentation and (in this case) Causation (2 points)
论证发展——使用目标历史思维技能，目标技能：论证与起因（2分）

Students must develop their argument by expanding upon the thesis. Students can earn up to two points in this section. One point would be granted if the student successfully describes the long-term and short-term causes of the Mexican War. A second point would be granted if the student explains the reasons why particular factors contributed to the war. Long-term factors could include the idea of "manifest destiny," which refers to the movement of individuals to the West, as well as to the political extension of U.S. territory. The term captured the fervor of the westward expansion movement, implying that it was God's plan that the United States take over and settle the entire continent. The United States was also interested in expanding its trade with Asia. Such trade would be greatly enhanced by the acquisition of the northern states of Mexico, giving the United States access to the Pacific Ocean. Finally, students could mention cultural factors that paved the way for war, including a belief in Anglo-Saxon superiority. Many Americans felt that it was their duty to bring civilization and democratic principles to the lands controlled by Mexico.

In terms of short-term causes of the war, students would certainly mention the border dispute between the United States and Mexico. Texas had recently (1844) been annexed by the United States. Mexico said the border between Texas and Mexico was at the Nueces River. However, the United States insisted it was at the Rio Grande, 150 miles to the south. This conflict led to skirmishes, and then to war. Students could also mention the election of the expansionist James K. Polk as president in 1844.

Argument Development: Using Evidence—Targeted Skill: Argumentation (2 points) 论证发展，使用史料——目标技能：论证（2分）

In addition to citing causes of the Mexican War, students must also use evidence to support their argument. Students can earn one point by addressing the topic of the question—short-term and long-term causes of the Mexican War—with specific examples of relevant evidence. A second point can be earned by utilizing this evidence to fully and effectively substantiate the stated thesis or a relevant argument. The specific evidence the student chooses will vary depending on the approach of the essay. Students, for instance, might mention the opposition of Abraham Lincoln, then a member of the House of Representatives, to going to war with Mexico. He challenged President Polk's assertion that "American blood has been shed on American soil." He repeatedly challenged the president to show him the spot where American blood had been shed. This specific evidence could be used to substantiate claims of political tensions on the eve of the war between Whigs and Democrats. These tensions were played out in the election of 1844, which Polk won, ensuring a more aggressive foreign policy in terms of western expansion.

Synthesis—Targeted Skill: Synthesis (1 point) 整合——目标技能：信息整合（1分）

The sixth and final point on the long essay can be earned for demonstrating the historical thinking skill of synthesis. A student can earn this point by extending the argument to explain the connections between the argument of the essay and ONE of the following: a development in a different historical period, situation, era, or geographical area, or a course theme and/or approach to history that is not the focus of the essay (such as political, economic, social, cultural, or intellectual history). In this case, the student could draw connections between the lead-up to the Mexican War and lead-up to any other war in American history. Such connections could focus on the significance of economic factors in explaining the push toward war. The student could draw comparisons between the desire for expanded trade with Asia in the lead-up to the Mexican War and concerns about American sugar production in Cuba in the lead-up to the Spanish-American War.

Question 2

What good responses will include:

A good response to long-essay question #2 will discuss the long-term and short-term causes of the Spanish-American War and to analyze the relative importance of the different causes of the war.

Thesis—Targeted skill: Argumentation (1 point) 整合——目标技能：论证（1分）

Students will earn one point for presenting a thesis that makes a historically defensible claim and responds to all parts of the question. The thesis, which must consist of one or more sentences and must be located either in the introduction or the conclusion, must make a convincing claim about the relative importance of the causes of the Spanish-American War (1898). A convincing thesis can, for example, argue that one cause is more important than others or that two causes worked in tandem with one another to set the stage for war. In addition, the student should explain why the cause or causes chosen were most significant in understanding the war.

Argument development: Using the Targeted Historical Thinking Skill—Targeted skills: Argumentation and (in this case) Causation (2 points)
论证发展，使用目标历史思维技能——目标技能：论证与起因（2分）

Students must develop their argument by expanding upon the thesis. Students can earn up to two points in this section. One point would be granted if the student successfully describes the long-term and short-term causes of the Spanish-American War. A second point would be granted if the student explains the reasons why particular factors contributed to the war. Long-term factors could include the push for imperial expansion. By the late nineteenth century, United States political leaders were looking beyond the nation's borders to expand its influence and power. The United States was expanding trade with Asia and Hawaii. Earlier in the 1890s, American businessmen had wrested control of the island of Hawaii from local leaders. Acquiring parts of Spain's empire was on the radar of American political and economic leaders.

In terms of short-term causes of the war, students would certainly mention the conflict in Cuba over independence from Spain. Rebels had been struggling with Spain for decades. By the 1890s, the fighting in Cuba had become front-page news in the United States with lurid accounts of Spanish atrocities. The conflict in Cuba highlights another cause for U.S. concern. American-owned sugar plantations were suffering damage due to the fighting in Cuba. Economic interests supplemented humanitarian interests. In 1898, the U.S. ship, the *Maine*, exploded and sunk in the harbor of Havana, Cuba. Many in the United States thought that the destruction of the ship was the work of Spain, especially after American newspapers bluntly accused Spain of the crime, despite the scarcity of evidence. This sensationalistic, irresponsible coverage of events is known as *yellow journalism*. Finally, an intercepted correspondence between Spanish officials, the De Lôme letter, revealed unflattering views of President William McKinley.

Argument development: Using Evidence—Targeted skill: Argumentation (2 points) 论证发展，使用史料——目标技能：论证（2分）

In addition to citing causes of the Spanish-American War, students must also use evidence to support their argument. Students can earn one point by addressing the topic of the question—short-term and long term causes of the Spanish-American War —with specific examples of relevant evidence. A second point can be earned by utilizing this evidence to fully and effectively substantiate the stated thesis or a relevant argument. The specific evidence the student chooses will vary depending on the approach of the essay. Students, for instance, might mention José Martí, the history of the Cuban independence movement, "yellow journalism," William Randolph Hearst, Joseph Pulitzer, Governor Valeriano Weyler, concentration camps, sugar production, the political background of President William McKinley, the American Anti-Imperialist League, Mark Twain, Josiah Strong and racial justifications for imperialism, Alfred Mahan and naval power, or a host of other details.

Synthesis—Targeted skill: Synthesis (1 point) 整合——目标技能：信息整合（1分）

The sixth and final point on the long essay can be earned for demonstrating the historical thinking skill of synthesis. A student can earn this point by extending the argument to explain the connections between the argument of the essay and ONE of the following: A development in a different historical period, situation, era, or geographical area, or a course theme and/ or approach to history that is not the focus of the essay (such as political, economic, social, cultural, or intellectual history). In this case, the student could draw connections between the lead-up to the Spanish-American War and the lead-up to any other war in American History. Connections could also focus on the mixture of altruistic and self-serving rationales put forward on the eve of military conflicts. Alternately, an essay might explore another approach to history, such as looking at the Spanish-American War through the lens of cultural history. This synthesis could focus on notions of racial hierarchies that shaped American thinking at the time, and could make connections between the *Plessy v. Ferguson* decision (1896) and the war two years later. Both at home and abroad, American policy was shaped by a belief in the inferiority of non-white people and a conviction that non-white people were not ready for self-government.

ANSWER SHEET
Practice Test 2
答题纸
模拟测试二

SECTION I: PART A—MULTIPLE-CHOICE 第一部分：A——选择题

1. Ⓐ Ⓑ Ⓒ Ⓓ
2. Ⓐ Ⓑ Ⓒ Ⓓ
3. Ⓐ Ⓑ Ⓒ Ⓓ
4. Ⓐ Ⓑ Ⓒ Ⓓ
5. Ⓐ Ⓑ Ⓒ Ⓓ
6. Ⓐ Ⓑ Ⓒ Ⓓ
7. Ⓐ Ⓑ Ⓒ Ⓓ
8. Ⓐ Ⓑ Ⓒ Ⓓ
9. Ⓐ Ⓑ Ⓒ Ⓓ
10. Ⓐ Ⓑ Ⓒ Ⓓ
11. Ⓐ Ⓑ Ⓒ Ⓓ
12. Ⓐ Ⓑ Ⓒ Ⓓ
13. Ⓐ Ⓑ Ⓒ Ⓓ
14. Ⓐ Ⓑ Ⓒ Ⓓ
15. Ⓐ Ⓑ Ⓒ Ⓓ
16. Ⓐ Ⓑ Ⓒ Ⓓ
17. Ⓐ Ⓑ Ⓒ Ⓓ
18. Ⓐ Ⓑ Ⓒ Ⓓ
19. Ⓐ Ⓑ Ⓒ Ⓓ
20. Ⓐ Ⓑ Ⓒ Ⓓ

21. Ⓐ Ⓑ Ⓒ Ⓓ
22. Ⓐ Ⓑ Ⓒ Ⓓ
23. Ⓐ Ⓑ Ⓒ Ⓓ
24. Ⓐ Ⓑ Ⓒ Ⓓ
25. Ⓐ Ⓑ Ⓒ Ⓓ
26. Ⓐ Ⓑ Ⓒ Ⓓ
27. Ⓐ Ⓑ Ⓒ Ⓓ
28. Ⓐ Ⓑ Ⓒ Ⓓ
29. Ⓐ Ⓑ Ⓒ Ⓓ
30. Ⓐ Ⓑ Ⓒ Ⓓ
31. Ⓐ Ⓑ Ⓒ Ⓓ
32. Ⓐ Ⓑ Ⓒ Ⓓ
33. Ⓐ Ⓑ Ⓒ Ⓓ
34. Ⓐ Ⓑ Ⓒ Ⓓ
35. Ⓐ Ⓑ Ⓒ Ⓓ
36. Ⓐ Ⓑ Ⓒ Ⓓ
37. Ⓐ Ⓑ Ⓒ Ⓓ
38. Ⓐ Ⓑ Ⓒ Ⓓ
39. Ⓐ Ⓑ Ⓒ Ⓓ
40. Ⓐ Ⓑ Ⓒ Ⓓ

41. Ⓐ Ⓑ Ⓒ Ⓓ
42. Ⓐ Ⓑ Ⓒ Ⓓ
43. Ⓐ Ⓑ Ⓒ Ⓓ
44. Ⓐ Ⓑ Ⓒ Ⓓ
45. Ⓐ Ⓑ Ⓒ Ⓓ
46. Ⓐ Ⓑ Ⓒ Ⓓ
47. Ⓐ Ⓑ Ⓒ Ⓓ
48. Ⓐ Ⓑ Ⓒ Ⓓ
49. Ⓐ Ⓑ Ⓒ Ⓓ
50. Ⓐ Ⓑ Ⓒ Ⓓ
51. Ⓐ Ⓑ Ⓒ Ⓓ
52. Ⓐ Ⓑ Ⓒ Ⓓ
53. Ⓐ Ⓑ Ⓒ Ⓓ
54. Ⓐ Ⓑ Ⓒ Ⓓ
55. Ⓐ Ⓑ Ⓒ Ⓓ

Question 1 问题1

SECTION I: PART B—SHORT ANSWER 第一部分：B——简答题
Use dark blue or black ink only for the short-answer questions. Do not write outside of the box.

Question 2 问题2

SECTION I: PART B—SHORT ANSWER 第一部分：B——简答题
Use dark blue or black ink only for the short-answer questions. Do not write outside of the box.

Question 3 问题3

SECTION I: PART B—SHORT ANSWER 第一部分：B——简答题
Use dark blue or black ink only for the short-answer questions. Do not write outside of the box.

Question 4 问题4

Circle the number of the Essay that you are answering on this page.	Mandatory: 1	Circle one: 2 or 3

Practice Test 2　模拟测试二

SECTION I　第一部分

Part A: Multiple-Choice Questions　选择题

> **Directions:** The questions in this section are grouped in sets of 2–4. Each set is organized around a primary source, secondary source, or historical issue. Select the best answer for each of the questions in this section. (55 minutes)

Questions 1–3 refer to the following image:

"FIRE!"

—Herblock, *Washington Post*, 1949

1. Which of the following statements most accurately describes the main point of this cartoon?

   (A) The need to extinguish the communist threat justified swift and severe government action.
   (B) The freedoms of Americans were at risk because of an overreaction to the perceived threat of communism after World War II.
   (C) The existence of communists in the United States was a simple problem to solve.
   (D) There was no need to panic in the face of the communist threat.

2. Which other historical time period could have elicited a similar political cartoon?

   (A) The Panic of 1873.
   (B) The Progressive Era.
   (C) The Great Awakening.
   (D) The Quasi-War with France in 1798.

3. Which of the following actions would this cartoonist most likely have criticized?

   (A) Congressional passage of the McCarran Internal Security Act (over President Harry S. Truman's veto).
   (B) President Dwight D. Eisenhower's warning in regard to the "military-industrial complex" in his Farewell Address.
   (C) Vice President Richard Nixon's "Kitchen Debate" with Soviet Premier Khrushchev in Moscow.
   (D) The implementation of the Truman Doctrine to contain Soviet expansion.

Questions 4–6 refer to the following passage:

"I know that whenever the subject has occurred in conversation where I have been present, it has appeared to be the opinion of every one that we could not be taxed by a Parliament wherein we were not represented. But the payment of duties laid by an act of Parliament as regulations of commerce was never disputed. . . . An *external* tax is a duty laid on commodities imported; that duty is added to the first cost and other charges on the commodity, and, when it is offered for sale, makes a part of the price. If the people do not like it at that price, they refuse it; they are not obliged to pay it. But an *internal* tax is forced from the people without their consent if not laid by their own representatives. The Stamp Act says we shall have no commerce, make no exchange of property with each other, neither purchase nor grant, nor recover debts; we shall neither marry nor make our wills, unless we pay such and such sums; and thus it is intended to extort our money from us or ruin us by the consequence of refusing to pay it."

—Benjamin Franklin, *Examination before Parliament*, 1766

4. Which Enlightenment political ideal is best represented in this passage?

   (A) Governments derive their powers from the consent of the governed.
   (B) Governmental power should be divided among three branches.
   (C) The general will, or majority, should determine the rules of society.
   (D) The free market is the best way to determine the economic course of a society.

5. Prime Minister George Grenville later challenged Benjamin Franklin's statements that the American colonists should have representation in Parliament by claiming

   (A) the colonists had virtual representation in Parliament, meaning that Parliament represented all subjects of the British king.
   (B) the Stamp Act would be only the first of many internal taxes that the Americans would be expected to pay.
   (C) no subject of the king had the right to challenge Parliament's authority.
   (D) by refusing to pay the taxes imposed by Parliament, the Americans were committing treason.

6. Which of the following actions most closely mirrors the arguments presented in this quotation by Benjamin Franklin?

   (A) Antifederalist arguments in favor of adding a Bill of Rights to the U.S. Constitution.
   (B) Representatives of the colonies convening the Stamp Act Congress to protest the laws of Parliament.
   (C) South Carolina implementing the doctrine of nullification in the 1830s.
   (D) The business-friendly policies of Presidents Calvin Coolidge and Herbert Hoover in the 1930s.

Questions 7–9 refer to the following passage:

"As a means of effecting this end I suggest for your consideration the propriety of setting apart an ample district west of the Mississippi, and without the limit of any State or Territory now formed, to be guaranteed to the Indian tribes as long as they shall occupy it. . . . There they may be secured in the enjoyment of governments of their own choice, subject to no other control from the United States than such as may be necessary to preserve peace on the frontier and between the several tribes. There the benevolent may endeavor to teach them the arts of civilization. . . .

"This emigration would be voluntary, for it would be as cruel and unjust to compel the aborigines to abandon the graves of their fathers and seek a home in a distant land. But they should be distinctly informed that if they remain within the limits of the States they must be subject to their laws. . . ."

—President Andrew Jackson, 1829

7. Which author was most critical of the policy being described here by President Jackson?

   (A) Rachel Carson in *Silent Spring.*
   (B) Ralph Ellison in *Invisible Man.*
   (C) Helen Hunt Jackson in *A Century of Dishonor.*
   (D) William Lloyd Garrison in *The Liberator.*

8. The policy described most immediately led to

   (A) peace between Indian tribes and white settlers.
   (B) the forced removal of the Cherokee from their homeland.
   (C) the first Treaty of Fort Laramie, which guaranteed Indian possession of lands west of the Mississippi River.
   (D) a negotiated settlement between the tribes of the Southeast and the U.S. government, by which the tribes were allowed to remain on their lands for ten years.

9. President Jackson's policy was later altered by the

   (A) Homestead Act of 1862.
   (B) Immigration Act of 1921.
   (C) Supreme Court decision in *Plessy v. Ferguson*.
   (D) Dawes Act of 1887.

Questions 10–12 refer to the following passage:

"I am in Birmingham because injustice is here. . . . Moreover, I am cognizant of the interrelatedness of all communities and states. I cannot sit idly by in Atlanta and not be concerned about what happens in Birmingham. Injustice anywhere is a threat to justice everywhere. We are caught in an inescapable network of mutuality, tied in a single garment of destiny. Whatever affects one directly affects all indirectly. Never again can we afford to live with the narrow, provincial 'outside agitator' idea. Anyone who lives inside the United States can never be considered an outsider anywhere in this country. . . ."

—Martin Luther King, Jr., "Letter from a Birmingham Jail," April 16, 1963

10. Based on this quotation, what can you infer about the efforts of Martin Luther King and others in the civil rights movement of the 1950s?

    (A) The civil rights movement was not finding success through nonviolent methods.
    (B) Advocates for civil rights were coordinating their efforts to raise awareness of racial segregation across the country.
    (C) King was focused on ending segregation in Birmingham only.
    (D) King was willing to compromise his principles and would be a violent agitator if necessary.

11. Which of the following Supreme Court decisions was the primary contributor to the system of segregation that Martin Luther King and others were trying to end?

    (A) *Dred Scott v. Sanford* (1857).
    (B) *Brown v. Board of Education of Topeka, Kansas* (1954).
    (C) *Worcester v. Georgia* (1831).
    (D) *Plessy v. Ferguson* (1896).

12. Martin Luther King was in jail in Birmingham, Alabama, because of his belief in protesting injustice through the use of

    (A) targeted assassinations of segregationist public officials.
    (B) massive letter-writing campaigns denouncing segregated businesses.
    (C) violent self-defense.
    (D) nonviolent direct action.

Questions 13–16 refer to the following passage.

"One-half of the people of this nation to-day are utterly powerless to blot from the statute books an unjust law, or to write there a new and a just one. The women, dissatisfied as they are with this form of government, that enforces taxation without representation,—that compels them to obey laws to which they have never given their consent,—that imprisons and hangs them without a trial by a jury of their peers, that robs them, in marriage, of the custody of their own persons, wages and children,—are this half of the people left wholly at the mercy of the other half, in direct violation of the spirit and letter of the declarations of the framers of this government, every one of which was based on the immutable principle of equal rights to all."

—Susan B. Anthony, "I Stand Before You Under Indictment" (speech), 1873

13. On which of these documents is Susan B. Anthony basing her appeal for women's equality?

    (A) Articles of Confederation.
    (B) Proclamation of Amnesty and Reconstruction.
    (C) Compromise of 1850.
    (D) Declaration of Independence.

14. Which other nineteenth-century reform movement made similar arguments to those written here by Susan B. Anthony?

    (A) The temperance movement.
    (B) Utopian communities.
    (C) The abolition movement.
    (D) Public school advocates.

15. Susan B. Anthony and others in the women's rights movement had a major influence on the ratification of which of the following?

    (A) The Nineteenth Amendment.
    (B) The Equal Rights Amendment.
    (C) The Fifteenth Amendment.
    (D) The Twenty-sixth Amendment.

16. The language of this passage by Susan B. Anthony demonstrates which of the following continuities in U.S. history?

(A) Debates over free speech.
(B) Debates over voting rights.
(C) Debates over federal power and states' rights.
(D) Debates over the procedures of amending the Constitution.

Questions 17–20 refer to the following image:

FORTY-MILLIONAIRE CARNEGIE IN HIS GREAT DOUBLE ROLE.
AS THE TIGHT-FISTED EMPLOYER HE REDUCES WAGES THAT HE MAY PLAY PHILANTHROPIST AND GIVE AWAY LIBRARIES, ETC.

17. Which of the following statements best represents the criticism of Andrew Carnegie found in this cartoon?

(A) Carnegie was able to give away a great deal of money only because he violated his workers' rights.
(B) Carnegie did not give enough of his considerable fortune to charity.
(C) Carnegie was dividing his attention and was therefore not as successful in either of his main endeavors.
(D) Carnegie's ruthless business practices were causing him to lose touch with his working-class origins.

18. Which of the following was another common criticism of Andrew Carnegie?

(A) As an immigrant, Carnegie had no right to own controlling interests in major American industries.
(B) Carnegie did nothing to prevent the use of violence against his workers when they asked for better wages and working conditions.
(C) Carnegie was seen as the epitome of American success, but he was not even the richest man in America.
(D) Too much of Carnegie's philanthropic efforts were concentrated on his homeland of Scotland, denying Americans the benefits of his charity.

19. Which of the following was NOT designed to empower the government to regulate the increasing wealth and power of the industrialists in the late nineteenth and early twentieth centuries?

(A) Sherman Anti-Trust Act (1890).
(B) Interstate Commerce Act (1887).
(C) Federal Trade Commission Act (1914).
(D) Newlands Reclamation Act (1902).

20. The actions taken by Andrew Carnegie that were critiqued in the cartoon reflected the thinking of which of the following concepts?

(A) The Social Gospel.
(B) "Survival of the Fittest."
(C) The Gospel of Wealth.
(D) "Rugged individualism."

Questions 21–23 refer to the following passage:

"Wherever I go—the street, the shop, the house, or the steamboat—I hear the people talk in such a way as to indicate that they are yet unable to conceive of the Negro as possessing any rights at all. Men who are honorable in their dealings with their white neighbors will cheat a Negro without feeling a single twinge of their honor. To kill a Negro they do not deem murder; to debauch a Negro woman they do not think fornication; to take the property away from a Negro they do not consider robbery. The people boast that when they get freedmen affairs in their own hands, to use their own classic expression, 'the niggers will catch hell.'

"The reason of all this is simple and manifest. The whites esteem the blacks their property by natural right, and however much they may admit that the individual relations of masters and slaves have been destroyed by the war and the President's emancipation proclamation, they still have an ingrained feeling that the blacks at large belong to the whites at large, and whenever opportunity serves they treat the colored people just as their profit, caprice or passion may dictate."

—Congressional testimony of Col. Samuel Thomas, Assistant Commissioner,
Bureau of Refugees, Freedmen and Abandoned Lands, 1865

21. According to this official from the Freedmen's Bureau, how had southern society reacted to the end of the Civil War?

(A) Blacks were able to freely travel around the country without fear of reprisal.
(B) The only way for southern whites to demonstrate their manhood was to mistreat freed slaves.
(C) Southern whites were willing to accept the freedom of slaves as long as the slaves did not ask for voting rights.
(D) The freed slaves were experiencing discrimination and limitations on their rights similar to their treatment under slavery.

22. The Fourteenth Amendment attempted to eliminate the societal conditions described in this passage by

(A) revoking the voting rights of all known members of the Confederate government and soldiers of the Confederate Army.

(B) granting citizenship and guaranteeing equal protection under the law to former slaves.

(C) creating a special appeals process that expedited civil rights claims directly to the Supreme Court.

(D) ensuring that former slaves received the 40 acres of land promised to them by General William Sherman and the Freedmen's Bureau Bill of 1866.

23. Which of the following events of the twentieth century reflects a continuation of the attitudes of southern whites as described in this passage?

(A) The Great Migration.

(B) Jim Crow legislation.

(C) The Civil Rights Act of 1957.

(D) The March on Washington for Jobs and Freedom.

Questions 24–26 refer to the following passage:

"We may... be said to have reached almost the last stage of national humiliation. There is scarcely any thing that can wound the pride or degrade the character of an independent nation which we do not experience... Do we owe debts to foreigners and to our citizens...? There remains without any proper or satisfactory provision for their discharge. Is commerce of importance to national wealth? Ours is at the lowest point of declension."

—Alexander Hamilton, *Federalist* #15, 1787

24. Which of the following factors did Alexander Hamilton believe was a source for the problems in the excerpt from *Federalist* #15?

(A) economic class divisions among the American people that prevented them from forging a unified vision.

(B) a failure of American policy-makers to abandon mercantilist principles and to embrace a laissez-faire approach to trade.

(C) a weak central government without the powers to address pressing issues.

(D) an unhealthy obsession among the American people with religion and individual salvation, at the expense of interest in solving practical national problems.

25. Which of the following specific developments contributed to the general sentiment expressed in *Federalist* #15?

(A) Great Britain refused to evacuate forts in the Great Lakes region.

(B) Spanish forces retook Florida from the United States.

(C) French forces aided American Indians in conducting raids on New England.

(D) Dutch traders forced American ships to extend tribute payments in order to dock in Holland.

26. To address the problems identified in *Federalist* #15, Hamilton proposed

    (A) abandoning an isolationist approach to foreign policy and adopting a more aggressive and interventionist stance.
    (B) adopting a new constitution in order to create a more national government.
    (C) forging alliances with American Indian nations to present a united front to European powers.
    (D) increasing spending on military forces and cutting spending on social programs.

Questions 27–29 refer to the following passage:

"Lincoln was strongly anti-slavery, but he was not an abolitionist or a Radical Republican and never claimed to be one. He made a sharp distinction between his frequently reiterated personal wish that 'all men everywhere could be free' and his official duties as a legislator, congressman, and president in a legal and constitutional system that recognized the South's right to property in slaves. Even after issuing the Emancipation Proclamation he continued to declare his preference for gradual abolition. While his racial views changed during the Civil War, he never became a principled egalitarian in the manner of abolitionists such as Frederick Douglass or Wendell Phillips or Radical Republicans like Charles Sumner."

—Eric Foner, *The Fiery Trial*, 2010

27. Which of the following statements best describes Eric Foner's argument about President Abraham Lincoln's views on slavery?

    (A) President Lincoln was a consistent supporter of the abolitionist cause.
    (B) President Lincoln was reluctant to be ideologically associated with advocates like Frederick Douglass.
    (C) In his ambition to become president, Abraham Lincoln declared his desire to use his constitutional powers to end slavery.
    (D) President Lincoln had continually changing views on slavery and abolition that did not always fit into the prevailing political categories.

28. How did President Lincoln's issuance of the Emancipation Proclamation alter the course of the Civil War?

    (A) The war came to a swift conclusion because the Proclamation made the Confederacy realize the futility of their cause.
    (B) The war grew in scope because the Proclamation caused Great Britain to join the fight on the side of the Union.
    (C) President Jefferson Davis of the Confederacy vowed massive resistance to any Union effort to free the slaves.
    (D) The war aims of the United States were no longer exclusively focused on the preservation of the Union.

29. Which of these statements best describes the Emancipation Proclamation?

   (A) It guaranteed the freedom of all slaves living within the boundaries of the United States at the conclusion of the Civil War.

   (B) It freed only the slaves in states and portions of states in rebellion against the United States at the time it was issued.

   (C) It declared that the freedom of the slaves was conditional upon the agreement of individual southern states to sign a peace treaty with the U.S. government.

   (D) It prohibited the use of slaves in combat in both the Union and Confederate Armies.

Questions 30–31 refer to the following passage:

"The only force which is strong enough to break down social convention is economic necessity. . . . The economic necessity which has forced women out of the home and into the world of business has completely annihilated the old idea that a woman should eat only in the privacy of her household or in the homes of her friends, has created the absolutely new social phenomenon of women eating in public, unescorted by men, by the tens of thousands, and has given rise to a wholly new phase of the restaurant business."

—*The New York Times*, October 15, 1905

30. Which of the following groups would have most likely supported the scenario described in this passage?

   (A) Ku Klux Klan.
   (B) American Temperance Union.
   (C) National Woman Suffrage Association.
   (D) Southern Christian Leadership Conference.

31. The scenario described in the passage above is most directly reflected in the ideas of which of the following?

   (A) Civil Rights Act of 1964.
   (B) Equal Rights Amendment.
   (C) Pure Food and Drug Act.
   (D) Interstate Commerce Act.

Questions 32–34 refer to the following political image:

"Pull away, pull away my Son. Don't fear. I'll give you all my assistance."

"Oh! I fear it is stronger rooted than I expected but with the assistance of my old friend and a little more brandy I will bring it down."

—"Mad Tom in a Rage," unknown cartoonist, circa 1802

32. The above cartoon illustrates which of the following?

    (A) The growing political partisanship after the election of Thomas Jefferson as president.

    (B) A governmental effort to regulate excessive drinking.

    (C) An effort on the part of the British government to subvert American democracy.

    (D) The pessimistic outlook of many Americans concerning the ability of the nation to survive its formative years.

33. The development of political parties led to which of the following amendments to the Constitution of the United States?

    (A) The elected president would appoint the vice president after the election to ensure that members of the same political party filled both positions.

    (B) The majority party in Congress would have the authority to choose the vice president.

    (C) Distinct ballots would be cast for president and vice president, avoiding a situation in which one person from each political party would serve in those posts.

    (D) The Electoral College was abolished, and the winner of the popular vote would be declared president, with the vice president being chosen by the officials of the president's political party.

34. How does this cartoon demonstrate the political viewpoint of the Federalist Party?

(A) The Devil is coming to the assistance of Thomas Jefferson in his efforts to tear down the federal government.

(B) Thomas Paine is attempting to hold back the efforts of the Devil to destroy the national government.

(C) Alexander Hamilton is working with the Devil to dismantle the Constitutional principle of federalism.

(D) John Adams and George Washington were unable to successfully argue against the negative attitudes of the Republican press.

Questions 35–38 refer to the following passage:

"The economic ills we suffer have come upon us over several decades. They will not go away in days, weeks, or months, but they will go away. They will go away because we as Americans have the capacity now, as we've had in the past, to do whatever needs to be done to preserve this last and greatest bastion of freedom. In this present crisis, government is not the solution to our problem; government is the problem. . . .

"It is my intention to curb the size and influence of the Federal establishment and to demand recognition of the distinction between the powers granted to the Federal Government and those reserved to the States or to the people. All of us need to be reminded that the Federal Government did not create the States; the States created the Federal Government."

—Ronald Reagan, First Inaugural Address, January 21, 1981

35. The conservative political revival that led to President Ronald Reagan's election in 1980 held the view that

(A) political leaders in the 1960s and 1970s did not do enough to challenge the racial and economic status quo.

(B) the United States had relied too heavily on military solutions and needed to pursue a more isolationist foreign policy.

(C) religious leaders had become too assertive in governmental policy and had blurred the separation of church and state.

(D) liberal laws and court decisions in the 1960s and a general moral decline were undermining the United States.

36. Which of the following would have most likely agreed with President Reagan's statement that the federal government was created by the states and the federal government's role should be limited?

(A) The Anti-Federalists.

(B) The Whig Party.

(C) The Mugwumps.

(D) The Progressives.

37. Which of the following ongoing debates in U.S. history is expressed in the quotation?

   (A) Debates over the powers of the president.
   (B) Debates over participation in elections.
   (C) Debates over federal power over the economy.
   (D) Debates over federal power over international affairs.

38. One way in which President Reagan acted on his rhetoric in the passage was to

   (A) increase the military budget.
   (B) work with Congress to cut taxes and government spending.
   (C) eliminate the Department of Housing and Urban Development.
   (D) prohibit pay increases for government workers.

Questions 39–40 refer to the following passage:

"Our energy plan will also include a number of specific goals, to measure our progress toward a stable energy system. These are the goals we set for 1985:

- Reduce the annual growth rate in our energy demand to less than two percent.
- Reduce gasoline consumption by ten percent below its current level.
- Cut in half the portion of U.S. oil which is imported, from a potential level of 16 million barrels to six million barrels a day.
- Establish a strategic petroleum reserve of one billion barrels, more than six months' supply.
- Increase our coal production by about two thirds to more than 1 billion tons a year.
- Insulate 90 percent of American homes and all new buildings.
- Use solar energy in more than two and one-half million houses."

—President Jimmy Carter, speech on April 18, 1977

39. The passage above reflects which of the following continuities of U.S. history?

   (A) Concern for working-class Americans.
   (B) The shifting role of the federal government.
   (C) Concern for natural resources and their environmental impact.
   (D) The role of the United States in world diplomacy.

40. President Jimmy Carter's speech, excerpted above, was primarily a reaction to which of the following events?

   (A) The Soviet Union's invasion of Afghanistan.
   (B) The Iran hostage crisis.
   (C) A series of embargoes enacted by the Middle East-dominated organization known as OPEC.
   (D) Terrorist bombings that targeted U.S. military personnel.

Questions 41–43 refer to the following image:

—William Carson, "A Bigger Job Than He Thought For,"
Sunday Globe (Utica, NY), 1899

41. The 1899 cartoon shown above makes the point that

   (A) insurgents in Cuba were being manipulated by Spain into resisting the presence of American troops.
   (B) native Hawaiians behaved in a childlike manner when the Hawaiian islands were annexed by the United States.
   (C) the United States misread the reaction of the Filipino people when it acquired the Philippines following the Spanish-American War.
   (D) the task of completing the Panama Canal was more time consuming, and more costly, than the United States had originally anticipated.

42. The cartoon reflects which of the following continuities in U.S. history?

   (A) Debates over extending constitutional rights to peoples in territories acquired by the United States.
   (B) Debates over the wisdom of asserting American control over foreign possessions.
   (C) Debates over the morality of tactics used by the United States in wars of colonial independence.
   (D) Debates over allowing the Central Intelligence Agency to engage in covert operations in foreign countries.

43. The event depicted in the cartoon represents which of the following?

    (A) A shift in American foreign policy from "gunboat diplomacy" to "dollar diplomacy."
    (B) The beginning of a period of isolation from world affairs.
    (C) A shift from "brinksmanship" to détente.
    (D) The beginning of a period of imperialistic activities by the United States.

Questions 44–45 refer to the following passage:

"I marvel not a little, right worshipful, that since the first discovery of America (which is now full four score and ten years), after so great conquests and plantings of the Spaniards and Portuguese there, that we of England could never have the grace to set fast footing in such fertile and temperate places as are left as yet unpossessed of them. But . . . I conceive great hope that the time approacheth and now is that we of England may share and part stakes [divide the prize] (if we will ourselves) both with the Spaniard and the Portuguese in part of America and other regions as yet undiscovered.

"And surely if there were in us that desire to advance the honor of our country which ought to be in every good man, we would not all this while have [neglected] the possessing of these lands which of equity and right appertain unto us, as by the discourses that follow shall appear most plainly."

—Richard Hakluyt, *Divers Voyages Touching the Discovery of America and the Islands Adjacent*, 1582

44. The ideas expressed in the passage above most closely reflect the influence of which of the following?

    (A) The Enlightenment philosophy of natural rights.
    (B) The economic policy of mercantilism.
    (C) The religious philosophy of predestination.
    (D) The social contract theory.

45. By following the ideas of Richard Hakluyt, England was eventually able to

    (A) drive the French and Portuguese governments into bankruptcy.
    (B) conquer large parts of Africa in the eighteenth century.
    (C) establish several colonies along the Atlantic coastline of North America.
    (D) destroy the Dutch commercial empire.

Questions 46–49 refer to the following passage:

"The God that holds you over the pit of hell, much as one holds a spider, or some loathsome insect, over the fire, abhors you, and is dreadfully provoked; his wrath towards you burns like fire; he looks upon you as worthy of nothing else, but to be cast into the fire; he is of purer eyes than to bear to have you in his sight; you are ten thousand times so abominable in his eyes as the most hateful venomous serpent is in ours. You have offended him infinitely more than ever a stubborn rebel did his prince: and yet 'tis nothing but his hand that holds you from falling into the fire every moment: 'tis to be ascribed to nothing else, that you did not go to hell the last night; that you was suffered to awake again in this world, after you closed your eyes to sleep: and there is no other reason to be given why you have not dropped into hell since you arose in the morning, but that God's hand has held you up: there is no other reason to be given why you ha[ve]n't gone to hell since you have sat here in the house of God, provoking his pure eyes by your sinful wicked manner of attending his solemn worship: yea, there is nothing else that is to be given as a reason why you don't this very moment drop down into hell."

—Jonathan Edwards, "Sinners in the Hands of an Angry God," 1741 (excerpt).

46. An important point that Jonathan Edwards is making in the sermon, excerpted above, is that

   (A) despite the sinful nature of humanity, God has given individuals a chance to rectify their sins.
   (B) human beings are born inherently good, but are corrupted by the evils of society.
   (C) God is merciless, allowing sinners and saints alike to suffer in the fires of hell.
   (D) it is not important what you believe in life, just as long as you live your life in a moral and ethical manner.

47. The sermon by Jonathan Edwards was a central text of

   (A) Transcendentalism.
   (B) Mormonism.
   (C) the Great Awakening.
   (D) the Social Gospel.

48. Which of the following describes the context that Jonathan Edwards was preaching in?

   (A) There had been a marked decline in piety in Puritan New England; Edwards hoped to rekindle the fires of New England church members.
   (B) The government of Massachusetts had disestablished the Congregational Church, forcing preachers like Edwards to travel from town to town in search of adherents.
   (C) New England had experienced a wave of immigrants from all over Europe, including many Catholics, Jews, Protestants from a variety of sects, and non-believers; Edwards hope to convert them to teachings of the Congregational Church.
   (D) New England was recently devastated by war with American Indians; Edwards sought to reassure the survivors that God did, indeed, exist.

49. Jonathan Edwards was part of a broader religious movement that impacted colonial American society by

   (A) encouraging colonists to question and challenge the legitimacy of British authorities.
   (B) citing the immorality of slavery and stressing the importance of ending the institution.
   (C) asserting the importance of developing amicable relations with American Indians.
   (D) fostering changes in colonists' understandings of God, themselves, and the world around them.

Questions 50–52 refer to the following image:

50. What does the above image reflect about the decade of the 1920s?

   (A) Consumer safety was the primary concern of leading manufacturing companies.
   (B) Automobiles were a rare commodity and therefore extremely expensive.
   (C) New technologies such as automobiles were unproven and unsafe, requiring extensive propaganda in order to make consumers interested in them.
   (D) Consumer products were increasingly affordable and highly desired by the public as a sign of status.

51. Like other consumer products such as radios and home electric appliances, automobiles were often offered to consumers through

(A) payment plans, which allowed consumers to spread full payment over time.
(B) self-manufacturing kits, which reduced the costs for the companies selling the products.
(C) exclusive retail stores, which prevented consumers from buying products at the lowest possible price.
(D) incentives such as rebates, which consumers could acquire by agreeing to sell products for the manufacturer.

52. The consumer economy of the 1920s most directly shows the influence of which of the following?

(A) Manifest destiny and territorial expansion.
(B) The Industrial Revolution and a spirit of entrepreneurship.
(C) Reconstruction and the "Redemption" of the South.
(D) World War I and international cooperation.

Questions 53–55 refer to the following table:

Wholesale Price Index of Farm Products (Based on 1910–1914 = 100)	
1866	140
1870	112
1876	89
1880	80
1882	99
1886	68
1890	71
1896	56
1900	71

53. Which of the following describes an important reason for the trend reflected in the figures in the table above?

(A) The number of family farms increased in the 1870s and 1880s, as thousands of "new immigrant" families settled in the rural Midwest.
(B) Population stagnated as the spread of birth control and the growth of the middle class led to falling birthrates.
(C) Mechanization of agriculture, improved techniques, and an increase in acres under cultivation created agricultural surpluses.
(D) American expansion into Latin America resulted in surplus agricultural products from Central and South America flooding American markets.

54. Which of the following was a demand of the Populist Party in the 1880s and 1890s to address the situation reflected in the figures in the table?

(A) A national sales tax.

(B) Government funding for the purchase of agricultural machinery.

(C) "Internal improvements" in the West, including railroads and canals.

(D) An end to the gold standard and a shift to currency backed by silver as well as gold.

55. Which of the following describes developments in the 1870s, 1880s, and 1890s that occurred, in part, as a result of the trend indicated in the chart?

(A) The federal government established agencies that oversaw agricultural production in the United States, limiting production of certain products.

(B) The United States lowered import tariffs in order to stimulate international trade and reduce surpluses of agricultural products.

(C) Farmers created local and regional networks to challenge and resist corporate control of agricultural markets.

(D) Major agricultural producers invested in the establishment of a transcontinental railroad network to more effectively transport agricultural goods to urban markets.

STOP

If there is still time remaining, you may review your answers.

Part B: Short-Answer Questions 简答题

> **Directions:** The following section contains four questions. Answer each of the questions, using the source material and your knowledge of American history. Note: students are not required to develop and support a thesis statement in responding to these questions. (50 minutes)

Question 1 is based on the following two passages:

"Our greatest danger is that in the great leap from slavery to freedom we may overlook the fact that the masses of us are to live by the productions of our hands, and fail to keep in mind that we shall prosper in proportion as we learn to dignify and glorify common labour, and put brains and skill into the common occupations of life; shall prosper in proportion as we learn to draw the line between the superficial and the substantial, the ornamental gewgaws of life and the useful. No race can prosper till it learns that there is as much dignity in tilling a field as in writing a poem. It is at the bottom of life we must begin, and not at the top. Nor should we permit our grievances to overshadow our opportunities. . . . The opportunity to earn a dollar in a factory just now is worth infinitely more than the opportunity to spend a dollar in an opera-house."

—Booker T. Washington, "Atlanta Compromise Speech," 1895

"Mr. Washington distinctly asks that black people give up, at least for the present, three things—
First, political power,
Second, insistence on civil rights
Third, higher education of Negro youth, ––
and concentrate all their energies on industrial education, and accumulation of wealth, and the conciliation of the South. This policy has been courageously and insistently advocated for over fifteen years, and has been triumphant for perhaps ten years. As a result of this tender of the palm-branch, what has been the return? In these years there have occurred:

1. The disfranchisement of the Negro.
2. The legal creation of a distinct status of civil inferiority for the Negro.
3. The steady withdrawal of aid from institutions for the higher training of the Negro."

"His doctrine has tended to make the whites, North and South, shift the burden of the Negro problem to the Negro's shoulders and stand aside as critical and rather pessimistic spectators; when in fact the burden belongs to the nation, and the hands of none of us are clean if we bend not our energies to righting these great wrongs."

—Excerpt from W. E. B. Du Bois, *The Souls of Black Folk* (1903)

1. Use the excerpts above and your knowledge of U.S. history to answer parts A, B, and C.

   (A) Briefly explain the main idea of the first passage.
   (B) Briefly explain the main idea of the second passage.
   (C) Explain which set of ideas was more influential in shaping the approach of the civil rights movements of the 1950s and 1960s.

2. Use the excerpts above and your knowledge of U.S. history to answer parts A, B, and C.

   (A) Provide evidence from the 1930s of public support for New Deal programs.
   (B) Provide evidence from the 1930s of public opposition to New Deal programs.
   (C) In the decades since the 1930s, discuss how the New Deal has been employed in domestic policy debates.

Question 3 is based on the following two passages:

"The first requirement for the acquisition of power by the Positive Woman is to understand the differences between men and women. . . . She understands that men and women are different, and that those very differences provide the key to her success as a person and fulfillment as a woman. . . . The Positive Woman looks upon her femaleness and her fertility as part of her purpose, her potential, and her power. She rejoices that she has a capability for creativity that men can never have. . . .

"The overriding psychological need of a woman is to love something alive. A baby fulfills this need in the lives of most women. If a baby is not available to fill that need, women search for a baby-substitute. This is the reason why women have traditionally gone into teaching and nursing careers. They are doing what comes naturally to the female psyche."

—Phyllis Schlafly, *The Power of the Positive Woman*, 1977

"I don't think most women want to pick up briefcases and march off to meaningless, depersonalized jobs. . . . We want to liberate men from those inhuman roles as well. We want to share the work and the responsibility, and to have men share equal responsibility for the children. Probably the ultimate myth is that children must have fulltime mothers, and that liberated women make bad ones. The truth is that most American children seem to be suffering from too much mother and too little father. . . . [W]e need free universal daycare. With that aid, as in Scandinavian countries, and with laws that permit women equal work and equal pay, man will be relieved of his role as sole breadwinner and stranger to his own children. . . . Women's Liberation really is Men's Liberation too. . . .

"The point is that Women's Liberation is not destroying the American family. It is trying to build a human compassionate alternative out of its ruins."

—Gloria Steinem, Commencement Address, Vassar College, 1970

3. Use the excerpts above and your knowledge of U.S. history to complete parts A, B, and C.

   (A) Explain the point of view of the first passage.
   (B) Explain the point of view of the second passage.
   (C) Choose a specific person or movement from U.S. history and explain how that person or event represents a continuity with the point of view of ONE of the passages.

Question 4 is based on the following passage:

"I would like to talk on behalf of all those veterans. . . . In our opinion and from our experience, there is nothing in South Vietnam which could happen that realistically threatens the United States of America. And to attempt to justify the loss of one American life in Vietnam, Cambodia or Laos by linking such loss to the preservation of freedom . . . is to us the height of criminal hypocrisy, and it is that kind of hypocrisy which we feel has torn this country apart. . . .

"Each day . . . someone has to give up his life so that the United States doesn't have to admit something that the entire world already knows, so that we can't say that we have made a mistake. Someone has to die so that President Nixon won't be, and these are his words, 'the first President to lose a war.'

"We are asking Americans to think about that because how do you ask a man to be the last man to die in Vietnam? How do you ask a man to be the last man to die for a mistake?"

—John Kerry, testimony before the Senate Foreign Relations Committee, April 23, 1971

4. Use the excerpt above and your knowledge of U.S. history to answer parts A, B, and C.

   (A) Explain the main point John Kerry is making in the passage.
   (B) Provide evidence, not included in the passage, that could be used to support Kerry's point of view.
   (C) Choose ONE of the following conflicts from U.S. history and explain how the passage's argument could also be used in relationship to that conflict. Cite at least one piece of specific information about your chosen conflict to support your argument.

   War of 1812
   Mexican-American War
   World War I

Part A: Document-Based Question 材料分析题

> **Directions:** The following question is based on the accompanying Documents 1–7. This question is designed to test your ability to apply the historical thinking skills of **continuity and change over time**, in conjunction with **argumentation, analyzing evidence, contextualization,** and **synthesis**. Your response should be based on your analysis of the documents and your knowledge of the topic. (55 minutes)

Write a well-integrated essay that does the following:

- States an appropriate thesis that directly addresses all parts of the question.
- Supports the thesis or an appropriate argument with evidence from all or all but one of the documents AND your knowledge of U.S. history beyond/outside the documents.
- Analyzes a majority of the documents in terms of such features as their intended audience, purpose, point of view, format, argument, limitations, and/or social context as appropriate to the argument.
- Places the argument in the context of broader regional, national, or global processes.

Question 1

Analyze major continuities and changes in the ways in which Americans addressed and debated immigration policy in two different time periods—in the period 1750–1800 and in the period 1875–1925.

DOCUMENT 1

Source: Benjamin Franklin, *Observations Concerning the Increase of Mankind, Peopling of Countries, etc.* (1753).

Why should the [*Germans*] be suffered to swarm into our Settlements, and by herding together establish their Language and Manners to the Exclusion of ours? Why should *Pennsylvania*, founded by the *English*, become a Colony of *Aliens*, who will shortly be so numerous as to Germanize us instead of our Anglifying them, and will never adopt our Language or Customs, any more than they can acquire our Complexion.

DOCUMENT 2

Source: J. Hector St. John De Crevecoeur, *Letters From An American Farmer*, Letter III (1782).

What then is the American, this new man? He is either an European, or the descendant of an European, hence that strange mixture of blood, which you will find in no other country. I could point out to you a family whose grandfather was an Englishman, whose wife was Dutch, whose son married a French woman, and whose present four sons have now four wives of different nations. *He* is an American, who leaving behind him all his ancient prejudices and manners, receives new ones from the new mode of life he has embraced, the new government he obeys, and the new rank he holds. He becomes an American by being received in the broad lap of our great *Alma Mater.* Here individuals of all nations are melted into a new race of men, whose labours and posterity will one day cause great changes in the world. Americans are the western pilgrims, who are carrying along with them that great mass of arts, sciences, vigour, and industry which began long since in the east; they will finish the great circle. The Americans were once scattered all over Europe; here they are incorporated into one of the finest systems of population which has ever appeared, and which will hereafter become distinct by the power of the different climates they inhabit. The American ought therefore to love this country much better than that wherein either he or his forefathers were born.

DOCUMENT 3

Source: Theodore Sedgwick, from debate in the House of Representatives over Naturalization Bill, 1794.

And shall we alone adopt the rash theory that the subjects of all governments despotic, monarchical, and aristocratical are, as soon as they set foot on American ground, qualified to participate in administering the sovereignty of our country? Shall we hold the benefits of American citizenship so cheap as to invite, nay, almost bribe, the discontented, the ambitious, and the avaricious of every country to accept them?...

A war, the most cruel and dreadful which has been known for centuries, was now raging in those in all those countries from which emigrants were to be expected. The most fierce and unrelenting passions were engaged in a conflict, which shock to their foundations all the ancient political structures of Europe. . . . Could any reasonable man believe, that men who, actuated by such passions, had fought on grounds so opposite, almost equally distant from the happy mean we had chosen, would here mingle in social affections with each other, or with us? That their passions and prejudices would subside as soon as they should set foot in America? or that, possessing those passions and prejudices, they were qualified to make or to be made the governors of Americans?

Source: Joseph McDonnell, *Labor Standard*, June 30, 1878.

The cry that the "Chinese must go" is both narrow and unjust. It represents no broad or universal principle. It is merely a repetition of the cry that was raised years ago by American Indians against the immigration of Irishmen, Englishmen, Germans and others from European nations. It now ill becomes those, or the descendants of those, against whom this cry was raised in past years, to raise a similar tocsin against a class of foreigners who have been degraded by ages of oppression. . . .

The feeling at the bottom of the "Know Nothing" movement IN ITS EARLY DAYS was certainly a general one against low wages, and if it had raised the cry:

No low wages.
No cheap labor!

Instead of sounding the intolerant, silly, and shameful cry against Irishmen, Englishmen, Germans and all other "foreigners," it would have accomplished incalculable good. As it was it fell into the hands of infamous, scheming politicians, who pandered to the worst prejudices of the masses by raising a cry against men of various religious faiths and foreign nationalities. This policy suited them; it raised them to prominence and office and allowed what they IN THEIR HEARTS desired, the onward march of low wages.

Source: Joseph Keppler, "Welcome to All!" *Puck*, 1880.

WELCOME TO ALL!

Credit: Granger Collection

Source: Madison Grant, *The Passing of the Great Race* (1916).

These new immigrants were no longer exclusively members of the Nordic race as were the earlier ones who came of their own impulse to improve their social conditions. The transportation lines advertised America as a land flowing with milk and honey, and the European governments took the opportunity to unload upon careless, wealthy, and hospitable America the sweepings of their jails and asylums. The result was that the new immigration, while it still included many strong elements from the north of Europe, contained a large and increasing number of the weak, the broken, and the mentally crippled of all races drawn from the lowest stratum of the Mediterranean basin and the Balkans, together with hordes of the wretched, submerged populations of the Polish Ghettos.

DOCUMENT 7

Source: Billy Ireland, "We Can't Digest the Scum," *Columbus Dispatch*, 1919.

Credit: Billy Ireland Cartoon Library and Museum, Ohio State University

Part B: Long-Essay Questions 论述题

Choose ONE of the following questions and write an analytical essay that uses specific, relevant evidence to support your thesis and to demonstrate the specified historical thinking skills. *Historical Thinking Skills: **Causation**, used in conjunction with **Argumentation**, **Use of Evidence**, and **Synthesis**. Thematic Learning Objective: **Culture and Society**, #3—Explain how ideas about women's rights and gender roles have affected society and politics (for question 1); Geography and the Environment, #1—Explain how geographic and environmental factors shaped the development of various communities, and analyze how competition for and debates over natural resources have affected both interactions among different groups and the development of government policies (for question 2); and **Politics and Power**, #2—Explain how popular movements, reform efforts, and political activists have sought to change American society and institutions (for both questions).* (35 minutes)

1. At different times in American history, individuals and groups have challenged commonly held ideas about the proper role of women in society and have worked to redefine prevailing ideas about gender. Such a process occurred in the period 1910–1930 and also in the period 1960–1980. Compare the efforts to challenge ideas about gender in the period 1910–1930 with the period 1960–1980 with respect to tactics, goals, and level of success.

2. At different times in American history, individuals and groups have pushed for changes in values and policies on the natural environment. Such a process occurred in the period 1900–1915 and also in the period 1960–1980. Compare the efforts to change values and policies on the natural environment in the period 1900–1915 with the period 1960–1975 with respect to tactics, goals, and level of success.

SCORING THE TEST　估分

The AP United States History test is composed of four parts grouped into two sections. The multiple-choice test is scored with one point given for each correct answer.

- *There is no penalty for guessing,* so you should answer every question on the test.
- The DBQ is given a score from 0–7.
- The long essay is given a score from 0 to 6.

To attain your final AP score, the following method should be used:

Multiple-Choice Score × 1.31 = _____

+

Short-Answer Score × 3.0 = _____

+

DBQ Score × 6.43 = _____

+

Long Essay Score × 4.5 = _____

Total of all above scores is composite score = _____(round it)

Score Range	AP Score
111-180	5
91-110	4
76-90	3
57-75	2
>56	1

To get a final score for the test, compare your composite score to the chart directly above.

Following are four separate guides to scoring each section of this test. Once you have scored each piece of the test, place the score on the appropriate line above. When you are done, do the computations to get your final score. Remember that this test is designed to mimic the AP exam, but you will not take it in the same conditions that you will during the real test, and it is not scored by professionals who are reading 1,000 or more essays daily. While this test is a good predictor of success, it is only as good as the student using it, so do not stop studying just because you got a good score here.

ANSWER KEY　答案

Practice Test 2　模拟测试二

1. **(B)**	11. **(D)**	21. **(D)**	31. **(B)**	41. **(C)**	51. **(A)**
2. **(D)**	12. **(D)**	22. **(B)**	32. **(A)**	42. **(B)**	52. **(B)**
3. **(A)**	13. **(D)**	23. **(B)**	33. **(C)**	43. **(D)**	53. **(C)**
4. **(A)**	14. **(C)**	24. **(C)**	34. **(A)**	44. **(B)**	54. **(D)**
5. **(A)**	15. **(A)**	25. **(A)**	35. **(D)**	45. **(C)**	55. **(C)**
6. **(B)**	16. **(B)**	26. **(B)**	36. **(A)**	46. **(A)**	
7. **(C)**	17. **(A)**	27. **(D)**	37. **(C)**	47. **(C)**	
8. **(B)**	18. **(B)**	28. **(D)**	38. **(B)**	48. **(A)**	
9. **(D)**	19. **(D)**	29. **(B)**	39. **(C)**	49. **(D)**	
10. **(B)**	20. **(C)**	30. **(C)**	40. **(C)**	50. **(D)**	

ANSWERS AND EXPLANATIONS　答案与解析

Section I　第一部分

PART A: MULTIPLE-CHOICE QUESTIONS　选择题

1. **(B)** The cartoonist Herblock was pointing out that the growing anticommunist sentiment in the United States following World War II could become a threat to the civil liberties of Americans. The hysterical figure climbing the ladder is about to extinguish the torch of liberty. This question addresses the Learning Objective "Politics and Power" and the Historical Thinking Skills "Using Historical Evidence" and "Interpretation."

2. **(D)** In 1798, President John Adams and the Federalist Party in Congress were concerned that Americans supportive of France and French immigrants in America were working to undermine the U.S. government. This led to the passage of the Alien and Sedition Acts, which were criticized as violations of the liberties guaranteed by the Bill of Rights. This question addresses the Learning Objectives "Politics and Power" and "American in the World" and the Historical Thinking Skill "Comparison."

3. **(A)** After President Harry S. Truman vetoed the McCarran Internal Act in 1950, Congress overrode his veto. Truman criticized the act saying it represented "the greatest danger to freedom of speech, press, and assembly since the Alien and Sedition Laws of 1798." The act required groups deemed to be "subversive" to register with the federal government, prohibited some members of these groups from becoming American citizens, created an investigatory agency to find people suspected of engaging in subversive activities, and gave the president the power to detain suspected subversive people in the event of an emergency. Critics of the act echoed the sentiment of the cartoonist—that the act was an overreaction to perceived threats.

4. **(A)** John Locke's contract theory was well known among the American colonial elites such as Franklin and was a foundational principle of American democracy. The concept is integral to both the Declaration of Independence and the Constitution of the United States.

5. **(A)** Grenville's argument that the colonies of the British Empire had virtual representation was criticized in both Parliament and the American colonies as illogical and not at all founded in British law. The backlash against Grenville's policies led to the repeal of the Stamp Act later in 1766.

6. **(B)** Benjamin Franklin was an early proponent of colonial unity, often arguing that the 13 British colonies in America should work together for the betterment of all. A prime example of this type of advocacy was Franklin's famous "Join or Die" political cartoon from the French and Indian War era. His testimony to British officials in 1766 was directly related to the Stamp Act and colonial actions to protest against the stamp tax, such as the Stamp Act Congress. Franklin and other colonial leaders argued that the colonies should be given representation in Parliament if Parliament was going to tax the colonies.

7. **(C)** Published in 1881, Helen Hunt Jackson's book, *A Century of Dishonor*, was a scathing indictment of U.S. policy toward Indian tribes over the previous century. Jackson sent the book to every member of Congress, but it did not have as immediate an impact as she had hoped.

8. **(B)** The Indian Removal Act put Jackson's policy request into law in 1830. It took several years of political and legal maneuvering, but the Indian Removal act was eventually implemented during the presidency of Jackson's successor, Martin Van Buren. The Cherokee tribe, unlike the other affected tribes, resisted the pressure to sign a treaty that would cede their ancestral lands. The result of their resistance was their forcible removal, leading to the deaths of thousands of Cherokee.

9. **(D)** The Dawes Act established a system of land allotments to Indian tribes, granting 160 acres to the head of a family, and allowed for a method by which Indians could receive U.S. citizenship. The Dawes Act ended the reservation system of community ownership of land for Indian tribes and made the assimilation of Indians into American culture a matter of national policy.

10. **(B)** Martin Luther King, Jr., was only one of many civil rights leaders across the country, but he was probably the most prominent by the end of the 1950s. King coordinated his activist effort for civil rights with many of those civil rights leaders, culminating with the March on Washington for Jobs and Freedom in August 1963, which was organized by King, labor leader A. Phillip Randolph, and various other activist groups.

11. **(D)** Racial segregation was given the endorsement of the Supreme Court with the 1896 *Plessy v. Ferguson* decision, which established the "separate but equal" doctrine. Using that allowance, many states continued and expanded the Jim Crow laws that disenfranchised and discriminated against African Americans.

12. **(D)** Martin Luther King, Jr. followed the precedent set by Henry David Thoreau and Mohandas Gandhi and practiced nonviolent protest methods. King knew that in order to win the struggle for civil rights, advocates for racial equality must occupy the moral high ground. That meant that he did not support the use of violence as a means to achieve the end of segregation or to acquire voting rights.

13. **(D)** Susan B. Anthony and other advocates for women's rights often appealed to America's founding documents in their arguments for equality. In this quote, she echoes the list of grievances against the king of England found in the Declaration of Independence—taxa-

tion without representation, withholding trial by jury, depriving them of property without due process—as a way to connect the women's rights movement to the leaders of the Revolution and their struggle for freedom.

14. **(C)** Abolitionists sought freedom for slaves and felt that the promises outlined in the Declaration of Independence, namely that "all men are created equal," should and did apply to all people. Those promises could not be fulfilled until slaves were granted their freedom.

15. **(A)** The Nineteenth Amendment, ratified in 1920, gave women the right to vote on a nationwide basis. It was the result of at least 72 years of effort on the part of women's rights advocates, who had been arguing for equal suffrage since the adoption of the Declaration of Rights and Sentiments at the Seneca Falls Convention in 1848.

16. **(B)** Susan B. Anthony was, along with Elizabeth Cady Stanton, a founder of the National Woman Suffrage Association in 1869. Anthony was arrested for voting in the 1872 presidential election and refused to pay the fine imposed on her by a judge. In addition to women like Susan B. Anthony, other groups that have fought for voting rights include African Americans (Fifteenth Amendment) and young people (Twenty-sixth Amendment).

17. **(A)** Andrew Carnegie made sizable philanthropic contributions in both the United States and his homeland of Scotland. The cartoonist draws attention to Carnegie's cash donations and his monetary grants to build libraries while he was simultaneously cutting the wages of the workers in his steel plants. The dichotomous nature of Carnegie's wealth has often been used as a symbol of the "Gilded Age" of the late nineteenth century.

18. **(B)** Workers went on strike at Andrew Carnegie's Homestead Steel plant near Pittsburgh in 1892. Carnegie and his operations manager Henry Clay Frick hired the Pinkerton Detective Agency to defend the plant and the newly hired non-union workers. The strikers and the Pinkertons clashed violently, with the striking workers winning the battle. Pennsylvania state militia later arrived to restore order, allowing Frick to reopen the plant with the non-union workers.

19. **(D)** The Newlands Reclamation Act was part of the environmental legislation of the Progressive era. The law gave the federal government authority over water rights in much of the nation, which paved the way for federal construction of dams and irrigation projects. All of the other choices were federal attempts to regulate or limit the abusive practices of big businesses.

20. **(C)** Andrew Carnegie wrote "Wealth" (also known as "The Gospel of Wealth") in 1889, in which he argued that the newly rich class of industrialists and entrepreneurs had a responsibility to give back to the community. He thought that wealthy people, rather than the government, should administer funds for public-minded projects. He argued that the wealthy should live modest lifestyles and avoid extravagances.

21. **(D)** Despite the freedom former slaves obtained via the Thirteenth Amendment, this representative of the Freedmen's Bureau said that southern whites were slow to accept the new social conditions brought about by the amendment. Many southern states began to pass restrictive laws in an attempt to continue their dominance.

22. **(B)** In an effort to integrate the freed slaves into American political and social life, and to deny individual states the ability to legally discriminate against blacks, the Fourteenth Amendment declared, "No state shall make or enforce any law which shall abridge the privileges or immunities of citizens of the United States; nor shall any state deprive any person of life, liberty, or property, without due process of law; nor deny to any person within its jurisdiction the equal protection of the laws."

23. **(B)** Jim Crow legislation was a term used to describe laws passed to disenfranchise blacks and to systematize racial segregation. Some examples of Jim Crow laws include the poll tax, literacy tests, and separate facilities, including schools, for whites and blacks. The Jim Crow system was eroded by several Supreme Court decisions in the 1950s, most famously *Brown v. Board of Education* in 1954, and Congressional legislation in the 1960s such as the Civil Rights Act of 1964. Additionally, the Twenty-fourth Amendment prohibited the poll tax.

24. **(C)** Alexander Hamilton came to believe that many of the problems facing the United States could be traced to the inadequacy of the structure of government under the Articles of Confederation. He was instrumental in writing a new document, the Constitution, and in pushing for its ratification. He, James Madison, and John Jay wrote a series of articles under the collective pseudonym, Publius, in defense of the new Constitution. The 85 numbered articles, including the one excerpted in the question, were later collected as *The Federalist Papers*. Hamilton believed that a government that allowed for more power on the national level would be more effective in carrying out an assertive agenda and would be given greater respect on the world stage.

25. **(A)** Many Americans were alarmed that Great Britain would not evacuate forts in the Great Lakes region, even after the signing of the Treaty of Paris (1783). In the treaty, Great Britain recognized the independence of the United States, but it maintained that it would not leave the forts in the West until the United States compensated Loyalists for property losses. The presence of a foreign power on U.S. soil was an embarrassment to Hamilton. He came to believe that the structure of the government itself needed to be changed in order for the United States to gain respect on the world stage.

26. **(B)** A series of events in the 1780s led Hamilton to believe that a new form of government was necessary in order for the United States to thrive. He was part of a group of political leaders who met in Philadelphia from May to September, 1787, with the goal of framing a new governing document. They wrote the Constitution, and then sent it to state ratifying conventions. The Constitution represented a marked departure from the Articles of Confederation. The Constitution created a centralized national government. States still retained certain powers, but the Constitution stated that the national government would be supreme.

27. **(D)** Historian Eric Foner's 2010 Pulitzer Prize-winning book, *The Fiery Trial*, traces Abraham Lincoln's changing perspectives on slavery and abolition from his youth in Kentucky and Illinois all the way through his assassination in 1865. Foner's book argues that it is difficult to place labels on Lincoln's beliefs on these subjects because Lincoln did not hold a consistent belief throughout his life. Instead, Lincoln's thoughts on slavery changed as he gathered more information on the subject, met new people in his public and private life, and gained power as a politician.

28. **(D)** Until the summer of 1862, when President Abraham Lincoln began contemplating the way he could legally emancipate slaves in the South, he had been repeatedly stating publicly that his primary goal in the war was to save the Union. President Lincoln used the Emancipation Proclamation to marry the freedom of the slaves to the plan of preserving the Union, declaring that the Proclamation was a "military necessity," and allowed for black men to serve in the U.S. Army.

29. **(B)** The Emancipation Proclamation, despite being a groundbreaking document in U.S. history, was intentionally limited in its scope. President Abraham Lincoln was careful to stay within what he believed to be his Constitutional powers in issuing the document. He did so by only applying the document to the emancipation of slaves who were in states that were in rebellion on the date the Proclamation went into effect—January 1, 1863. President Lincoln had been stating, even before he was president, that he did not believe that the federal government had the authority to abolish slavery. But the Civil War was a special circumstance and President Lincoln believed that his interpretation of the Constitution allowed him special powers in the event of an insurrection. There were also political considerations that President Lincoln needed to take into account, especially the need to keep the slaveholding "Border States" of Delaware, Maryland, Kentucky, and Missouri in the Union. As such, the Emancipation Proclamation exempted those states from its decrees.

30. **(C)** The National Woman Suffrage Association (NWSA) was formed in 1869 and was active in women's rights causes until its merger with the American Woman Suffrage Association in 1890; among its leaders were Elizabeth Cady Stanton and Susan B. Anthony. NWSA advocated an amendment to the U.S. Constitution that would grant women the right to vote on a national basis. In addition to suffrage, NWSA campaigned for a broad-based platform of women's equality including political, social, and cultural issues.

31. **(B)** Women's suffrage activist Alice Paul first wrote the Equal Rights Amendment in 1923, when it was also first introduced in Congress. The proposed amendment's language guaranteed that the "Equality of rights under the law shall not be denied or abridged by the United States or by any State on account of sex." It was re-introduced in Congress every year until it finally passed in 1970. Congress imposed a time limit for ratification on the Amendment, originally 1979 but later extended until 1982. The Equal Rights Amendment fell short of ratification by eight states (or three, if the rescission of ratification of five states is not counted).

32. **(A)** This cartoon, drawn by an unknown artist sometime in 1801 or 1802, shows two Revolutionary leaders, Thomas Jefferson and Thomas Paine, coordinating their efforts to pull down the federal government that had been led by Jefferson's predecessors as president, George Washington and John Adams. Paine is shown with radical writings in his pockets and is depicted as a heavy drinker, while Jefferson, the new president, was shown as the Devil. The Federalist Party, led by Alexander Hamilton, had been in nominal control of the national government ever since the adoption of the Constitution in 1788 and escalated its written and verbal attacks on Thomas Jefferson's Republican (or Democratic-Republican) Party.

33. **(C)** The Twelfth Amendment altered the procedure by which the Electoral College voted for president and vice president. Previous to the amendment's ratification, the winner of the electoral vote became president and the second-place candidate became vice

president. With the advent of the party system, it was obvious that having the top two executive branch officials come from different political parties would cause problems of governance. The Twelfth Amendment says, "[the Electors] shall name in their ballots the person voted for as President, and in distinct ballots the person voted for as Vice-President. . . ." This change meant that members of the Electoral College would now be voting for party tickets for the two high offices, not just voting for first and second choices for the office of president.

34. **(A)** The Federalist Party, led by Alexander Hamilton, had long been suspicious of Thomas Jefferson's political viewpoints and often characterized Jefferson as a radical and an atheist. Here he is depicted as working in consort with the devil. The political press in the period of the early Republic was not shy about outright attacks on the characters of public officials, and being the author of the Declaration of Independence did not in any way shield Jefferson from those attacks. Thomas Paine, the pamphleteer responsible for *Common Sense*, was also the subject of Federalist attacks because of his support for the radical revolutionaries in France.

35. **(D)** There were many factors that led to the election of Ronald Reagan as president, but one of the largest factors was the conservative reaction to the growth of government spending on social welfare programs under President Lyndon B. Johnson in the 1960s. President Johnson's "Great Society" agenda included new or expanded government spending to combat poverty, housing shortages, and nutritional needs for millions of Americans. Conservatives like President Reagan believed that issues such as those were not under the purview of the federal government, but rather should be handled by the individual states. In addition, conservatives sought to undo some of the Supreme Court decisions during the period that Earl Warren was the chief justice (1953-1969), especially decisions that hindered law enforcement. Conservatives were also critical of what they perceived to be a moral decline in the United States, as reflected in protest movements, drug use, promiscuity, and rock music.

36. **(A)** During the debate over the ratification of the Constitution of the United States in 1787 and 1788, many people, generally categorized as the Anti-Federalists, argued that the new nation would be best served by a limited national government, with a larger role for the individual states, which would allow for the states to respond to the needs of their people on a local level. The Anti-Federalists were satisfied with the structure of the U.S. government under the Articles of Confederation, which had limited the powers of Congress and guaranteed the equality and sovereignty of each state.

37. **(C)** President Ronald Reagan ran on a platform of shrinking the size and spending of the federal government, and his inaugural address takes on that issue directly. President Reagan and the Republican Party had vowed to change the way the federal government interacted with the economic system of the United States, primarily promising to cut taxes, cut spending, and to reduce or eliminate regulations on businesses. This was a reversal of policy from much of the twentieth century, where presidents such as Franklin Roosevelt, Dwight Eisenhower, and Lyndon Johnson had used the federal government to shape a changing U.S. economy.

38. **(B)** President Ronald Reagan's economic policies, commonly called supply-side or "trickle-down" economics were intended to cut taxes and regulations while also cutting government spending in order to reduce the growing national debt. The theory behind

much of President Reagan's economic plans was that the wealthy and business owners, with their taxes lowered and restrictions loosened, would be able to invest more money and spur job growth, thereby allowing working-class Americans to have more earning potential.

39. **(C)** President Jimmy Carter's 1977 speech on the energy crisis was part of an ongoing debate in the United States about how best to use natural resources such as petroleum and natural gas. President Carter urged Americans to change their energy consumption habits and advocated for national policies that would protect the environment, help the economy, and promote national defense.

40. **(C)** Starting with the presidential administration of Richard Nixon, the United States had been subjected to several oil embargoes enacted by the Organization of Petroleum Exporting Countries (OPEC). The embargoes had resulted in gasoline shortages, higher fuel prices, and other economic consequences. President Jimmy Carter was hoping to ease some of the threat of those embargoes by enacting a new national energy policy that would make the United States less reliant on imported petroleum.

41. **(C)** The 1899 cartoon makes the point that the United States misread the situation in the Philippines following the Spanish-American War (1898). Under the provisions of the Treaty of Paris (1898), the United States assumed several of Spain's possessions following the war, including the Philippines, Guam, and Puerto Rico. The United States stated that it would grant the Philippines independence sometime in the future, but for the time being, it held on to the Philippines. Many Filipinos were deeply disappointed in this outcome, hoping to attain independence, as Cuba had following the war. A resistance movement developed in the Philippines and a bloody three-year war, known as the Philippine-American War ensued. Filipino forces were led by Emilio Aguinaldo. The infantilization of the Filipino people in the image can be read on two levels. It serves as a visual pun, comparing Uncle Sam to a parent coming to the realization that a baby is more work than originally thought. Also, it reflects racist attitudes toward the Filipino people.

42. **(B)** The cartoon questions the wisdom of American involvement in the Philippines. It does not reject the morality of such involvement. After all, the portrayal of Filipino rebel leader Emilio Aguinaldo as an infant seems to imply that the Philippines was not ready for self-rule. However, the cartoon wonders if the effort is worth it. Similar questions were raised during the war in Vietnam and during other American interventions.

43. **(D)** The cartoon depicts the war in the Philippines, with rebels following the American victory in the Spanish-American War. Many Filipino people expected to gain independence after Spain's defeat. They were deeply disappointed that the United States decided to hold on to the Philippines. This move by the United States marks a turn toward a more imperialistic policy.

44. **(B)** Mercantilism, as practiced by European nations in the sixteenth through the eighteenth centuries, was an economic system by which nations attempted to accumulate wealth by creating a trade surplus, especially by founding colonies on other continents. Mercantilism served to strengthen the power of monarchs and led to intense competition for land and resources between the European nations. Here, the Englishman Richard Hakluyt advocated for English participation in that competition by striving to establish colonies on the Atlantic coast of America.

45. **(C)** Richard Hakluyt wrote extensively on the benefits of establishing colonies in the New World. The arguments he presented in favor of doing so included economic, spiritual, political, and nationalistic benefits for England. England's first permanent colony was established at Jamestown in Virginia in 1607 and by 1732 there were 13 colonies along the Atlantic Coast of North America, as well as an English foothold in Canada and island possessions in the Caribbean Sea.

46. **(A)** Edwards is asserting that God gives individuals a chance to rectify their sins because he is merciful. The sermon presents a dark view of humanity, but Edwards offers hope to those who find their way to Jesus. This sermon is one of the central texts of the Great Awakening. The idea that human beings are inherently good, but are corrupted by the evils of society (B) is associated with Jean-Jacques Rousseau, one of the great philosophers of the French enlightenment. Edwards has a dimmer view of human nature. In Edwards's view, God is angry, but he is not merciless (C). It is his action, after all, that is preventing us from descending into the fires of hell. Choice (D) describes a more modern view of ethics and morality; Edwards certainly argued that it is important that one believes in the saving grace of Jesus.

47. **(C)** Edwards was a central figure in the Great Awakening. In the face of declining membership in the Congregational Church of New England, preachers such as Edwards attempted to revive flagging piety. By the 1730s, several charismatic ministers attempted to infuse a new passion into religious practice. These ministers, and their followers, were part of a religious resurgence known as the Great Awakening. The movement took a more emotional, and less cerebral, approach to religion. The other choices identify nineteenth-century religious movements.

48. **(A)** By the early 1700s, the white-hot piety of Puritanism had dimmed considerably. The succeeding generations of New England became increasingly interested in commerce and matters of this world, rather than spiritual things. They had not endured religious suppression in England, nor had they suffered through the difficulties of settling in the New World. The Great Awakening hoped to revive the intense religious feeling of the previous century. Disestablishment—the severing of links between the church and the state—occurred in many states in the early nineteenth century (B). New England remained fairly homogeneous throughout the colonial period. It failed to attract immigrants from outside of England (C). There were devastating wars with American Indians in New England, such as King Philip's War, but those wars occurred in the seventeenth century (D).

49. **(D)** Edwards was part of the Great Awakening, and the Great Awakening contributed to changes in colonists' understanding of God, themselves, and the world around them. Specifically, it led to questioning of traditional authorities and encouraged colonists to see themselves as agents for change. It did not specifically encourage a questioning of British policies (A); this did not occur until after the French and Indian War, well after the height of the Great Awakening. Great Awakening ministers did not, for the most part, condemn slavery (B), nor did they encourage better treatment of American Indians (C).

50. **(D)** The Ford Motor Company was known for the policy of its chairman, Henry Ford, to pay his workers well enough to be able to afford the product they were making. American consumers of the 1920s were able to buy more products at affordable prices, but were

also subjected to a great deal of advertising that attempted to convince them of the necessity of those purchases in order to increase or maintain their status in society.

51. **(A)** Credit-buying plans offered by companies like the Ford Motor Company allowed consumers to purchase products that they otherwise may not have been able to afford if they had been required to pay the entire purchase price up front. Many consumers were willing to use credit to buy the new products as a way to demonstrate their status in an increasingly status-centered culture. However, the growth of consumer debt was a significant harbinger of the approaching economic calamity of the Great Depression.

52. **(B)** The Industrial Revolution in the United States began in the late 1700s and grew along with the nation throughout the 1800s. American manufacturing had become one of the world's leading exporters of manufactured goods, in no small part because of the contributions of numerous inventors and entrepreneurs like Eli Whitney, Charles Goodyear, John Deere, Cyrus McCormick, and Henry Ford himself.

53. **(C)** The numbers in the table illustrate a major problem for farmers in the post–Civil War period. Commodity prices for agricultural products were falling; in other words, farmers were getting less and less for their produce. It reached a point where it was hardly worth growing crops. The costs of production were almost more than the price they received for their goods. A primary culprit in this situation was mechanization and improved agricultural techniques. These created surpluses that pushed down prices. Another important cause was the tight money supply, which contributed to deflation. An important demand of the movement was to base currency on silver as well as gold.

54. **(D)** Farmers' organizations, such as the Grange and the Populist Party, wanted more money in circulation so that there would be inflation. Inflation would lead to higher prices for agricultural commodities. The populists demanded an end to the gold standard and a shift to currency backed by silver as well as gold.

55. **(C)** In the last decades of the nineteenth century, farmers organized groups to challenge the corporate-driven policies that were reducing their profitability and potential markets. The Populist Party became a formidable force in the 1890s. The movement challenged the concentration of wealth and power among eastern industrialists and bankers. It supported a national income tax so that those with higher incomes would pay more than the poor. It also supported free and unlimited coinage of silver. The Populist Party wanted the United States to get off the gold standard and to issue money backed by silver as well. This would increase the amount of money in circulation and would lead to inflation. Farmers supported inflationary policies so that the prices they received for their produce would increase.

PART B: SHORT-ANSWER QUESTIONS 简答题

Good responses to question #1

A. A good response would explain the main idea of the first passage.

... Booker T. Washington was arguing that it would be a mistake for African Americans to focus, in the immediate future, on struggling for equality in the United States. "It is at the bottom of life we must begin." Rather, he urged African Americans to learn useful and productive trades. He argued that there was dignity in common labor. He urged African Americans to take a "go slow" approach in terms of struggling against an oppressive system. A more demanding approach, he warned, could lead to a backlash by whites against African Americans.

B. A good response would explain the main idea of the first passage.

... W. E. B. Du Bois argued that Booker T. Washington's approach to the African American struggle for progress and justice was misguided. Du Bois wrote that it was not enough to urge African Americans to simply acquire vocational training. He believed that Washington was ignoring the larger problems in society—the lack of voting rights for African Americans and the creation of the Jim Crow system. He argued that, first and foremost, society must change.

C. A good response would explain which set of ideas was more influential in shaping the approach of the civil rights movement of the 1950s and 1960s.

... In many ways, the approach of W. E. B. Du Bois resonated more with the civil rights activists of the 1950s and 1960s. The goal of the movement was social change—not vocational training. It is true that early on in the civil rights struggle, activists focused on issues of education and schooling, but this was a tactic to end segregation in the South. It was one of many tactics used to change society. Others included sitting in at lunch counters, marching in cities across the South, riding in integrated interstate busses into the South, and pushing for more African Americans to register to vote.

... The approaches and ideas of both W. E. B. Du Bois and Booker T. Washington both can be seen in the activism of the 1960s. The debate between caution and militancy that was evident in their exchange around the turn of the twentieth century was evident in the 1950s and 1960s. Martin Luther King and the Southern Christian Leadership Conference were accused by the Student Nonviolent Coordinating Committee of being too cautious in challenging white supremacy in the South.

Good responses to question #2

A. A good response would describe evidence of public support for the New Deal in the 1930s, such as:

... The reelection of President Franklin D. Roosevelt in 1936 and 1940. The 1936 election was one of the most lopsided elections in history, with Roosevelt getting over 60 percent of the popular vote, and all but eight electoral votes.

. . . Participation rates in New Deal programs. The Works Progress Administration employed over 8 million people during its years of operations (1935–1943). The Social Security Administration (1935) was immediately popular with the public—over 20 million Social Security cards were issued in the first year of the cards' existence (1937).

. . . Democrats held dominant majorities in the House of Representatives and in the Senate in the 1930s.

. . . Roosevelt was able to connect with the public in the immensely popular fireside on the radio.

B. A good response would describe evidence of public opposition to New Deal programs, such as:

. . . The popularity of Senator Huey Long, who denounced the rich and argued that the New Deal did not go far enough in creating a just society. His Share Our Wealth program was extremely popular.

. . . The persistence of conservative condemnations of the New Deal by organizations such as the American Liberty League. Conservative critics insisted that Roosevelt was pushing the American economy toward socialism.

. . . Father Charles Coughlin, who used his popular national radio show to attack Roosevelt as being a communist and a dictator.

C. A good response would describe the place of the New Deal in public policy debates that have occurred in the decades since the 1930s.

. . . In the 1960s, Lyndon Johnson and the Democratic Party invoked the legacy of the New Deal in promoting the programs of the Great Society. Republicans, on the other hand, invoked the conservative arguments of the 1930s to accuse President Johnson of socialistic tendencies.

. . . In the 1990s, the Republican Party's agenda, the "Contract with America," criticized the legacy of the New Deal. It hoped to reduce the costs and scope of federal social programs. Democratic president Bill Clinton did agree to sign legislation ending welfare as a federal entitlement program. Clinton proclaimed that he was "ending welfare as we know it" and replacing it with block grants to states. Some liberal critics, invoking the legacy of the New Deal, criticized Clinton's shift toward a more conservative direction.

Good responses to question #3

A. A good response would present an explanation of the point of view of the first passage. Such an explanation might include:

. . . Phyllis Schlafly is arguing against calls for greater gender equality in American society. She is contrasting the "Positive Woman" with the women who were participating in the women's liberation movement of the 1960s and 1970s.

. . . Schlafly starts with the assumption that men and women are essentially different. She is emphasizing a woman's love of babies and her desire to cultivate "femaleness."

Schlafly's assertions of the essential differences between men and women differed markedly from the claims of the women's liberation movement of the 1960s and 1970s.

B. A good response would present an explanation of the point of view of the second passage. Such an explanation might include:

. . . Gloria Steinem is trying to challenge some of the cultural assumptions that led many people to oppose the women's liberation movement. She is arguing for both mothers and fathers to be active in parenting. She is urging changes in society that will create greater gender equality.

. . . Gloria Steinem is arguing that the women's liberation movement should not be seen as a threat by men. She is asserting that men would benefit (as much as women would) from a more egalitarian and humane society. She noted that the world of work is inhumane, and that a liberation movement would change the nature of the workplace as well as the nature of home life.

C. A good response would present a continuity between one of the writers and a person or movement in American history.

In terms of Phyllis Schlafly, one could cite continuities between her and one or more of the following people or movements:

. . . The "cult of domesticity" in the nineteenth century, urging women to accept their role as keepers of the home and primary caregivers of children.

. . . Resistance to women gaining the right to vote in the early twentieth century. In 1911, several women, including Josephine Dodge, founded the Association Opposed to Woman's Suffrage.

. . . The depiction of women in television shows in the 1950s, such as *Father Knows Best* and *Leave It To Beaver*. Such shows depicted women as homemakers and mothers.

In terms of Gloria Steinem, one could cite continuities between her and one or more of the following people or movements:

. . . The Seneca Falls Convention (1848). The gathering called attention to the whole structure of gender inequality in the United States, including issues relating to property rights, education, wages, child custody, divorce, and the overall legal status of women. Elizabeth Cady Stanton and Lucretia Mott were important organizers of the event.

. . . Susan B. Anthony, a tireless worker for women's rights. She was a link between the generation of activists who organized the Seneca Falls Convention and the women who successfully pushed for the ratification of the Nineteenth Amendment, guaranteeing women the right to vote.

. . . The National American Woman Suffrage Association (NAWSA), created in 1890, following the merger of two early suffrage organizations. The NAWSA, which had over 2 million members at its height, played a key role in the ratification of the Nineteenth Amendment (1920), which guaranteed women the right to vote.

Good responses to question #4

A. A good response would present an explanation of the point of view of the first passage. Such an explanation might include:

... John Kerry is asserting that U.S. policy in Vietnam is tragically misguided. He believes that Vietnam did not pose a threat to the United States and that the United States did not have a legitimate reason for fighting a war there.

... John Kerry is speaking in defense of the servicemen who have served in Vietnam. He thinks it is wrong that the American government sends young men to fight in Vietnam without legitimate objectives in mind. He believes the United States is being stubborn in its refusal to admit failure in Vietnam.

B. A good response would provide evidence, not included in the passage, to support John Kerry's argument, such as:

... The actions of American troops in the My Lai massacre.

... The burning of Vietnamese villages, such as Cam Ne. The burning of Cam Ne was captured by a television news crew.

... The bombing of Vietnamese villages, such as Ben Tre. About the bombing of that city, a U.S. Army major said, "It became necessary to destroy the town to save it."

... The use of dangerous chemicals such as Agent Orange and napalm.

... The failure of the United States to capture the "hearts and minds" of the Vietnamese people.

... The nature of the conflict in Vietnam; many argued that it was more of a civil war than a Cold War conflict.

C. A good response would choose one of the conflicts listed in the question and explain how critics might make an argument about that conflict that would be similar to the argument John Kerry made about the Vietnam War.

An explanation of continuities between Kerry's argument and arguments against the War of 1812 might include the following:

... Critics of the War of 1812 argued that the war was misguided and not in the interests of the United States. They cited the interruption of trade with Great Britain as an important reason for their opposition. Opponents of the war organized the Hartford Convention in 1814 to express their grievances.

An explanation of continuities between Kerry's argument and arguments against the Mexican War (1846–1848) might include the following:

... Critics of the Mexican War argued that the war was unjust and was provoked by the United States. Critics, such as Abraham Lincoln, insisted that the border dispute leading up to the war was invented by President James K. Polk. One opponent of the war, Henry David Thoreau, refused to pay taxes in protest.

An explanation of continuities between Kerry's argument and arguments against U.S. participation in World War I (1914–1918, with the United States joining the war in 1917) might include the following:

. . . Critics of World War I argued that the war did not involve American interests. They insisted that it reflected age-old rivalries in Europe and that the United States would be wise to avoid such conflicts. Some socialist critics of World War I argued that the war was being fought on behalf of the capitalist class.

Section II 第二部分

PART A: DOCUMENT-BASED QUESTION 材料分析题

What good responses will include:

A good response would draw on six or seven documents (that is, all or all but one of the documents provided) to present an analysis of each of the elements mentioned in the question: The continuities and changes in the ways in which Americans addressed immigration to America in two different periods. The first period is decades immediately before and after the United States achieved independence (1750–1800); the second period connects the era of the Gilded Age with the immediate aftermath of World War I (1875–1925).

Thesis and Argument Development—Targeted Skills: Argumentation and (in this case) Continuity and Change Over Time (2 points)
论点及论证发展——目标技能：论证、保持连贯性并能随时间变化（2分）

The thesis for this question should focus on the historical thinking skill of continuity and change over time. It should note key elements in debates and discussions around immigration in two different time periods, and note similarities and/or differences between the two periods. The thesis should make an assertion of continuities and/or changes over time. In regard to continuities, in both periods we see concerns over what it means to be an American, and who is qualified to become one. We see fears and prejudices toward certain groups in both periods. We also see, in both periods, Americans exhibiting a welcoming attitude toward immigration. Broadly speaking, in both periods Americans vigorously debated immigration policy; in both periods, Americans debated legislation to restrict immigration into the United States. In regard to changes, in the earlier period, concerns around immigration centered around identity, while in the later period, concerns included economic fears. The economic concerns of the Gilded Age around low wages and unemployment were not central to the thinking of Americans in the second half of the eighteenth century. A simple claim would earn one point. For the second point, the thesis should recognize and account for historical complexity by explicitly noting contradiction, corroboration, and/or qualification, as illustrated by historical evidence. For example, a more complex thesis might acknowledge that anti-immigrant sentiment existed in both periods, but it would qualify the tone of anti-immigrant sentiment in the two periods. In the earlier period, the opposition focused on the ability of immigrants to fit into the culture of the United States; in the later period and earlier period, we see outright racism toward entire groups.

Document Analysis—Targeted Skills: Analyzing Evidence: Content and Sourcing, and Argumentation (2 points)

材料分析——目标技能：分析史料的内容、来源并进行论证（2分）

It should be immediately apparent that the first three documents deal with the early period (1750–1800), while the last four documents deal with the later period (1875–1925). For the first period, one document (document 2) expresses a welcoming attitude. J. Hector St. John De Crevecoeur writes positively of the idea that anyone can leave behind his old ways and become an American. He sees great potential for the United States to exist as a multiethnic republic—"Here individuals of all nations are melted into a new race of men." Here, connections can be made between Crevecoeur and the idea of the United States as a "melting pot," popularized in the early twentieth century. Documents 1 and 3 are critical of the influx of immigrants in America. Benjamin Franklin (Document 1) worries that an influx of Germans to Pennsylvania would change that colony's English cultural "character." Theodore Sedgwick is concerned about the background of immigrants coming from the warring monarchies of the Old World (Document 3).

For the later period, Documents 4 and 5 are welcoming of new immigrants, while Documents 6 and 7 are harshly anti-immigrant. Document 4 is a sharp rebuttal to the anti-Chinese rhetoric of the 1870s. The cartoon by Joseph Keppler (himself Austrian-born) envisions the United States as Noah's ark—providing a refuge to immigrants from the troubled countries of Europe, which is shrouded in storm clouds (Document 5). Madison Grant, the anthropologist and founder of the American Museum of Natural History, employs racial theories to warn against the influx of non-Nordic peoples (Document 6). The last document, a cartoon by Billy Ireland, depicts a dour Uncle Sam looking at the "melting pot" of American society. He is unhappy with the "scum" that his risen to the top of the pot—"un-American" radicals with the "mad notions of Europe" (Document 7).

In order to receive credit for the first point, the essay should use the content of at least six of the documents to support the stated thesis or a relevant argument. For the second point the student must explain one of the following for at least four of the documents: author's point of view, author's purpose, historical context, or audience. Strong essays go beyond simple descriptions of the contents of the documents. Rather, a good essay should make connections between documents or sections of documents in crafting the essay into a convincing argument.

Using Evidence Beyond the Documents: Targeted Skills: Contextualization and Argumentation (2 points)

使用给定材料之外的材料——目标技能：联系有关背景进行论证（2分）

Essays should situate the argument in its historical context by explaining broader historical events, developments, or processes immediately relevant to the question. Such contextualization will earn the student one point; an additional point can be earned by providing specific examples and evidence beyond what is contained within the documents. In this case, students could establish a broader context by discussing the fact that war shaped debates in both periods. During the early period, there was war in Europe between France and an alliance of countries headed by Great Britain. This war occurred in the aftermath of the French Revolution. The conflict drew in the United States, which engaged in the "Quasi-War" with France. In the later period, World War I was the backdrop to much of the anti-immigrant sentiment of the late 1910s. In both cases, wartime anxieties led to legislation that restricted immigration. Toward the end of the early period, Congress passed the Alien and Sedition Acts; toward the end of the second period, Congress passed the Emergency Quota Act and the National Origins Act, establishing the quota system for immigration. Contextualization could also focus on the political debates in each period—between Federalists and Democratic Republicans in the first period, and between progressive reformers and isolationist jingoists in the second period.

Synthesis—Targeted Skill: Synthesis (1 point)　整合——目标技能：信息整合（1分）

The final point of the document-based question requires the student to extend the argument of the essay, by explaining connections between the argument and one of the following: a development in a different historical period, situation, or geographical area; or a theme and/ or approach to history that is not the focus of the essay (such as political, economic, social, cultural, or intellectual history). In this case, students might want to extend the argument of the essay to economic conditions in both periods and develop a conclusion about connections between the economy and attitudes toward immigration. Or students might want to extend the essay to a discussion of anti-Irish sentiment in the middle of the nineteenth century or to political clashes over immigration in the late twentieth and early twenty-first centuries.

PART B: THE LONG-ESSAY QUESTIONS　论述题

Question 1
What good responses will include:

A good response to long-essay question #1 will point out similarities and differences between the women's rights movement of the earlier period (1910 to 1930) and of the later period (1960 to 1980). It would address at least one of the categories of analysis listed in the question—goals, tactic, and levels of success.

Thesis—Targeted Skill: Argumentation (1 point)　整合——目标技能：论证（1分）

Students will earn one point for presenting a thesis that makes a historically defensible claim and responds to all parts of the question. The thesis, which must consist of one or more sentences and must be located either in the introduction or the conclusion, must make a convincing claim about similarities or differences between the movement to redefine gender in the two periods under discussion. In terms of goals, a student could focus on differences: "The women's rights movement of the 1910s and 1920s was more focused on political issues, while the movement of the 1960s and 1970s was more focused on economic issues." A different thesis could focus on similarities, in tactics: "Neither of the two major movements for women's rights—in the early twentieth century and in the 1960s and 1970s—reached out to African American women or working-class women; both were white middle-class movements." There are a number of historically defensible claims that students could make in responding to the question.

Argument Development: Using the Targeted Historical Thinking Skill— Targeted Skills: Argumentation and (in this case) Comparison (2 points)
论证发展，使用目标历史思维技能——目标技能：论证并比较（2分）

Students must develop their argument by expanding upon the thesis. Students can earn up to two points in this section. One point would be granted if the student successfully describes similarities *and* differences among historical individuals, events, developments, or processes.

And a second point can be earned if the essay explains the reasons for similarities *and* differences among historical individuals, events, developments, or processes. Students here can flesh out their theses with different factors or elements. If a student puts forth the first thesis—about the political nature of the earlier reform movement, and the economic focus of the latter movement—the student could describe a number of goals of each movement, some pointing toward similarities and some pointing toward difference. These goals could include the relaxation of formal dress codes, the promotion of women in higher-level occupations, the push toward fairness in the legal system, the acceptance of the idea that the "personal is political," and greater access to reproductive rights. Students must also describe why the movements were similar to one another, or why they were different.

Argument Development: Using Evidence—Targeted Skill: Argumentation (2 points) 论证发展，使用史料——目标技能：论证（2分）

In addition to citing similarities and/or differences between the two movements under question, students must also use evidence to support their argument. Students can earn one point by addressing the topic of the question with specific examples of relevant evidence. A second point can be earned by utilizing this evidence to fully and effectively substantiate the stated thesis or a relevant argument. The specific evidence the student chooses will vary depending on the approach of the essay. Students, for instance, might mention (for the first period) some of the following as evidence: Susan B. Anthony, the National American Woman Suffrage Association, World War I, restrictive clothing, smoking in public, birth control, opposition to the Nineteenth Amendment, or voting patterns after ratification of the Nineteenth Amendment, to name a few. In the later period, students could mention Betty Friedan, Gloria Steinem, the National Organization for Women, "bra burning," protests at the 1968 Miss America Pageant, the Equal Rights Amendment, or the "glass ceiling." The evidence chosen, and the connection to the thesis, would vary from essay to essay.

Synthesis—Targeted Skill: Synthesis (1 point) 整合——目标技能：信息整合（1分）

The sixth and final point on the long essay can be earned for demonstrating the historical thinking skill of synthesis. A student can earn this point by extending the argument to explain the connections between the argument of the essay and *one* of the following: a development in a different historical period, situation, era, or geographical area, or a course theme and/or approach to history that is not the focus of the essay (such as political, economic, social, cultural, or intellectual history). In this case, the student could draw connections between the two different women's rights movements and different civil rights movements. Students could look at the rise of the National Association for the Advancement of Colored People in the 1910s and the Student Non-Violent Coordinating Committee in the 1960s. Or students could compare the struggles of women in the two periods under discussion with gender-related struggles earlier in American history, from Jane Addams's request to "remember the ladies," to the Seneca Falls Convention of 1848. Students could then qualify or corroborate their theses by extending them beyond the parameters of the essay.

Question 2

What good responses will include:

A good response to long-essay question #2 will point out similarities and differences between the environmental movement of the earlier period (1900 to 1915) and of the later period (1960 to 1980). It would address at least one of the categories of analysis listed in the question—goals, tactic, and levels of success.

Thesis—Targeted Skill: Argumentation (1 point)　整合——目标技能：论证（1分）

Students will earn one point for presenting a thesis that makes a historically defensible claim and responds to all parts of the question. The thesis, which must consist of one or more sentences and must be located in either the introduction or the conclusion, must make a convincing claim about similarities or differences between the environmental movements in the two periods under discussion. In terms of goals, a student could focus on differences: "The environmental movement of the early twentieth century was more focused on regulation and wise use of resources, while the movement of the 1960s and 1970s was focused on changing the ways humans live on earth." A different thesis could focus on similarities, in terms of their level of success: "Both of the environmental movements, of the early twentieth century and the 1960s and 1970s, had limited success; both movements ran up against the stumbling blocks of corporate power and human nature." There are a number of historically defensible claims that students could make in responding to the question.

Argument Development: Using the Targeted Historical Thinking Skill—Targeted Skills: Argumentation and (in this case) Comparison (2 points)
论证发展，使用目标历史思维技能——目标技能：论证并比较（2分）

Students must develop their argument by expanding upon the thesis. Students can earn up to two points in this section. One point would be granted if the student successfully describes similarities *and* differences among historical individuals, events, developments, or processes. And a second can be earned if the essay explains the reasons for similarities *and* differences among historical individuals, events, developments, or processes. Students here can flesh out their theses with different factors or elements in their argument. If students put forth the first thesis about the early environmental movement focusing on regulatory goals and the later movement focusing on changing behavior, they could discuss the setting aside of forested land in the early period and the push for fuel efficiency and the reduction of waste in the second period.

Argument Development: Using Evidence—Targeted Skill: Argumentation (2 points)　论证发展，使用史料——目标技能：论证（2分）

In addition to citing similarities and/or differences between the two movements under question, students must also use evidence to support their argument. Students can earn one point by addressing the topic of the question with specific examples of relevant evidence. A second point can be earned by utilizing this evidence to fully and effectively substantiate the stated thesis or a relevant argument. The specific evidence the student chooses will vary depending on the approach of the essay. Students, for instance, might mention (for the first period) Theodore Roosevelt, Gifford Pinchot, preservationism, national parks, John Muir, conservationism, or the Hetch Hetchy water controversy in California. For the later period, the student could mention Rachel Carson's *Silent Spring*, the chemical DDT, Earth Day, The Clean Air Act, Three Mile Island, or the energy crisis of the 1970s. The key is connecting this evidence to the thesis of the essay.

Synthesis—Targeted Skill: Synthesis (1 point) 整合——目标技能：信息整合（1分）

The sixth and final point on the long essay can be earned for demonstrating the historical thinking skill of synthesis. A student can earn this point by extending the argument to explain the connections between the argument of the essay and *one* of the following: a development in a different historical period, situation, era, or geographical area, or a course theme and/or approach to history that is not the focus of the essay (such as political, economic, social, cultural, or intellectual history). In this case, the student could draw connections between the two different environmental movements and the broader reform movements of the two eras. The environmental movement of the early twentieth century could be discussed in the context of the progressive movement. An essay could explore the influence of Frederick Winslow Taylor's scientific management theories on environmental reform. This could help explain the push toward the rational use of resources and development of scientific plans for regulation. For the environmental movement of the 1960s, an essay could explore the backdrop of the New Left and the civil rights movement. One could connect the militant tactics and broad vision of these movements with the more sweeping nature on the environmental movement of the era. Students could then qualify or corroborate their thesis by extending it beyond the parameters of the essay.

Index 索引

Washington Conference, 299–300

Watergate, 344

Webster-Ashburton Treaty, 158

Wesley, John, 140

West Bank, 376

Western Hemisphere, 153–160

West Indies, 62–63, 65, 121

Westward expansion, 150, 158–159, 173–177, 225–230

Whigs, 133–135

Whiskey Rebellion, 113–114, 118

"White Man's Burden, The," 281

White superiority, 42

White supremacy, 261

Whitney, Eli, 145, 151

Wilderness protection, 260–261

Williams, Roger, 59

Wilmot Proviso, 175, 182

Wilson, Woodrow, 257–259, 261, 286–292

Witch trials, 60–61

Women
    in American Revolution, 96

in antebellum society, 149

domesticity of, 143, 149, 236–237

Equal Rights Amendment, 344

in Great Depression, 271

in labor force, 213–214

liberation movement by, 336

in professions, 371

Progressive movement and, 254

rights movement by, 143–144, 192–193

"Rosie the Riveter," 297–298

suffrage movement, 263

in twentieth century, 251

Women's Army Auxiliary Corps, 297

Wool Act, 71

Worcester v. Georgia, 133, 159

Work, exchange, and technology, 11

Working class, 211, 214, 221–222

Works Progress Administration, 268

World Trade Organization, 364

World War I, 248, 287–295, 303, 315

World War II, 248–249, 279, 294–303, 315, 331

Wounded Knee massacre, 230–231

X

XYZ affair, 122–123

Y

Yalta Conference, 302

"Yellow Journalism," 283

Yom Kippur War, 328

Yugoslavia, 376

Z

Zenger, John Peter, 79

Zimmerman note, 289–290

How to Use the CD-ROM

The software is not installed on your computer; it runs directly from the CD-ROM. Barron's CD-ROM includes an "autorun" feature that automatically launches the application when the CD is inserted into the CD-ROM drive. In the unlikely event that the autorun feature is disabled, follow the manual launching instructions below.

Windows®
1. Click on the Start button and choose "My Computer."
2. Double-click on the CD-ROM drive, which will be named **AP_US_History**.
3. Double-click **AP_US_History.exe** to launch the program.

Mac®
2. Double-click the CD-ROM icon.
3. Double-click the **AP_US_History** icon to start the program.

SYSTEM REQUIREMENTS

Microsoft® Windows®
2.33GHz or faster x86-compatible
processor, or Intel Atom™
(1.6GHz or faster processor for
netbook class devices)
Microsoft® Windows® Server 2008,
Windows 7, Windows 8.1 Classic,
or WIndows 10
512MB of RAM
(1GB recommended)

MAC® OS X
Intel® Core™ Duo 1.83GHz
or faster processor
Mac OS X v10.7 and above
512MB of RAM
(1GB recommended)